# GARFIELD
## FAT CAT 3-PACK
### VOLUME 23

# FAT CAT 3-PACK

## VOLUME 23

BY
JIM DAVIS

**BALLANTINE BOOKS · NEW YORK**

2021 Ballantine Books Trade Paperback Edition



Published in the United States by Ballantine Books, an imprint of Random House,
a division of Penguin Random House LLC, New York.

BALLANTINE and the HOUSE colophon are registered trademarks of Penguin Random House LLC.

NICKELODEON is a Trademark of Viacom International, Inc.

GARFIELD SLURPS AND BURPS and GARFIELD BELLY LAUGHS were each published separately by Ballantine Books, an imprint of Random House, a division of Penguin Random House LLC, in 2019. GARFIELD EASY AS PIE was published separately by Ballantine Books, an imprint of Random House, a division of Penguin Random House LLC, New York, in 2020.

ISBN 978-0-593-15639-1

Printed in China on acid-free paper

randomhousebooks.com

9 8 7 6 5 4 3 2 1

# Garfield
# SLURPS and BURPS

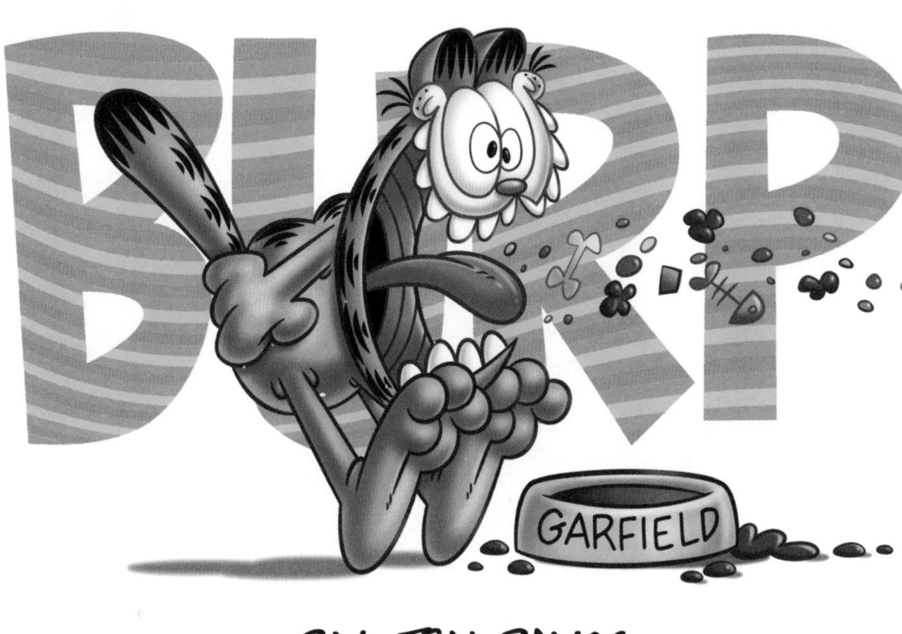
GARFIELD

BY JIM DAVIS

**Ballantine Books • New York**

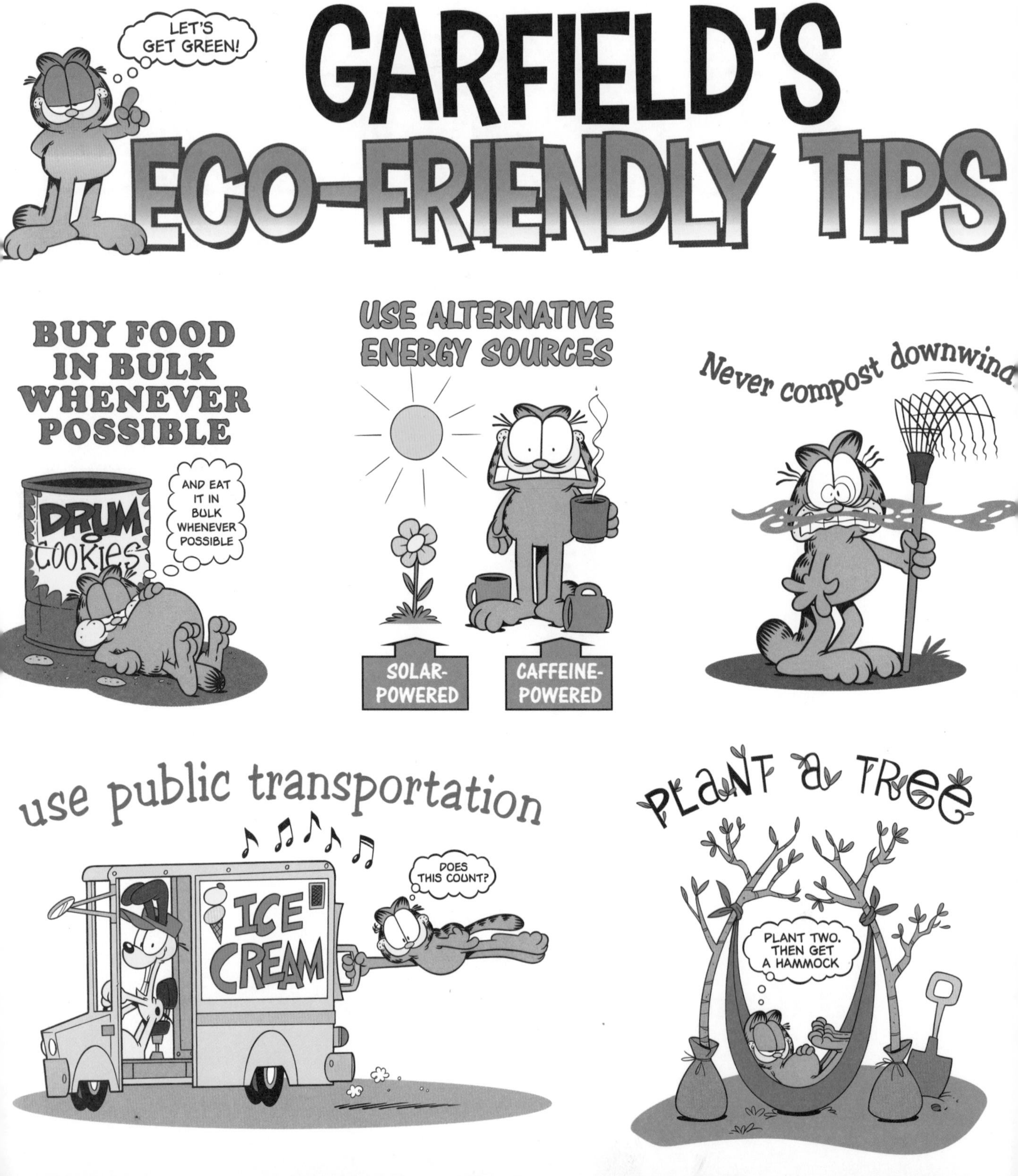
LET'S GET GREEN!
GARFIELD'S
ECO-FRIENDLY TIPS
BUY FOOD IN BULK WHENEVER POSSIBLE
DRUM COOKIES
AND EAT IT IN BULK WHENEVER POSSIBLE
USE ALTERNATIVE ENERGY SOURCES
SOLAR-POWERED
CAFFEINE-POWERED
Never compost downwind
use public transportation
ICE CREAM
DOES THIS COUNT?
PLANT a TREE
PLANT TWO. THEN GET A HAMMOCK

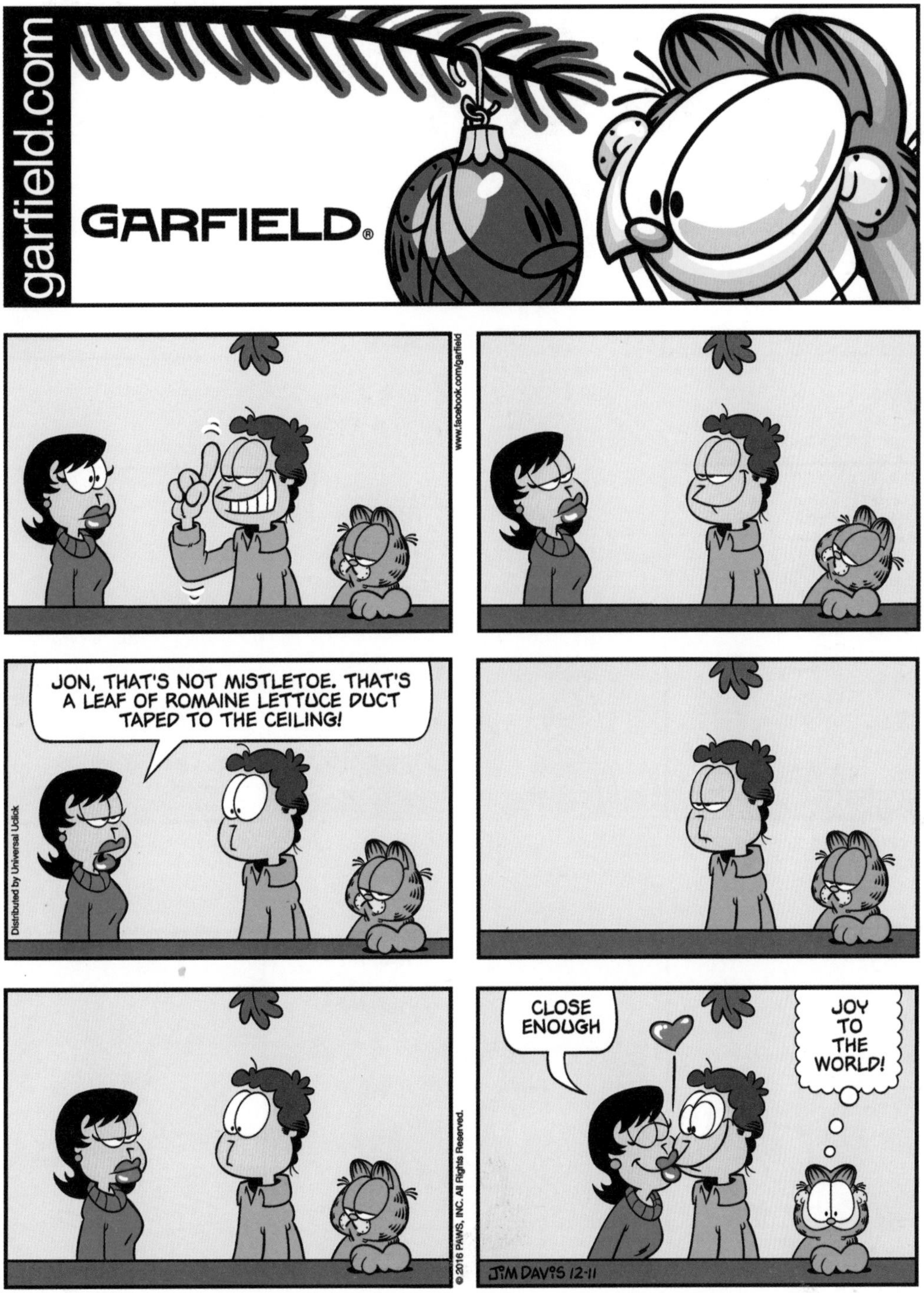
garfield.com
GARFIELD®
www.facebook.com/garfield
JON, THAT'S NOT MISTLETOE. THAT'S A LEAF OF ROMAINE LETTUCE DUCT TAPED TO THE CEILING!
Distributed by Universal Uclick
CLOSE ENOUGH
JOY TO THE WORLD!
© 2016 PAWS, INC. All Rights Reserved.
JIM DAVIS 12-11

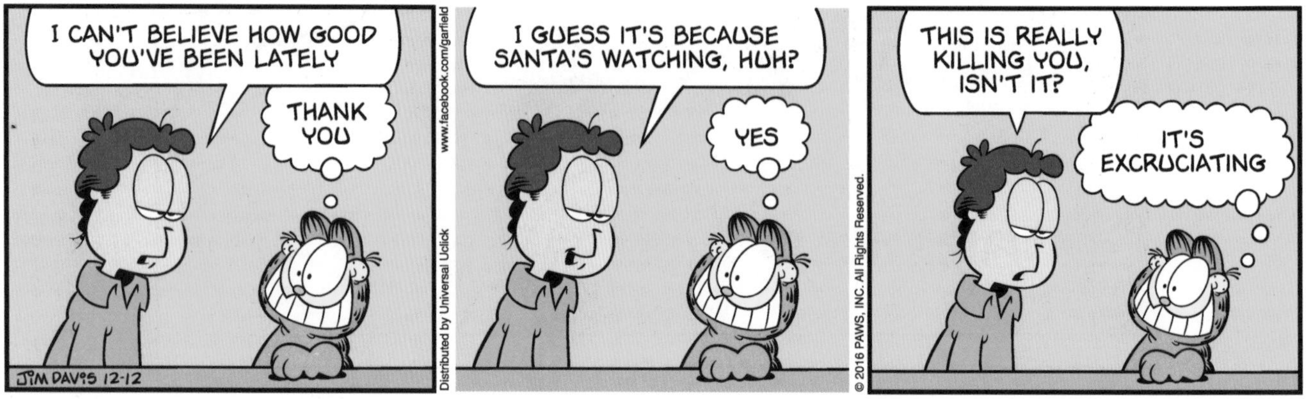
I CAN'T BELIEVE HOW GOOD YOU'VE BEEN LATELY
THANK YOU
I GUESS IT'S BECAUSE SANTA'S WATCHING, HUH?
YES
THIS IS REALLY KILLING YOU, ISN'T IT?
IT'S EXCRUCIATING
JIM DAVIS 12-12
Distributed by Universal Uclick www.facebook.com/garfield
© 2016 PAWS, INC. All Rights Reserved.

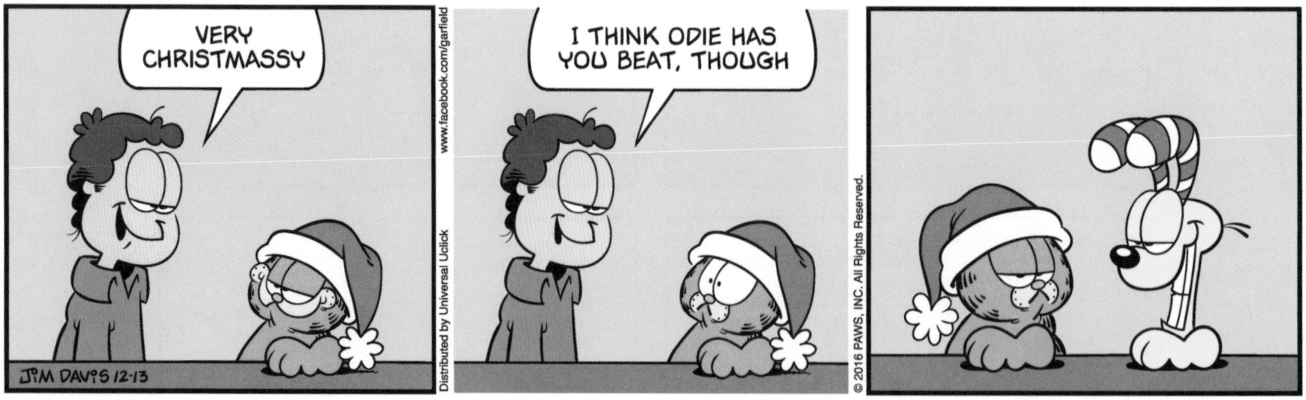
VERY CHRISTMASSY
I THINK ODIE HAS YOU BEAT, THOUGH
JIM DAVIS 12-13
Distributed by Universal Uclick www.facebook.com/garfield
© 2016 PAWS, INC. All Rights Reserved.

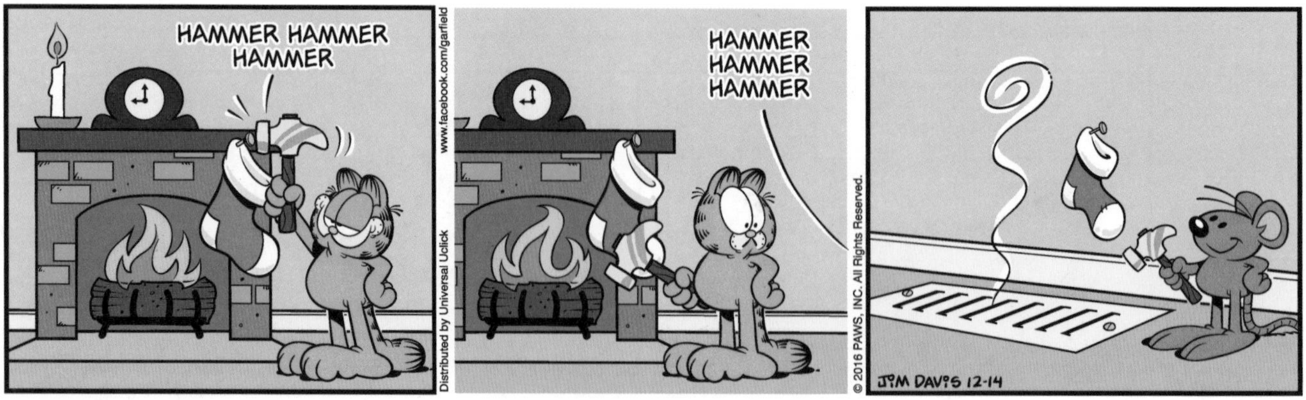
HAMMER HAMMER HAMMER
HAMMER HAMMER HAMMER
JIM DAVIS 12-14
Distributed by Universal Uclick www.facebook.com/garfield
© 2016 PAWS, INC. All Rights Reserved.

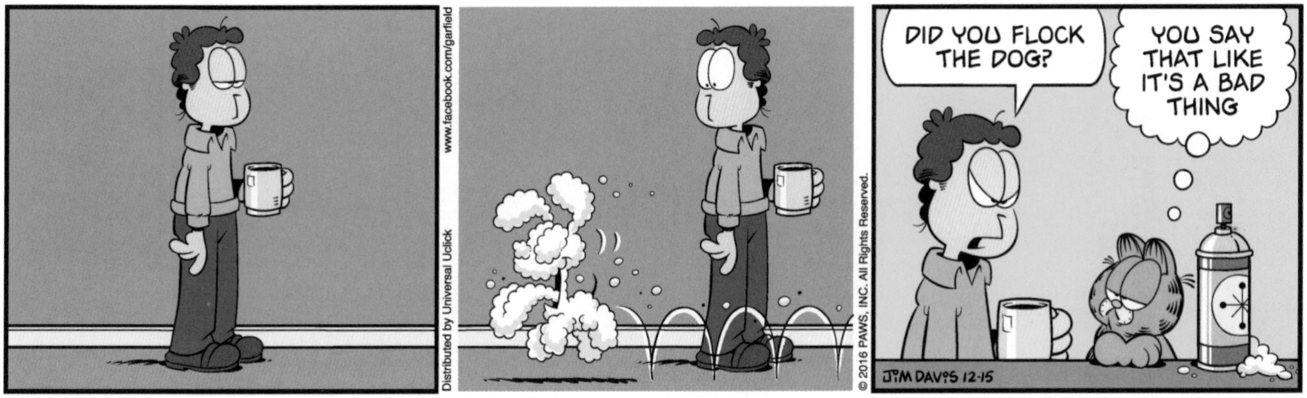
www.facebook.com/garfield
Distributed by Universal Uclick
© 2016 PAWS, INC. All Rights Reserved.
DID YOU FLOCK THE DOG?
YOU SAY THAT LIKE IT'S A BAD THING
JIM DAVIS 12-15

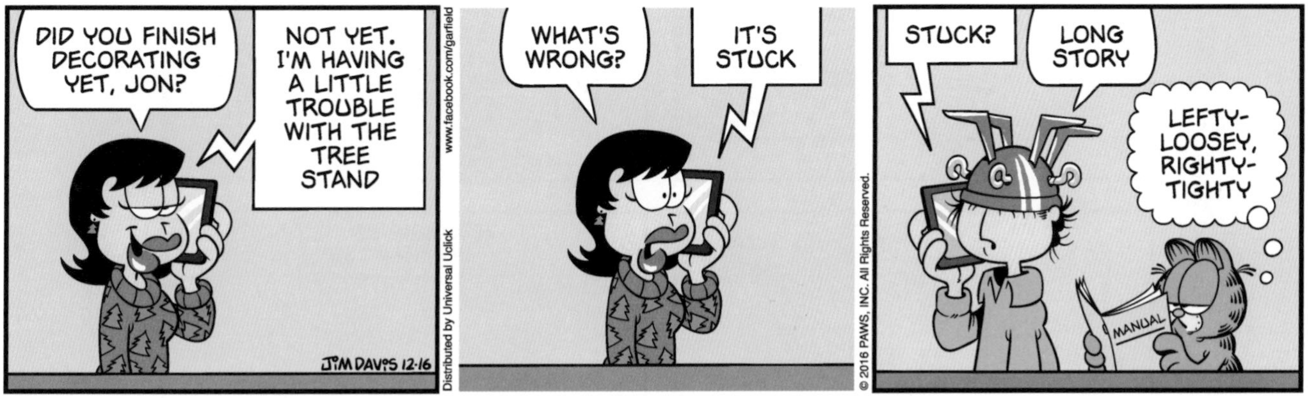
DID YOU FINISH DECORATING YET, JON?
NOT YET. I'M HAVING A LITTLE TROUBLE WITH THE TREE STAND
JIM DAVIS 12-16
www.facebook.com/garfield
Distributed by Universal Uclick
WHAT'S WRONG?
IT'S STUCK
© 2016 PAWS, INC. All Rights Reserved.
STUCK?
LONG STORY
LEFTY-LOOSEY, RIGHTY-TIGHTY
MANUAL

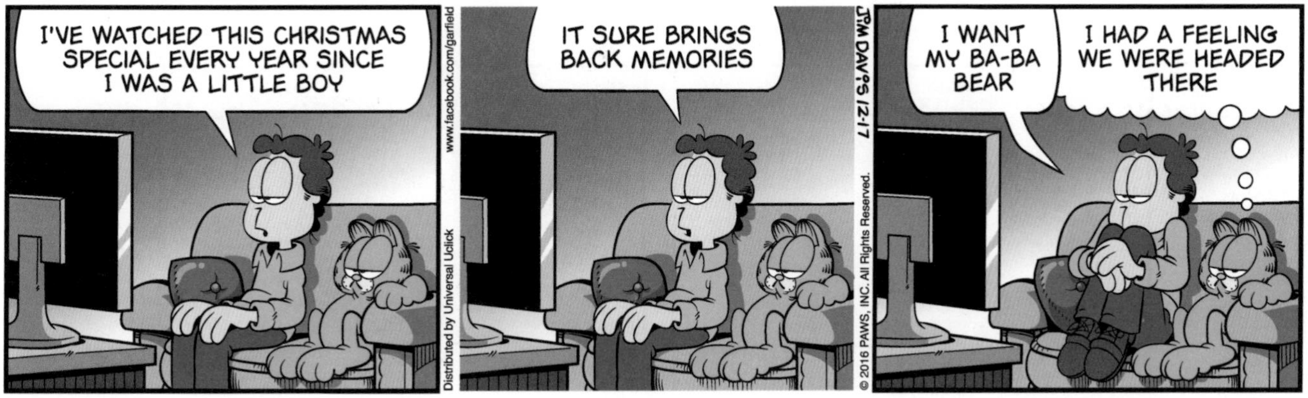
I'VE WATCHED THIS CHRISTMAS SPECIAL EVERY YEAR SINCE I WAS A LITTLE BOY
www.facebook.com/garfield
Distributed by Universal Uclick
IT SURE BRINGS BACK MEMORIES
JIM DAVIS 12-17
© 2016 PAWS, INC. All Rights Reserved.
I WANT MY BA-BA BEAR
I HAD A FEELING WE WERE HEADED THERE

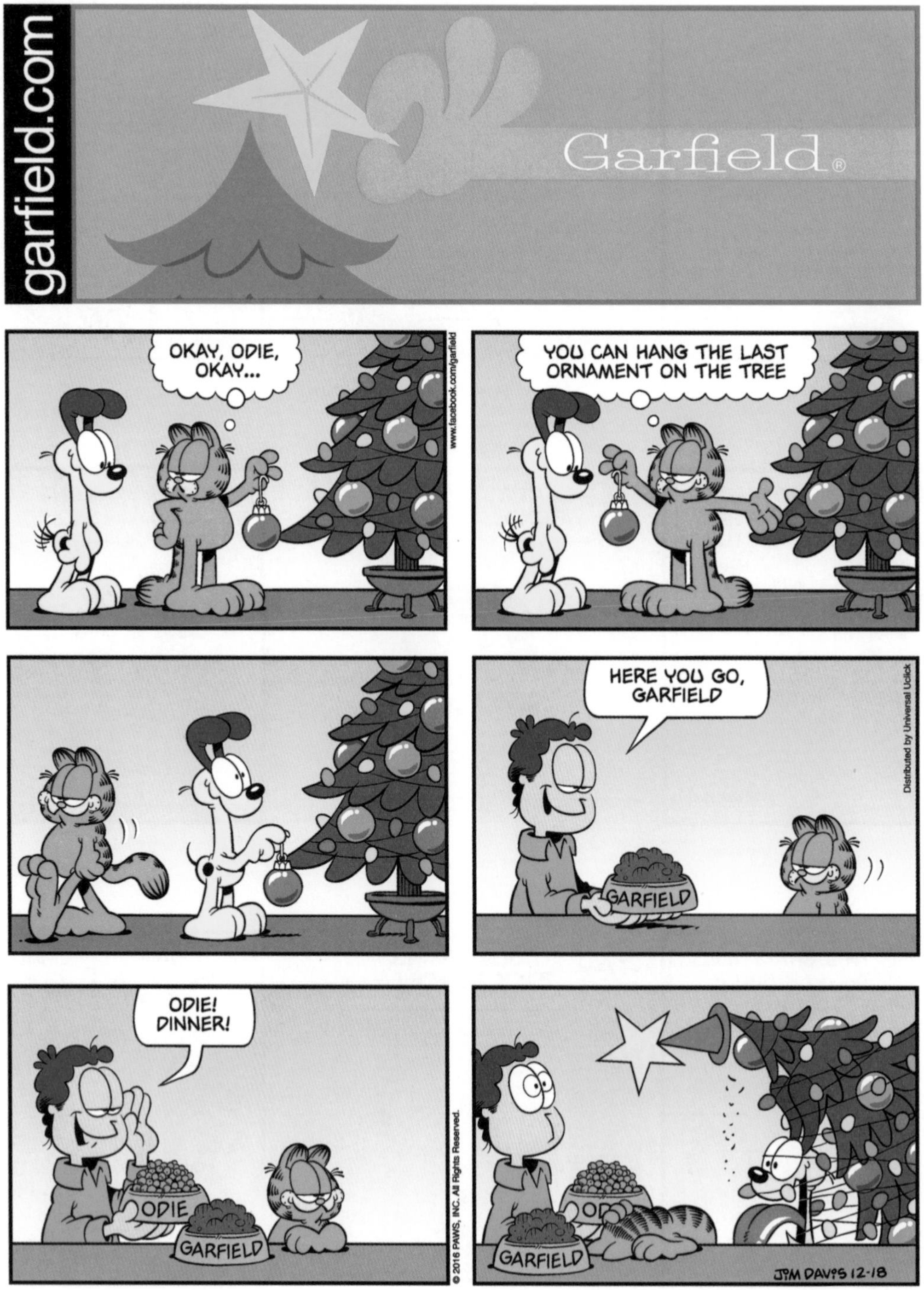
garfield.com
Garfield®
OKAY, ODIE, OKAY...
www.facebook.com/garfield
YOU CAN HANG THE LAST ORNAMENT ON THE TREE
HERE YOU GO, GARFIELD
Distributed by Universal Uclick
GARFIELD
ODIE! DINNER!
ODIE
GARFIELD
© 2016 PAWS, INC. All Rights Reserved.
GARFIELD
JIM DAVIS 12-18

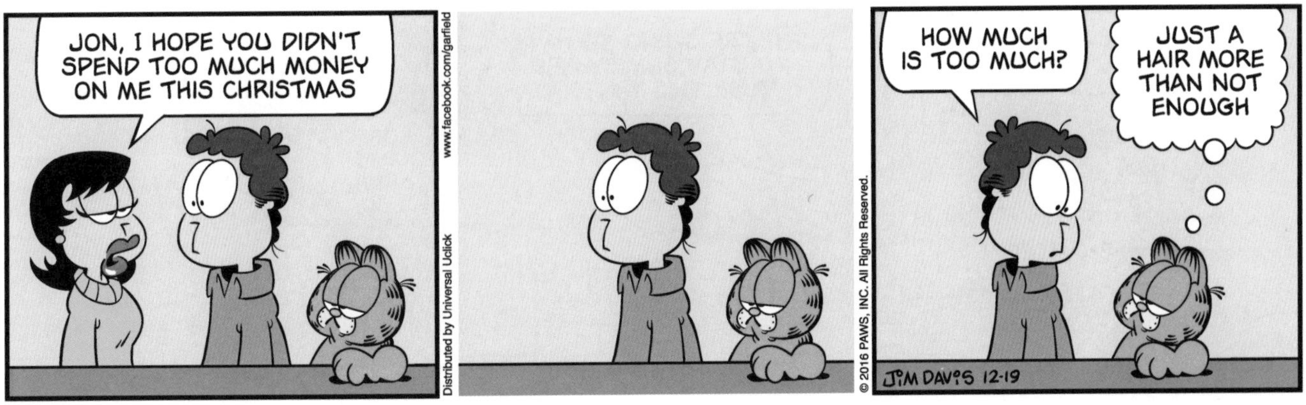
JON, I HOPE YOU DIDN'T SPEND TOO MUCH MONEY ON ME THIS CHRISTMAS
Distributed by Universal Uclick www.facebook.com/garfield
HOW MUCH IS TOO MUCH?
JUST A HAIR MORE THAN NOT ENOUGH
© 2016 PAWS, INC. All Rights Reserved.
JIM DAVIS 12-19

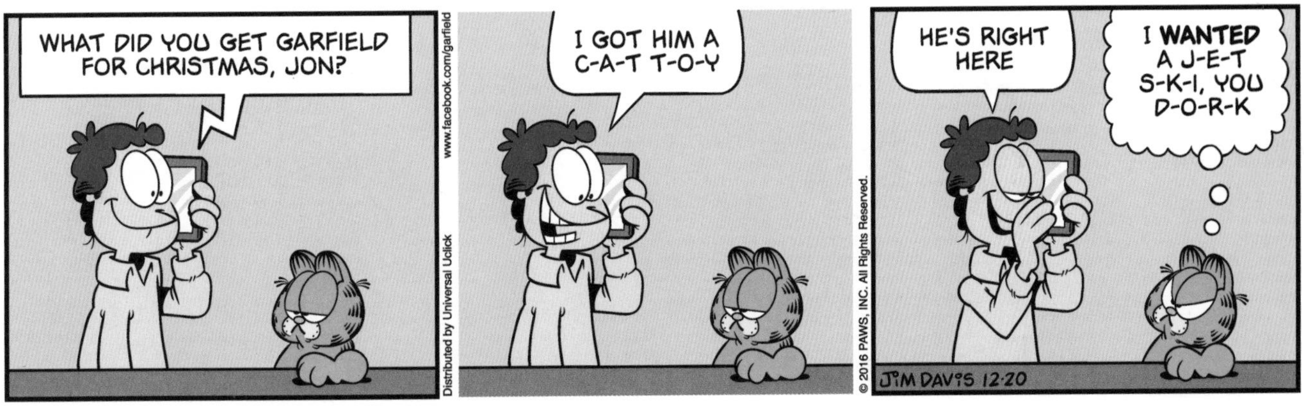
WHAT DID YOU GET GARFIELD FOR CHRISTMAS, JON?
Distributed by Universal Uclick www.facebook.com/garfield
I GOT HIM A C-A-T T-O-Y
HE'S RIGHT HERE
I **WANTED** A J-E-T S-K-I, YOU D-O-R-K
© 2016 PAWS, INC. All Rights Reserved.
JIM DAVIS 12-20

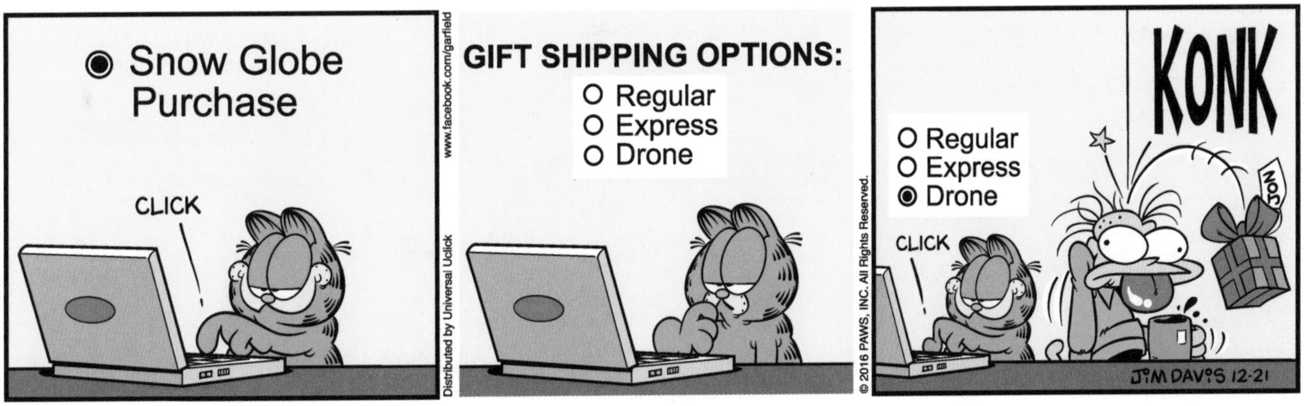
Snow Globe Purchase
CLICK
Distributed by Universal Uclick www.facebook.com/garfield
GIFT SHIPPING OPTIONS:
Regular
Express
Drone
© 2016 PAWS, INC. All Rights Reserved.
KONK
Regular
Express
Drone
CLICK
JON
JIM DAVIS 12-21

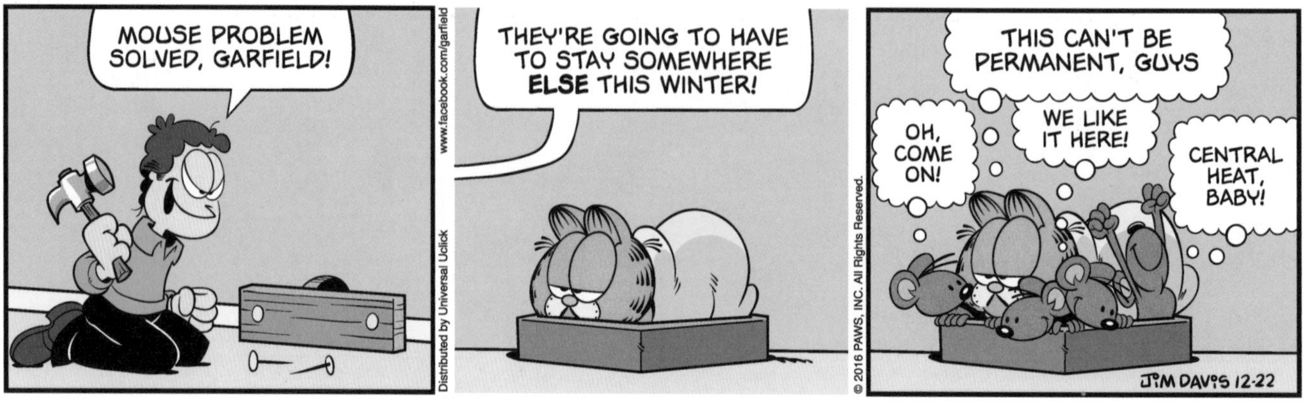
MOUSE PROBLEM SOLVED, GARFIELD!
www.facebook.com/garfield
Distributed by Universal Uclick
THEY'RE GOING TO HAVE TO STAY SOMEWHERE **ELSE** THIS WINTER!
© 2016 PAWS, INC. All Rights Reserved.
THIS CAN'T BE PERMANENT, GUYS
OH, COME ON!
WE LIKE IT HERE!
CENTRAL HEAT, BABY!
JIM DAVIS 12-22

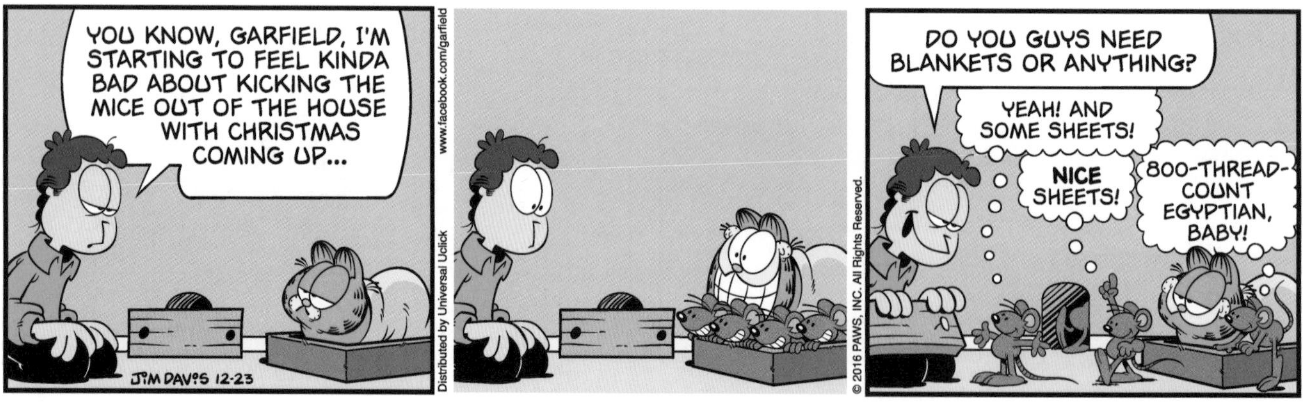
YOU KNOW, GARFIELD, I'M STARTING TO FEEL KINDA BAD ABOUT KICKING THE MICE OUT OF THE HOUSE WITH CHRISTMAS COMING UP...
JIM DAVIS 12-23
www.facebook.com/garfield
Distributed by Universal Uclick
© 2016 PAWS, INC. All Rights Reserved.
DO YOU GUYS NEED BLANKETS OR ANYTHING?
YEAH! AND SOME SHEETS!
**NICE** SHEETS!
800-THREAD-COUNT EGYPTIAN, BABY!

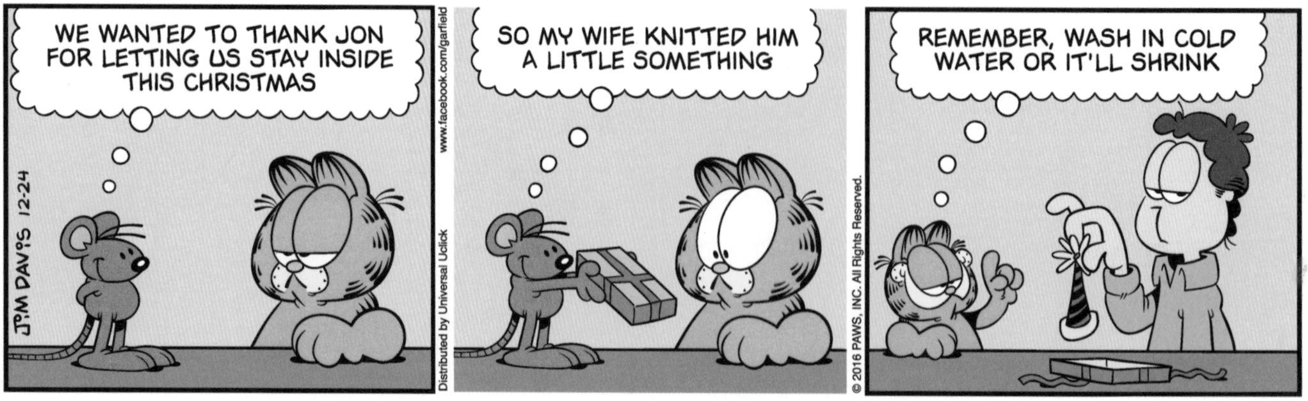
WE WANTED TO THANK JON FOR LETTING US STAY INSIDE THIS CHRISTMAS
JIM DAVIS 12-24
www.facebook.com/garfield
Distributed by Universal Uclick
SO MY WIFE KNITTED HIM A LITTLE SOMETHING
© 2016 PAWS, INC. All Rights Reserved.
REMEMBER, WASH IN COLD WATER OR IT'LL SHRINK

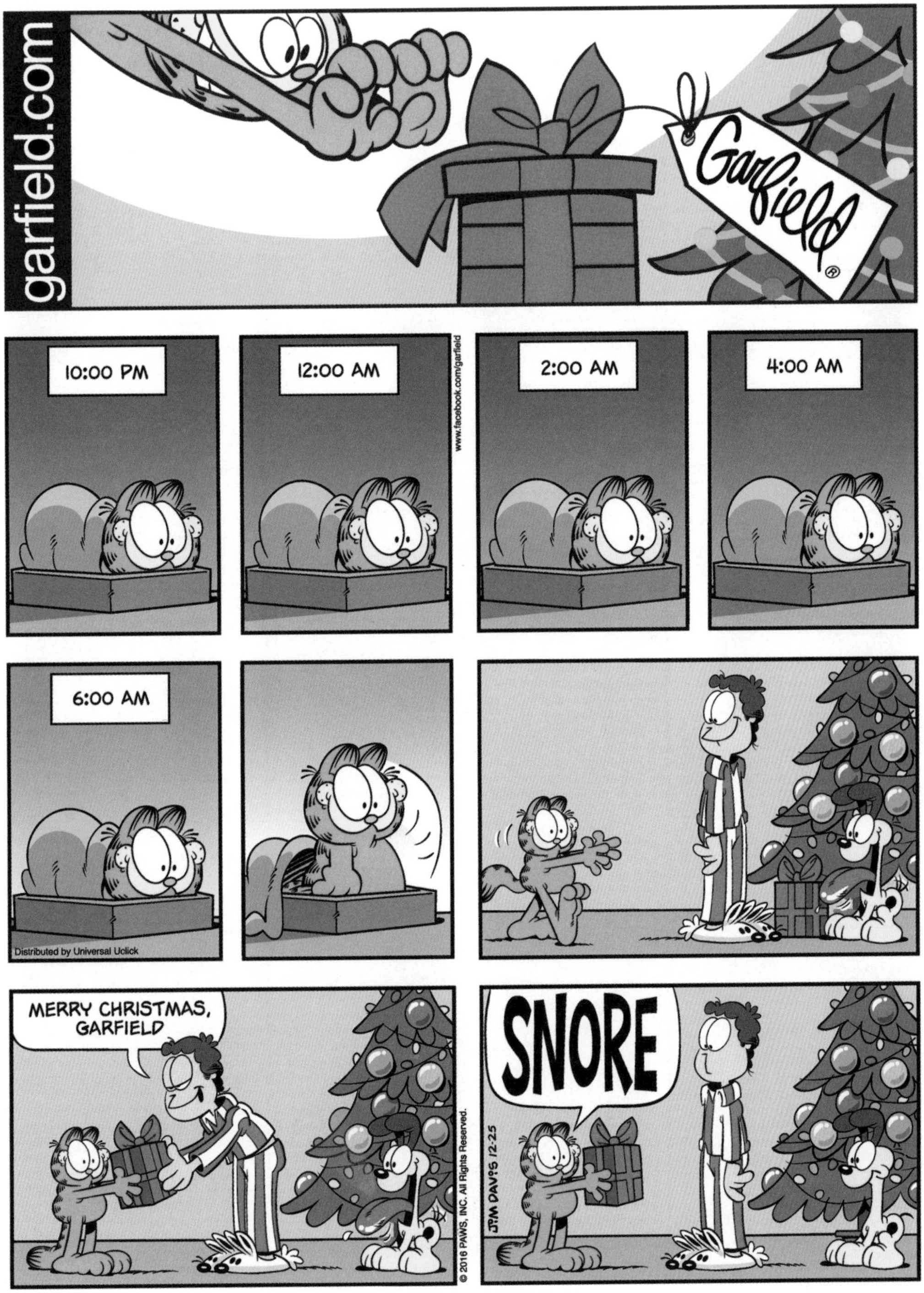

garfield.com
Garfield®
10:00 PM
12:00 AM
2:00 AM
4:00 AM
6:00 AM
MERRY CHRISTMAS, GARFIELD
SNORE
JPM DAVPS 12-25
www.facebook.com/garfield
Distributed by Universal Uclick
© 2016 PAWS, INC. All Rights Reserved.

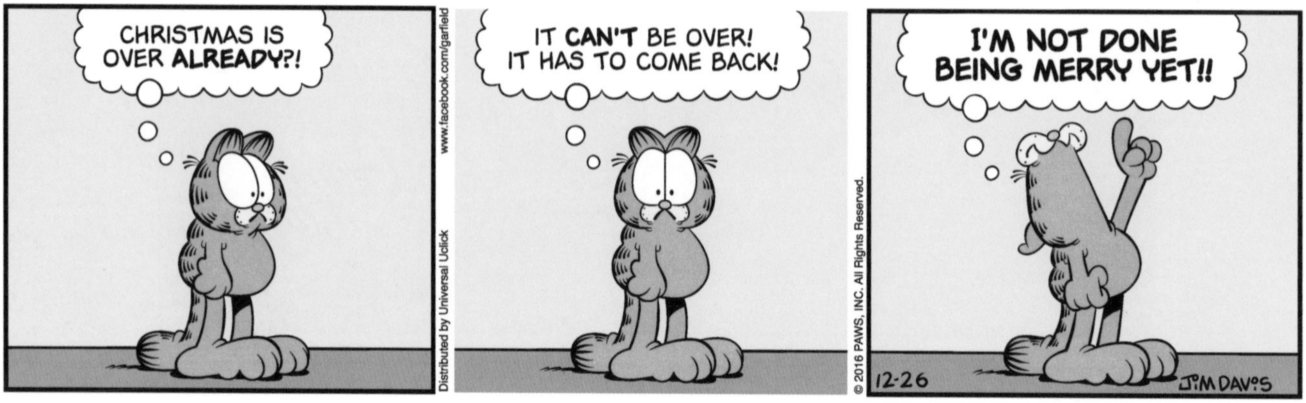

CHRISTMAS IS OVER ALREADY?!
IT CAN'T BE OVER! IT HAS TO COME BACK!
I'M NOT DONE BEING MERRY YET!!
www.facebook.com/garfield
Distributed by Universal Uclick
© 2016 PAWS, INC. All Rights Reserved.
12-26
JIM DAVIS


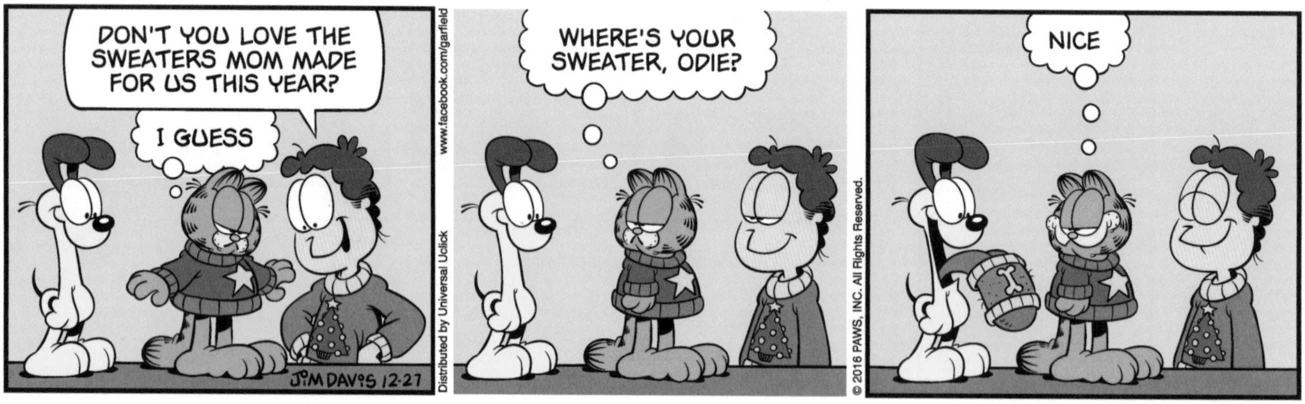

DON'T YOU LOVE THE SWEATERS MOM MADE FOR US THIS YEAR?
I GUESS
JIM DAVIS 12-27
WHERE'S YOUR SWEATER, ODIE?
NICE
www.facebook.com/garfield
Distributed by Universal Uclick
© 2016 PAWS, INC. All Rights Reserved.


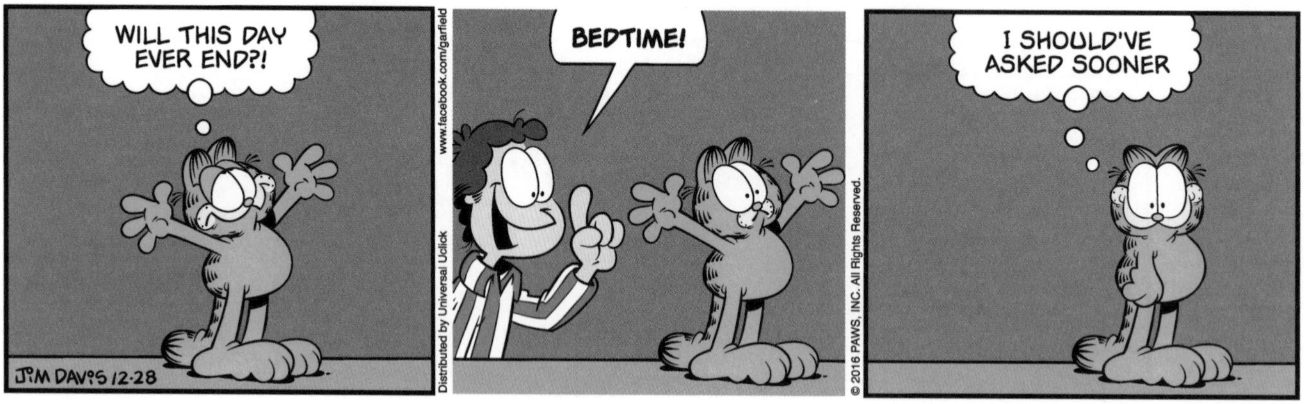

WILL THIS DAY EVER END?!
JIM DAVIS 12-28
BEDTIME!
I SHOULD'VE ASKED SOONER
www.facebook.com/garfield
Distributed by Universal Uclick
© 2016 PAWS, INC. All Rights Reserved.

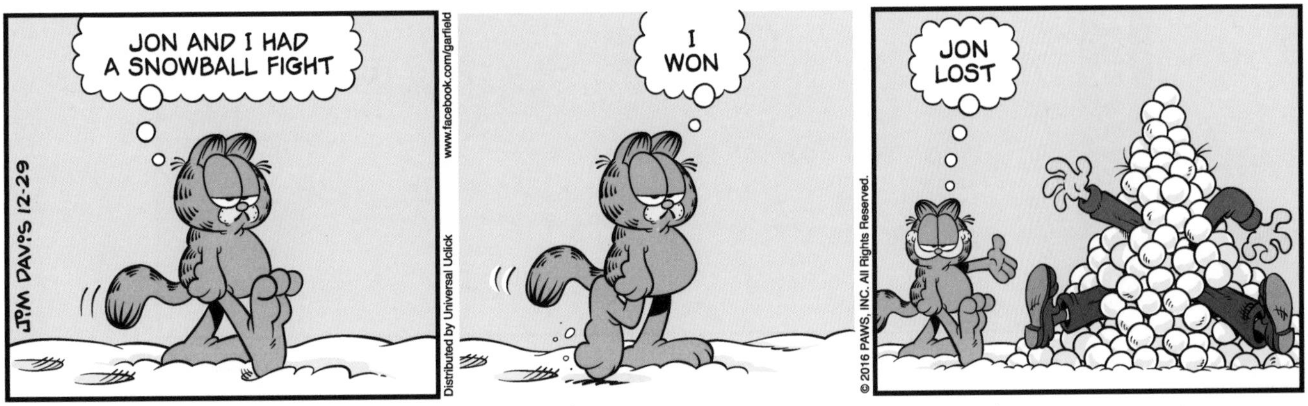
JON AND I HAD A SNOWBALL FIGHT
JIM DAVIS 12-29
I WON
JON LOST
Distributed by Universal Uclick
www.facebook.com/garfield
© 2016 PAWS, INC. All Rights Reserved.

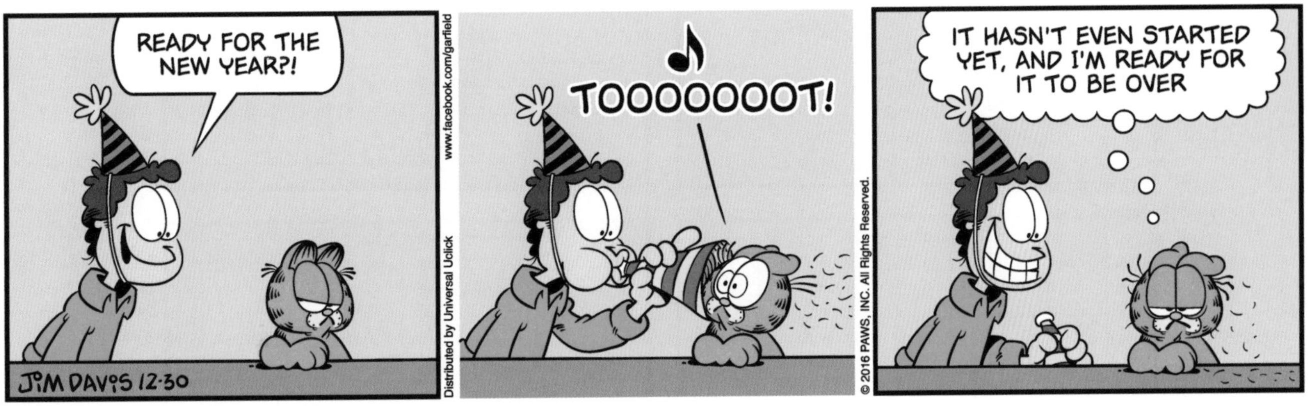
READY FOR THE NEW YEAR?!
JIM DAVIS 12-30
TOOOOOOOT!
IT HASN'T EVEN STARTED YET, AND I'M READY FOR IT TO BE OVER
Distributed by Universal Uclick
www.facebook.com/garfield
© 2016 PAWS, INC. All Rights Reserved.

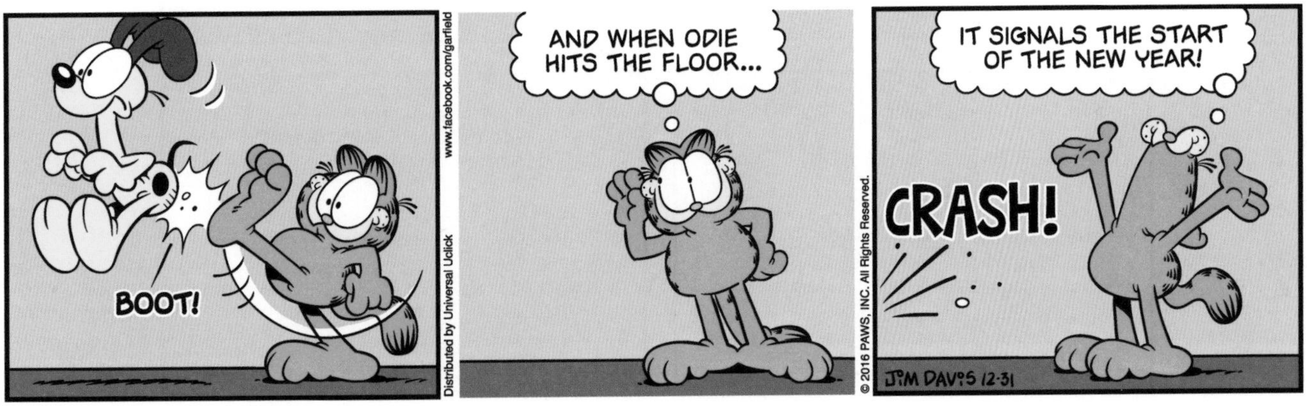
BOOT!
AND WHEN ODIE HITS THE FLOOR...
IT SIGNALS THE START OF THE NEW YEAR!
CRASH!
JIM DAVIS 12-31
Distributed by Universal Uclick
www.facebook.com/garfield
© 2016 PAWS, INC. All Rights Reserved.

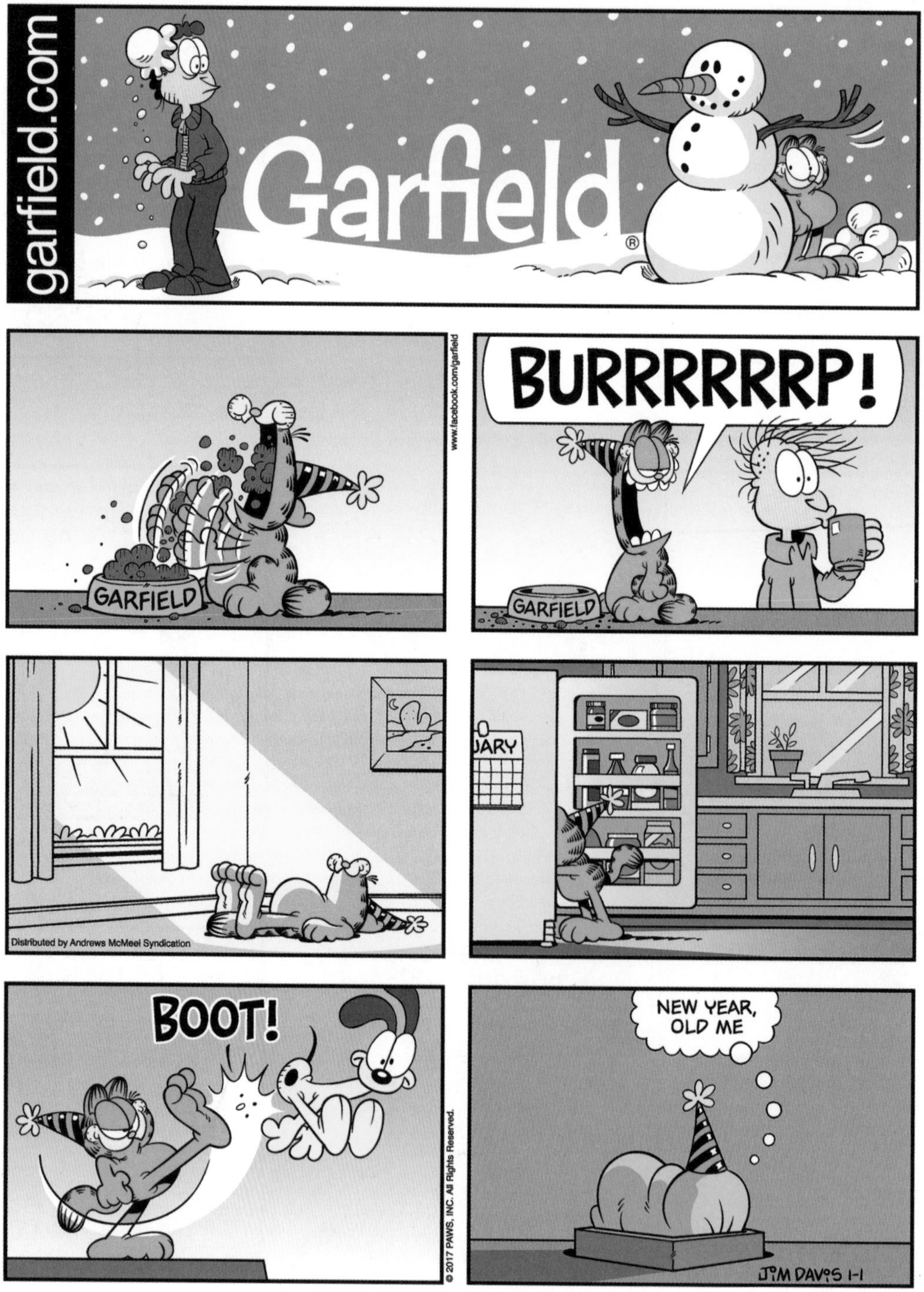
garfield.com
Garfield ®
www.facebook.com/garfield
GARFIELD
BURRRRRRP!
GARFIELD
JARY
Distributed by Andrews McMeel Syndication
BOOT!
© 2017 PAWS, INC. All Rights Reserved.
NEW YEAR, OLD ME
JIM DAVIS 1-1

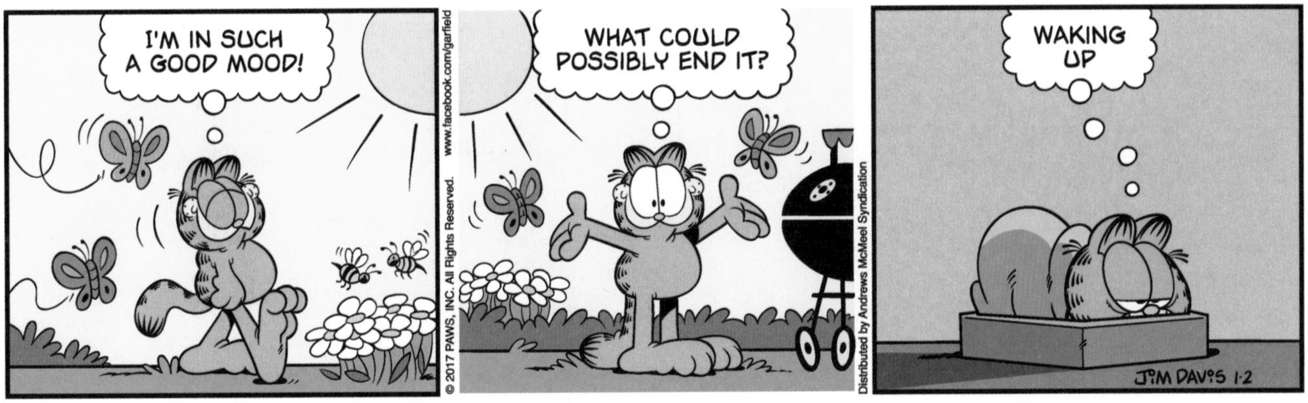
I'M IN SUCH A GOOD MOOD!
WHAT COULD POSSIBLY END IT?
WAKING UP
JIM DAVIS 1-2


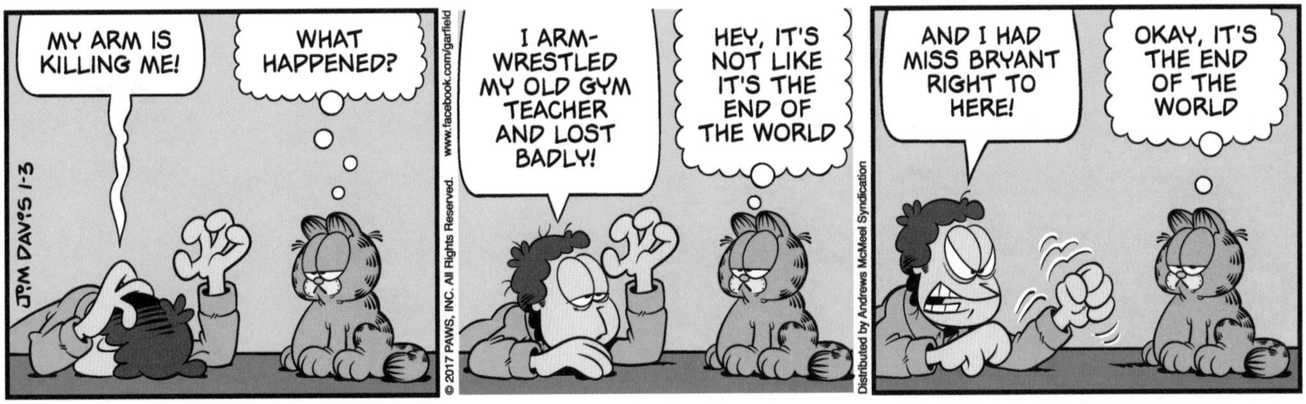
MY ARM IS KILLING ME!
WHAT HAPPENED?
JIM DAVIS 1-3
I ARM-WRESTLED MY OLD GYM TEACHER AND LOST BADLY!
HEY, IT'S NOT LIKE IT'S THE END OF THE WORLD
AND I HAD MISS BRYANT RIGHT TO HERE!
OKAY, IT'S THE END OF THE WORLD


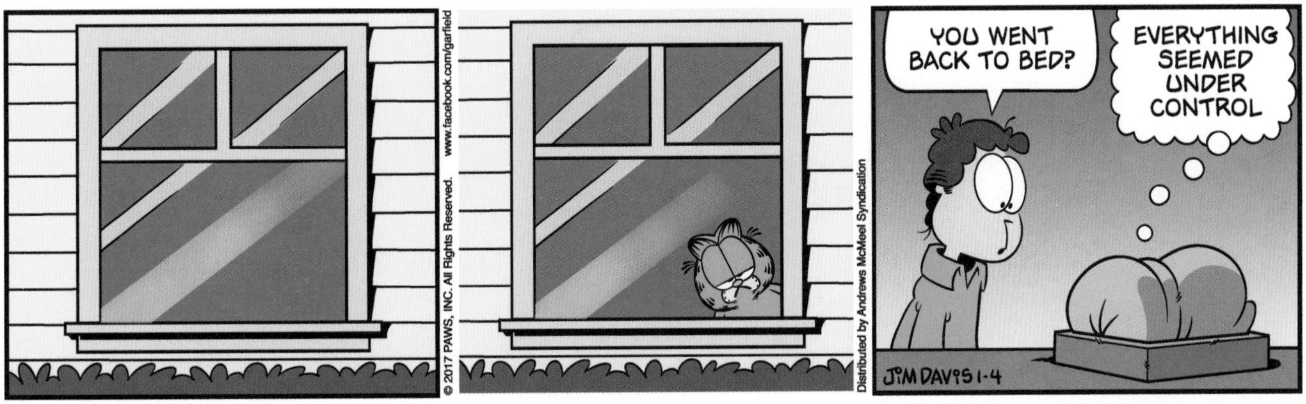
YOU WENT BACK TO BED?
EVERYTHING SEEMED UNDER CONTROL
JIM DAVIS 1-4

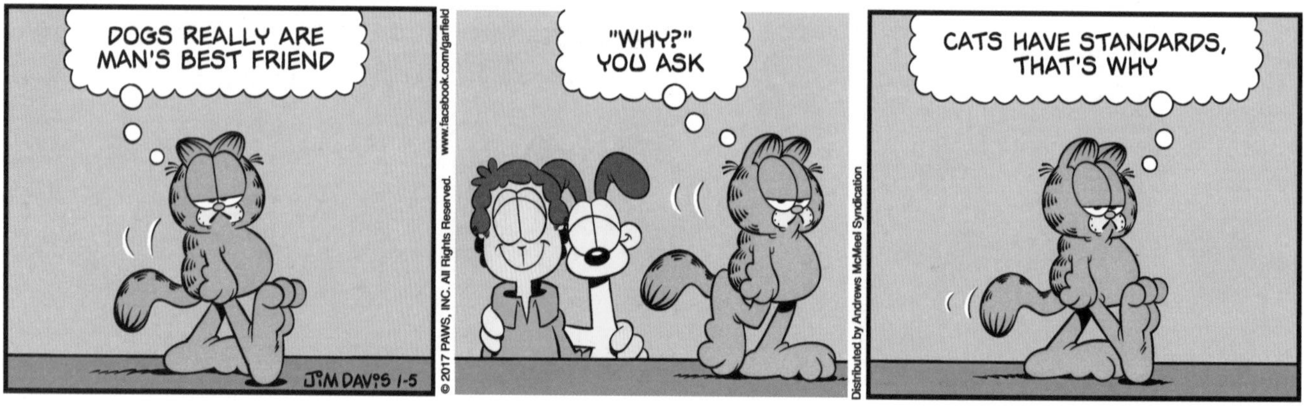
DOGS REALLY ARE MAN'S BEST FRIEND
JIM DAVIS 1-5
© 2017 PAWS, INC. All Rights Reserved. www.facebook.com/garfield
"WHY?" YOU ASK
Distributed by Andrews McMeel Syndication
CATS HAVE STANDARDS, THAT'S WHY

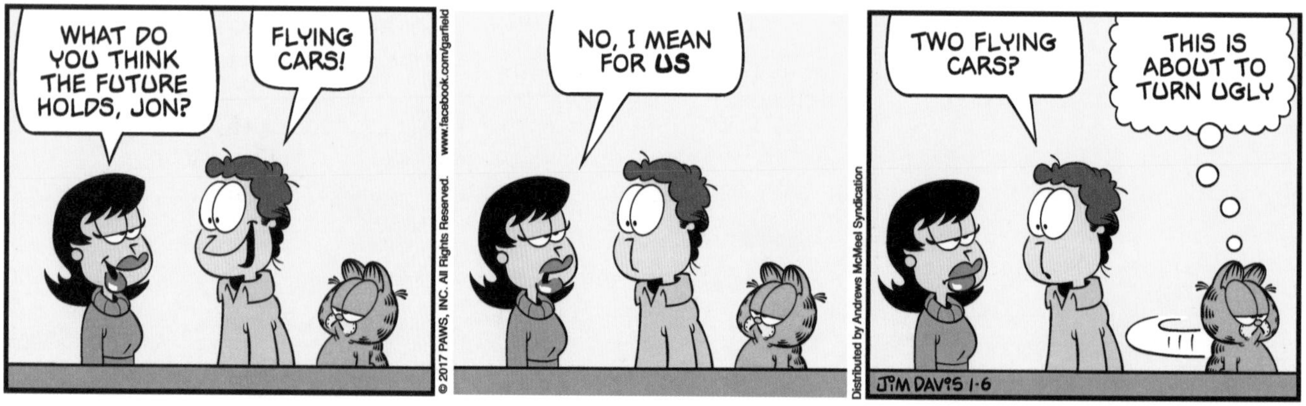
WHAT DO YOU THINK THE FUTURE HOLDS, JON?
FLYING CARS!
© 2017 PAWS, INC. All Rights Reserved. www.facebook.com/garfield
NO, I MEAN FOR **US**
Distributed by Andrews McMeel Syndication
TWO FLYING CARS?
THIS IS ABOUT TO TURN UGLY
JIM DAVIS 1-6

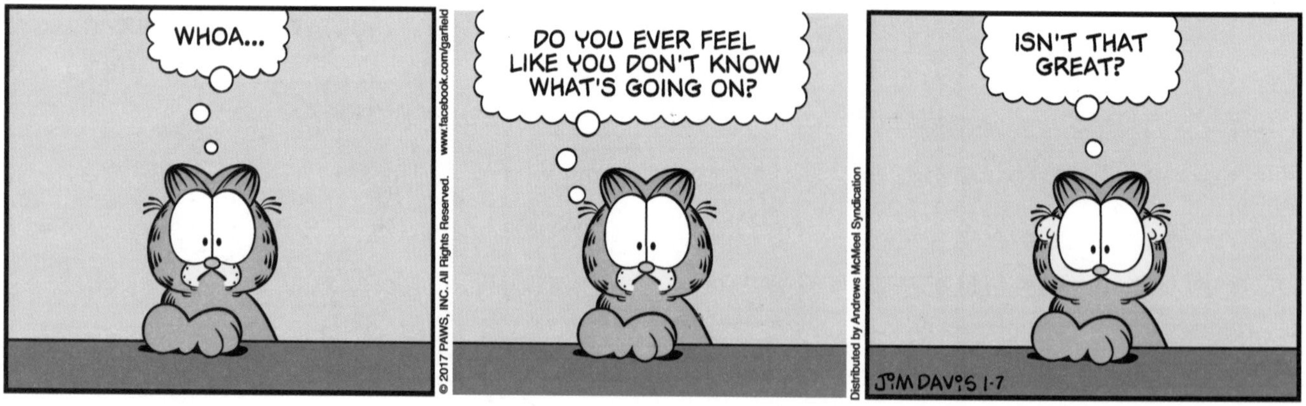
WHOA...
© 2017 PAWS, INC. All Rights Reserved. www.facebook.com/garfield
DO YOU EVER FEEL LIKE YOU DON'T KNOW WHAT'S GOING ON?
Distributed by Andrews McMeel Syndication
ISN'T THAT GREAT?
JIM DAVIS 1-7

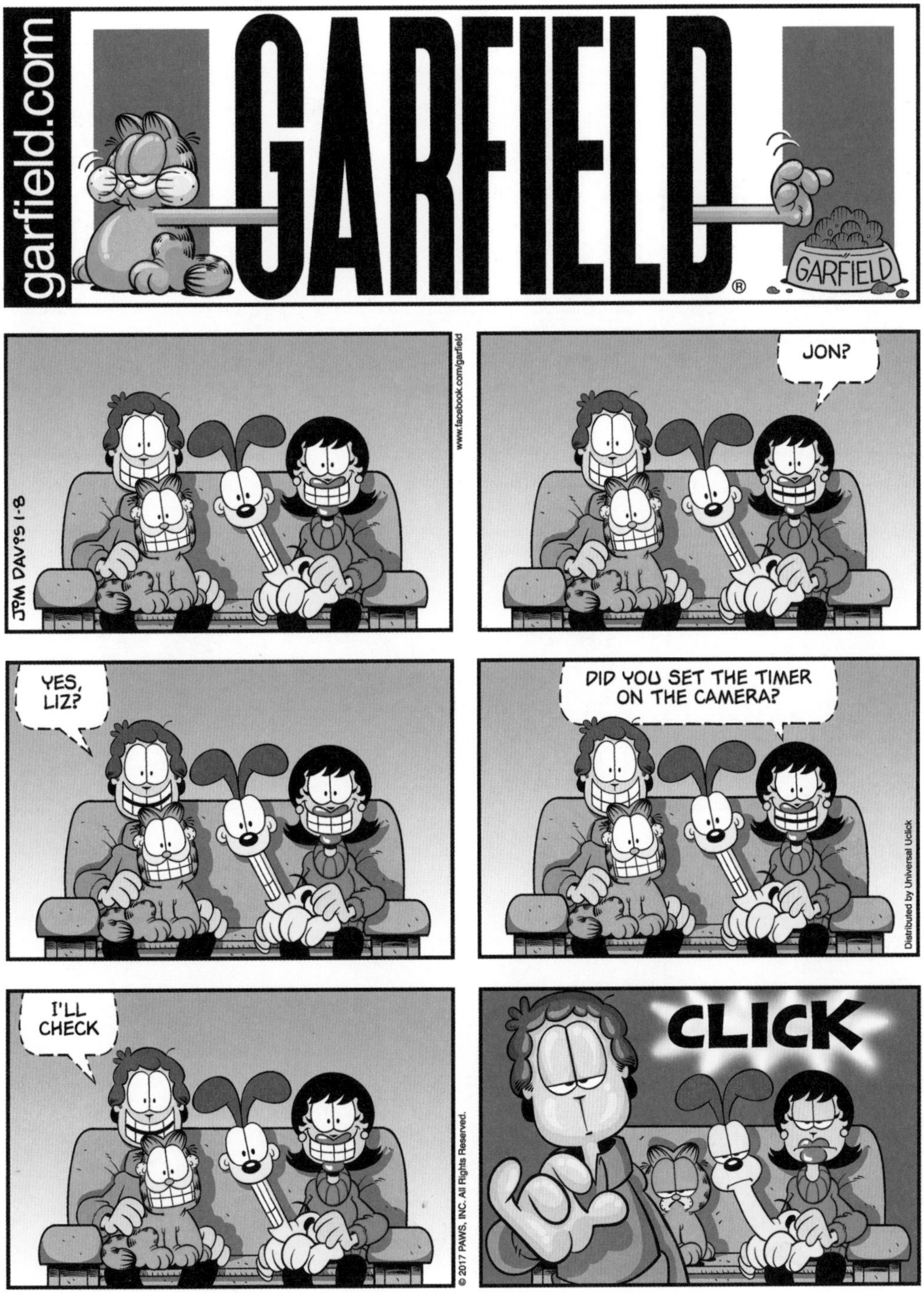

garfield.com
GARFIELD
GARFIELD
JIM DAVIS 1-8
www.facebook.com/garfield
JON?
YES, LIZ?
DID YOU SET THE TIMER ON THE CAMERA?
Distributed by Universal Uclick
I'LL CHECK
© 2017 PAWS, INC. All Rights Reserved.
CLICK

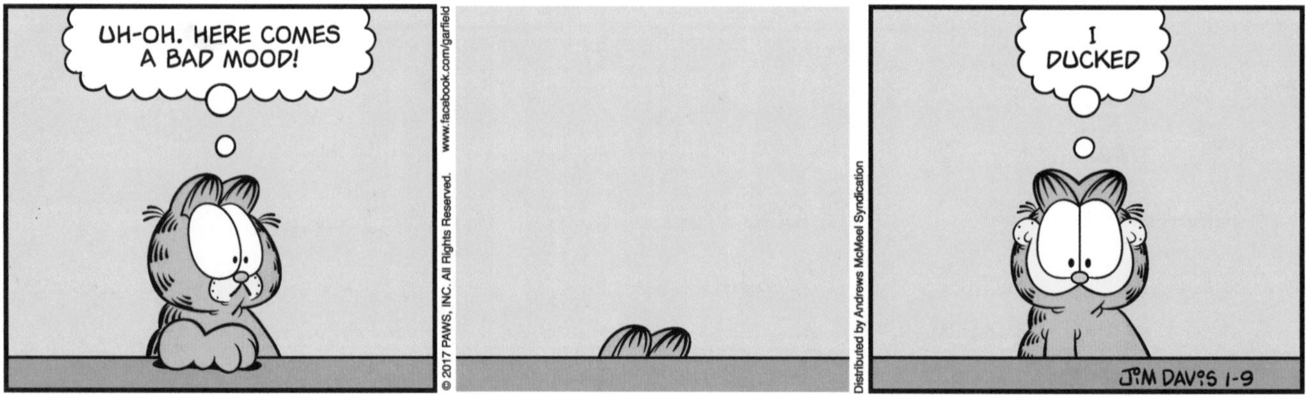
UH-OH. HERE COMES A BAD MOOD!
© 2017 PAWS, INC. All Rights Reserved. www.facebook.com/garfield
Distributed by Andrews McMeel Syndication
I DUCKED
JIM DAVIS 1-9

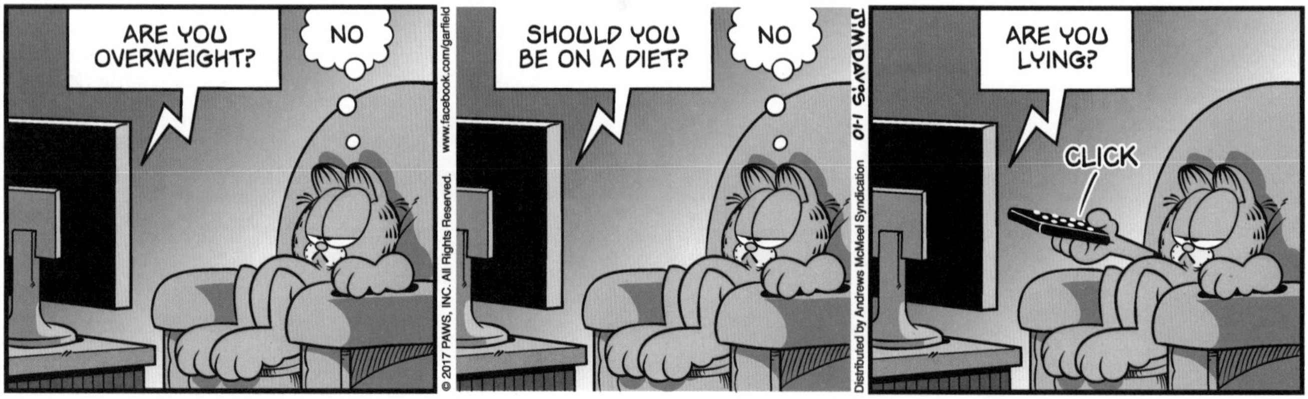
ARE YOU OVERWEIGHT?
NO
© 2017 PAWS, INC. All Rights Reserved. www.facebook.com/garfield
SHOULD YOU BE ON A DIET?
NO
JIM DAVIS 1-10
Distributed by Andrews McMeel Syndication
ARE YOU LYING?
CLICK

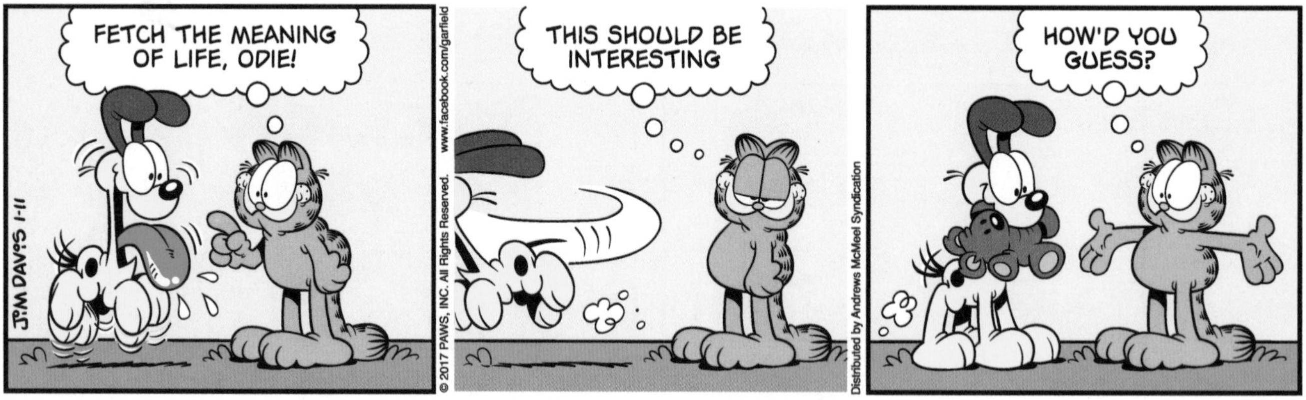
FETCH THE MEANING OF LIFE, ODIE!
JIM DAVIS 1-11
© 2017 PAWS, INC. All Rights Reserved. www.facebook.com/garfield
THIS SHOULD BE INTERESTING
Distributed by Andrews McMeel Syndication
HOW'D YOU GUESS?

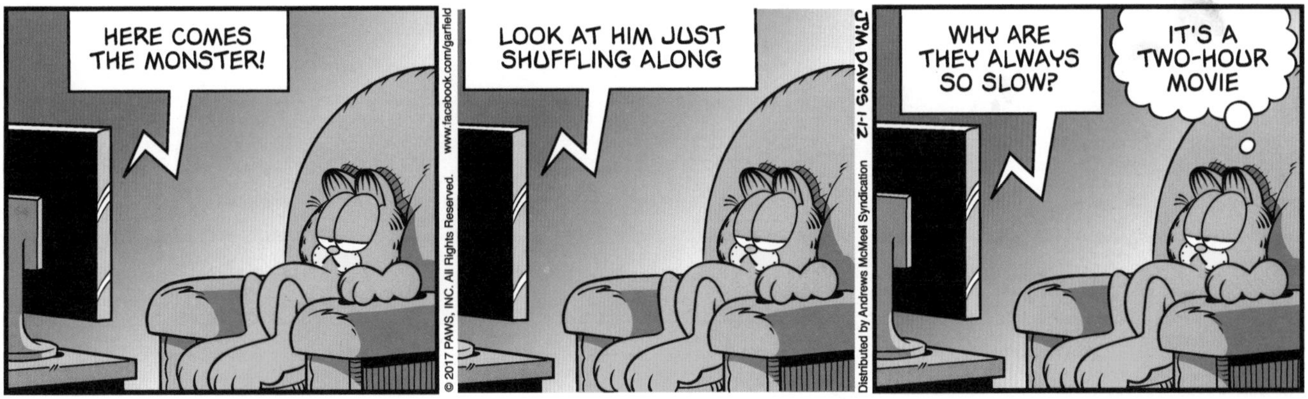
HERE COMES THE MONSTER!
LOOK AT HIM JUST SHUFFLING ALONG
WHY ARE THEY ALWAYS SO SLOW?
IT'S A TWO-HOUR MOVIE
© 2017 PAWS, INC. All Rights Reserved. www.facebook.com/garfield
JIM DAVIS 1-12
Distributed by Andrews McMeel Syndication

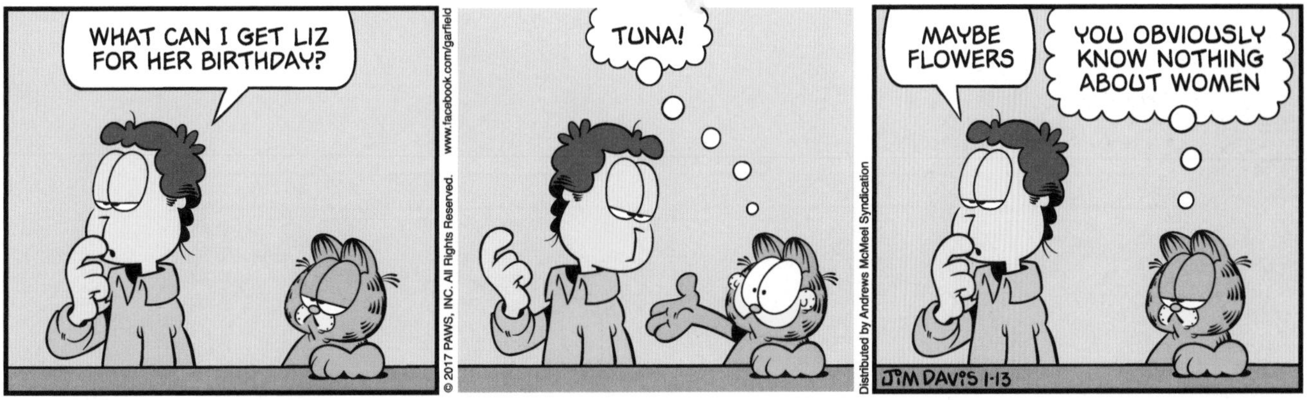
WHAT CAN I GET LIZ FOR HER BIRTHDAY?
TUNA!
MAYBE FLOWERS
YOU OBVIOUSLY KNOW NOTHING ABOUT WOMEN
© 2017 PAWS, INC. All Rights Reserved. www.facebook.com/garfield
Distributed by Andrews McMeel Syndication
JIM DAVIS 1-13

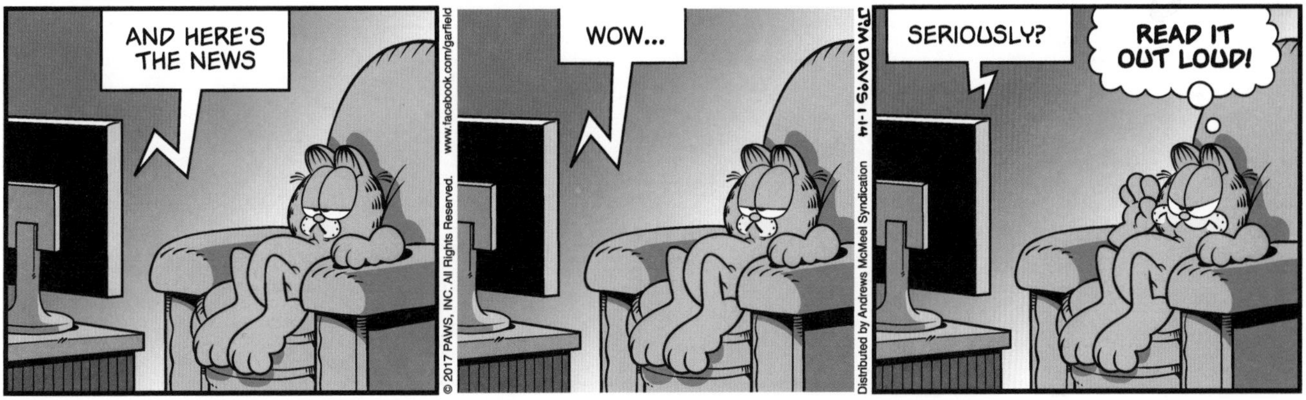
AND HERE'S THE NEWS
WOW...
SERIOUSLY?
READ IT OUT LOUD!
© 2017 PAWS, INC. All Rights Reserved. www.facebook.com/garfield
JIM DAVIS 1-14
Distributed by Andrews McMeel Syndication

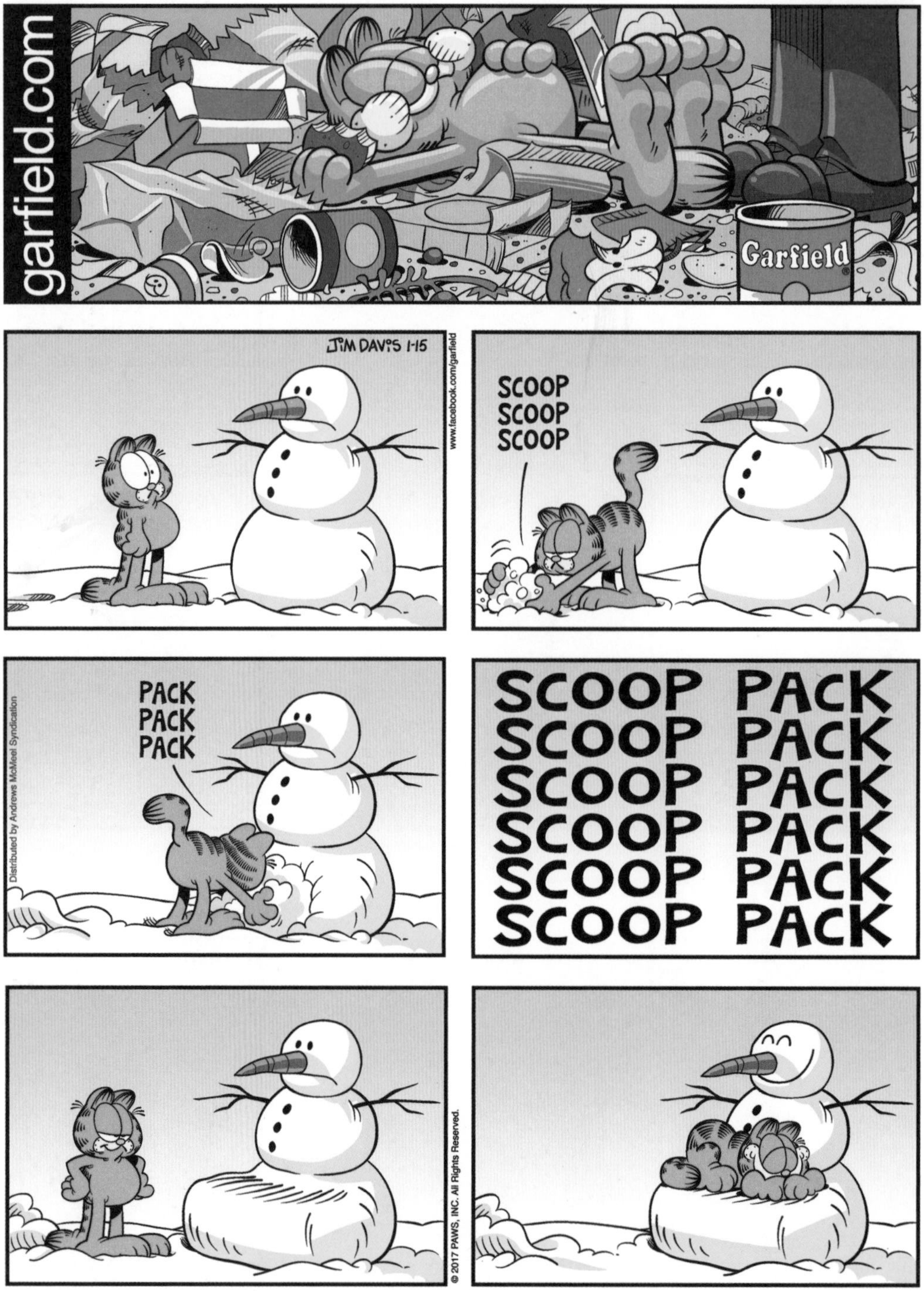
garfield.com
Garfield
JIM DAVIS 1-15
www.facebook.com/garfield
SCOOP
SCOOP
SCOOP
Distributed by Andrews McMeel Syndication
PACK
PACK
PACK
SCOOP PACK
SCOOP PACK
SCOOP PACK
SCOOP PACK
SCOOP PACK
SCOOP PACK
© 2017 PAWS, INC. All Rights Reserved.

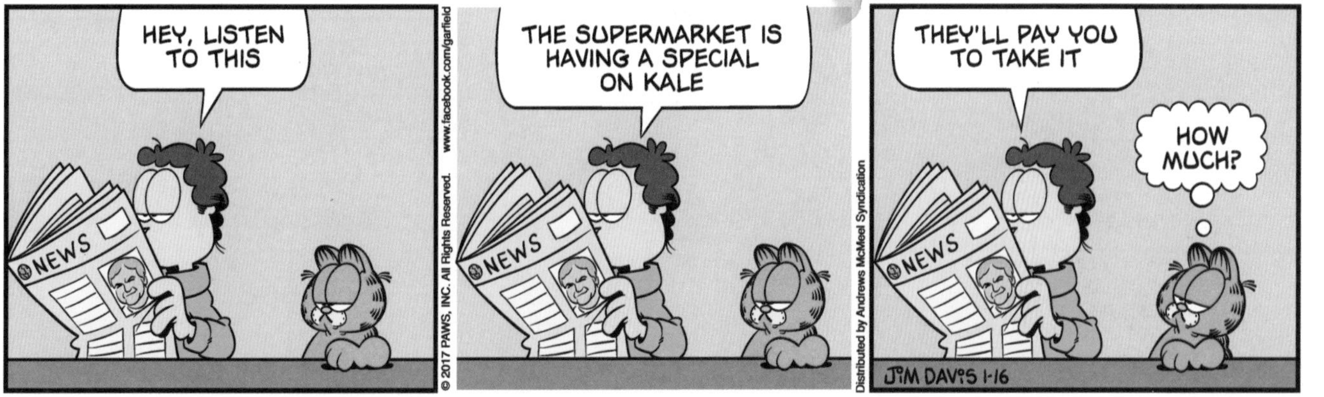
HEY, LISTEN TO THIS
NEWS
© 2017 PAWS, INC. All Rights Reserved. www.facebook.com/garfield
THE SUPERMARKET IS HAVING A SPECIAL ON KALE
NEWS
Distributed by Andrews McMeel Syndication
THEY'LL PAY YOU TO TAKE IT
HOW MUCH?
NEWS
JIM DAVIS 1-16

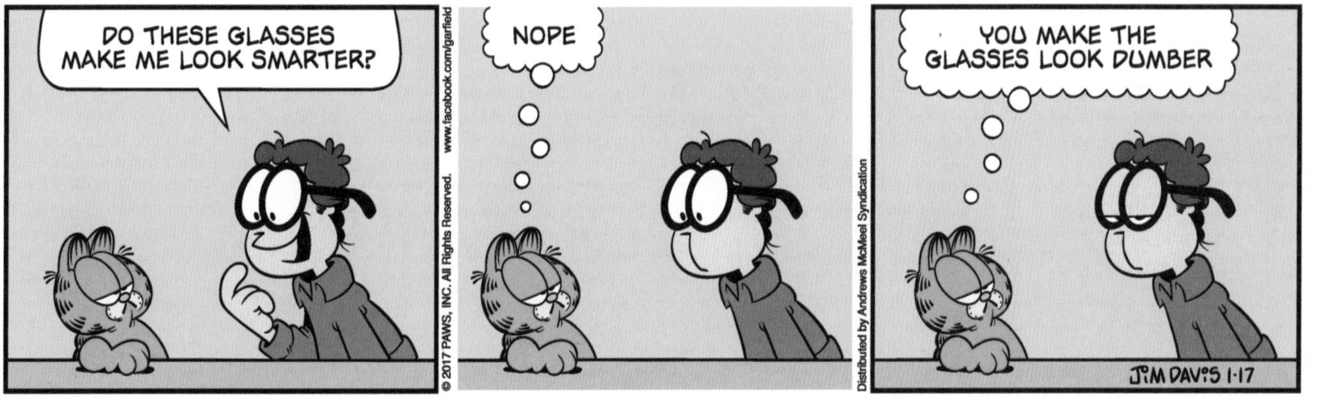
DO THESE GLASSES MAKE ME LOOK SMARTER?
© 2017 PAWS, INC. All Rights Reserved. www.facebook.com/garfield
NOPE
Distributed by Andrews McMeel Syndication
YOU MAKE THE GLASSES LOOK DUMBER
JIM DAVIS 1-17

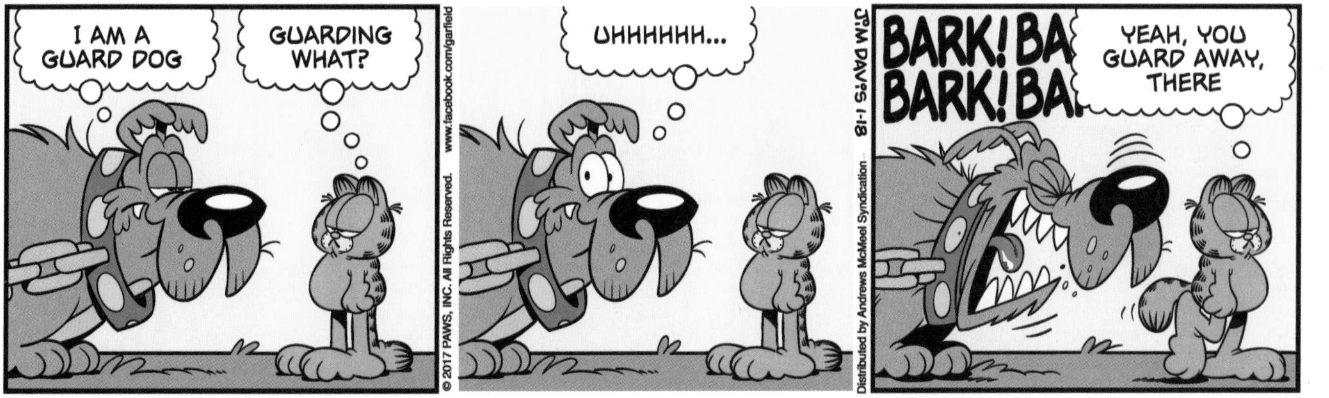
I AM A GUARD DOG
GUARDING WHAT?
© 2017 PAWS, INC. All Rights Reserved. www.facebook.com/garfield
UHHHHHH...
JIM DAVIS 1-18
Distributed by Andrews McMeel Syndication
BARK! BA
BARK! BA
YEAH, YOU GUARD AWAY, THERE

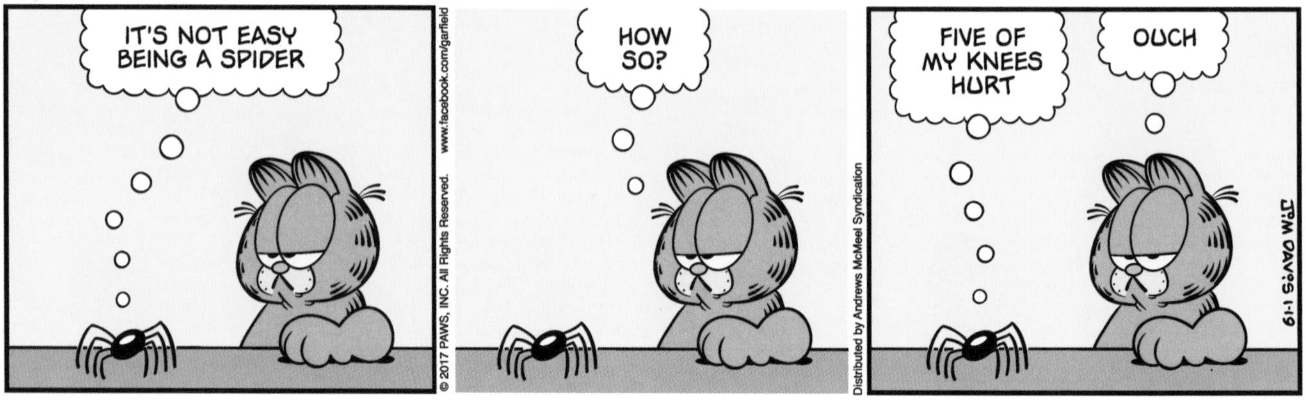
IT'S NOT EASY BEING A SPIDER
HOW SO?
FIVE OF MY KNEES HURT
OUCH
JIM DAVIS 1-19
© 2017 PAWS, INC. All Rights Reserved. www.facebook.com/garfield
Distributed by Andrews McMeel Syndication

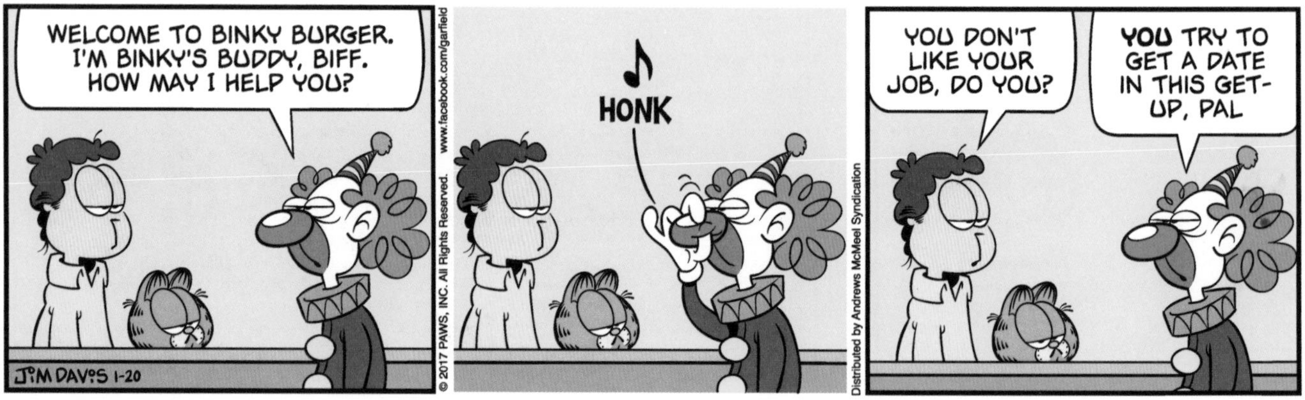
WELCOME TO BINKY BURGER. I'M BINKY'S BUDDY, BIFF. HOW MAY I HELP YOU?
JIM DAVIS 1-20
HONK
YOU DON'T LIKE YOUR JOB, DO YOU?
YOU TRY TO GET A DATE IN THIS GET-UP, PAL
© 2017 PAWS, INC. All Rights Reserved. www.facebook.com/garfield
Distributed by Andrews McMeel Syndication

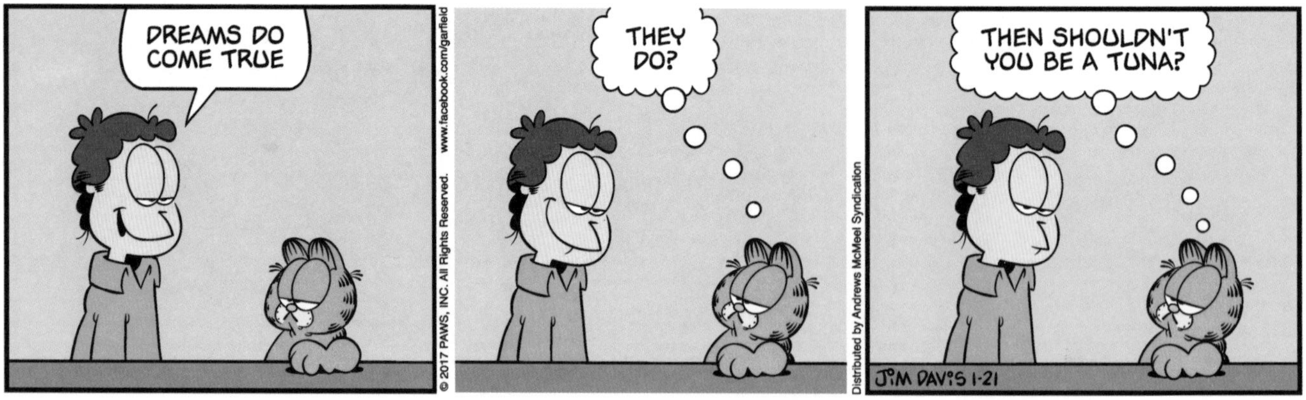
DREAMS DO COME TRUE
THEY DO?
THEN SHOULDN'T YOU BE A TUNA?
JIM DAVIS 1-21
© 2017 PAWS, INC. All Rights Reserved. www.facebook.com/garfield
Distributed by Andrews McMeel Syndication

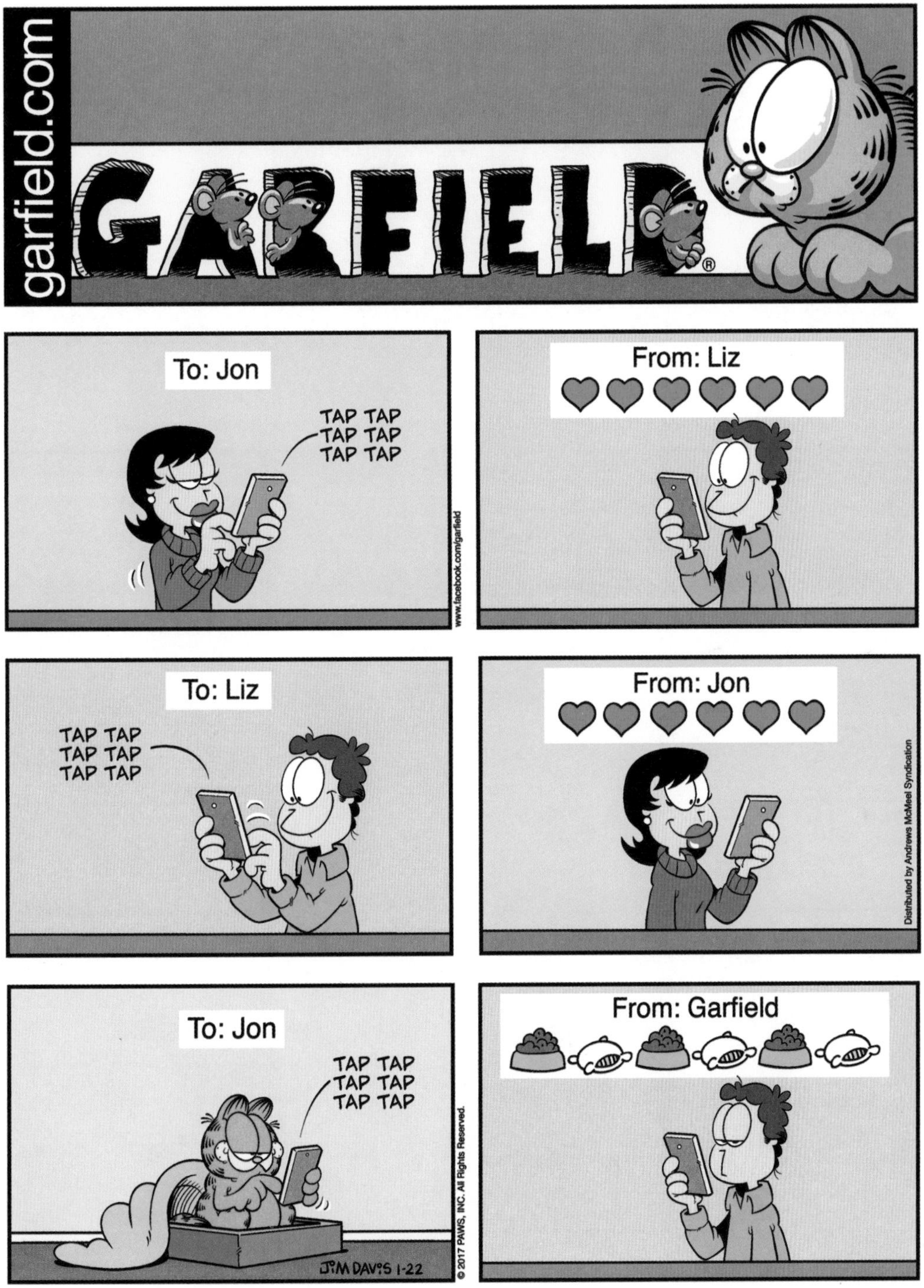
garfield.com
GARFIELD®
To: Jon
TAP TAP
TAP TAP
TAP TAP
www.facebook.com/garfield
From: Liz
To: Liz
TAP TAP
TAP TAP
TAP TAP
From: Jon
Distributed by Andrews McMeel Syndication
To: Jon
TAP TAP
TAP TAP
TAP TAP
JIM DAVIS 1-22
© 2017 PAWS, INC. All Rights Reserved.
From: Garfield

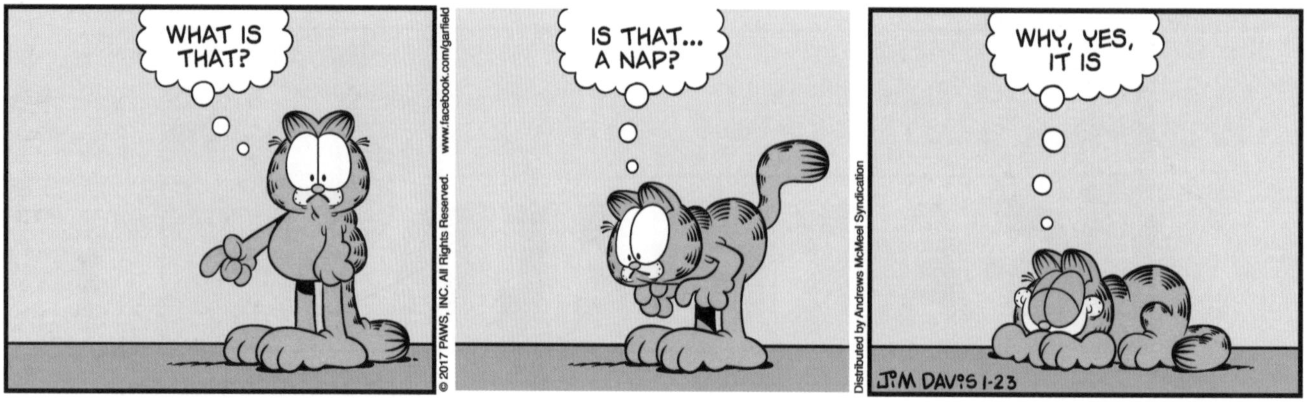
WHAT IS THAT?
© 2017 PAWS, INC. All Rights Reserved. www.facebook.com/garfield
IS THAT... A NAP?
Distributed by Andrews McMeel Syndication
WHY, YES, IT IS
JIM DAVIS 1-23

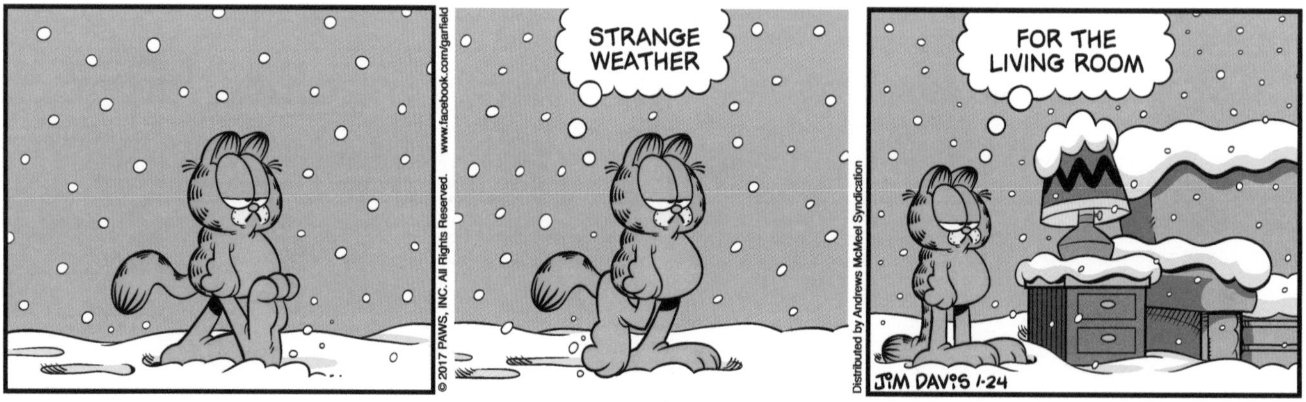
© 2017 PAWS, INC. All Rights Reserved. www.facebook.com/garfield
STRANGE WEATHER
Distributed by Andrews McMeel Syndication
FOR THE LIVING ROOM
JIM DAVIS 1-24

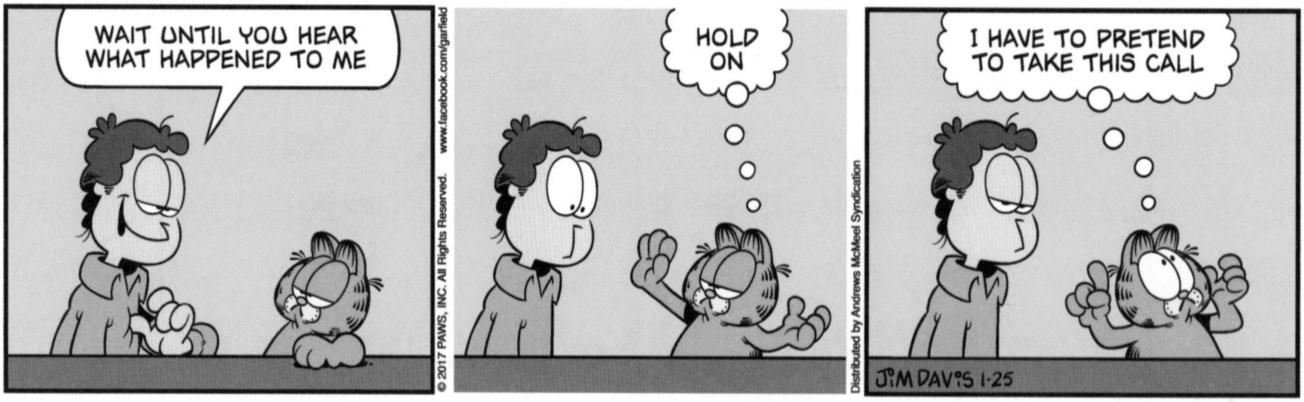
WAIT UNTIL YOU HEAR WHAT HAPPENED TO ME
© 2017 PAWS, INC. All Rights Reserved. www.facebook.com/garfield
HOLD ON
Distributed by Andrews McMeel Syndication
I HAVE TO PRETEND TO TAKE THIS CALL
JIM DAVIS 1-25

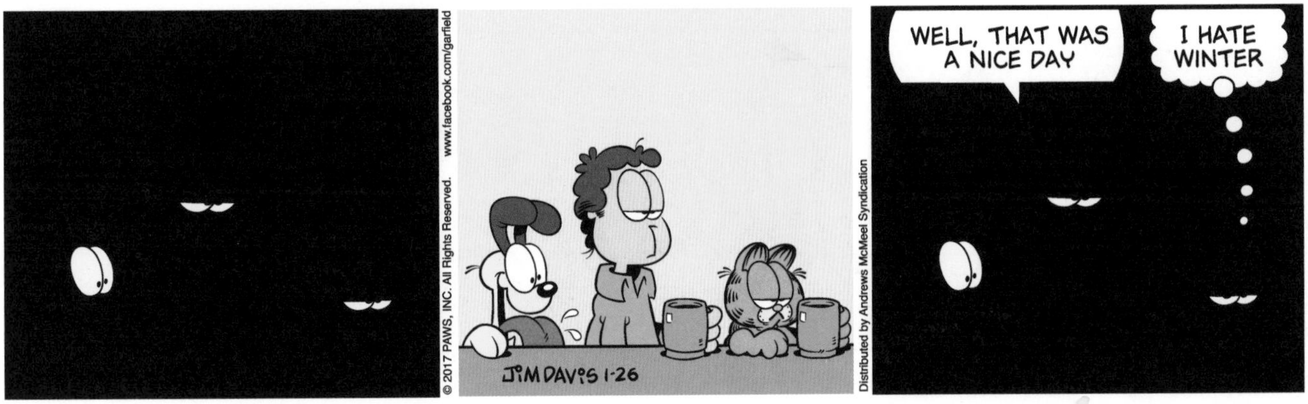
© 2017 PAWS, INC. All Rights Reserved. www.facebook.com/garfield
JIM DAVIS 1-26
Distributed by Andrews McMeel Syndication
WELL, THAT WAS A NICE DAY
I HATE WINTER

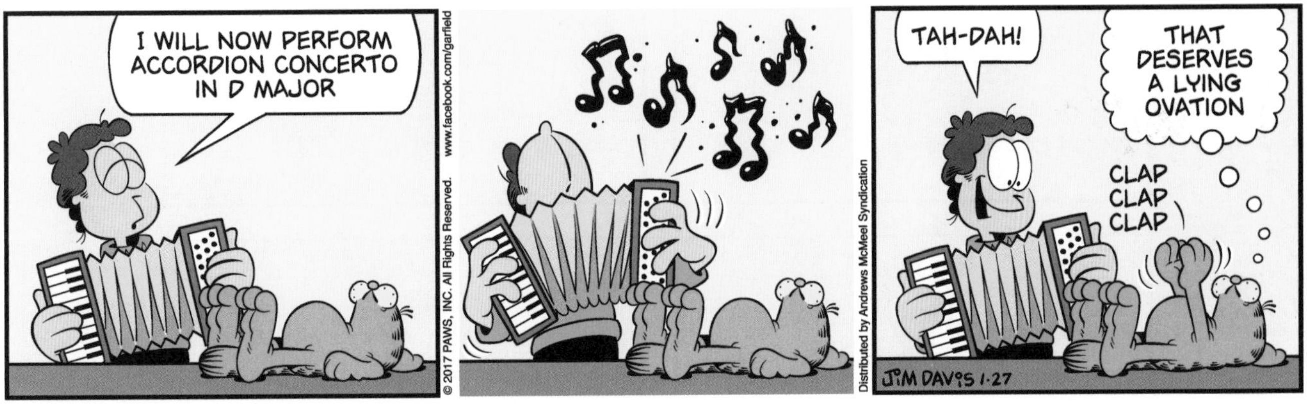
I WILL NOW PERFORM ACCORDION CONCERTO IN D MAJOR
© 2017 PAWS, INC. All Rights Reserved. www.facebook.com/garfield
Distributed by Andrews McMeel Syndication
TAH-DAH!
THAT DESERVES A LYING OVATION
CLAP CLAP CLAP
JIM DAVIS 1-27

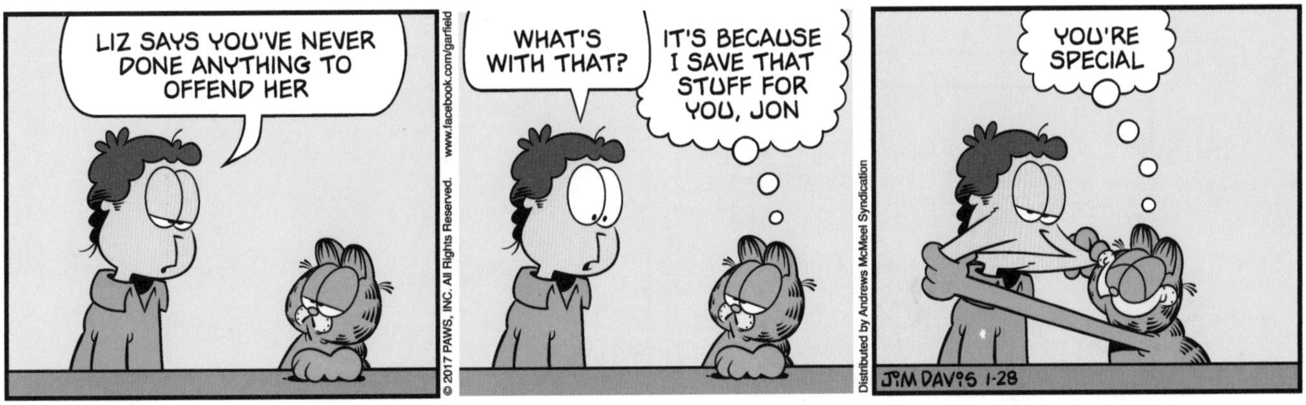
LIZ SAYS YOU'VE NEVER DONE ANYTHING TO OFFEND HER
© 2017 PAWS, INC. All Rights Reserved. www.facebook.com/garfield
WHAT'S WITH THAT?
IT'S BECAUSE I SAVE THAT STUFF FOR YOU, JON
Distributed by Andrews McMeel Syndication
YOU'RE SPECIAL
JIM DAVIS 1-28

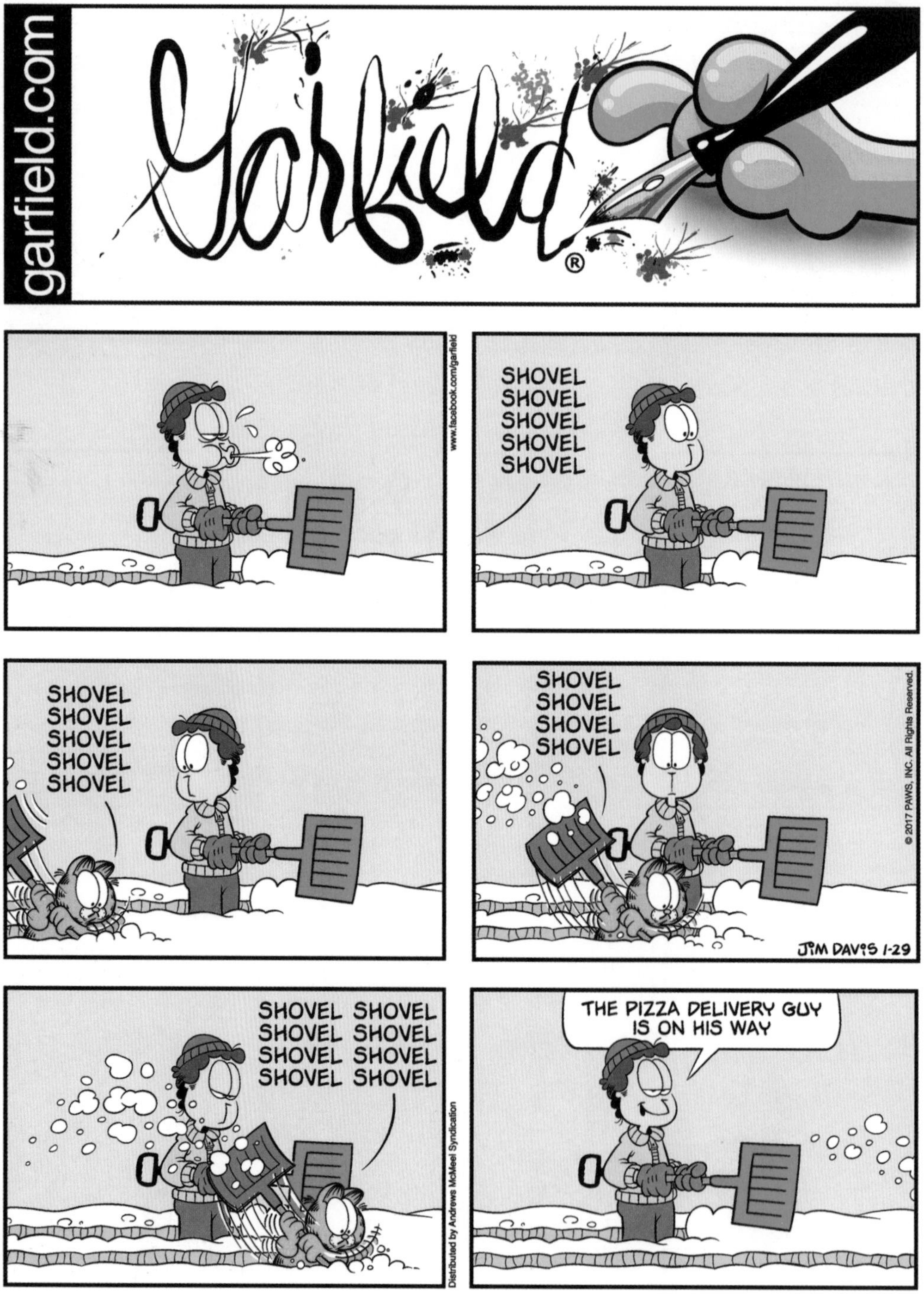
garfield.com
Garfield
www.facebook.com/garfield
SHOVEL
SHOVEL
SHOVEL
SHOVEL
SHOVEL
SHOVEL
SHOVEL
SHOVEL
SHOVEL
SHOVEL
SHOVEL
SHOVEL
SHOVEL
SHOVEL
© 2017 PAWS, INC. All Rights Reserved.
JIM DAVIS 1-29
SHOVEL SHOVEL
SHOVEL SHOVEL
SHOVEL SHOVEL
SHOVEL SHOVEL
Distributed by Andrews McMeel Syndication
THE PIZZA DELIVERY GUY IS ON HIS WAY

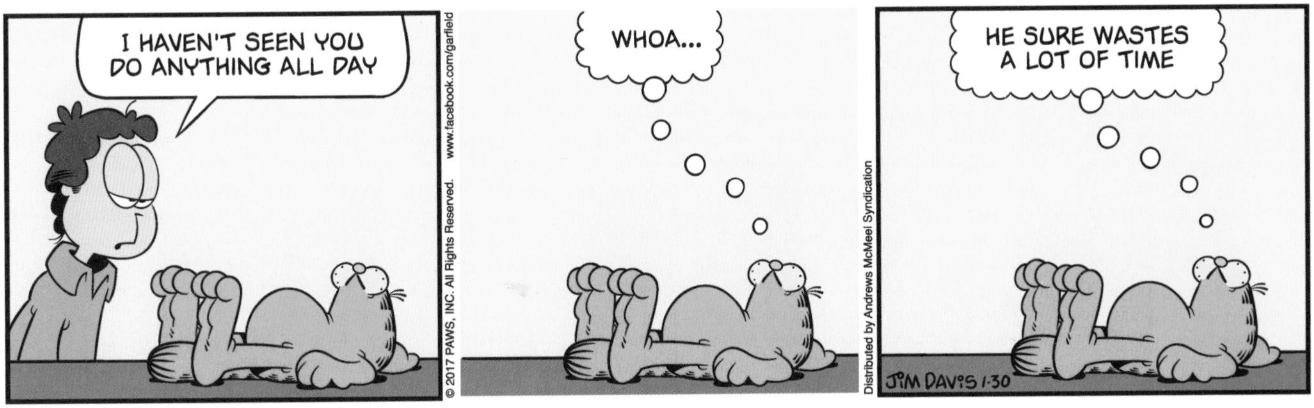
I HAVEN'T SEEN YOU DO ANYTHING ALL DAY
WHOA...
HE SURE WASTES A LOT OF TIME
© 2017 PAWS, INC. All Rights Reserved. www.facebook.com/garfield
Distributed by Andrews McMeel Syndication
JIM DAVIS 1-30

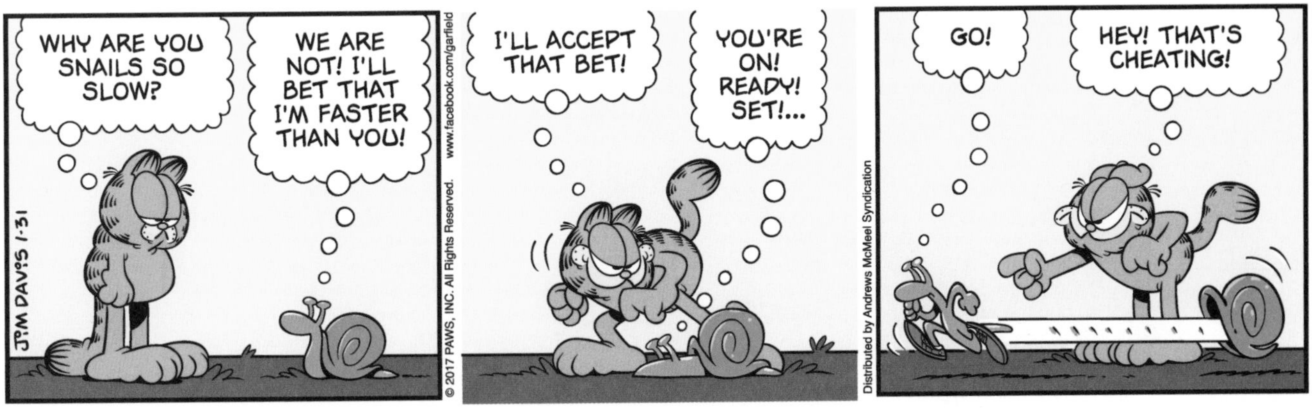
WHY ARE YOU SNAILS SO SLOW?
WE ARE NOT! I'LL BET THAT I'M FASTER THAN YOU!
I'LL ACCEPT THAT BET!
YOU'RE ON! READY! SET!...
GO!
HEY! THAT'S CHEATING!
JIM DAVIS 1-31
© 2017 PAWS, INC. All Rights Reserved. www.facebook.com/garfield
Distributed by Andrews McMeel Syndication

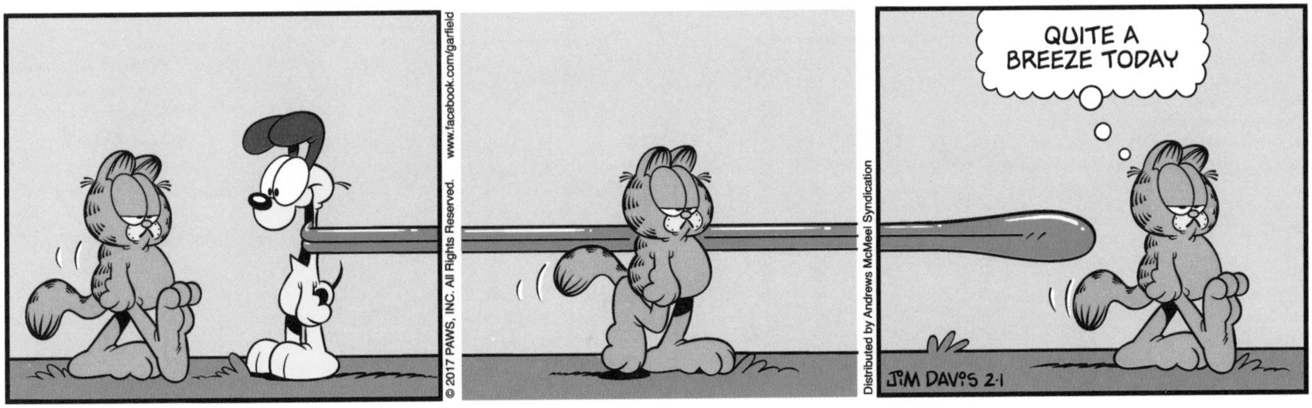
QUITE A BREEZE TODAY
© 2017 PAWS, INC. All Rights Reserved. www.facebook.com/garfield
Distributed by Andrews McMeel Syndication
JIM DAVIS 2-1

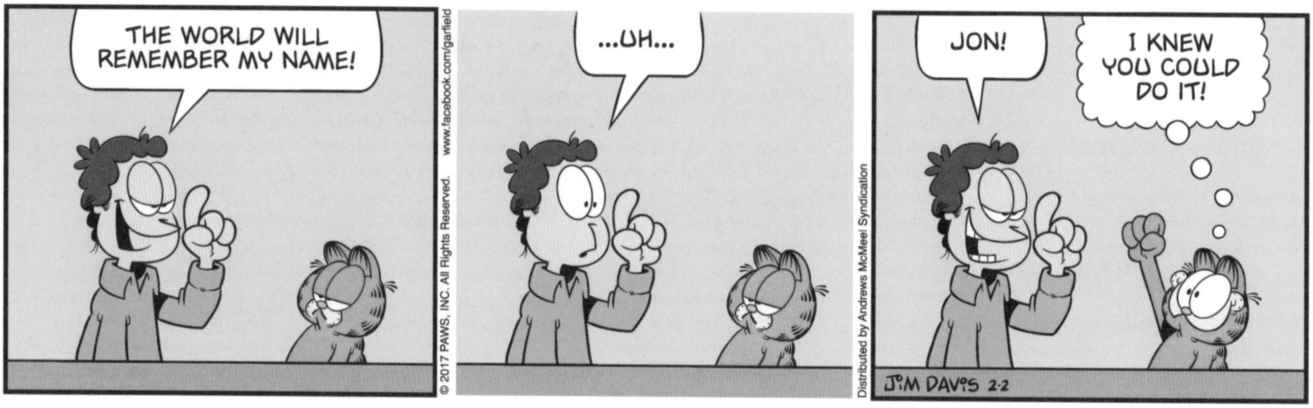
THE WORLD WILL REMEMBER MY NAME!
...UH...
JON!
I KNEW YOU COULD DO IT!
JIM DAVIS 2-2


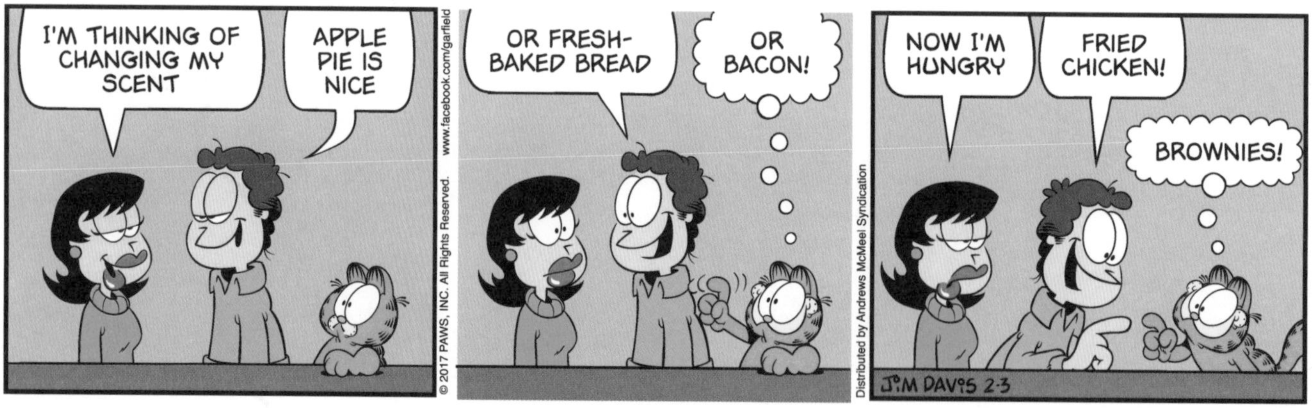
I'M THINKING OF CHANGING MY SCENT
APPLE PIE IS NICE
OR FRESH-BAKED BREAD
OR BACON!
NOW I'M HUNGRY
FRIED CHICKEN!
BROWNIES!
JIM DAVIS 2-3


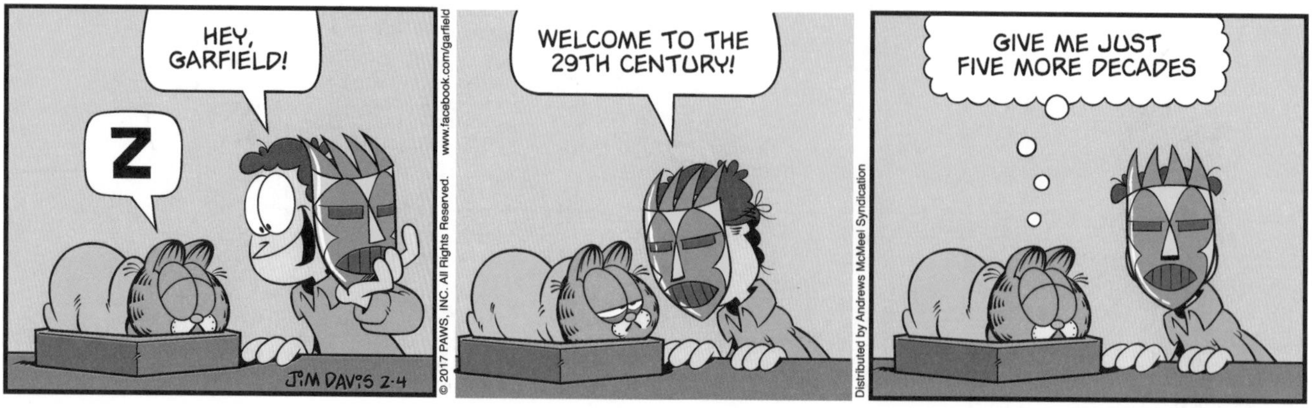
Z
HEY, GARFIELD!
JIM DAVIS 2-4
WELCOME TO THE 29TH CENTURY!
GIVE ME JUST FIVE MORE DECADES

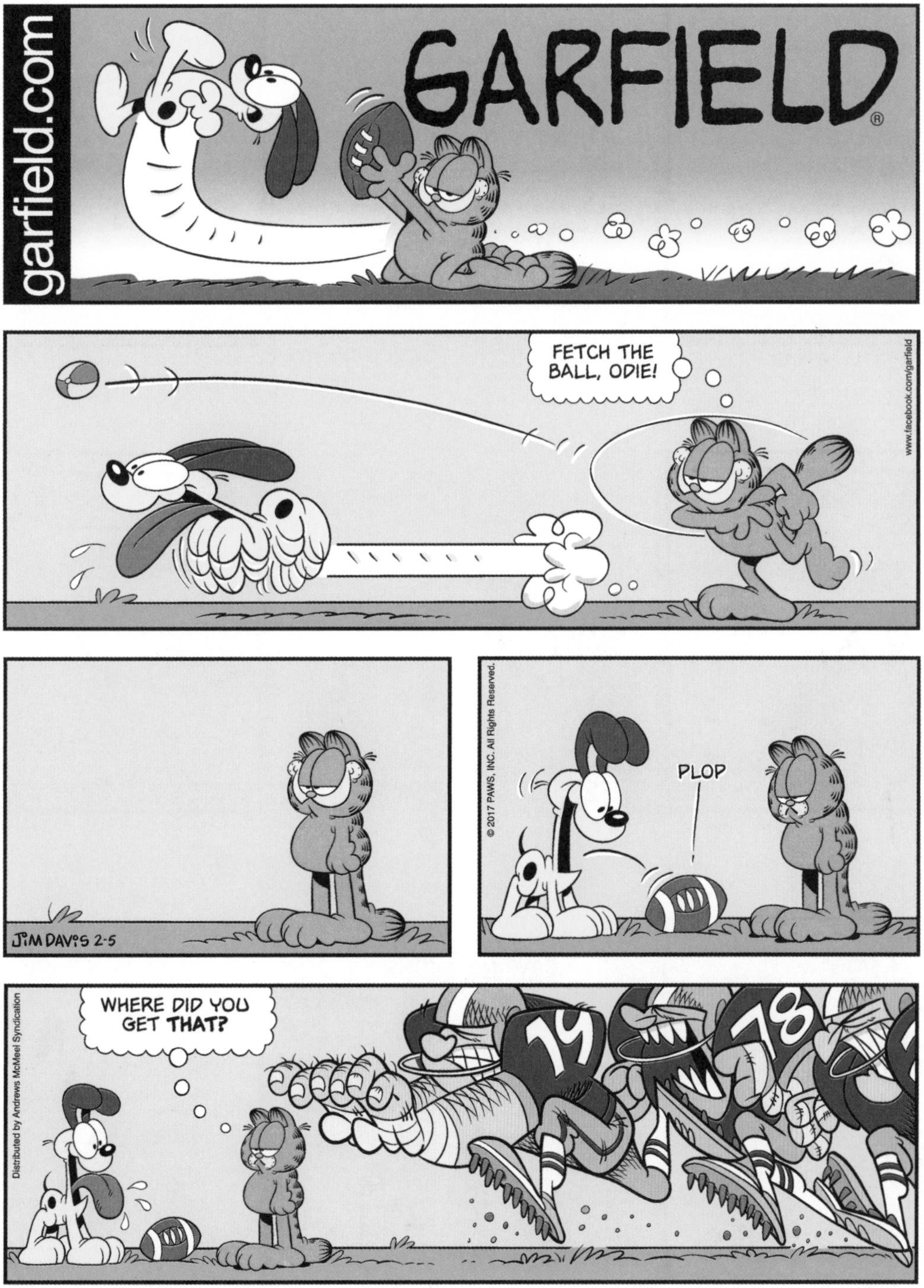
garfield.com
GARFIELD®
FETCH THE BALL, ODIE!
www.facebook.com/garfield
JIM DAVIS 2-5
© 2017 PAWS, INC. All Rights Reserved.
PLOP
Distributed by Andrews McMeel Syndication
WHERE DID YOU GET THAT?
19
78

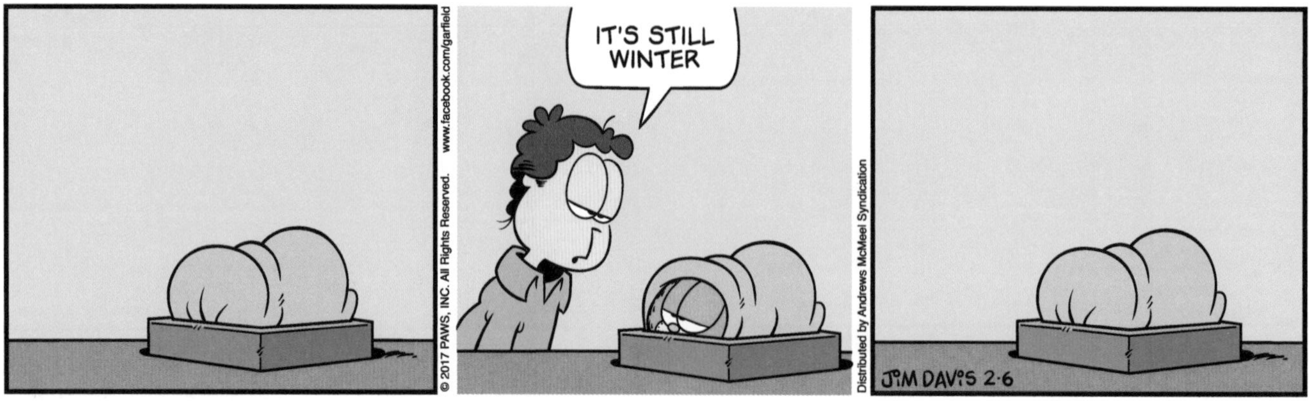
IT'S STILL WINTER
JIM DAVIS 2-6
© 2017 PAWS, INC. All Rights Reserved. www.facebook.com/garfield
Distributed by Andrews McMeel Syndication

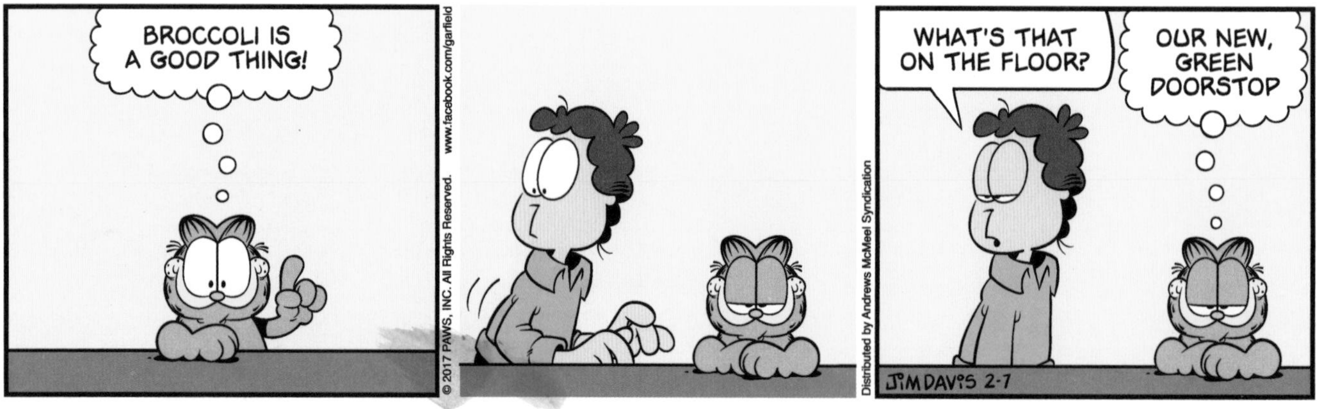
BROCCOLI IS A GOOD THING!
WHAT'S THAT ON THE FLOOR?
OUR NEW, GREEN DOORSTOP
JIM DAVIS 2-7
© 2017 PAWS, INC. All Rights Reserved. www.facebook.com/garfield
Distributed by Andrews McMeel Syndication

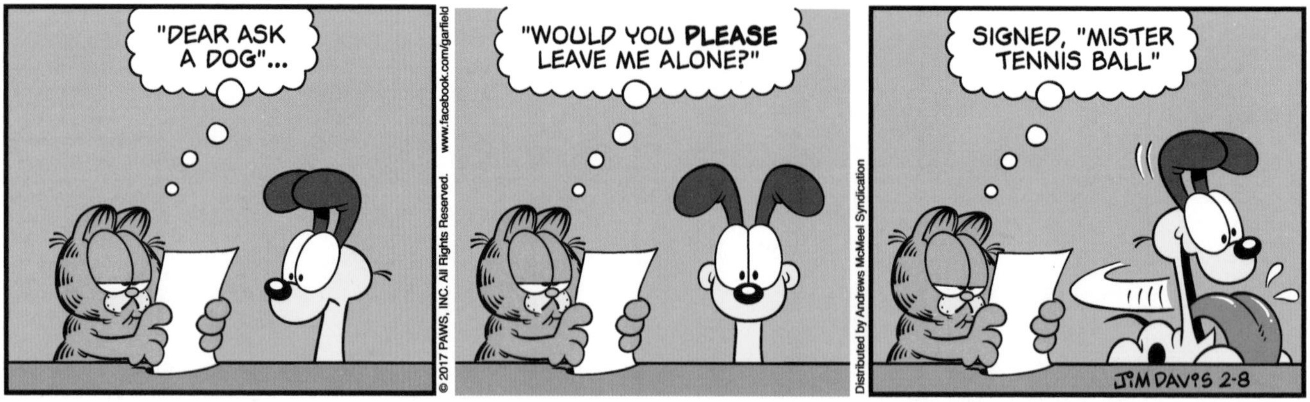
"DEAR ASK A DOG"...
"WOULD YOU **PLEASE** LEAVE ME ALONE?"
SIGNED, "MISTER TENNIS BALL"
JIM DAVIS 2-8
© 2017 PAWS, INC. All Rights Reserved. www.facebook.com/garfield
Distributed by Andrews McMeel Syndication

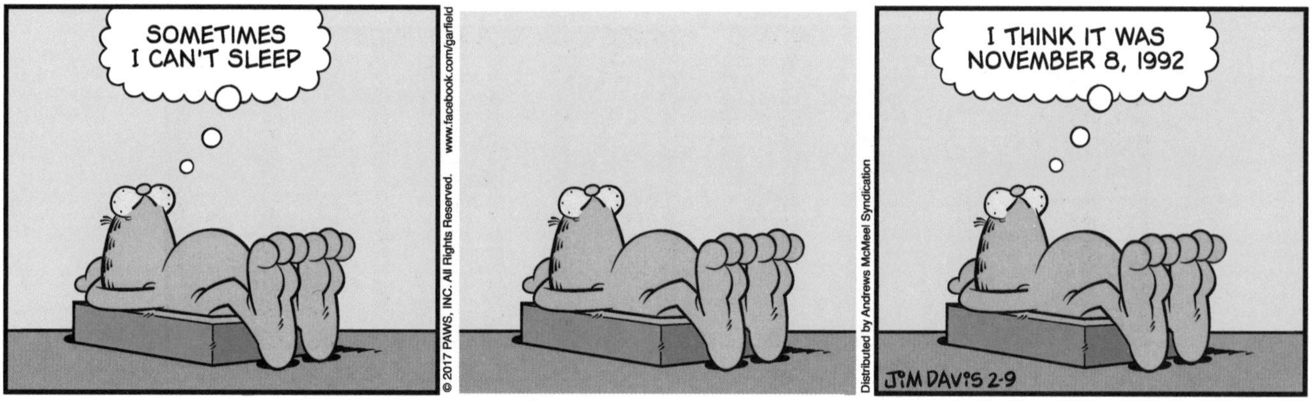
SOMETIMES I CAN'T SLEEP
© 2017 PAWS, INC. All Rights Reserved. www.facebook.com/garfield
I THINK IT WAS NOVEMBER 8, 1992
Distributed by Andrews McMeel Syndication
JIM DAVIS 2-9

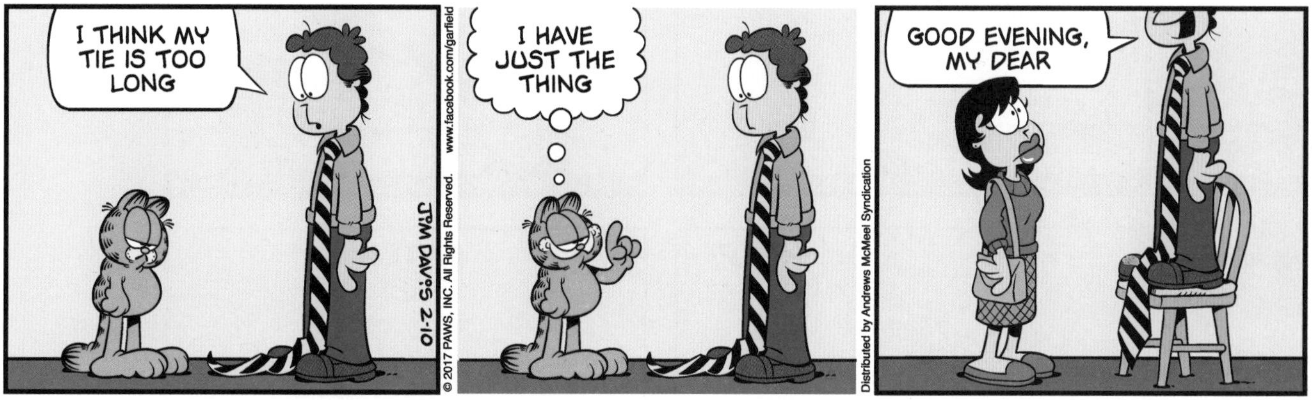
I THINK MY TIE IS TOO LONG
JIM DAVIS 2-10
© 2017 PAWS, INC. All Rights Reserved. www.facebook.com/garfield
I HAVE JUST THE THING
Distributed by Andrews McMeel Syndication
GOOD EVENING, MY DEAR

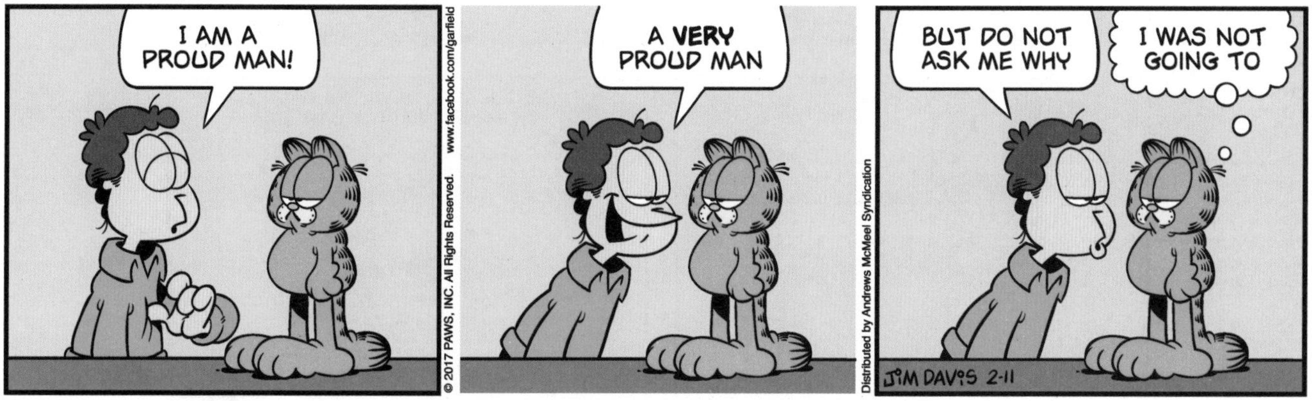
I AM A PROUD MAN!
© 2017 PAWS, INC. All Rights Reserved. www.facebook.com/garfield
A **VERY** PROUD MAN
Distributed by Andrews McMeel Syndication
BUT DO NOT ASK ME WHY
I WAS NOT GOING TO
JIM DAVIS 2-11

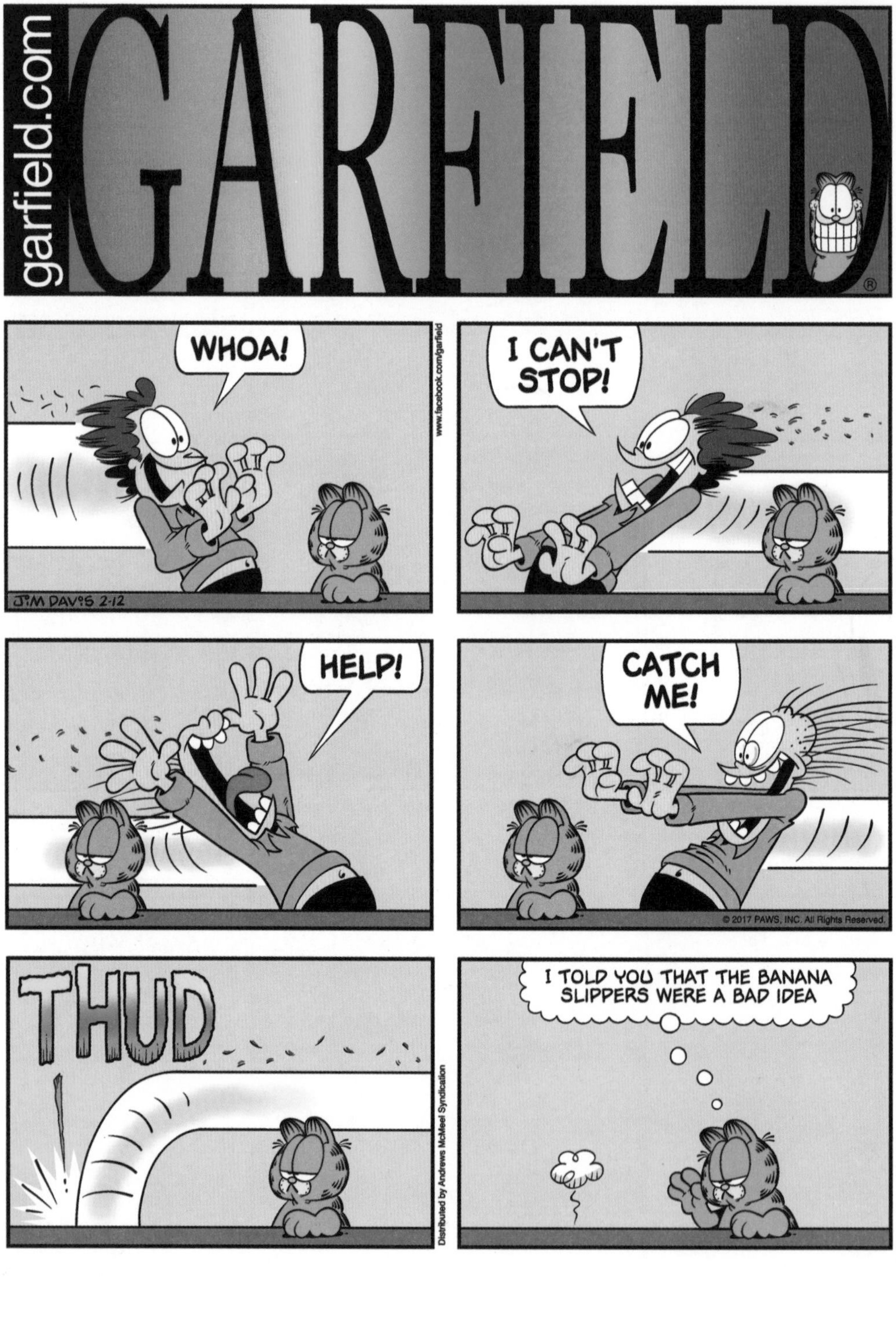

garfield.com
GARFIELD
WHOA!
JIM DAVIS 2-12
www.facebook.com/garfield
I CAN'T STOP!
HELP!
CATCH ME!
© 2017 PAWS, INC. All Rights Reserved.
THUD
Distributed by Andrews McMeel Syndication
I TOLD YOU THAT THE BANANA SLIPPERS WERE A BAD IDEA

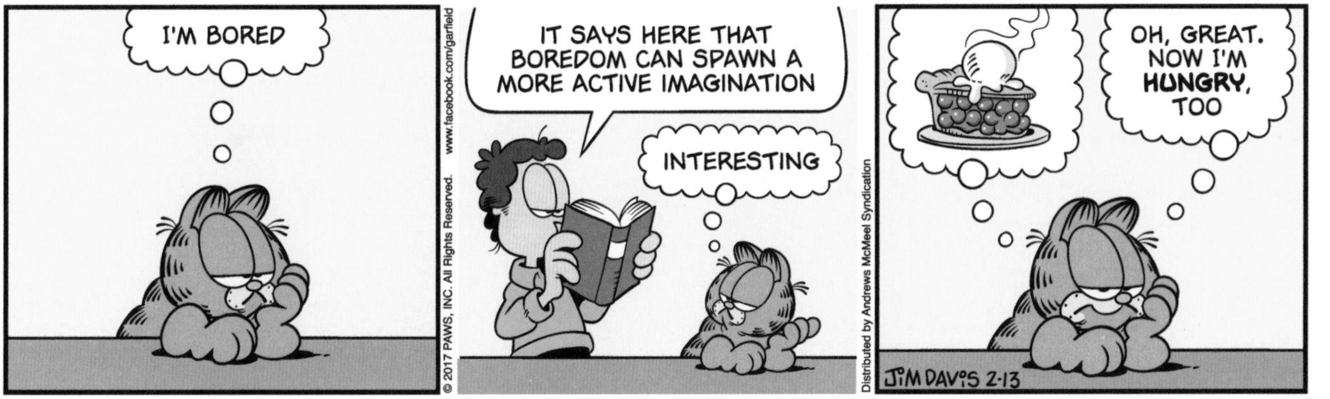
I'M BORED
© 2017 PAWS, INC. All Rights Reserved. www.facebook.com/garfield
IT SAYS HERE THAT BOREDOM CAN SPAWN A MORE ACTIVE IMAGINATION
INTERESTING
Distributed by Andrews McMeel Syndication
OH, GREAT. NOW I'M **HUNGRY**, TOO
JIM DAVIS 2-13

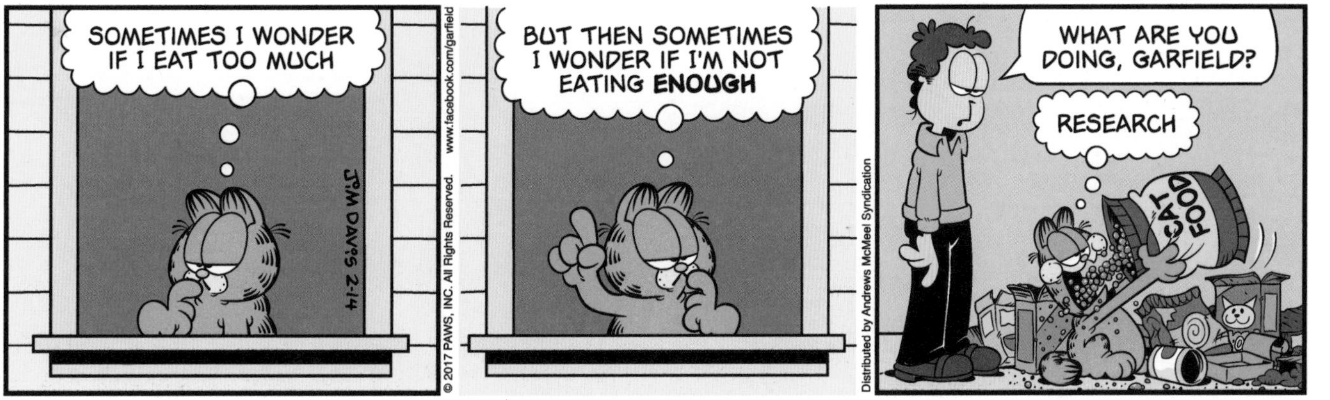
SOMETIMES I WONDER IF I EAT TOO MUCH
JIM DAVIS 2-14
© 2017 PAWS, INC. All Rights Reserved. www.facebook.com/garfield
BUT THEN SOMETIMES I WONDER IF I'M NOT EATING **ENOUGH**
Distributed by Andrews McMeel Syndication
WHAT ARE YOU DOING, GARFIELD?
RESEARCH
CAT FOOD

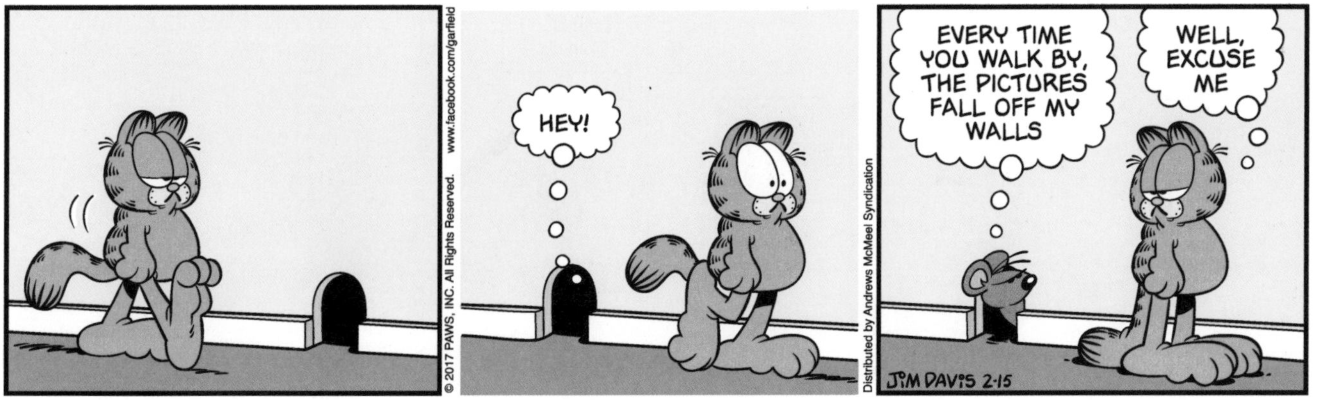
© 2017 PAWS, INC. All Rights Reserved. www.facebook.com/garfield
HEY!
Distributed by Andrews McMeel Syndication
EVERY TIME YOU WALK BY, THE PICTURES FALL OFF MY WALLS
WELL, EXCUSE ME
JIM DAVIS 2-15

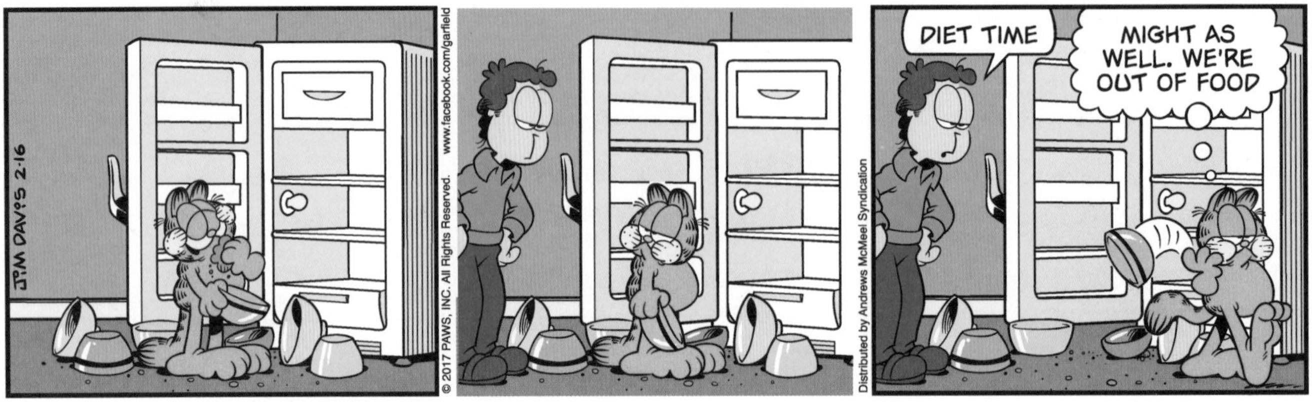
JIM DAVIS 2·16
© 2017 PAWS, INC. All Rights Reserved. www.facebook.com/garfield
Distributed by Andrews McMeel Syndication
DIET TIME
MIGHT AS WELL. WE'RE OUT OF FOOD

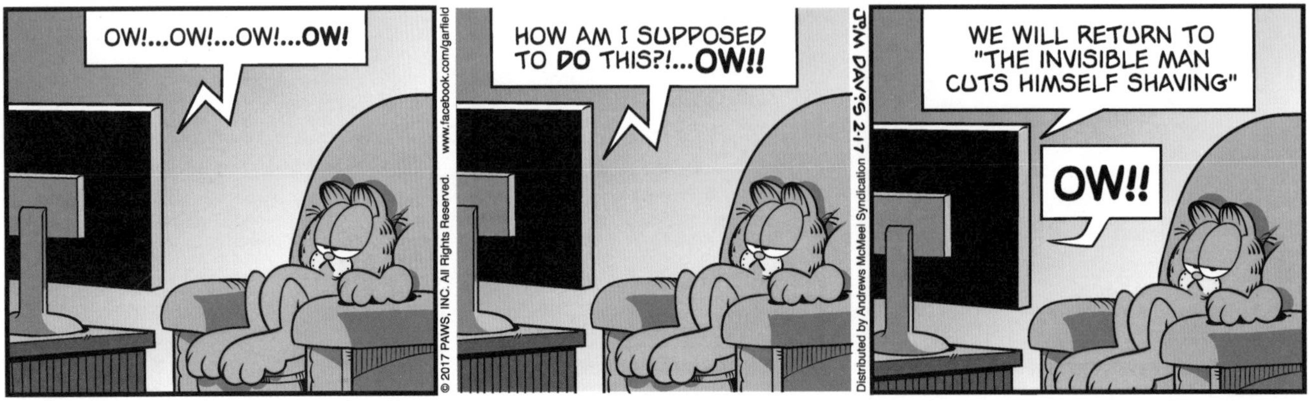
OW!...OW!...OW!...**OW!**
© 2017 PAWS, INC. All Rights Reserved. www.facebook.com/garfield
HOW AM I SUPPOSED TO **DO** THIS?!...**OW!!**
JIM DAVIS 2·17
Distributed by Andrews McMeel Syndication
WE WILL RETURN TO "THE INVISIBLE MAN CUTS HIMSELF SHAVING"
**OW!!**

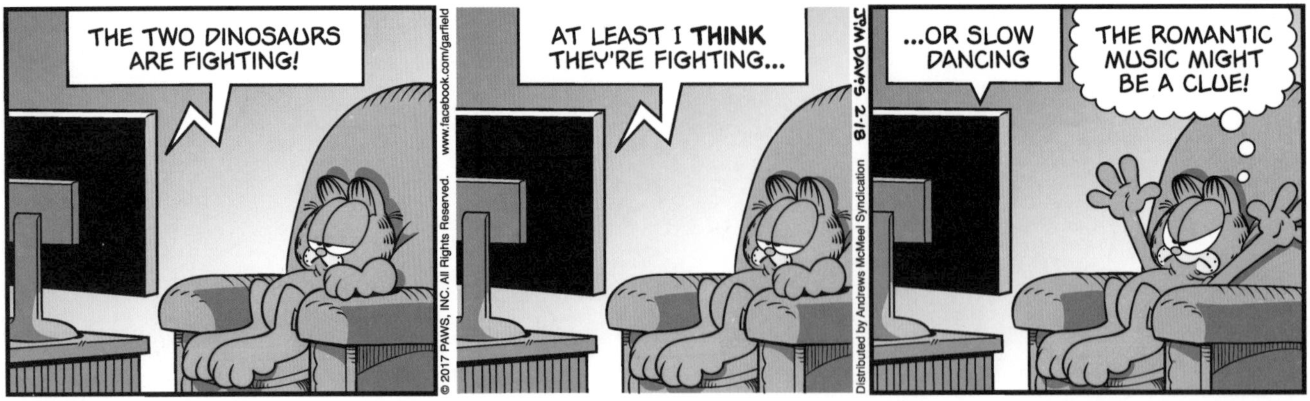
THE TWO DINOSAURS ARE FIGHTING!
© 2017 PAWS, INC. All Rights Reserved. www.facebook.com/garfield
AT LEAST I **THINK** THEY'RE FIGHTING...
JIM DAVIS 2·18
Distributed by Andrews McMeel Syndication
...OR SLOW DANCING
THE ROMANTIC MUSIC MIGHT BE A CLUE!

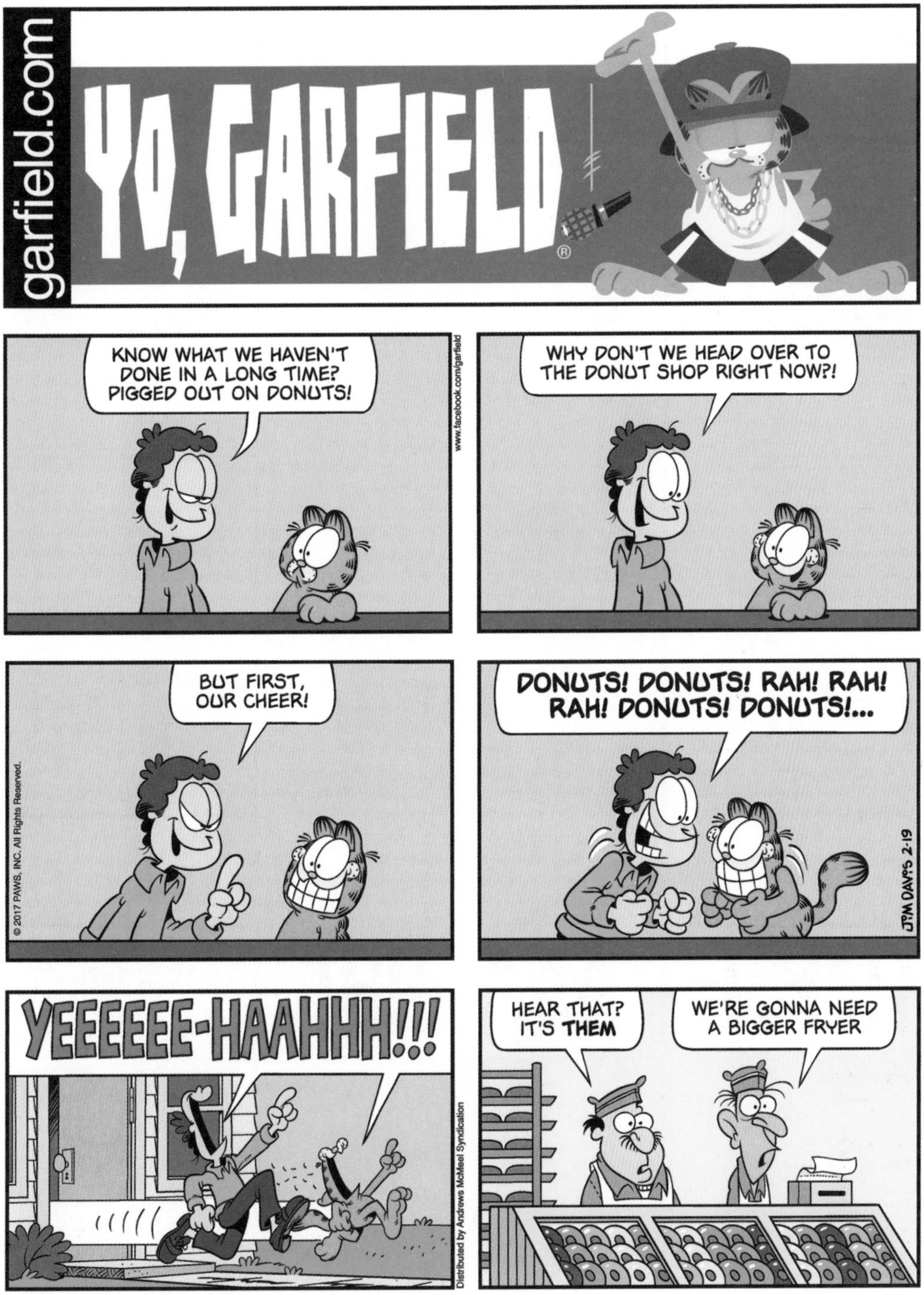

garfield.com
YO, GARFIELD
KNOW WHAT WE HAVEN'T DONE IN A LONG TIME? PIGGED OUT ON DONUTS!
www.facebook.com/garfield
WHY DON'T WE HEAD OVER TO THE DONUT SHOP RIGHT NOW?!
BUT FIRST, OUR CHEER!
© 2017 PAWS, INC. All Rights Reserved.
DONUTS! DONUTS! RAH! RAH! RAH! DONUTS! DONUTS!...
JPM DAVPS 2-19
YEEEEEE-HAAHHH!!!
Distributed by Andrews McMeel Syndication
HEAR THAT? IT'S **THEM**
WE'RE GONNA NEED A BIGGER FRYER

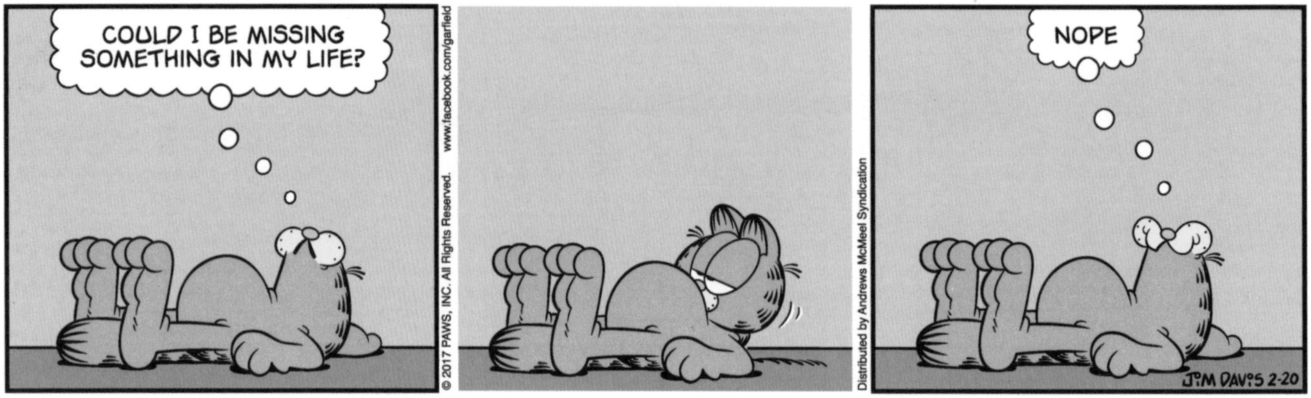
COULD I BE MISSING SOMETHING IN MY LIFE?
© 2017 PAWS, INC. All Rights Reserved. www.facebook.com/garfield
Distributed by Andrews McMeel Syndication
NOPE
JIM DAVIS 2-20

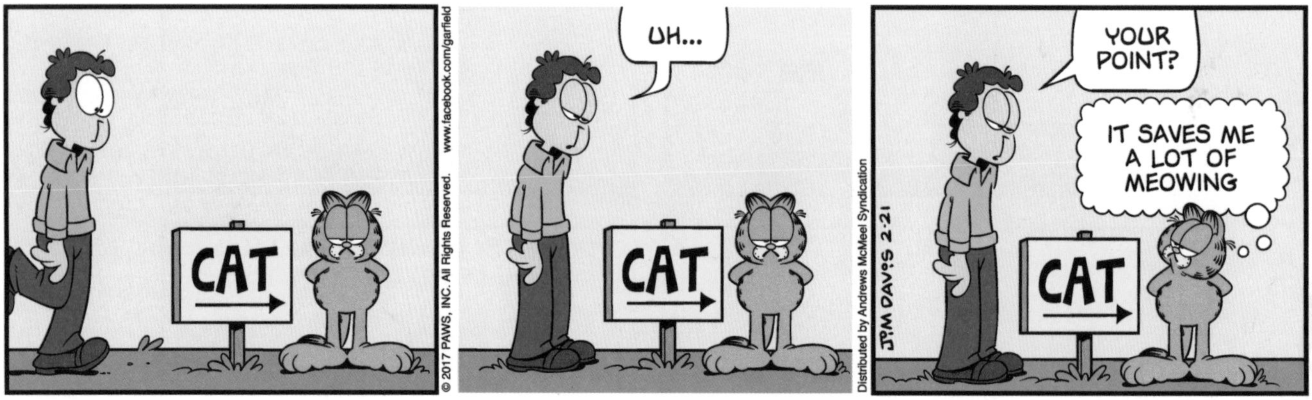
CAT
© 2017 PAWS, INC. All Rights Reserved. www.facebook.com/garfield
UH...
CAT
Distributed by Andrews McMeel Syndication
JIM DAVIS 2-21
YOUR POINT?
IT SAVES ME A LOT OF MEOWING
CAT

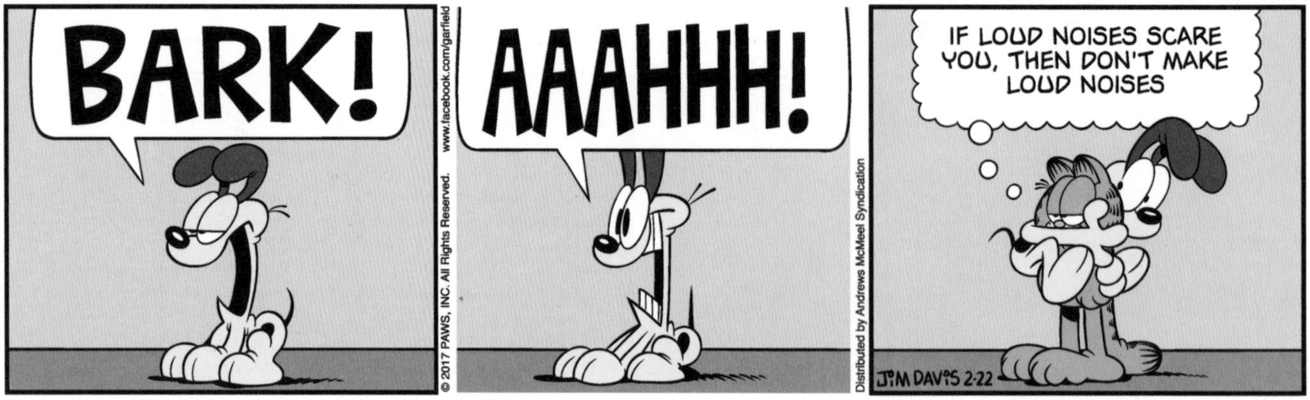
BARK!
© 2017 PAWS, INC. All Rights Reserved. www.facebook.com/garfield
AAAHHH!
Distributed by Andrews McMeel Syndication
IF LOUD NOISES SCARE YOU, THEN DON'T MAKE LOUD NOISES
JIM DAVIS 2-22

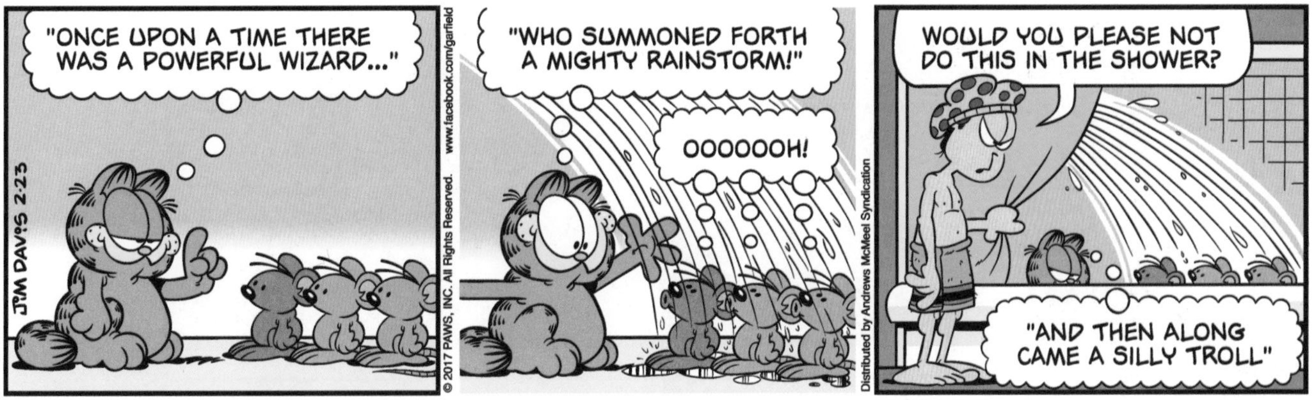
JIM DAVIS 2·23
"ONCE UPON A TIME THERE WAS A POWERFUL WIZARD..."
© 2017 PAWS, INC. All Rights Reserved. www.facebook.com/garfield
"WHO SUMMONED FORTH A MIGHTY RAINSTORM!"
OOOOOOH!
Distributed by Andrews McMeel Syndication
WOULD YOU PLEASE NOT DO THIS IN THE SHOWER?
"AND THEN ALONG CAME A SILLY TROLL"

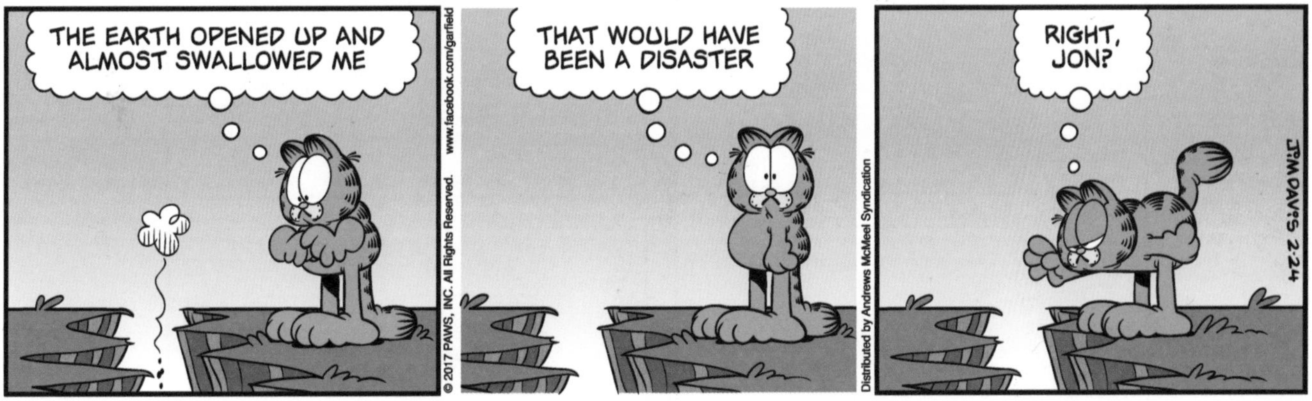
THE EARTH OPENED UP AND ALMOST SWALLOWED ME
© 2017 PAWS, INC. All Rights Reserved. www.facebook.com/garfield
THAT WOULD HAVE BEEN A DISASTER
Distributed by Andrews McMeel Syndication
RIGHT, JON?
JIM DAVIS 2·24

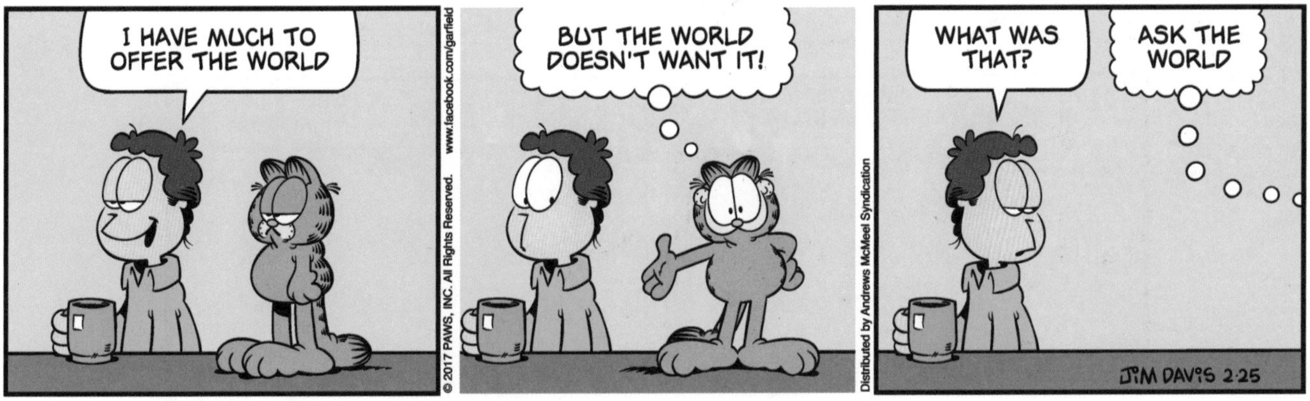
I HAVE MUCH TO OFFER THE WORLD
© 2017 PAWS, INC. All Rights Reserved. www.facebook.com/garfield
BUT THE WORLD DOESN'T WANT IT!
Distributed by Andrews McMeel Syndication
WHAT WAS THAT?
ASK THE WORLD
JIM DAVIS 2·25

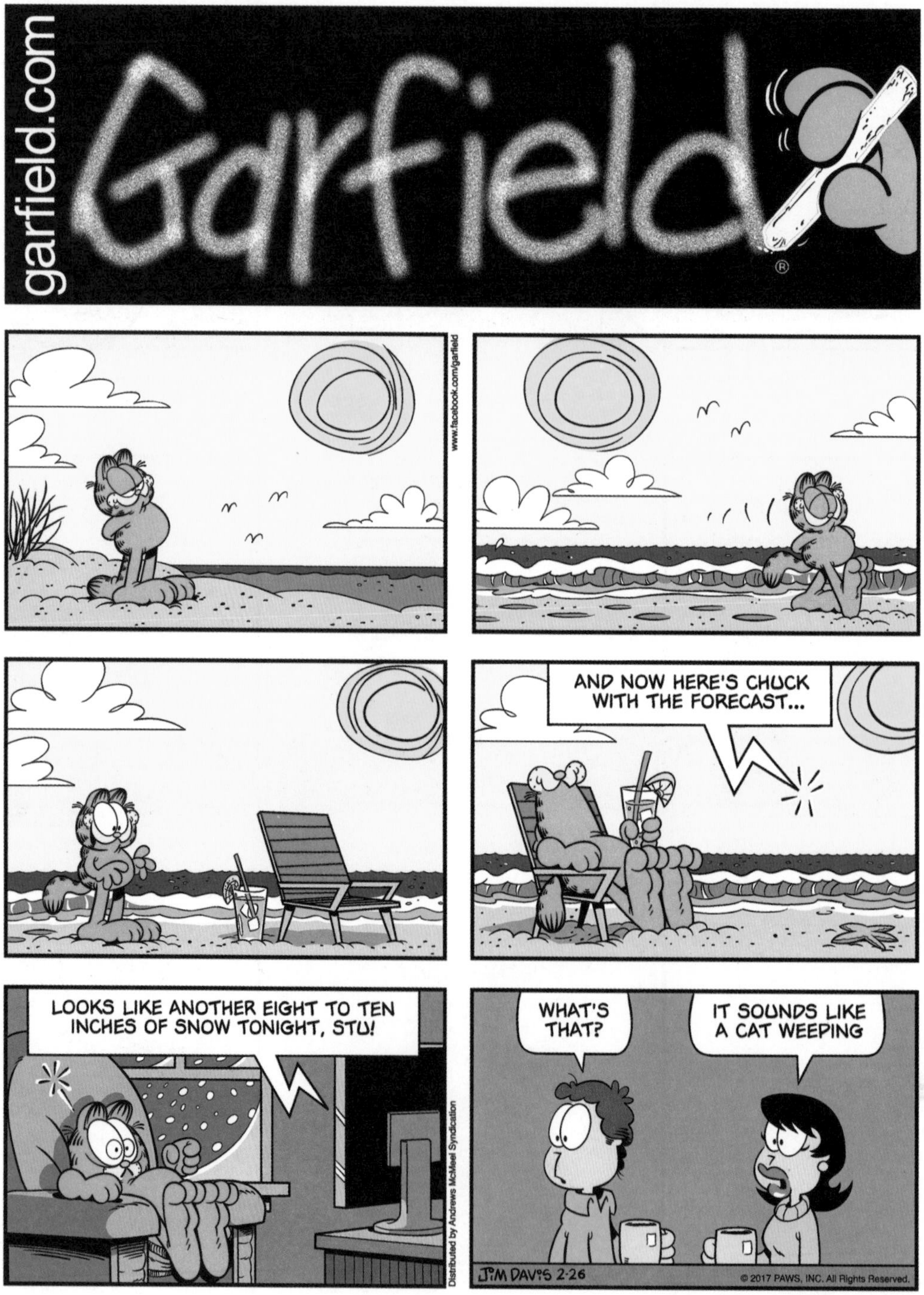
garfield.com
Garfield
www.facebook.com/garfield
AND NOW HERE'S CHUCK WITH THE FORECAST...
LOOKS LIKE ANOTHER EIGHT TO TEN INCHES OF SNOW TONIGHT, STU!
Distributed by Andrews McMeel Syndication
WHAT'S THAT?
IT SOUNDS LIKE A CAT WEEPING
JIM DAVIS 2-26
© 2017 PAWS, INC. All Rights Reserved.

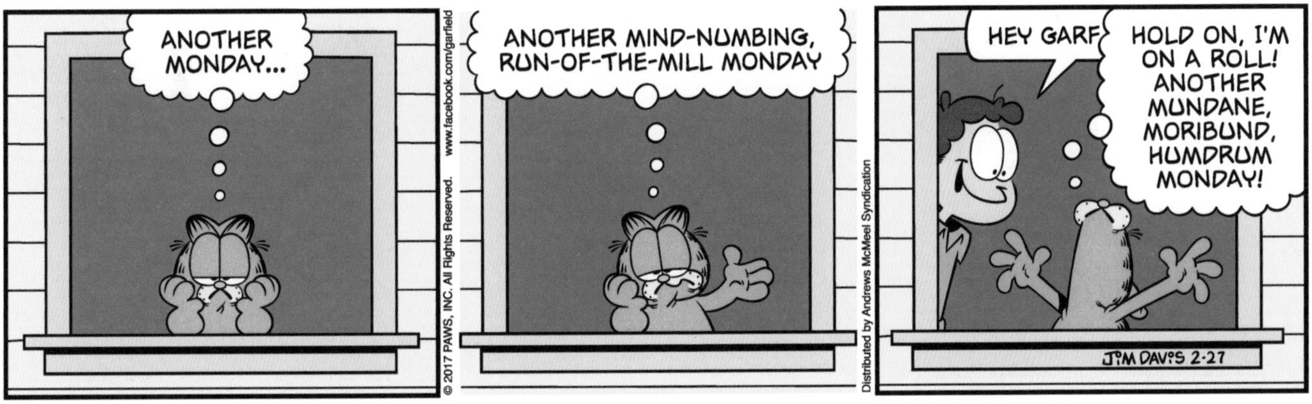
ANOTHER MONDAY...
ANOTHER MIND-NUMBING, RUN-OF-THE-MILL MONDAY
HEY GARF
HOLD ON, I'M ON A ROLL! ANOTHER MUNDANE, MORIBUND, HUMDRUM MONDAY!
JIM DAVIS 2-27
© 2017 PAWS, INC. All Rights Reserved. www.facebook.com/garfield
Distributed by Andrews McMeel Syndication

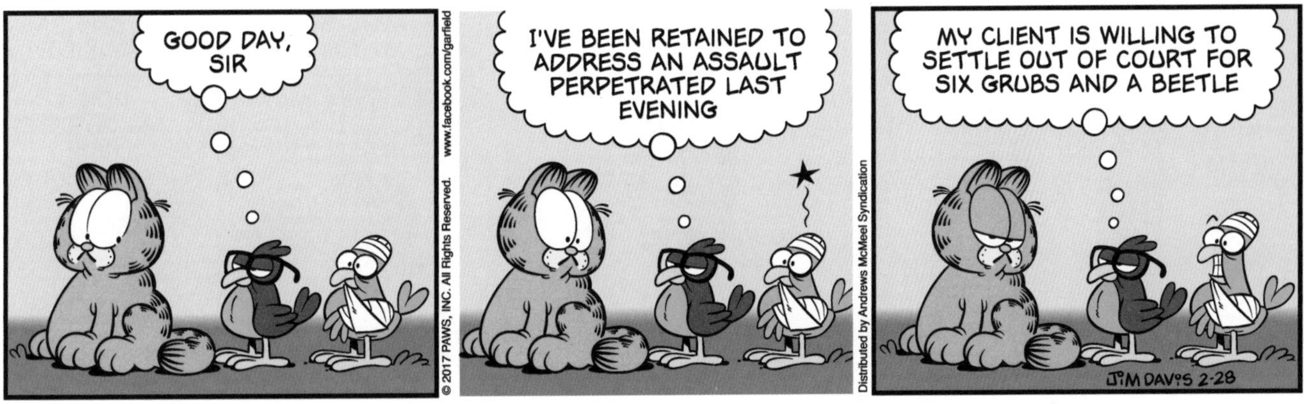
GOOD DAY, SIR
I'VE BEEN RETAINED TO ADDRESS AN ASSAULT PERPETRATED LAST EVENING
MY CLIENT IS WILLING TO SETTLE OUT OF COURT FOR SIX GRUBS AND A BEETLE
JIM DAVIS 2-28
© 2017 PAWS, INC. All Rights Reserved. www.facebook.com/garfield
Distributed by Andrews McMeel Syndication

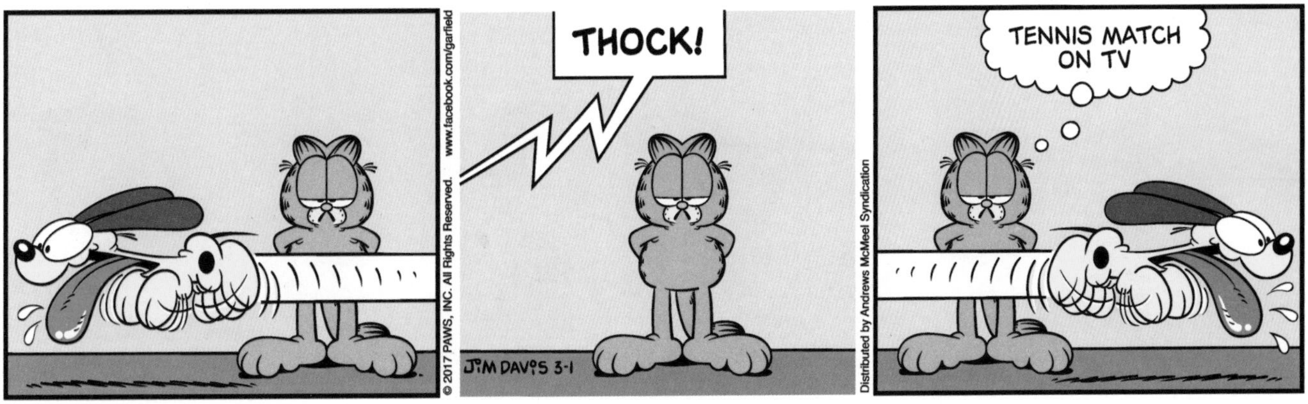
THOCK!
JIM DAVIS 3-1
TENNIS MATCH ON TV
© 2017 PAWS, INC. All Rights Reserved. www.facebook.com/garfield
Distributed by Andrews McMeel Syndication

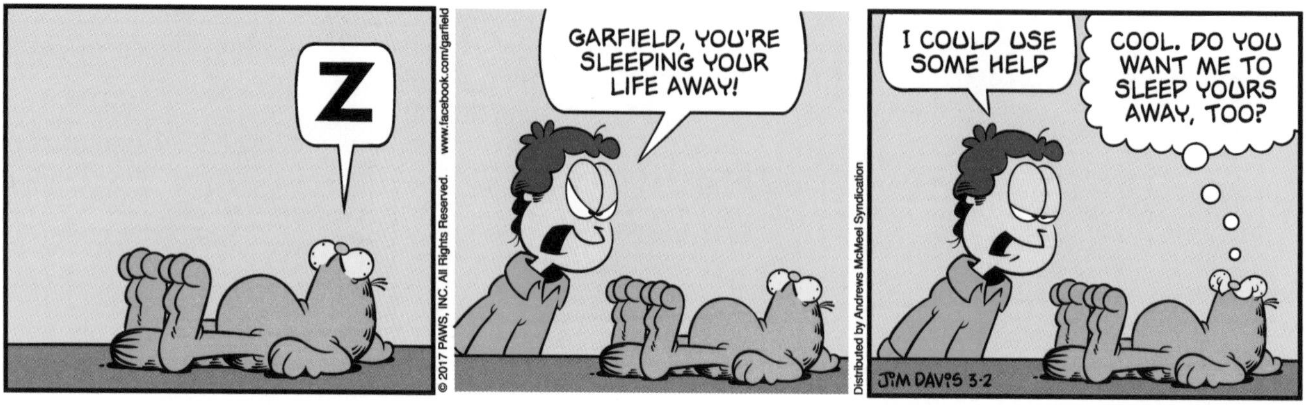

Z
GARFIELD, YOU'RE SLEEPING YOUR LIFE AWAY!
I COULD USE SOME HELP
COOL. DO YOU WANT ME TO SLEEP YOURS AWAY, TOO?
JIM DAVIS 3-2
© 2017 PAWS, INC. All Rights Reserved. www.facebook.com/garfield
Distributed by Andrews McMeel Syndication


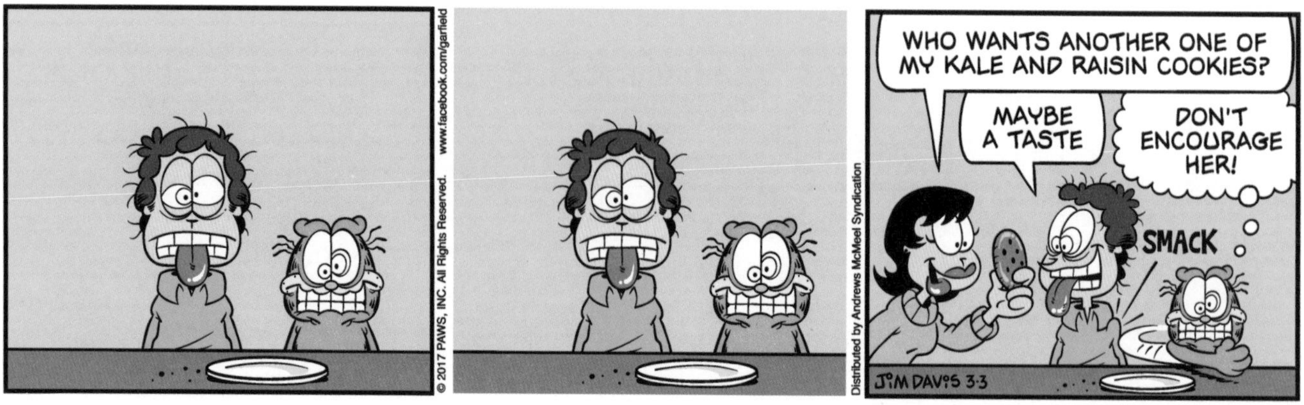

WHO WANTS ANOTHER ONE OF MY KALE AND RAISIN COOKIES?
MAYBE A TASTE
DON'T ENCOURAGE HER!
SMACK
JIM DAVIS 3-3
© 2017 PAWS, INC. All Rights Reserved. www.facebook.com/garfield
Distributed by Andrews McMeel Syndication


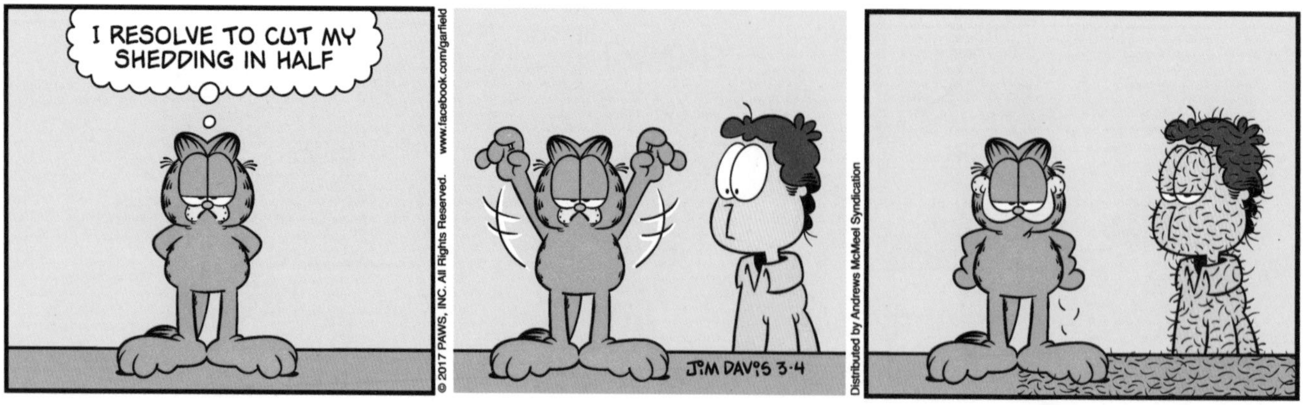

I RESOLVE TO CUT MY SHEDDING IN HALF
JIM DAVIS 3-4
© 2017 PAWS, INC. All Rights Reserved. www.facebook.com/garfield
Distributed by Andrews McMeel Syndication

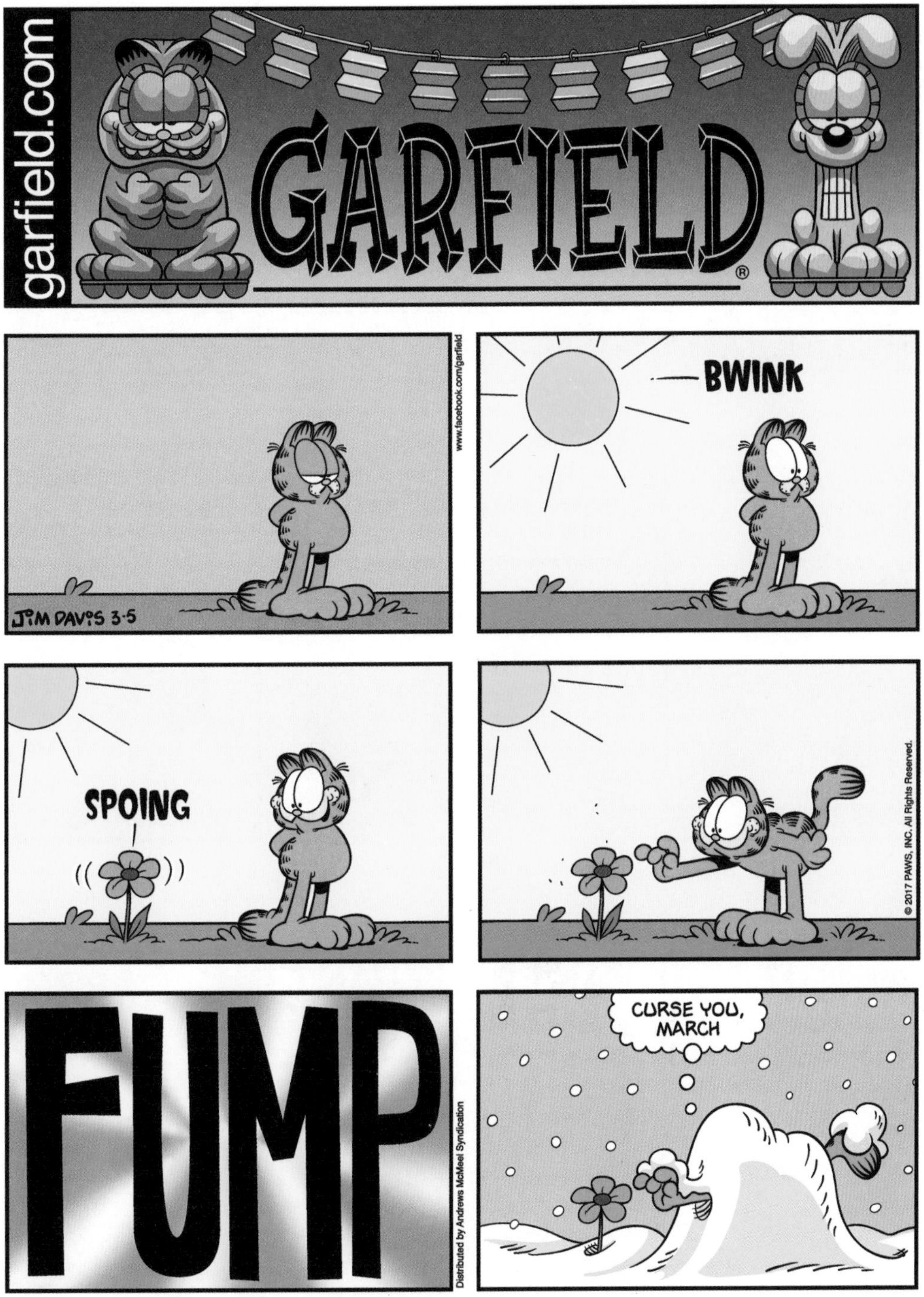
garfield.com
GARFIELD®
www.facebook.com/garfield
JIM DAVIS 3-5
BWINK
SPOING
© 2017 PAWS, INC. All Rights Reserved.
FUMP
Distributed by Andrews McMeel Syndication
CURSE YOU, MARCH

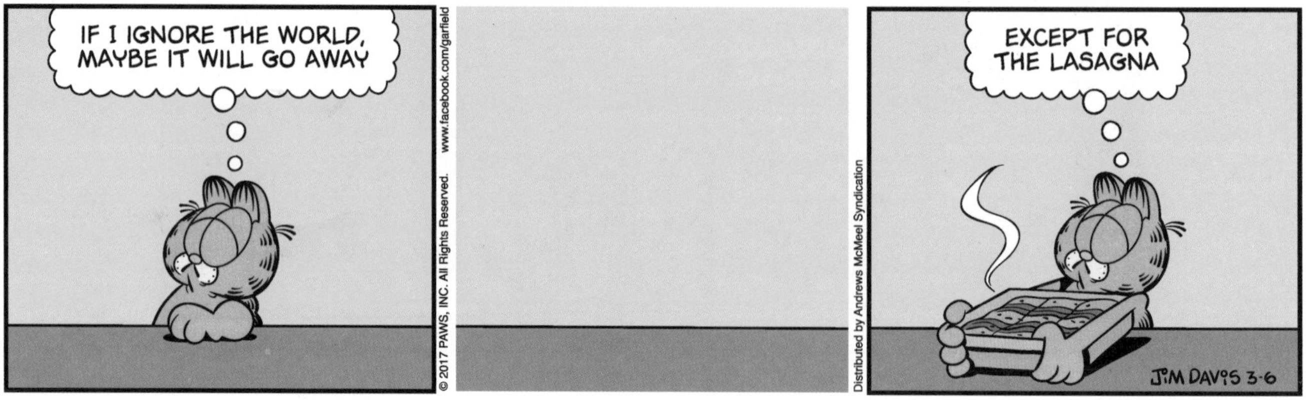
IF I IGNORE THE WORLD, MAYBE IT WILL GO AWAY
EXCEPT FOR THE LASAGNA
JIM DAVIS 3-6
© 2017 PAWS, INC. All Rights Reserved. www.facebook.com/garfield
Distributed by Andrews McMeel Syndication

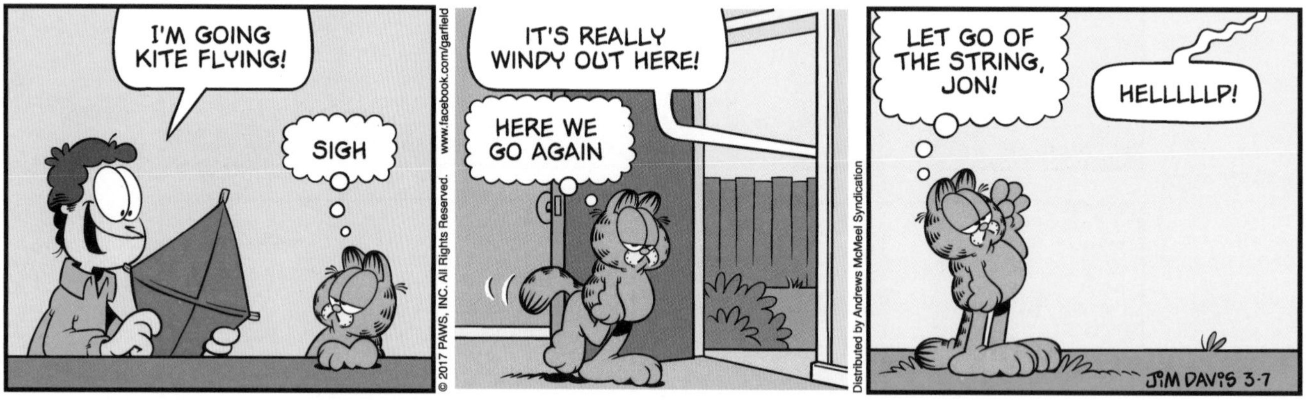
I'M GOING KITE FLYING!
SIGH
IT'S REALLY WINDY OUT HERE!
HERE WE GO AGAIN
LET GO OF THE STRING, JON!
HELLLLLP!
JIM DAVIS 3-7
© 2017 PAWS, INC. All Rights Reserved. www.facebook.com/garfield
Distributed by Andrews McMeel Syndication

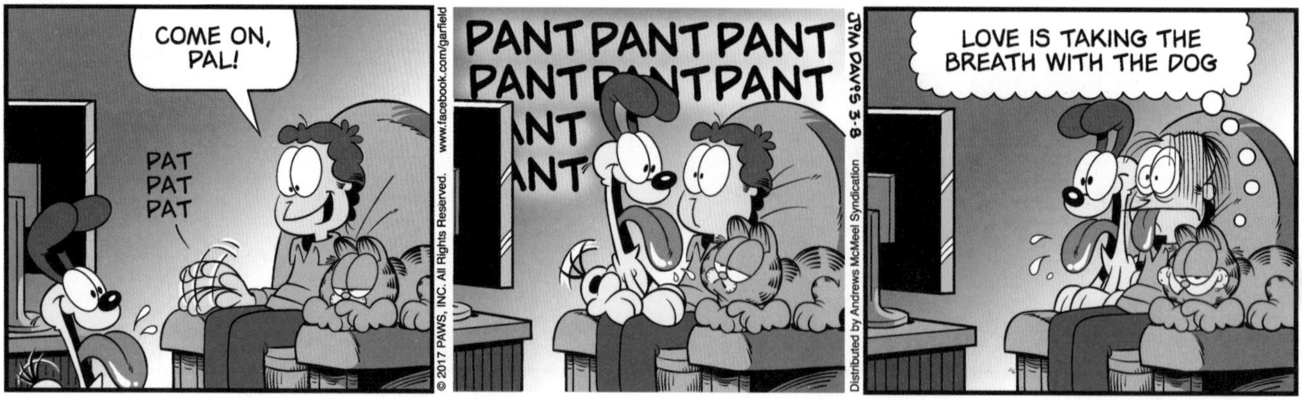
COME ON, PAL!
PAT PAT PAT
PANT PANT PANT
JIM DAVIS 3-8
LOVE IS TAKING THE BREATH WITH THE DOG
© 2017 PAWS, INC. All Rights Reserved. www.facebook.com/garfield
Distributed by Andrews McMeel Syndication

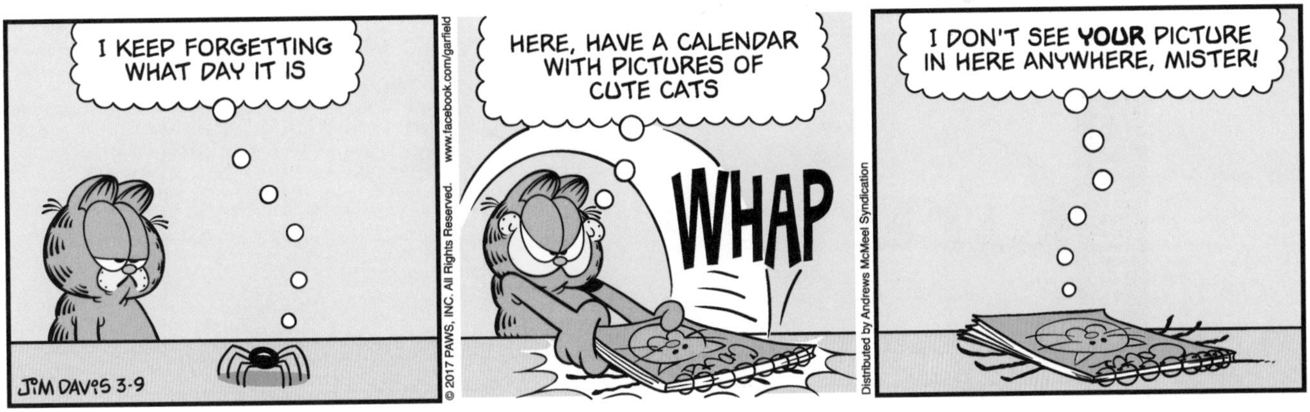
I KEEP FORGETTING WHAT DAY IT IS
JIM DAVIS 3-9
© 2017 PAWS, INC. All Rights Reserved. www.facebook.com/garfield
HERE, HAVE A CALENDAR WITH PICTURES OF CUTE CATS
WHAP
Distributed by Andrews McMeel Syndication
I DON'T SEE **YOUR** PICTURE IN HERE ANYWHERE, MISTER!

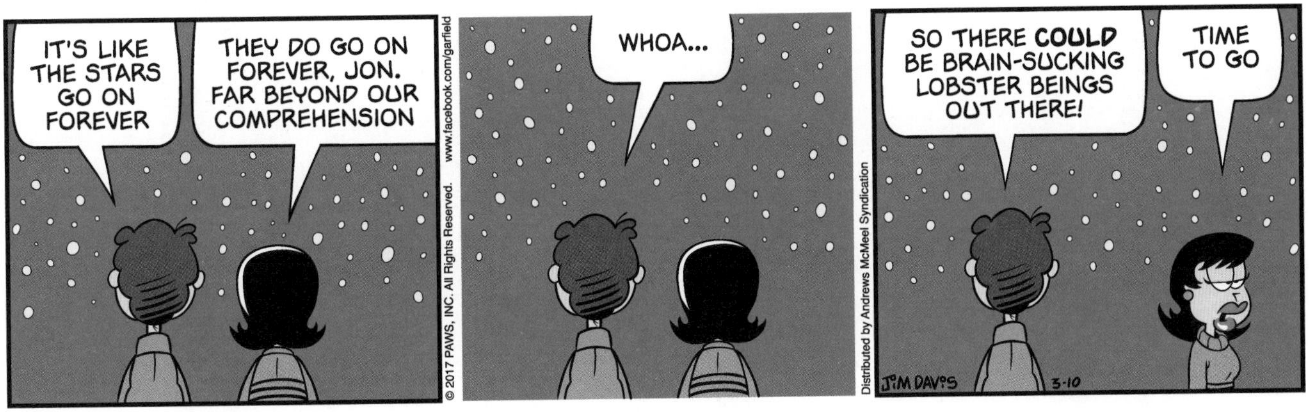
IT'S LIKE THE STARS GO ON FOREVER
THEY DO GO ON FOREVER, JON. FAR BEYOND OUR COMPREHENSION
© 2017 PAWS, INC. All Rights Reserved. www.facebook.com/garfield
WHOA...
Distributed by Andrews McMeel Syndication
SO THERE **COULD** BE BRAIN-SUCKING LOBSTER BEINGS OUT THERE!
TIME TO GO
JIM DAVIS 3-10

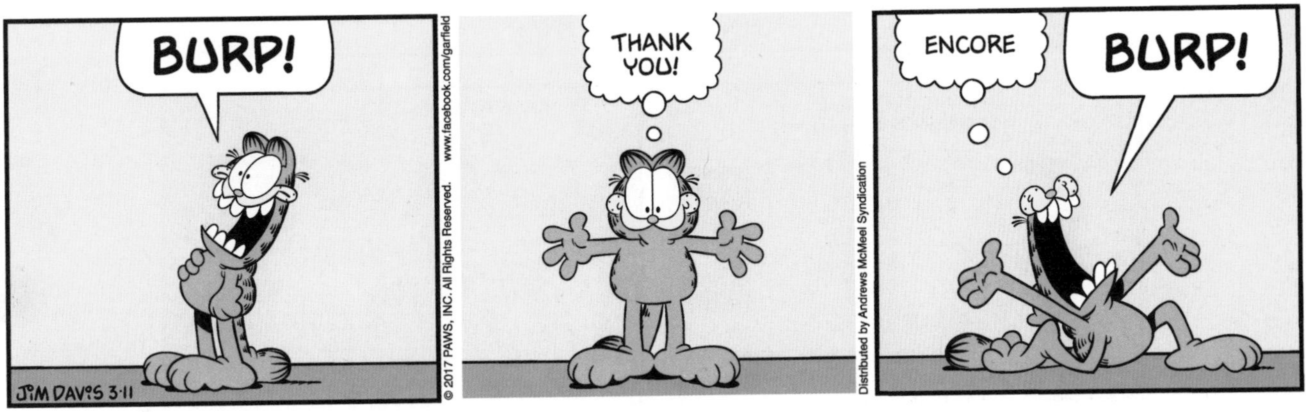
BURP!
JIM DAVIS 3-11
© 2017 PAWS, INC. All Rights Reserved. www.facebook.com/garfield
THANK YOU!
Distributed by Andrews McMeel Syndication
ENCORE
BURP!

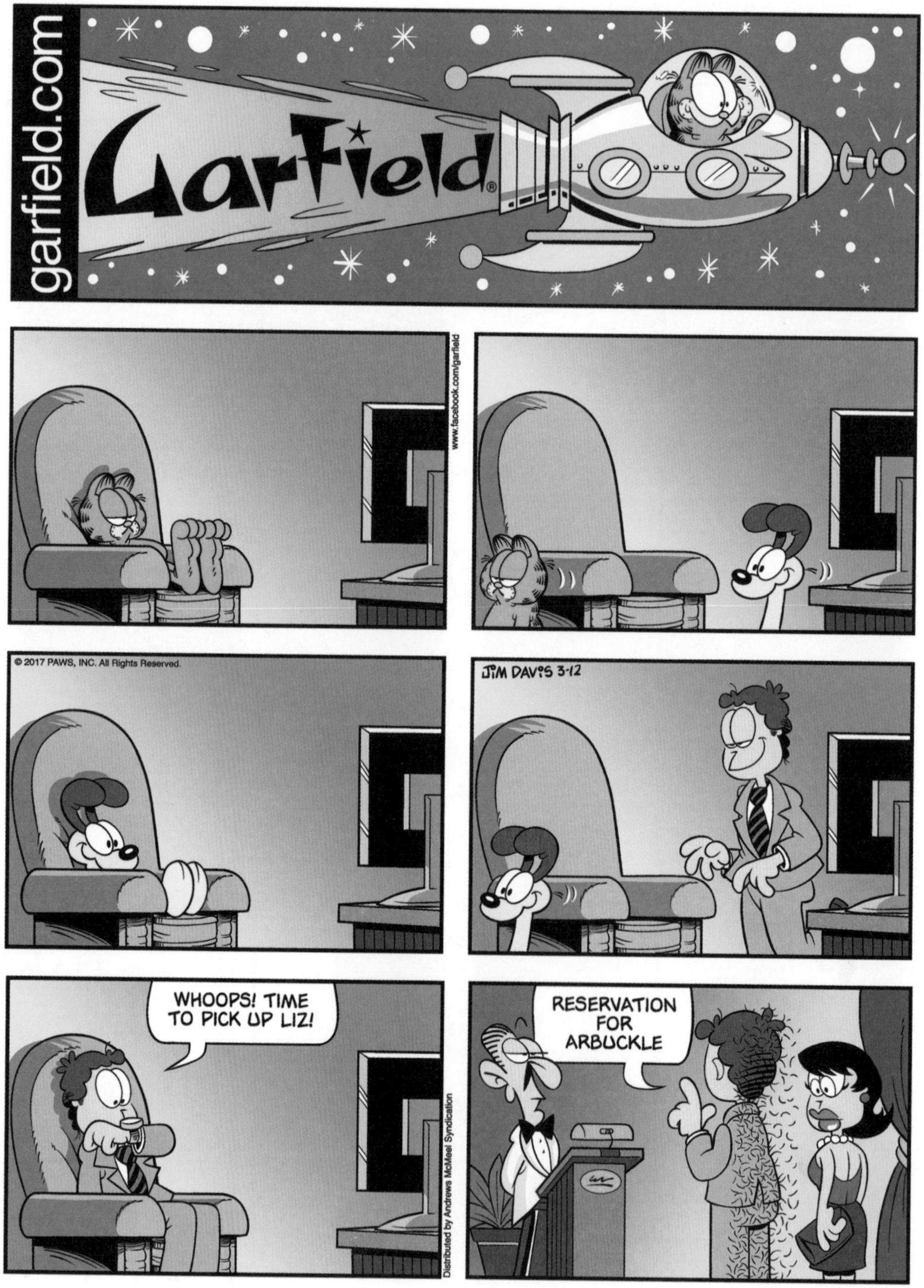
garfield.com
Garfield®
www.facebook.com/garfield
© 2017 PAWS, INC. All Rights Reserved.
JIM DAVIS 3-12
WHOOPS! TIME TO PICK UP LIZ!
Distributed by Andrews McMeel Syndication
RESERVATION FOR ARBUCKLE

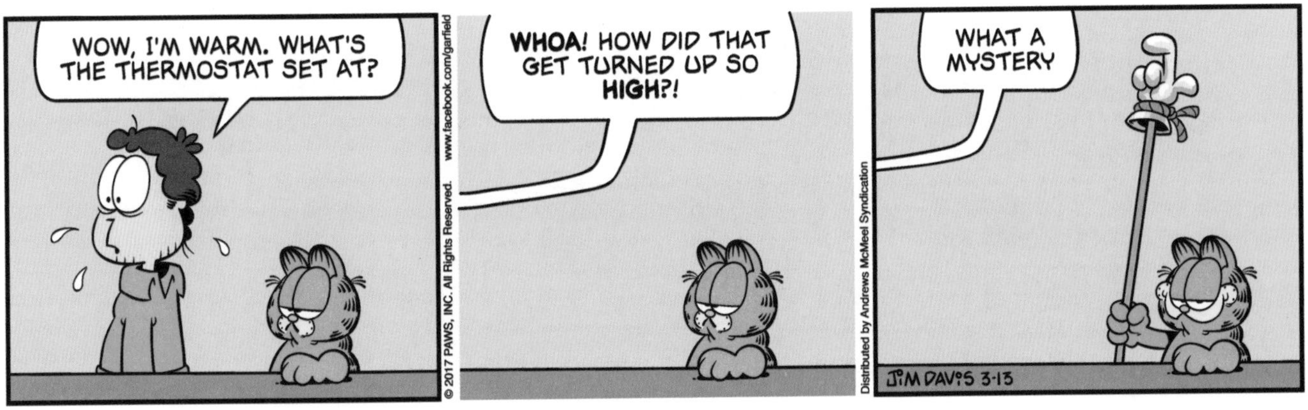
WOW, I'M WARM. WHAT'S THE THERMOSTAT SET AT?
WHOA! HOW DID THAT GET TURNED UP SO HIGH?!
WHAT A MYSTERY
© 2017 PAWS, INC. All Rights Reserved. www.facebook.com/garfield
Distributed by Andrews McMeel Syndication
JIM DAVIS 3-13

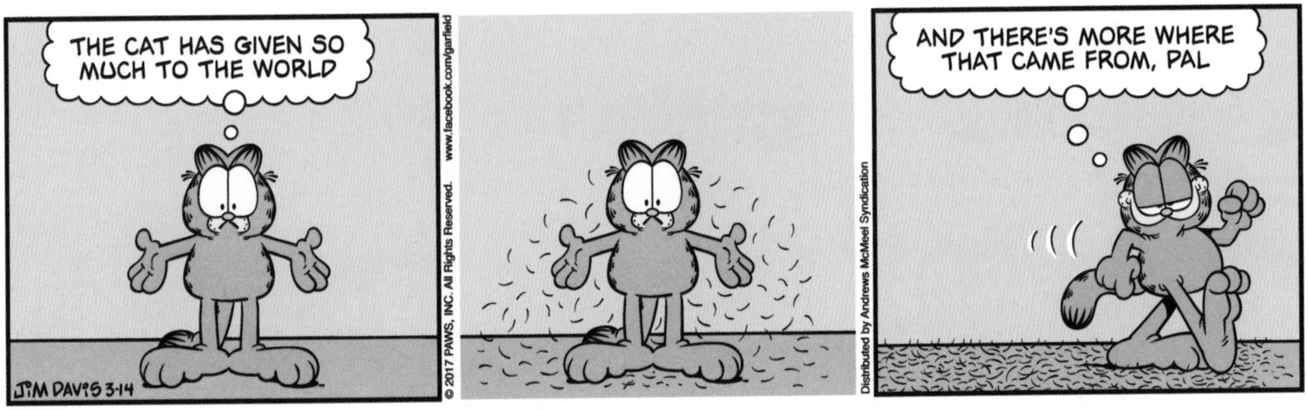
THE CAT HAS GIVEN SO MUCH TO THE WORLD
AND THERE'S MORE WHERE THAT CAME FROM, PAL
© 2017 PAWS, INC. All Rights Reserved. www.facebook.com/garfield
Distributed by Andrews McMeel Syndication
JIM DAVIS 3-14

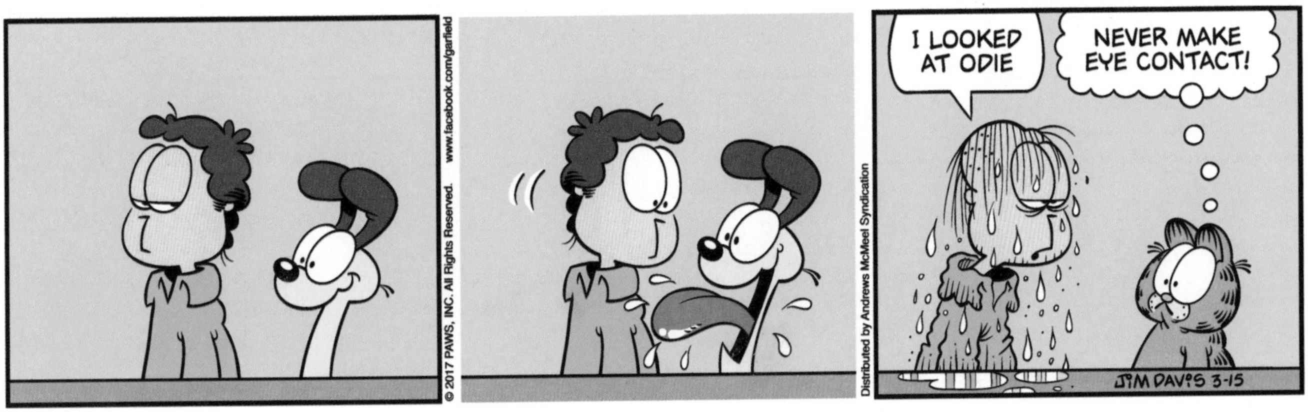
I LOOKED AT ODIE
NEVER MAKE EYE CONTACT!
© 2017 PAWS, INC. All Rights Reserved. www.facebook.com/garfield
Distributed by Andrews McMeel Syndication
JIM DAVIS 3-15

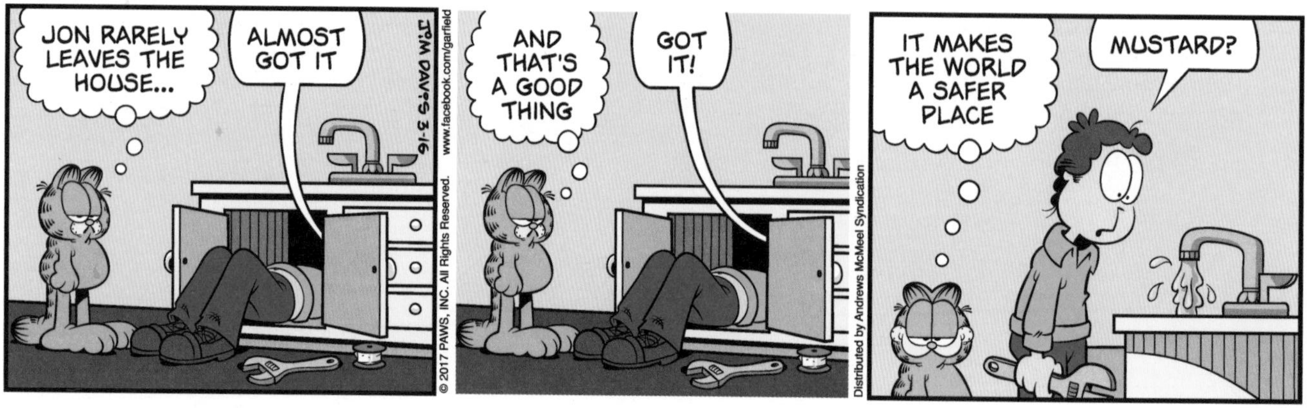
JON RARELY LEAVES THE HOUSE...
ALMOST GOT IT
JIM DAVIS 3-16
AND THAT'S A GOOD THING
GOT IT!
IT MAKES THE WORLD A SAFER PLACE
MUSTARD?
© 2017 PAWS, INC. All Rights Reserved. www.facebook.com/garfield
Distributed by Andrews McMeel Syndication

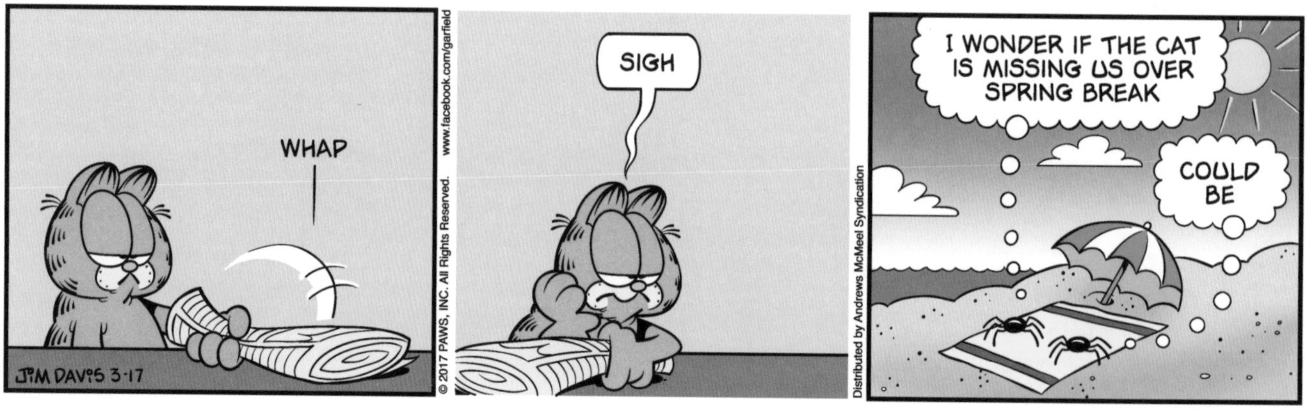
WHAP
JIM DAVIS 3-17
SIGH
I WONDER IF THE CAT IS MISSING US OVER SPRING BREAK
COULD BE
© 2017 PAWS, INC. All Rights Reserved. www.facebook.com/garfield
Distributed by Andrews McMeel Syndication

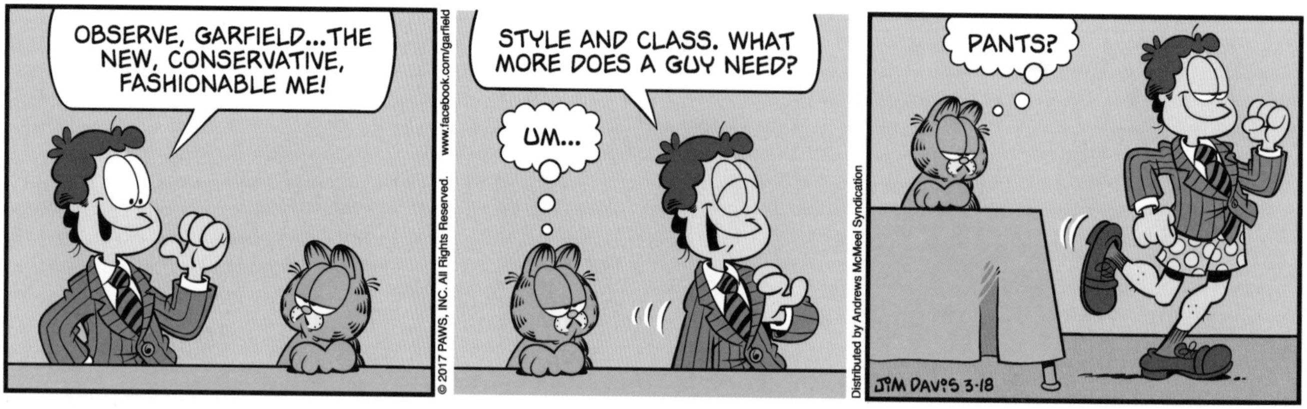
OBSERVE, GARFIELD...THE NEW, CONSERVATIVE, FASHIONABLE ME!
STYLE AND CLASS. WHAT MORE DOES A GUY NEED?
UM...
PANTS?
JIM DAVIS 3-18
© 2017 PAWS, INC. All Rights Reserved. www.facebook.com/garfield
Distributed by Andrews McMeel Syndication

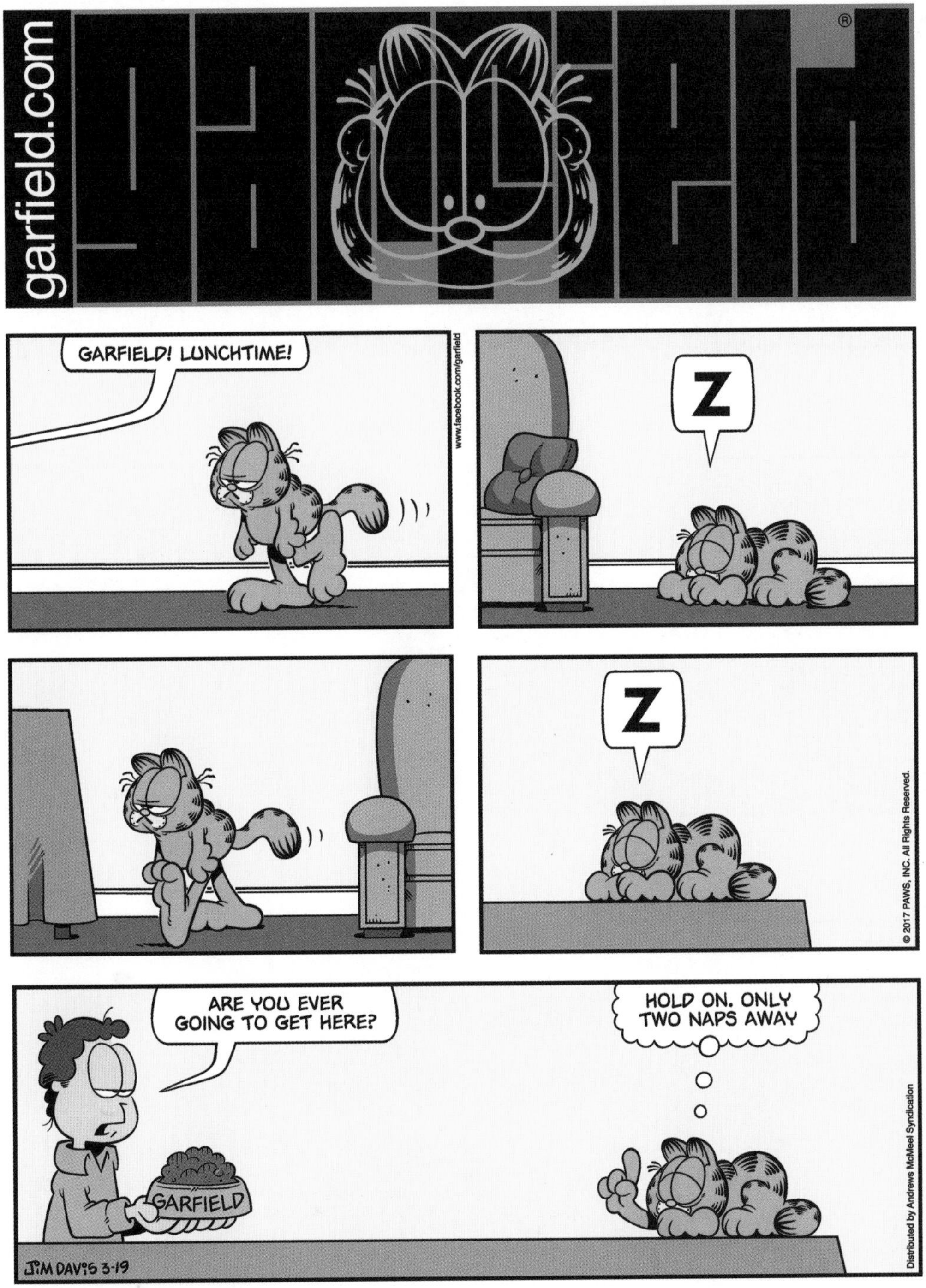

garfield.com
GARFIELD! LUNCHTIME!
www.facebook.com/garfield
Z
Z
© 2017 PAWS, INC. All Rights Reserved.
ARE YOU EVER GOING TO GET HERE?
HOLD ON. ONLY TWO NAPS AWAY
GARFIELD
JIM DAVIS 3-19
Distributed by Andrews McMeel Syndication

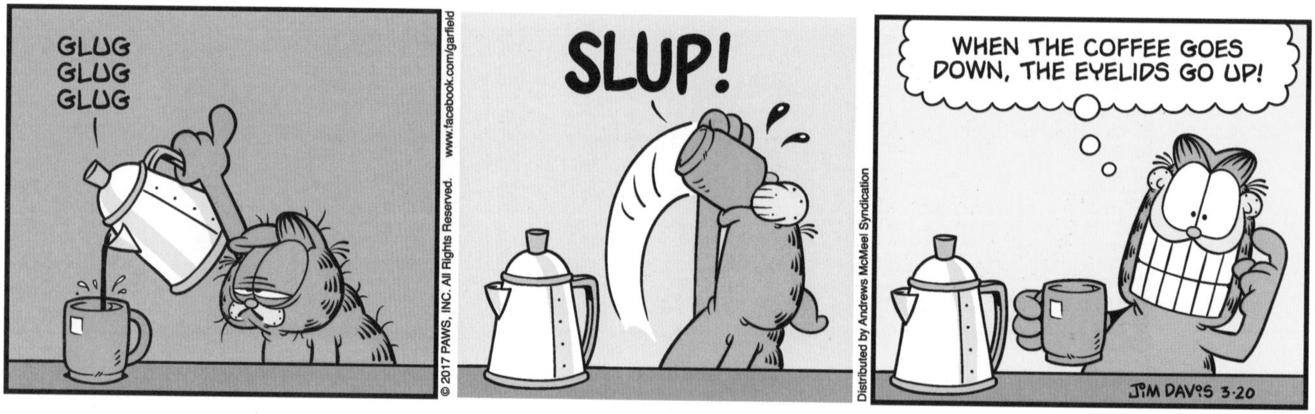
GLUG GLUG GLUG
SLUP!
WHEN THE COFFEE GOES DOWN, THE EYELIDS GO UP!
© 2017 PAWS, INC. All Rights Reserved. www.facebook.com/garfield
Distributed by Andrews McMeel Syndication
JIM DAVIS 3-20

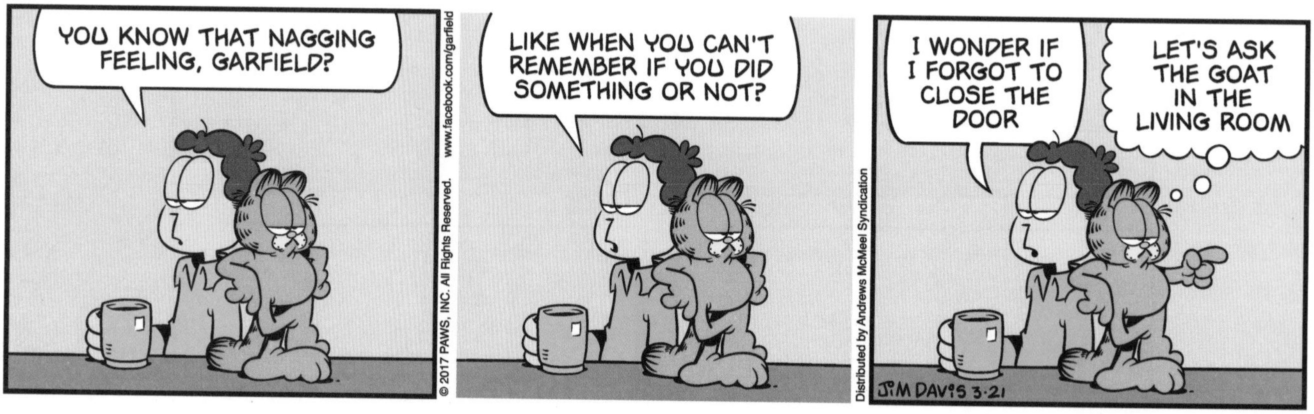
YOU KNOW THAT NAGGING FEELING, GARFIELD?
LIKE WHEN YOU CAN'T REMEMBER IF YOU DID SOMETHING OR NOT?
I WONDER IF I FORGOT TO CLOSE THE DOOR
LET'S ASK THE GOAT IN THE LIVING ROOM
© 2017 PAWS, INC. All Rights Reserved. www.facebook.com/garfield
Distributed by Andrews McMeel Syndication
JIM DAVIS 3-21

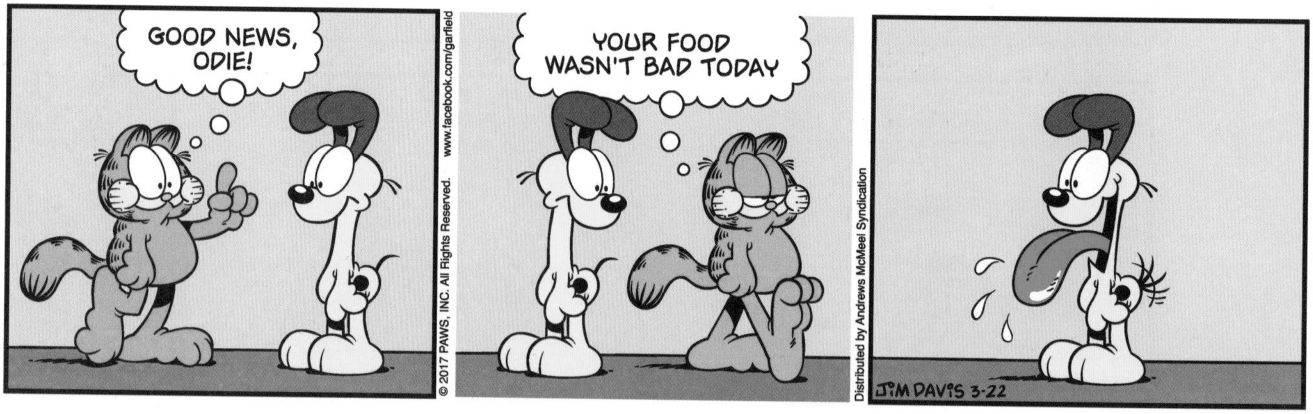
GOOD NEWS, ODIE!
YOUR FOOD WASN'T BAD TODAY
© 2017 PAWS, INC. All Rights Reserved. www.facebook.com/garfield
Distributed by Andrews McMeel Syndication
JIM DAVIS 3-22

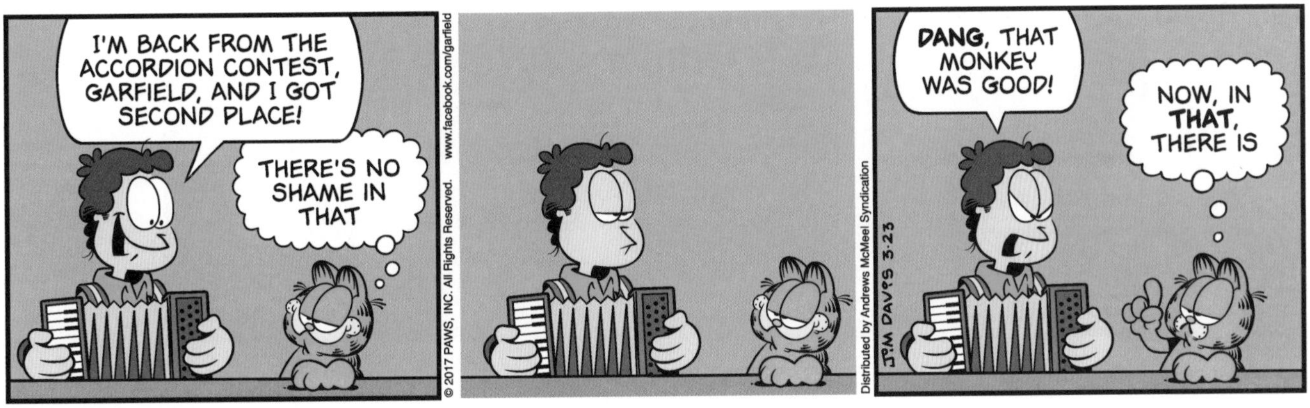
I'M BACK FROM THE ACCORDION CONTEST, GARFIELD, AND I GOT SECOND PLACE!
THERE'S NO SHAME IN THAT
DANG, THAT MONKEY WAS GOOD!
NOW, IN THAT, THERE IS
JIM DAVIS 3-23
© 2017 PAWS, INC. All Rights Reserved. www.facebook.com/garfield
Distributed by Andrews McMeel Syndication

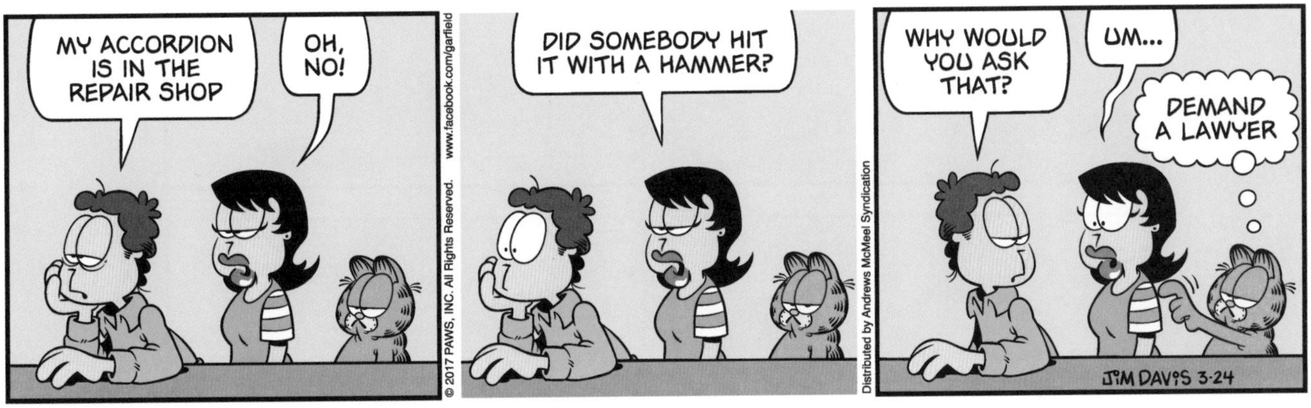
MY ACCORDION IS IN THE REPAIR SHOP
OH, NO!
DID SOMEBODY HIT IT WITH A HAMMER?
WHY WOULD YOU ASK THAT?
UM...
DEMAND A LAWYER
JIM DAVIS 3-24
© 2017 PAWS, INC. All Rights Reserved. www.facebook.com/garfield
Distributed by Andrews McMeel Syndication

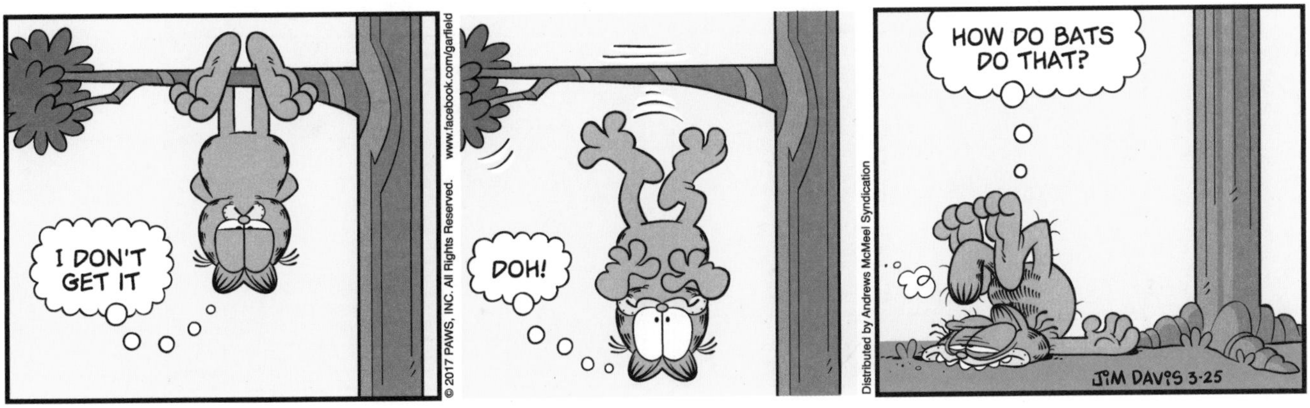
I DON'T GET IT
DOH!
HOW DO BATS DO THAT?
JIM DAVIS 3-25
© 2017 PAWS, INC. All Rights Reserved. www.facebook.com/garfield
Distributed by Andrews McMeel Syndication

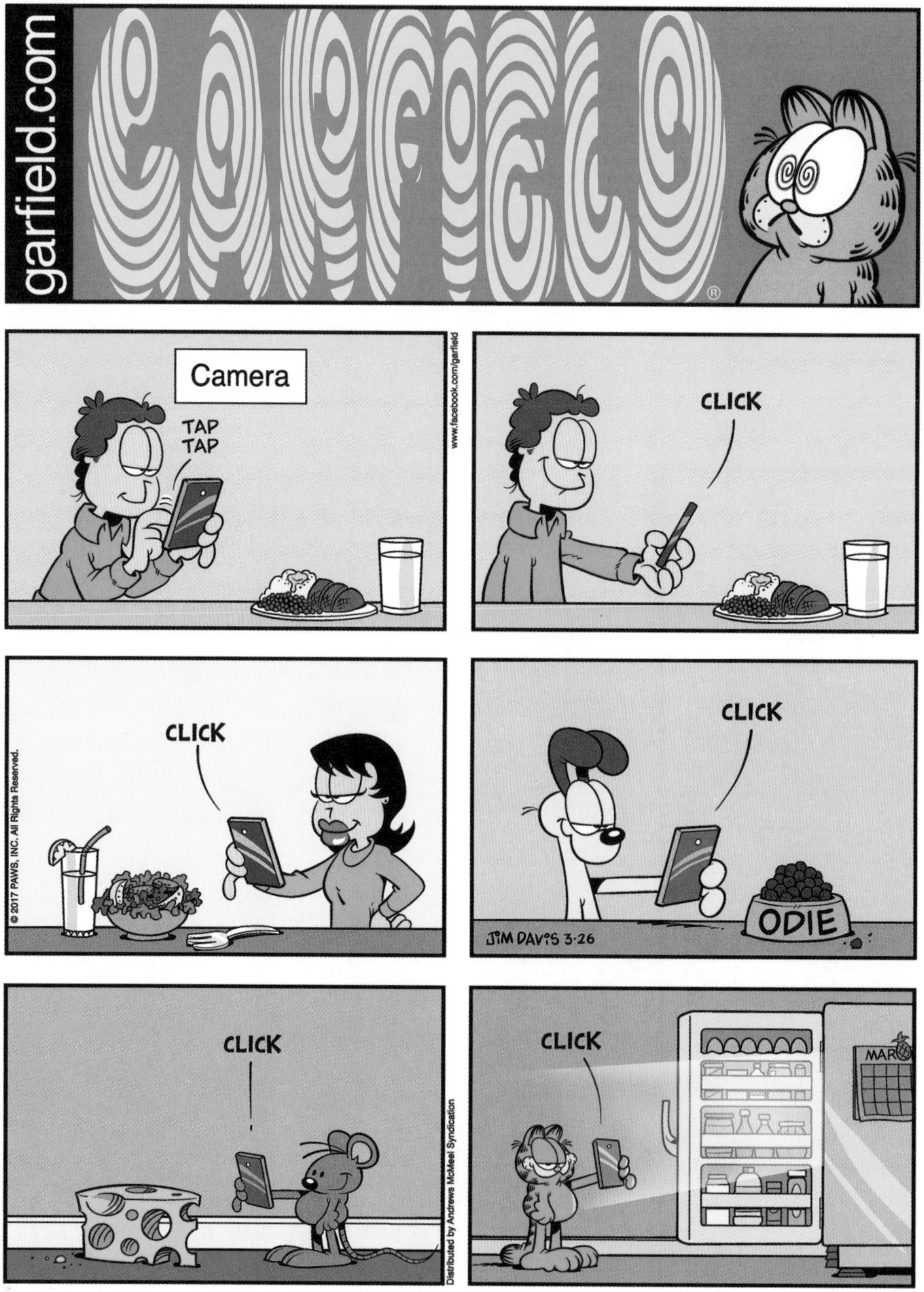
garfield.com
www.facebook.com/garfield
Camera
TAP
TAP
CLICK
© 2017 PAWS, INC. All Rights Reserved.
CLICK
CLICK
JIM DAVIS 3-26
ODIE
CLICK
Distributed by Andrews McMeel Syndication
CLICK
MAR

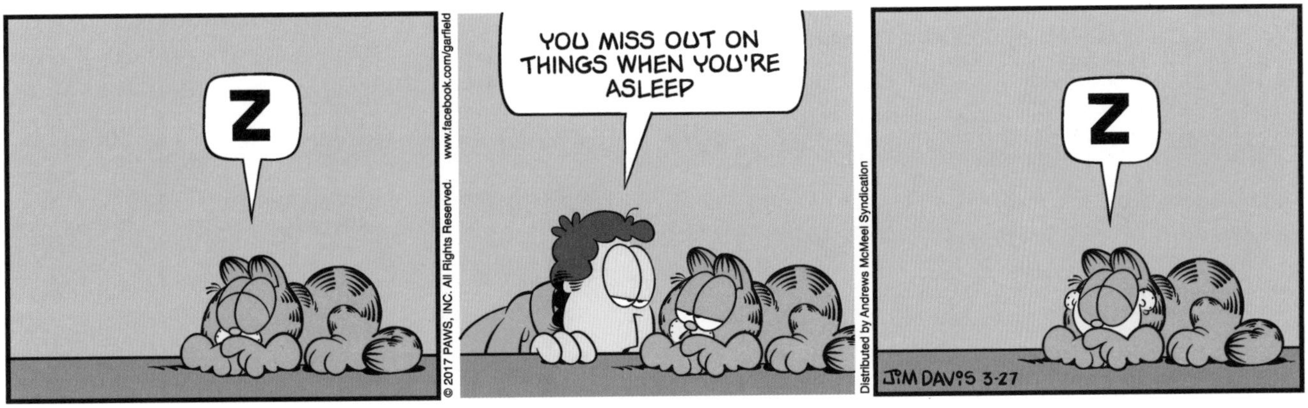
Z
YOU MISS OUT ON THINGS WHEN YOU'RE ASLEEP
Z
JIM DAVIS 3-27
© 2017 PAWS, INC. All Rights Reserved. www.facebook.com/garfield
Distributed by Andrews McMeel Syndication

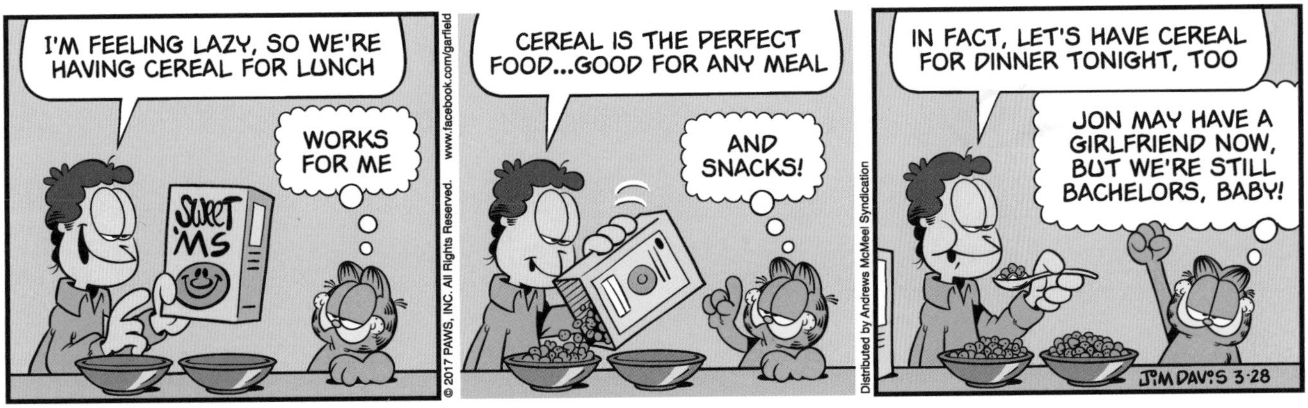
I'M FEELING LAZY, SO WE'RE HAVING CEREAL FOR LUNCH
SWEET 'MS
WORKS FOR ME
CEREAL IS THE PERFECT FOOD...GOOD FOR ANY MEAL
AND SNACKS!
IN FACT, LET'S HAVE CEREAL FOR DINNER TONIGHT, TOO
JON MAY HAVE A GIRLFRIEND NOW, BUT WE'RE STILL BACHELORS, BABY!
JIM DAVIS 3-28
© 2017 PAWS, INC. All Rights Reserved. www.facebook.com/garfield
Distributed by Andrews McMeel Syndication

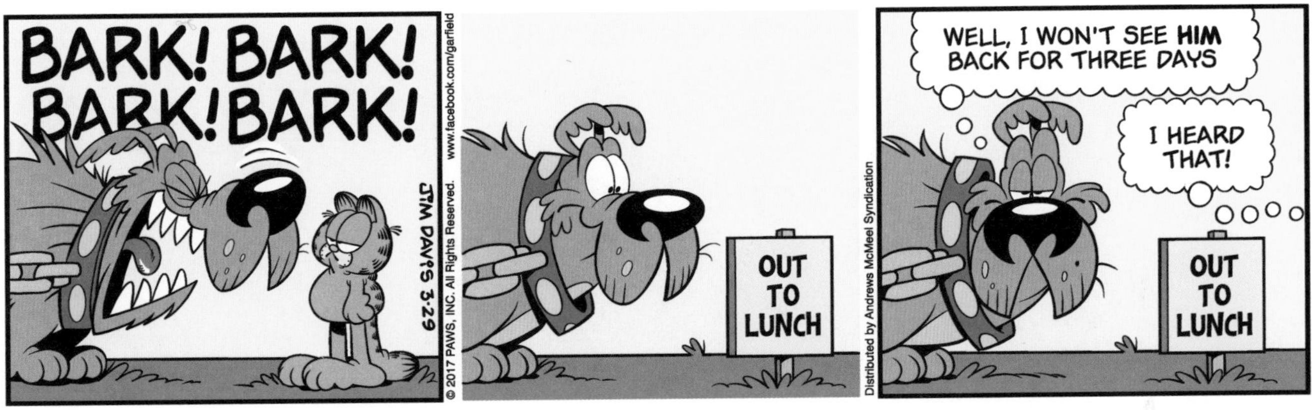
BARK! BARK! BARK! BARK!
JIM DAVIS 3-29
OUT TO LUNCH
WELL, I WON'T SEE HIM BACK FOR THREE DAYS
I HEARD THAT!
OUT TO LUNCH
© 2017 PAWS, INC. All Rights Reserved. www.facebook.com/garfield
Distributed by Andrews McMeel Syndication

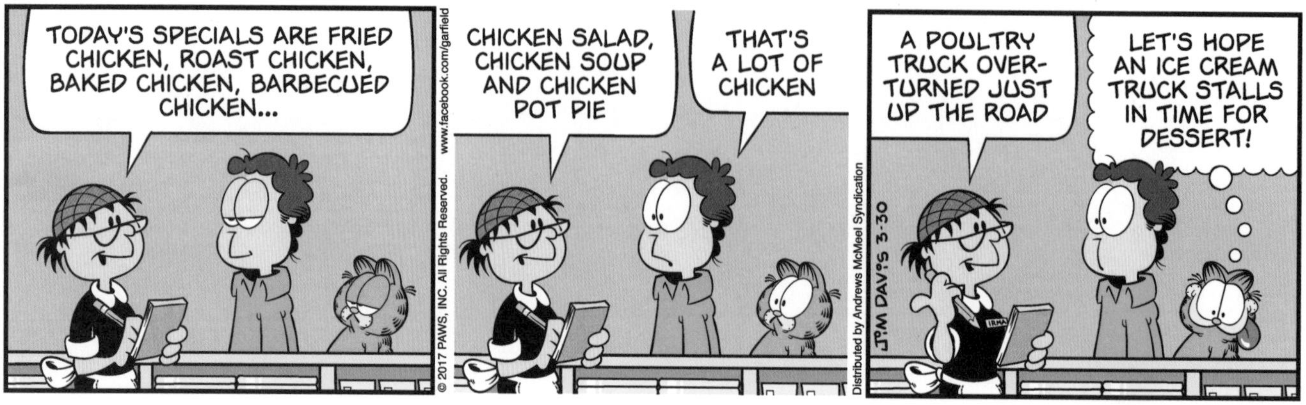
TODAY'S SPECIALS ARE FRIED CHICKEN, ROAST CHICKEN, BAKED CHICKEN, BARBECUED CHICKEN...
© 2017 PAWS, INC. All Rights Reserved. www.facebook.com/garfield
CHICKEN SALAD, CHICKEN SOUP AND CHICKEN POT PIE
THAT'S A LOT OF CHICKEN
Distributed by Andrews McMeel Syndication
A POULTRY TRUCK OVER-TURNED JUST UP THE ROAD
IRMA
LET'S HOPE AN ICE CREAM TRUCK STALLS IN TIME FOR DESSERT!
JIM DAVIS 3-30

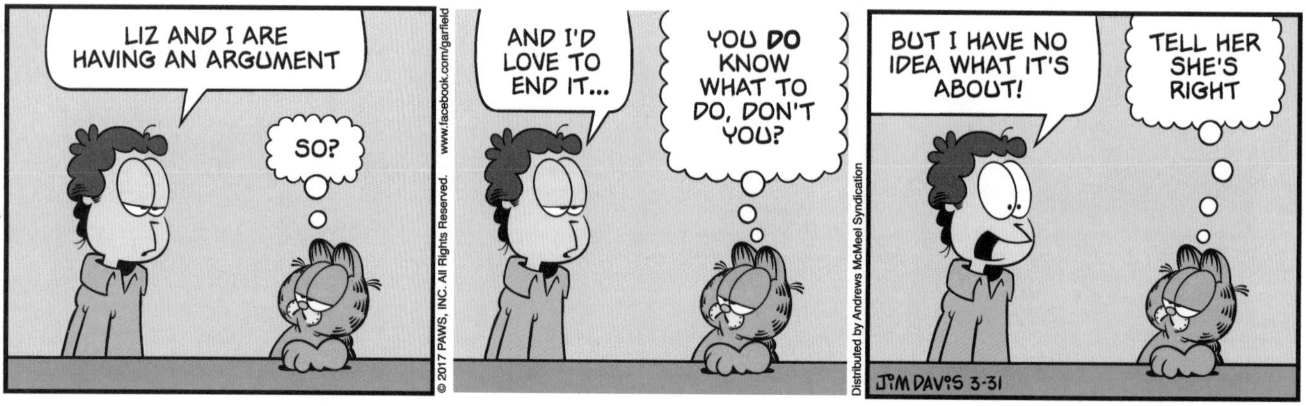
LIZ AND I ARE HAVING AN ARGUMENT
SO?
© 2017 PAWS, INC. All Rights Reserved. www.facebook.com/garfield
AND I'D LOVE TO END IT...
YOU DO KNOW WHAT TO DO, DON'T YOU?
Distributed by Andrews McMeel Syndication
BUT I HAVE NO IDEA WHAT IT'S ABOUT!
TELL HER SHE'S RIGHT
JIM DAVIS 3-31

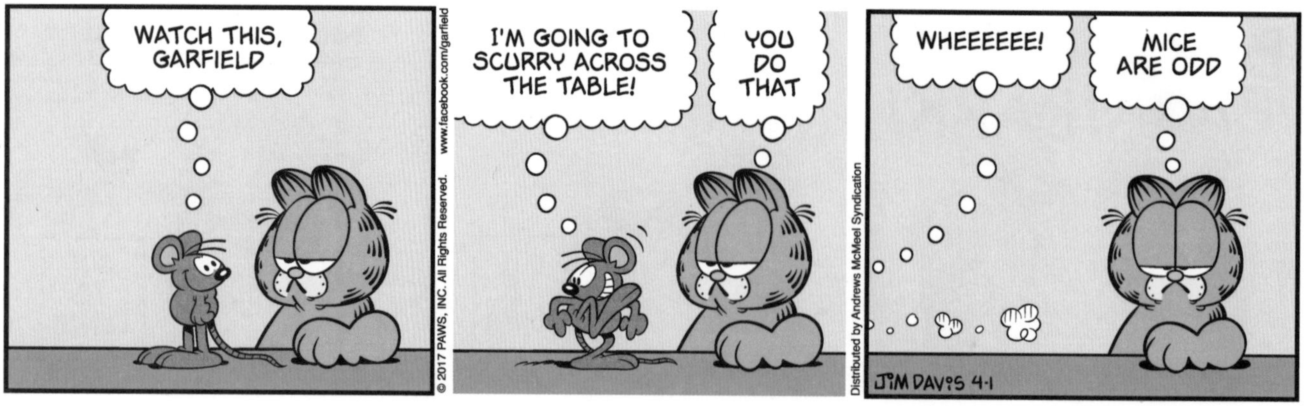
WATCH THIS, GARFIELD
© 2017 PAWS, INC. All Rights Reserved. www.facebook.com/garfield
I'M GOING TO SCURRY ACROSS THE TABLE!
YOU DO THAT
Distributed by Andrews McMeel Syndication
WHEEEEEE!
MICE ARE ODD
JIM DAVIS 4-1

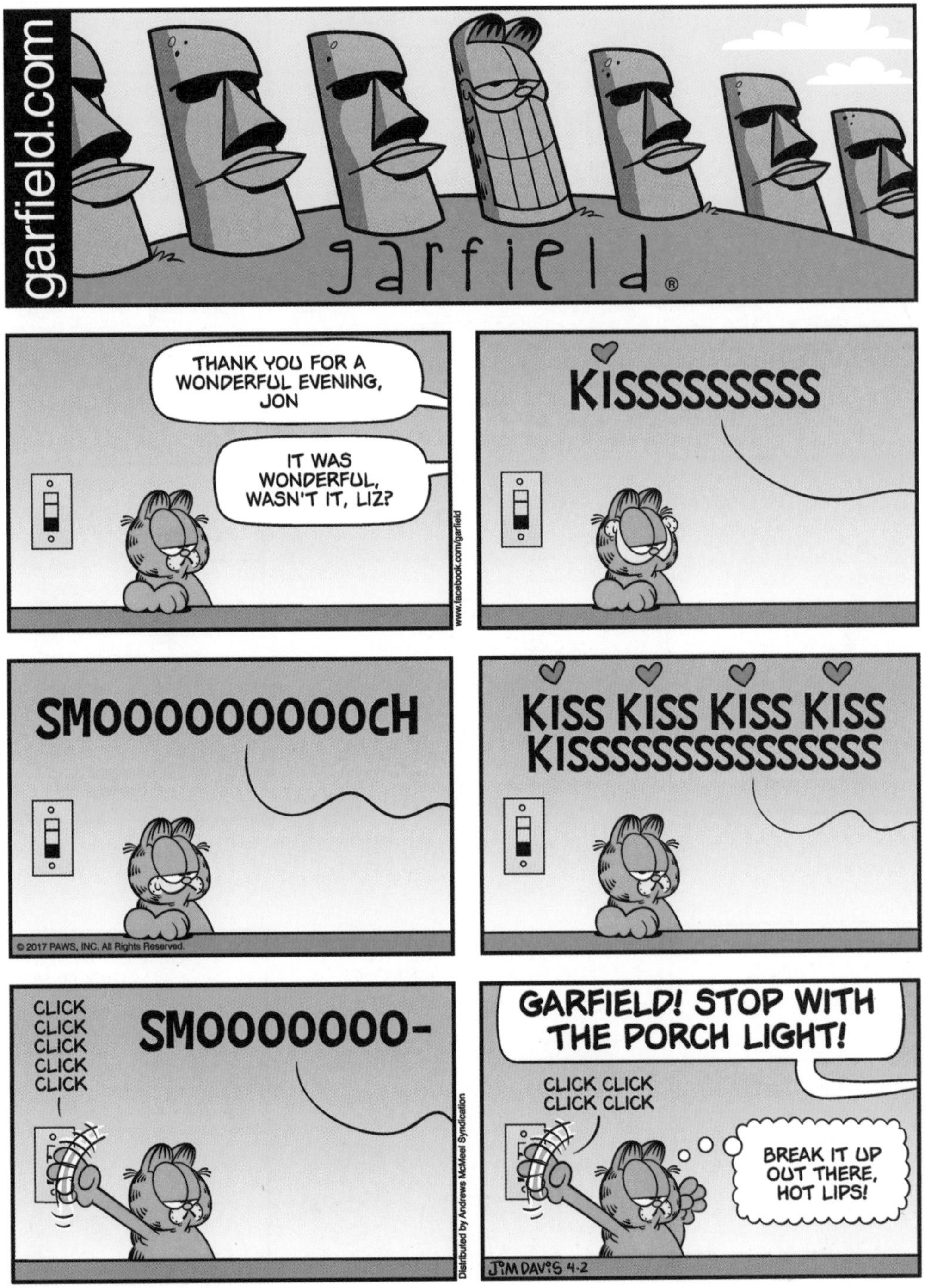
garfield.com
garfield®
THANK YOU FOR A WONDERFUL EVENING, JON
IT WAS WONDERFUL, WASN'T IT, LIZ?
www.facebook.com/garfield
KISSSSSSSSS
SMOOOOOOOOOCH
© 2017 PAWS, INC. All Rights Reserved.
KISS KISS KISS KISS KISSSSSSSSSSSSSSS
CLICK CLICK CLICK CLICK CLICK
SMOOOOOOO-
Distributed by Andrews McMeel Syndication
GARFIELD! STOP WITH THE PORCH LIGHT!
CLICK CLICK CLICK CLICK
BREAK IT UP OUT THERE, HOT LIPS!
JIM DAVIS 4-2

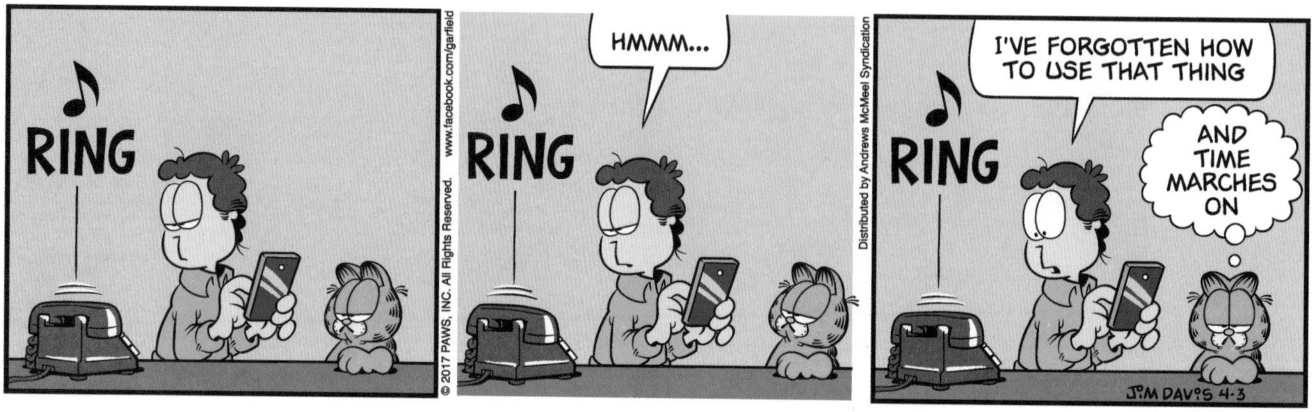
RING
RING
HMMM...
RING
I'VE FORGOTTEN HOW TO USE THAT THING
AND TIME MARCHES ON
JIM DAVIS 4-3
© 2017 PAWS, INC. All Rights Reserved. www.facebook.com/garfield
Distributed by Andrews McMeel Syndication

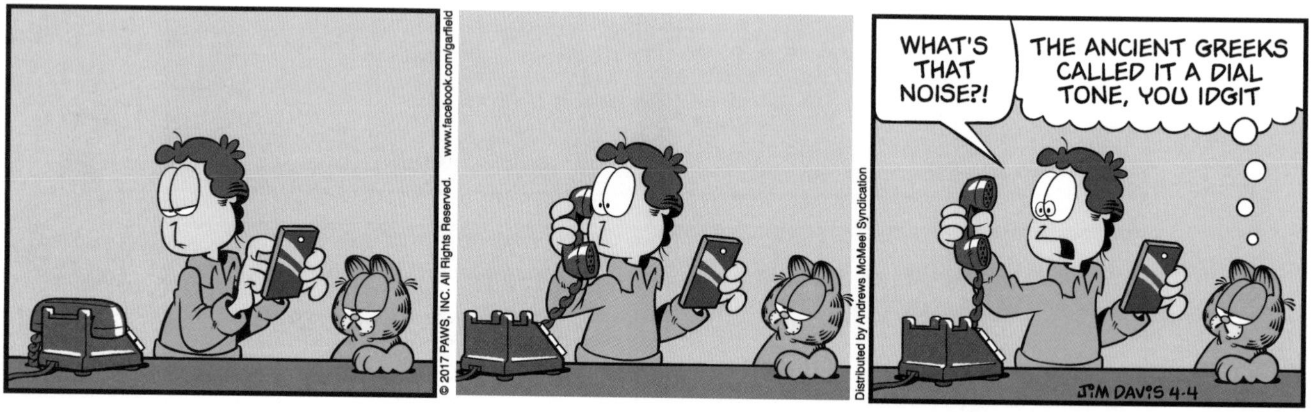
WHAT'S THAT NOISE?!
THE ANCIENT GREEKS CALLED IT A DIAL TONE, YOU IDGIT
JIM DAVIS 4-4
© 2017 PAWS, INC. All Rights Reserved. www.facebook.com/garfield
Distributed by Andrews McMeel Syndication

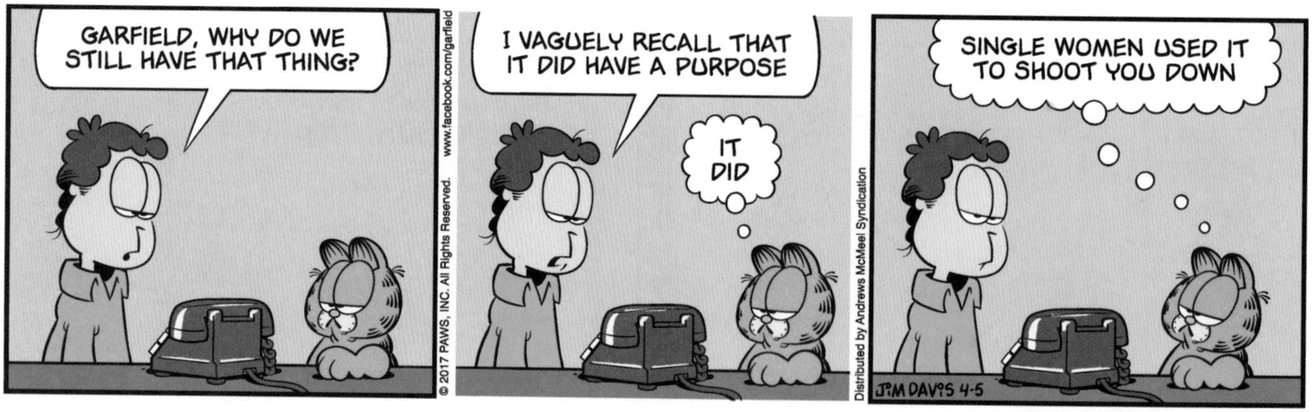
GARFIELD, WHY DO WE STILL HAVE THAT THING?
I VAGUELY RECALL THAT IT DID HAVE A PURPOSE
IT DID
SINGLE WOMEN USED IT TO SHOOT YOU DOWN
JIM DAVIS 4-5
© 2017 PAWS, INC. All Rights Reserved. www.facebook.com/garfield
Distributed by Andrews McMeel Syndication

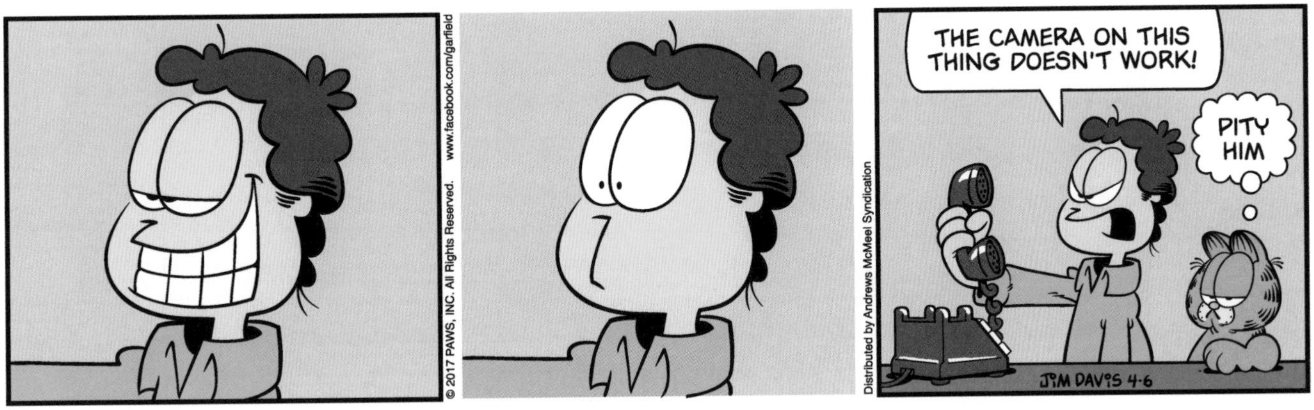
© 2017 PAWS, INC. All Rights Reserved. www.facebook.com/garfield
Distributed by Andrews McMeel Syndication
THE CAMERA ON THIS THING DOESN'T WORK!
PITY HIM
JIM DAVIS 4-6

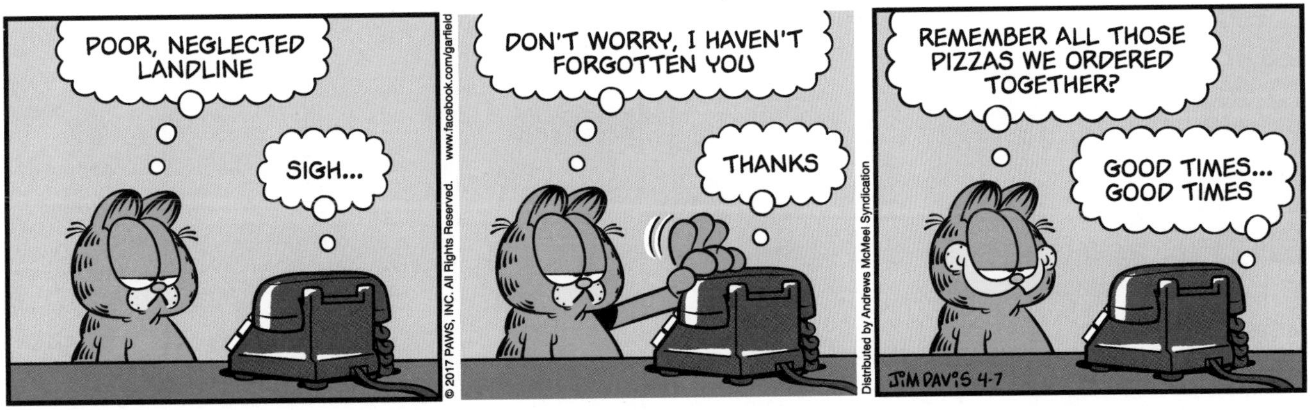
POOR, NEGLECTED LANDLINE
SIGH...
© 2017 PAWS, INC. All Rights Reserved. www.facebook.com/garfield
DON'T WORRY, I HAVEN'T FORGOTTEN YOU
THANKS
Distributed by Andrews McMeel Syndication
REMEMBER ALL THOSE PIZZAS WE ORDERED TOGETHER?
GOOD TIMES... GOOD TIMES
JIM DAVIS 4-7

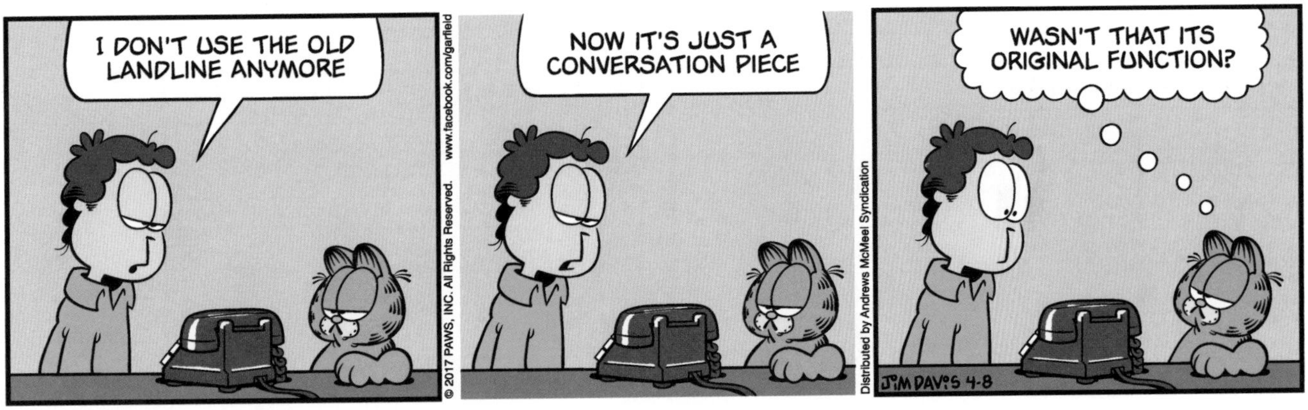
I DON'T USE THE OLD LANDLINE ANYMORE
© 2017 PAWS, INC. All Rights Reserved. www.facebook.com/garfield
NOW IT'S JUST A CONVERSATION PIECE
Distributed by Andrews McMeel Syndication
WASN'T THAT ITS ORIGINAL FUNCTION?
JIM DAVIS 4-8

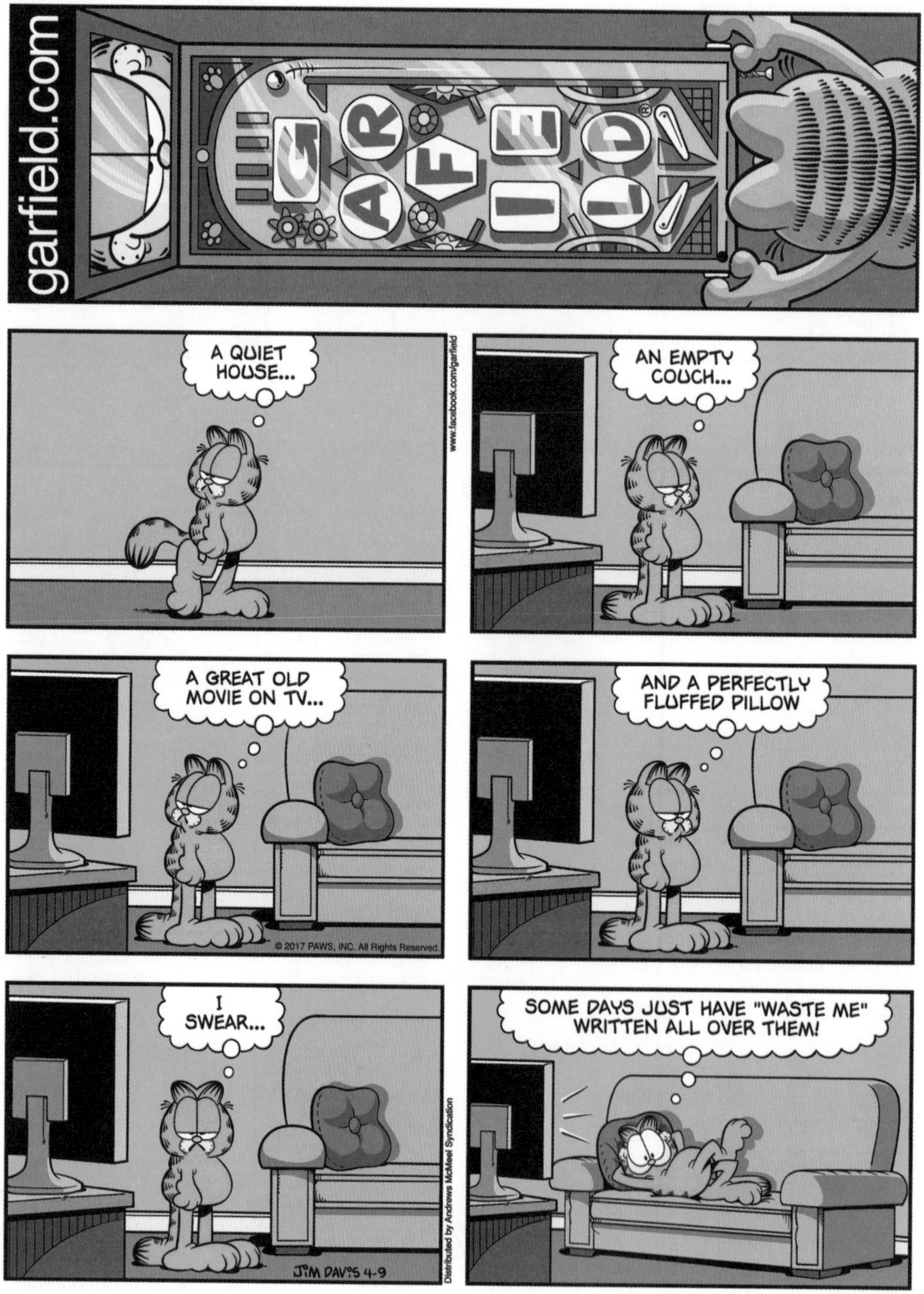
garfield.com
GARFIELD
A QUIET HOUSE...
www.facebook.com/garfield
AN EMPTY COUCH...
A GREAT OLD MOVIE ON TV...
© 2017 PAWS, INC. All Rights Reserved.
AND A PERFECTLY FLUFFED PILLOW
I SWEAR...
JIM DAVIS 4-9
Distributed by Andrews McMeel Syndication
SOME DAYS JUST HAVE "WASTE ME" WRITTEN ALL OVER THEM!

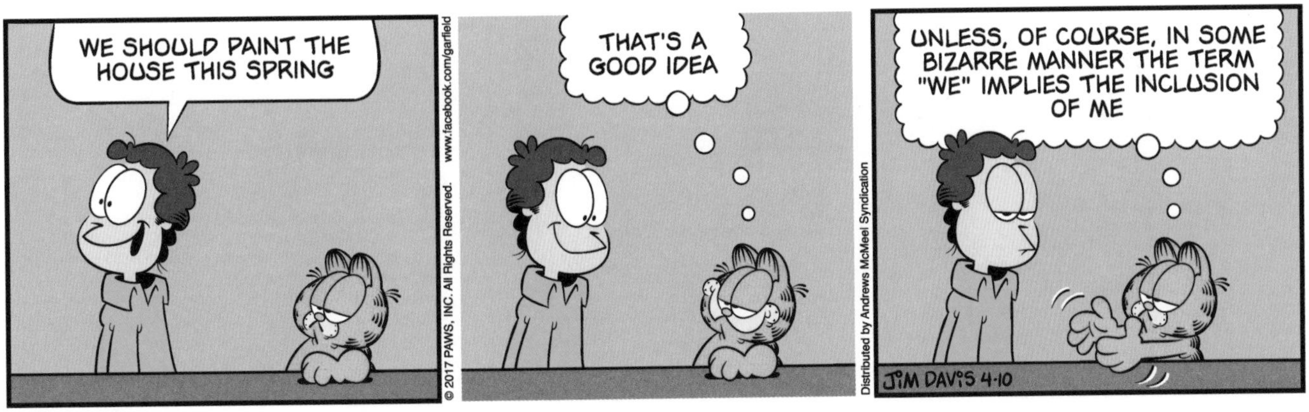
WE SHOULD PAINT THE HOUSE THIS SPRING
THAT'S A GOOD IDEA
UNLESS, OF COURSE, IN SOME BIZARRE MANNER THE TERM "WE" IMPLIES THE INCLUSION OF ME
JIM DAVIS 4-10
© 2017 PAWS, INC. All Rights Reserved. www.facebook.com/garfield
Distributed by Andrews McMeel Syndication

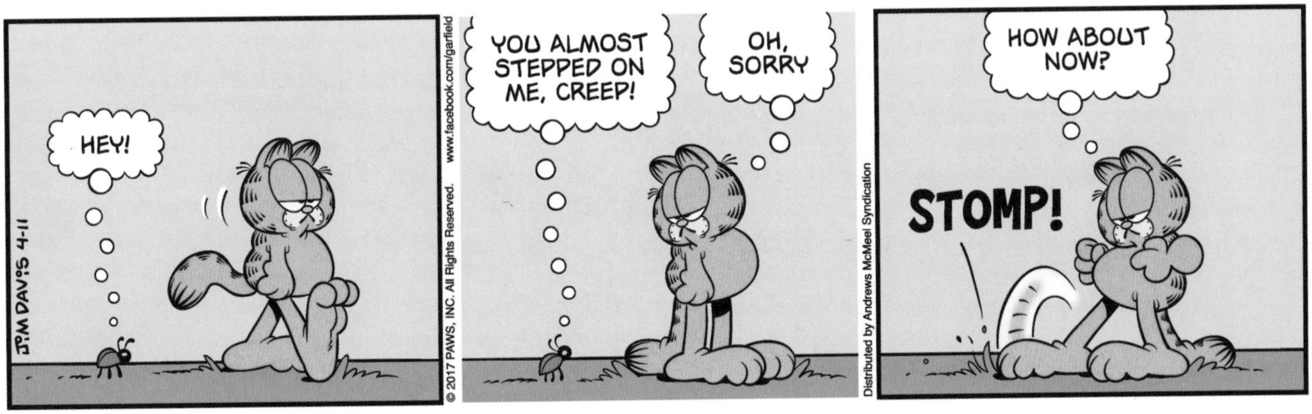
HEY!
JIM DAVIS 4-11
YOU ALMOST STEPPED ON ME, CREEP!
OH, SORRY
STOMP!
HOW ABOUT NOW?
© 2017 PAWS, INC. All Rights Reserved. www.facebook.com/garfield
Distributed by Andrews McMeel Syndication

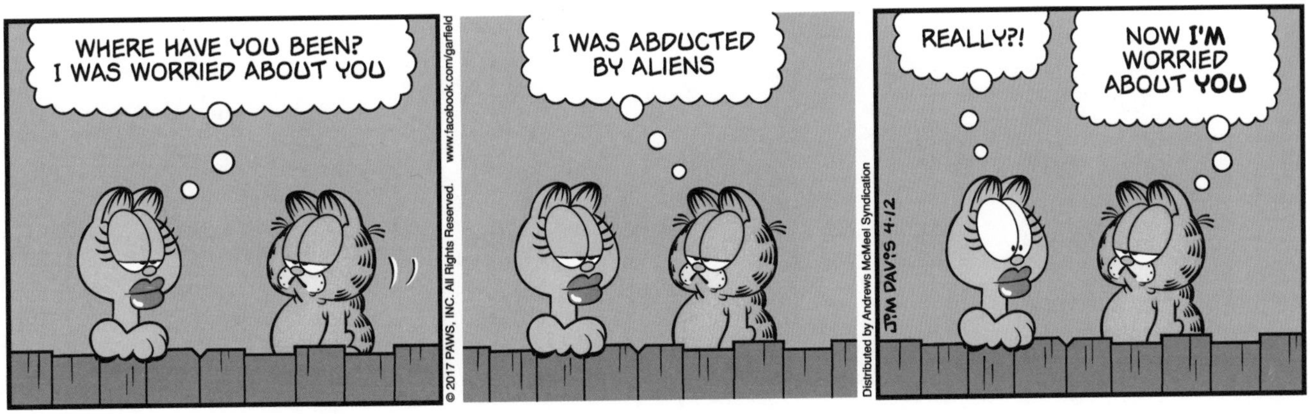
WHERE HAVE YOU BEEN? I WAS WORRIED ABOUT YOU
I WAS ABDUCTED BY ALIENS
REALLY?!
NOW I'M WORRIED ABOUT YOU
JIM DAVIS 4-12
© 2017 PAWS, INC. All Rights Reserved. www.facebook.com/garfield
Distributed by Andrews McMeel Syndication

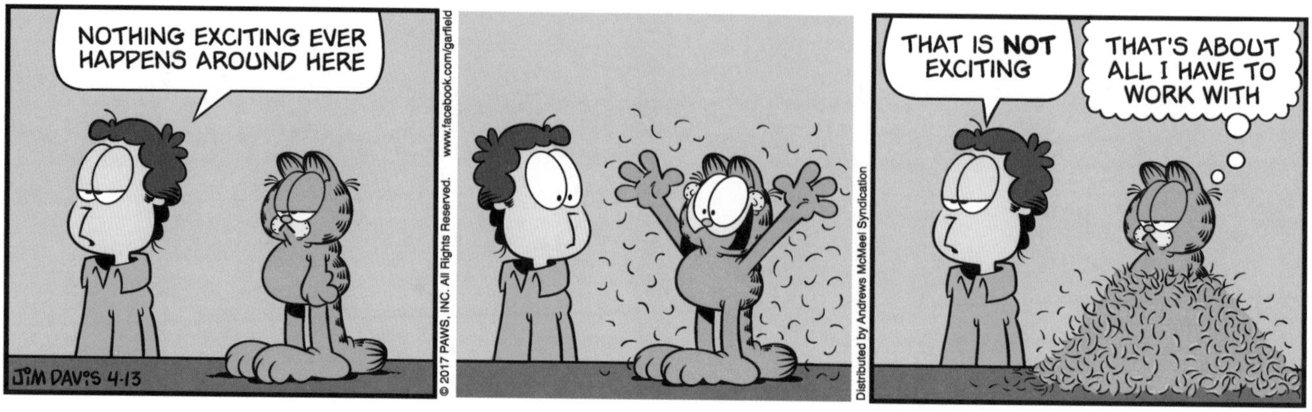
NOTHING EXCITING EVER HAPPENS AROUND HERE
JIM DAVIS 4-13
© 2017 PAWS, INC. All Rights Reserved. www.facebook.com/garfield
THAT IS **NOT** EXCITING
THAT'S ABOUT ALL I HAVE TO WORK WITH
Distributed by Andrews McMeel Syndication

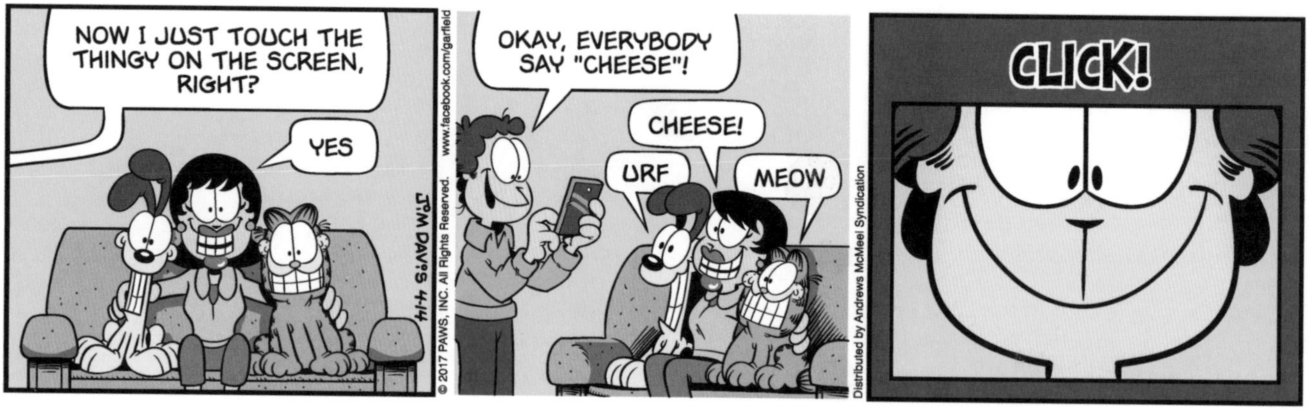
NOW I JUST TOUCH THE THINGY ON THE SCREEN, RIGHT?
YES
JIM DAVIS 4-14
© 2017 PAWS, INC. All Rights Reserved. www.facebook.com/garfield
OKAY, EVERYBODY SAY "CHEESE"!
CHEESE!
URF
MEOW
Distributed by Andrews McMeel Syndication
CLICK!

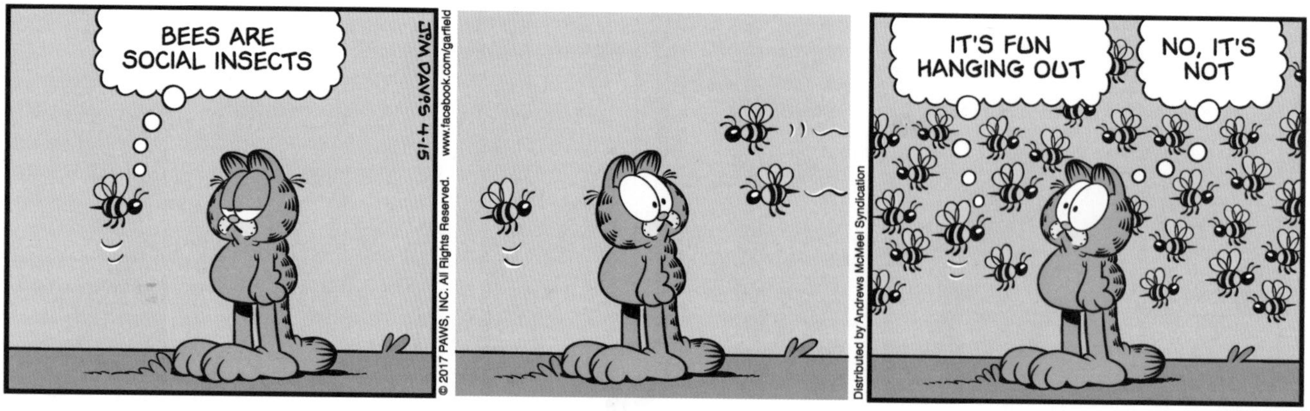
BEES ARE SOCIAL INSECTS
JIM DAVIS 4-15
© 2017 PAWS, INC. All Rights Reserved. www.facebook.com/garfield
Distributed by Andrews McMeel Syndication
IT'S FUN HANGING OUT
NO, IT'S NOT

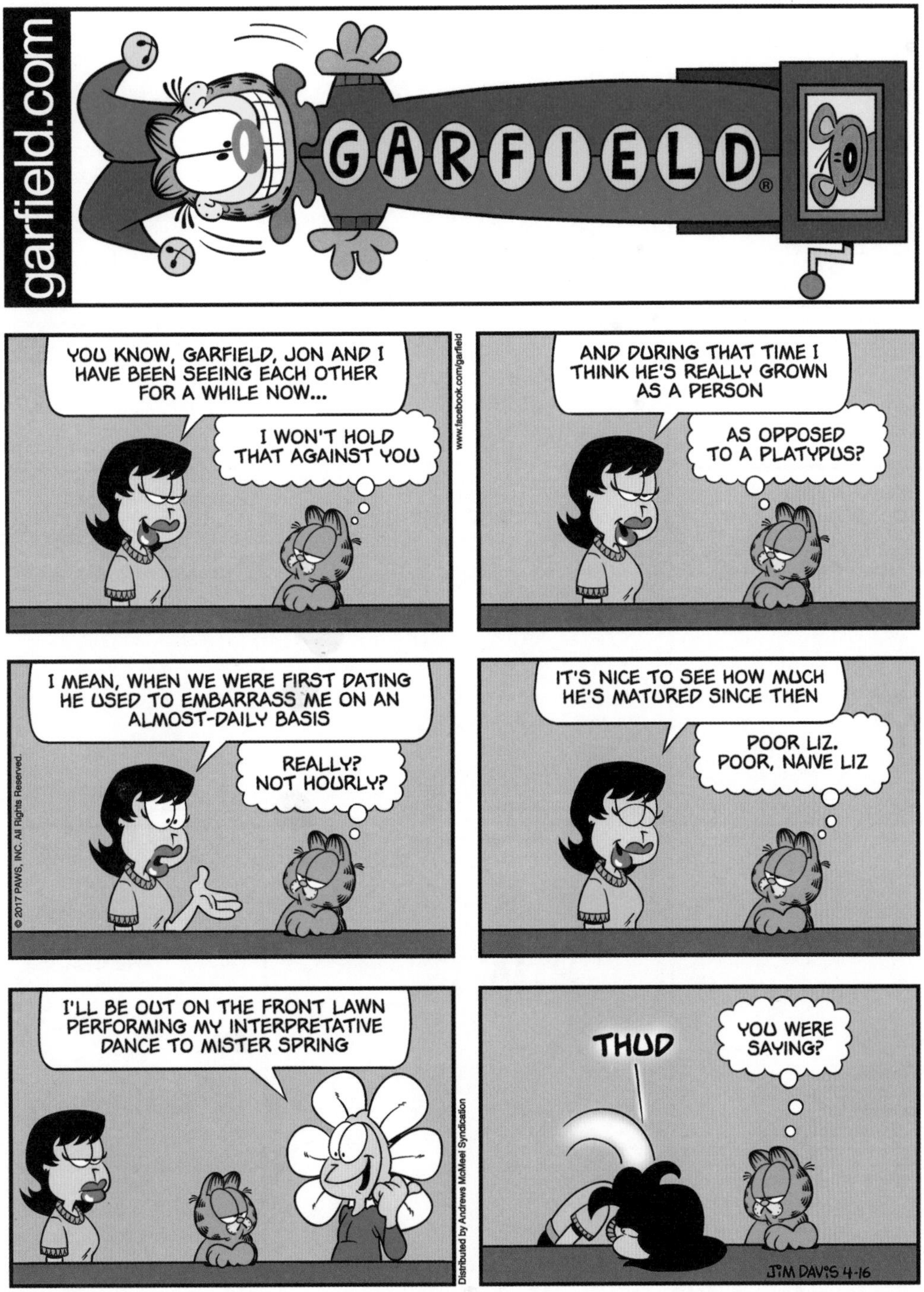
garfield.com
GARFIELD®
www.facebook.com/garfield
YOU KNOW, GARFIELD, JON AND I HAVE BEEN SEEING EACH OTHER FOR A WHILE NOW...
I WON'T HOLD THAT AGAINST YOU
AND DURING THAT TIME I THINK HE'S REALLY GROWN AS A PERSON
AS OPPOSED TO A PLATYPUS?
© 2017 PAWS, INC. All Rights Reserved.
I MEAN, WHEN WE WERE FIRST DATING HE USED TO EMBARRASS ME ON AN ALMOST-DAILY BASIS
REALLY? NOT HOURLY?
IT'S NICE TO SEE HOW MUCH HE'S MATURED SINCE THEN
POOR LIZ. POOR, NAIVE LIZ
I'LL BE OUT ON THE FRONT LAWN PERFORMING MY INTERPRETATIVE DANCE TO MISTER SPRING
Distributed by Andrews McMeel Syndication
THUD
YOU WERE SAYING?
JIM DAVIS 4-16

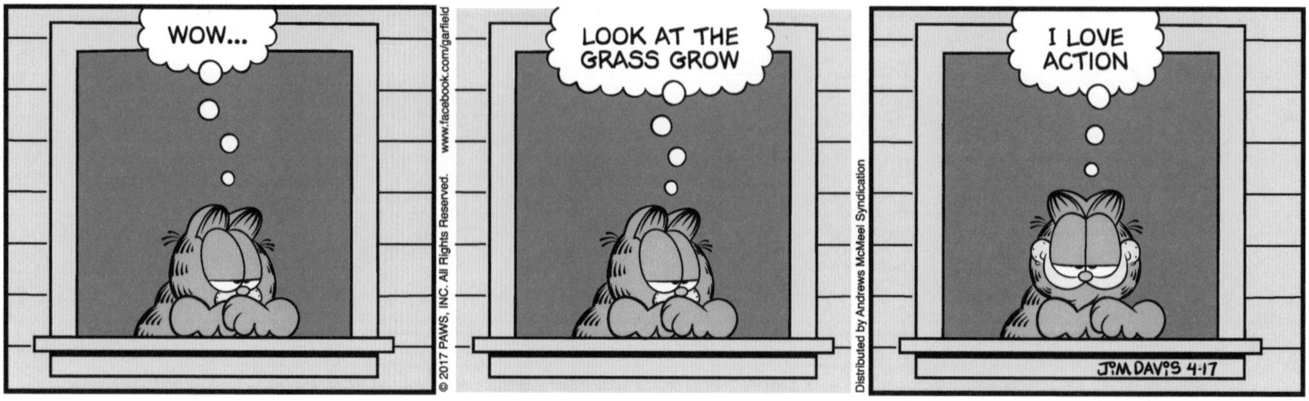
WOW...
LOOK AT THE GRASS GROW
I LOVE ACTION
JIM DAVIS 4-17


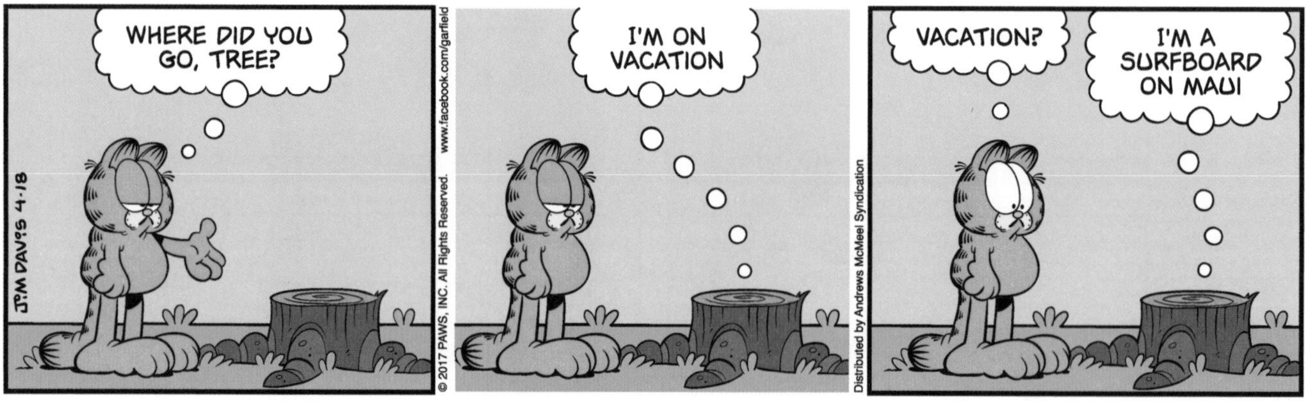
WHERE DID YOU GO, TREE?
I'M ON VACATION
VACATION?
I'M A SURFBOARD ON MAUI
JIM DAVIS 4-18


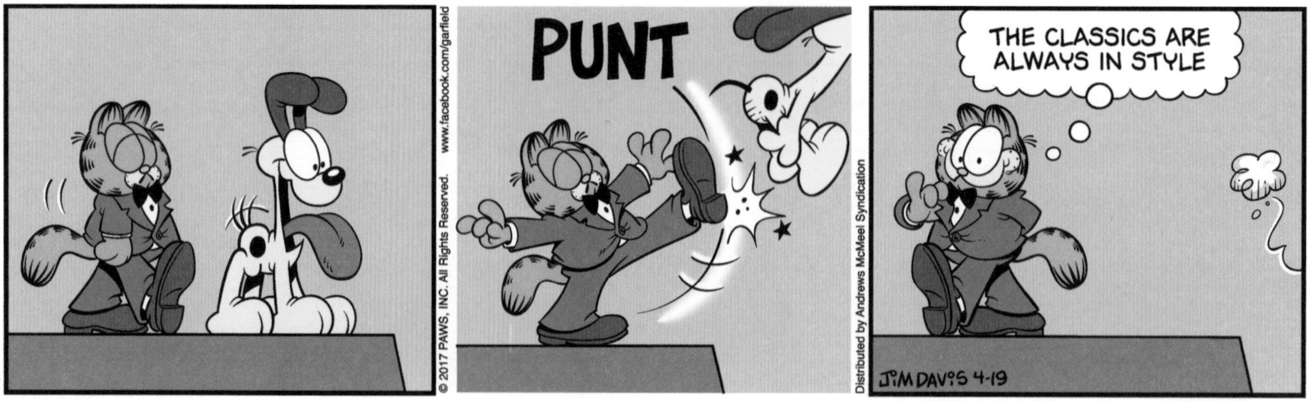
PUNT
THE CLASSICS ARE ALWAYS IN STYLE
JIM DAVIS 4-19

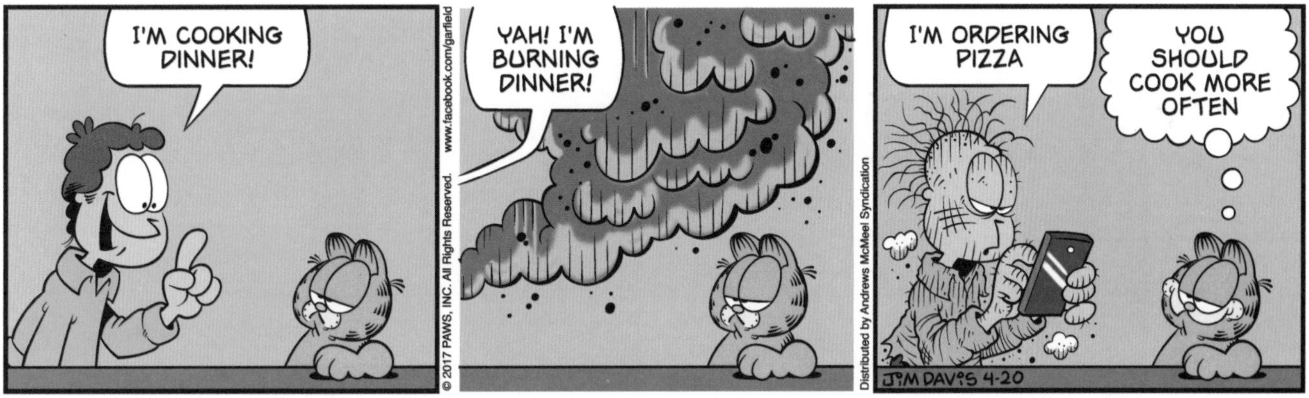
I'M COOKING DINNER!
YAH! I'M BURNING DINNER!
I'M ORDERING PIZZA
YOU SHOULD COOK MORE OFTEN
JIM DAVIS 4-20


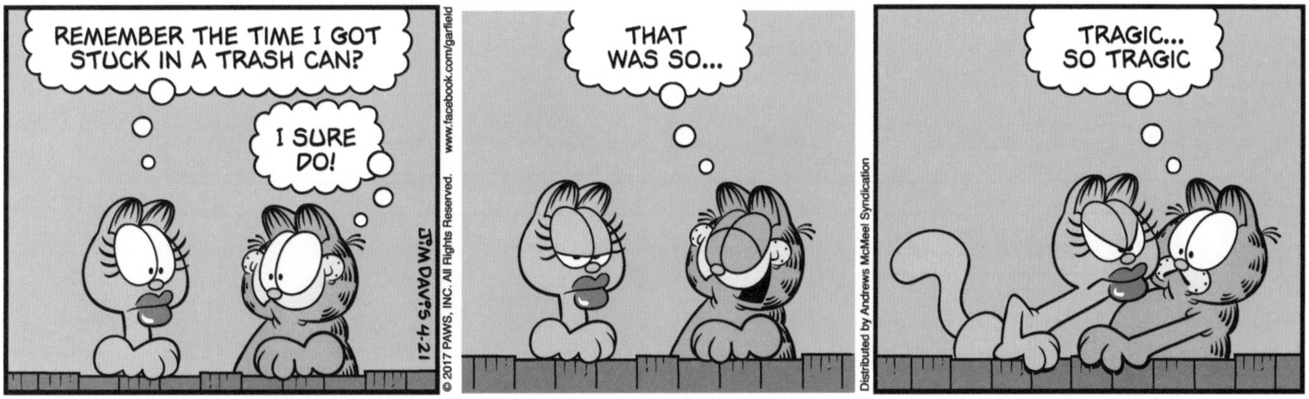
REMEMBER THE TIME I GOT STUCK IN A TRASH CAN?
I SURE DO!
JIM DAVIS 4-21
THAT WAS SO...
TRAGIC... SO TRAGIC


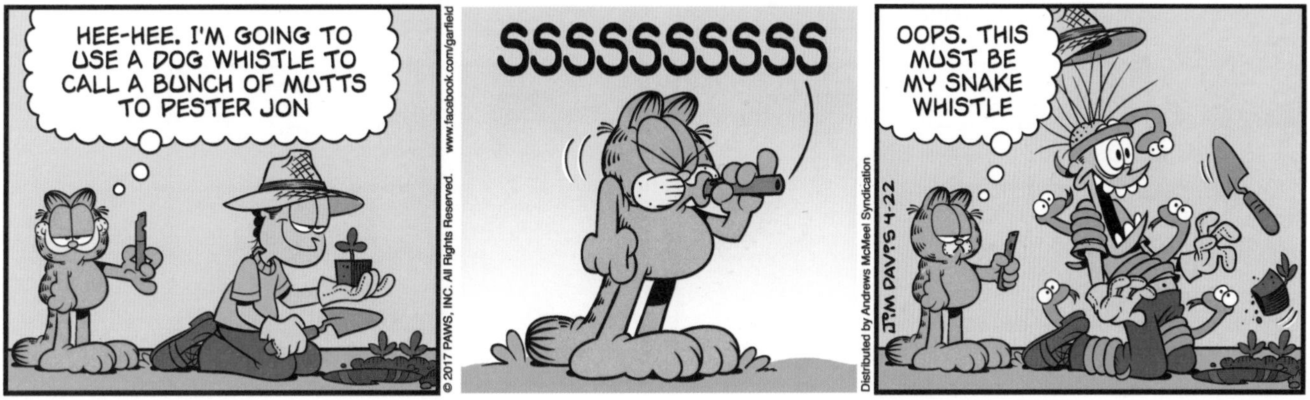
HEE-HEE. I'M GOING TO USE A DOG WHISTLE TO CALL A BUNCH OF MUTTS TO PESTER JON
SSSSSSSSSS
OOPS. THIS MUST BE MY SNAKE WHISTLE
JIM DAVIS 4-22

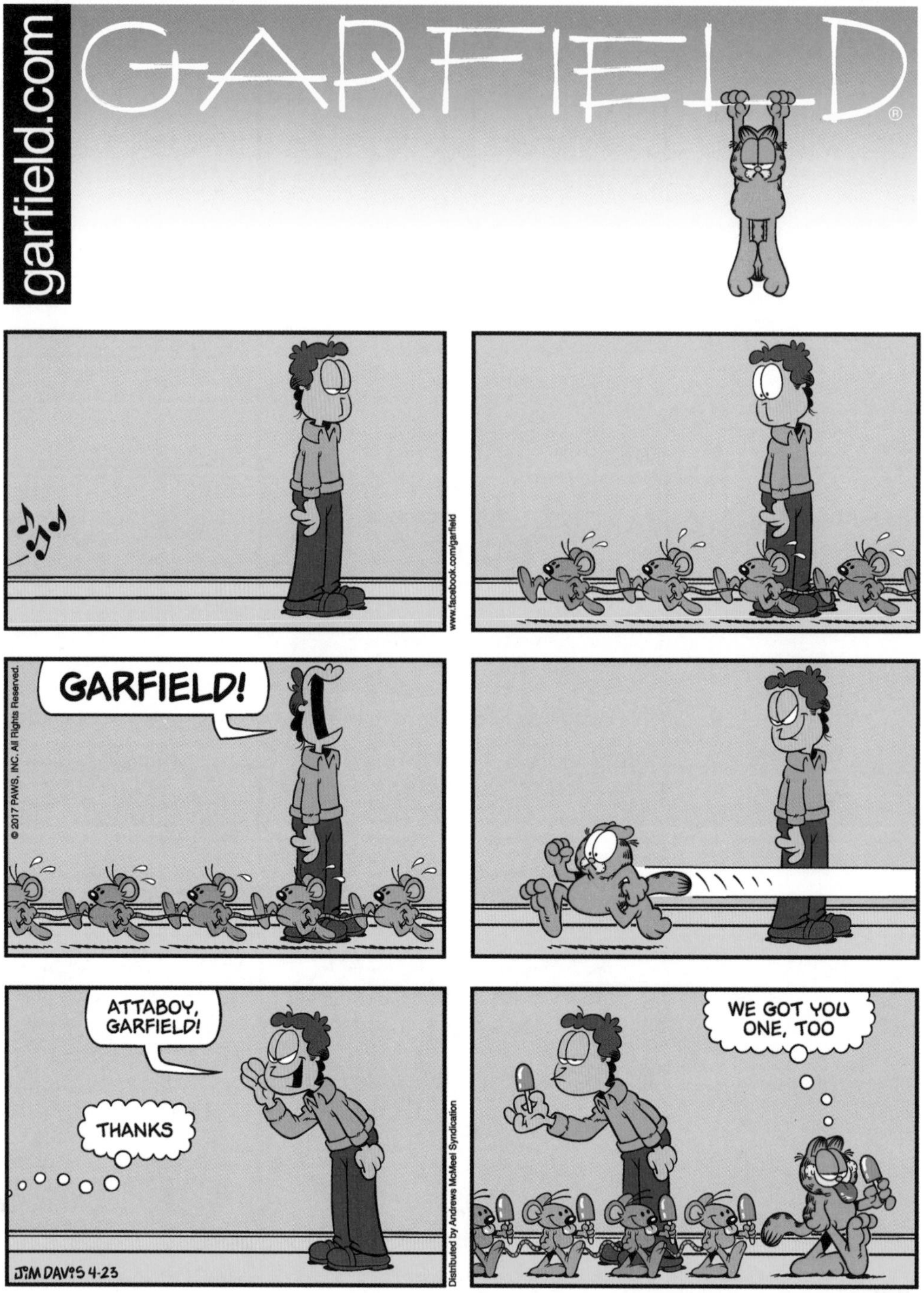
garfield.com
GARFIELD
GARFIELD!
ATTABOY, GARFIELD!
THANKS
WE GOT YOU ONE, TOO
JIM DAVIS 4-23
© 2017 PAWS, INC. All Rights Reserved.
www.facebook.com/garfield
Distributed by Andrews McMeel Syndication

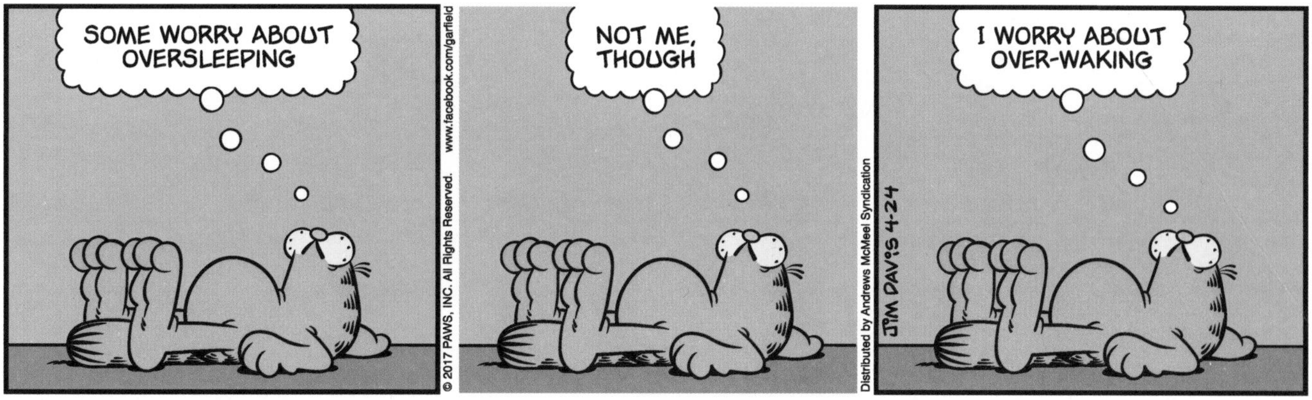
SOME WORRY ABOUT OVERSLEEPING
NOT ME, THOUGH
I WORRY ABOUT OVER-WAKING
© 2017 PAWS, INC. All Rights Reserved. www.facebook.com/garfield
Distributed by Andrews McMeel Syndication
JIM DAVIS 4-24

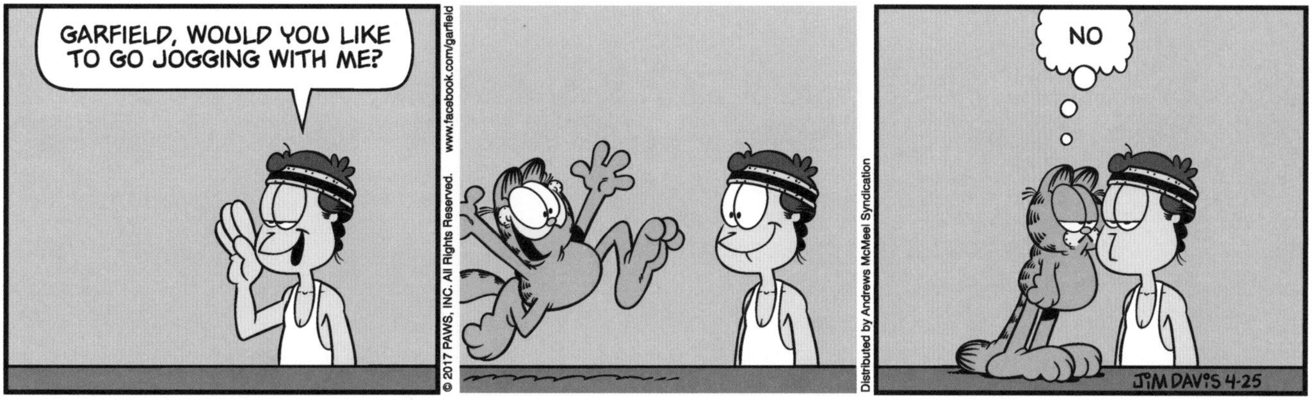
GARFIELD, WOULD YOU LIKE TO GO JOGGING WITH ME?
NO
© 2017 PAWS, INC. All Rights Reserved. www.facebook.com/garfield
Distributed by Andrews McMeel Syndication
JIM DAVIS 4-25

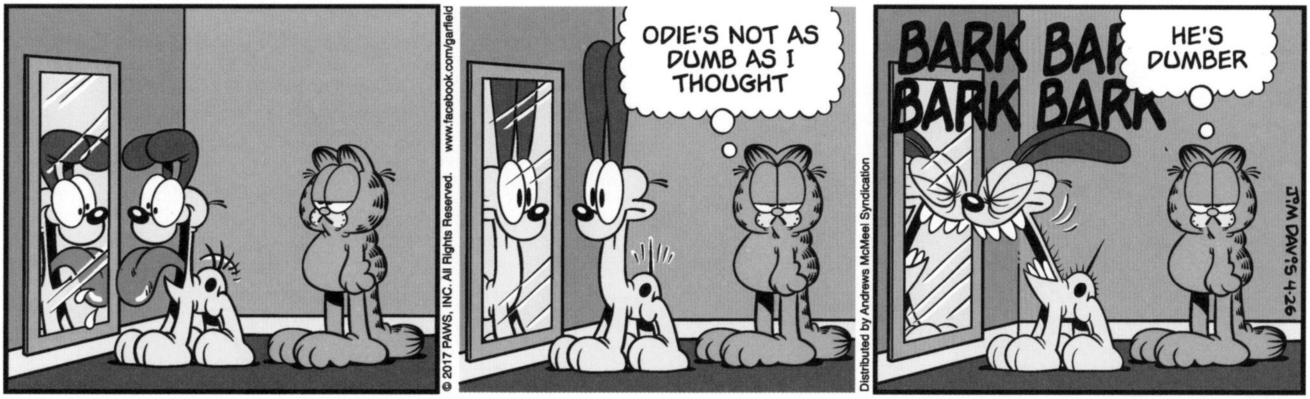
ODIE'S NOT AS DUMB AS I THOUGHT
BARK BARK BARK BARK
HE'S DUMBER
© 2017 PAWS, INC. All Rights Reserved. www.facebook.com/garfield
Distributed by Andrews McMeel Syndication
JIM DAVIS 4-26

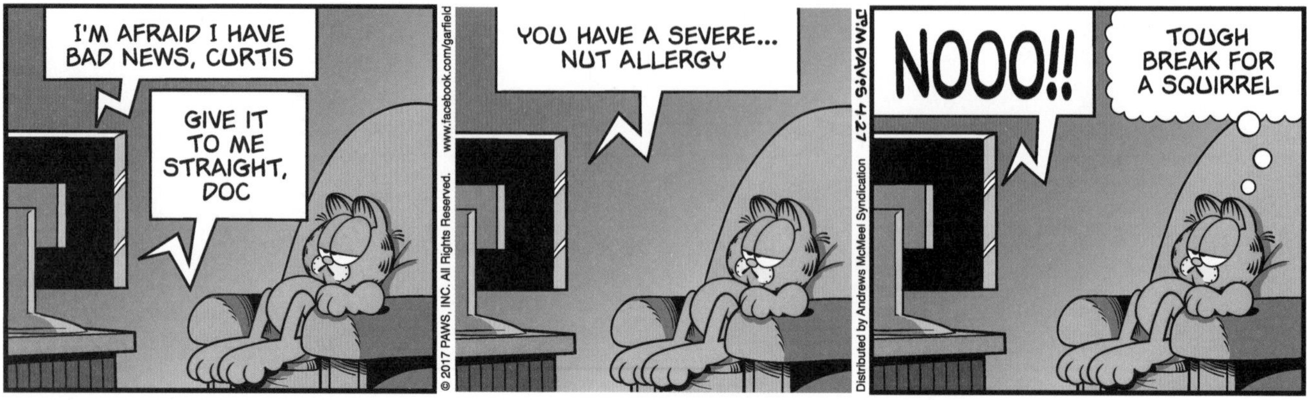
I'M AFRAID I HAVE BAD NEWS, CURTIS
GIVE IT TO ME STRAIGHT, DOC
© 2017 PAWS, INC. All Rights Reserved. www.facebook.com/garfield
YOU HAVE A SEVERE... NUT ALLERGY
JIM DAVIS 4-27
Distributed by Andrews McMeel Syndication
NOOO!!
TOUGH BREAK FOR A SQUIRREL

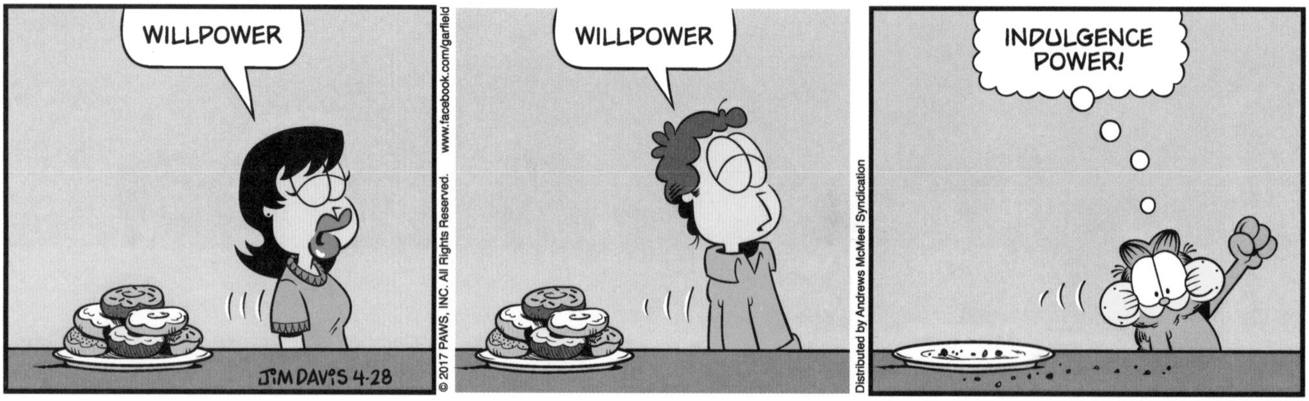
WILLPOWER
JIM DAVIS 4-28
© 2017 PAWS, INC. All Rights Reserved. www.facebook.com/garfield
WILLPOWER
Distributed by Andrews McMeel Syndication
INDULGENCE POWER!

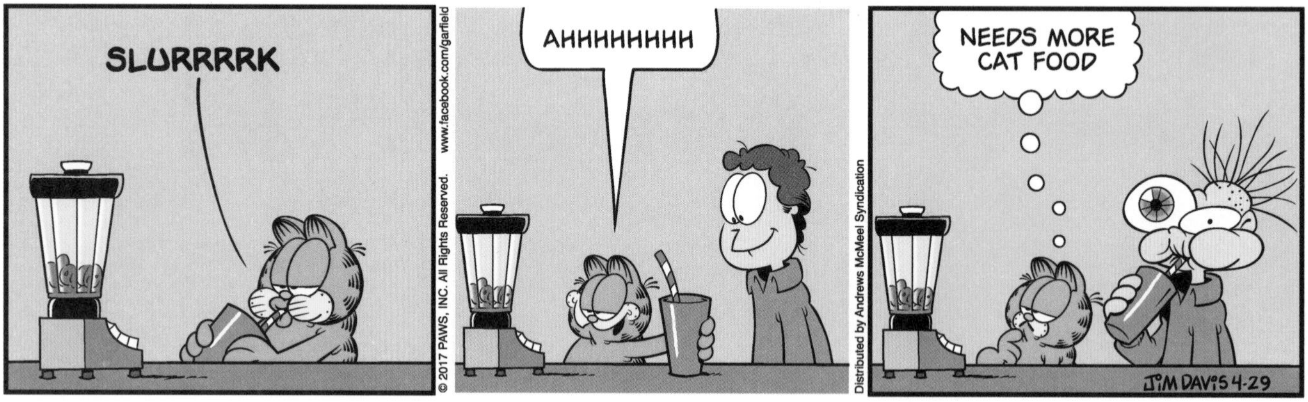
SLURRRRK
© 2017 PAWS, INC. All Rights Reserved. www.facebook.com/garfield
AHHHHHHHH
Distributed by Andrews McMeel Syndication
NEEDS MORE CAT FOOD
JIM DAVIS 4-29

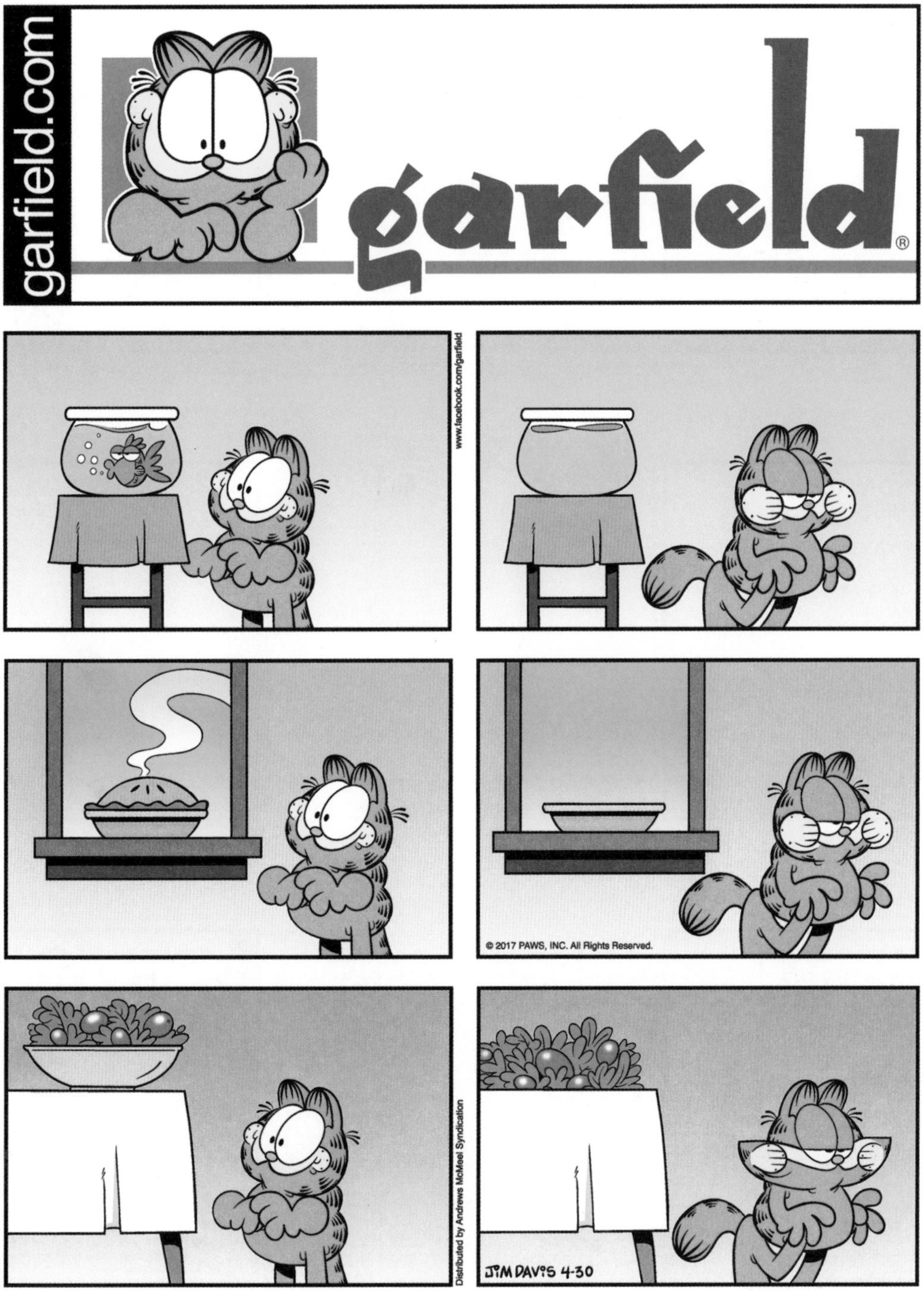
garfield.com
garfield
www.facebook.com/garfield
© 2017 PAWS, INC. All Rights Reserved.
Distributed by Andrews McMeel Syndication
JIM DAVIS 4-30

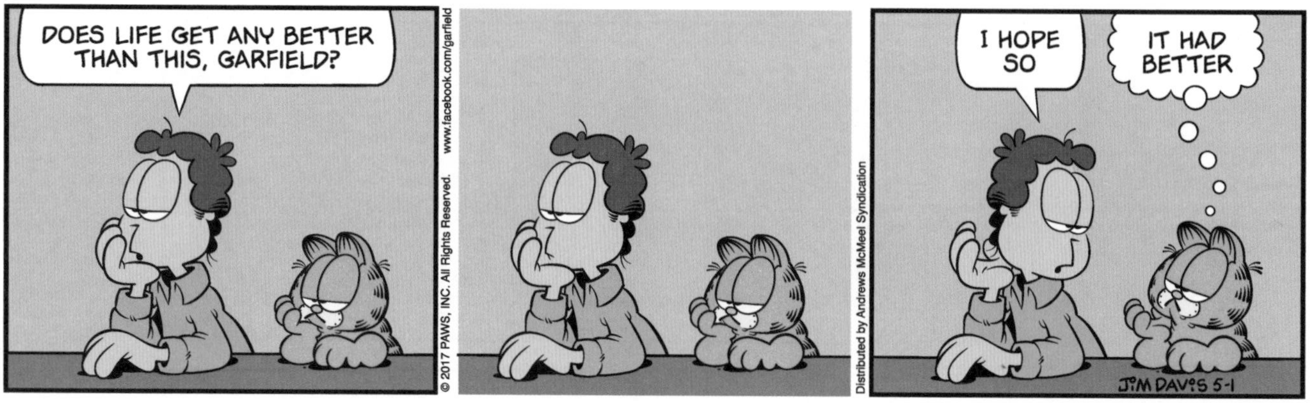
DOES LIFE GET ANY BETTER THAN THIS, GARFIELD?
I HOPE SO
IT HAD BETTER
JIM DAVIS 5-1
© 2017 PAWS, INC. All Rights Reserved. www.facebook.com/garfield
Distributed by Andrews McMeel Syndication

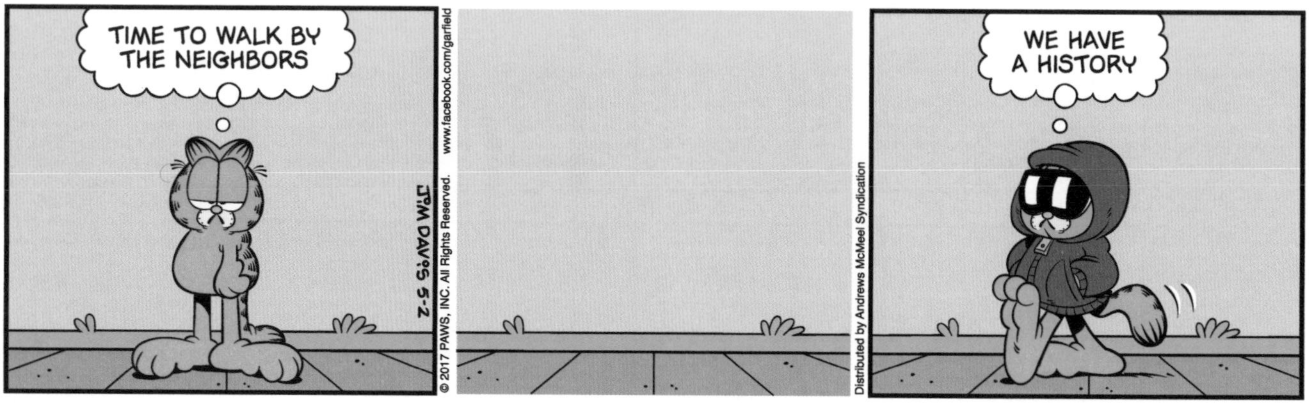
TIME TO WALK BY THE NEIGHBORS
JIM DAVIS 5-2
WE HAVE A HISTORY
© 2017 PAWS, INC. All Rights Reserved. www.facebook.com/garfield
Distributed by Andrews McMeel Syndication

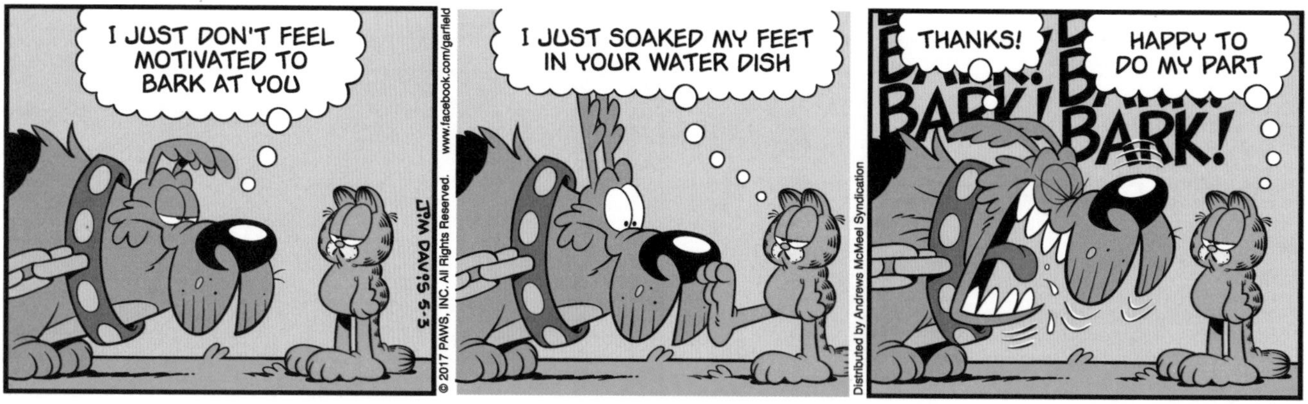
I JUST DON'T FEEL MOTIVATED TO BARK AT YOU
JIM DAVIS 5-3
I JUST SOAKED MY FEET IN YOUR WATER DISH
THANKS!
HAPPY TO DO MY PART
BARK!
© 2017 PAWS, INC. All Rights Reserved. www.facebook.com/garfield
Distributed by Andrews McMeel Syndication

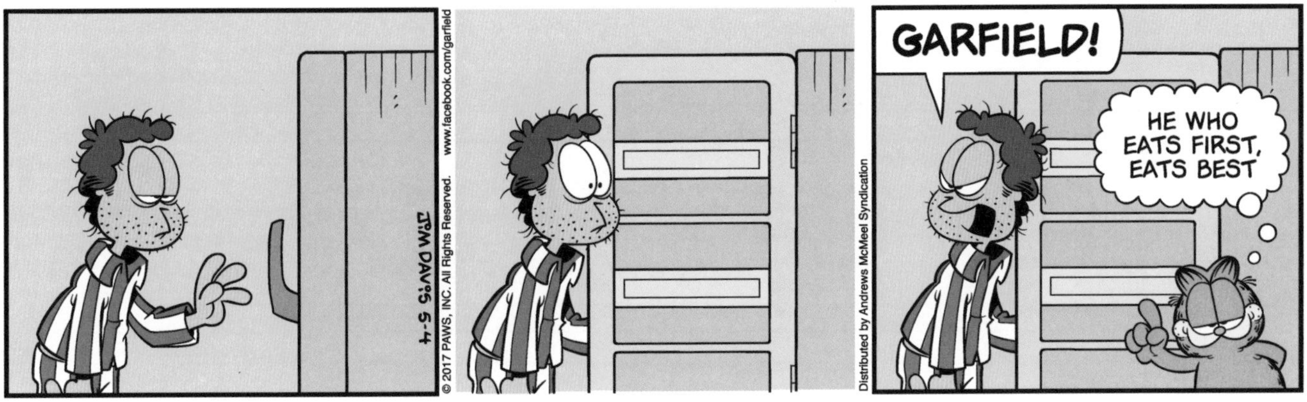
JIM DAVIS 5-4
© 2017 PAWS, INC. All Rights Reserved. www.facebook.com/garfield
GARFIELD!
HE WHO EATS FIRST, EATS BEST
Distributed by Andrews McMeel Syndication

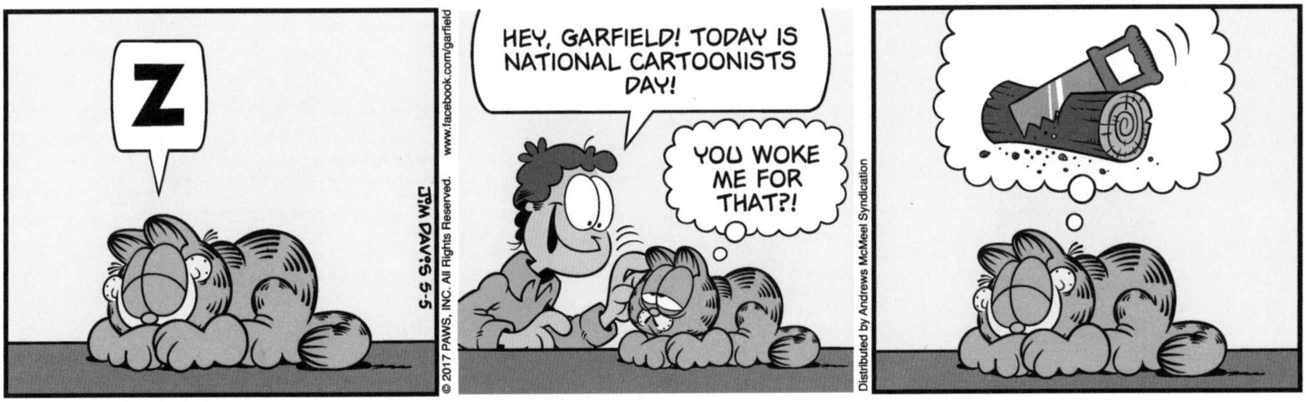
Z
JIM DAVIS 5-5
© 2017 PAWS, INC. All Rights Reserved. www.facebook.com/garfield
HEY, GARFIELD! TODAY IS NATIONAL CARTOONISTS DAY!
YOU WOKE ME FOR THAT?!
Distributed by Andrews McMeel Syndication

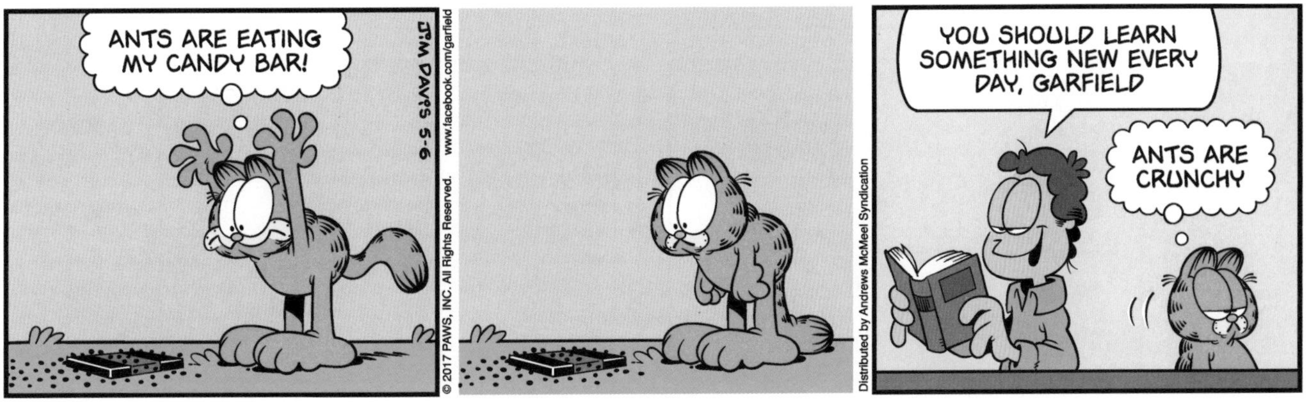
ANTS ARE EATING MY CANDY BAR!
JIM DAVIS 5-6
© 2017 PAWS, INC. All Rights Reserved. www.facebook.com/garfield
Distributed by Andrews McMeel Syndication
YOU SHOULD LEARN SOMETHING NEW EVERY DAY, GARFIELD
ANTS ARE CRUNCHY

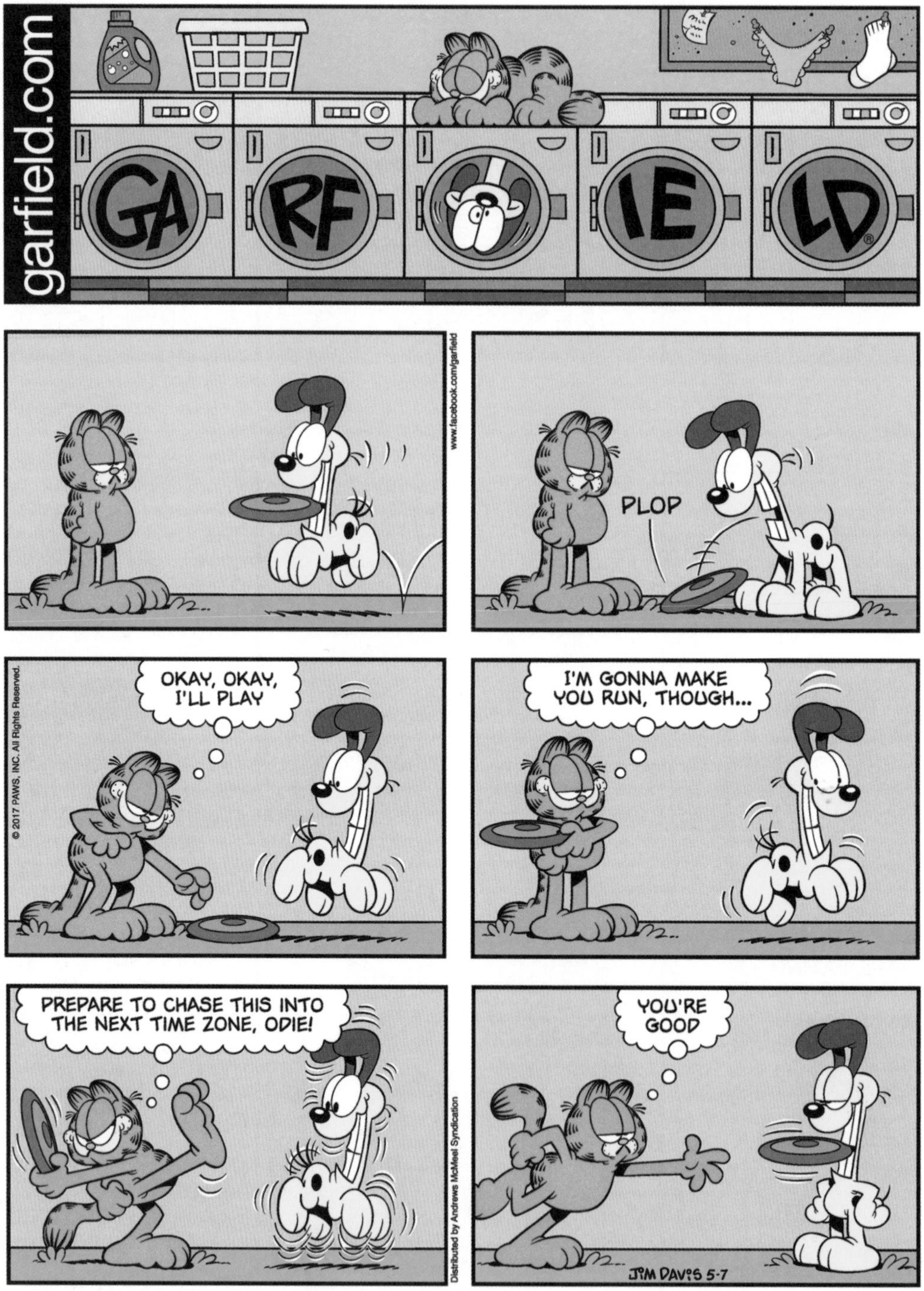
garfield.com
GARFIELD®
www.facebook.com/garfield
PLOP
© 2017 PAWS, INC. All Rights Reserved.
OKAY, OKAY, I'LL PLAY
I'M GONNA MAKE YOU RUN, THOUGH...
PREPARE TO CHASE THIS INTO THE NEXT TIME ZONE, ODIE!
Distributed by Andrews McMeel Syndication
YOU'RE GOOD
JIM DAVIS 5-7

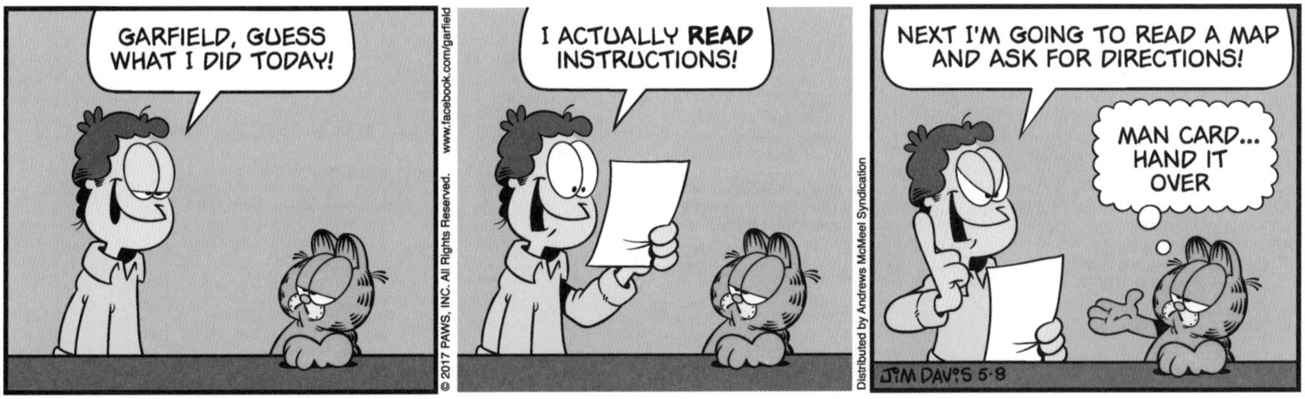
GARFIELD, GUESS WHAT I DID TODAY!
© 2017 PAWS, INC. All Rights Reserved. www.facebook.com/garfield
I ACTUALLY **READ** INSTRUCTIONS!
Distributed by Andrews McMeel Syndication
NEXT I'M GOING TO READ A MAP AND ASK FOR DIRECTIONS!
MAN CARD... HAND IT OVER
JIM DAVIS 5-8

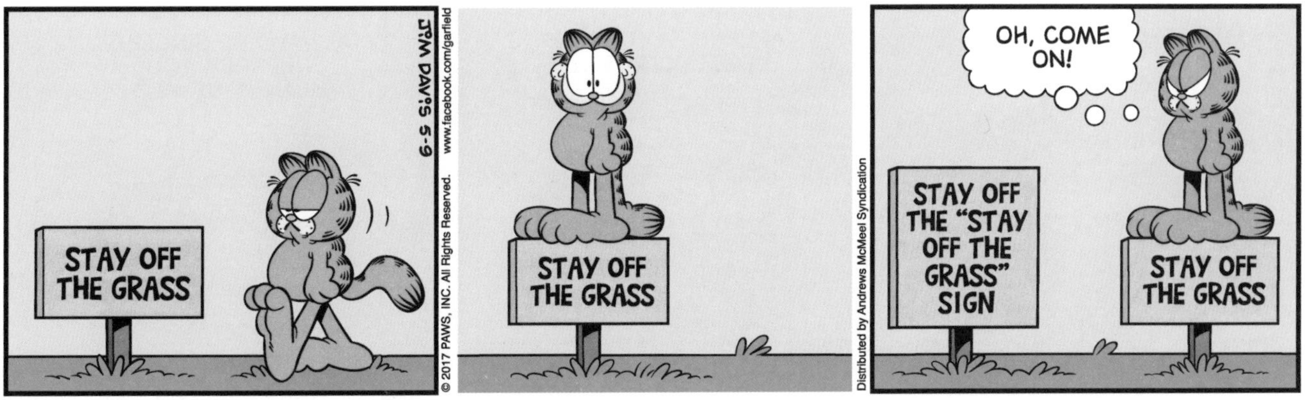
STAY OFF THE GRASS
JIM DAVIS 5-9
© 2017 PAWS, INC. All Rights Reserved. www.facebook.com/garfield
STAY OFF THE GRASS
Distributed by Andrews McMeel Syndication
OH, COME ON!
STAY OFF THE "STAY OFF THE GRASS" SIGN
STAY OFF THE GRASS

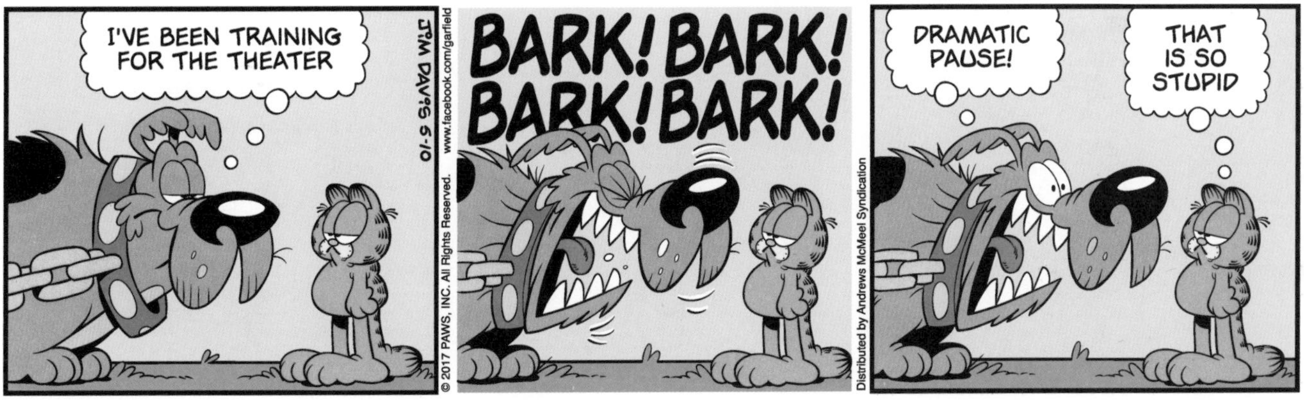
I'VE BEEN TRAINING FOR THE THEATER
JIM DAVIS 5-10
© 2017 PAWS, INC. All Rights Reserved. www.facebook.com/garfield
BARK! BARK! BARK! BARK!
Distributed by Andrews McMeel Syndication
DRAMATIC PAUSE!
THAT IS SO STUPID

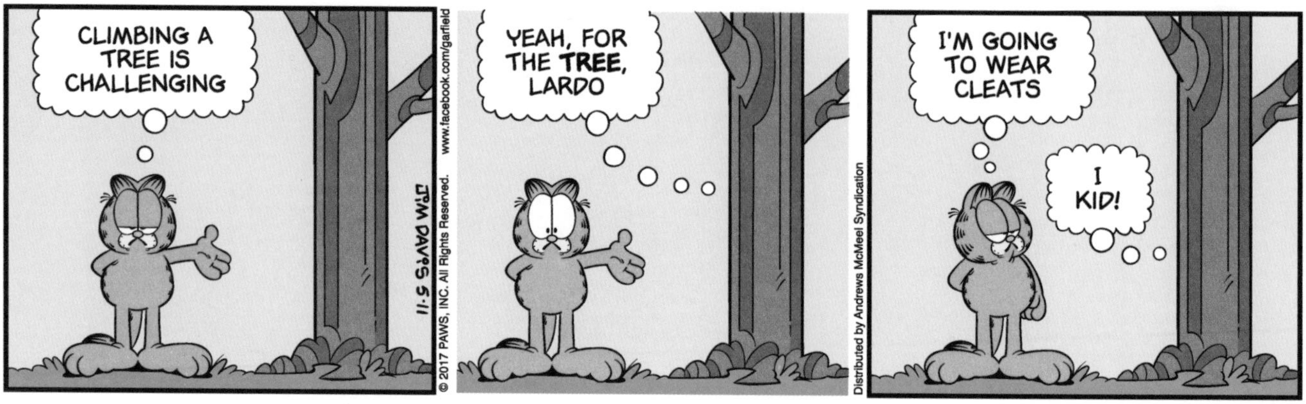
CLIMBING A TREE IS CHALLENGING
YEAH, FOR THE **TREE**, LARDO
I'M GOING TO WEAR CLEATS
I KID!
JIM DAVIS 5-11
© 2017 PAWS, INC. All Rights Reserved. www.facebook.com/garfield
Distributed by Andrews McMeel Syndication

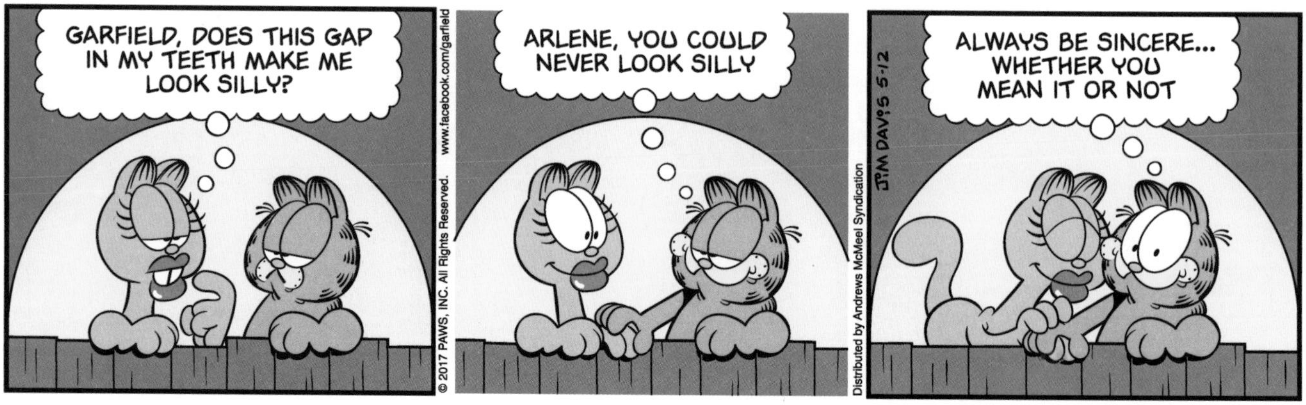
GARFIELD, DOES THIS GAP IN MY TEETH MAKE ME LOOK SILLY?
ARLENE, YOU COULD NEVER LOOK SILLY
ALWAYS BE SINCERE... WHETHER YOU MEAN IT OR NOT
JIM DAVIS 5-12
© 2017 PAWS, INC. All Rights Reserved. www.facebook.com/garfield
Distributed by Andrews McMeel Syndication

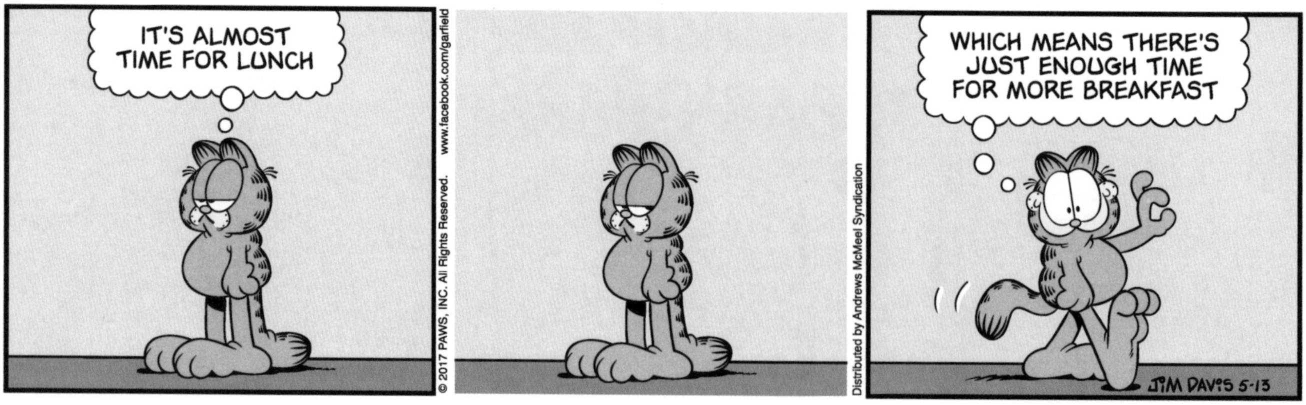
IT'S ALMOST TIME FOR LUNCH
WHICH MEANS THERE'S JUST ENOUGH TIME FOR MORE BREAKFAST
JIM DAVIS 5-13
© 2017 PAWS, INC. All Rights Reserved. www.facebook.com/garfield
Distributed by Andrews McMeel Syndication

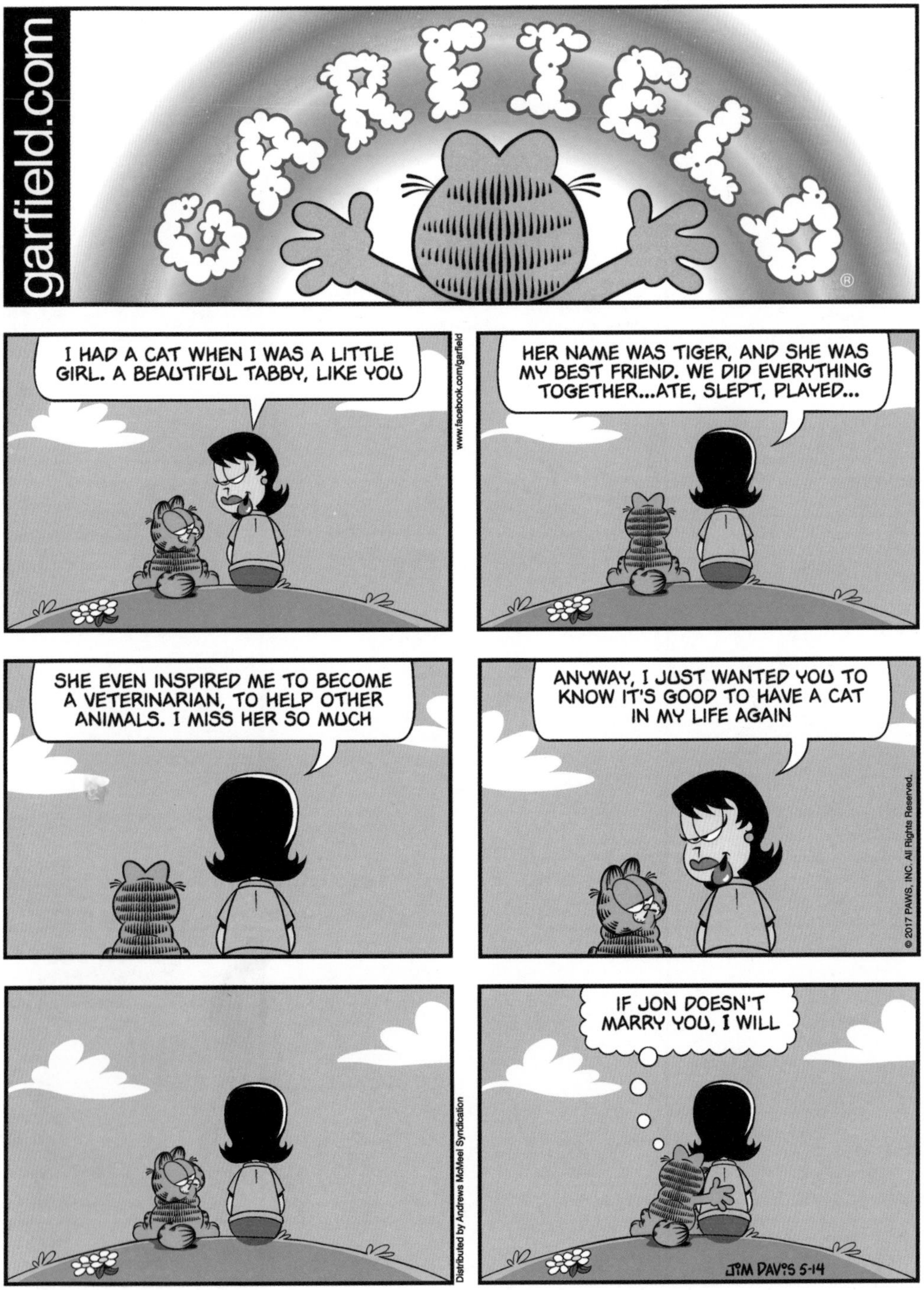
garfield.com
GARFIELD
I HAD A CAT WHEN I WAS A LITTLE GIRL. A BEAUTIFUL TABBY, LIKE YOU
www.facebook.com/garfield
HER NAME WAS TIGER, AND SHE WAS MY BEST FRIEND. WE DID EVERYTHING TOGETHER...ATE, SLEPT, PLAYED...
SHE EVEN INSPIRED ME TO BECOME A VETERINARIAN, TO HELP OTHER ANIMALS. I MISS HER SO MUCH
ANYWAY, I JUST WANTED YOU TO KNOW IT'S GOOD TO HAVE A CAT IN MY LIFE AGAIN
© 2017 PAWS, INC. All Rights Reserved.
Distributed by Andrews McMeel Syndication
IF JON DOESN'T MARRY YOU, I WILL
JIM DAVIS 5-14

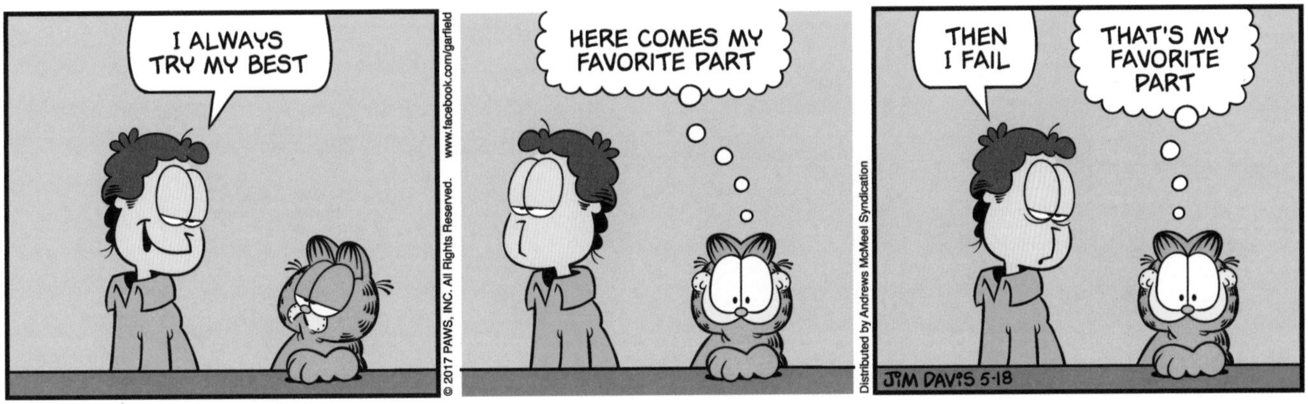
I ALWAYS TRY MY BEST
HERE COMES MY FAVORITE PART
THEN I FAIL
THAT'S MY FAVORITE PART
© 2017 PAWS, INC. All Rights Reserved. www.facebook.com/garfield
Distributed by Andrews McMeel Syndication
JIM DAVIS 5-18

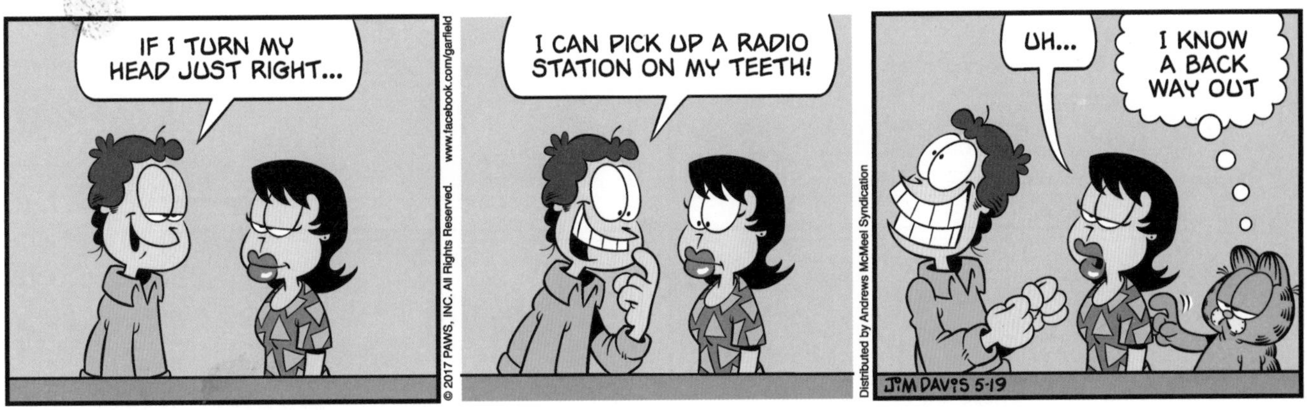
IF I TURN MY HEAD JUST RIGHT...
I CAN PICK UP A RADIO STATION ON MY TEETH!
UH...
I KNOW A BACK WAY OUT
© 2017 PAWS, INC. All Rights Reserved. www.facebook.com/garfield
Distributed by Andrews McMeel Syndication
JIM DAVIS 5-19

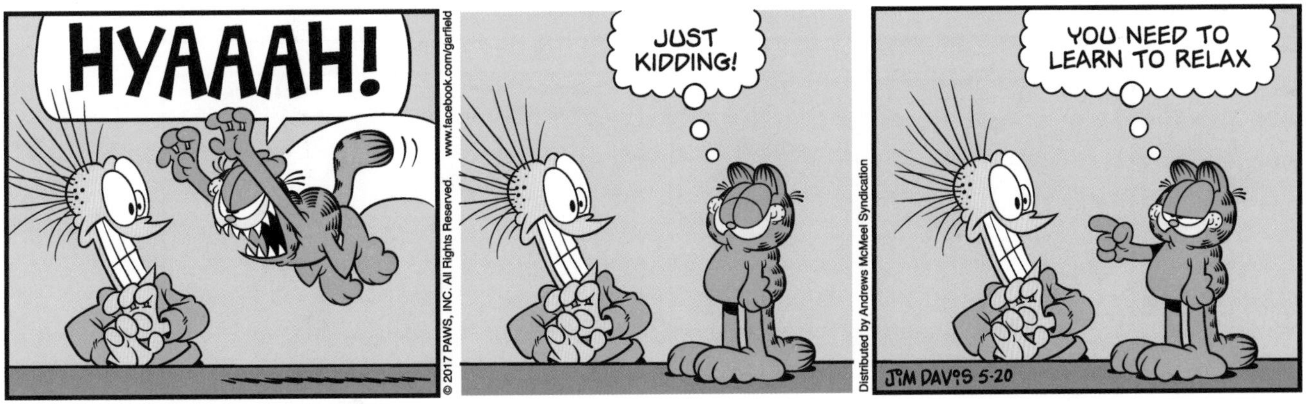
HYAAAH!
JUST KIDDING!
YOU NEED TO LEARN TO RELAX
© 2017 PAWS, INC. All Rights Reserved. www.facebook.com/garfield
Distributed by Andrews McMeel Syndication
JIM DAVIS 5-20

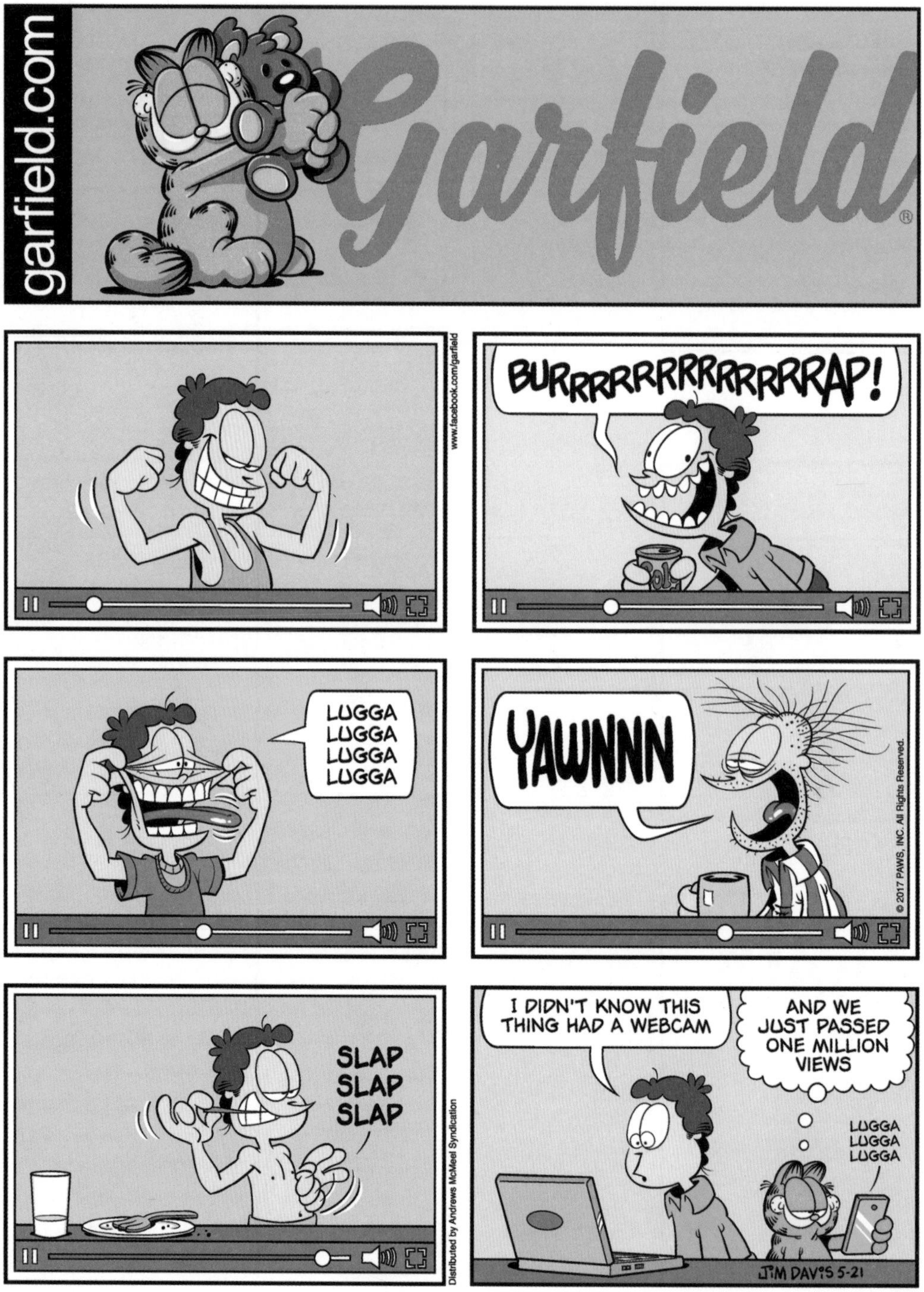
garfield.com
Garfield®
www.facebook.com/garfield
BURRRRRRRRRRRRRAP!
LUGGA LUGGA LUGGA LUGGA
YAWNNN
© 2017 PAWS, INC. All Rights Reserved.
SLAP SLAP SLAP
Distributed by Andrews McMeel Syndication
I DIDN'T KNOW THIS THING HAD A WEBCAM
AND WE JUST PASSED ONE MILLION VIEWS
LUGGA LUGGA LUGGA
JIM DAVIS 5-21

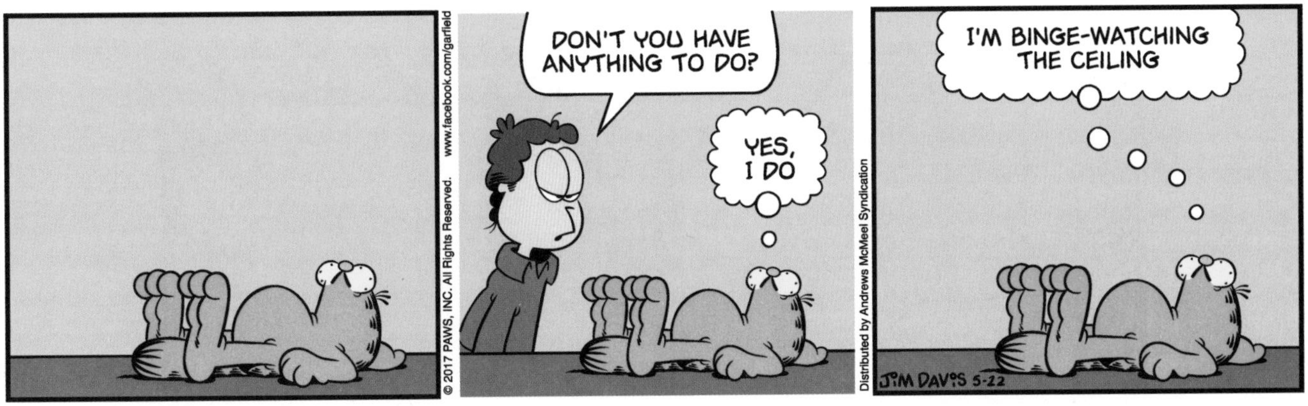
© 2017 PAWS, INC. All Rights Reserved. www.facebook.com/garfield
DON'T YOU HAVE ANYTHING TO DO?
YES, I DO
Distributed by Andrews McMeel Syndication
I'M BINGE-WATCHING THE CEILING
JIM DAVIS 5-22

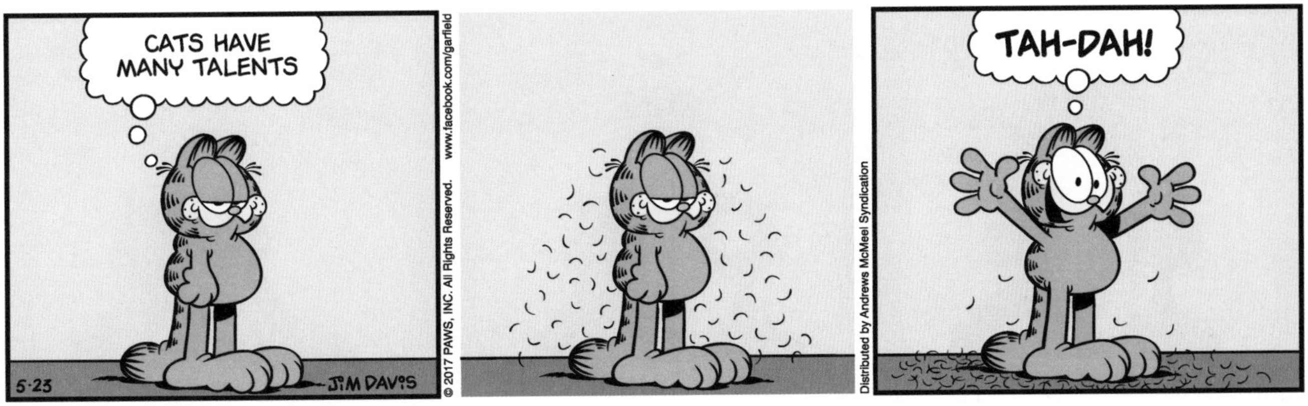
CATS HAVE MANY TALENTS
5-23
JIM DAVIS
© 2017 PAWS, INC. All Rights Reserved. www.facebook.com/garfield
Distributed by Andrews McMeel Syndication
TAH-DAH!

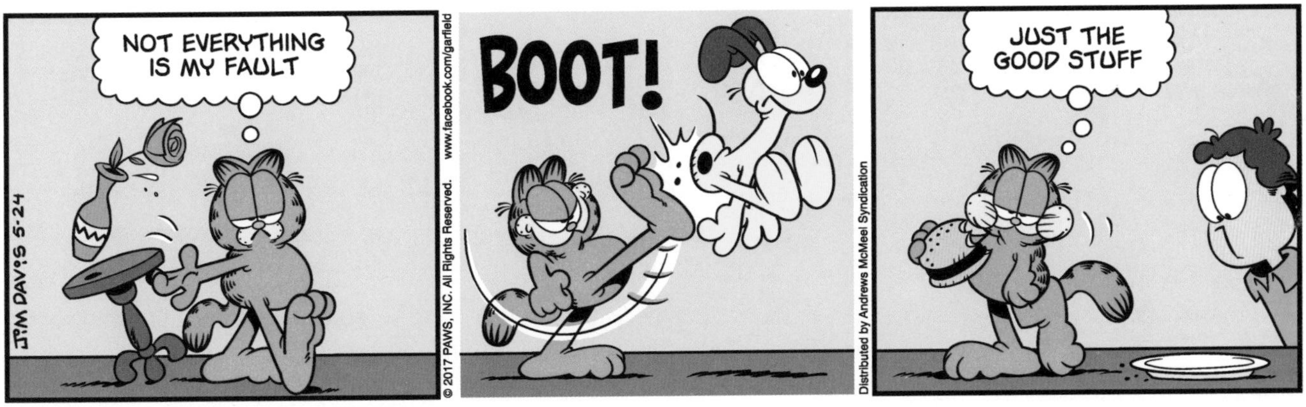
NOT EVERYTHING IS MY FAULT
JIM DAVIS 5-24
© 2017 PAWS, INC. All Rights Reserved. www.facebook.com/garfield
BOOT!
Distributed by Andrews McMeel Syndication
JUST THE GOOD STUFF

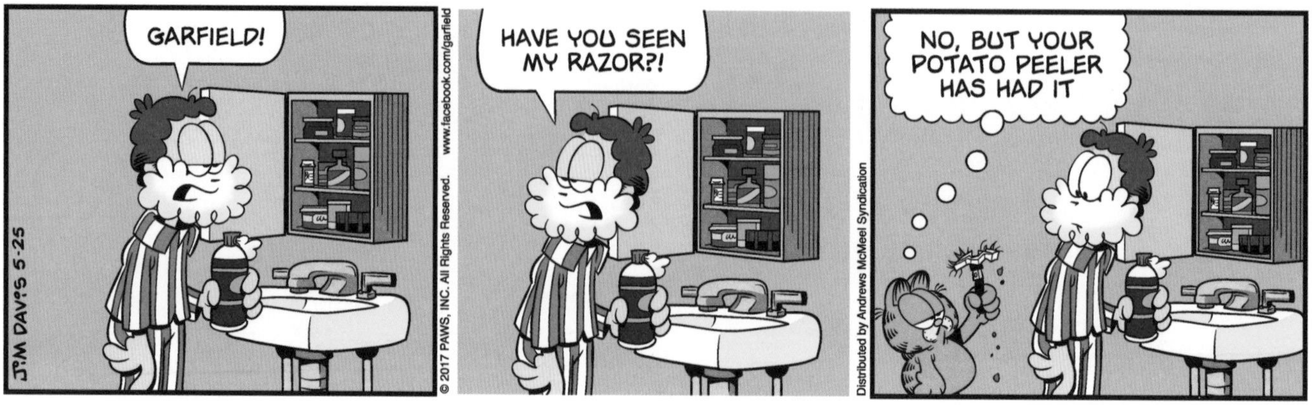
GARFIELD!
HAVE YOU SEEN MY RAZOR?!
NO, BUT YOUR POTATO PEELER HAS HAD IT
JIM DAVIS 5-25
© 2017 PAWS, INC. All Rights Reserved. www.facebook.com/garfield
Distributed by Andrews McMeel Syndication

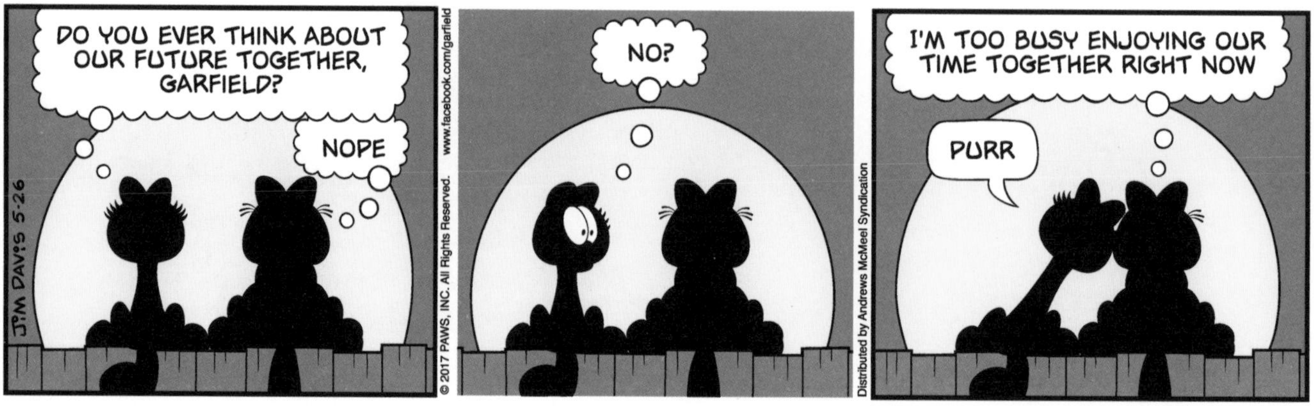
DO YOU EVER THINK ABOUT OUR FUTURE TOGETHER, GARFIELD?
NOPE
NO?
I'M TOO BUSY ENJOYING OUR TIME TOGETHER RIGHT NOW
PURR
JIM DAVIS 5-26
© 2017 PAWS, INC. All Rights Reserved. www.facebook.com/garfield
Distributed by Andrews McMeel Syndication

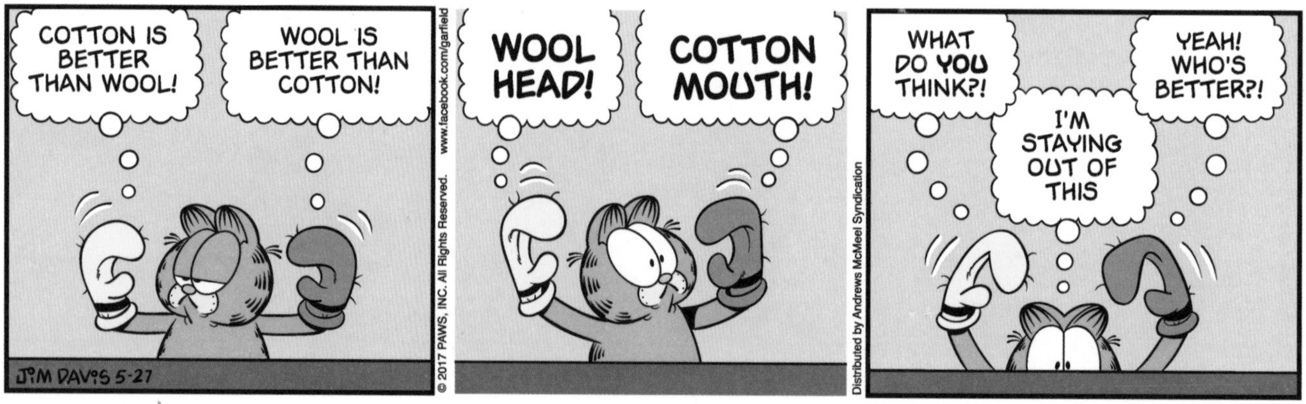
COTTON IS BETTER THAN WOOL!
WOOL IS BETTER THAN COTTON!
WOOL HEAD!
COTTON MOUTH!
WHAT DO YOU THINK?!
YEAH! WHO'S BETTER?!
I'M STAYING OUT OF THIS
JIM DAVIS 5-27
© 2017 PAWS, INC. All Rights Reserved. www.facebook.com/garfield
Distributed by Andrews McMeel Syndication

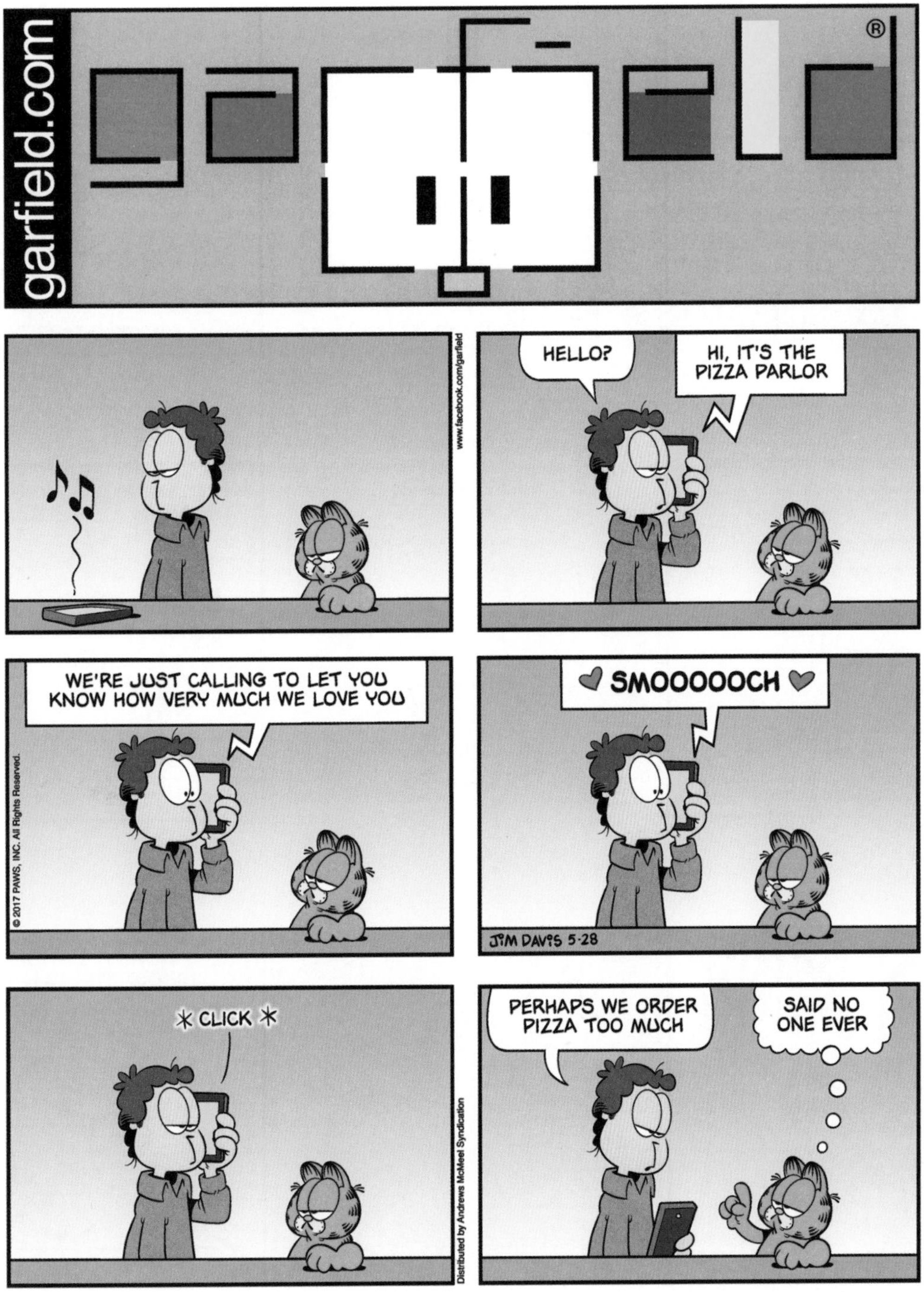
garfield.com
garfield
www.facebook.com/garfield
HELLO?
HI, IT'S THE PIZZA PARLOR
WE'RE JUST CALLING TO LET YOU KNOW HOW VERY MUCH WE LOVE YOU
© 2017 PAWS, INC. All Rights Reserved.
SMOOOOOCH
JIM DAVIS 5-28
* CLICK *
Distributed by Andrews McMeel Syndication
PERHAPS WE ORDER PIZZA TOO MUCH
SAID NO ONE EVER

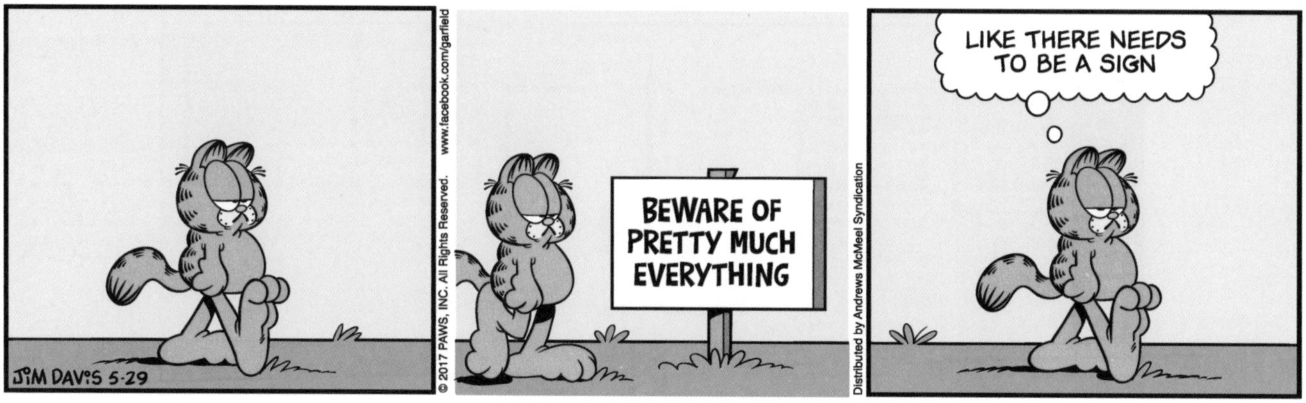
JIM DAVIS 5-29
© 2017 PAWS, INC. All Rights Reserved. www.facebook.com/garfield
BEWARE OF PRETTY MUCH EVERYTHING
Distributed by Andrews McMeel Syndication
LIKE THERE NEEDS TO BE A SIGN

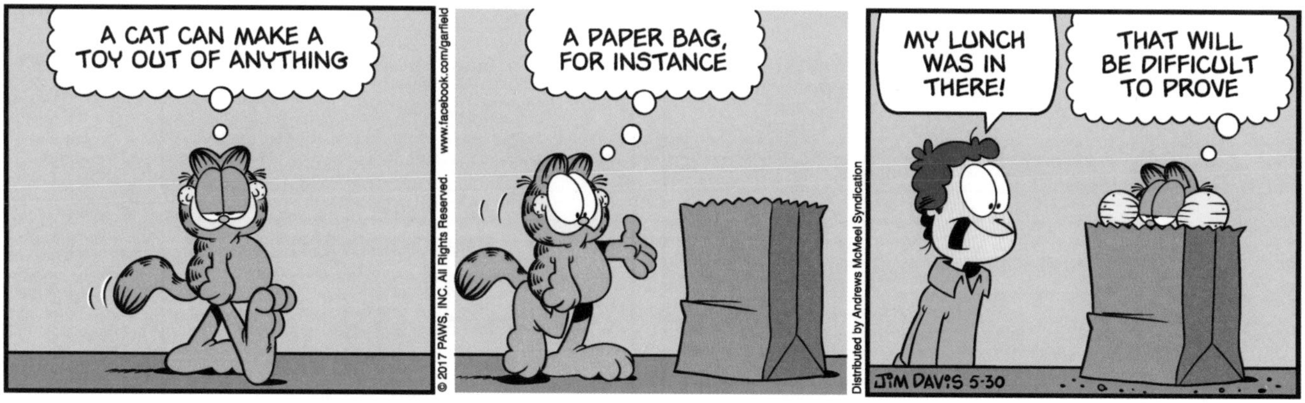
A CAT CAN MAKE A TOY OUT OF ANYTHING
© 2017 PAWS, INC. All Rights Reserved. www.facebook.com/garfield
A PAPER BAG, FOR INSTANCE
Distributed by Andrews McMeel Syndication
MY LUNCH WAS IN THERE!
THAT WILL BE DIFFICULT TO PROVE
JIM DAVIS 5-30

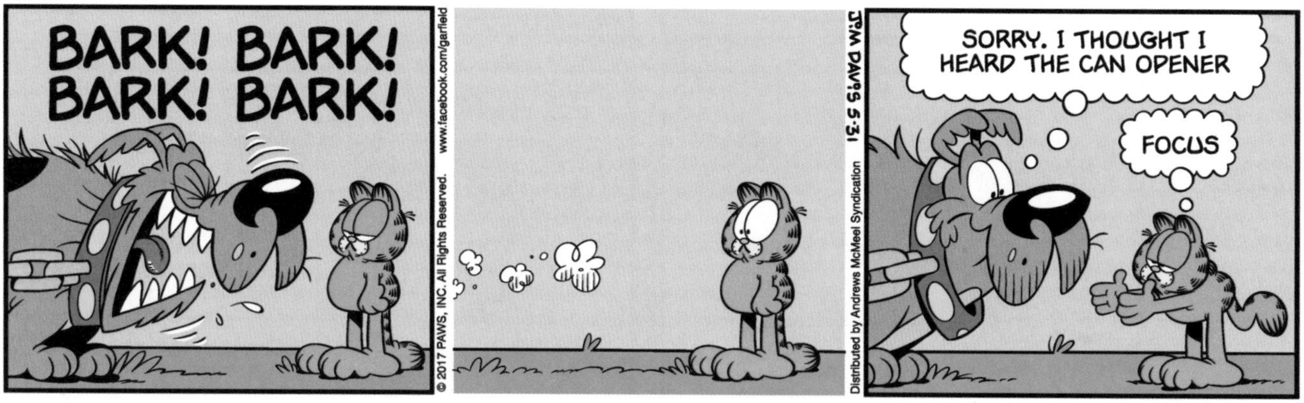
BARK! BARK! BARK! BARK!
© 2017 PAWS, INC. All Rights Reserved. www.facebook.com/garfield
JIM DAVIS 5-31
Distributed by Andrews McMeel Syndication
SORRY. I THOUGHT I HEARD THE CAN OPENER
FOCUS

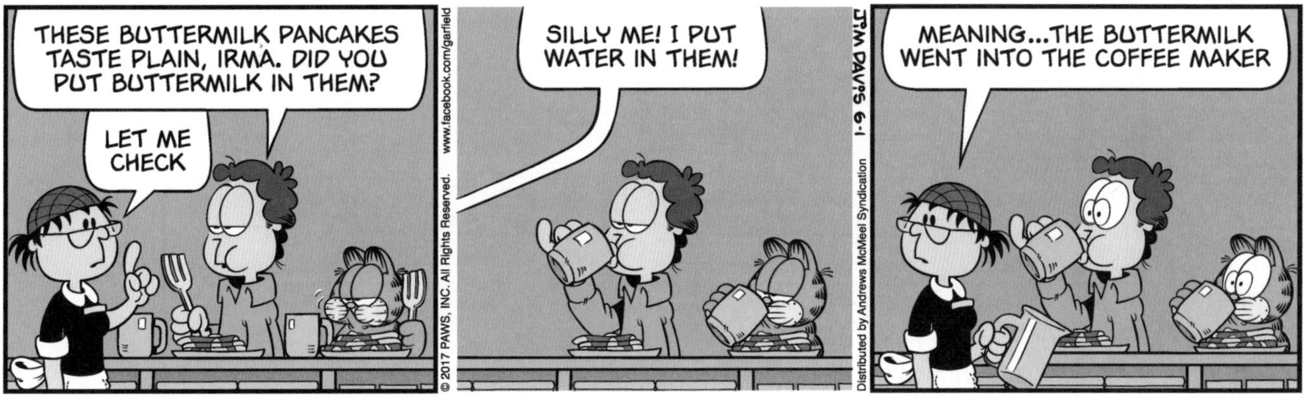
THESE BUTTERMILK PANCAKES TASTE PLAIN, IRMA. DID YOU PUT BUTTERMILK IN THEM?
LET ME CHECK
SILLY ME! I PUT WATER IN THEM!
MEANING...THE BUTTERMILK WENT INTO THE COFFEE MAKER
© 2017 PAWS, INC. All Rights Reserved. www.facebook.com/garfield
JIM DAVIS 6-1
Distributed by Andrews McMeel Syndication

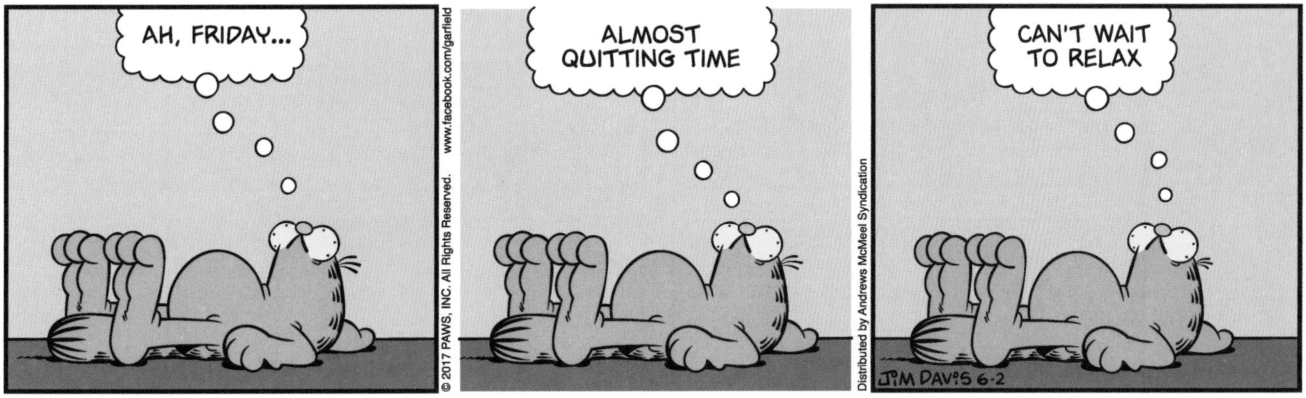
AH, FRIDAY...
ALMOST QUITTING TIME
CAN'T WAIT TO RELAX
© 2017 PAWS, INC. All Rights Reserved. www.facebook.com/garfield
Distributed by Andrews McMeel Syndication
JIM DAVIS 6-2

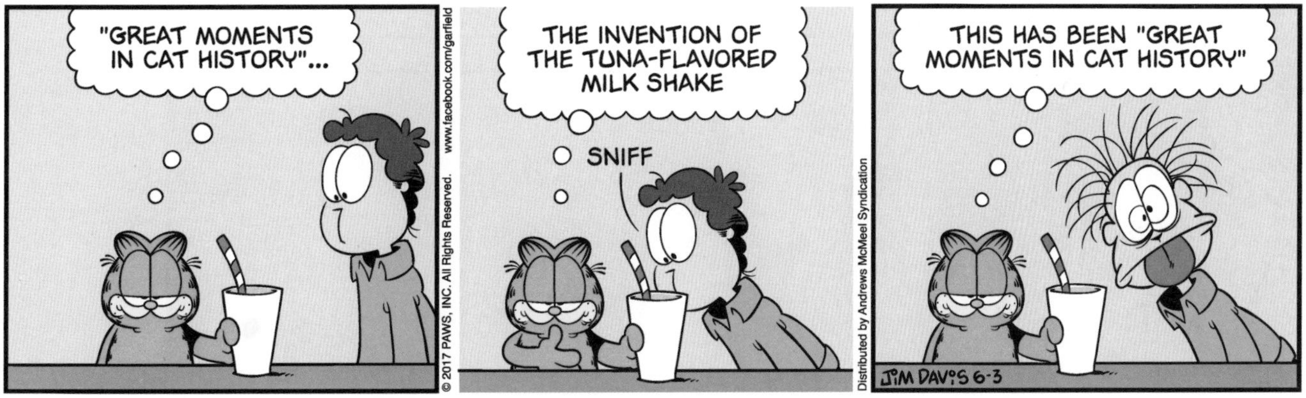
"GREAT MOMENTS IN CAT HISTORY"...
THE INVENTION OF THE TUNA-FLAVORED MILK SHAKE
SNIFF
THIS HAS BEEN "GREAT MOMENTS IN CAT HISTORY"
© 2017 PAWS, INC. All Rights Reserved. www.facebook.com/garfield
Distributed by Andrews McMeel Syndication
JIM DAVIS 6-3

garfield.com
Garfield
JIM DAVIS 6-4
ARE YOU QUITE DONE?!
JUST ONE MORE

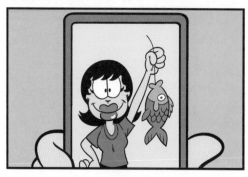

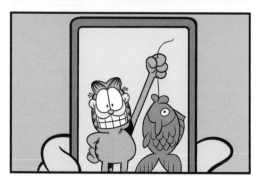

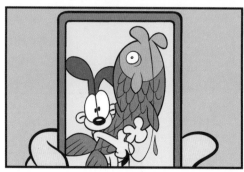

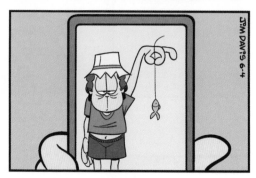

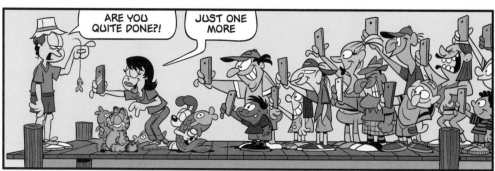

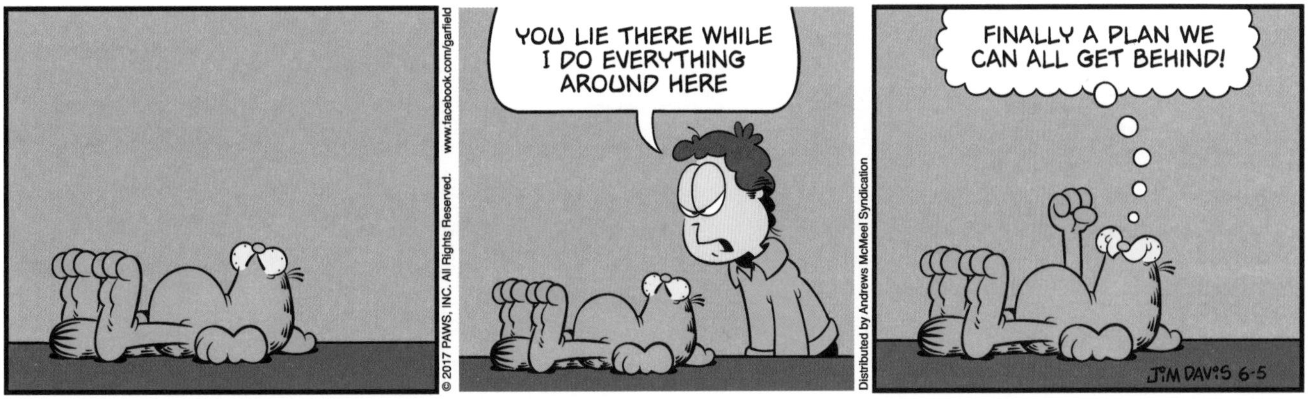
© 2017 PAWS, INC. All Rights Reserved. www.facebook.com/garfield
YOU LIE THERE WHILE I DO EVERYTHING AROUND HERE
Distributed by Andrews McMeel Syndication
FINALLY A PLAN WE CAN ALL GET BEHIND!
JIM DAVIS 6-5

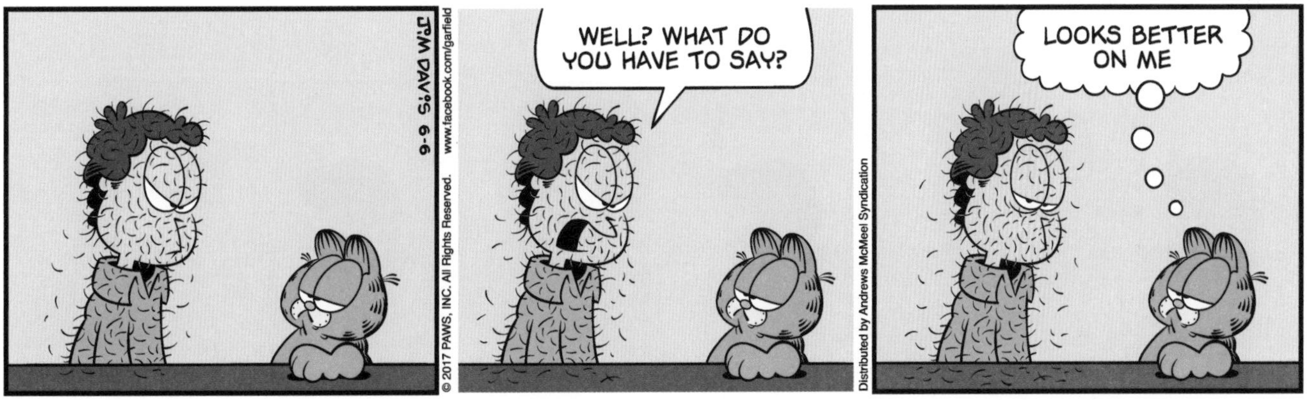
JIM DAVIS 6-6
© 2017 PAWS, INC. All Rights Reserved. www.facebook.com/garfield
WELL? WHAT DO YOU HAVE TO SAY?
Distributed by Andrews McMeel Syndication
LOOKS BETTER ON ME

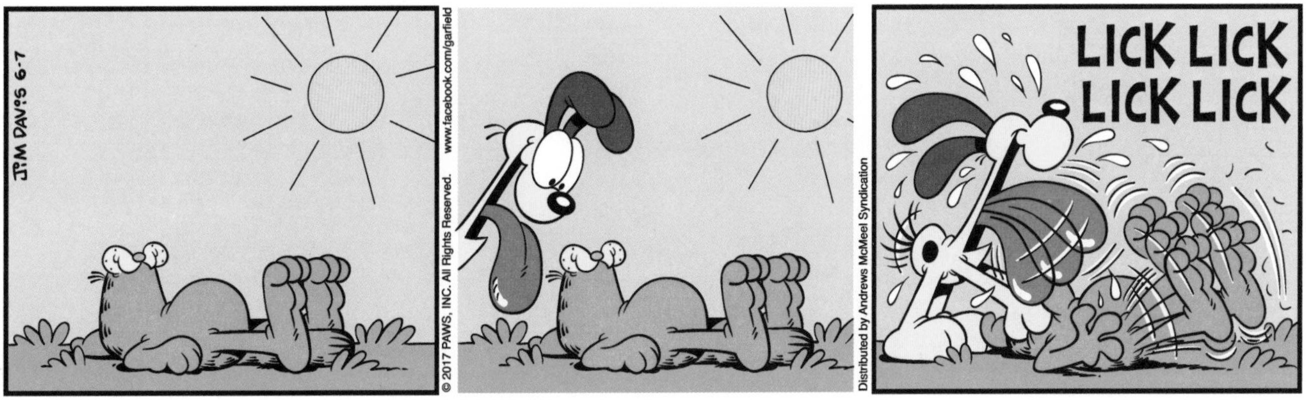
JIM DAVIS 6-7
© 2017 PAWS, INC. All Rights Reserved. www.facebook.com/garfield
Distributed by Andrews McMeel Syndication
LICK LICK
LICK LICK

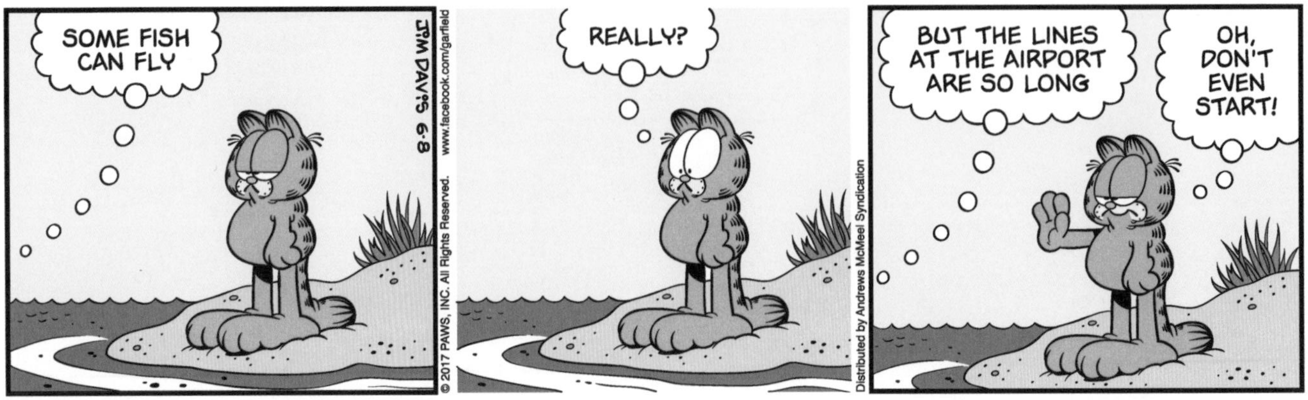
SOME FISH CAN FLY
JIM DAVIS 6-8
© 2017 PAWS, INC. All Rights Reserved. www.facebook.com/garfield
REALLY?
Distributed by Andrews McMeel Syndication
BUT THE LINES AT THE AIRPORT ARE SO LONG
OH, DON'T EVEN START!

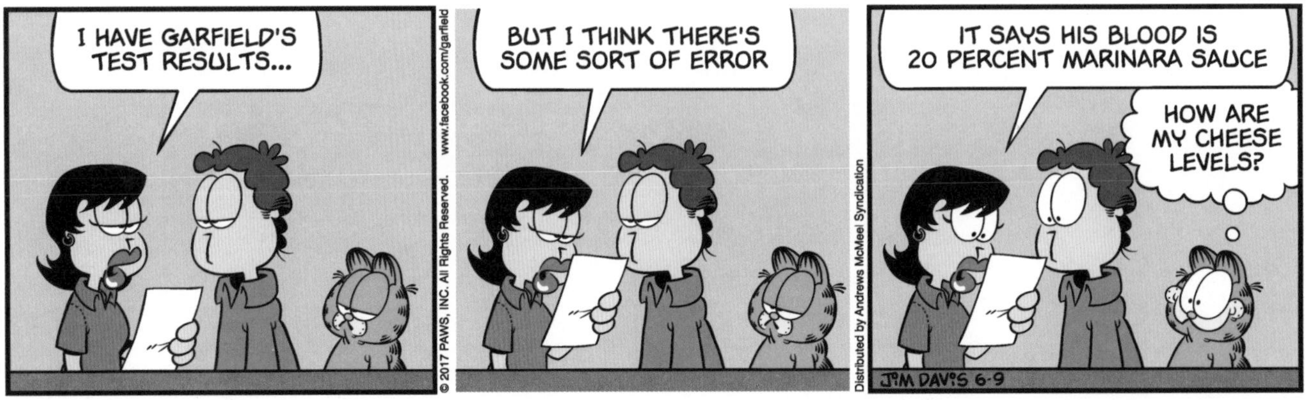
I HAVE GARFIELD'S TEST RESULTS...
© 2017 PAWS, INC. All Rights Reserved. www.facebook.com/garfield
BUT I THINK THERE'S SOME SORT OF ERROR
Distributed by Andrews McMeel Syndication
IT SAYS HIS BLOOD IS 20 PERCENT MARINARA SAUCE
HOW ARE MY CHEESE LEVELS?
JIM DAVIS 6-9

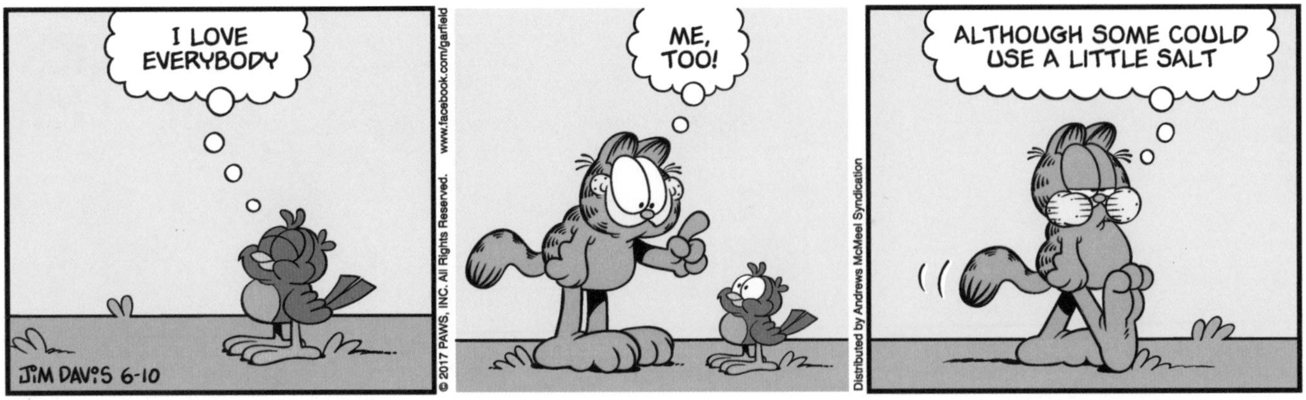
I LOVE EVERYBODY
JIM DAVIS 6-10
© 2017 PAWS, INC. All Rights Reserved. www.facebook.com/garfield
ME, TOO!
Distributed by Andrews McMeel Syndication
ALTHOUGH SOME COULD USE A LITTLE SALT

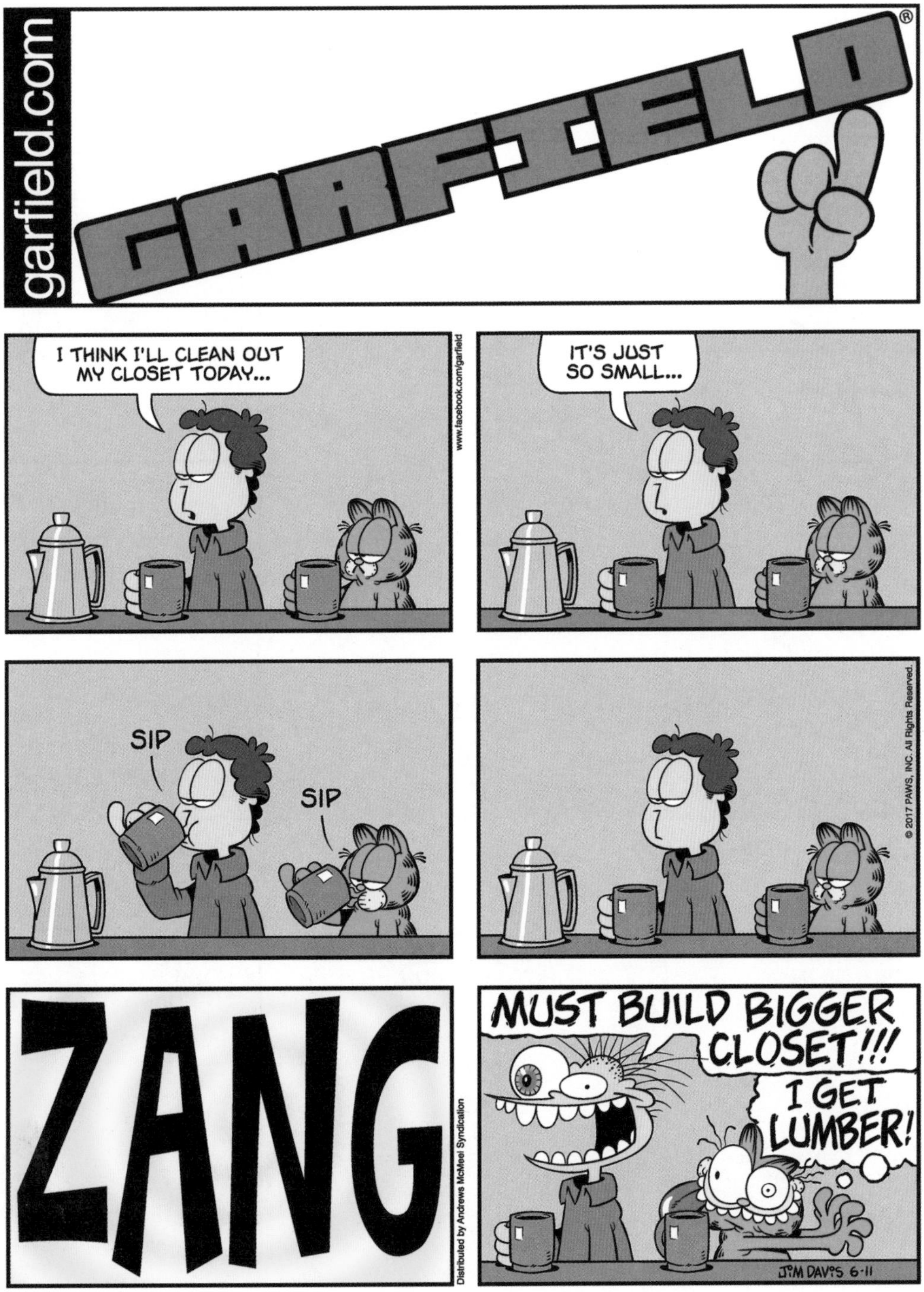
garfield.com
GARFIELD
I THINK I'LL CLEAN OUT MY CLOSET TODAY...
www.facebook.com/garfield
IT'S JUST SO SMALL...
SIP
SIP
© 2017 PAWS, INC. All Rights Reserved.
ZANG
Distributed by Andrews McMeel Syndication
MUST BUILD BIGGER CLOSET!!!
I GET LUMBER!
JIM DAVIS 6-11

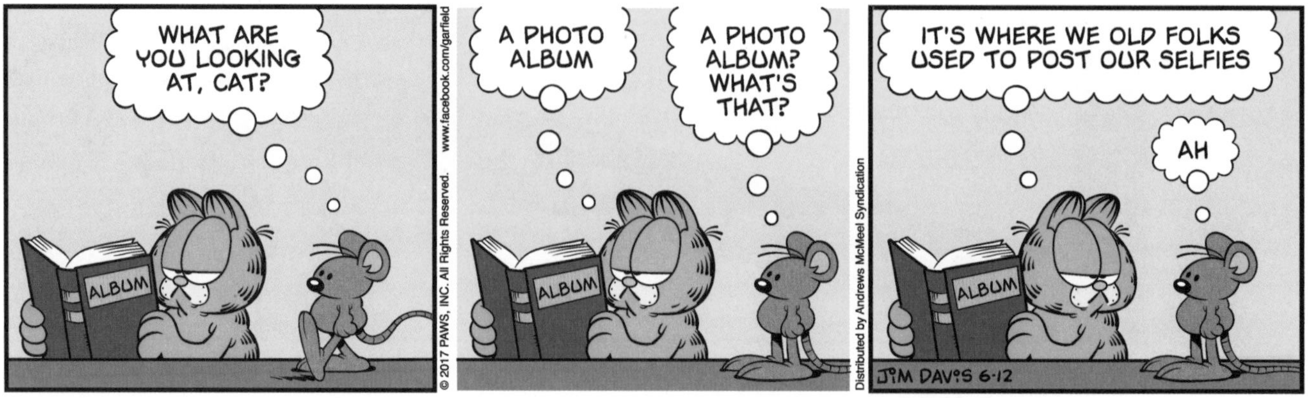
WHAT ARE YOU LOOKING AT, CAT?
ALBUM
© 2017 PAWS, INC. All Rights Reserved. www.facebook.com/garfield
A PHOTO ALBUM
A PHOTO ALBUM? WHAT'S THAT?
ALBUM
Distributed by Andrews McMeel Syndication
IT'S WHERE WE OLD FOLKS USED TO POST OUR SELFIES
AH
ALBUM
JIM DAVIS 6-12

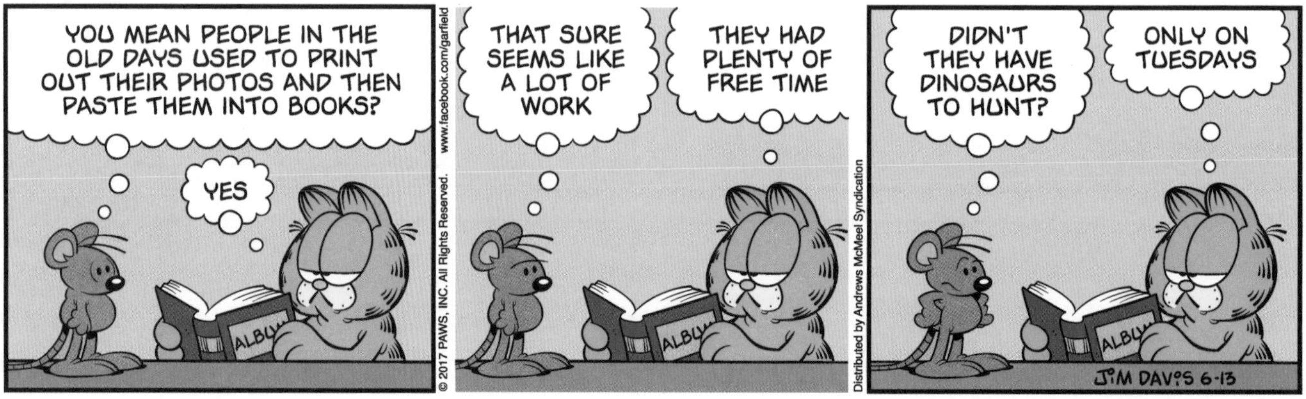
YOU MEAN PEOPLE IN THE OLD DAYS USED TO PRINT OUT THEIR PHOTOS AND THEN PASTE THEM INTO BOOKS?
YES
© 2017 PAWS, INC. All Rights Reserved. www.facebook.com/garfield
THAT SURE SEEMS LIKE A LOT OF WORK
THEY HAD PLENTY OF FREE TIME
Distributed by Andrews McMeel Syndication
DIDN'T THEY HAVE DINOSAURS TO HUNT?
ONLY ON TUESDAYS
JIM DAVIS 6-13

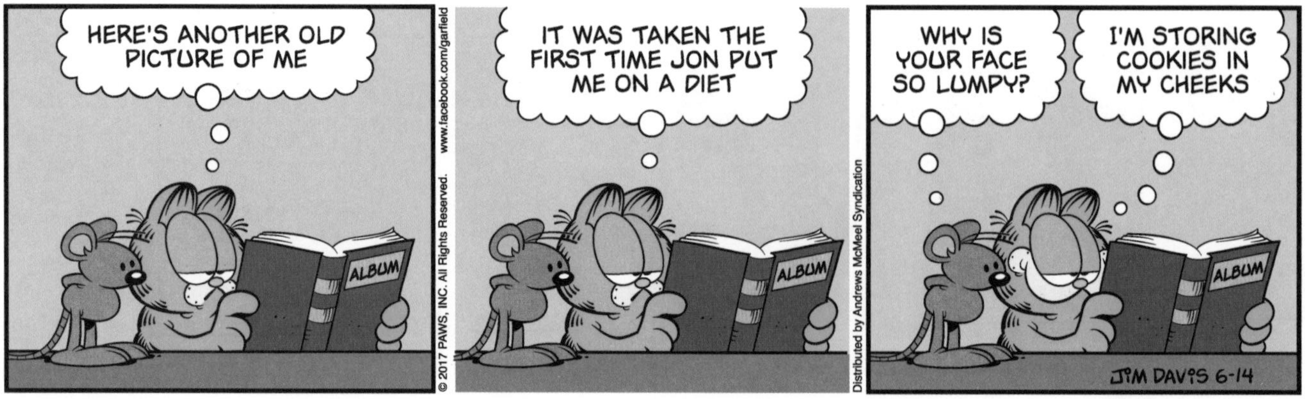
HERE'S ANOTHER OLD PICTURE OF ME
ALBUM
© 2017 PAWS, INC. All Rights Reserved. www.facebook.com/garfield
IT WAS TAKEN THE FIRST TIME JON PUT ME ON A DIET
ALBUM
Distributed by Andrews McMeel Syndication
WHY IS YOUR FACE SO LUMPY?
I'M STORING COOKIES IN MY CHEEKS
ALBUM
JIM DAVIS 6-14

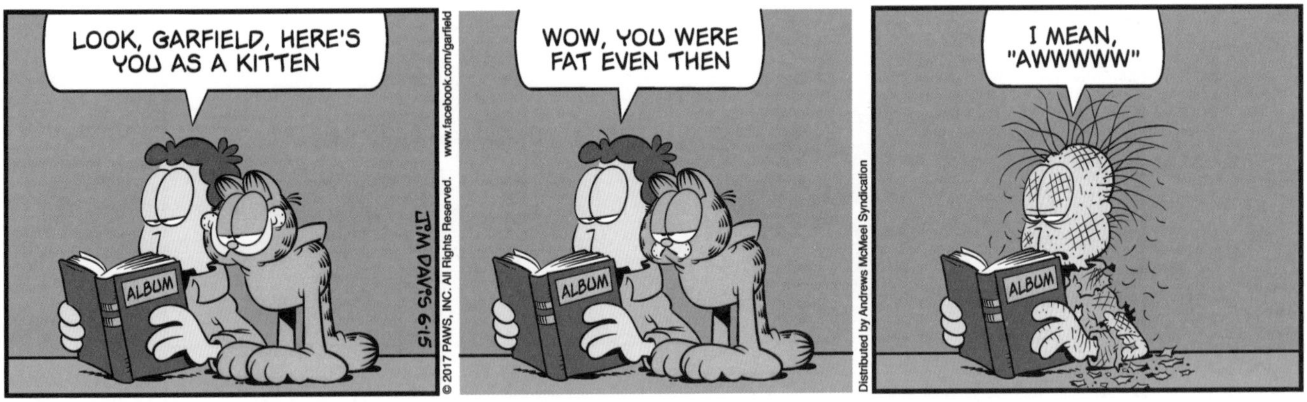
LOOK, GARFIELD, HERE'S YOU AS A KITTEN
ALBUM
JIM DAVIS 6-15
© 2017 PAWS, INC. All Rights Reserved. www.facebook.com/garfield
WOW, YOU WERE FAT EVEN THEN
ALBUM
Distributed by Andrews McMeel Syndication
I MEAN, "AWWWWW"
ALBUM

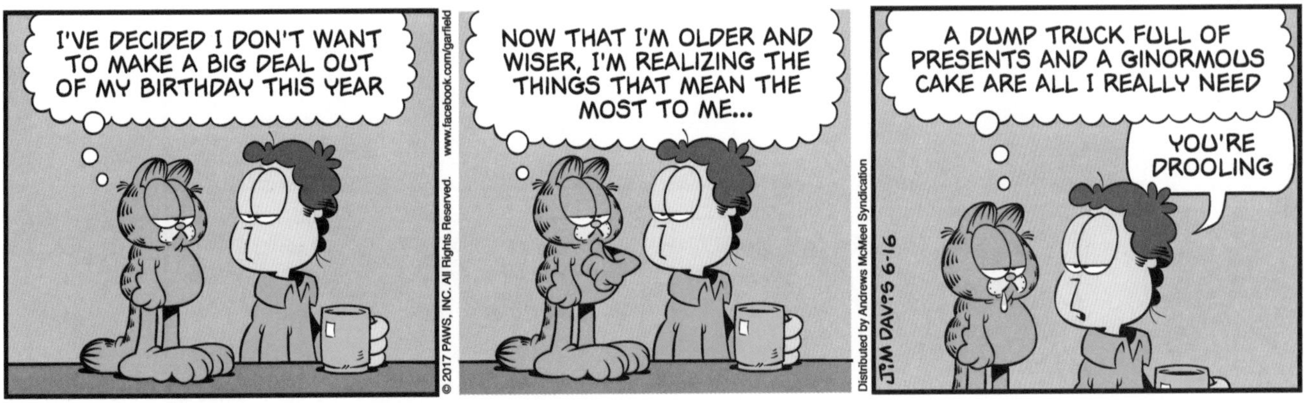
I'VE DECIDED I DON'T WANT TO MAKE A BIG DEAL OUT OF MY BIRTHDAY THIS YEAR
© 2017 PAWS, INC. All Rights Reserved. www.facebook.com/garfield
NOW THAT I'M OLDER AND WISER, I'M REALIZING THE THINGS THAT MEAN THE MOST TO ME...
Distributed by Andrews McMeel Syndication
JIM DAVIS 6-16
A DUMP TRUCK FULL OF PRESENTS AND A GINORMOUS CAKE ARE ALL I REALLY NEED
YOU'RE DROOLING

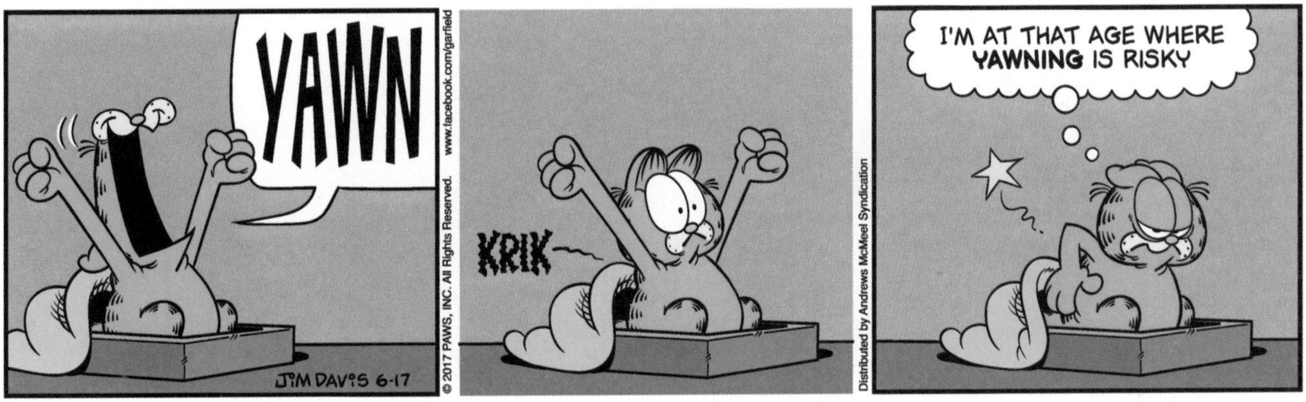
YAWN
JIM DAVIS 6-17
© 2017 PAWS, INC. All Rights Reserved. www.facebook.com/garfield
KRIK
Distributed by Andrews McMeel Syndication
I'M AT THAT AGE WHERE **YAWNING** IS RISKY

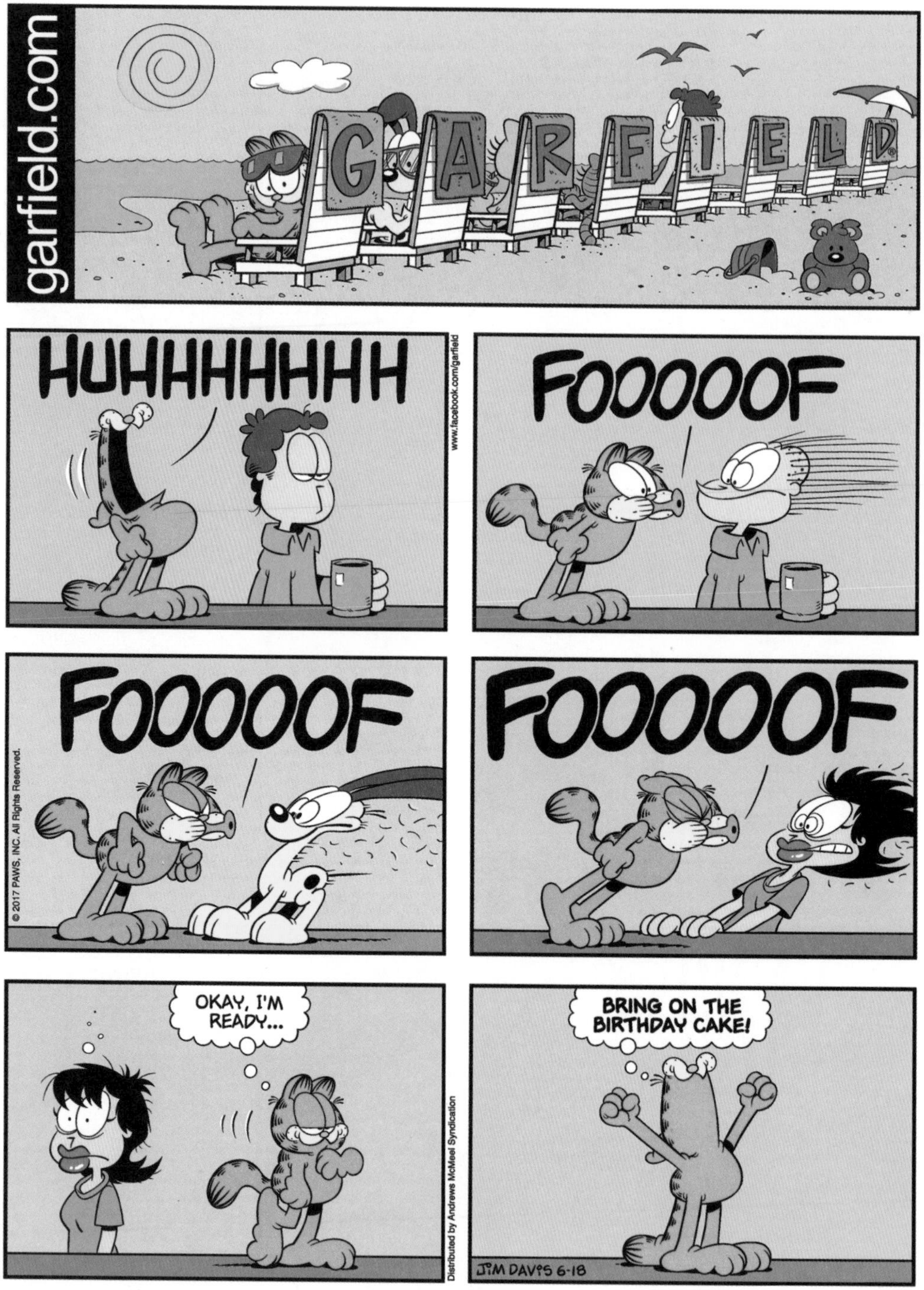
garfield.com
GARFIELD
www.facebook.com/garfield
HUHHHHHHH
FOOOOOF
© 2017 PAWS, INC. All Rights Reserved.
FOOOOOF
FOOOOOF
OKAY, I'M READY...
Distributed by Andrews McMeel Syndication
BRING ON THE BIRTHDAY CAKE!
JIM DAVIS 6-18

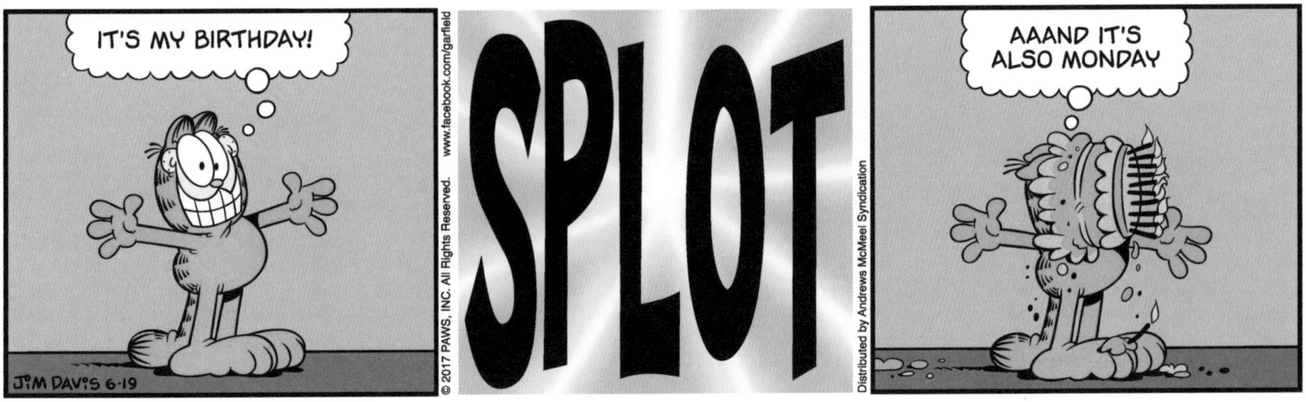
IT'S MY BIRTHDAY!
JIM DAVIS 6-19
© 2017 PAWS, INC. All Rights Reserved. www.facebook.com/garfield
SPLOT
Distributed by Andrews McMeel Syndication
AAAND IT'S ALSO MONDAY

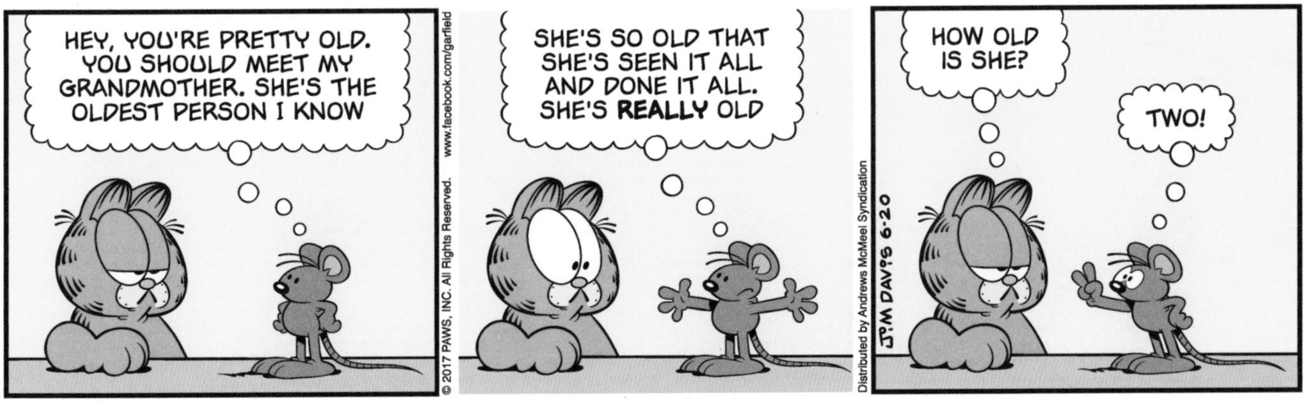
HEY, YOU'RE PRETTY OLD. YOU SHOULD MEET MY GRANDMOTHER. SHE'S THE OLDEST PERSON I KNOW
© 2017 PAWS, INC. All Rights Reserved. www.facebook.com/garfield
SHE'S SO OLD THAT SHE'S SEEN IT ALL AND DONE IT ALL. SHE'S **REALLY** OLD
Distributed by Andrews McMeel Syndication
JIM DAVIS 6-20
HOW OLD IS SHE?
TWO!

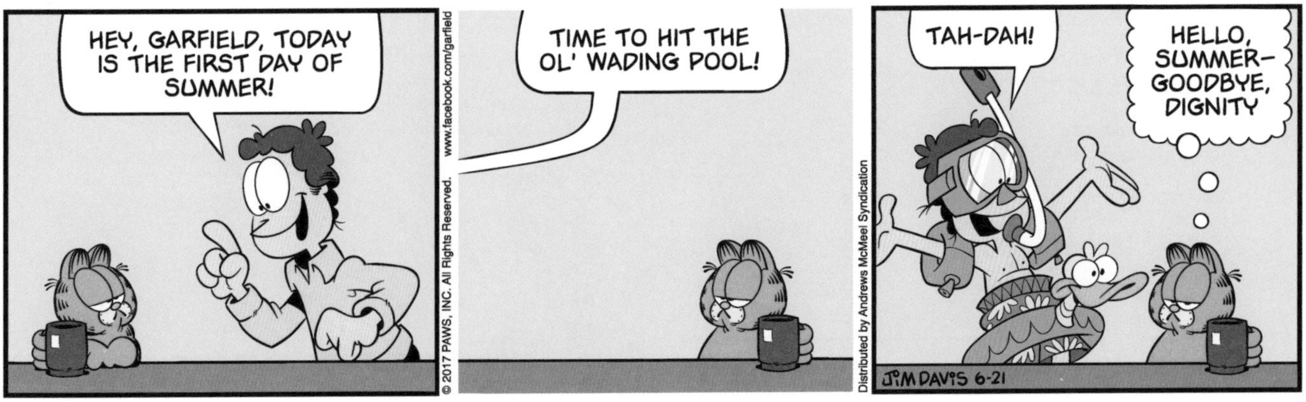
HEY, GARFIELD, TODAY IS THE FIRST DAY OF SUMMER!
© 2017 PAWS, INC. All Rights Reserved. www.facebook.com/garfield
TIME TO HIT THE OL' WADING POOL!
Distributed by Andrews McMeel Syndication
TAH-DAH!
HELLO, SUMMER— GOODBYE, DIGNITY
JIM DAVIS 6-21

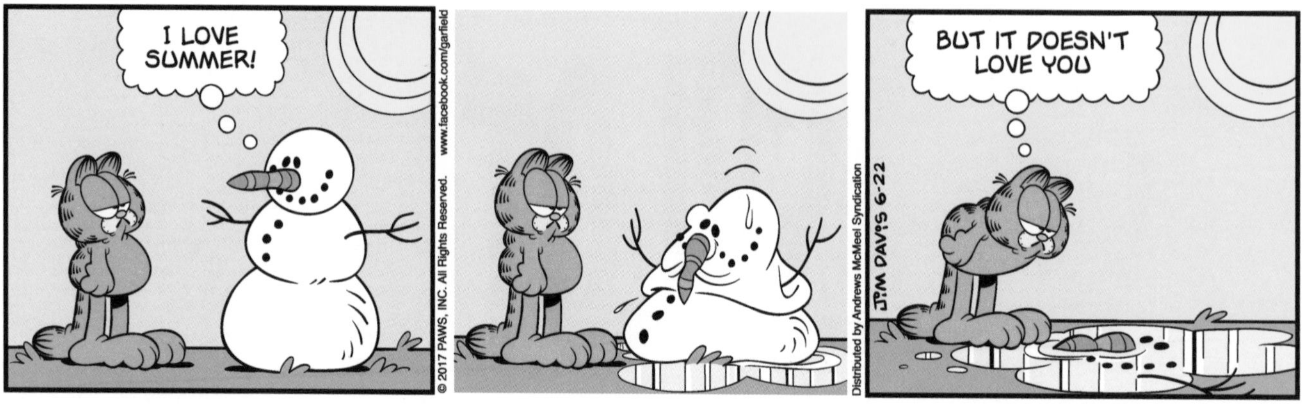
I LOVE SUMMER!
© 2017 PAWS, INC. All Rights Reserved. www.facebook.com/garfield
Distributed by Andrews McMeel Syndication
BUT IT DOESN'T LOVE YOU
JIM DAVIS 6-22

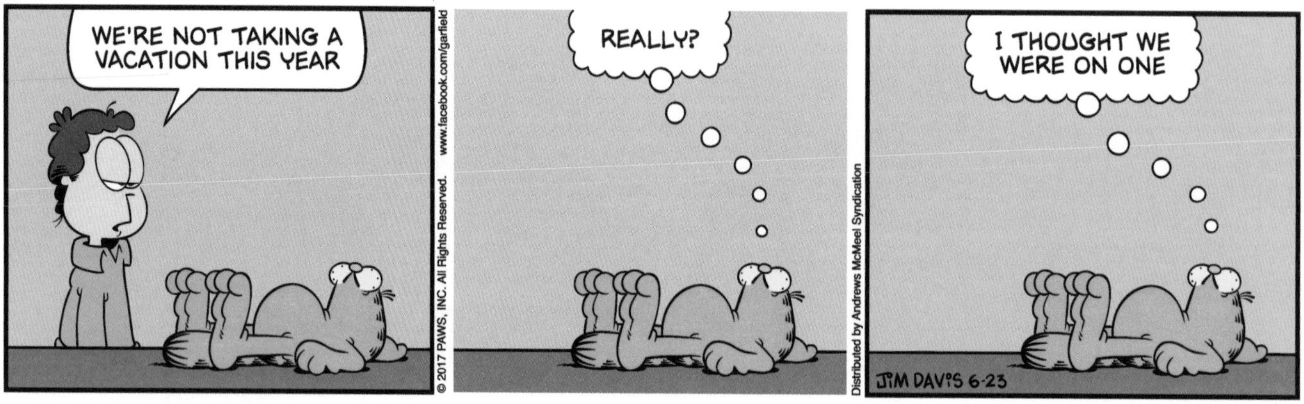
WE'RE NOT TAKING A VACATION THIS YEAR
© 2017 PAWS, INC. All Rights Reserved. www.facebook.com/garfield
REALLY?
Distributed by Andrews McMeel Syndication
I THOUGHT WE WERE ON ONE
JIM DAVIS 6-23

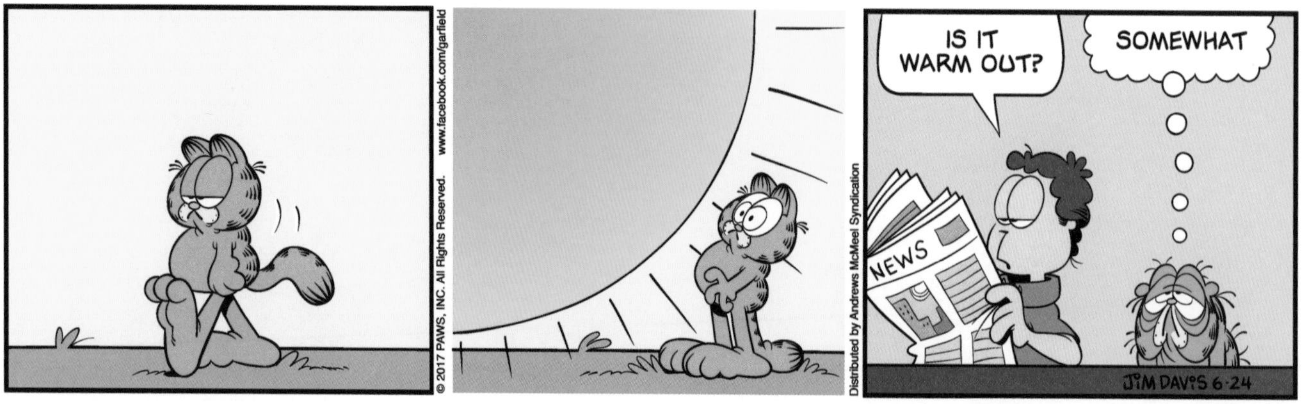
© 2017 PAWS, INC. All Rights Reserved. www.facebook.com/garfield
Distributed by Andrews McMeel Syndication
IS IT WARM OUT?
SOMEWHAT
NEWS
JIM DAVIS 6-24

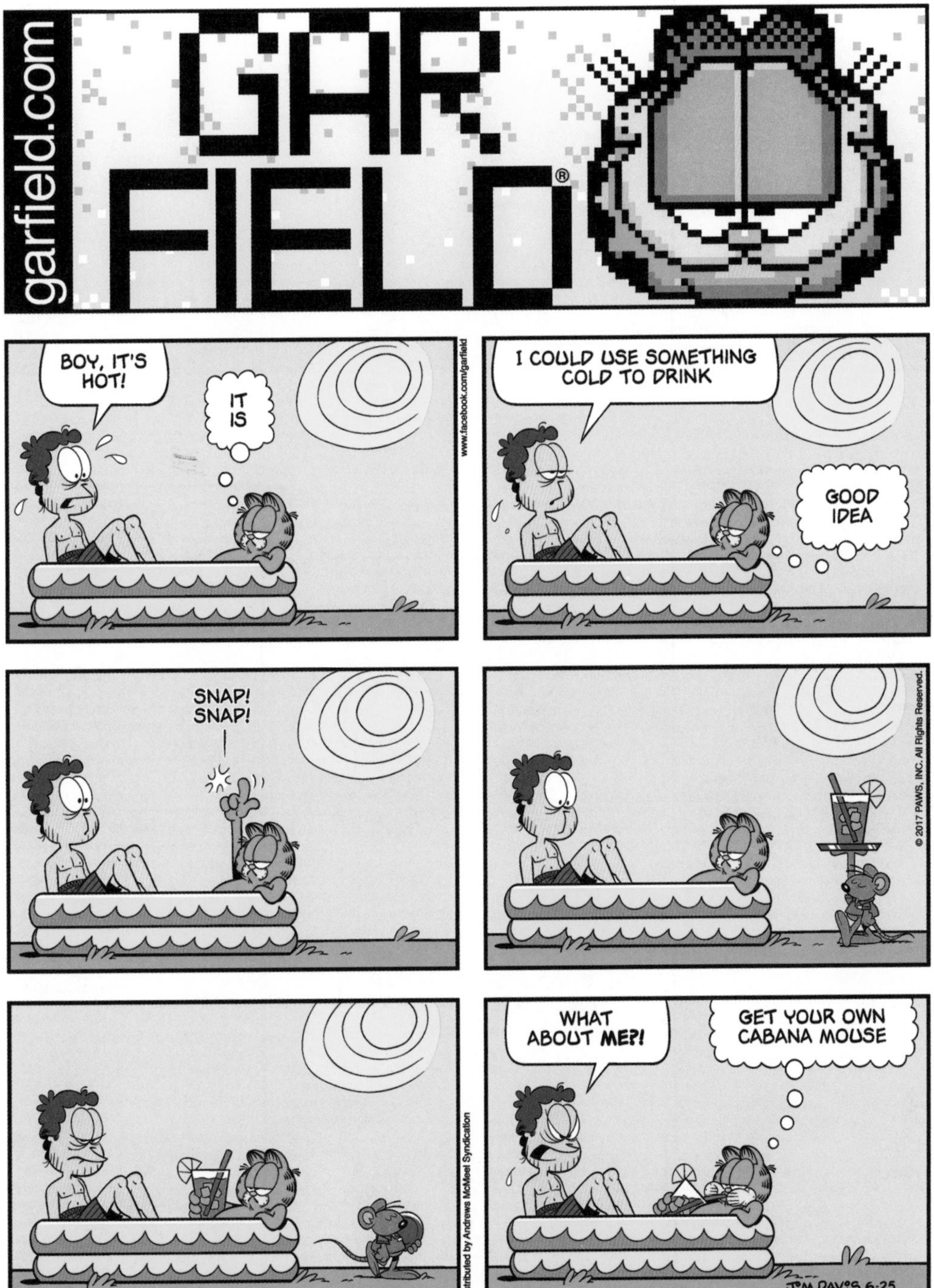
garfield.com
GARFIELD®
BOY, IT'S HOT!
IT IS
www.facebook.com/garfield
I COULD USE SOMETHING COLD TO DRINK
GOOD IDEA
SNAP! SNAP!
© 2017 PAWS, INC. All Rights Reserved.
Distributed by Andrews McMeel Syndication
WHAT ABOUT ME?!
GET YOUR OWN CABANA MOUSE
JIM DAVIS 6-25

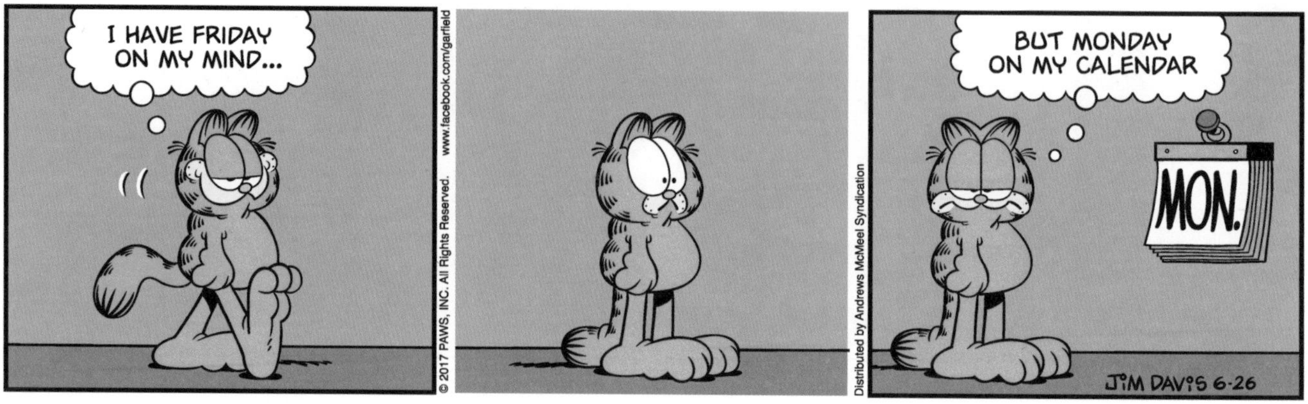
I HAVE FRIDAY ON MY MIND...
BUT MONDAY ON MY CALENDAR
MON.
JIM DAVIS 6-26


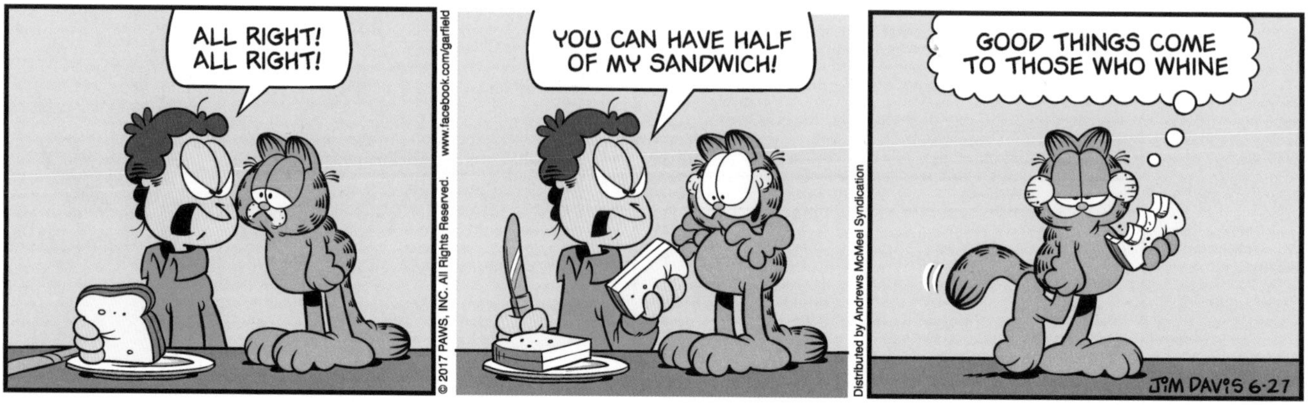
ALL RIGHT! ALL RIGHT!
YOU CAN HAVE HALF OF MY SANDWICH!
GOOD THINGS COME TO THOSE WHO WHINE
JIM DAVIS 6-27


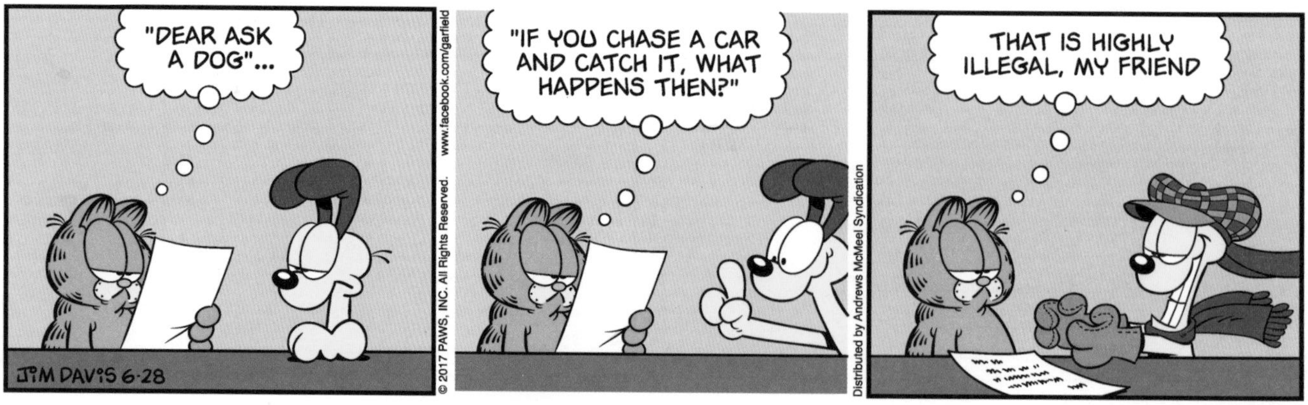
"DEAR ASK A DOG"...
"IF YOU CHASE A CAR AND CATCH IT, WHAT HAPPENS THEN?"
THAT IS HIGHLY ILLEGAL, MY FRIEND
JIM DAVIS 6-28

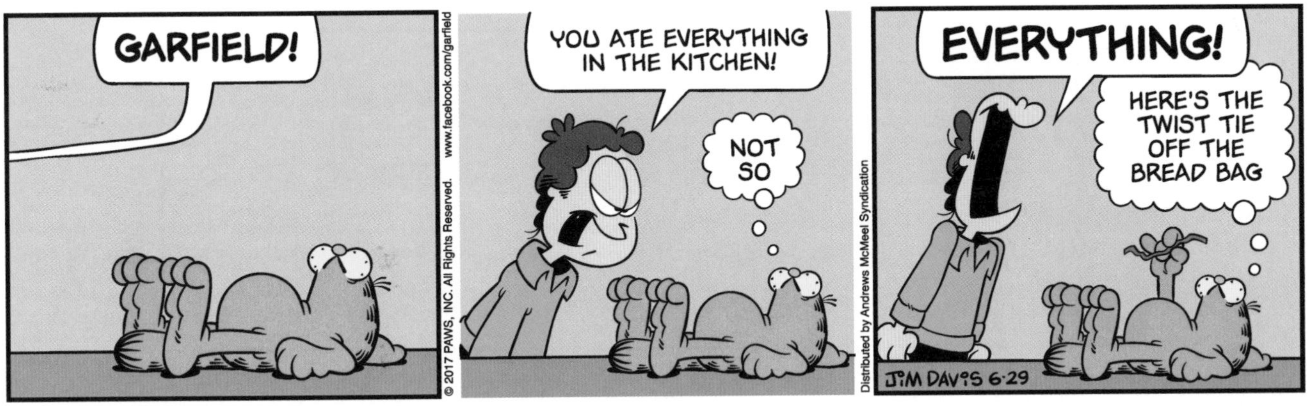
GARFIELD!
YOU ATE EVERYTHING IN THE KITCHEN!
NOT SO
EVERYTHING!
HERE'S THE TWIST TIE OFF THE BREAD BAG
© 2017 PAWS, INC. All Rights Reserved. www.facebook.com/garfield
Distributed by Andrews McMeel Syndication
JIM DAVIS 6-29

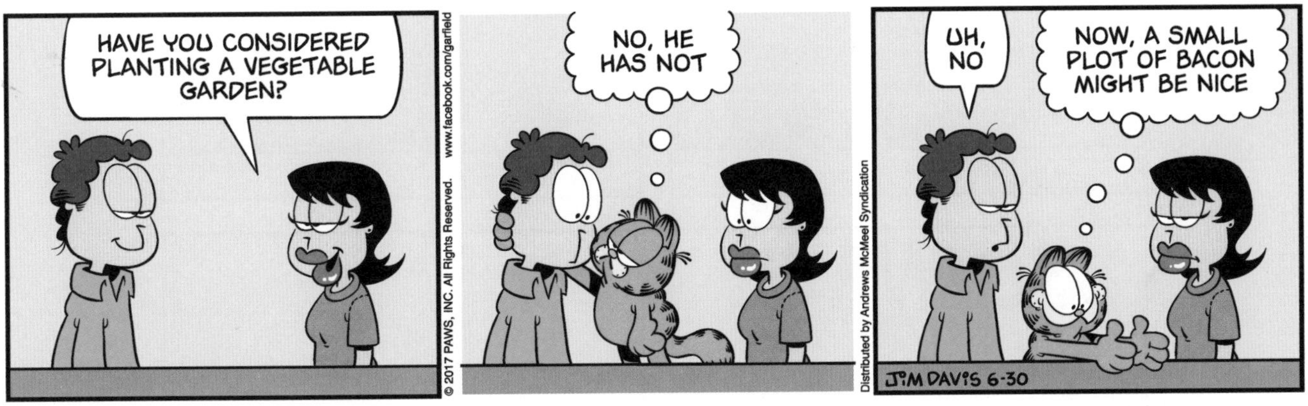
HAVE YOU CONSIDERED PLANTING A VEGETABLE GARDEN?
NO, HE HAS NOT
UH, NO
NOW, A SMALL PLOT OF BACON MIGHT BE NICE
© 2017 PAWS, INC. All Rights Reserved. www.facebook.com/garfield
Distributed by Andrews McMeel Syndication
JIM DAVIS 6-30

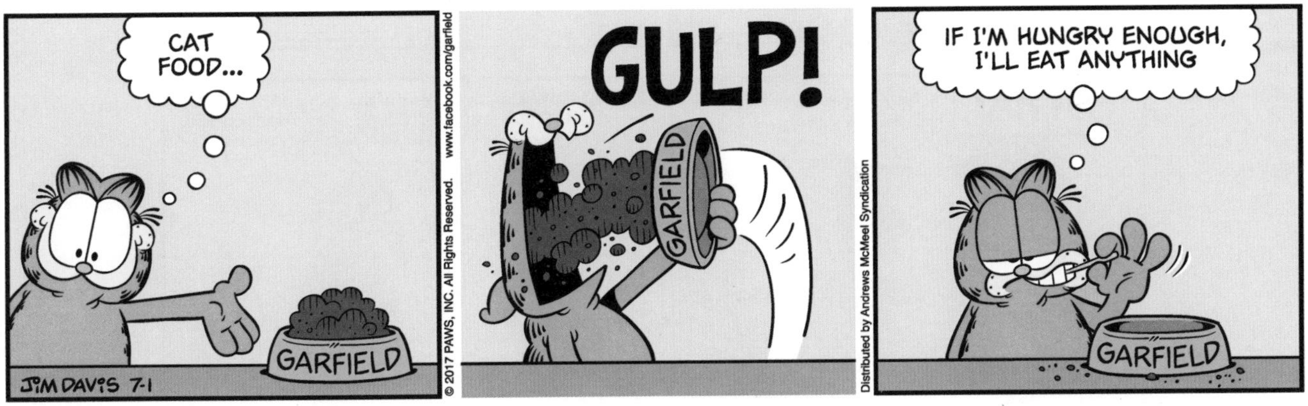
CAT FOOD...
GARFIELD
JIM DAVIS 7-1
GULP!
GARFIELD
IF I'M HUNGRY ENOUGH, I'LL EAT ANYTHING
GARFIELD
© 2017 PAWS, INC. All Rights Reserved. www.facebook.com/garfield
Distributed by Andrews McMeel Syndication

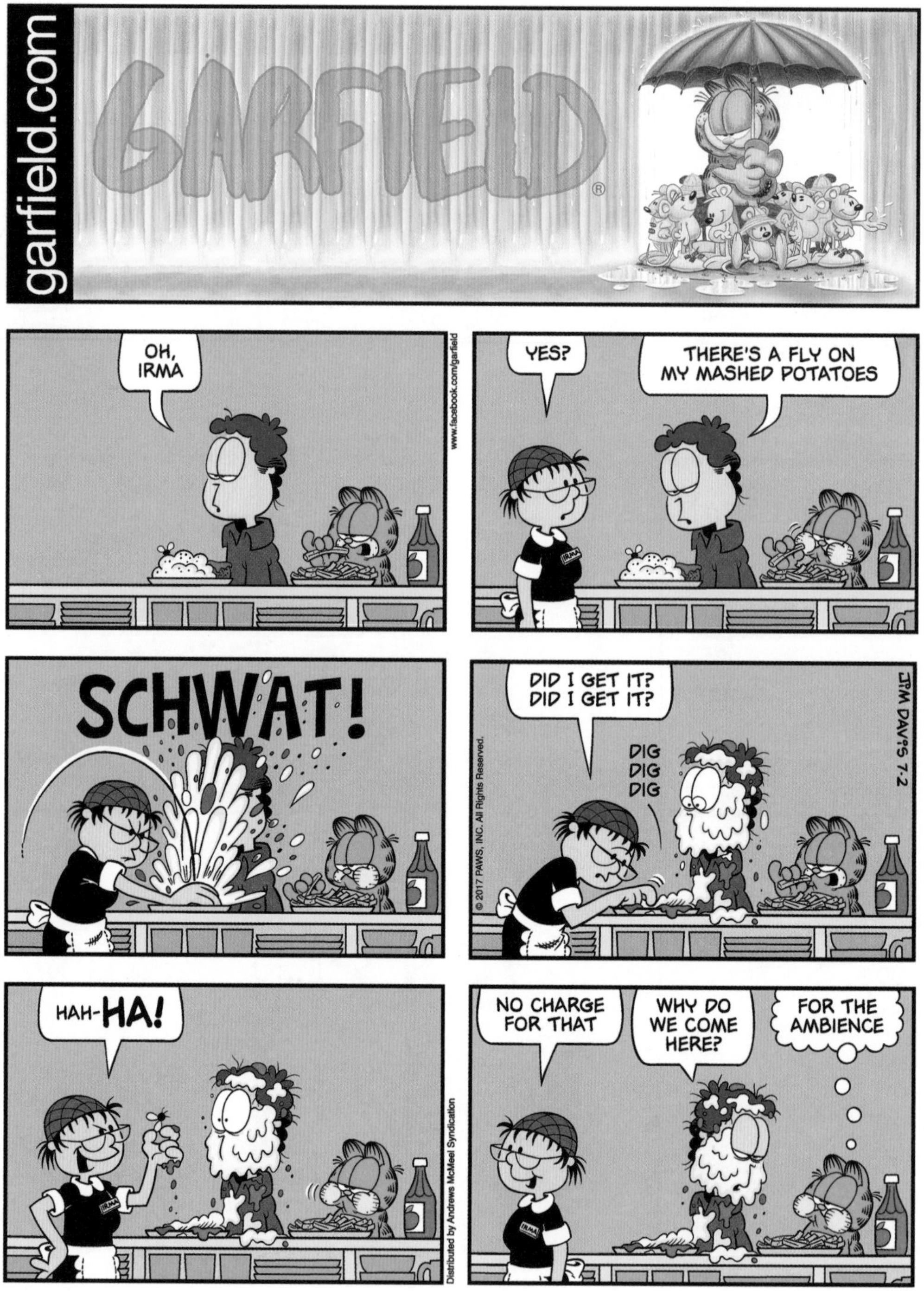
garfield.com
GARFIELD
OH, IRMA
www.facebook.com/garfield
YES?
THERE'S A FLY ON MY MASHED POTATOES
SCHWAT!
© 2017 PAWS, INC. All Rights Reserved.
DID I GET IT? DID I GET IT?
DIG DIG DIG
JIM DAVIS 7-2
HAH-HA!
Distributed by Andrews McMeel Syndication
NO CHARGE FOR THAT
WHY DO WE COME HERE?
FOR THE AMBIENCE

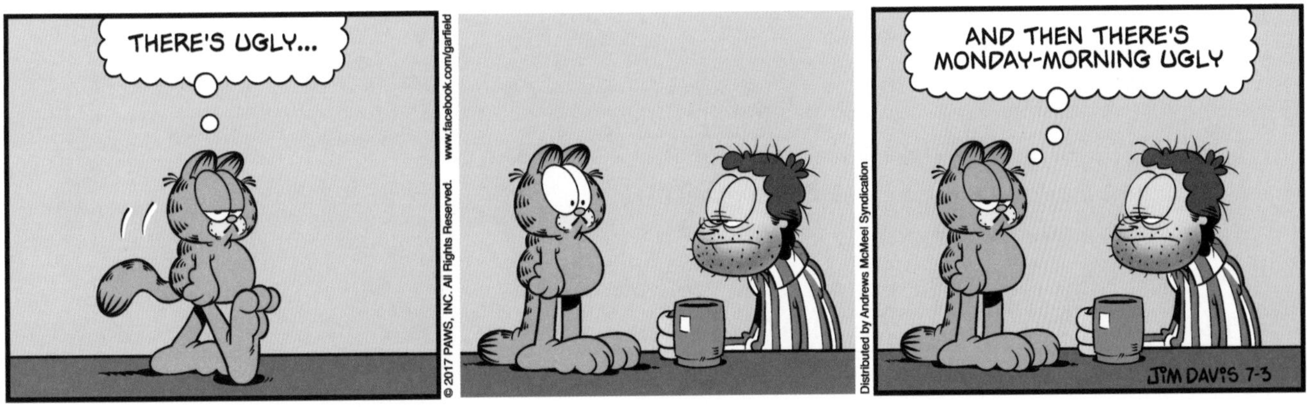
THERE'S UGLY...
AND THEN THERE'S MONDAY-MORNING UGLY
JIM DAVIS 7-3
© 2017 PAWS, INC. All Rights Reserved. www.facebook.com/garfield
Distributed by Andrews McMeel Syndication

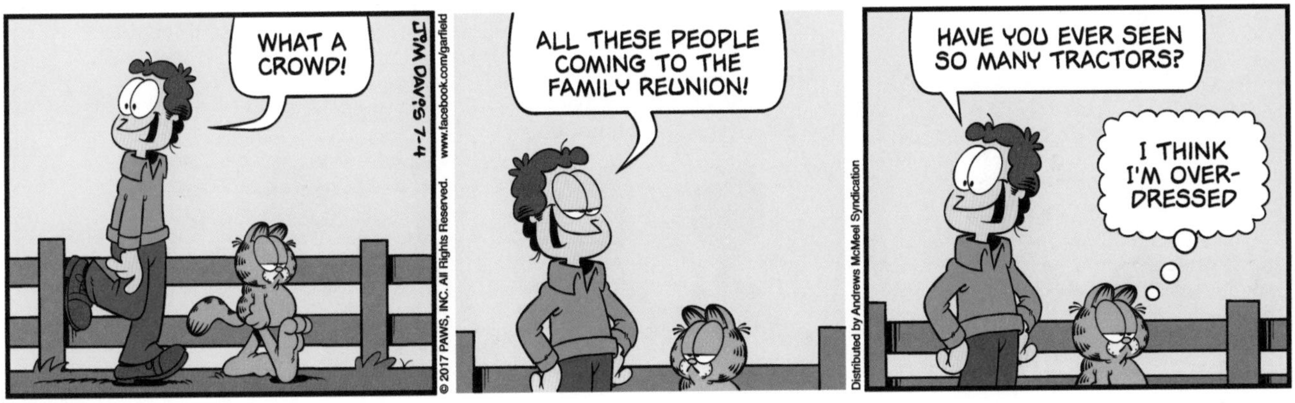
WHAT A CROWD!
ALL THESE PEOPLE COMING TO THE FAMILY REUNION!
HAVE YOU EVER SEEN SO MANY TRACTORS?
I THINK I'M OVER-DRESSED
JIM DAVIS 7-4
© 2017 PAWS, INC. All Rights Reserved. www.facebook.com/garfield
Distributed by Andrews McMeel Syndication

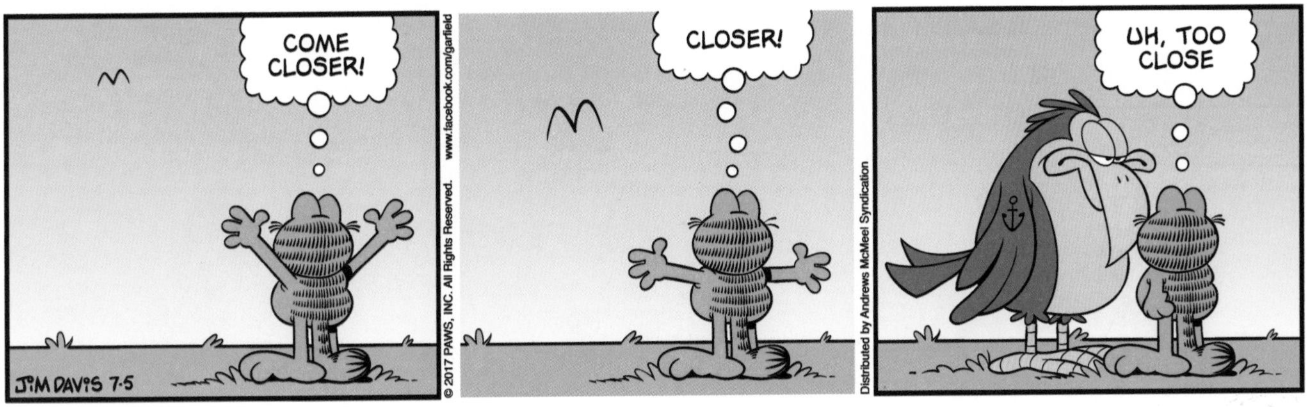
COME CLOSER!
CLOSER!
UH, TOO CLOSE
JIM DAVIS 7-5
© 2017 PAWS, INC. All Rights Reserved. www.facebook.com/garfield
Distributed by Andrews McMeel Syndication

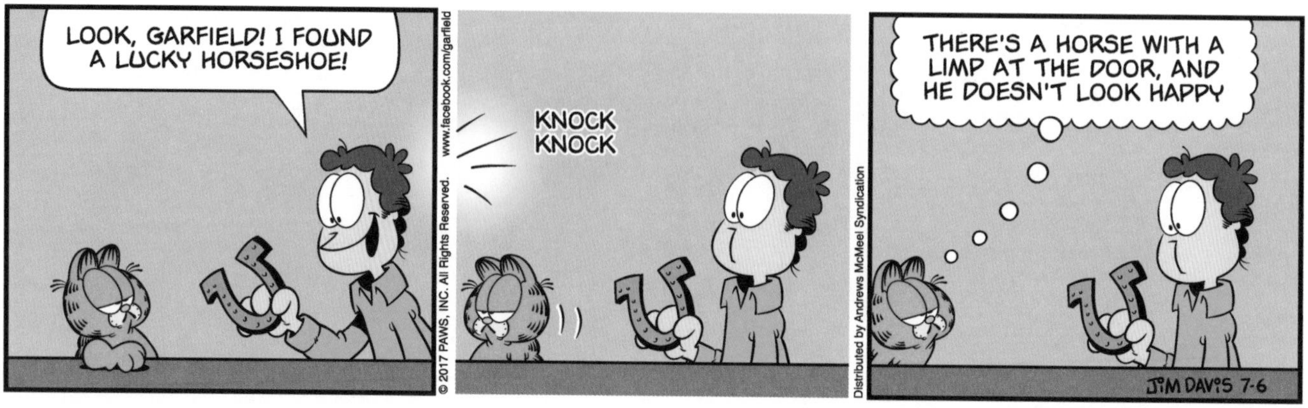
LOOK, GARFIELD! I FOUND A LUCKY HORSESHOE!
© 2017 PAWS, INC. All Rights Reserved. www.facebook.com/garfield
KNOCK KNOCK
Distributed by Andrews McMeel Syndication
THERE'S A HORSE WITH A LIMP AT THE DOOR, AND HE DOESN'T LOOK HAPPY
JIM DAVIS 7-6

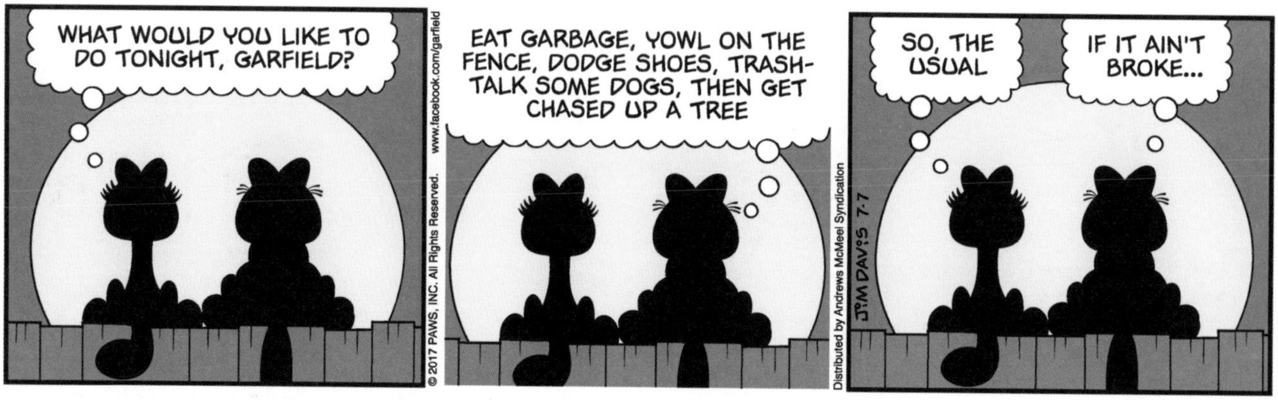
WHAT WOULD YOU LIKE TO DO TONIGHT, GARFIELD?
© 2017 PAWS, INC. All Rights Reserved. www.facebook.com/garfield
EAT GARBAGE, YOWL ON THE FENCE, DODGE SHOES, TRASH-TALK SOME DOGS, THEN GET CHASED UP A TREE
Distributed by Andrews McMeel Syndication
JIM DAVIS 7-7
SO, THE USUAL
IF IT AIN'T BROKE...

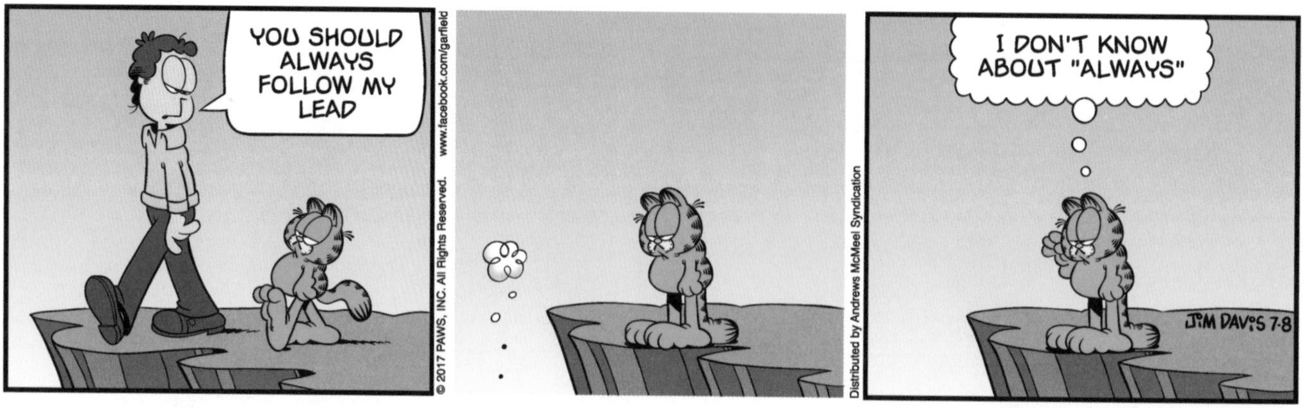
YOU SHOULD ALWAYS FOLLOW MY LEAD
© 2017 PAWS, INC. All Rights Reserved. www.facebook.com/garfield
Distributed by Andrews McMeel Syndication
I DON'T KNOW ABOUT "ALWAYS"
JIM DAVIS 7-8

# Garfield's Green Tips

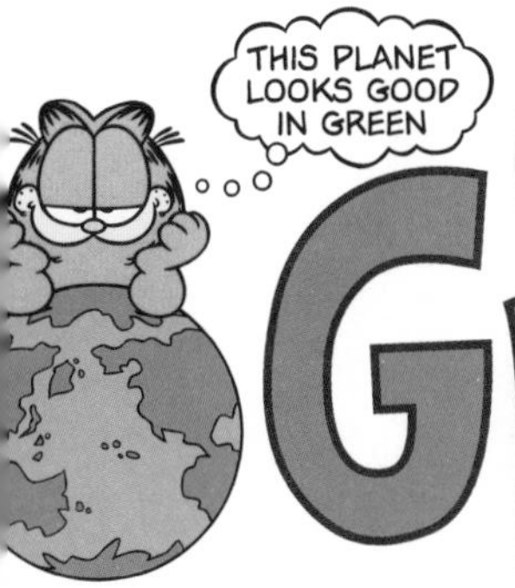
THIS PLANET LOOKS GOOD IN GREEN

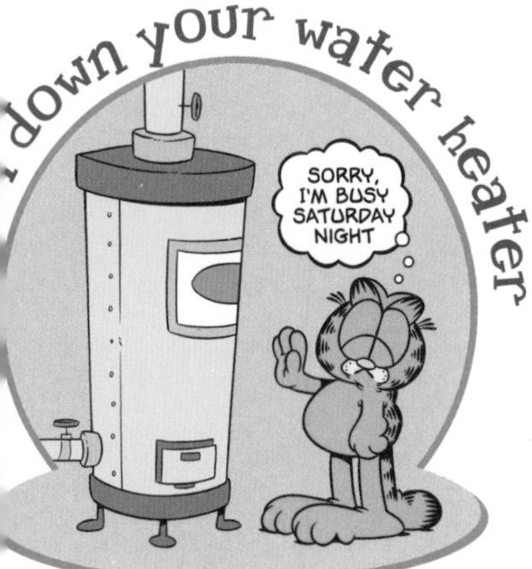
down your water heater
SORRY, I'M BUSY SATURDAY NIGHT

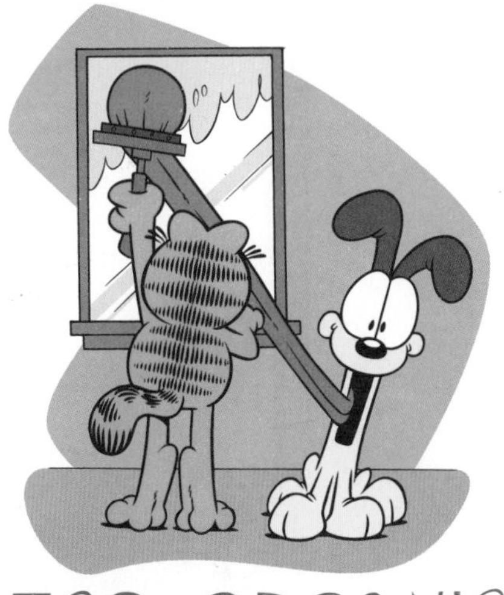

USE ORGANIC CLEANERS!

INSTEAD OF DISPOSABLE CUPS, USE A MUG

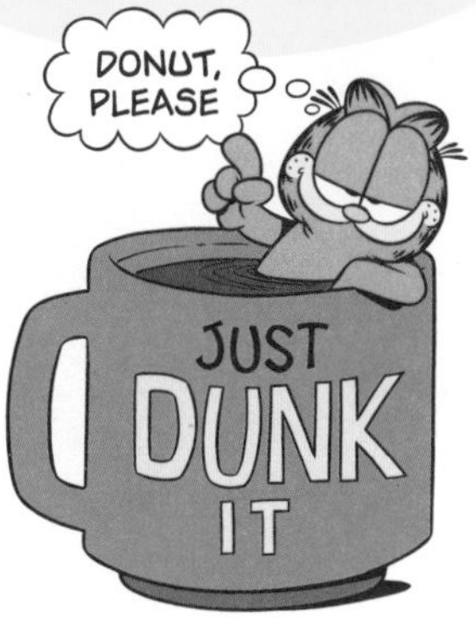
DONUT, PLEASE
JUST DUNK IT

Don't keep opening the refrigerator– empty it the first time

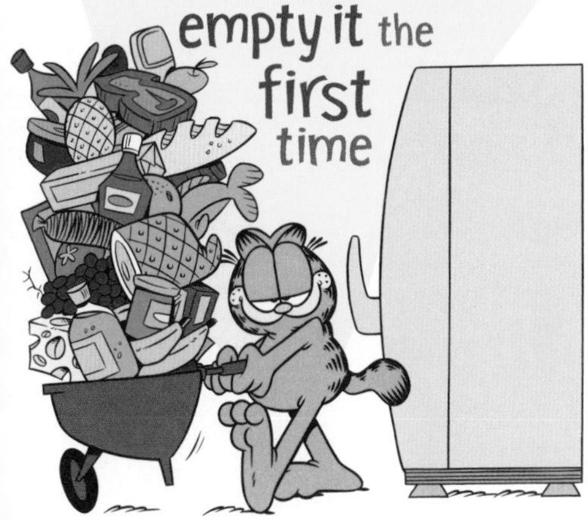

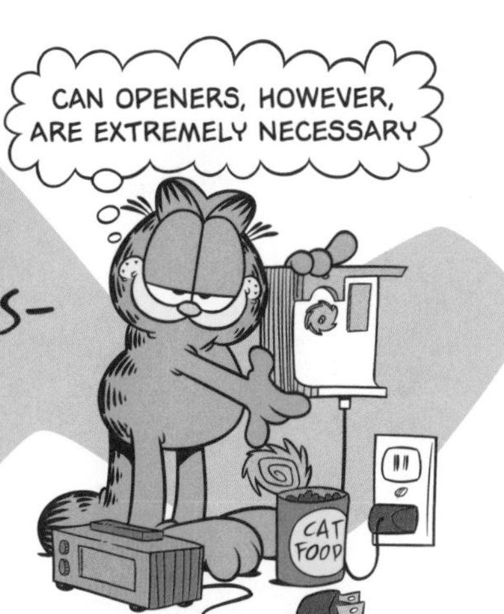
CAN OPENERS, HOWEVER, ARE EXTREMELY NECESSARY
CAT FOOD

UNPLUG ALL UNNECESSARY APPLIANCES– LIKE THE ALARM CLOCK

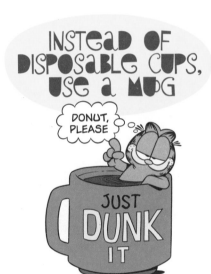

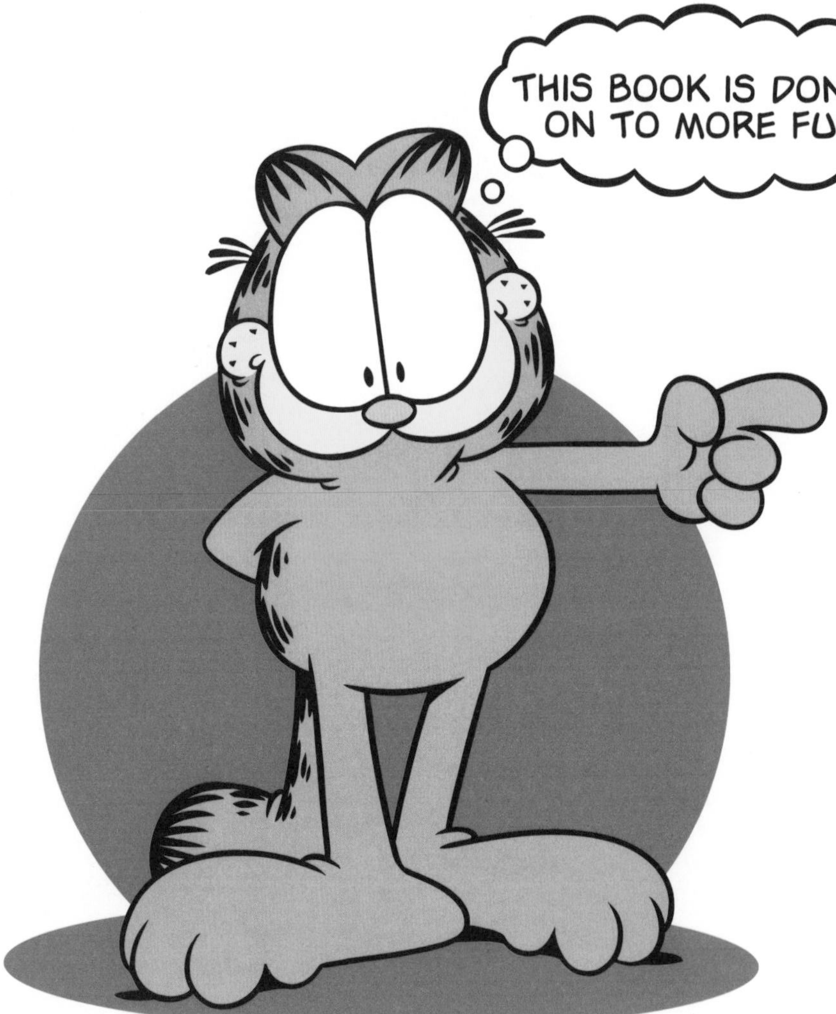
THIS BOOK IS DONE... ON TO MORE FUN!

# Garfield
# BELLY LAUGHS

BY JIM DAVIS

## Ballantine Books • New York

# WORDS TO LAUGH BY

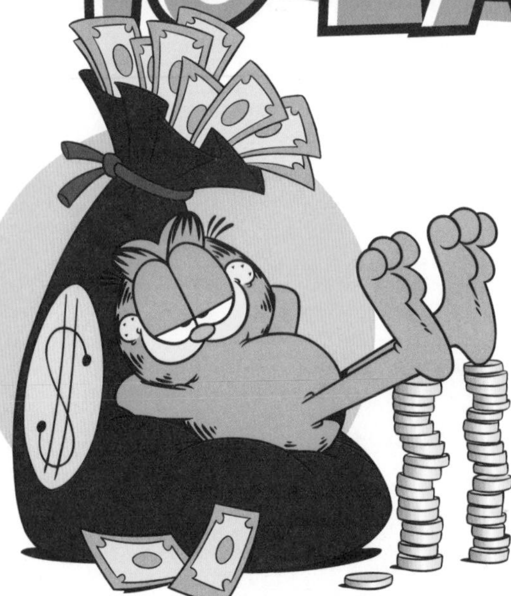

Always be yourself...unless you can be someone richer!

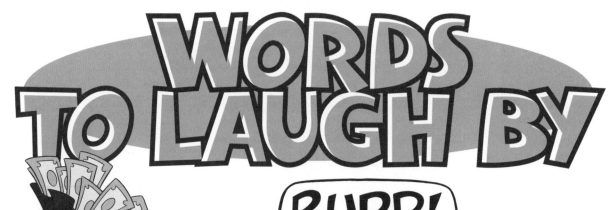

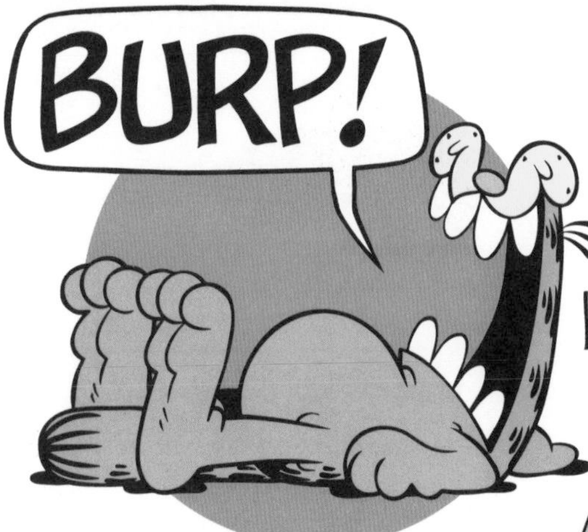
BURP!

Home is where you can be yourself.

You can't take it with you, so eat it now.

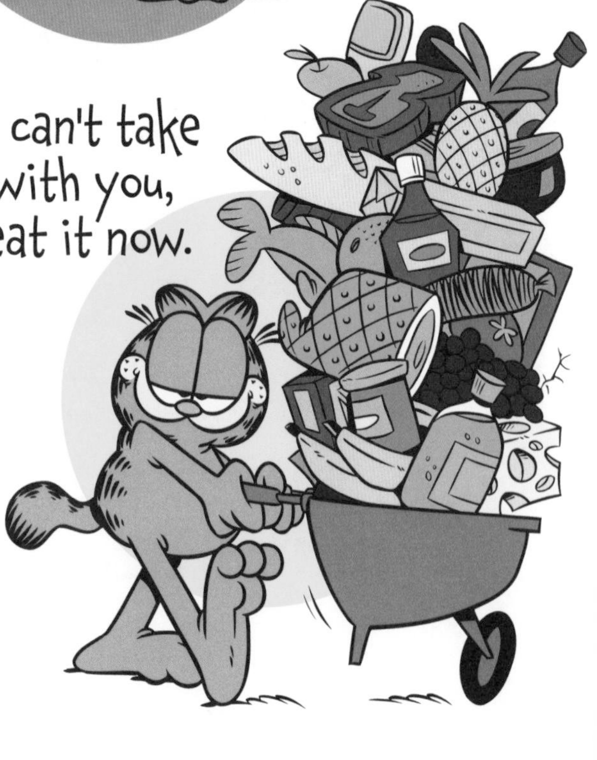

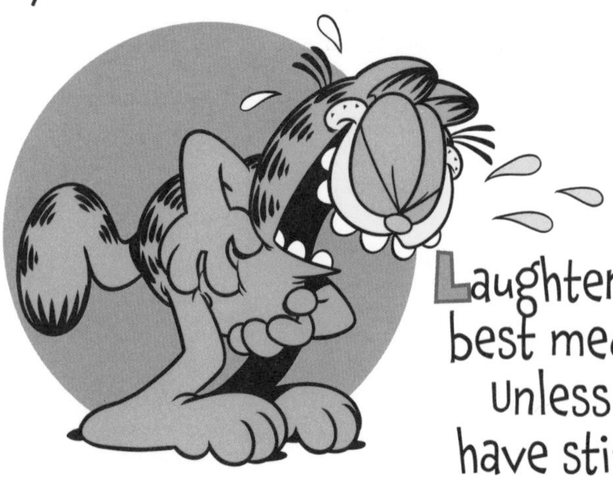

Laughter is the best medicine. Unless you have stitches.

garfield.com
Garfield®
© 2017 PAWS, INC. All Rights Reserved.
www.facebook.com/garfield
GARFIELD!
SHOOF
Distributed by Andrews McMeel Syndication
GARFIELD!
HUMMMMM
JIM DAVIS 7-9

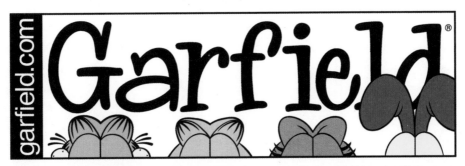

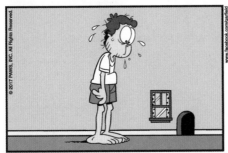

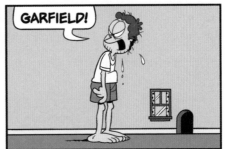

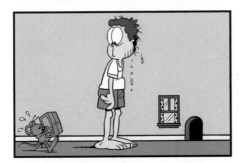

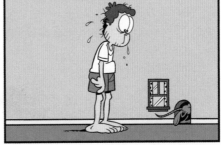

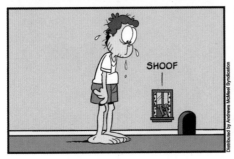

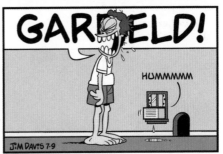

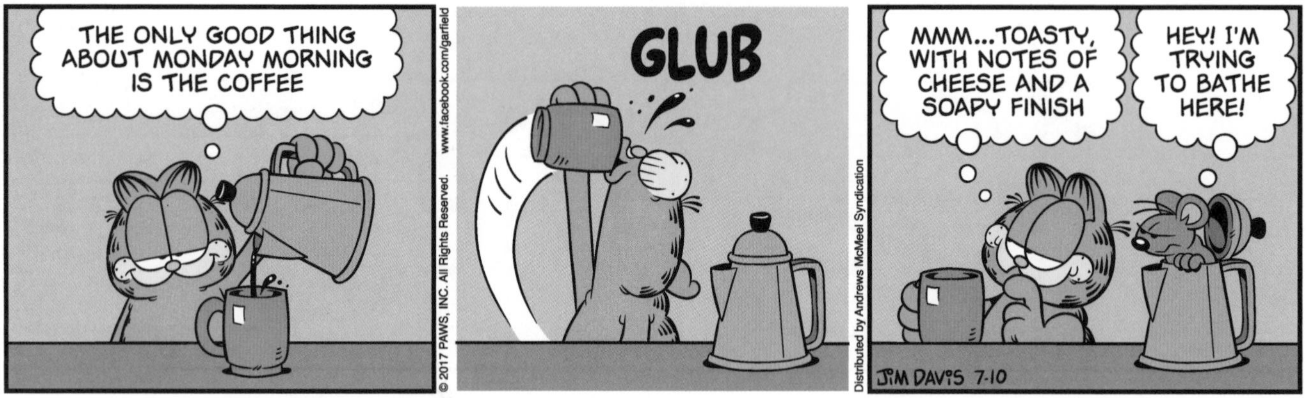
THE ONLY GOOD THING ABOUT MONDAY MORNING IS THE COFFEE
GLUB
MMM...TOASTY, WITH NOTES OF CHEESE AND A SOAPY FINISH
HEY! I'M TRYING TO BATHE HERE!
JIM DAVIS 7-10
© 2017 PAWS, INC. All Rights Reserved. www.facebook.com/garfield
Distributed by Andrews McMeel Syndication

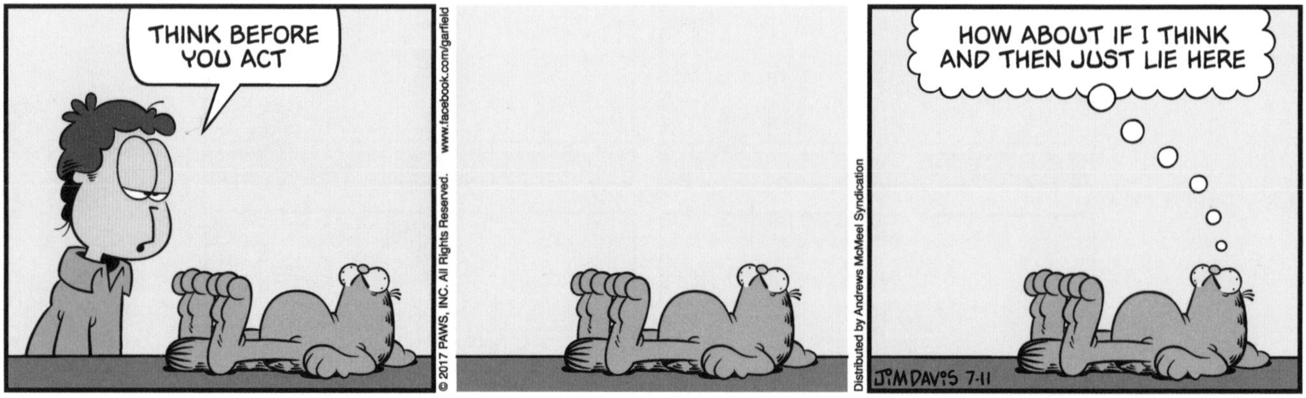
THINK BEFORE YOU ACT
HOW ABOUT IF I THINK AND THEN JUST LIE HERE
JIM DAVIS 7-11
© 2017 PAWS, INC. All Rights Reserved. www.facebook.com/garfield
Distributed by Andrews McMeel Syndication

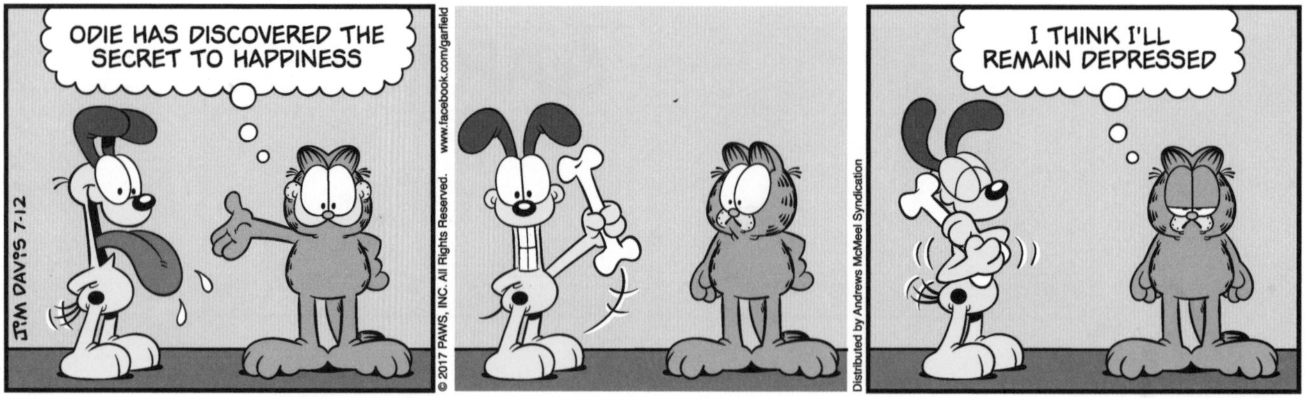
ODIE HAS DISCOVERED THE SECRET TO HAPPINESS
I THINK I'LL REMAIN DEPRESSED
JIM DAVIS 7-12
© 2017 PAWS, INC. All Rights Reserved. www.facebook.com/garfield
Distributed by Andrews McMeel Syndication

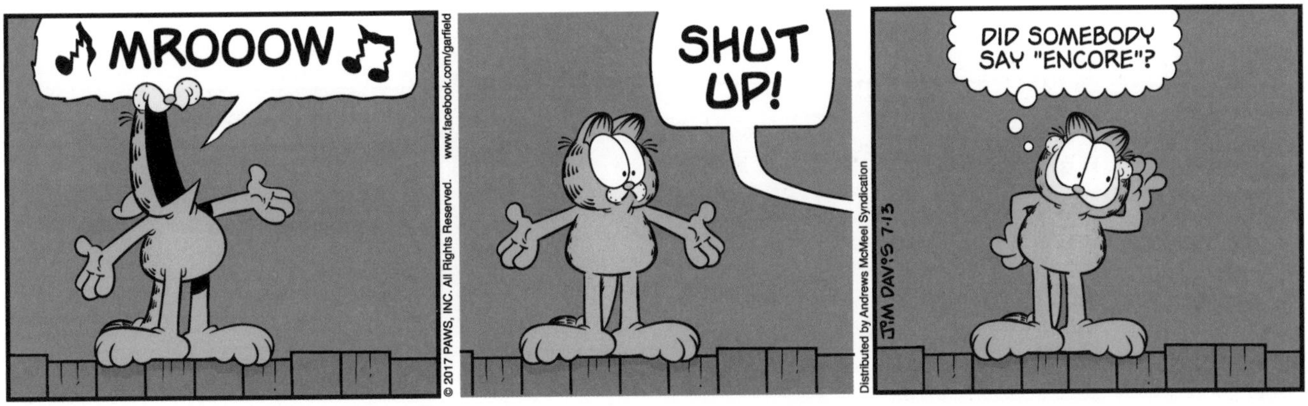
MROOOW
SHUT UP!
DID SOMEBODY SAY "ENCORE"?
© 2017 PAWS, INC. All Rights Reserved. www.facebook.com/garfield
Distributed by Andrews McMeel Syndication
JIM DAVIS 7-13

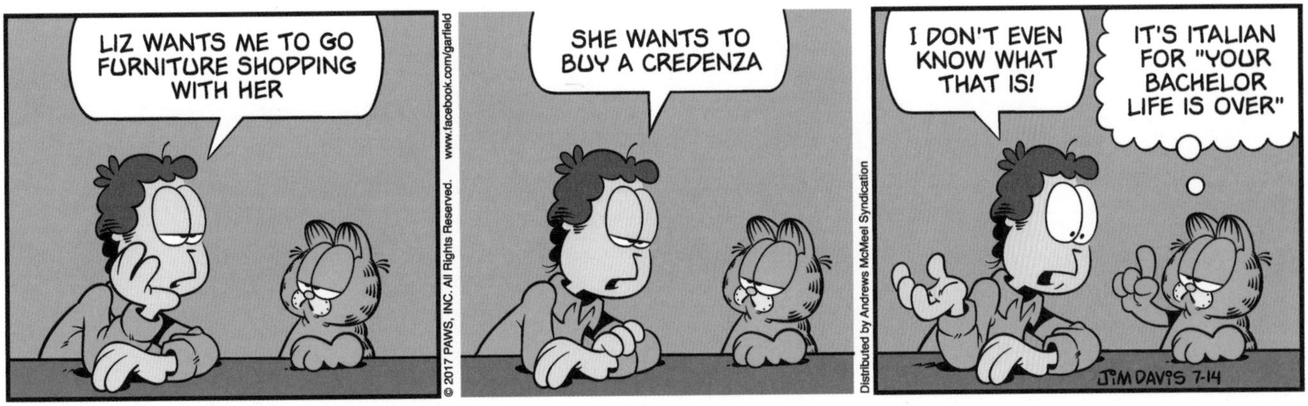
LIZ WANTS ME TO GO FURNITURE SHOPPING WITH HER
SHE WANTS TO BUY A CREDENZA
I DON'T EVEN KNOW WHAT THAT IS!
IT'S ITALIAN FOR "YOUR BACHELOR LIFE IS OVER"
© 2017 PAWS, INC. All Rights Reserved. www.facebook.com/garfield
Distributed by Andrews McMeel Syndication
JIM DAVIS 7-14

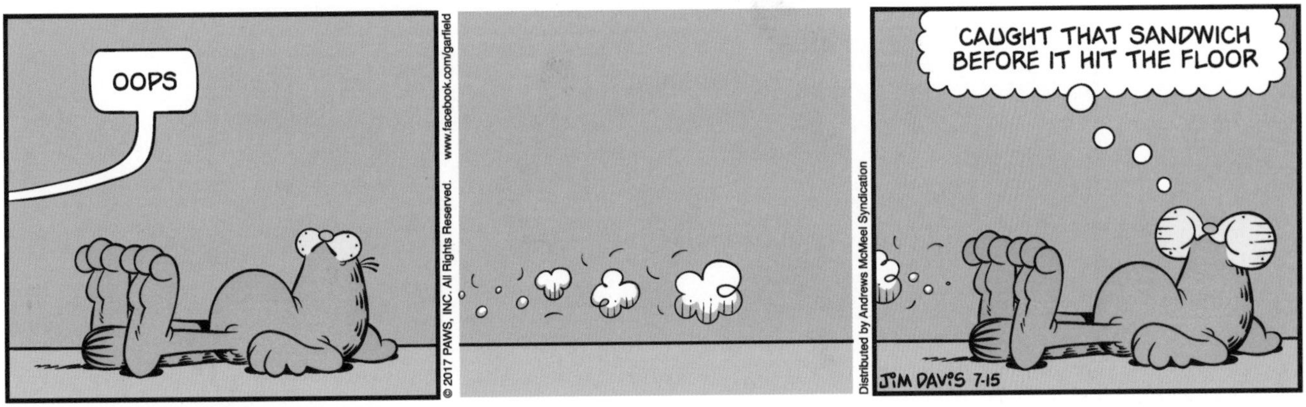
OOPS
CAUGHT THAT SANDWICH BEFORE IT HIT THE FLOOR
© 2017 PAWS, INC. All Rights Reserved. www.facebook.com/garfield
Distributed by Andrews McMeel Syndication
JIM DAVIS 7-15

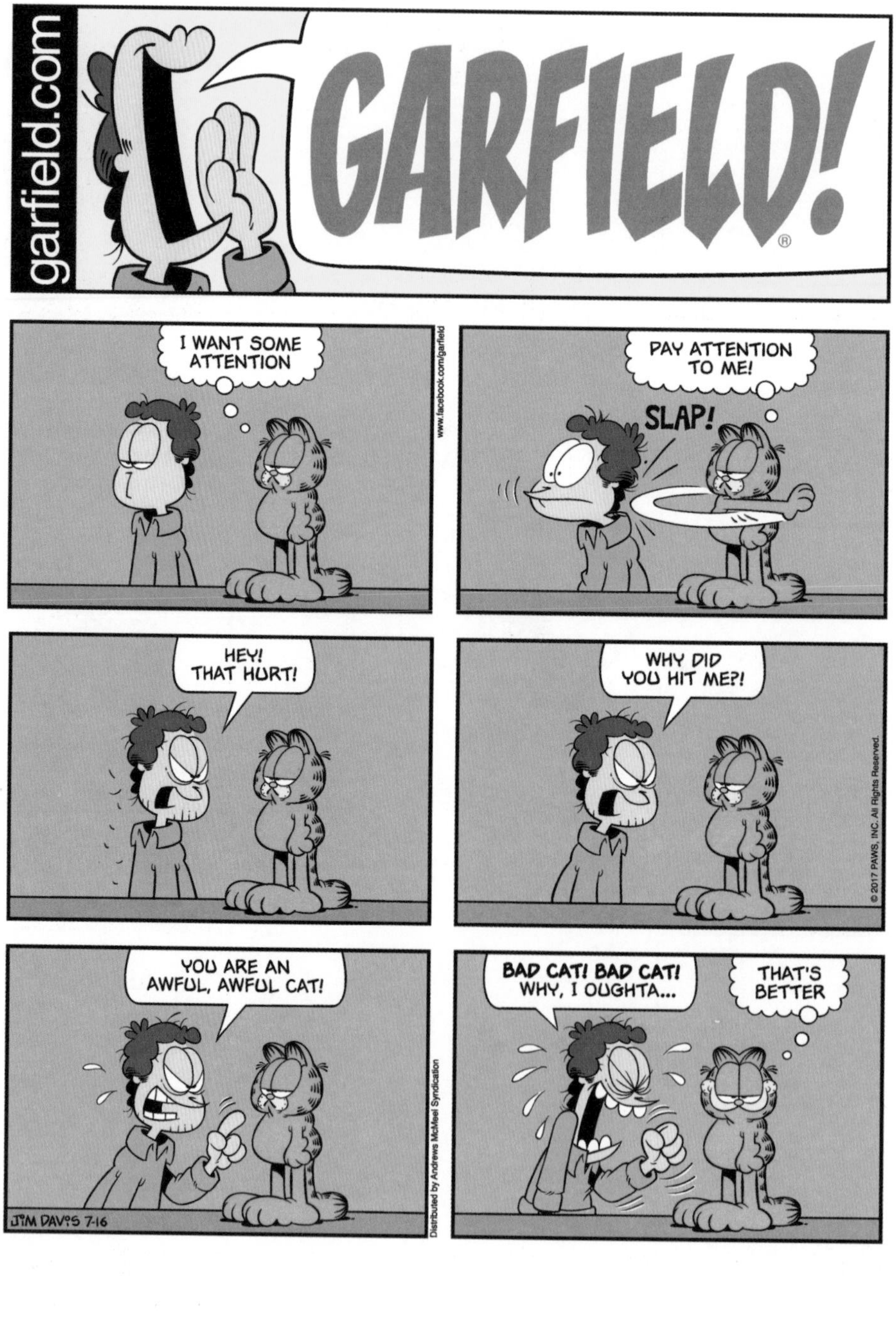
garfield.com
GARFIELD!
I WANT SOME ATTENTION
www.facebook.com/garfield
PAY ATTENTION TO ME!
SLAP!
HEY! THAT HURT!
WHY DID YOU HIT ME?!
© 2017 PAWS, INC. All Rights Reserved.
YOU ARE AN AWFUL, AWFUL CAT!
JIM DAVIS 7-16
Distributed by Andrews McMeel Syndication
BAD CAT! BAD CAT! WHY, I OUGHTA...
THAT'S BETTER

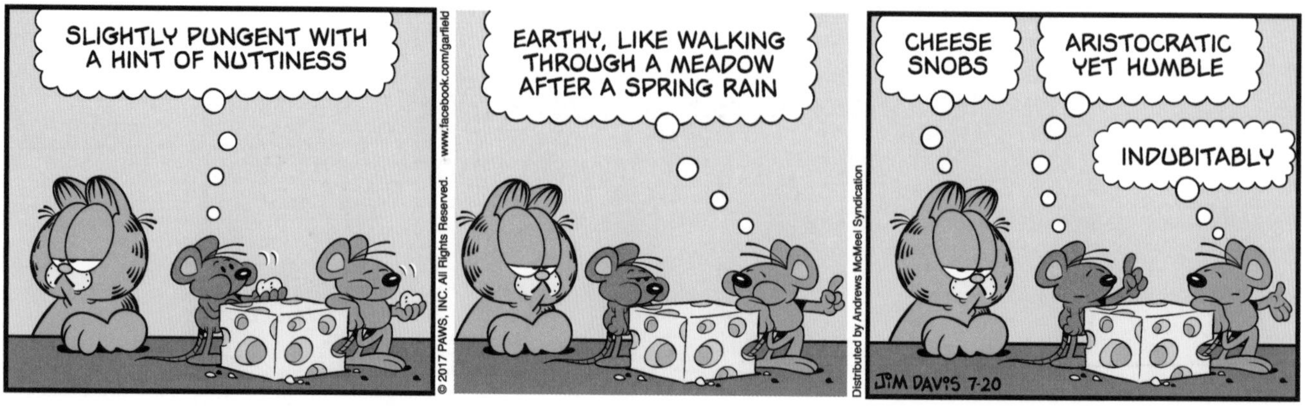
SLIGHTLY PUNGENT WITH A HINT OF NUTTINESS
EARTHY, LIKE WALKING THROUGH A MEADOW AFTER A SPRING RAIN
CHEESE SNOBS
ARISTOCRATIC YET HUMBLE
INDUBITABLY
© 2017 PAWS, INC. All Rights Reserved. www.facebook.com/garfield
Distributed by Andrews McMeel Syndication
JIM DAVIS 7-20

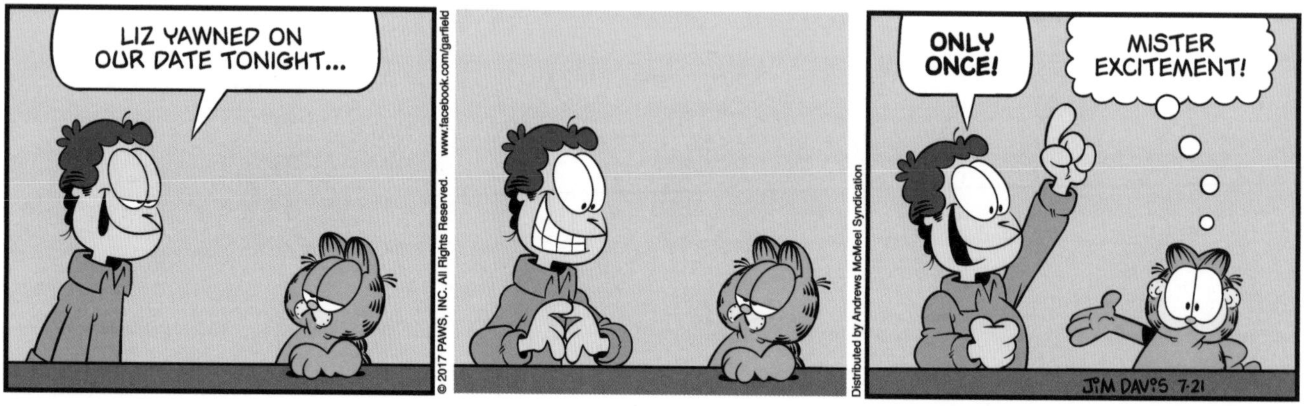
LIZ YAWNED ON OUR DATE TONIGHT...
ONLY ONCE!
MISTER EXCITEMENT!
© 2017 PAWS, INC. All Rights Reserved. www.facebook.com/garfield
Distributed by Andrews McMeel Syndication
JIM DAVIS 7-21

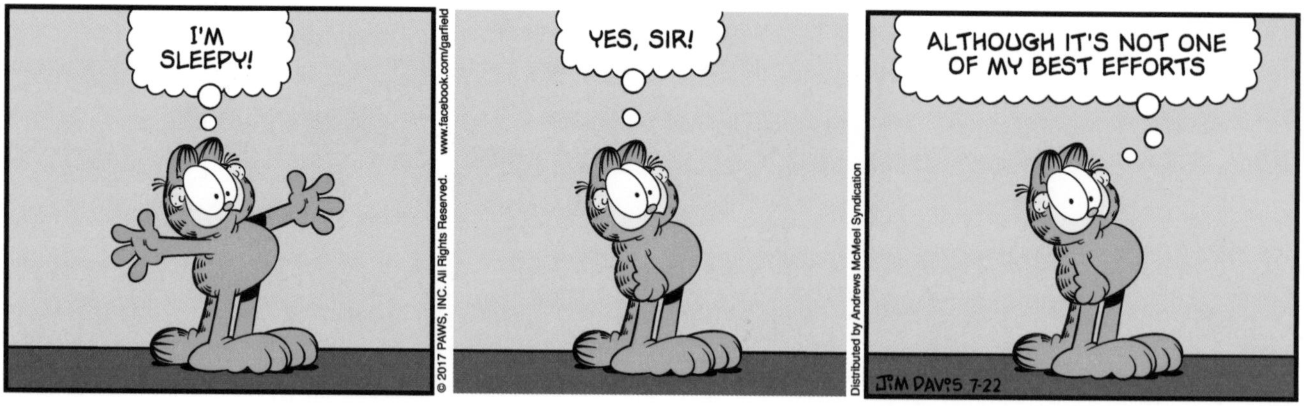
I'M SLEEPY!
YES, SIR!
ALTHOUGH IT'S NOT ONE OF MY BEST EFFORTS
© 2017 PAWS, INC. All Rights Reserved. www.facebook.com/garfield
Distributed by Andrews McMeel Syndication
JIM DAVIS 7-22

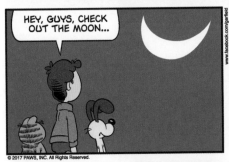

garfield.com
garfield
www.facebook.com/garfield
HEY, GUYS, CHECK OUT THE MOON...
IT LOOKS HAPPY, DOESN'T IT?
© 2017 PAWS, INC. All Rights Reserved.
WHEN I WAS A BOY, WE CALLED THAT A "SMILING MOON"
KIDS SURE DO THINK OF SOME FUNNY THINGS
Distributed by Andrews McMeel Syndication
JIM DAVIS 7-23

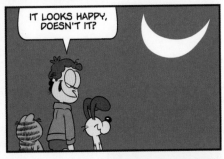

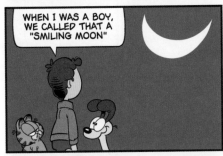

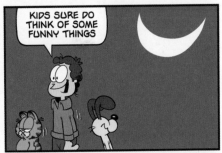

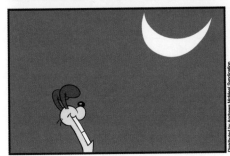

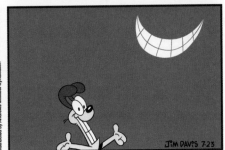

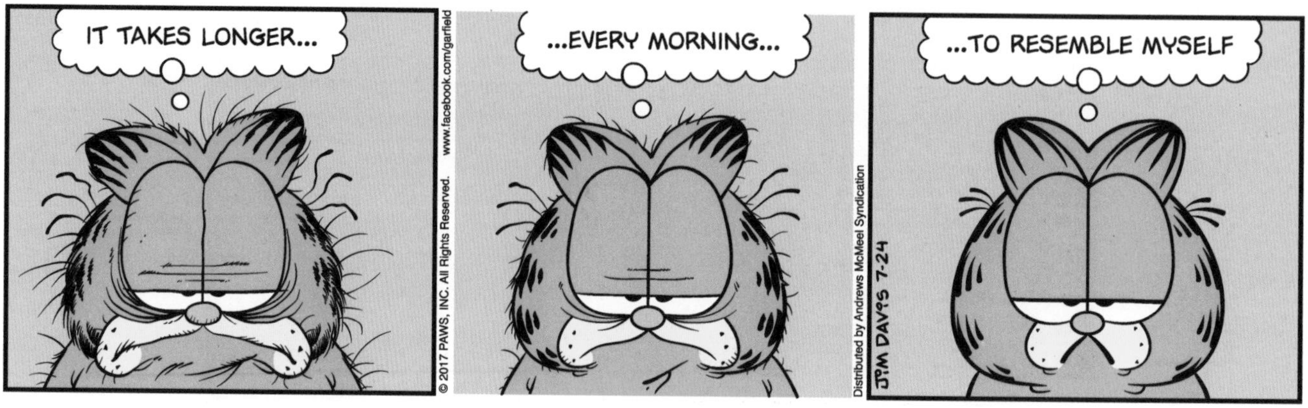
IT TAKES LONGER...
© 2017 PAWS, INC. All Rights Reserved. www.facebook.com/garfield
...EVERY MORNING...
Distributed by Andrews McMeel Syndication
JIM DAVIS 7-24
...TO RESEMBLE MYSELF

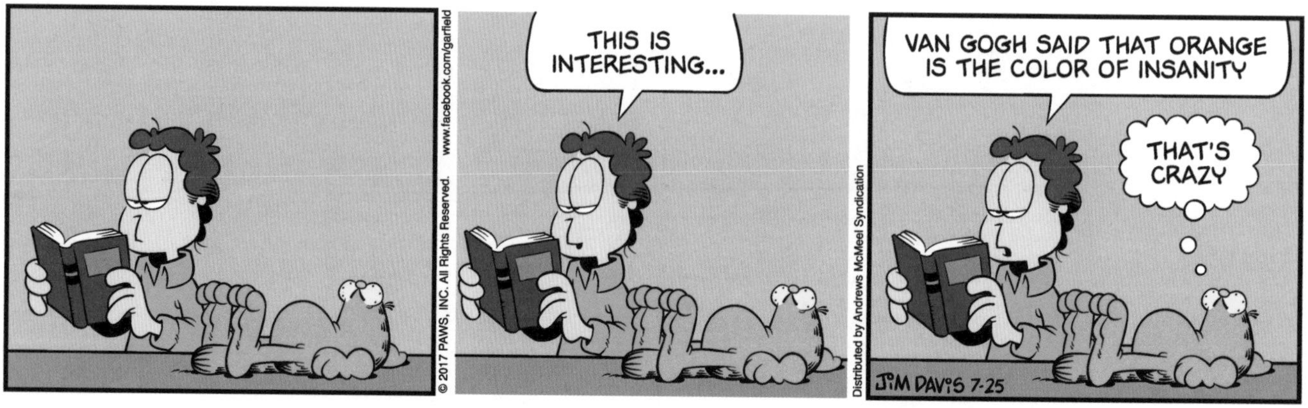
© 2017 PAWS, INC. All Rights Reserved. www.facebook.com/garfield
THIS IS INTERESTING...
Distributed by Andrews McMeel Syndication
VAN GOGH SAID THAT ORANGE IS THE COLOR OF INSANITY
THAT'S CRAZY
JIM DAVIS 7-25

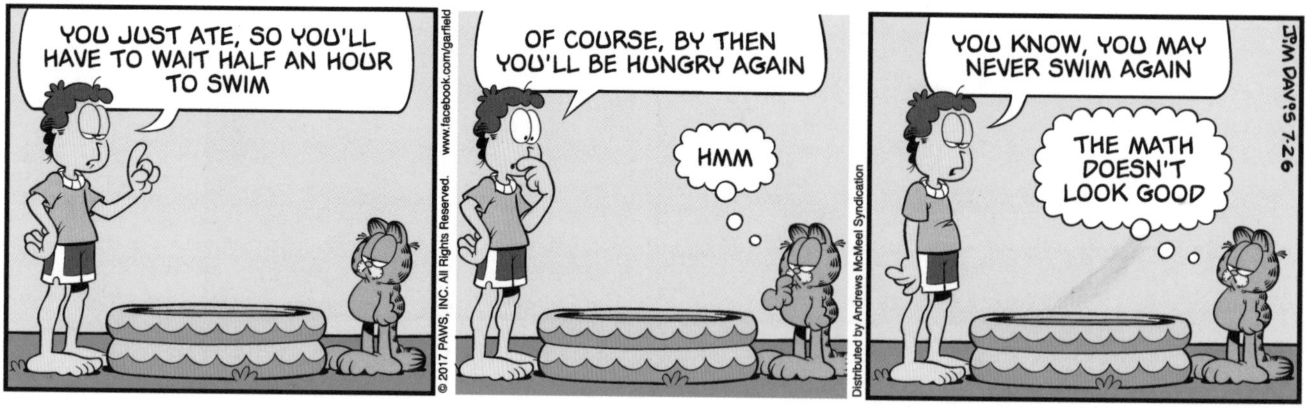
YOU JUST ATE, SO YOU'LL HAVE TO WAIT HALF AN HOUR TO SWIM
© 2017 PAWS, INC. All Rights Reserved. www.facebook.com/garfield
OF COURSE, BY THEN YOU'LL BE HUNGRY AGAIN
HMM
Distributed by Andrews McMeel Syndication
YOU KNOW, YOU MAY NEVER SWIM AGAIN
THE MATH DOESN'T LOOK GOOD
JIM DAVIS 7-26

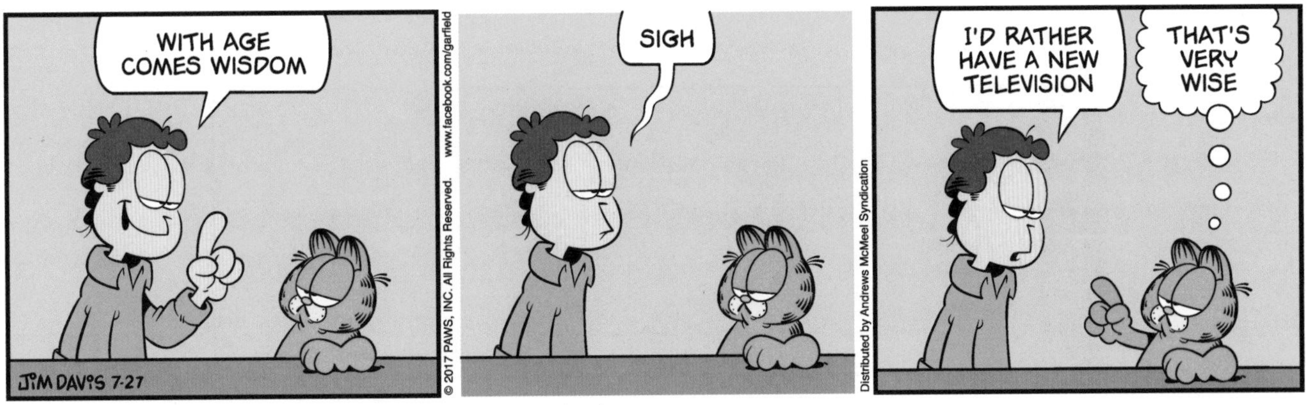
WITH AGE COMES WISDOM
SIGH
I'D RATHER HAVE A NEW TELEVISION
THAT'S VERY WISE
JIM DAVIS 7-27
© 2017 PAWS, INC. All Rights Reserved. www.facebook.com/garfield
Distributed by Andrews McMeel Syndication

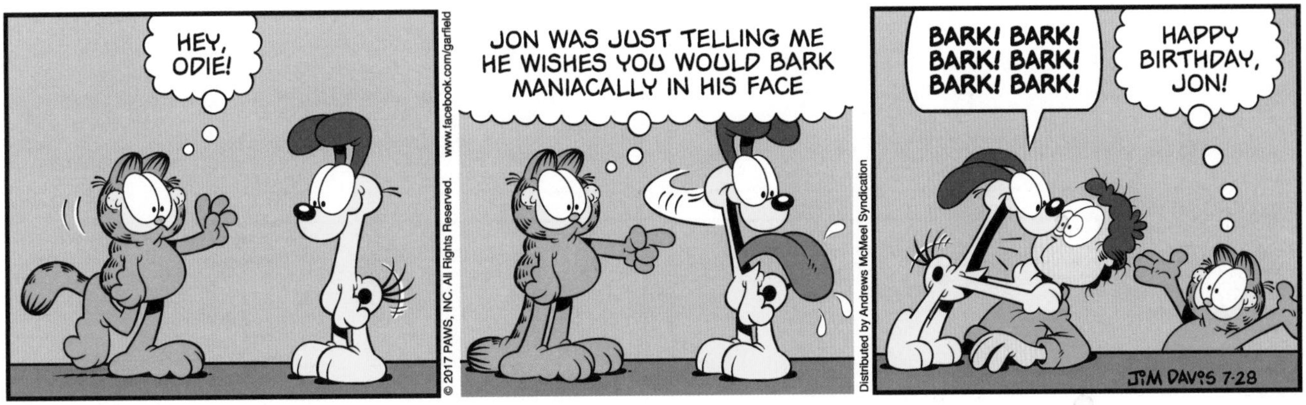
HEY, ODIE!
JON WAS JUST TELLING ME HE WISHES YOU WOULD BARK MANIACALLY IN HIS FACE
BARK! BARK! BARK! BARK! BARK! BARK!
HAPPY BIRTHDAY, JON!
JIM DAVIS 7-28
© 2017 PAWS, INC. All Rights Reserved. www.facebook.com/garfield
Distributed by Andrews McMeel Syndication

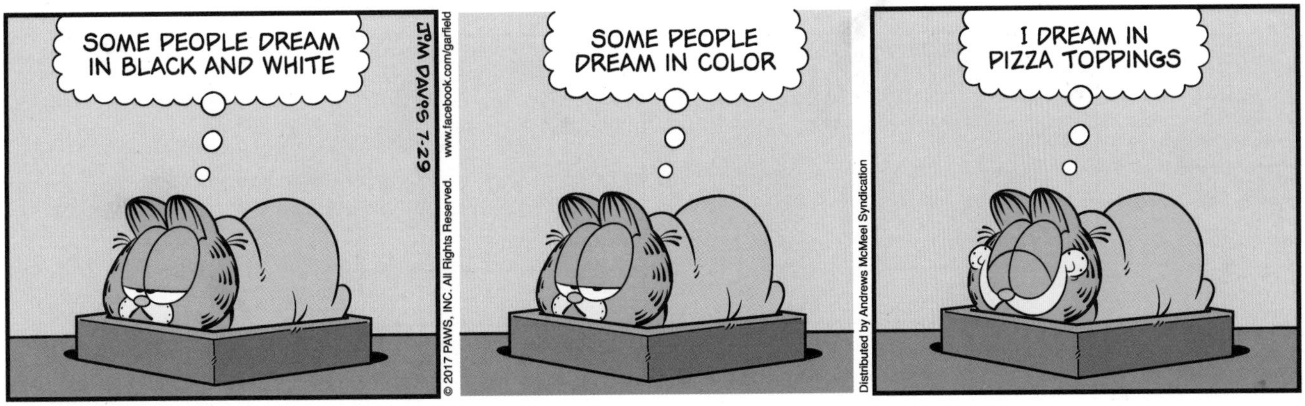
SOME PEOPLE DREAM IN BLACK AND WHITE
JIM DAVIS 7-29
SOME PEOPLE DREAM IN COLOR
I DREAM IN PIZZA TOPPINGS
© 2017 PAWS, INC. All Rights Reserved. www.facebook.com/garfield
Distributed by Andrews McMeel Syndication

garfield.com
Garfield®
www.facebook.com/garfield
JIM DAVIS 7-30
© 2017 PAWS, INC. All Rights Reserved.
Distributed by Andrews McMeel Syndication
SOME DAYS, YOU JUST GOTTA DANCE

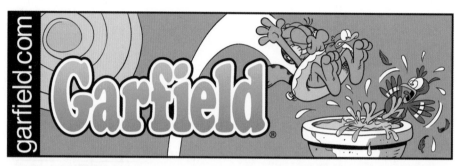

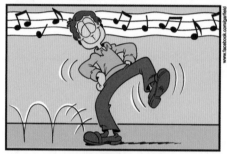

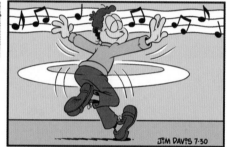

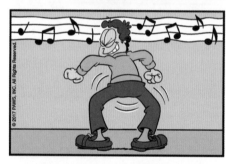

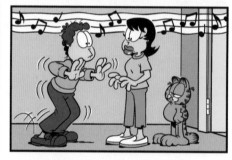

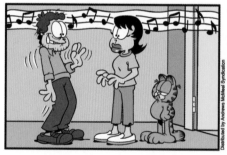

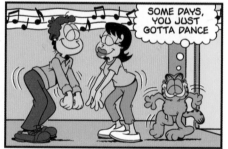

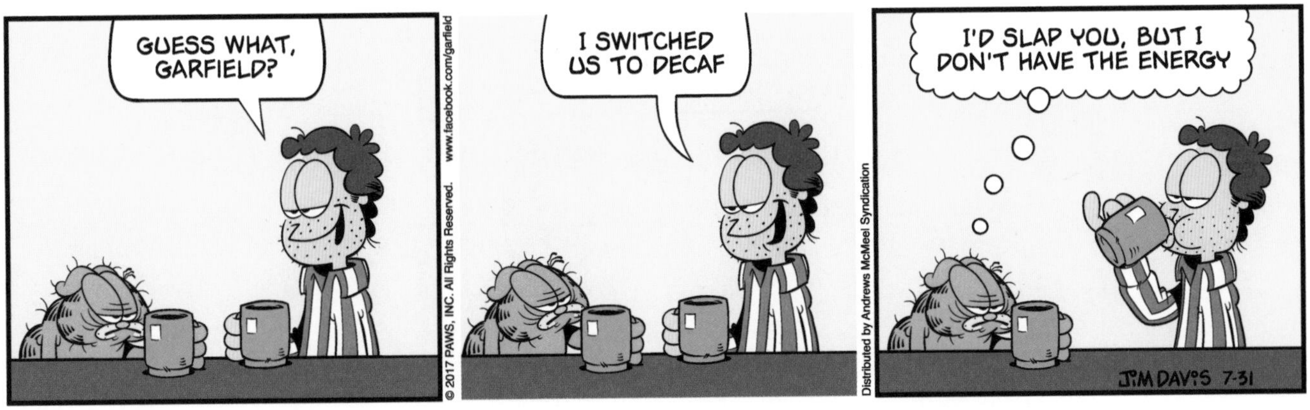
GUESS WHAT, GARFIELD?
© 2017 PAWS, INC. All Rights Reserved. www.facebook.com/garfield
I SWITCHED US TO DECAF
Distributed by Andrews McMeel Syndication
I'D SLAP YOU, BUT I DON'T HAVE THE ENERGY
JIM DAVIS 7-31

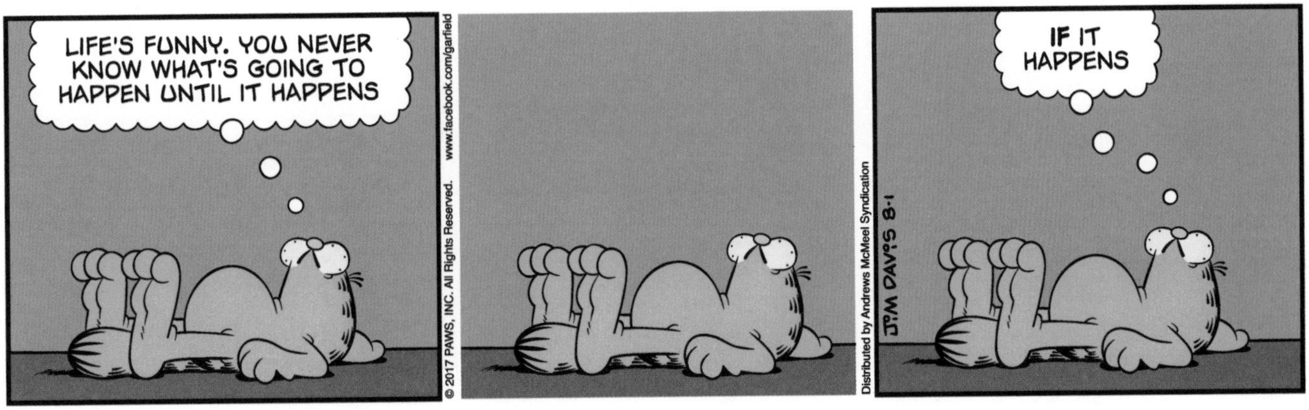
LIFE'S FUNNY. YOU NEVER KNOW WHAT'S GOING TO HAPPEN UNTIL IT HAPPENS
© 2017 PAWS, INC. All Rights Reserved. www.facebook.com/garfield
Distributed by Andrews McMeel Syndication
JIM DAVIS 8-1
IF IT HAPPENS

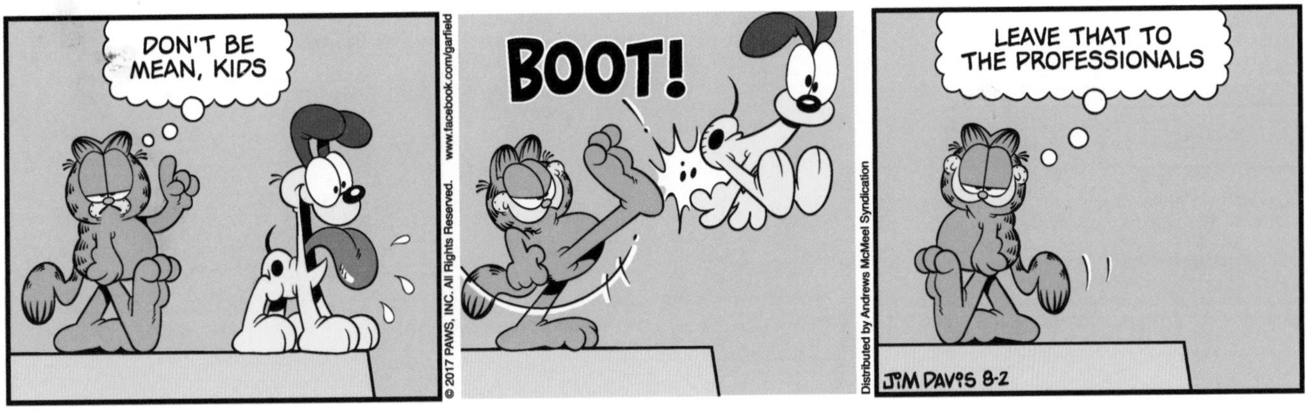
DON'T BE MEAN, KIDS
© 2017 PAWS, INC. All Rights Reserved. www.facebook.com/garfield
BOOT!
Distributed by Andrews McMeel Syndication
LEAVE THAT TO THE PROFESSIONALS
JIM DAVIS 8-2

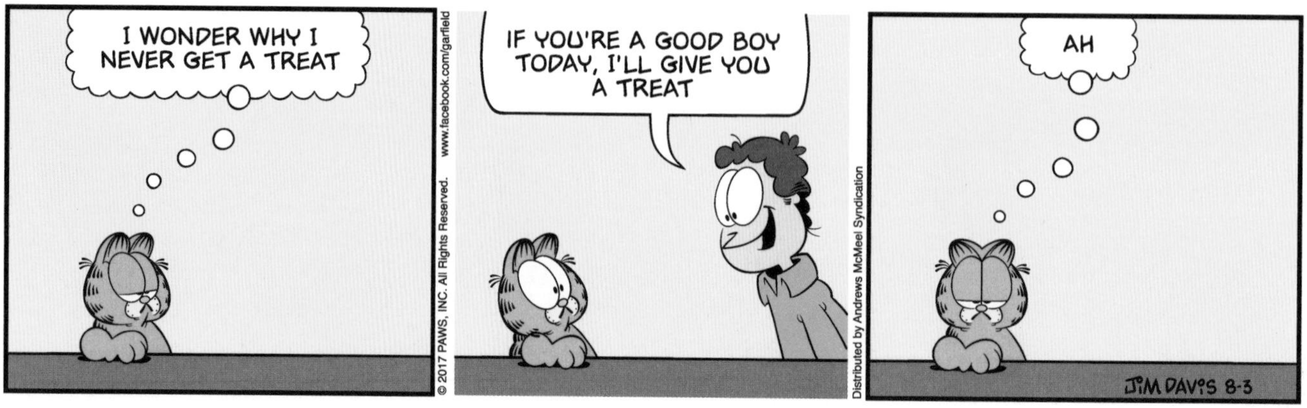
I WONDER WHY I NEVER GET A TREAT
IF YOU'RE A GOOD BOY TODAY, I'LL GIVE YOU A TREAT
AH
JIM DAVIS 8-3
© 2017 PAWS, INC. All Rights Reserved. www.facebook.com/garfield
Distributed by Andrews McMeel Syndication

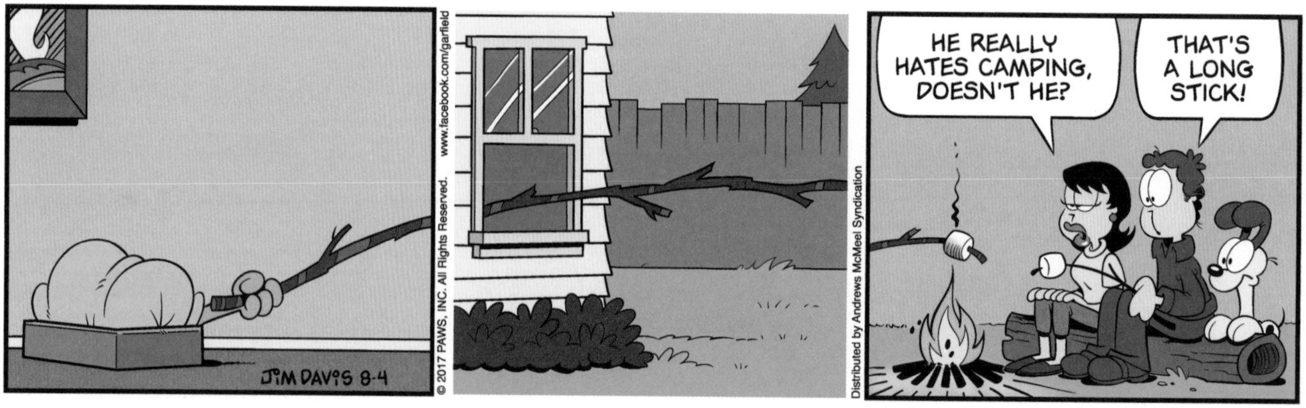
JIM DAVIS 8-4
HE REALLY HATES CAMPING, DOESN'T HE?
THAT'S A LONG STICK!
© 2017 PAWS, INC. All Rights Reserved. www.facebook.com/garfield
Distributed by Andrews McMeel Syndication

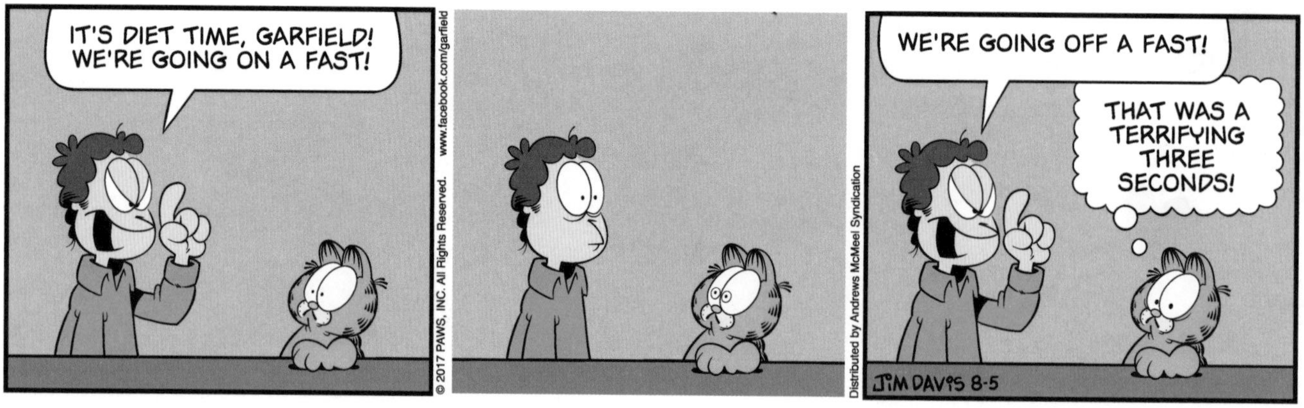
IT'S DIET TIME, GARFIELD! WE'RE GOING ON A FAST!
WE'RE GOING OFF A FAST!
THAT WAS A TERRIFYING THREE SECONDS!
JIM DAVIS 8-5
© 2017 PAWS, INC. All Rights Reserved. www.facebook.com/garfield
Distributed by Andrews McMeel Syndication

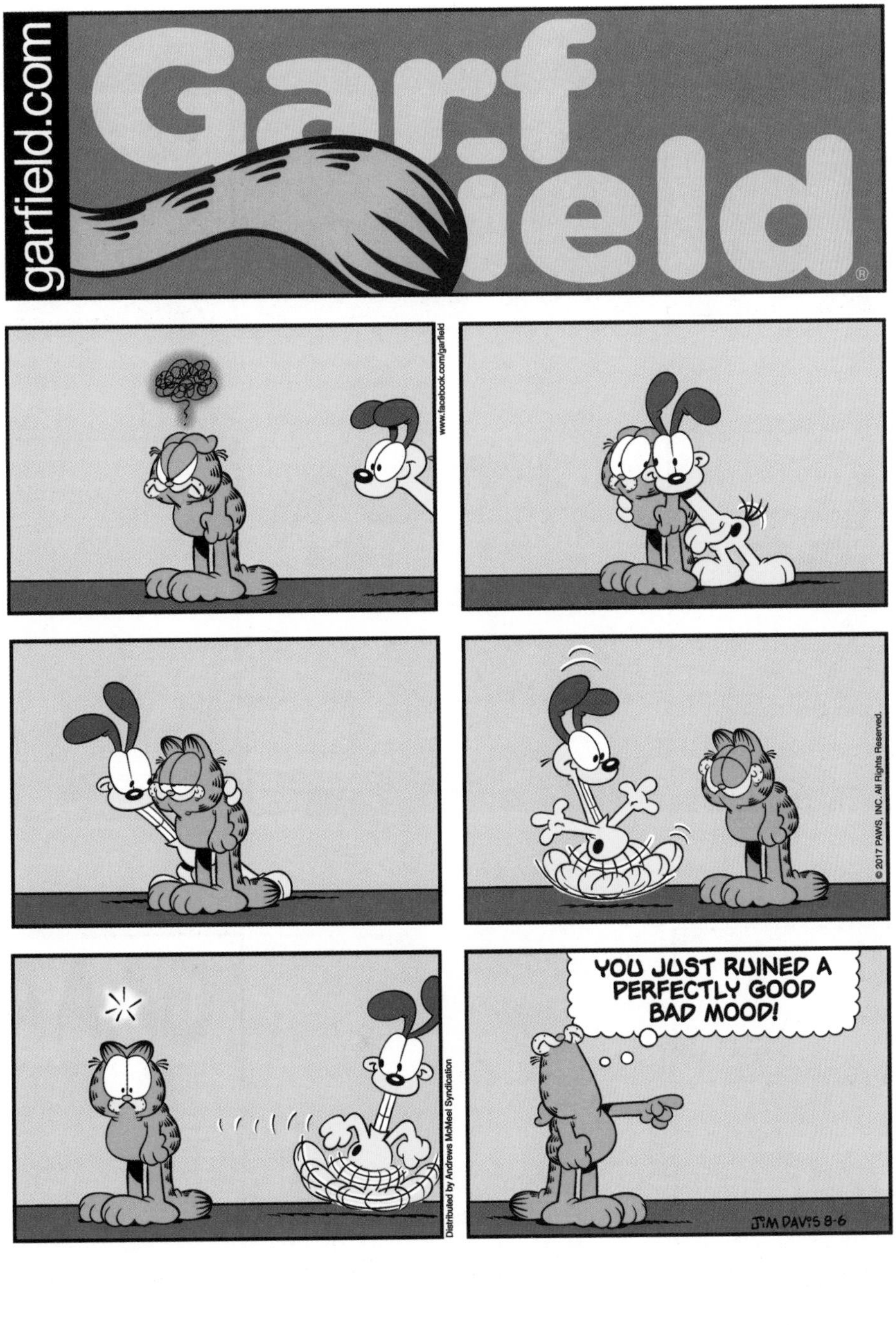
garfield.com
Garfield
www.facebook.com/garfield
© 2017 PAWS, INC. All Rights Reserved.
Distributed by Andrews McMeel Syndication
YOU JUST RUINED A PERFECTLY GOOD BAD MOOD!
JIM DAVIS 8-6

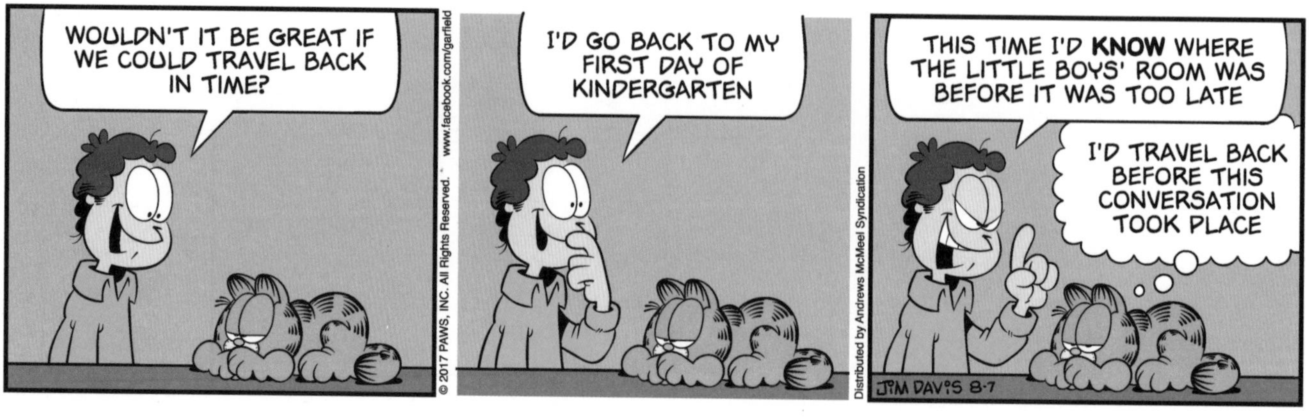
WOULDN'T IT BE GREAT IF WE COULD TRAVEL BACK IN TIME?
I'D GO BACK TO MY FIRST DAY OF KINDERGARTEN
THIS TIME I'D **KNOW** WHERE THE LITTLE BOYS' ROOM WAS BEFORE IT WAS TOO LATE
I'D TRAVEL BACK BEFORE THIS CONVERSATION TOOK PLACE
JIM DAVIS 8-7
© 2017 PAWS, INC. All Rights Reserved. www.facebook.com/garfield
Distributed by Andrews McMeel Syndication

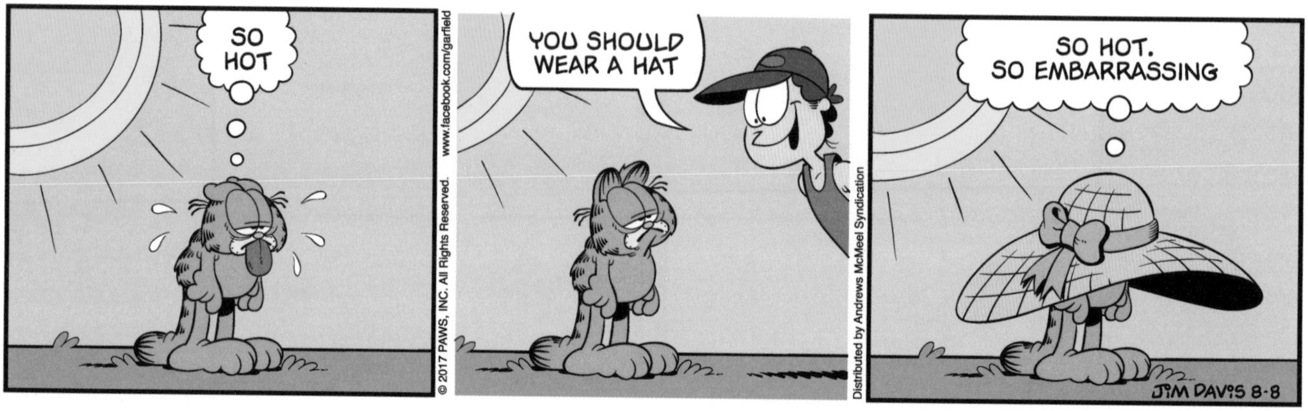
SO HOT
YOU SHOULD WEAR A HAT
SO HOT. SO EMBARRASSING
JIM DAVIS 8-8
© 2017 PAWS, INC. All Rights Reserved. www.facebook.com/garfield
Distributed by Andrews McMeel Syndication

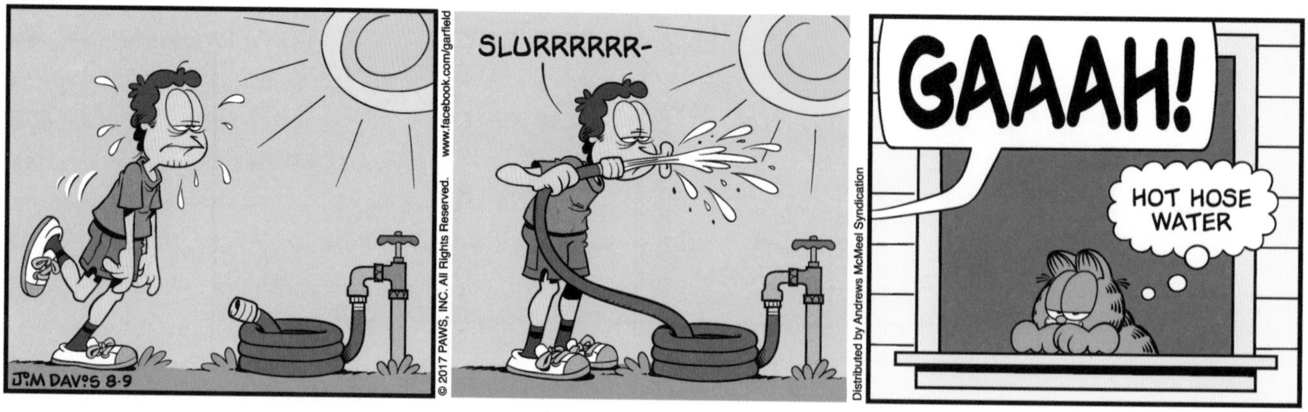
JIM DAVIS 8-9
SLURRRRRR-
GAAAH!
HOT HOSE WATER
© 2017 PAWS, INC. All Rights Reserved. www.facebook.com/garfield
Distributed by Andrews McMeel Syndication

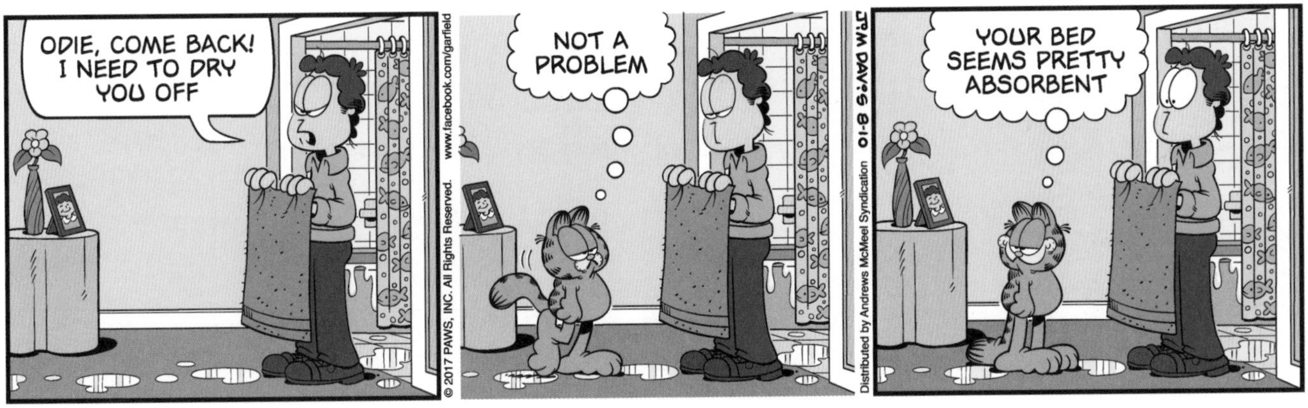
ODIE, COME BACK! I NEED TO DRY YOU OFF
NOT A PROBLEM
YOUR BED SEEMS PRETTY ABSORBENT
JIM DAVIS 8-10
© 2017 PAWS, INC. All Rights Reserved. www.facebook.com/garfield
Distributed by Andrews McMeel Syndication

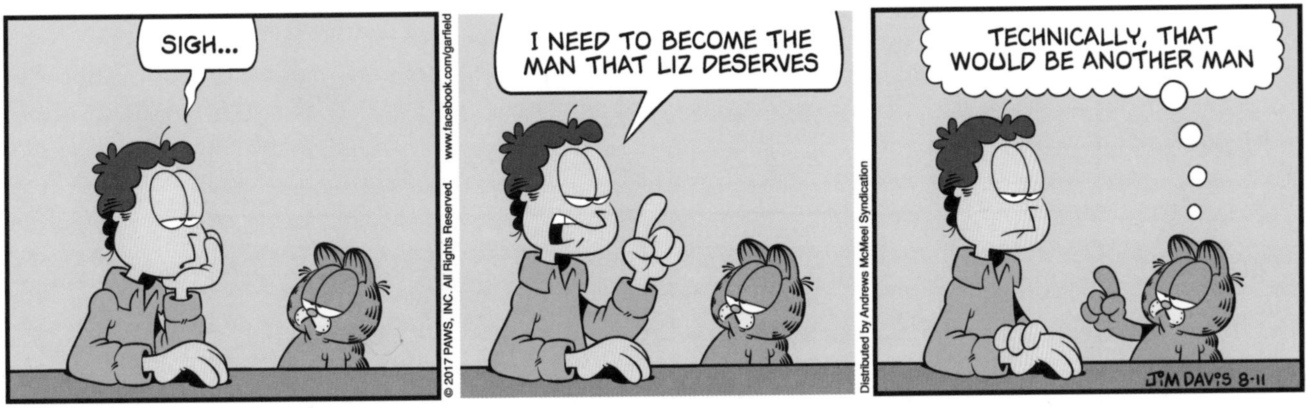
SIGH...
I NEED TO BECOME THE MAN THAT LIZ DESERVES
TECHNICALLY, THAT WOULD BE ANOTHER MAN
JIM DAVIS 8-11
© 2017 PAWS, INC. All Rights Reserved. www.facebook.com/garfield
Distributed by Andrews McMeel Syndication

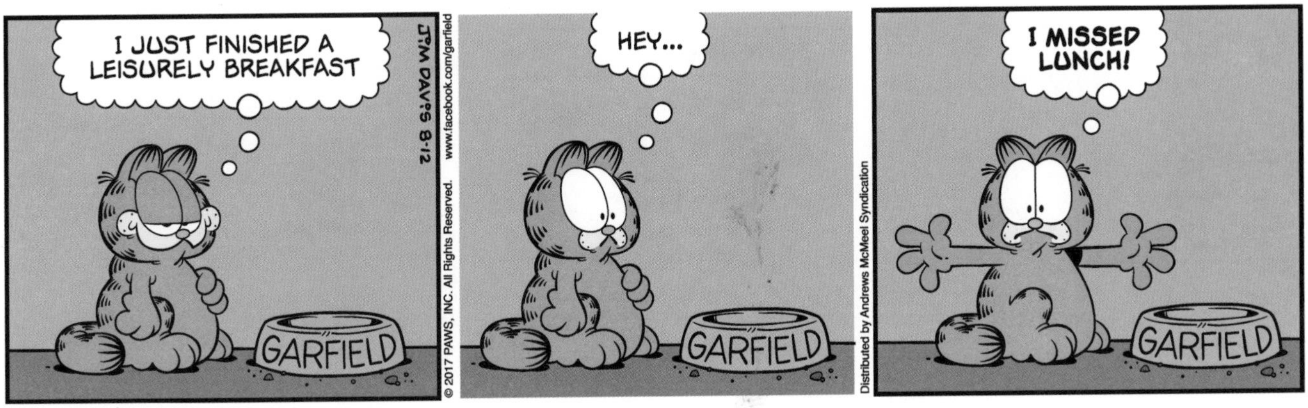
I JUST FINISHED A LEISURELY BREAKFAST
HEY...
I MISSED LUNCH!
GARFIELD
GARFIELD
GARFIELD
JIM DAVIS 8-12
© 2017 PAWS, INC. All Rights Reserved. www.facebook.com/garfield
Distributed by Andrews McMeel Syndication

garfield.com
NO LOITERING
GARFIELD
SO YOU WORKED IN THE YARD YESTERDAY WITHOUT A SHIRT ON?
www.facebook.com/garfield
YES
IT WAS PRETTY HOT AND SUNNY. DID YOU WEAR SUNSCREEN?
YEEES
ALL OVER?
© 2017 PAWS, INC. All Rights Reserved.
YES, MOTHEEER
REALLY? EVEN ON YOUR BACK?
SLAP!
YES!
Distributed by Andrews McMeel Syndication
BUST-ED
JIM DAVIS 8-13

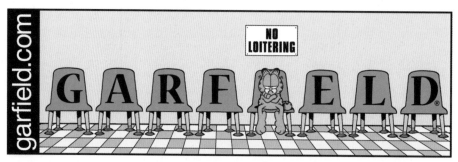

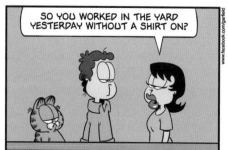

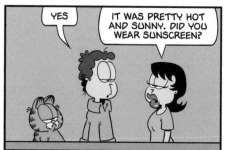

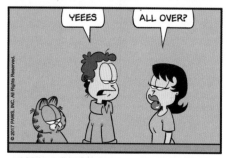

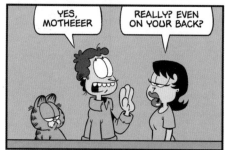

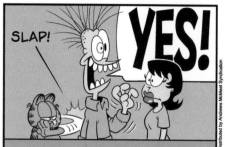

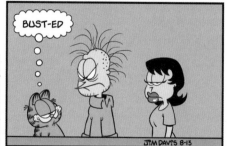

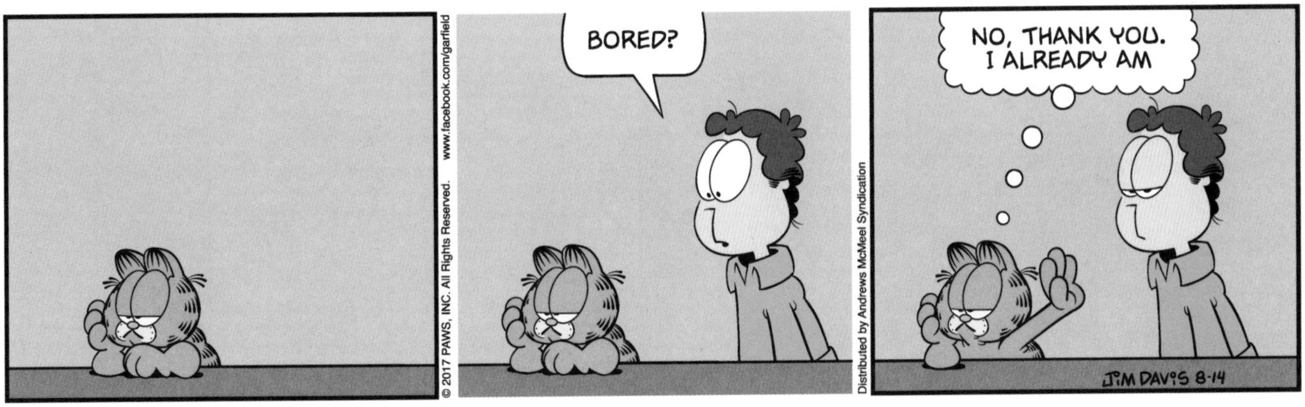
© 2017 PAWS, INC. All Rights Reserved. www.facebook.com/garfield
BORED?
Distributed by Andrews McMeel Syndication
NO, THANK YOU. I ALREADY AM
JIM DAVIS 8-14

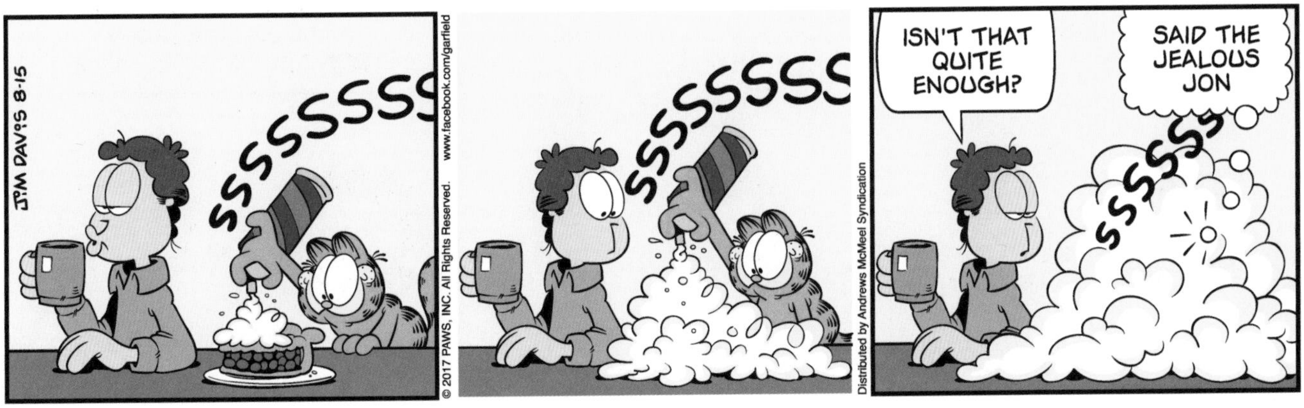
JIM DAVIS 8-15
SSSSSSSSS
© 2017 PAWS, INC. All Rights Reserved. www.facebook.com/garfield
SSSSSSSSS
Distributed by Andrews McMeel Syndication
ISN'T THAT QUITE ENOUGH?
SAID THE JEALOUS JON
SSSSSS

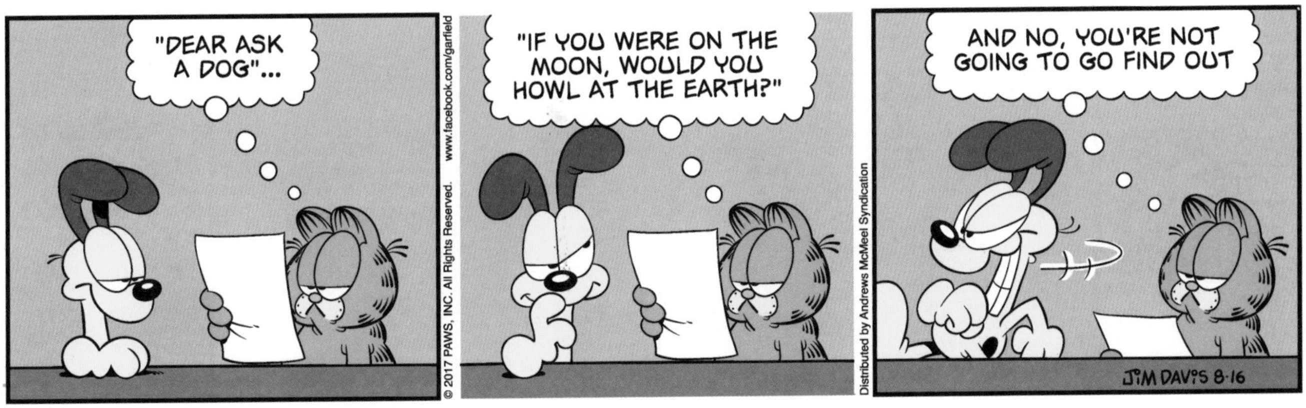
"DEAR ASK A DOG"...
© 2017 PAWS, INC. All Rights Reserved. www.facebook.com/garfield
"IF YOU WERE ON THE MOON, WOULD YOU HOWL AT THE EARTH?"
Distributed by Andrews McMeel Syndication
AND NO, YOU'RE NOT GOING TO GO FIND OUT
JIM DAVIS 8-16

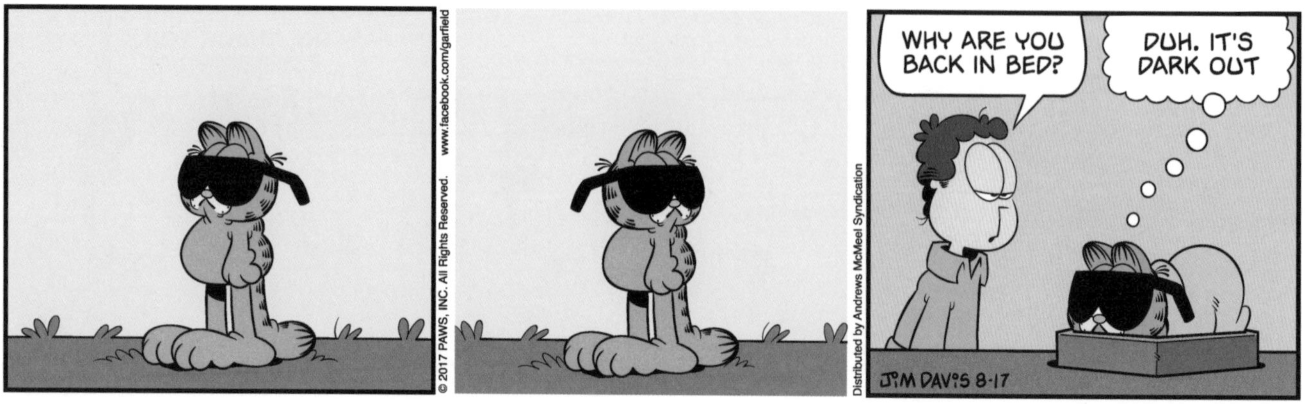
© 2017 PAWS, INC. All Rights Reserved. www.facebook.com/garfield
Distributed by Andrews McMeel Syndication
WHY ARE YOU BACK IN BED?
DUH. IT'S DARK OUT
JIM DAVIS 8-17

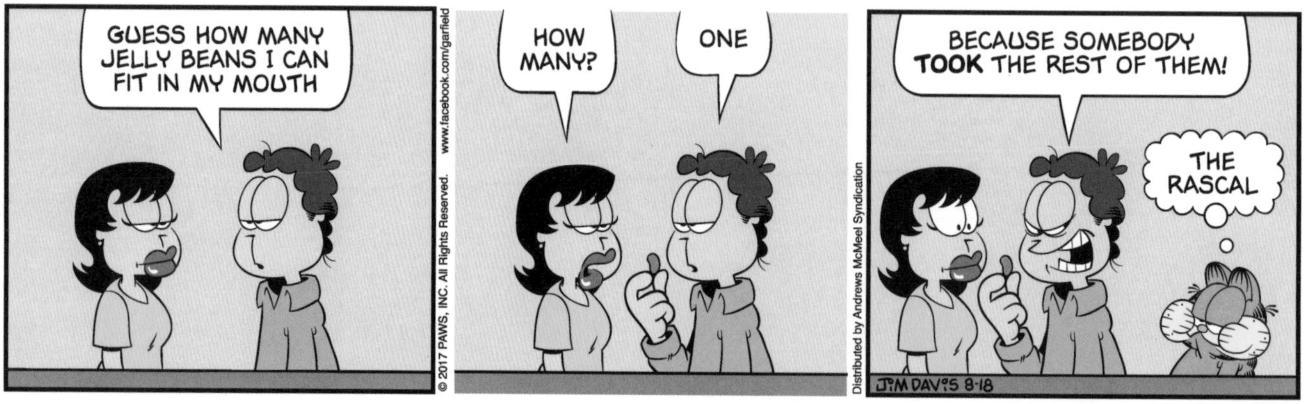
GUESS HOW MANY JELLY BEANS I CAN FIT IN MY MOUTH
© 2017 PAWS, INC. All Rights Reserved. www.facebook.com/garfield
HOW MANY?
ONE
Distributed by Andrews McMeel Syndication
BECAUSE SOMEBODY **TOOK** THE REST OF THEM!
THE RASCAL
JIM DAVIS 8-18

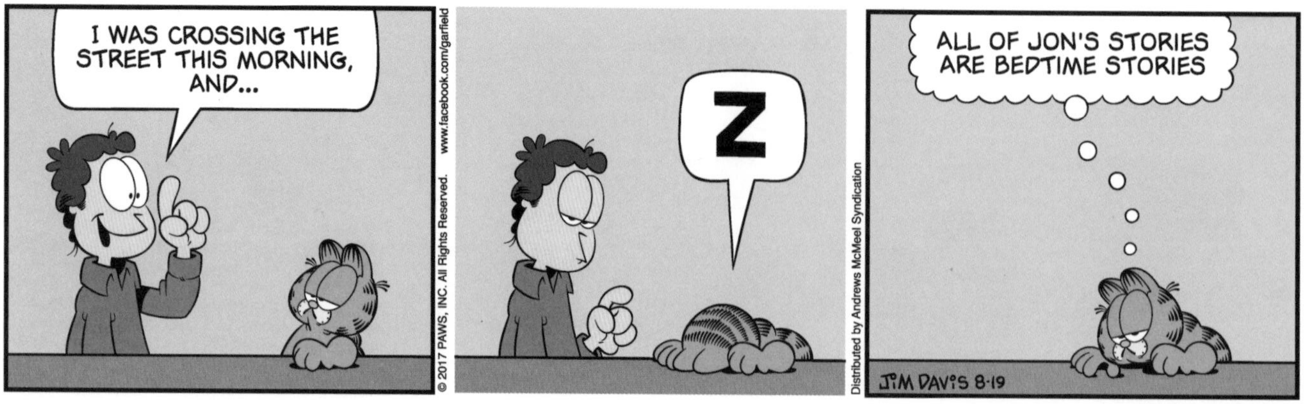
I WAS CROSSING THE STREET THIS MORNING, AND...
© 2017 PAWS, INC. All Rights Reserved. www.facebook.com/garfield
Z
Distributed by Andrews McMeel Syndication
ALL OF JON'S STORIES ARE BEDTIME STORIES
JIM DAVIS 8-19

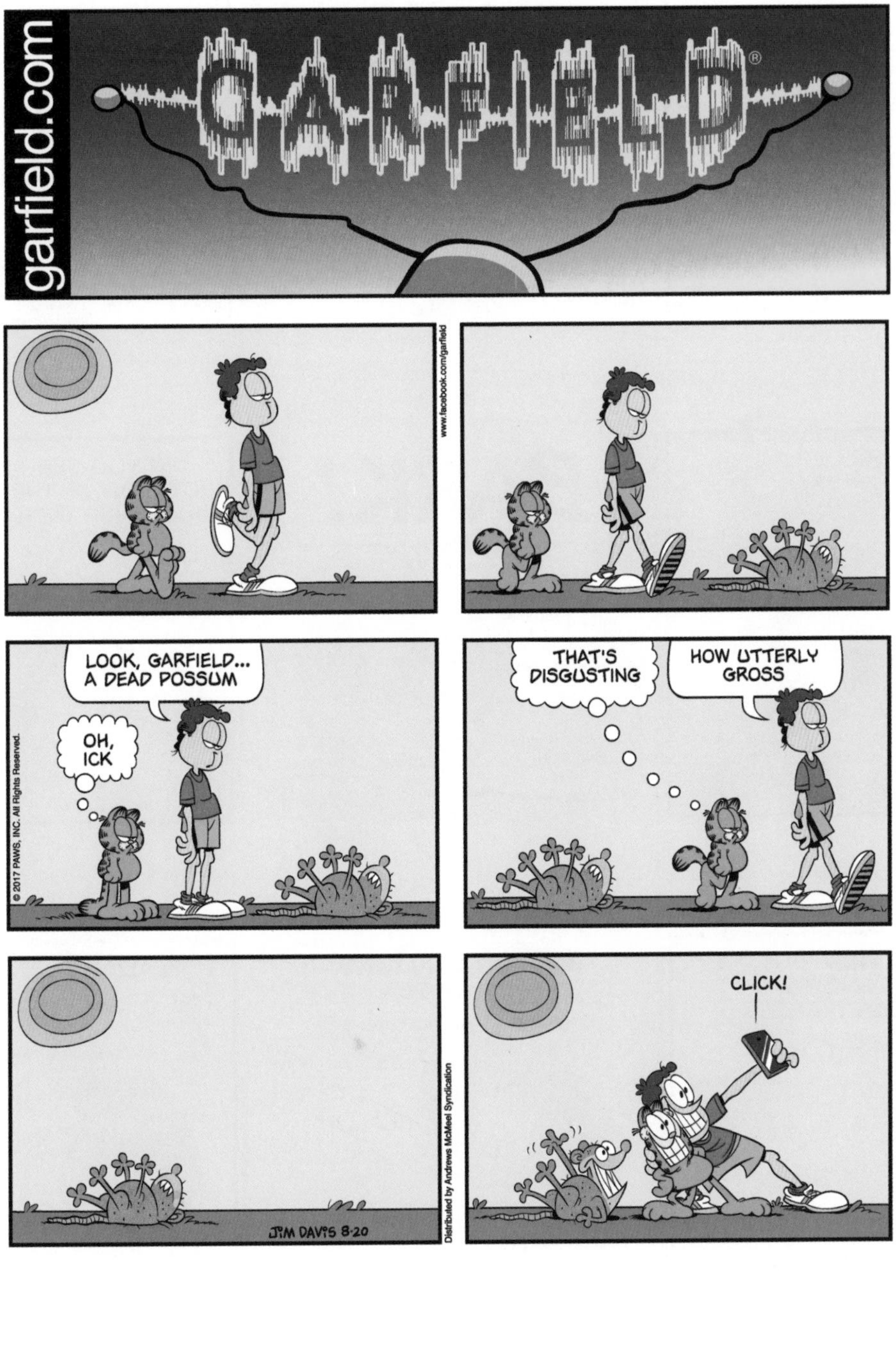
garfield.com
GARFIELD®
www.facebook.com/garfield
LOOK, GARFIELD... A DEAD POSSUM
OH, ICK
THAT'S DISGUSTING
HOW UTTERLY GROSS
© 2017 PAWS, INC. All Rights Reserved.
JIM DAVIS 8-20
Distributed by Andrews McMeel Syndication
CLICK!

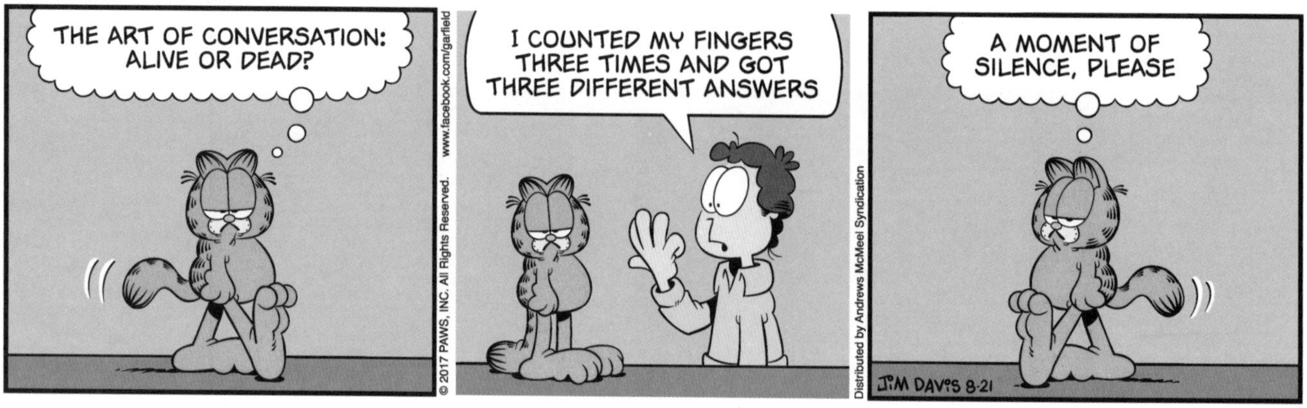
THE ART OF CONVERSATION: ALIVE OR DEAD?
I COUNTED MY FINGERS THREE TIMES AND GOT THREE DIFFERENT ANSWERS
A MOMENT OF SILENCE, PLEASE
© 2017 PAWS, INC. All Rights Reserved. www.facebook.com/garfield
Distributed by Andrews McMeel Syndication
JIM DAVIS 8-21

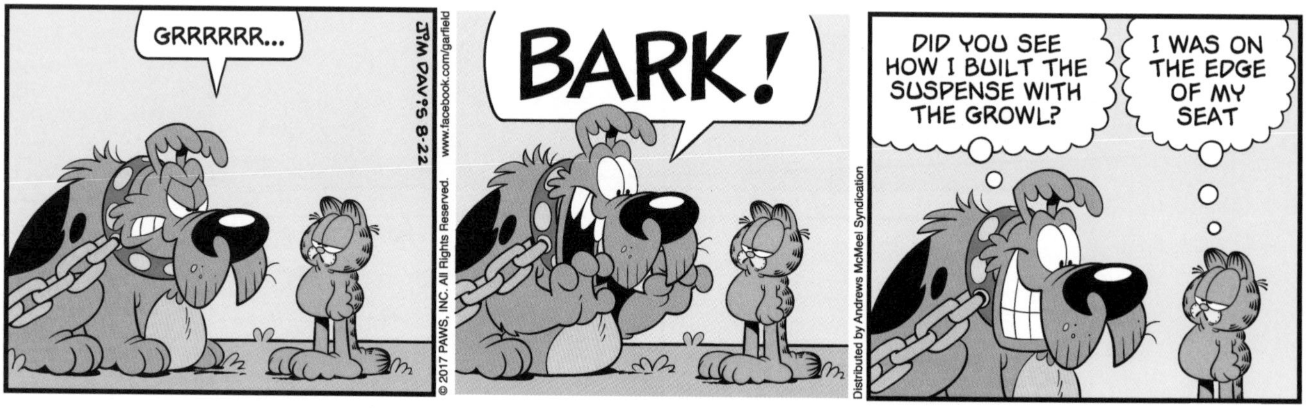
GRRRRRR...
JIM DAVIS 8-22
© 2017 PAWS, INC. All Rights Reserved. www.facebook.com/garfield
BARK!
Distributed by Andrews McMeel Syndication
DID YOU SEE HOW I BUILT THE SUSPENSE WITH THE GROWL?
I WAS ON THE EDGE OF MY SEAT

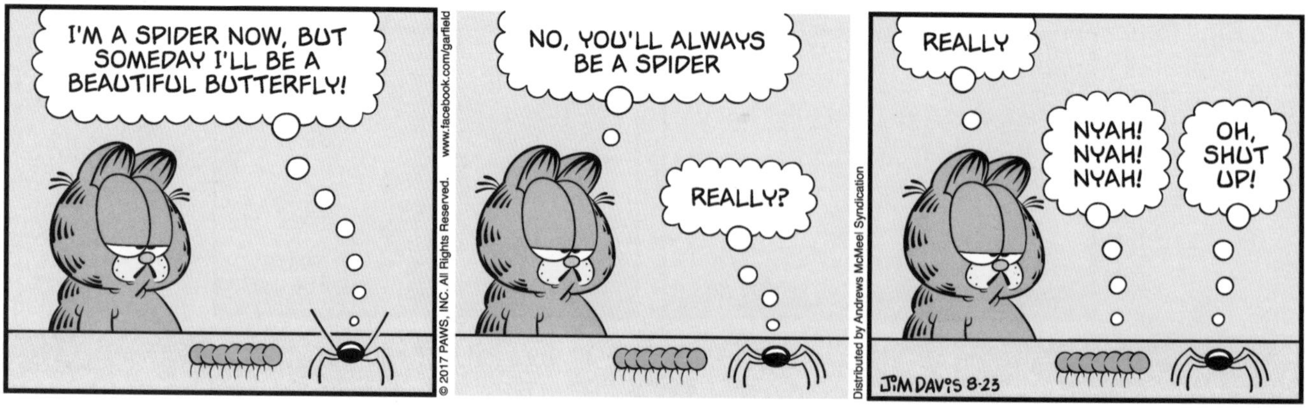
I'M A SPIDER NOW, BUT SOMEDAY I'LL BE A BEAUTIFUL BUTTERFLY!
© 2017 PAWS, INC. All Rights Reserved. www.facebook.com/garfield
NO, YOU'LL ALWAYS BE A SPIDER
REALLY?
Distributed by Andrews McMeel Syndication
REALLY
NYAH! NYAH! NYAH!
OH, SHUT UP!
JIM DAVIS 8-23

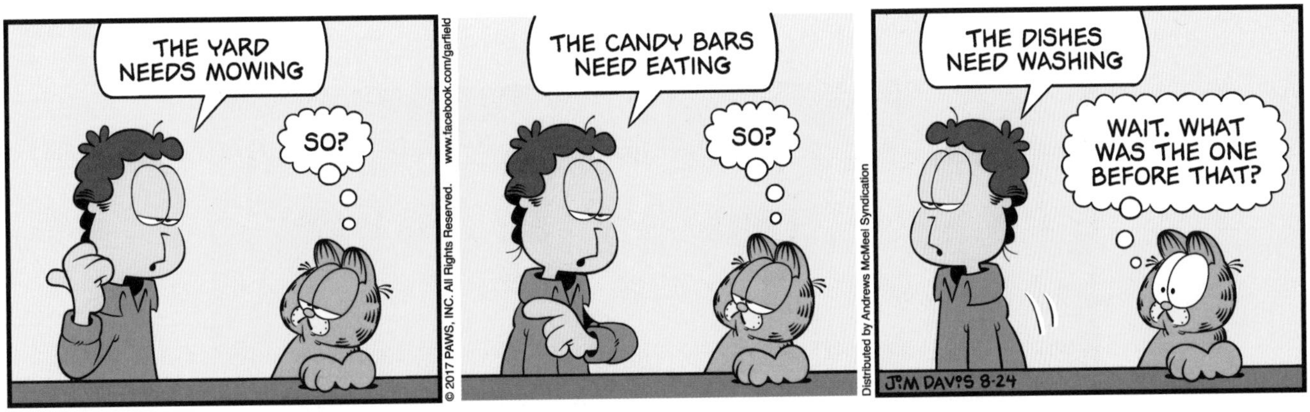
THE YARD NEEDS MOWING
SO?
© 2017 PAWS, INC. All Rights Reserved. www.facebook.com/garfield
THE CANDY BARS NEED EATING
SO?
Distributed by Andrews McMeel Syndication
THE DISHES NEED WASHING
WAIT. WHAT WAS THE ONE BEFORE THAT?
JIM DAVIS 8-24

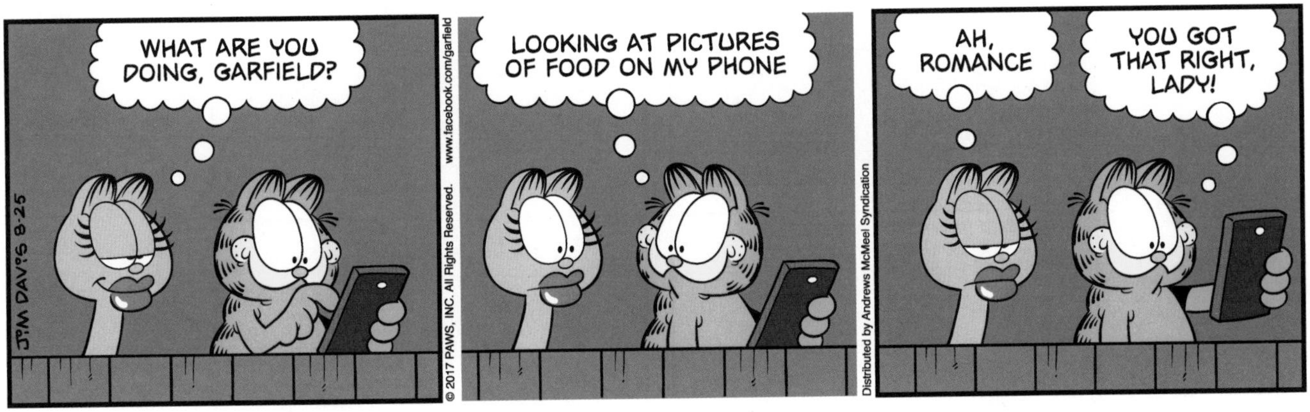
WHAT ARE YOU DOING, GARFIELD?
JIM DAVIS 8-25
© 2017 PAWS, INC. All Rights Reserved. www.facebook.com/garfield
LOOKING AT PICTURES OF FOOD ON MY PHONE
Distributed by Andrews McMeel Syndication
AH, ROMANCE
YOU GOT THAT RIGHT, LADY!

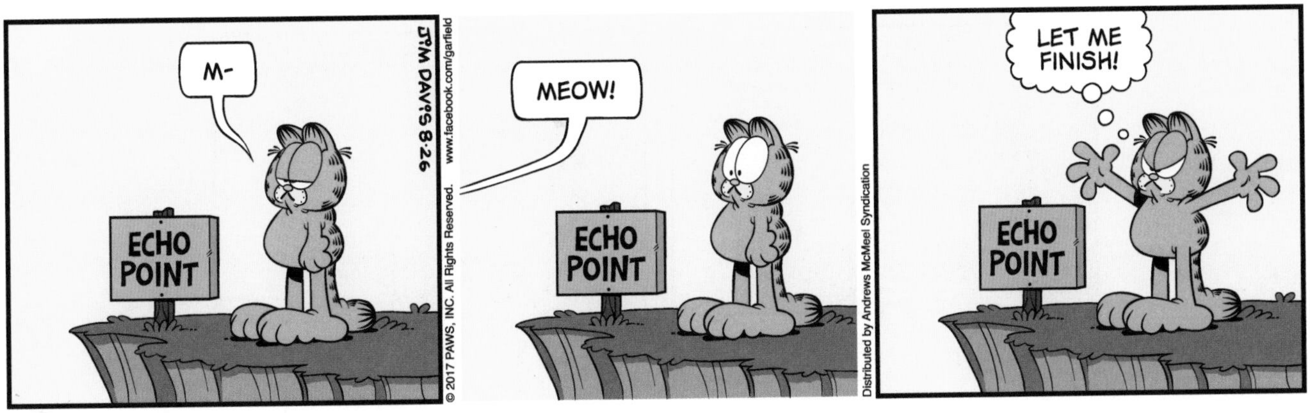
M-
ECHO POINT
JIM DAVIS 8-26
© 2017 PAWS, INC. All Rights Reserved. www.facebook.com/garfield
MEOW!
ECHO POINT
Distributed by Andrews McMeel Syndication
LET ME FINISH!
ECHO POINT

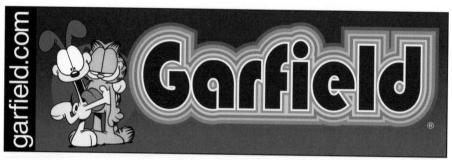

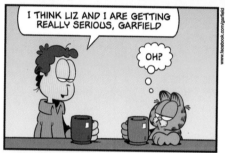

garfield.com
Garfield
I THINK LIZ AND I ARE GETTING REALLY SERIOUS, GARFIELD
OH?
www.facebook.com/garfield
TODAY WE WENT TO BINKY BURGER FOR LUNCH...
AND SHE ACTUALLY SHARED HER SOFT DRINK WITH ME!
WOW
© 2017 PAWS, INC. All Rights Reserved.
AND HER FRENCH FRIES!
THAT IS SERIOUS
MAYBE IT'S TIME TO TAKE OUR RELATIONSHIP TO THE NEXT LEVEL
I DON'T KNOW, JON...
Distributed by Andrews McMeel Syndication
ONION RINGS ARE A BIG STEP
JIM DAVIS 8-27

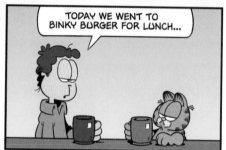

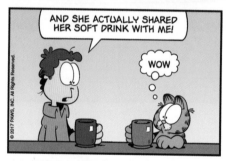

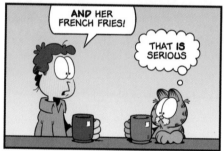

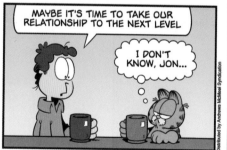

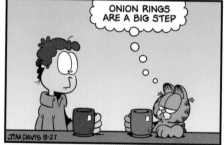

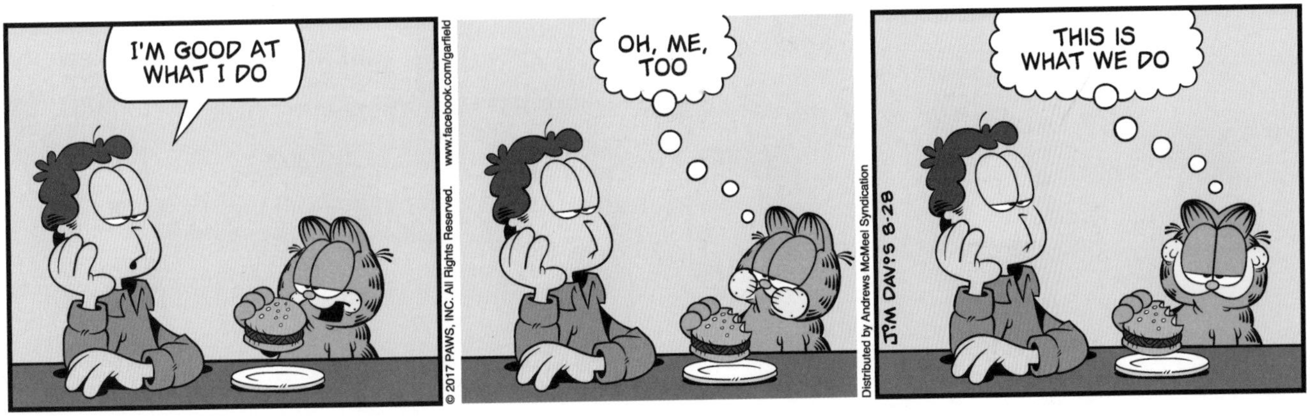
I'M GOOD AT WHAT I DO
© 2017 PAWS, INC. All Rights Reserved. www.facebook.com/garfield
OH, ME, TOO
Distributed by Andrews McMeel Syndication
JIM DAVIS 8-28
THIS IS WHAT WE DO

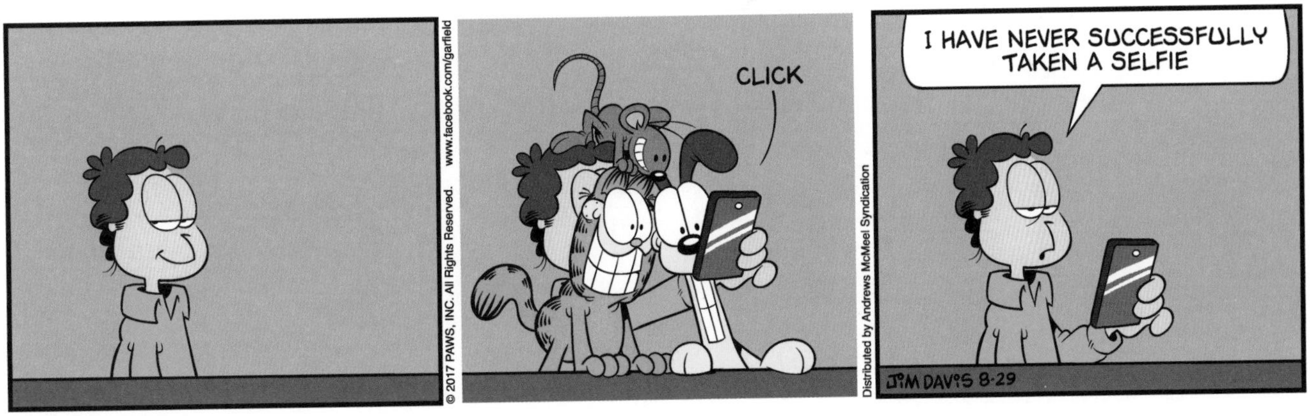
© 2017 PAWS, INC. All Rights Reserved. www.facebook.com/garfield
CLICK
Distributed by Andrews McMeel Syndication
I HAVE NEVER SUCCESSFULLY TAKEN A SELFIE
JIM DAVIS 8-29

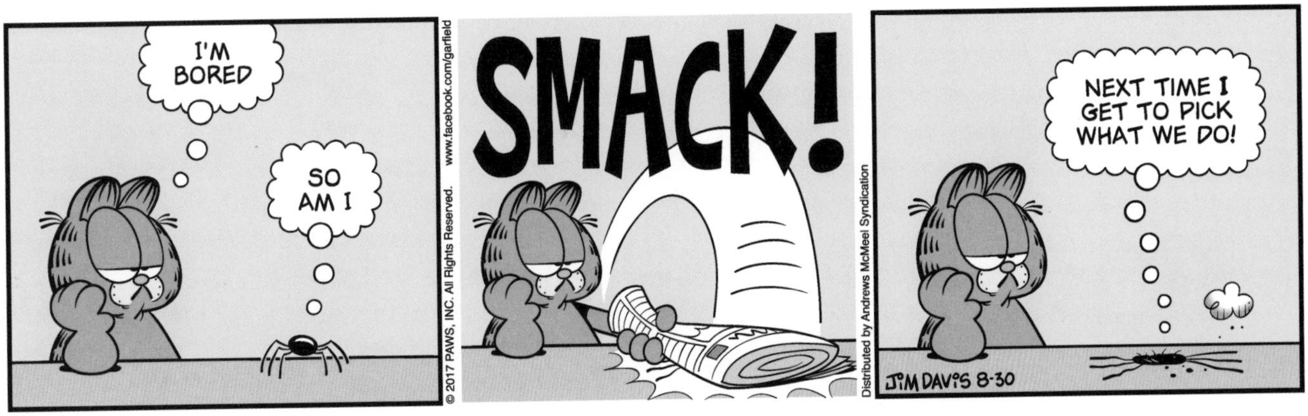
I'M BORED
SO AM I
© 2017 PAWS, INC. All Rights Reserved. www.facebook.com/garfield
SMACK!
Distributed by Andrews McMeel Syndication
NEXT TIME I GET TO PICK WHAT WE DO!
JIM DAVIS 8-30

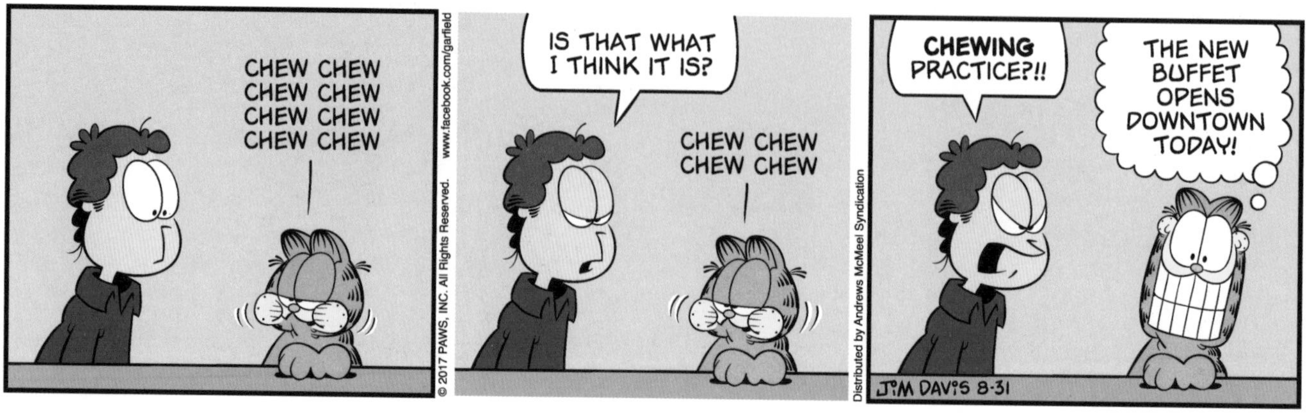
CHEW CHEW CHEW CHEW CHEW CHEW CHEW CHEW
© 2017 PAWS, INC. All Rights Reserved. www.facebook.com/garfield
IS THAT WHAT I THINK IT IS?
CHEW CHEW CHEW CHEW
Distributed by Andrews McMeel Syndication
CHEWING PRACTICE?!!
THE NEW BUFFET OPENS DOWNTOWN TODAY!
JIM DAVIS 8-31

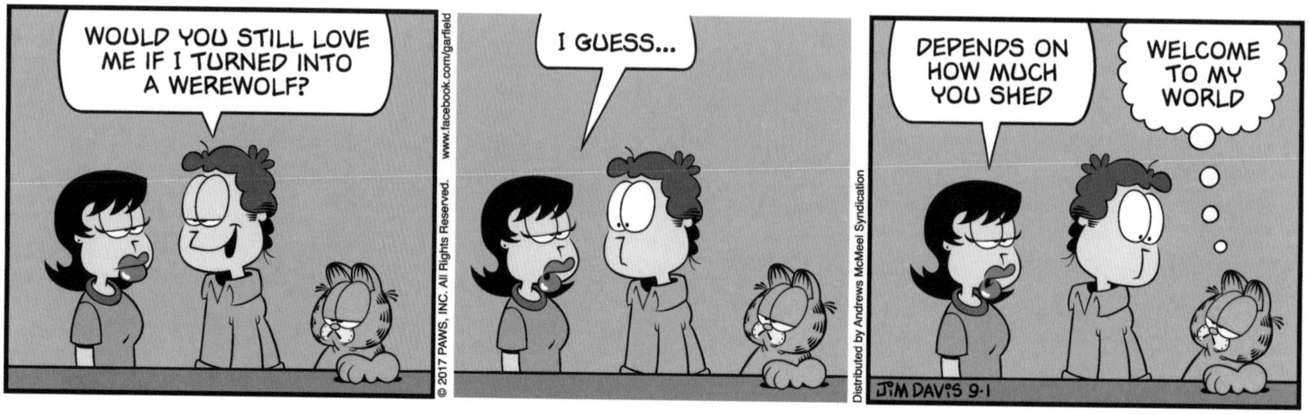
WOULD YOU STILL LOVE ME IF I TURNED INTO A WEREWOLF?
© 2017 PAWS, INC. All Rights Reserved. www.facebook.com/garfield
I GUESS...
Distributed by Andrews McMeel Syndication
DEPENDS ON HOW MUCH YOU SHED
WELCOME TO MY WORLD
JIM DAVIS 9-1

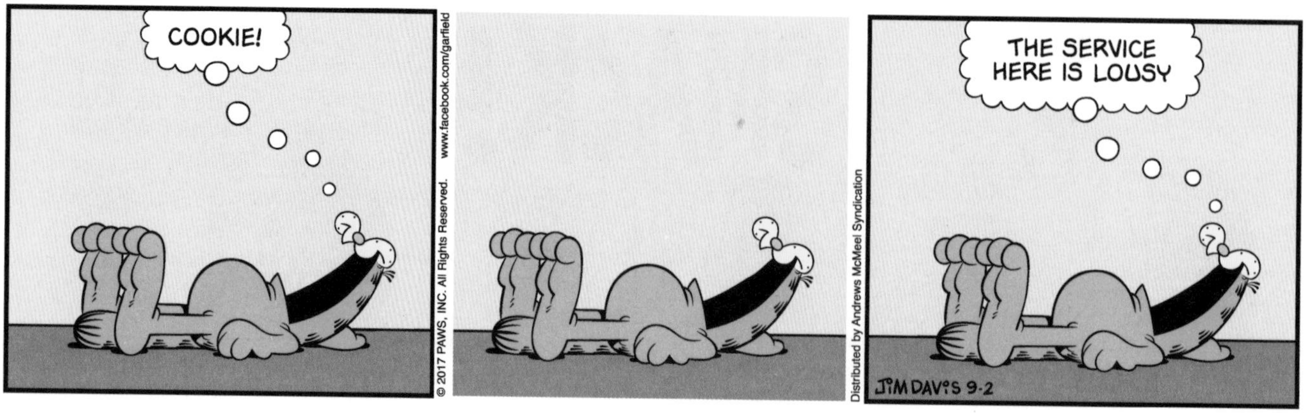
COOKIE!
© 2017 PAWS, INC. All Rights Reserved. www.facebook.com/garfield
Distributed by Andrews McMeel Syndication
THE SERVICE HERE IS LOUSY
JIM DAVIS 9-2

garfield.com
Garfield
CHARCOAL
CHARCOAL
www.facebook.com/garfield
LIGHTER FLUID
LIGHTER FLUID
MATCH
MATCH
SSSHICK!
© 2017 PAWS, INC. All Rights Reserved.
FOOOMF
Distributed by Andrews McMeel Syndication
EYEBROWS
THE GROCERY STORE WAS FRESH OUT
JIM DAVIS 9-3

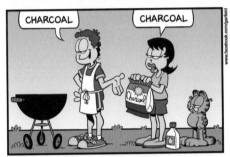

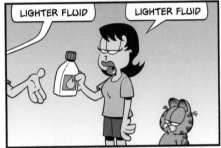

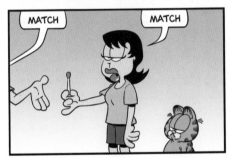

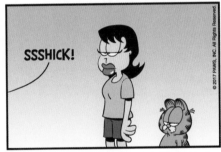

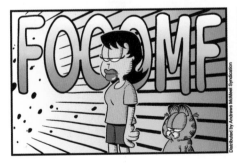

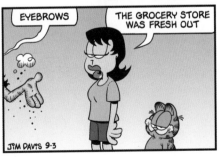

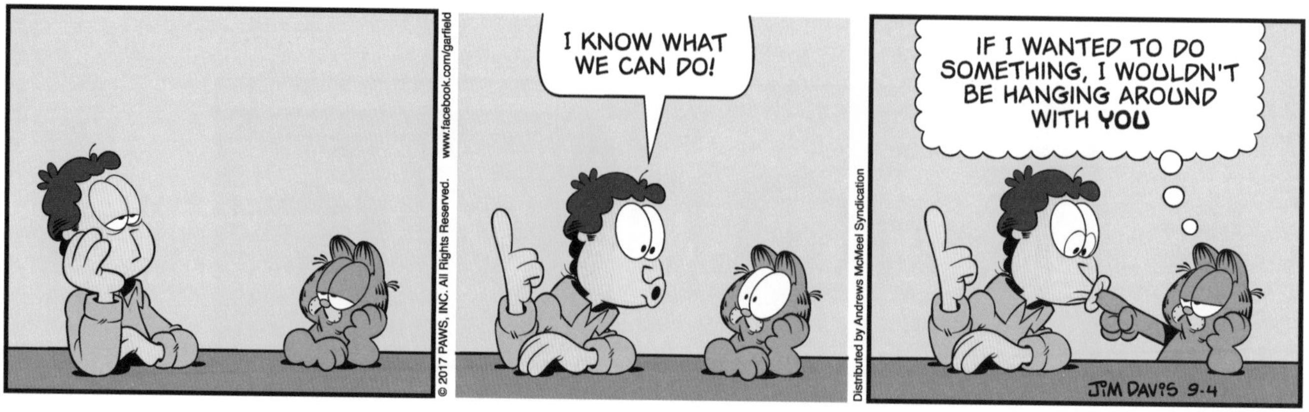
I KNOW WHAT WE CAN DO!
IF I WANTED TO DO SOMETHING, I WOULDN'T BE HANGING AROUND WITH YOU
© 2017 PAWS, INC. All Rights Reserved. www.facebook.com/garfield
Distributed by Andrews McMeel Syndication
JIM DAVIS 9-4

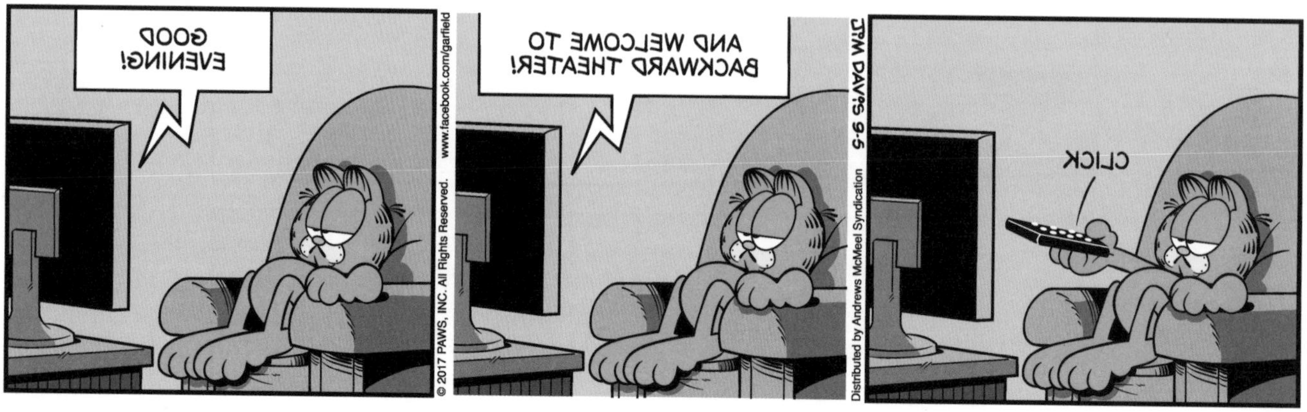
GOOD EVENING!
AND WELCOME TO BACKWARD THEATER!
CLICK
© 2017 PAWS, INC. All Rights Reserved. www.facebook.com/garfield
JIM DAVIS 9-5
Distributed by Andrews McMeel Syndication

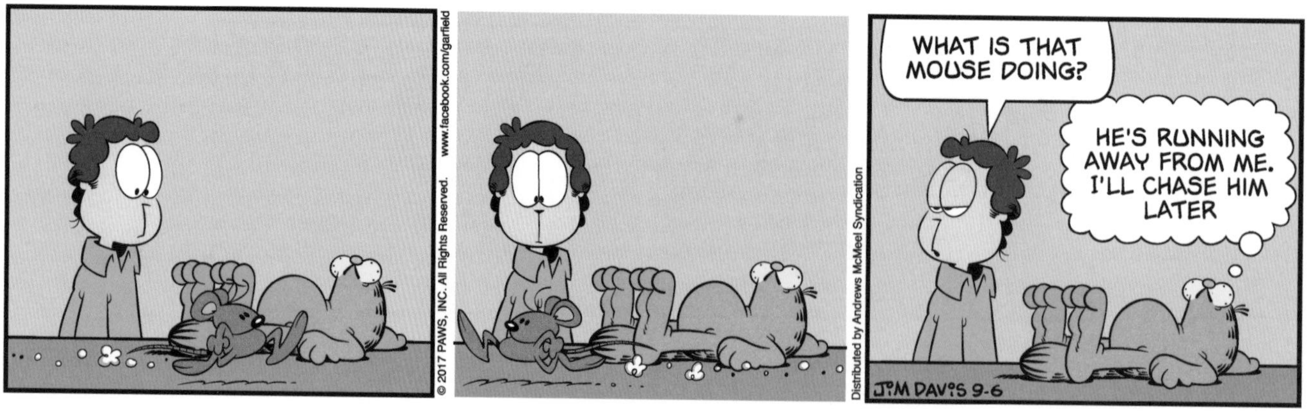
WHAT IS THAT MOUSE DOING?
HE'S RUNNING AWAY FROM ME. I'LL CHASE HIM LATER
© 2017 PAWS, INC. All Rights Reserved. www.facebook.com/garfield
Distributed by Andrews McMeel Syndication
JIM DAVIS 9-6

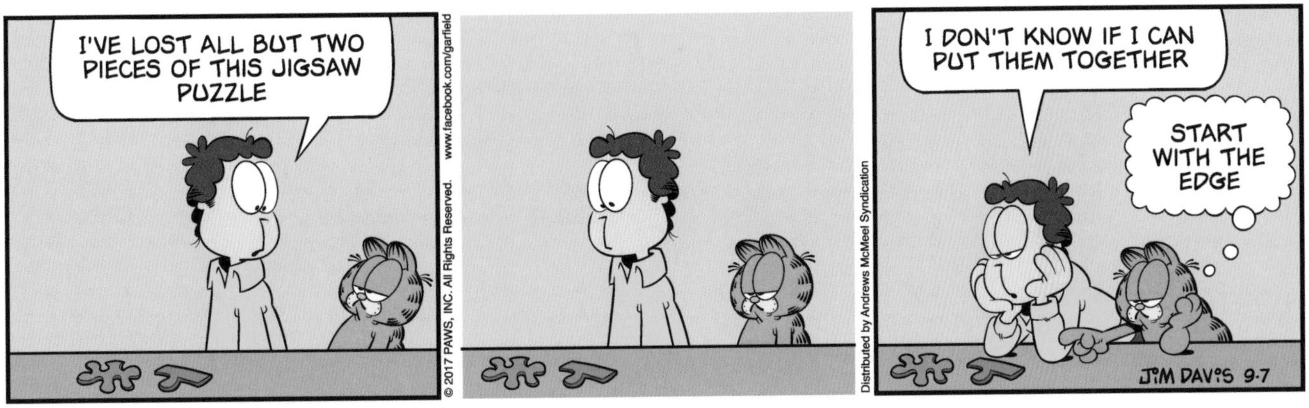
I'VE LOST ALL BUT TWO PIECES OF THIS JIGSAW PUZZLE
© 2017 PAWS, INC. All Rights Reserved. www.facebook.com/garfield
I DON'T KNOW IF I CAN PUT THEM TOGETHER
START WITH THE EDGE
Distributed by Andrews McMeel Syndication
JIM DAVIS 9-7

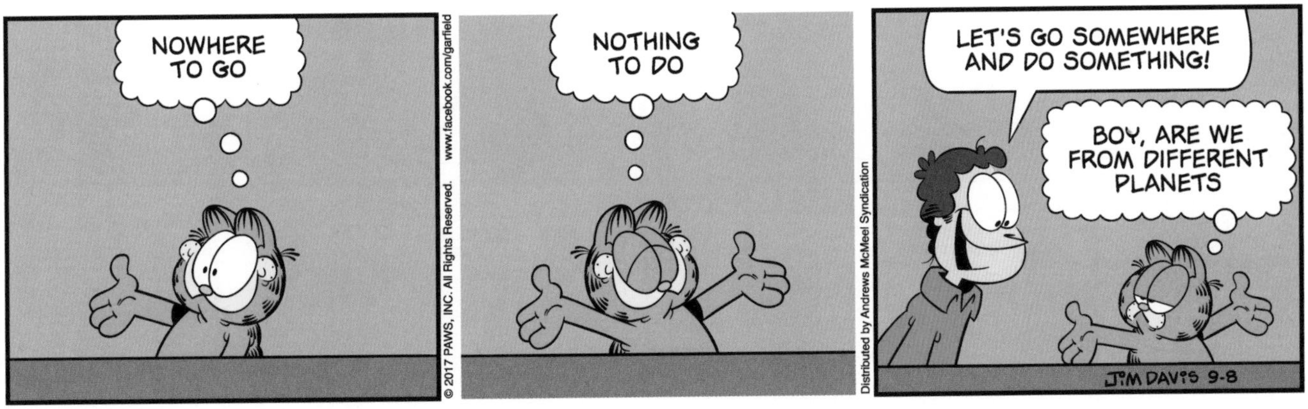
NOWHERE TO GO
© 2017 PAWS, INC. All Rights Reserved. www.facebook.com/garfield
NOTHING TO DO
LET'S GO SOMEWHERE AND DO SOMETHING!
BOY, ARE WE FROM DIFFERENT PLANETS
Distributed by Andrews McMeel Syndication
JIM DAVIS 9-8

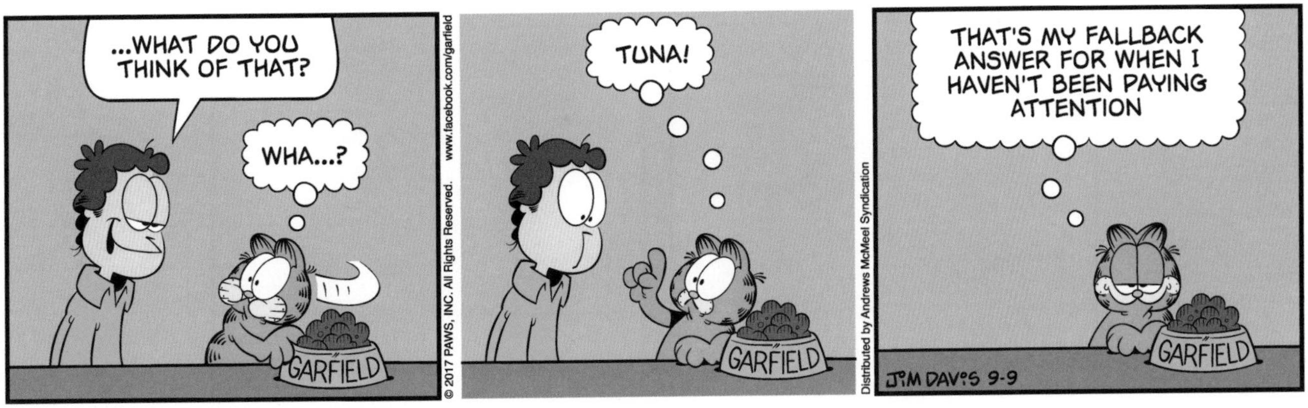
...WHAT DO YOU THINK OF THAT?
WHA...?
GARFIELD
© 2017 PAWS, INC. All Rights Reserved. www.facebook.com/garfield
TUNA!
GARFIELD
THAT'S MY FALLBACK ANSWER FOR WHEN I HAVEN'T BEEN PAYING ATTENTION
GARFIELD
Distributed by Andrews McMeel Syndication
JIM DAVIS 9-9

garfield.com
GARFIELD
www.facebook.com/garfield
GARFIELD
HI, THERE!
POO!
GARFIELD
OH! DID I STARTLE YOU?
GARFIELD
YOU REALLY JUMPED
GARFIELD
© 2017 PAWS, INC. All Rights Reserved.
THAT WAS PRETTY FUNNY!
GARFIELD
JIM DAVIS 9-10
Distributed by Andrews McMeel Syndication
SORT OF
GARFIELD

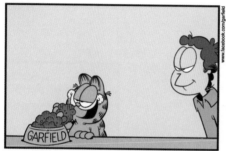

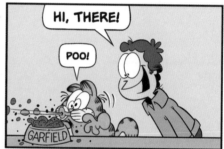

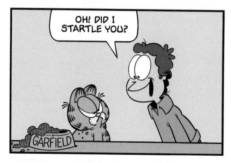

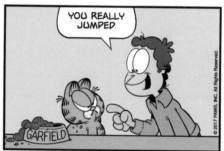

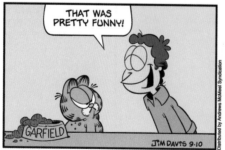

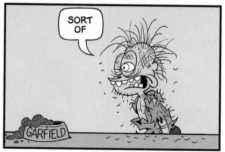

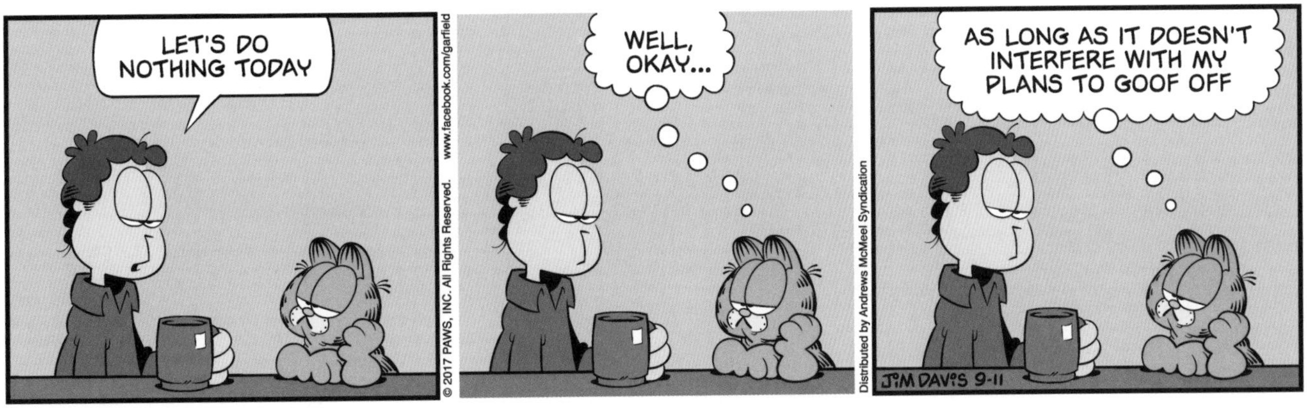
LET'S DO NOTHING TODAY
WELL, OKAY...
AS LONG AS IT DOESN'T INTERFERE WITH MY PLANS TO GOOF OFF
JIM DAVIS 9-11


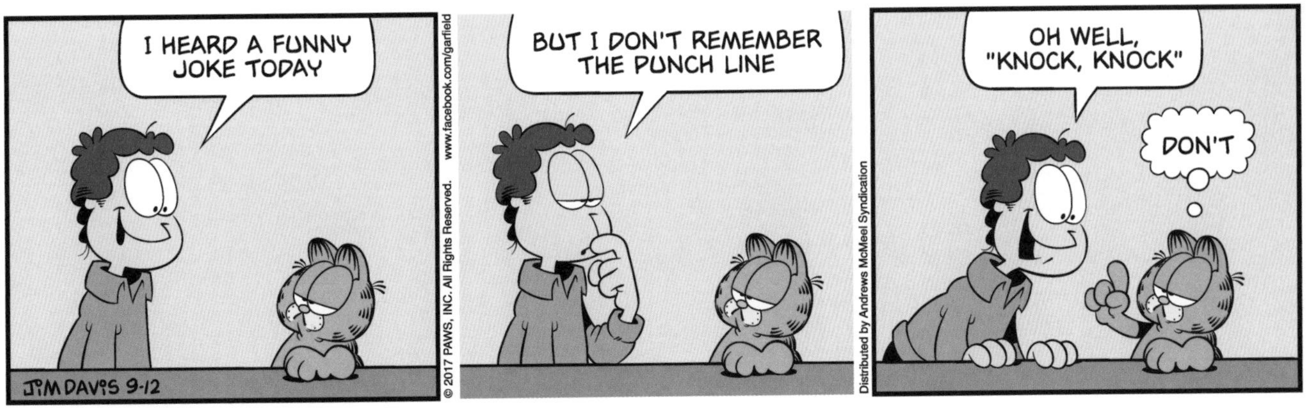
I HEARD A FUNNY JOKE TODAY
BUT I DON'T REMEMBER THE PUNCH LINE
OH WELL, "KNOCK, KNOCK"
DON'T
JIM DAVIS 9-12


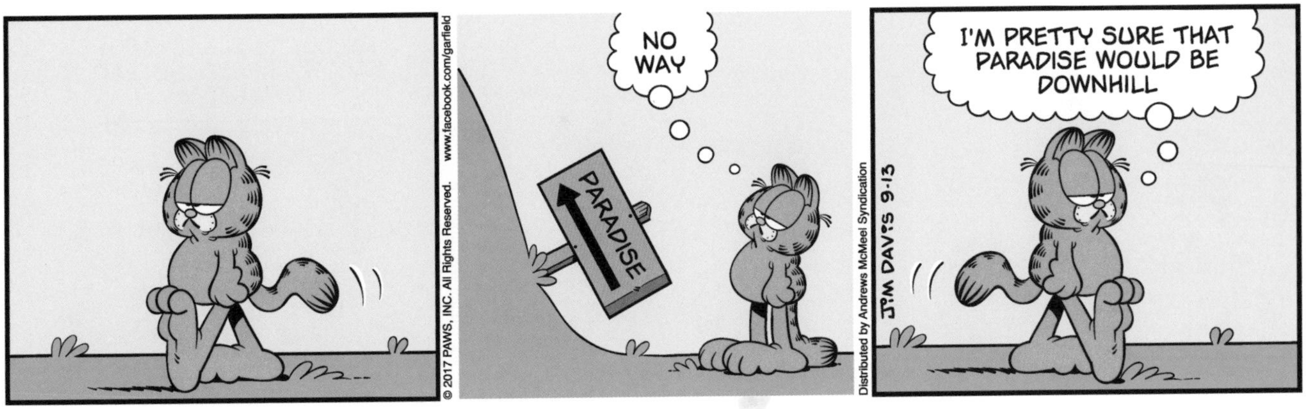
PARADISE
NO WAY
I'M PRETTY SURE THAT PARADISE WOULD BE DOWNHILL
JIM DAVIS 9-13

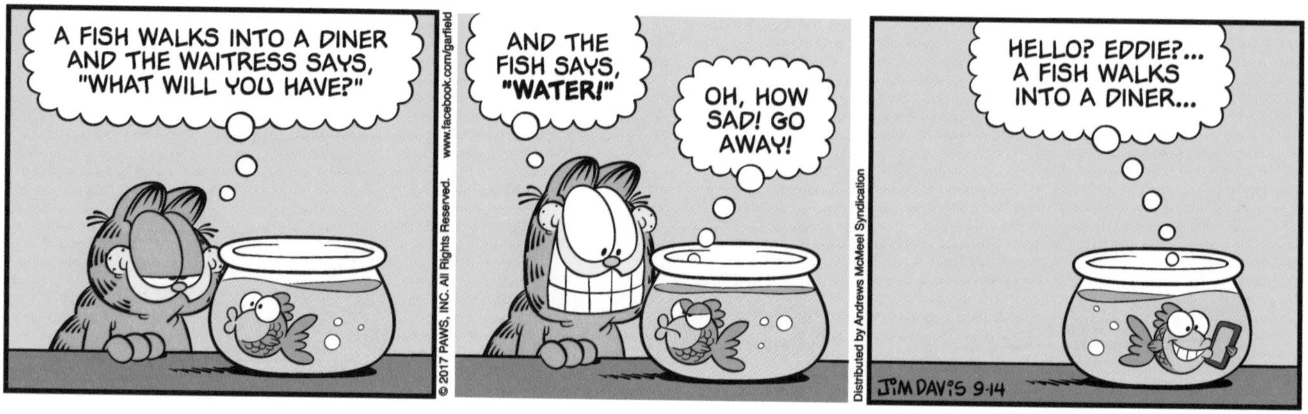
A FISH WALKS INTO A DINER AND THE WAITRESS SAYS, "WHAT WILL YOU HAVE?"
© 2017 PAWS, INC. All Rights Reserved. www.facebook.com/garfield
AND THE FISH SAYS, **"WATER!"**
OH, HOW SAD! GO AWAY!
Distributed by Andrews McMeel Syndication
HELLO? EDDIE?... A FISH WALKS INTO A DINER...
JIM DAVIS 9-14

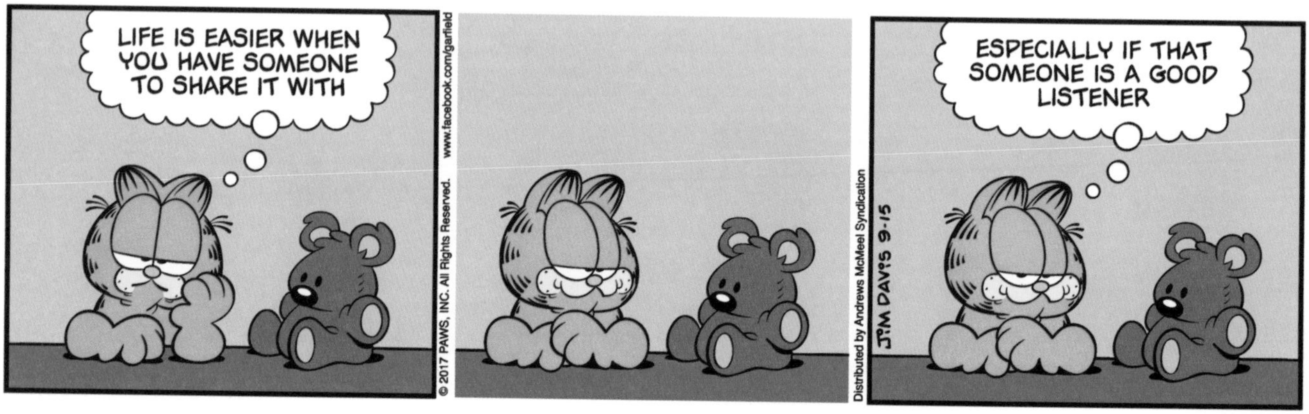
LIFE IS EASIER WHEN YOU HAVE SOMEONE TO SHARE IT WITH
© 2017 PAWS, INC. All Rights Reserved. www.facebook.com/garfield
Distributed by Andrews McMeel Syndication
JIM DAVIS 9-15
ESPECIALLY IF THAT SOMEONE IS A GOOD LISTENER

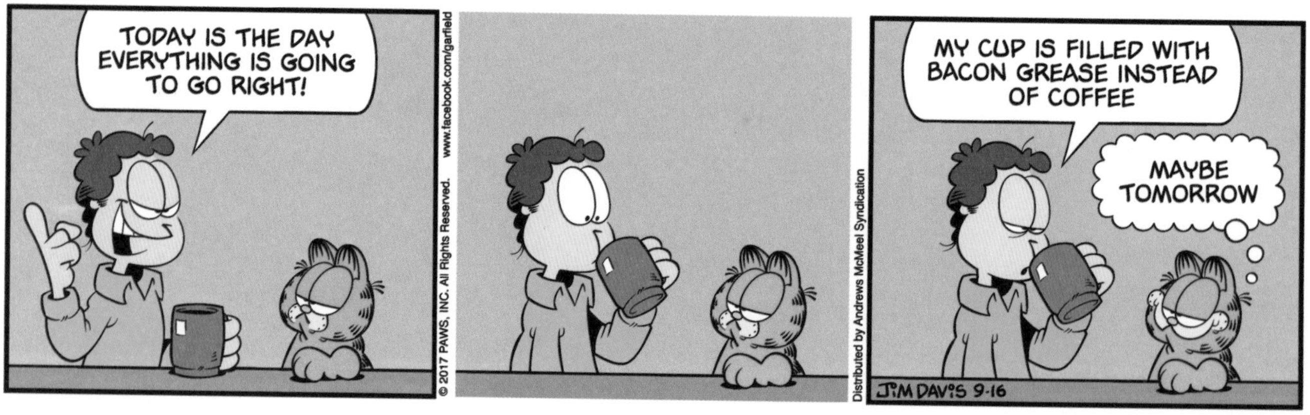
TODAY IS THE DAY EVERYTHING IS GOING TO GO RIGHT!
© 2017 PAWS, INC. All Rights Reserved. www.facebook.com/garfield
Distributed by Andrews McMeel Syndication
MY CUP IS FILLED WITH BACON GREASE INSTEAD OF COFFEE
MAYBE TOMORROW
JIM DAVIS 9-16

garfield.com
Garfield
www.facebook.com/garfield
Distributed by Andrews McMeel Syndication
SUMMER'S NOT OVER UNTIL THE LAST WET DOG HAS SHAKEN
GAAAHHH
JIM DAVIS 9-17
© 2017 PAWS, INC. All Rights Reserved.

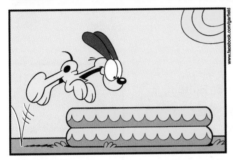

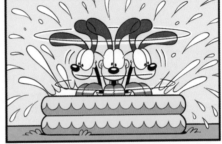

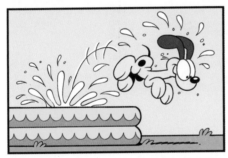

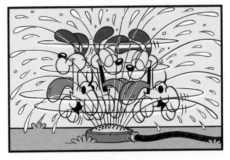

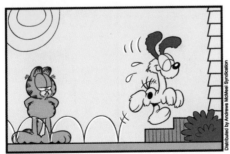

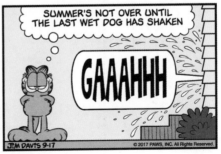

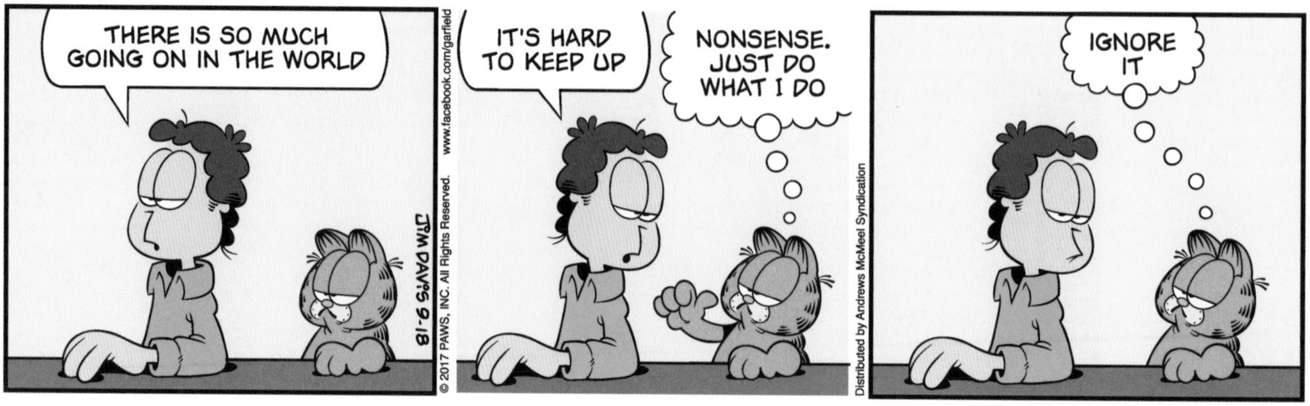
THERE IS SO MUCH GOING ON IN THE WORLD
JIM DAVIS 9-18
© 2017 PAWS, INC. All Rights Reserved. www.facebook.com/garfield
IT'S HARD TO KEEP UP
NONSENSE. JUST DO WHAT I DO
Distributed by Andrews McMeel Syndication
IGNORE IT

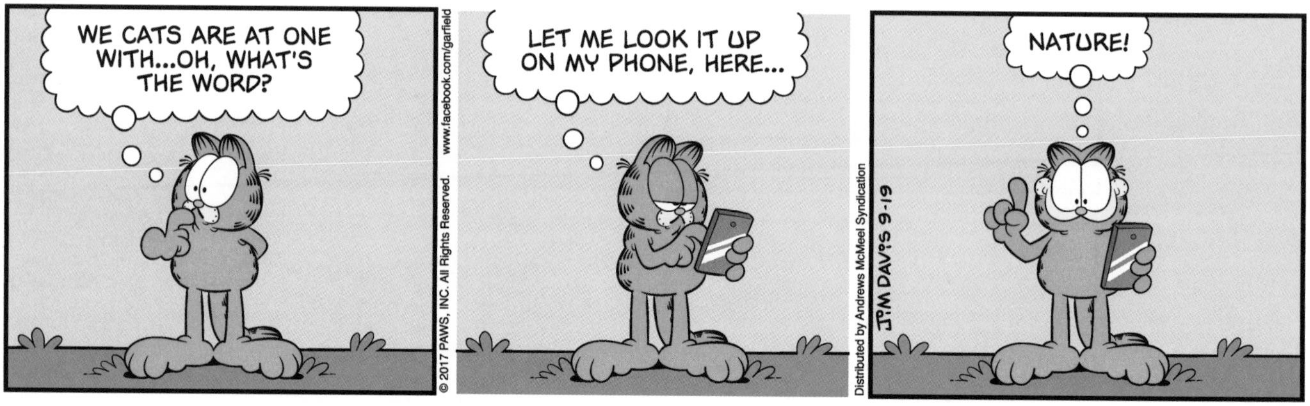
WE CATS ARE AT ONE WITH...OH, WHAT'S THE WORD?
© 2017 PAWS, INC. All Rights Reserved. www.facebook.com/garfield
LET ME LOOK IT UP ON MY PHONE, HERE...
Distributed by Andrews McMeel Syndication
JIM DAVIS 9-19
NATURE!

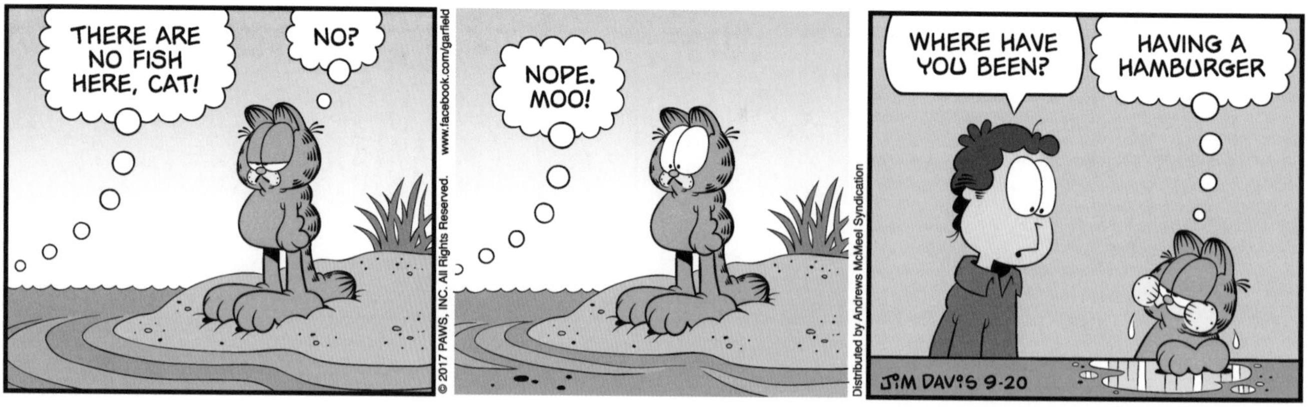
THERE ARE NO FISH HERE, CAT!
NO?
© 2017 PAWS, INC. All Rights Reserved. www.facebook.com/garfield
NOPE. MOO!
Distributed by Andrews McMeel Syndication
WHERE HAVE YOU BEEN?
HAVING A HAMBURGER
JIM DAVIS 9-20

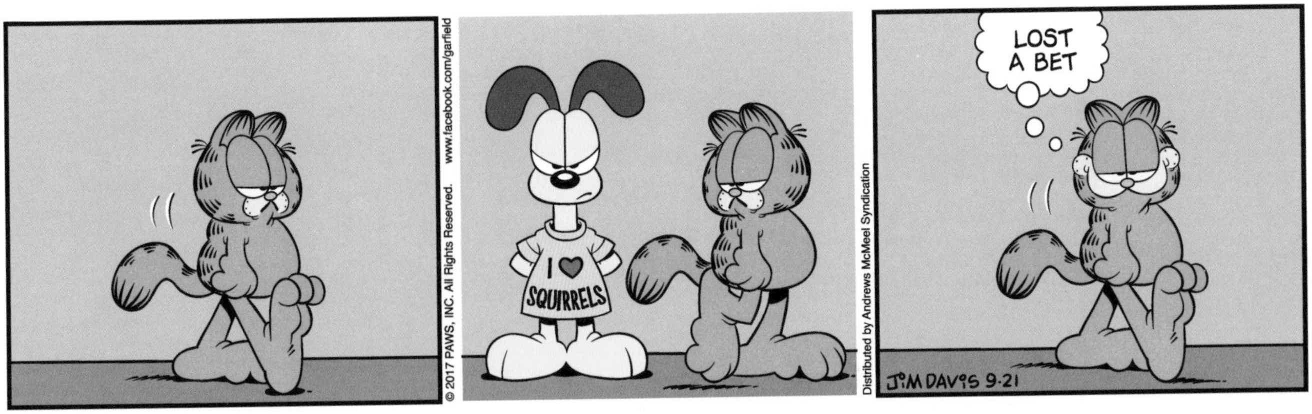
© 2017 PAWS, INC. All Rights Reserved. www.facebook.com/garfield
I ♥ SQUIRRELS
Distributed by Andrews McMeel Syndication
LOST A BET
JIM DAVIS 9-21

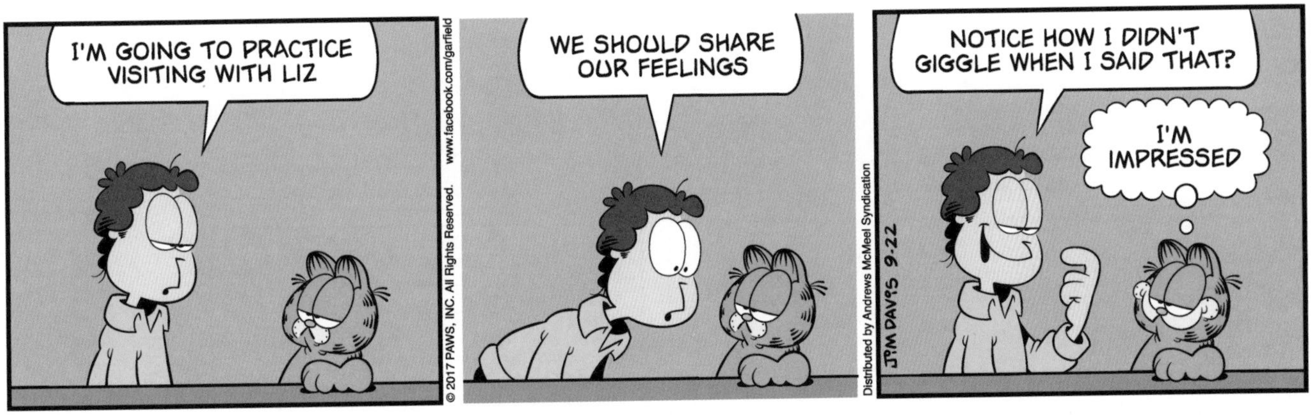
I'M GOING TO PRACTICE VISITING WITH LIZ
© 2017 PAWS, INC. All Rights Reserved. www.facebook.com/garfield
WE SHOULD SHARE OUR FEELINGS
Distributed by Andrews McMeel Syndication
JIM DAVIS 9-22
NOTICE HOW I DIDN'T GIGGLE WHEN I SAID THAT?
I'M IMPRESSED

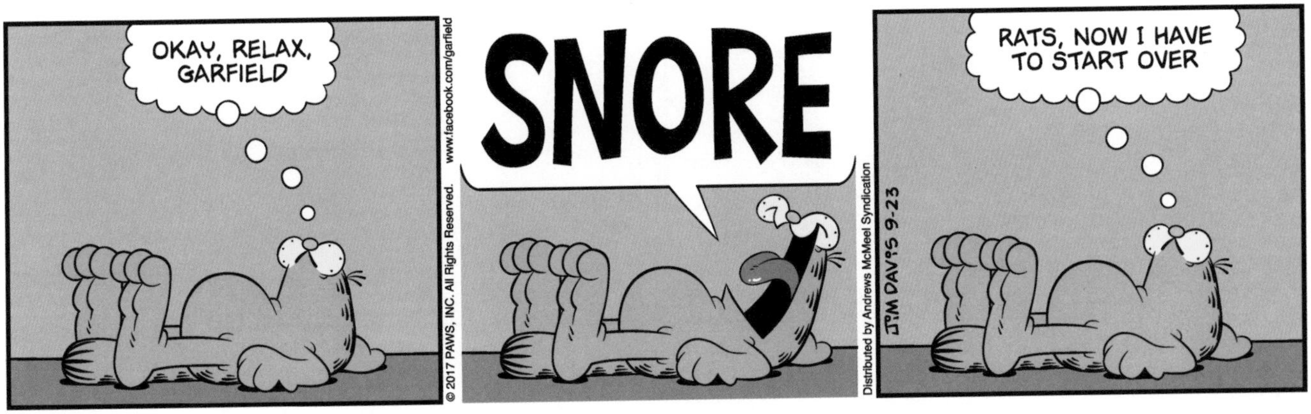
OKAY, RELAX, GARFIELD
© 2017 PAWS, INC. All Rights Reserved. www.facebook.com/garfield
SNORE
Distributed by Andrews McMeel Syndication
JIM DAVIS 9-23
RATS, NOW I HAVE TO START OVER

garfield.com
GARFIELD
www.facebook.com/garfield
WE HAVE A NEW COOK
HE JUST GRADUATED FROM A CULINARY SCHOOL
OH?
© 2017 PAWS, INC. All Rights Reserved.
WHICH SCHOOL?
THE INSTITUTE OF ADVANCED BACHELOR CUISINE
WOW
WHAT WILL YOU HAVE?
TWO SOUPS, PLEASE
Distributed by Andrews McMeel Syndication
JPM DAVPS 9-24
YUM

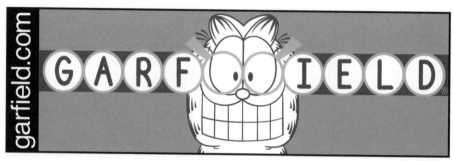

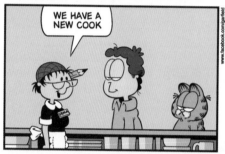

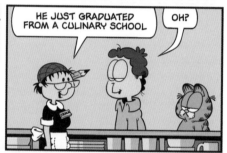

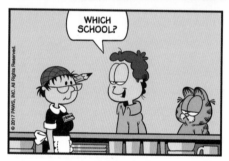

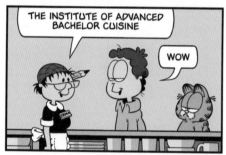

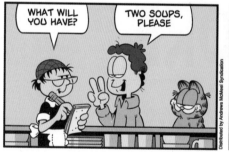

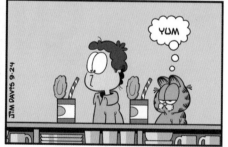

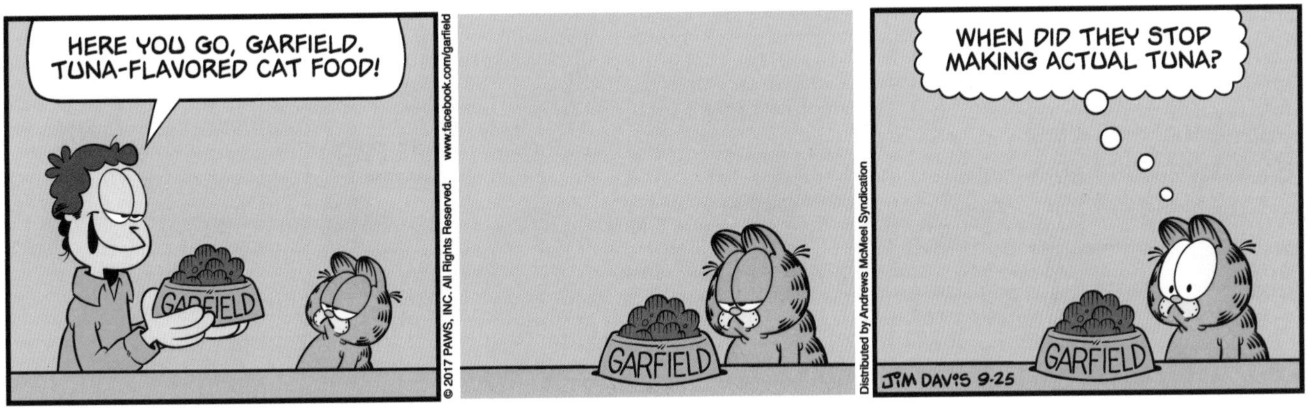
HERE YOU GO, GARFIELD. TUNA-FLAVORED CAT FOOD!
GARFIELD
© 2017 PAWS, INC. All Rights Reserved. www.facebook.com/garfield
GARFIELD
Distributed by Andrews McMeel Syndication
WHEN DID THEY STOP MAKING ACTUAL TUNA?
GARFIELD
JIM DAVIS 9-25

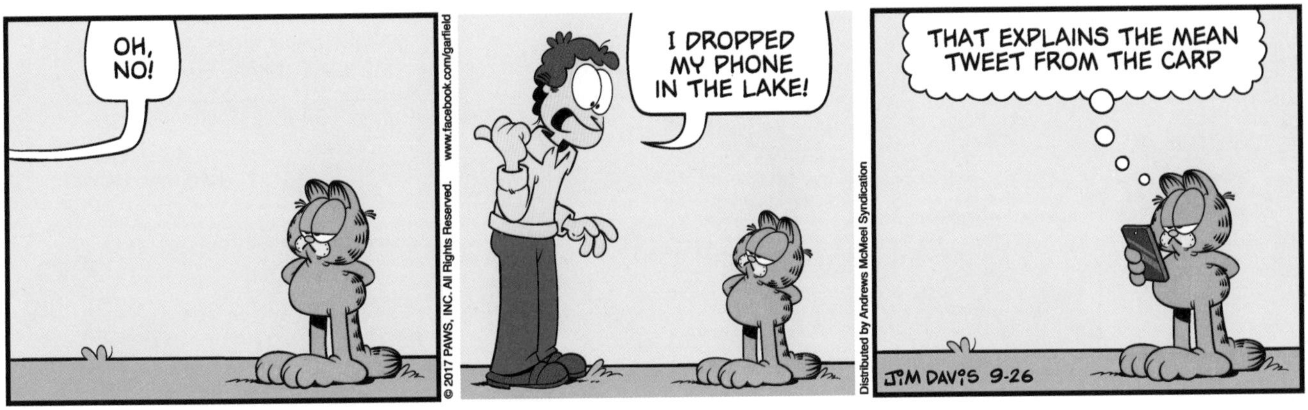
OH, NO!
© 2017 PAWS, INC. All Rights Reserved. www.facebook.com/garfield
I DROPPED MY PHONE IN THE LAKE!
Distributed by Andrews McMeel Syndication
THAT EXPLAINS THE MEAN TWEET FROM THE CARP
JIM DAVIS 9-26

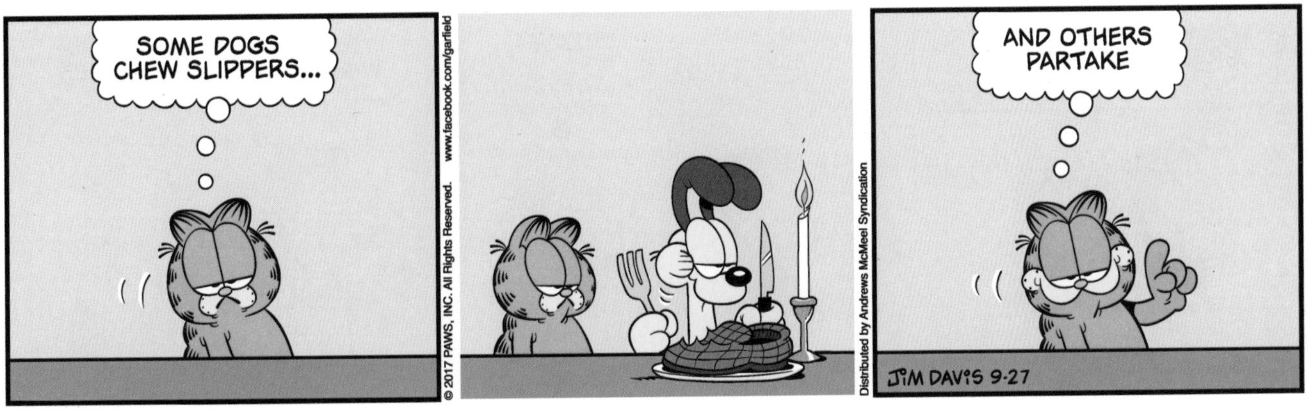
SOME DOGS CHEW SLIPPERS...
© 2017 PAWS, INC. All Rights Reserved. www.facebook.com/garfield
Distributed by Andrews McMeel Syndication
AND OTHERS PARTAKE
JIM DAVIS 9-27

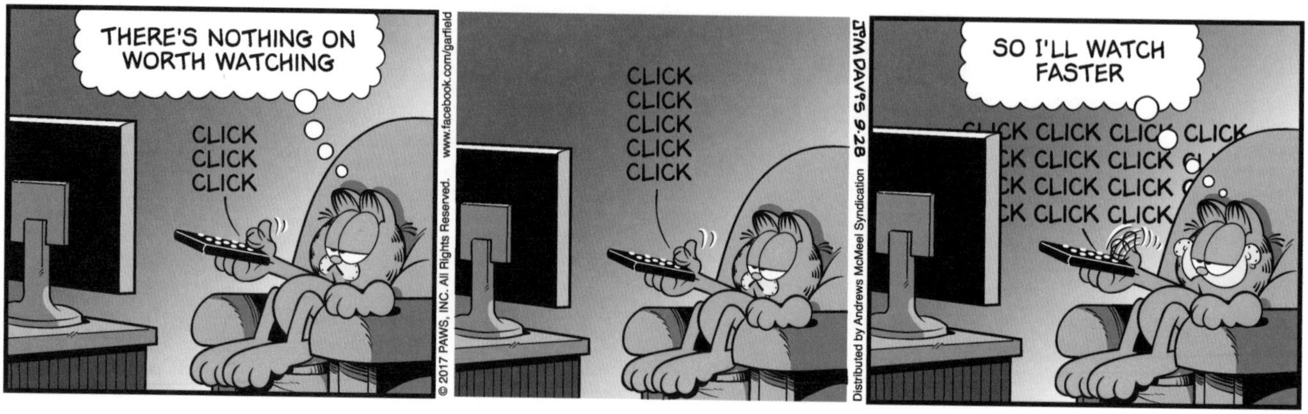
THERE'S NOTHING ON WORTH WATCHING
CLICK CLICK CLICK
© 2017 PAWS, INC. All Rights Reserved. www.facebook.com/garfield
CLICK CLICK CLICK CLICK CLICK
JIM DAVIS 9-28
Distributed by Andrews McMeel Syndication
SO I'LL WATCH FASTER

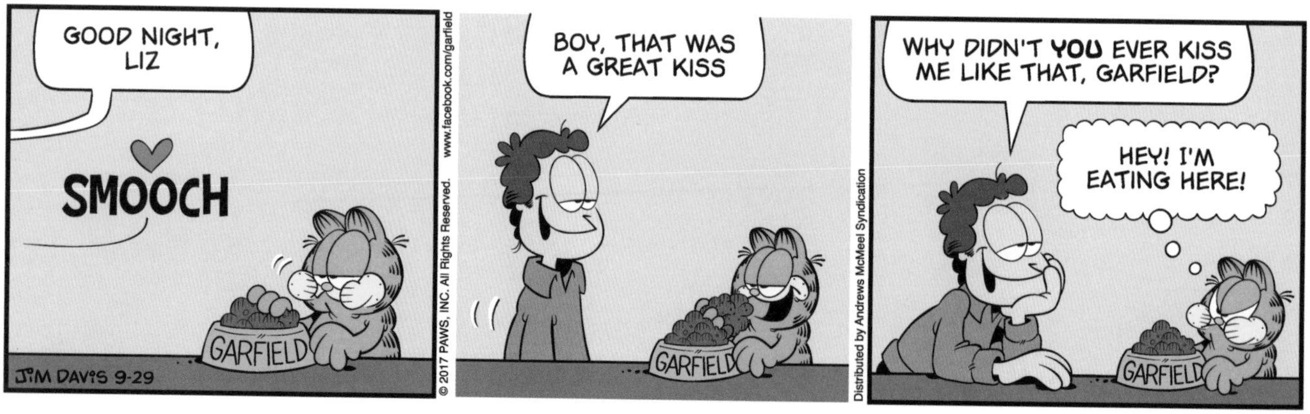
GOOD NIGHT, LIZ
SMOOCH
GARFIELD
JIM DAVIS 9-29
© 2017 PAWS, INC. All Rights Reserved. www.facebook.com/garfield
BOY, THAT WAS A GREAT KISS
GARFIELD
Distributed by Andrews McMeel Syndication
WHY DIDN'T **YOU** EVER KISS ME LIKE THAT, GARFIELD?
HEY! I'M EATING HERE!
GARFIELD

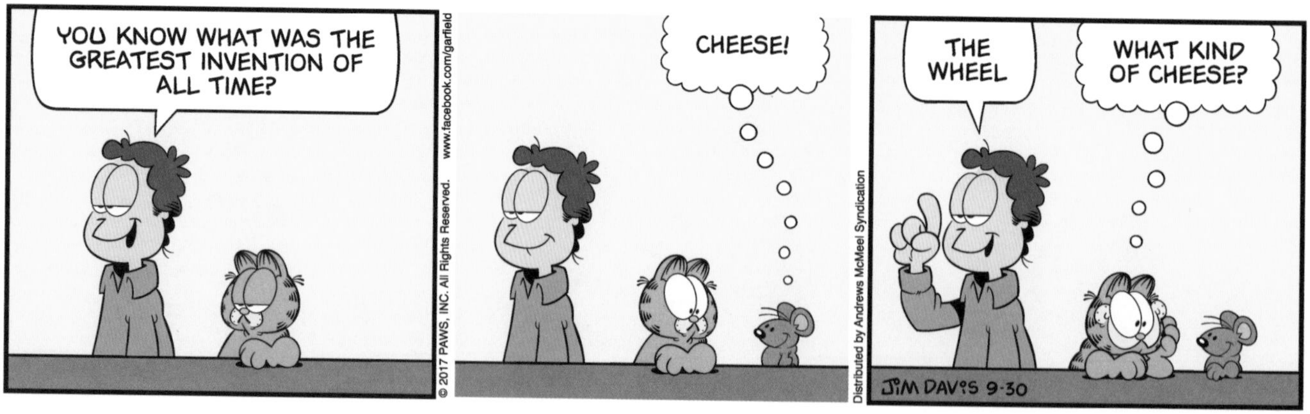
YOU KNOW WHAT WAS THE GREATEST INVENTION OF ALL TIME?
© 2017 PAWS, INC. All Rights Reserved. www.facebook.com/garfield
CHEESE!
Distributed by Andrews McMeel Syndication
THE WHEEL
WHAT KIND OF CHEESE?
JIM DAVIS 9-30

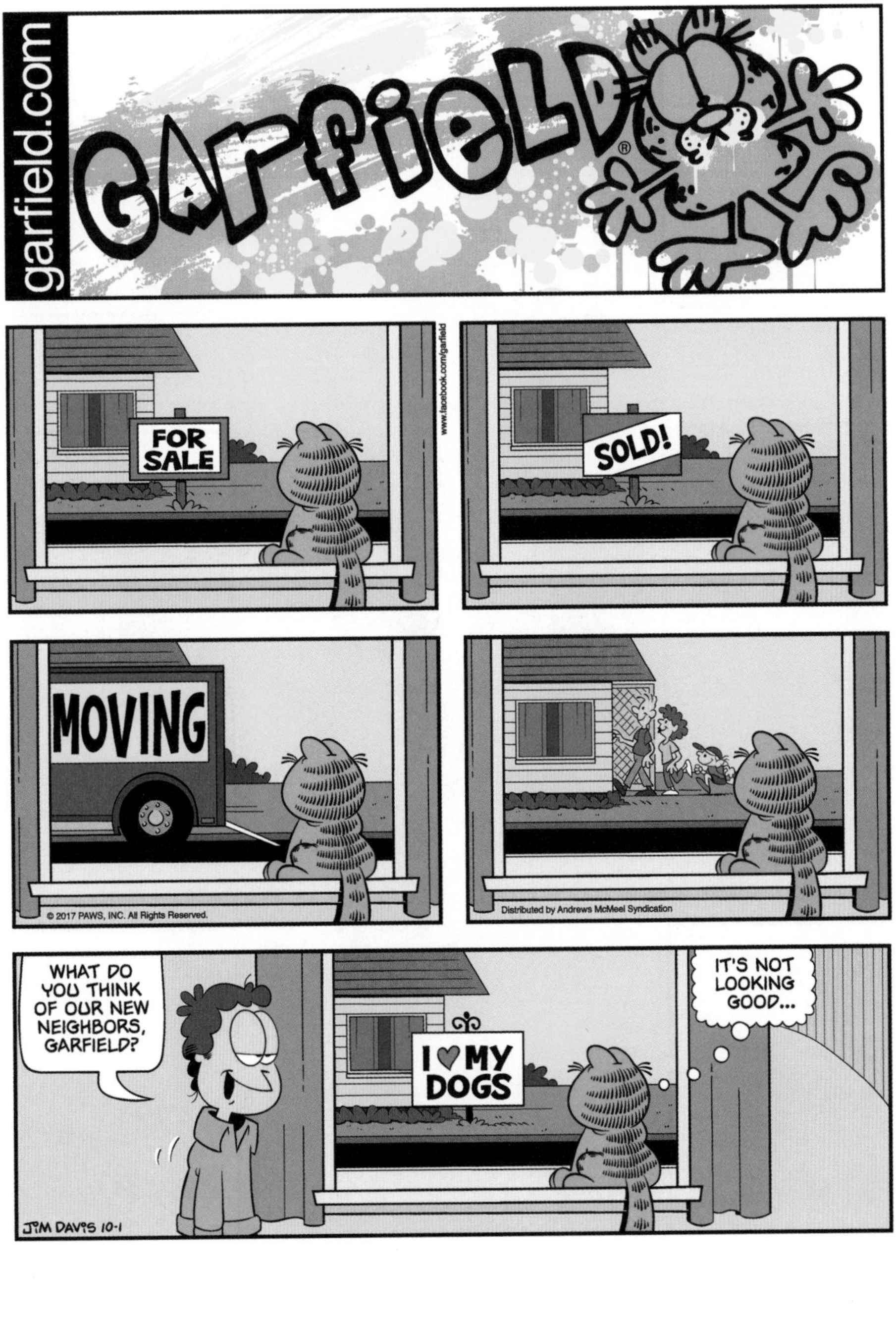

garfield.com
GARFIELD®
www.facebook.com/garfield
FOR SALE
SOLD!
MOVING
© 2017 PAWS, INC. All Rights Reserved.
Distributed by Andrews McMeel Syndication
WHAT DO YOU THINK OF OUR NEW NEIGHBORS, GARFIELD?
I ♥ MY DOGS
IT'S NOT LOOKING GOOD...
JIM DAVIS 10-1

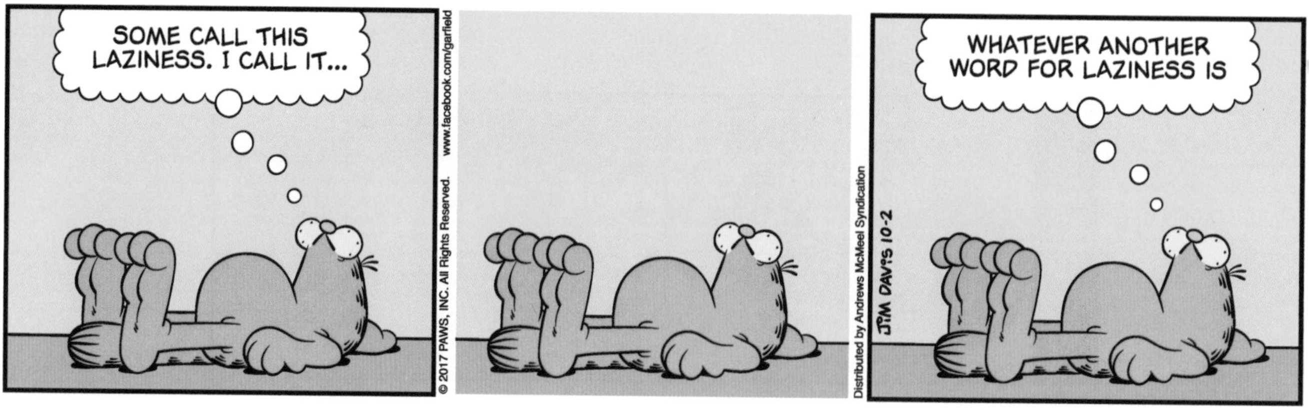
SOME CALL THIS LAZINESS. I CALL IT...
WHATEVER ANOTHER WORD FOR LAZINESS IS
© 2017 PAWS, INC. All Rights Reserved. www.facebook.com/garfield
Distributed by Andrews McMeel Syndication
JIM DAVIS 10-2

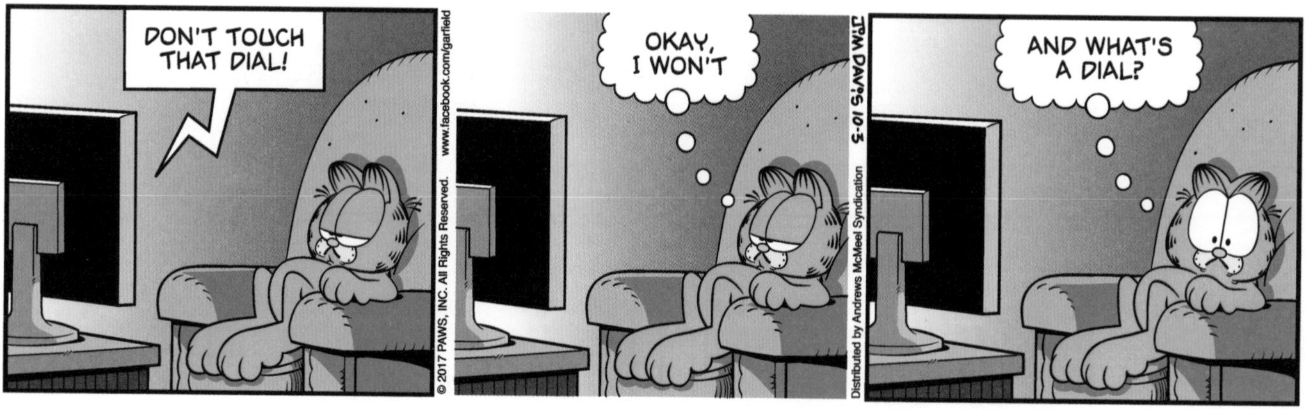
DON'T TOUCH THAT DIAL!
OKAY, I WON'T
AND WHAT'S A DIAL?
© 2017 PAWS, INC. All Rights Reserved. www.facebook.com/garfield
JIM DAVIS 10-3
Distributed by Andrews McMeel Syndication

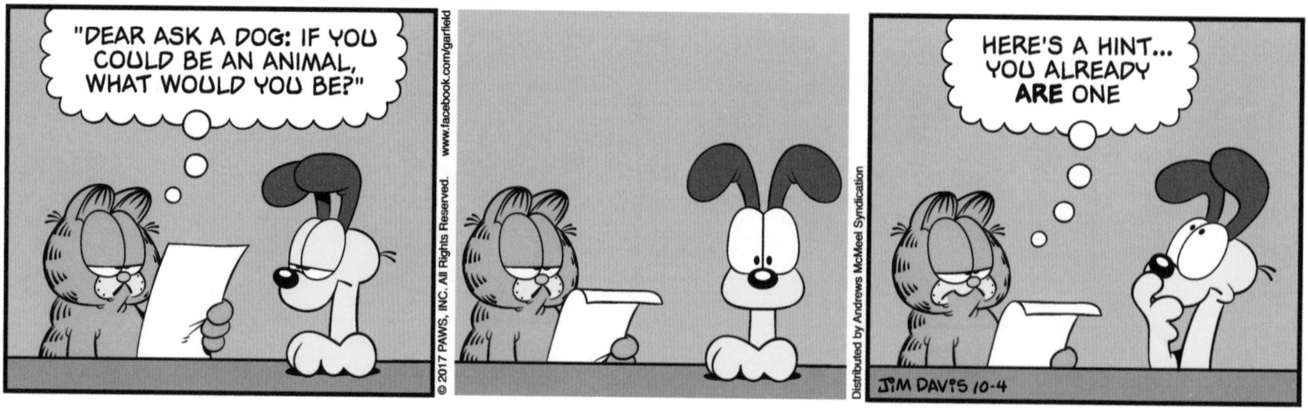
"DEAR ASK A DOG: IF YOU COULD BE AN ANIMAL, WHAT WOULD YOU BE?"
HERE'S A HINT... YOU ALREADY ARE ONE
© 2017 PAWS, INC. All Rights Reserved. www.facebook.com/garfield
Distributed by Andrews McMeel Syndication
JIM DAVIS 10-4

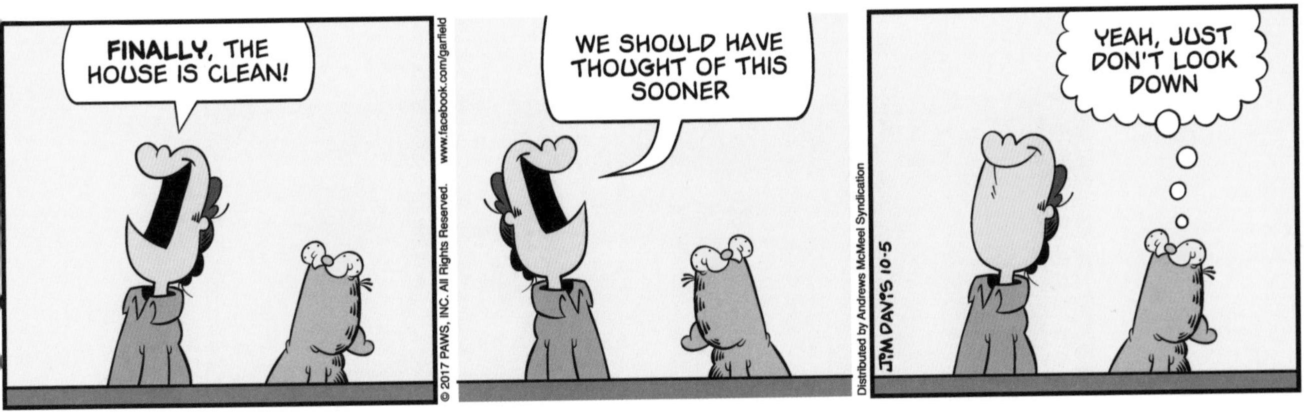
FINALLY, THE HOUSE IS CLEAN!
© 2017 PAWS, INC. All Rights Reserved. www.facebook.com/garfield
WE SHOULD HAVE THOUGHT OF THIS SOONER
Distributed by Andrews McMeel Syndication
JIM DAVIS 10-5
YEAH, JUST DON'T LOOK DOWN

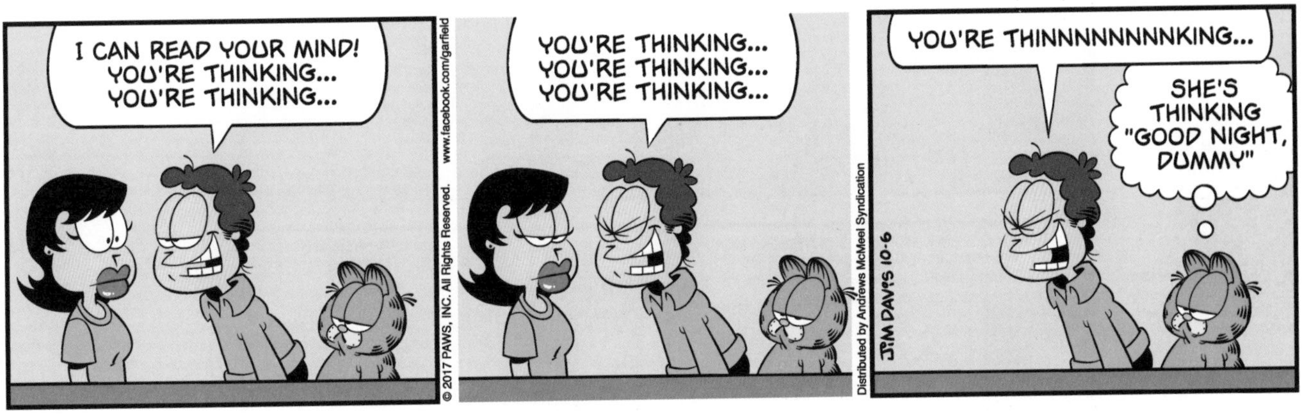
I CAN READ YOUR MIND! YOU'RE THINKING... YOU'RE THINKING...
© 2017 PAWS, INC. All Rights Reserved. www.facebook.com/garfield
YOU'RE THINKING... YOU'RE THINKING... YOU'RE THINKING...
Distributed by Andrews McMeel Syndication
JIM DAVIS 10-6
YOU'RE THINNNNNNNNNKING...
SHE'S THINKING "GOOD NIGHT, DUMMY"

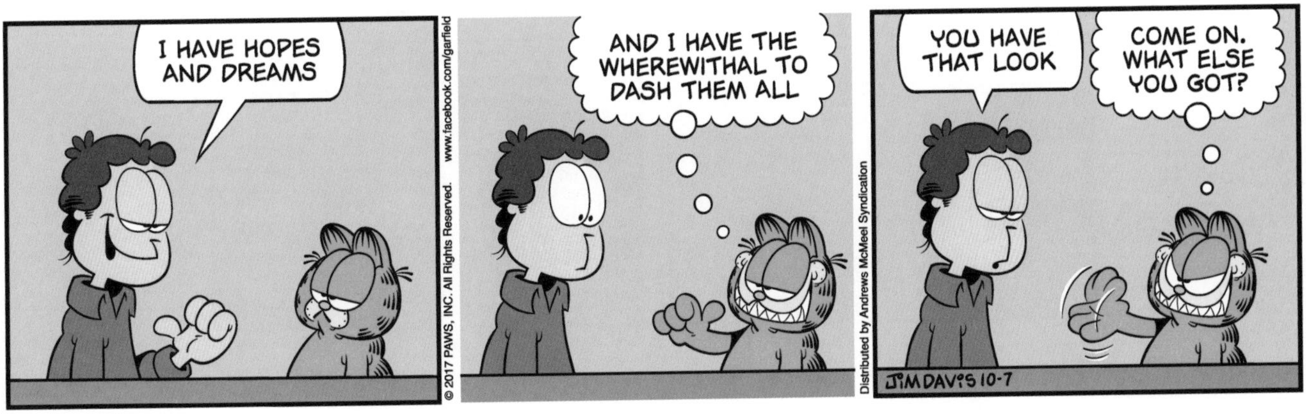
I HAVE HOPES AND DREAMS
© 2017 PAWS, INC. All Rights Reserved. www.facebook.com/garfield
AND I HAVE THE WHEREWITHAL TO DASH THEM ALL
Distributed by Andrews McMeel Syndication
YOU HAVE THAT LOOK
COME ON. WHAT ELSE YOU GOT?
JIM DAVIS 10-7

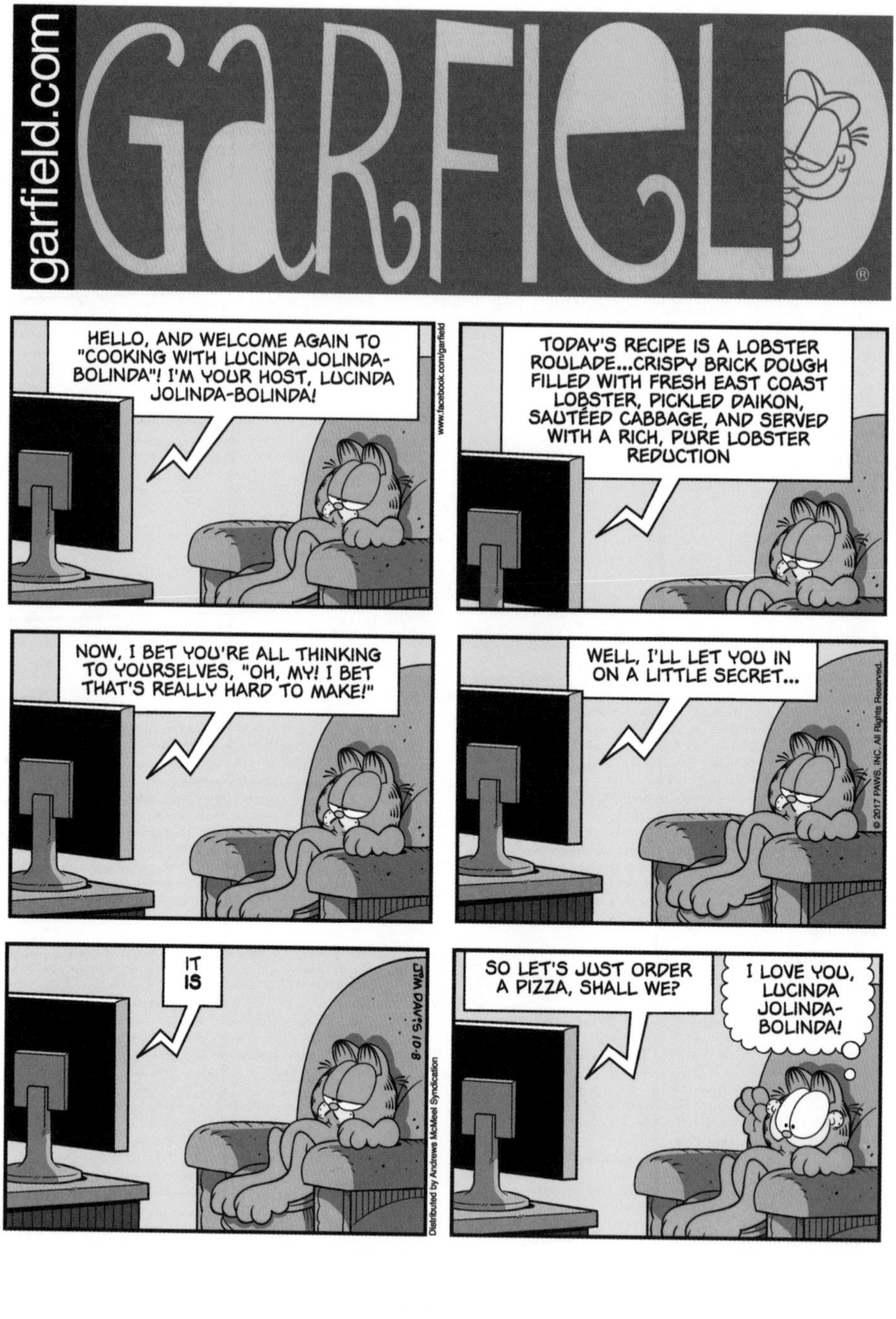
garfield.com
GARFIELD®
HELLO, AND WELCOME AGAIN TO "COOKING WITH LUCINDA JOLINDA-BOLINDA"! I'M YOUR HOST, LUCINDA JOLINDA-BOLINDA!
www.facebook.com/garfield
TODAY'S RECIPE IS A LOBSTER ROULADE...CRISPY BRICK DOUGH FILLED WITH FRESH EAST COAST LOBSTER, PICKLED DAIKON, SAUTÉED CABBAGE, AND SERVED WITH A RICH, PURE LOBSTER REDUCTION
NOW, I BET YOU'RE ALL THINKING TO YOURSELVES, "OH, MY! I BET THAT'S REALLY HARD TO MAKE!"
WELL, I'LL LET YOU IN ON A LITTLE SECRET...
© 2017 PAWS, INC. All Rights Reserved.
IT **IS**
JIM DAVIS 10-8
Distributed by Andrews McMeel Syndication
SO LET'S JUST ORDER A PIZZA, SHALL WE?
I LOVE YOU, LUCINDA JOLINDA-BOLINDA!

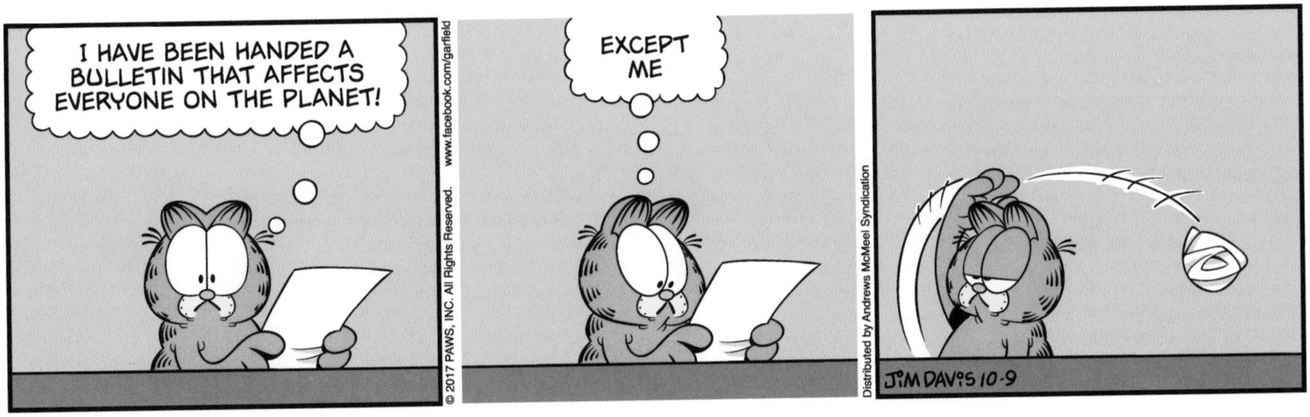
I HAVE BEEN HANDED A BULLETIN THAT AFFECTS EVERYONE ON THE PLANET!
EXCEPT ME
© 2017 PAWS, INC. All Rights Reserved. www.facebook.com/garfield
Distributed by Andrews McMeel Syndication
JIM DAVIS 10-9

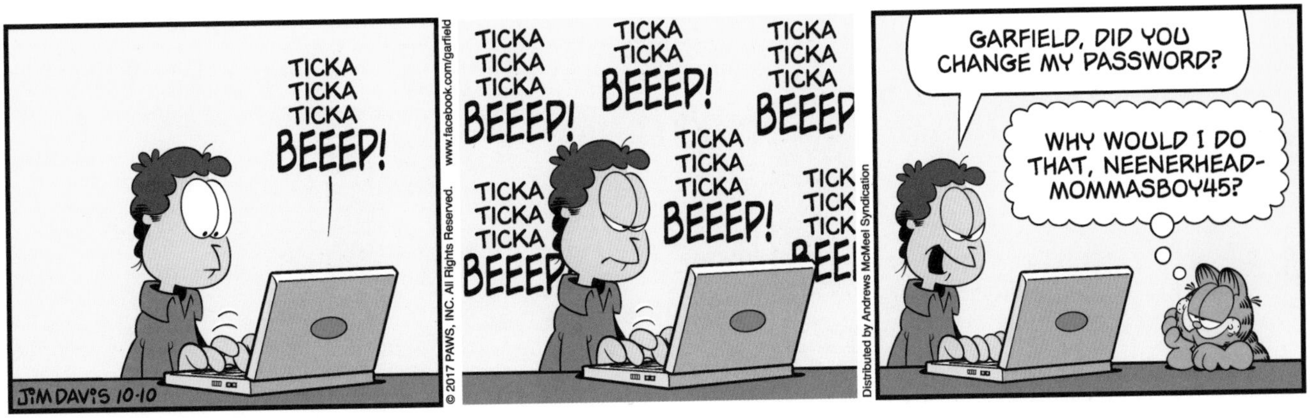
TICKA TICKA TICKA BEEEP!
JIM DAVIS 10-10
TICKA TICKA TICKA BEEEP!
TICKA TICKA BEEEP!
TICKA TICKA TICKA
TICKA TICKA TICKA BEEEP!
TICKA TICKA TICKA
© 2017 PAWS, INC. All Rights Reserved. www.facebook.com/garfield
GARFIELD, DID YOU CHANGE MY PASSWORD?
WHY WOULD I DO THAT, NEENERHEAD-MOMMASBOY45?
Distributed by Andrews McMeel Syndication

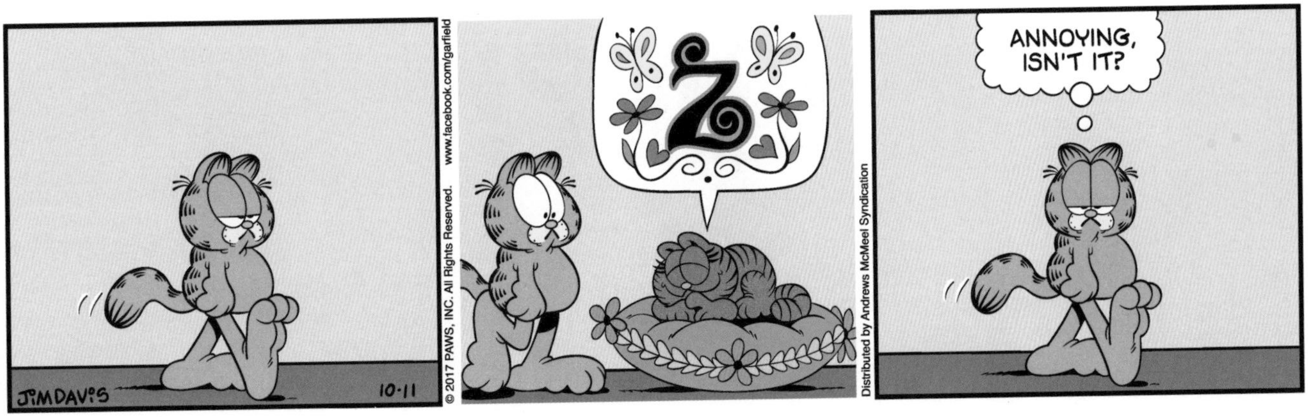
JIM DAVIS 10-11
© 2017 PAWS, INC. All Rights Reserved. www.facebook.com/garfield
Z
ANNOYING, ISN'T IT?
Distributed by Andrews McMeel Syndication

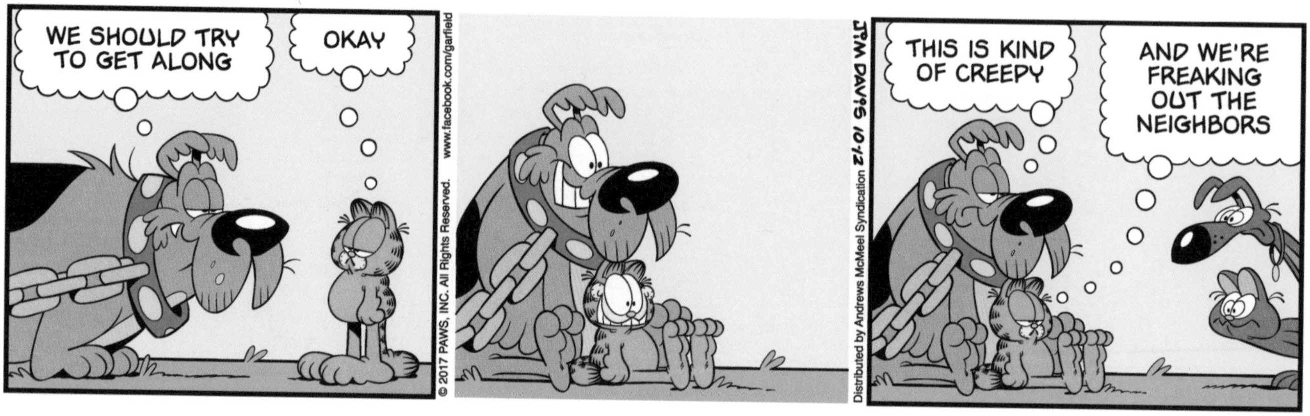
WE SHOULD TRY TO GET ALONG
OKAY
JIM DAVIS 10-12
THIS IS KIND OF CREEPY
AND WE'RE FREAKING OUT THE NEIGHBORS
© 2017 PAWS, INC. All Rights Reserved. www.facebook.com/garfield
Distributed by Andrews McMeel Syndication

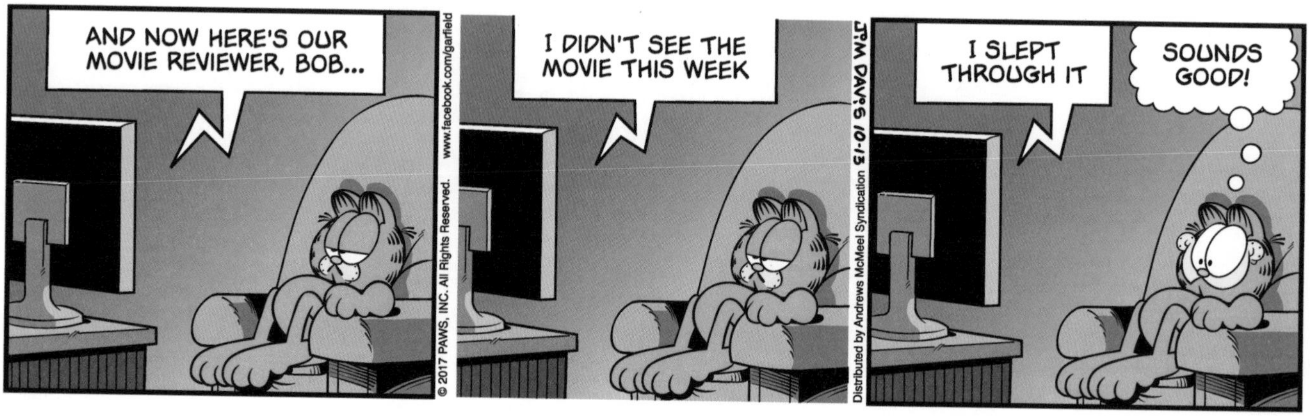
AND NOW HERE'S OUR MOVIE REVIEWER, BOB...
I DIDN'T SEE THE MOVIE THIS WEEK
JIM DAVIS 10-13
I SLEPT THROUGH IT
SOUNDS GOOD!
© 2017 PAWS, INC. All Rights Reserved. www.facebook.com/garfield
Distributed by Andrews McMeel Syndication

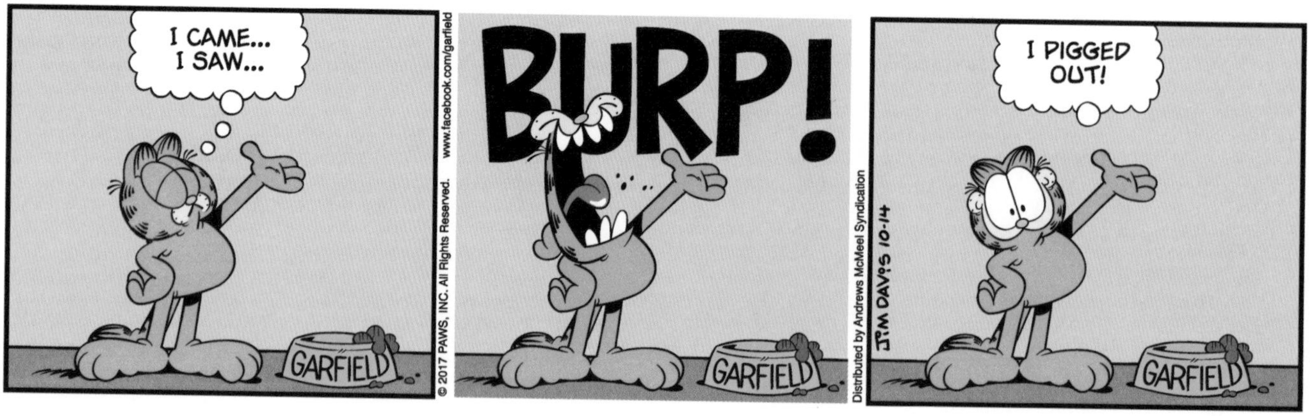
I CAME... I SAW...
GARFIELD
BURP!
GARFIELD
JIM DAVIS 10-14
I PIGGED OUT!
GARFIELD
© 2017 PAWS, INC. All Rights Reserved. www.facebook.com/garfield
Distributed by Andrews McMeel Syndication

garfield.com
garfield®
I LOVE FALL
www.facebook.com/garfield
I LOVE THE COLORS...
I LOVE THE COOL DAYS... I LOVE THE SMELLS...
© 2017 PAWS, INC. All Rights Reserved.
NYAAHHH
Distributed by Andrews McMeel Syndication
AND, OF COURSE, THERE'S JON'S ANNUAL RAKING MELTDOWN
WHAP!
WHAP!
WHAP!
WHAP!
WHAP!
JIM DAVIS 10-15

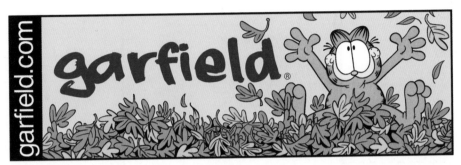

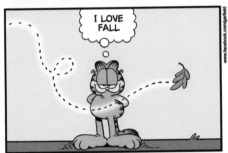

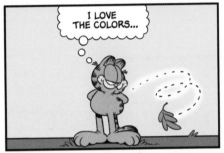

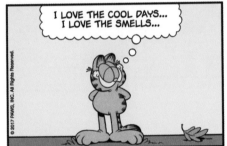

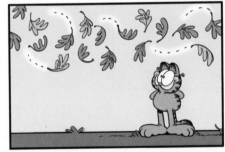

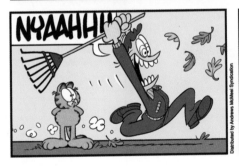

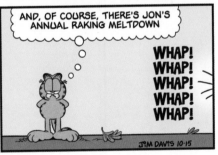

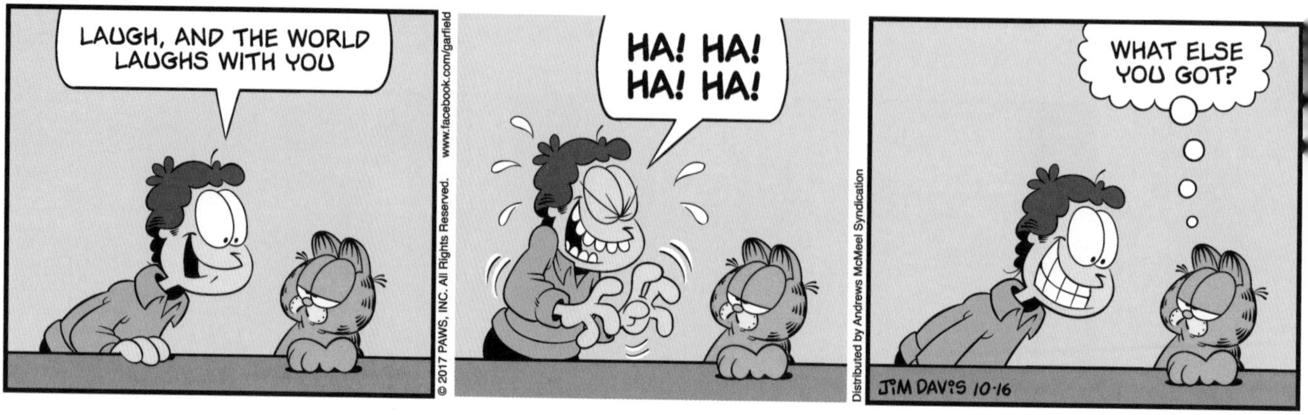
LAUGH, AND THE WORLD LAUGHS WITH YOU
© 2017 PAWS, INC. All Rights Reserved. www.facebook.com/garfield
HA! HA! HA! HA!
Distributed by Andrews McMeel Syndication
WHAT ELSE YOU GOT?
JIM DAVIS 10-16

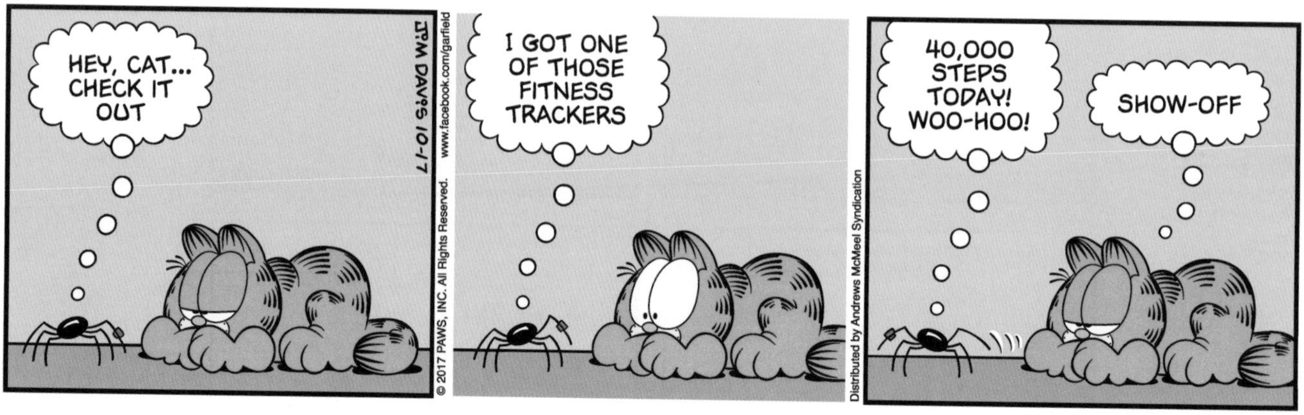
HEY, CAT... CHECK IT OUT
JIM DAVIS 10-17
© 2017 PAWS, INC. All Rights Reserved. www.facebook.com/garfield
I GOT ONE OF THOSE FITNESS TRACKERS
Distributed by Andrews McMeel Syndication
40,000 STEPS TODAY! WOO-HOO!
SHOW-OFF

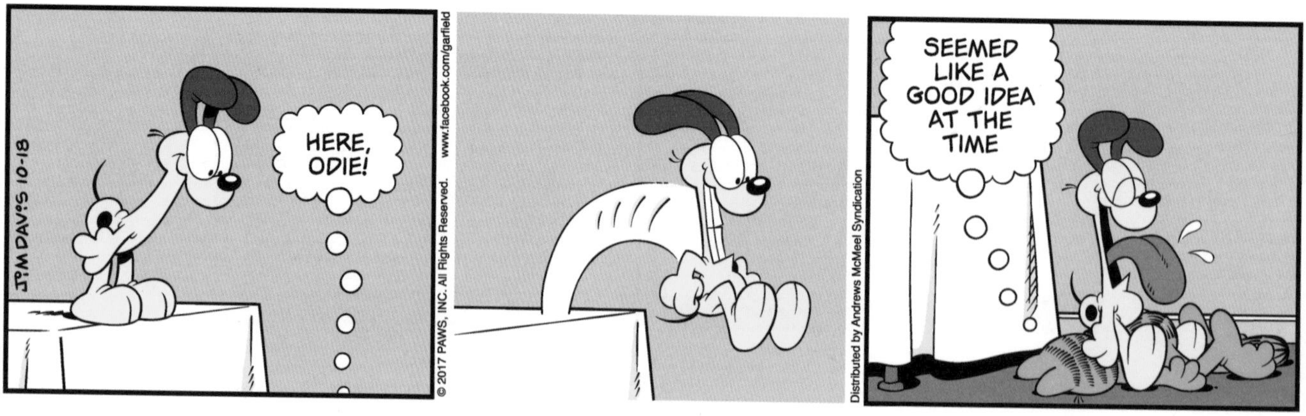
JIM DAVIS 10-18
HERE, ODIE!
© 2017 PAWS, INC. All Rights Reserved. www.facebook.com/garfield
Distributed by Andrews McMeel Syndication
SEEMED LIKE A GOOD IDEA AT THE TIME

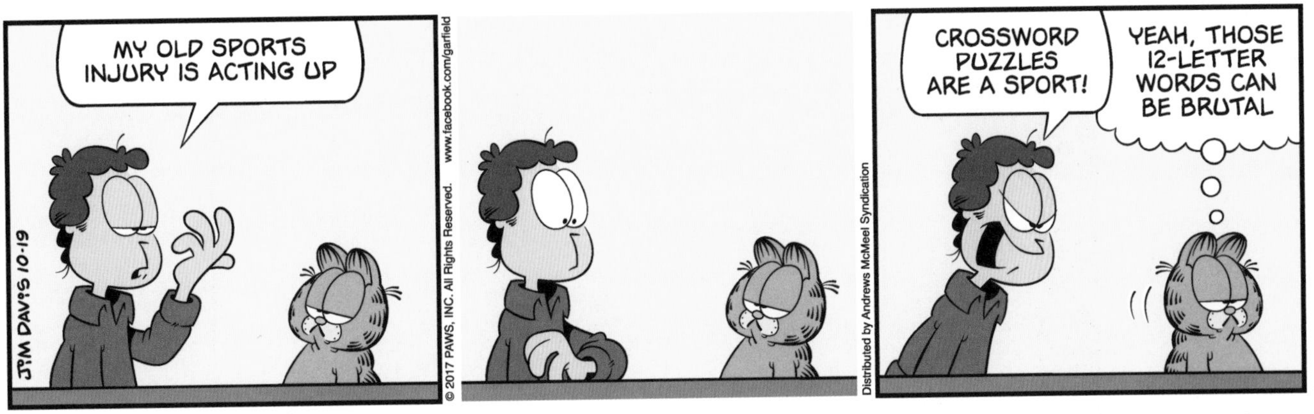
MY OLD SPORTS INJURY IS ACTING UP
CROSSWORD PUZZLES ARE A SPORT!
YEAH, THOSE 12-LETTER WORDS CAN BE BRUTAL
JIM DAVIS 10-19
© 2017 PAWS, INC. All Rights Reserved. www.facebook.com/garfield
Distributed by Andrews McMeel Syndication

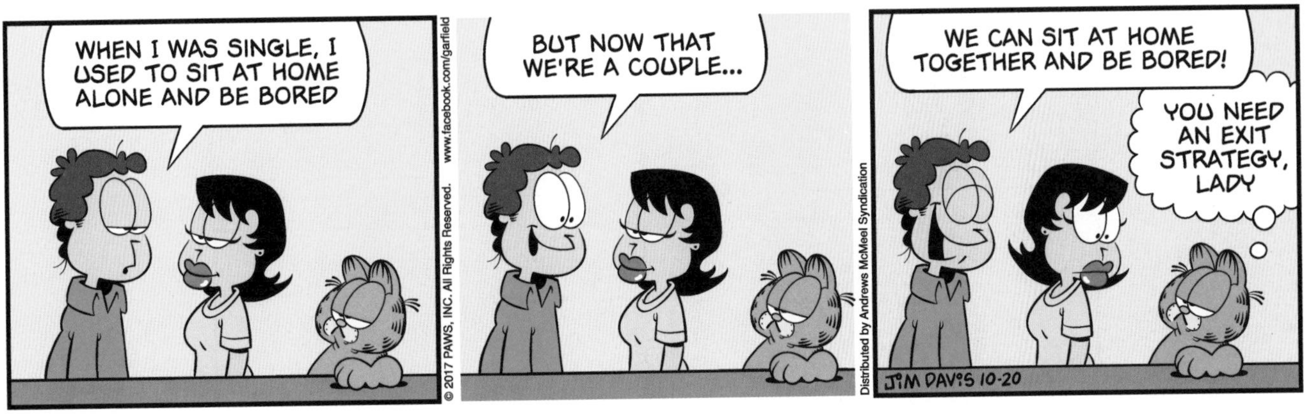
WHEN I WAS SINGLE, I USED TO SIT AT HOME ALONE AND BE BORED
BUT NOW THAT WE'RE A COUPLE...
WE CAN SIT AT HOME TOGETHER AND BE BORED!
YOU NEED AN EXIT STRATEGY, LADY
JIM DAVIS 10-20
© 2017 PAWS, INC. All Rights Reserved. www.facebook.com/garfield
Distributed by Andrews McMeel Syndication

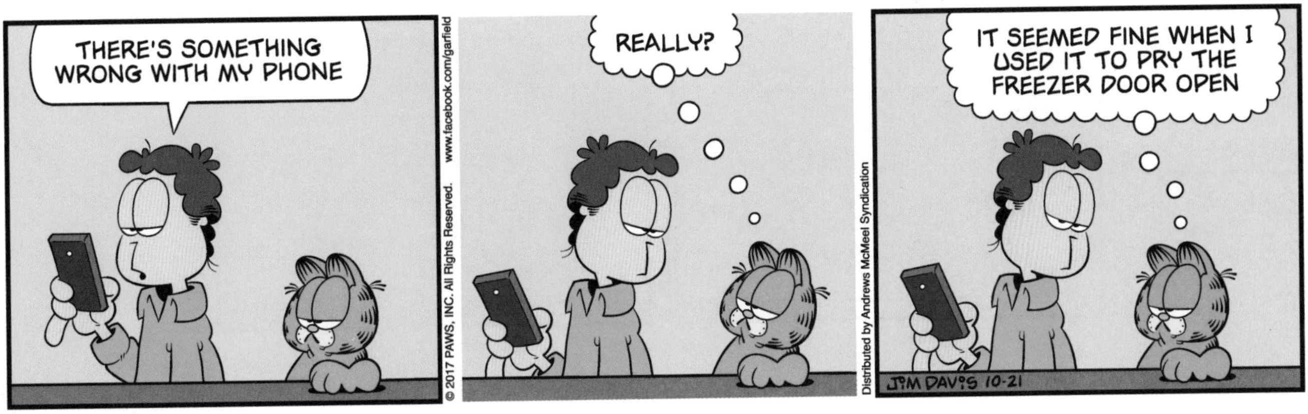
THERE'S SOMETHING WRONG WITH MY PHONE
REALLY?
IT SEEMED FINE WHEN I USED IT TO PRY THE FREEZER DOOR OPEN
JIM DAVIS 10-21
© 2017 PAWS, INC. All Rights Reserved. www.facebook.com/garfield
Distributed by Andrews McMeel Syndication

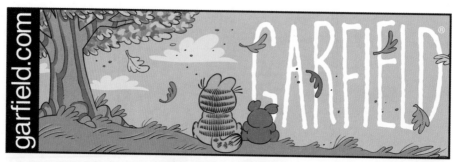

garfield.com
GARFIELD®
www.facebook.com/garfield
WHAT WERE WE FIGHTING ABOUT AGAIN?
UMMM...
I DON'T EVEN REMEMBER
NEITHER DO I
© 2017 PAWS, INC. All Rights Reserved.
THIS IS SILLY
I AGREE
WHATEVER IT WAS, I FORGIVE YOU
PAT PAT PAT
Distributed by Andrews McMeel Syndication
JIM DAVIS 10-22

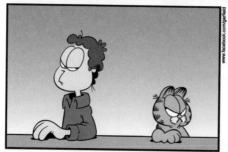

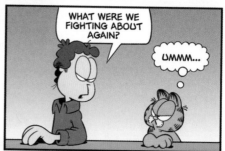

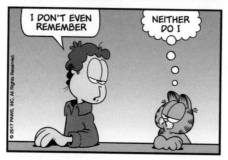

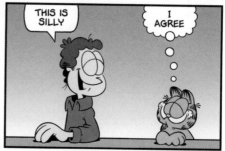

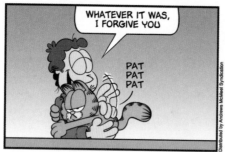

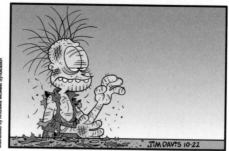

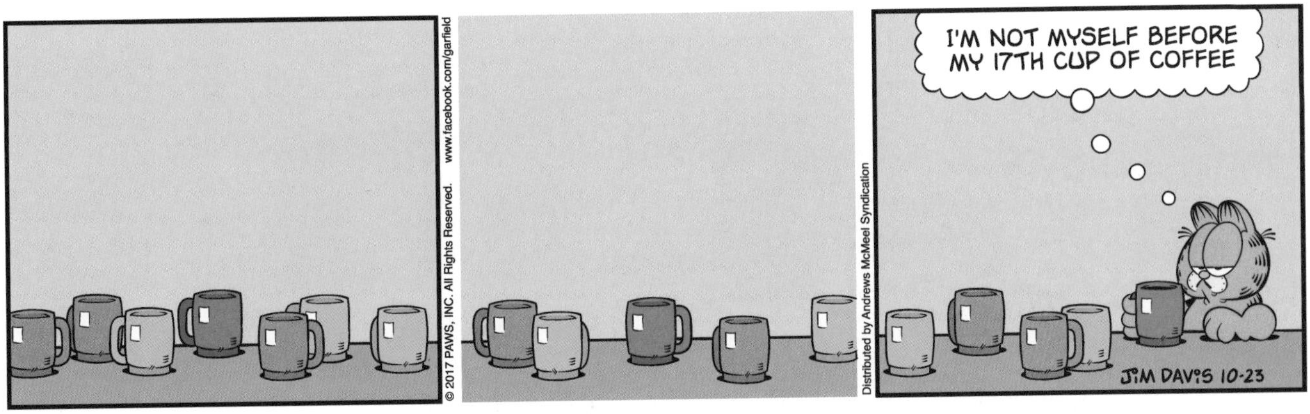

© 2017 PAWS, INC. All Rights Reserved. www.facebook.com/garfield
Distributed by Andrews McMeel Syndication
I'M NOT MYSELF BEFORE MY 17TH CUP OF COFFEE
JIM DAVIS 10-23


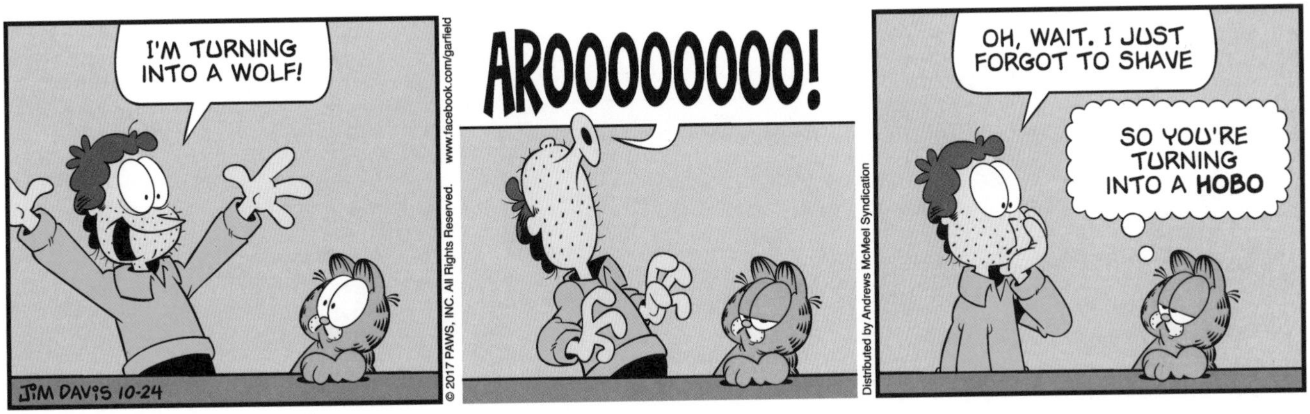

I'M TURNING INTO A WOLF!
JIM DAVIS 10-24
© 2017 PAWS, INC. All Rights Reserved. www.facebook.com/garfield
AROOOOOOOO!
Distributed by Andrews McMeel Syndication
OH, WAIT. I JUST FORGOT TO SHAVE
SO YOU'RE TURNING INTO A **HOBO**


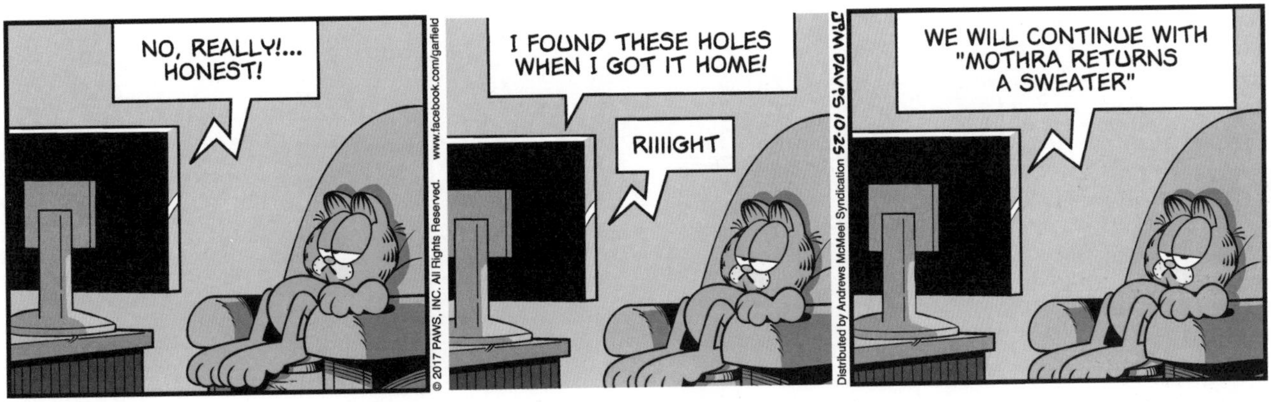

NO, REALLY!... HONEST!
© 2017 PAWS, INC. All Rights Reserved. www.facebook.com/garfield
I FOUND THESE HOLES WHEN I GOT IT HOME!
RIIIIGHT
JIM DAVIS 10-25
Distributed by Andrews McMeel Syndication
WE WILL CONTINUE WITH "MOTHRA RETURNS A SWEATER"

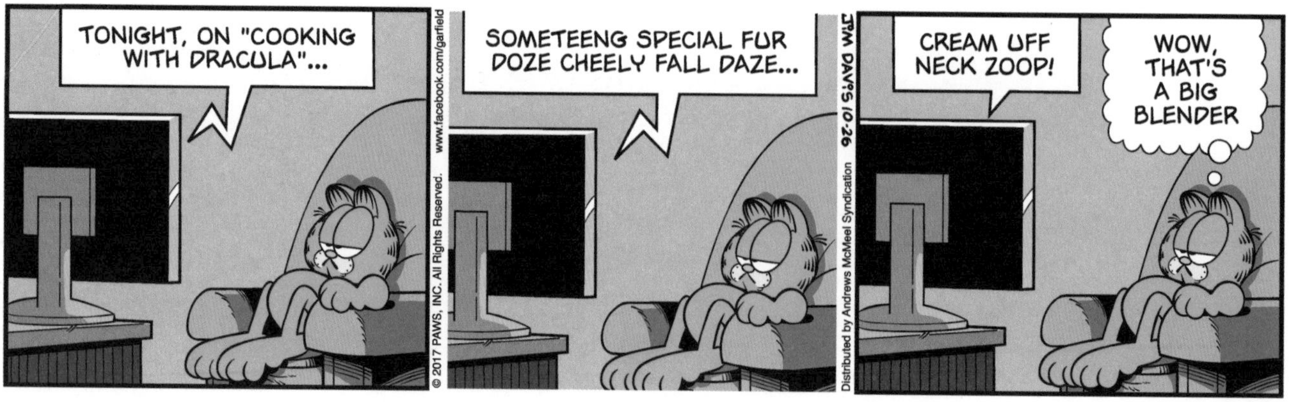
TONIGHT, ON "COOKING WITH DRACULA"...
© 2017 PAWS, INC. All Rights Reserved. www.facebook.com/garfield
SOMETEENG SPECIAL FUR DOZE CHEELY FALL DAZE...
JIM DAVIS 10-26
Distributed by Andrews McMeel Syndication
CREAM UFF NECK ZOOP!
WOW, THAT'S A BIG BLENDER

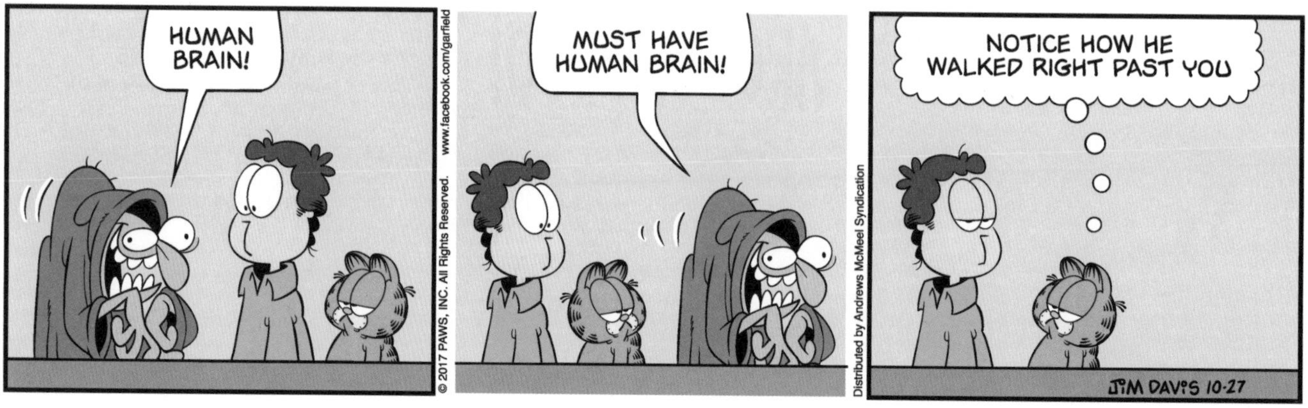
HUMAN BRAIN!
© 2017 PAWS, INC. All Rights Reserved. www.facebook.com/garfield
MUST HAVE HUMAN BRAIN!
Distributed by Andrews McMeel Syndication
NOTICE HOW HE WALKED RIGHT PAST YOU
JIM DAVIS 10-27

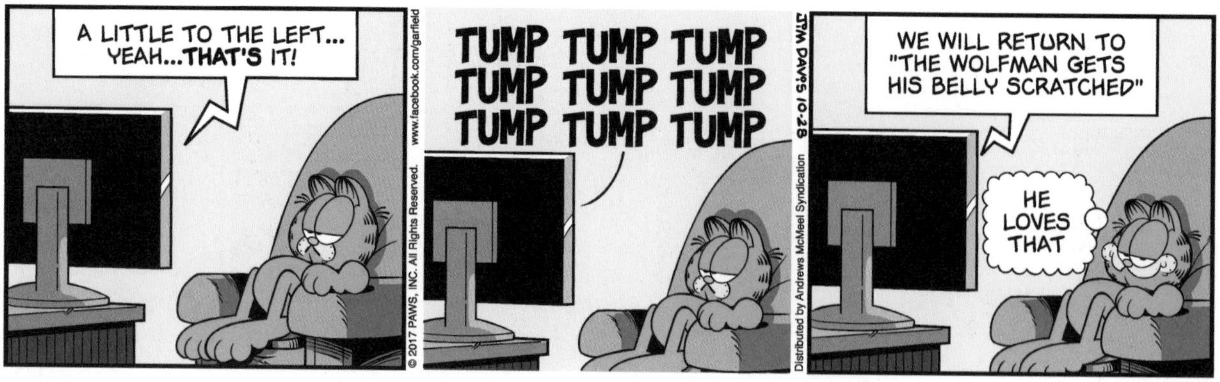
A LITTLE TO THE LEFT... YEAH...THAT'S IT!
© 2017 PAWS, INC. All Rights Reserved. www.facebook.com/garfield
TUMP TUMP TUMP TUMP TUMP TUMP TUMP TUMP TUMP
JIM DAVIS 10-28
Distributed by Andrews McMeel Syndication
WE WILL RETURN TO "THE WOLFMAN GETS HIS BELLY SCRATCHED"
HE LOVES THAT

garfield.com
GARFIELD
I'M ON MY WAY OVER TO PICK YOU UP FOR OUR DATE NOW, LIZ!
FINE. WHAT ARE YOU WEARING?
www.facebook.com/garfield
IT'S A SURPRISE!
UH-OH. MAYBE YOU SHOULD CHANGE
I LOOK **FINE**, LIZ! DON'T YOU TRUST ME?
PUT GARFIELD ON
© 2017 PAWS, INC. All Rights Reserved.
GARFIELD, HOW DOES HE LOOK?
HAAAACK!
Distributed by Andrews McMeel Syndication
HEY! YOU CLEAN UP THAT HAIRBALL!
CHANGE
JIM DAVIS 10-29

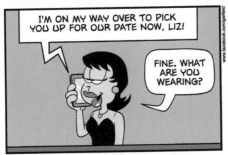

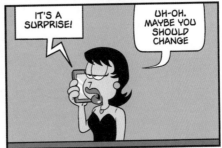

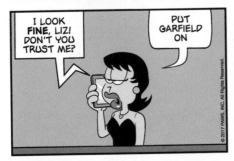

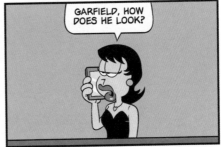

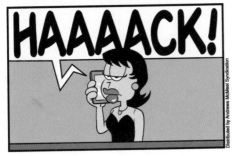

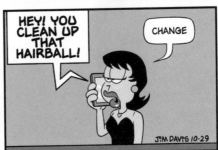

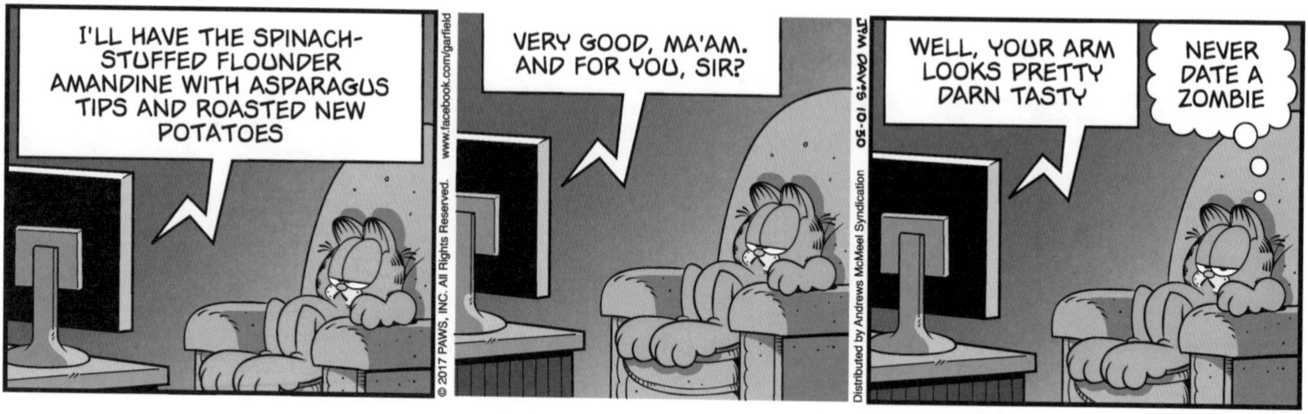
I'LL HAVE THE SPINACH-STUFFED FLOUNDER AMANDINE WITH ASPARAGUS TIPS AND ROASTED NEW POTATOES
VERY GOOD, MA'AM. AND FOR YOU, SIR?
WELL, YOUR ARM LOOKS PRETTY DARN TASTY
NEVER DATE A ZOMBIE
JIM DAVIS 10-30
© 2017 PAWS, INC. All Rights Reserved. www.facebook.com/garfield
Distributed by Andrews McMeel Syndication

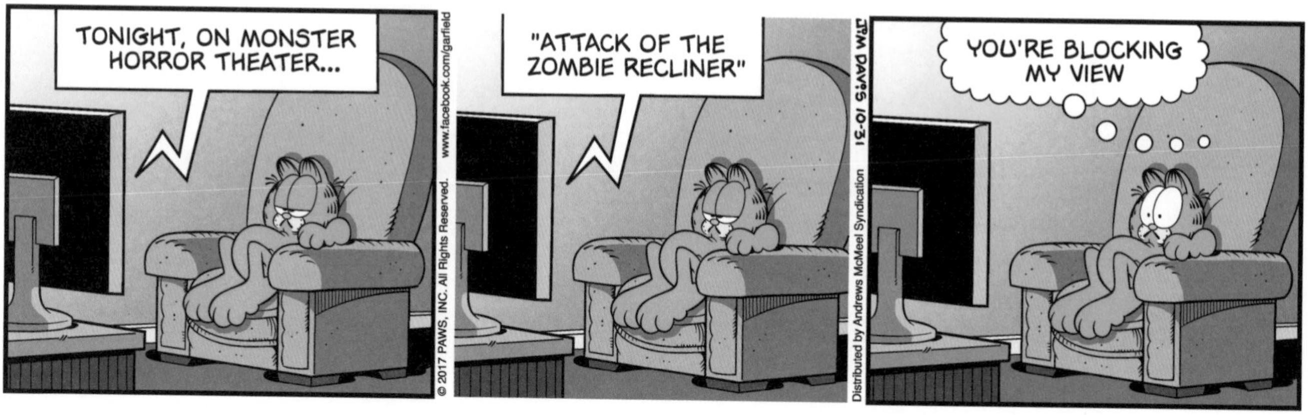
TONIGHT, ON MONSTER HORROR THEATER...
"ATTACK OF THE ZOMBIE RECLINER"
YOU'RE BLOCKING MY VIEW
JIM DAVIS 10-31
© 2017 PAWS, INC. All Rights Reserved. www.facebook.com/garfield
Distributed by Andrews McMeel Syndication

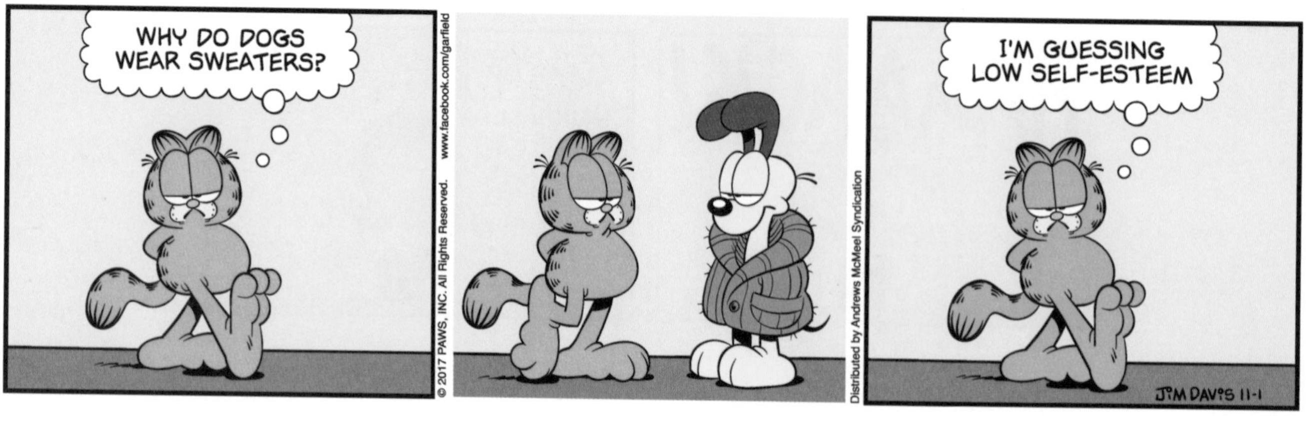
WHY DO DOGS WEAR SWEATERS?
I'M GUESSING LOW SELF-ESTEEM
JIM DAVIS 11-1
© 2017 PAWS, INC. All Rights Reserved. www.facebook.com/garfield
Distributed by Andrews McMeel Syndication

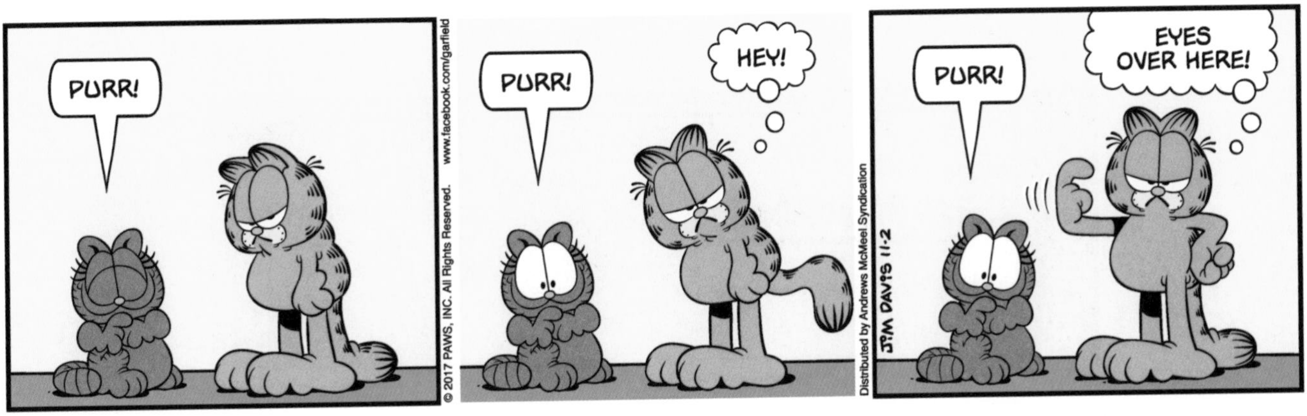
PURR!
© 2017 PAWS, INC. All Rights Reserved. www.facebook.com/garfield
PURR!
HEY!
Distributed by Andrews McMeel Syndication
JIM DAVIS 11-2
PURR!
EYES OVER HERE!

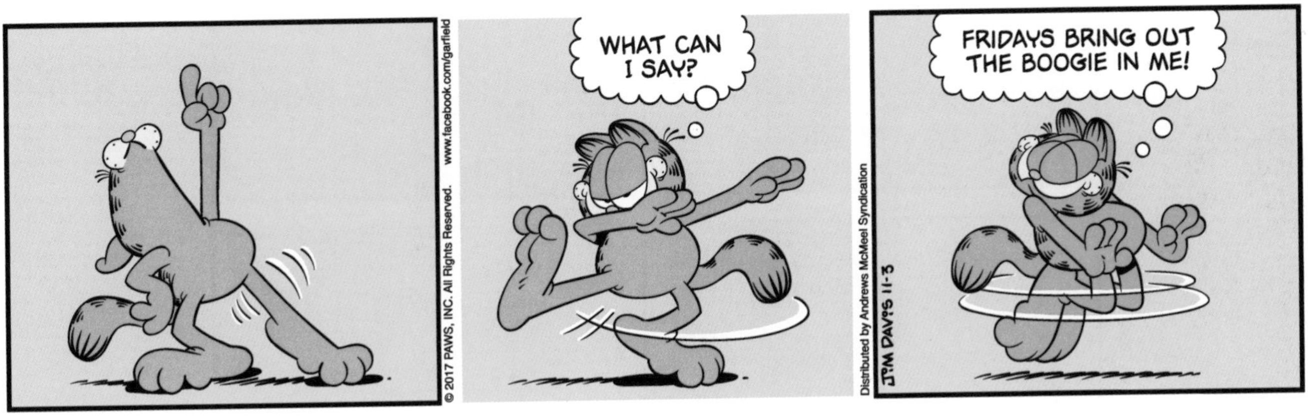
© 2017 PAWS, INC. All Rights Reserved. www.facebook.com/garfield
WHAT CAN I SAY?
Distributed by Andrews McMeel Syndication
JIM DAVIS 11-3
FRIDAYS BRING OUT THE BOOGIE IN ME!

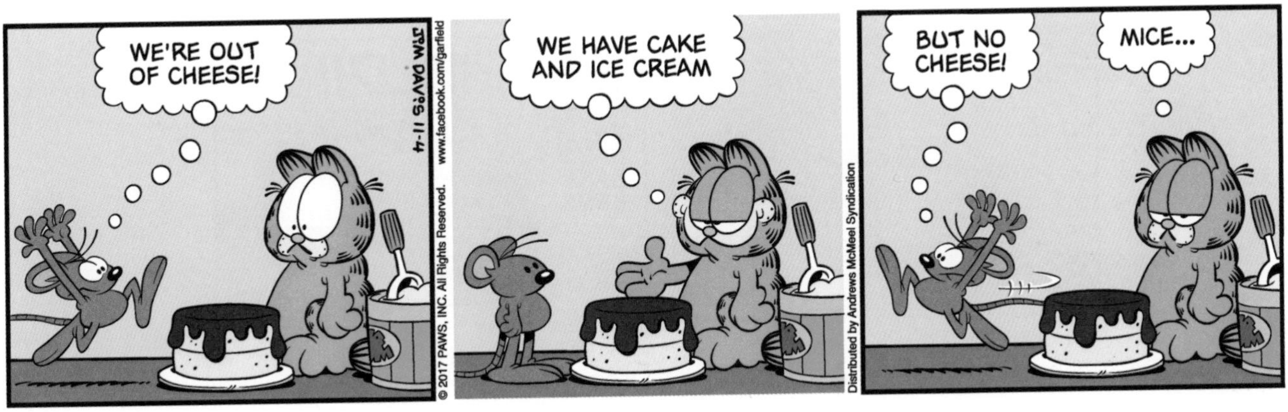
WE'RE OUT OF CHEESE!
JIM DAVIS 11-4
© 2017 PAWS, INC. All Rights Reserved. www.facebook.com/garfield
WE HAVE CAKE AND ICE CREAM
Distributed by Andrews McMeel Syndication
BUT NO CHEESE!
MICE...

garfield.com
Garfield®
© 2017 PAWS, INC. All Rights Reserved.
UH-OH
www.facebook.com/garfield
I THINK I FORGOT MY KEYS
PAT PAT PAT
LOOKS LIKE WE'RE LOCKED OUT, GUYS
GUYS?
JIM DAVIS 11-5
FLIP FLIP FLIP
Distributed by Andrews McMeel Syndication
GARFIELD!!
BANG! BANG! BANG!
ANOTHER PIE, ODIE?

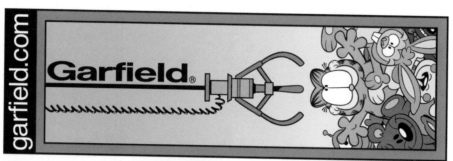

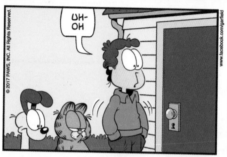

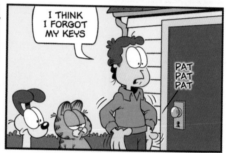

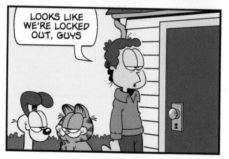

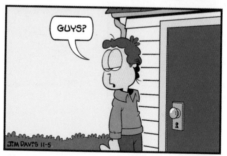

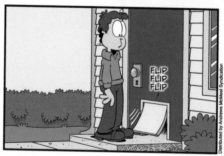

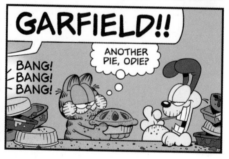

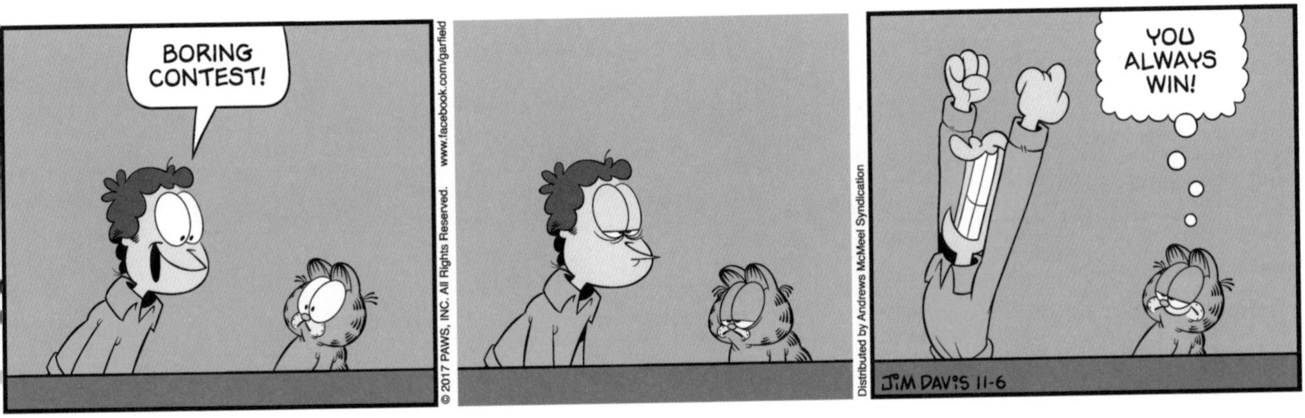
BORING CONTEST!
YOU ALWAYS WIN!
JIM DAVIS 11-6
© 2017 PAWS, INC. All Rights Reserved. www.facebook.com/garfield
Distributed by Andrews McMeel Syndication

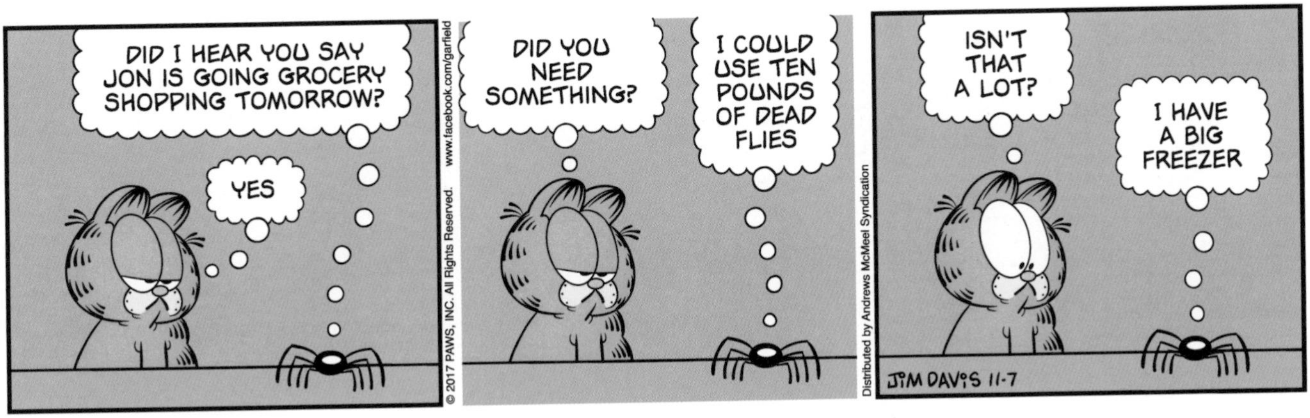
DID I HEAR YOU SAY JON IS GOING GROCERY SHOPPING TOMORROW?
YES
DID YOU NEED SOMETHING?
I COULD USE TEN POUNDS OF DEAD FLIES
ISN'T THAT A LOT?
I HAVE A BIG FREEZER
JIM DAVIS 11-7
© 2017 PAWS, INC. All Rights Reserved. www.facebook.com/garfield
Distributed by Andrews McMeel Syndication

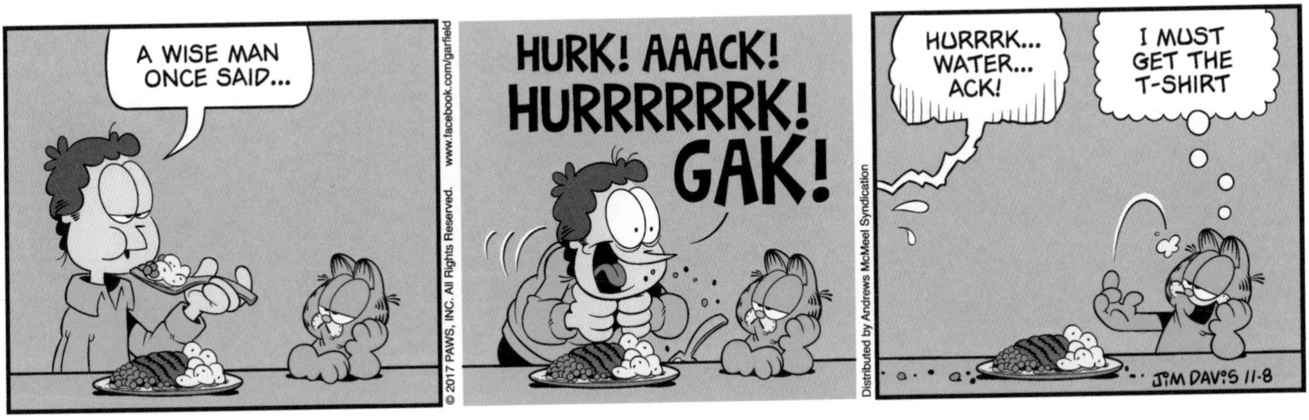
A WISE MAN ONCE SAID...
HURK! AAACK! HURRRRRRK! GAK!
HURRRK... WATER... ACK!
I MUST GET THE T-SHIRT
JIM DAVIS 11-8
© 2017 PAWS, INC. All Rights Reserved. www.facebook.com/garfield
Distributed by Andrews McMeel Syndication

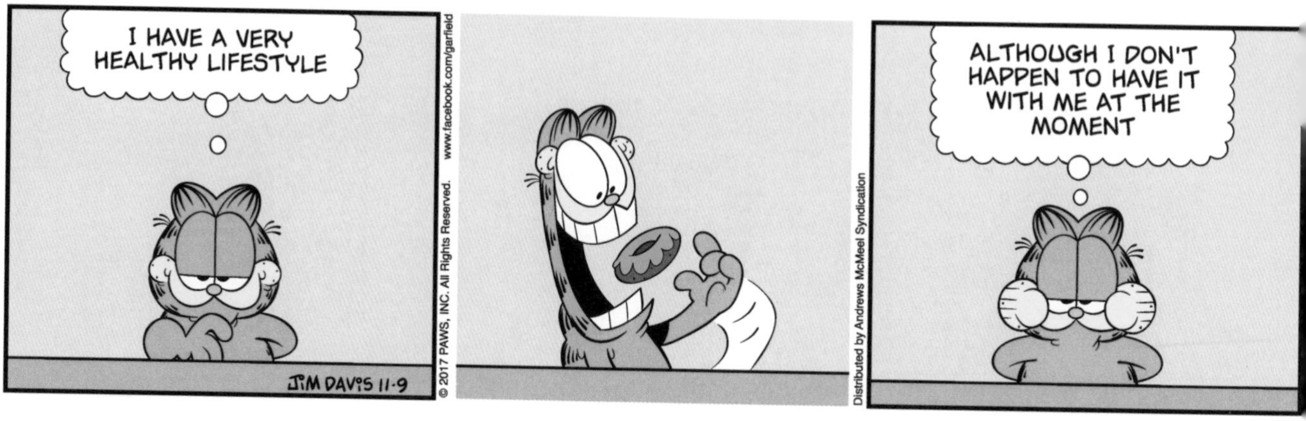
I HAVE A VERY HEALTHY LIFESTYLE
JIM DAVIS 11-9
© 2017 PAWS, INC. All Rights Reserved. www.facebook.com/garfield
Distributed by Andrews McMeel Syndication
ALTHOUGH I DON'T HAPPEN TO HAVE IT WITH ME AT THE MOMENT

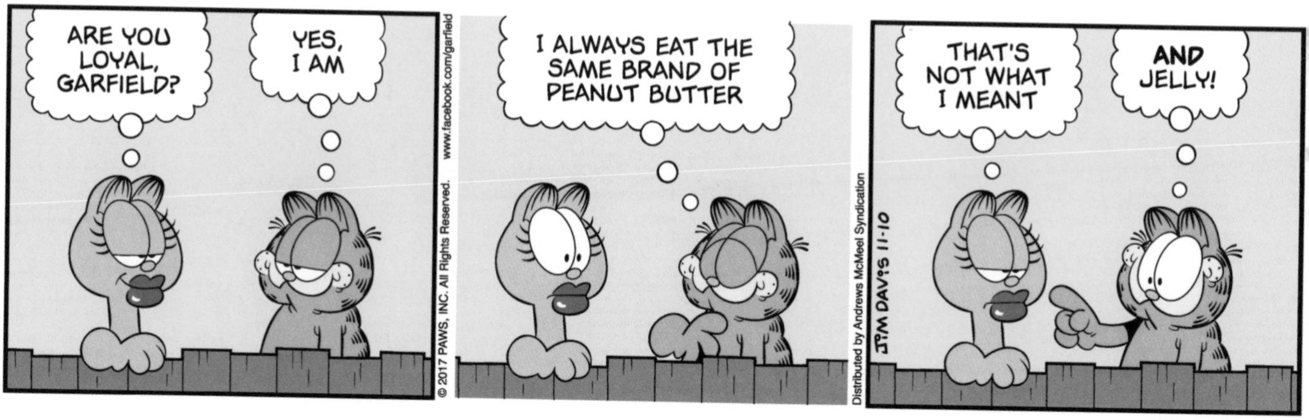
ARE YOU LOYAL, GARFIELD?
YES, I AM
© 2017 PAWS, INC. All Rights Reserved. www.facebook.com/garfield
I ALWAYS EAT THE SAME BRAND OF PEANUT BUTTER
Distributed by Andrews McMeel Syndication
JIM DAVIS 11-10
THAT'S NOT WHAT I MEANT
AND JELLY!

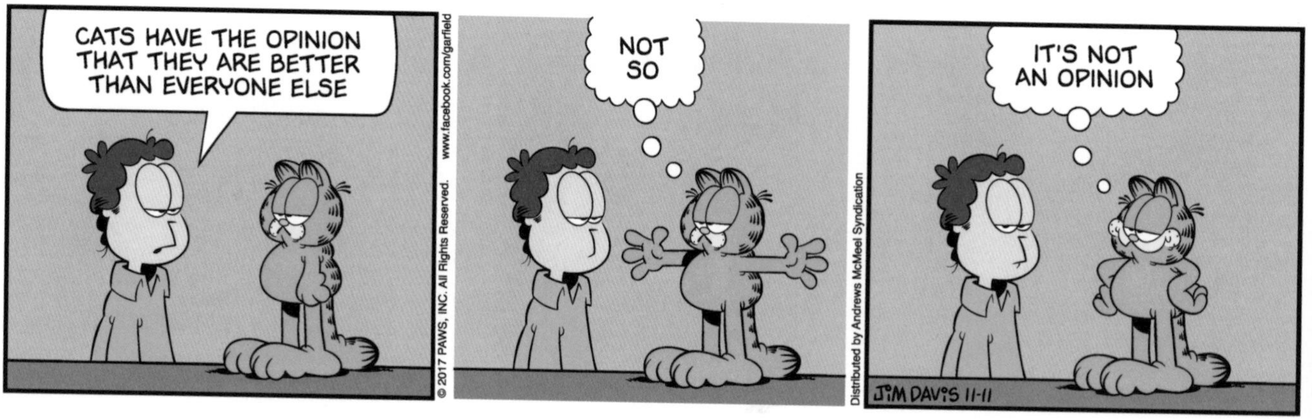
CATS HAVE THE OPINION THAT THEY ARE BETTER THAN EVERYONE ELSE
© 2017 PAWS, INC. All Rights Reserved. www.facebook.com/garfield
NOT SO
Distributed by Andrews McMeel Syndication
IT'S NOT AN OPINION
JIM DAVIS 11-11

garfield.com
GARFIELD
Activating Sleep Mode
JIM DAVIS 11-12
www.facebook.com/garfield
[redacted]
ALL DONE!
© 2017 PAWS, INC. All Rights Reserved.
WANT TO GO FOR A WALK?
Z
FLUMP
Distributed by Andrews McMeel Syndication
CATS DON'T HAVE A SLEEP MODE!
CATS **INVENTED** SLEEP MODE

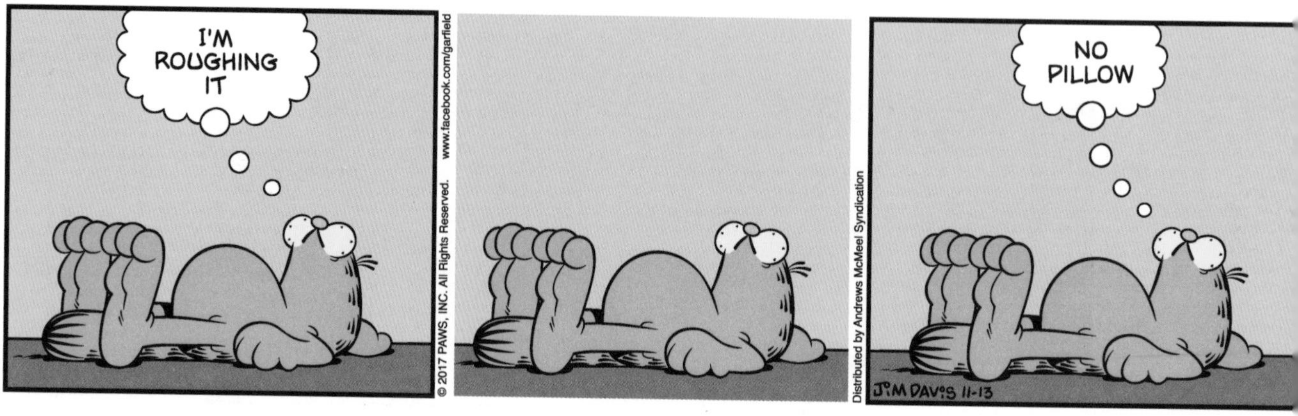
I'M ROUGHING IT
NO PILLOW
© 2017 PAWS, INC. All Rights Reserved. www.facebook.com/garfield
Distributed by Andrews McMeel Syndication
JIM DAVIS 11-13

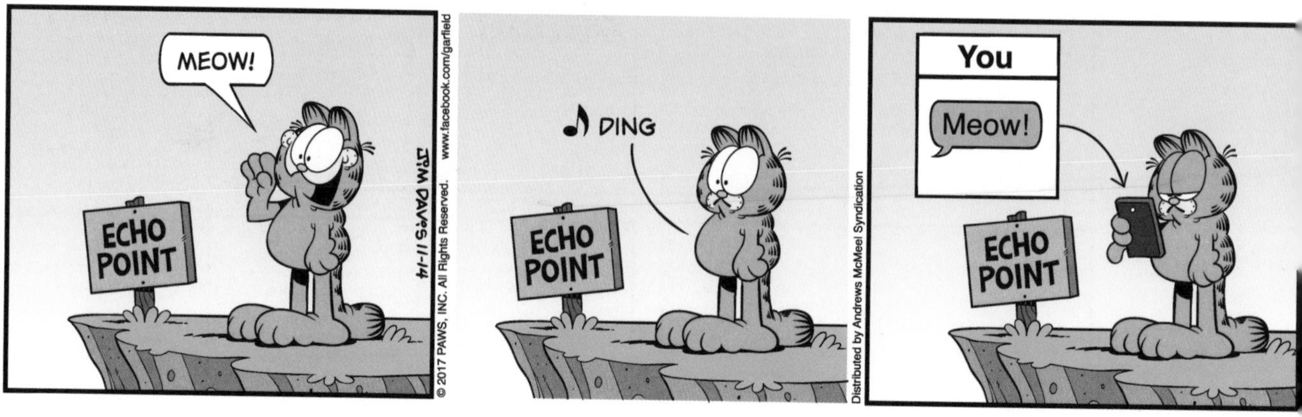
MEOW!
ECHO POINT
JIM DAVIS 11-14
© 2017 PAWS, INC. All Rights Reserved. www.facebook.com/garfield
DING
Distributed by Andrews McMeel Syndication
You
Meow!

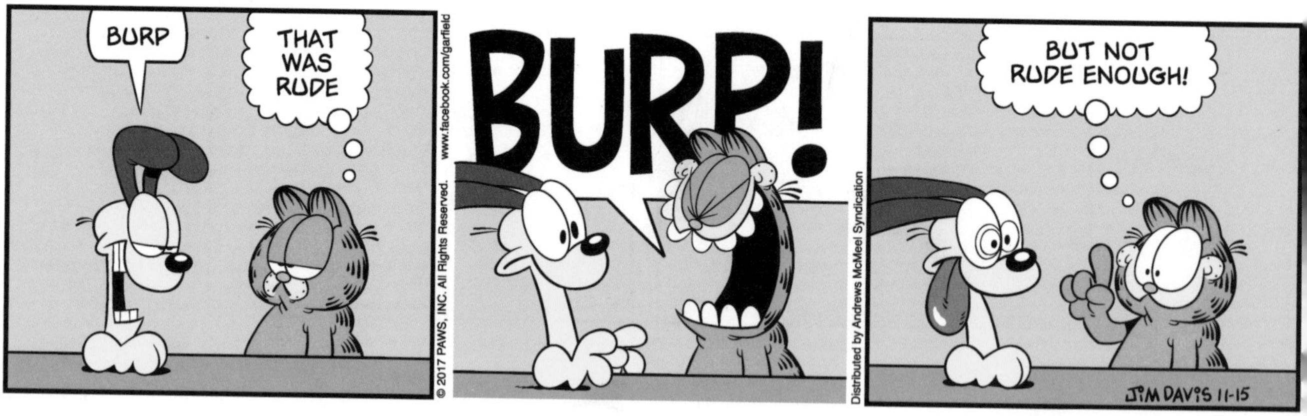
BURP
THAT WAS RUDE
© 2017 PAWS, INC. All Rights Reserved. www.facebook.com/garfield
BURP!
Distributed by Andrews McMeel Syndication
BUT NOT RUDE ENOUGH!
JIM DAVIS 11-15

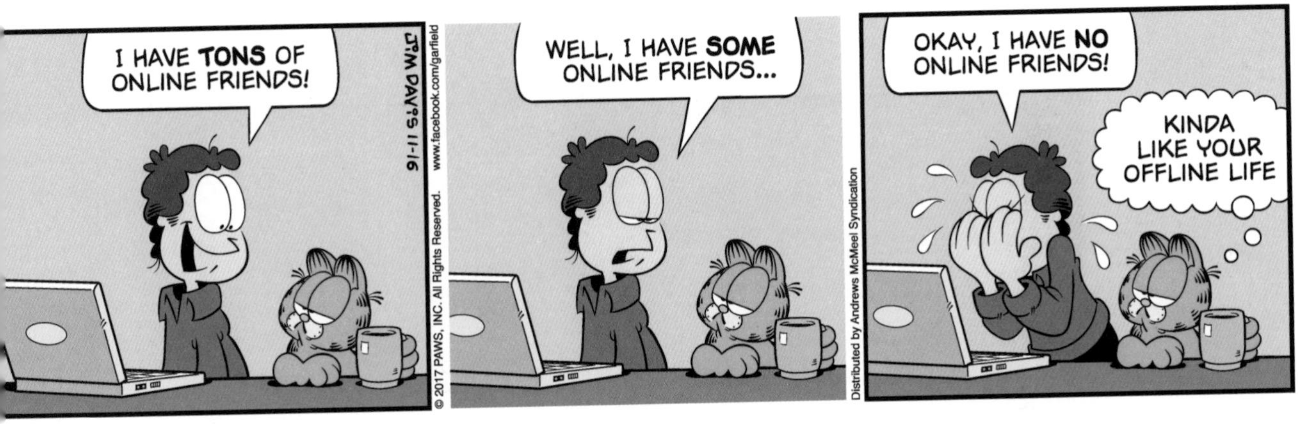
I HAVE **TONS** OF ONLINE FRIENDS!
JIM DAVIS 11-16
© 2017 PAWS, INC. All Rights Reserved. www.facebook.com/garfield
WELL, I HAVE **SOME** ONLINE FRIENDS...
Distributed by Andrews McMeel Syndication
OKAY, I HAVE **NO** ONLINE FRIENDS!
KINDA LIKE YOUR OFFLINE LIFE

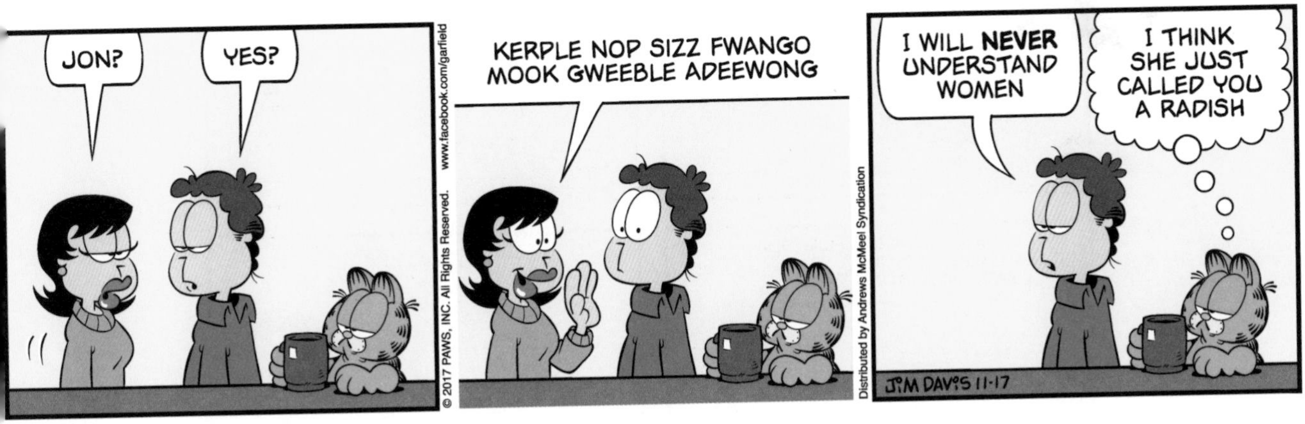
JON?
YES?
© 2017 PAWS, INC. All Rights Reserved. www.facebook.com/garfield
KERPLE NOP SIZZ FWANGO MOOK GWEEBLE ADEEWONG
Distributed by Andrews McMeel Syndication
I WILL **NEVER** UNDERSTAND WOMEN
I THINK SHE JUST CALLED YOU A RADISH
JIM DAVIS 11-17

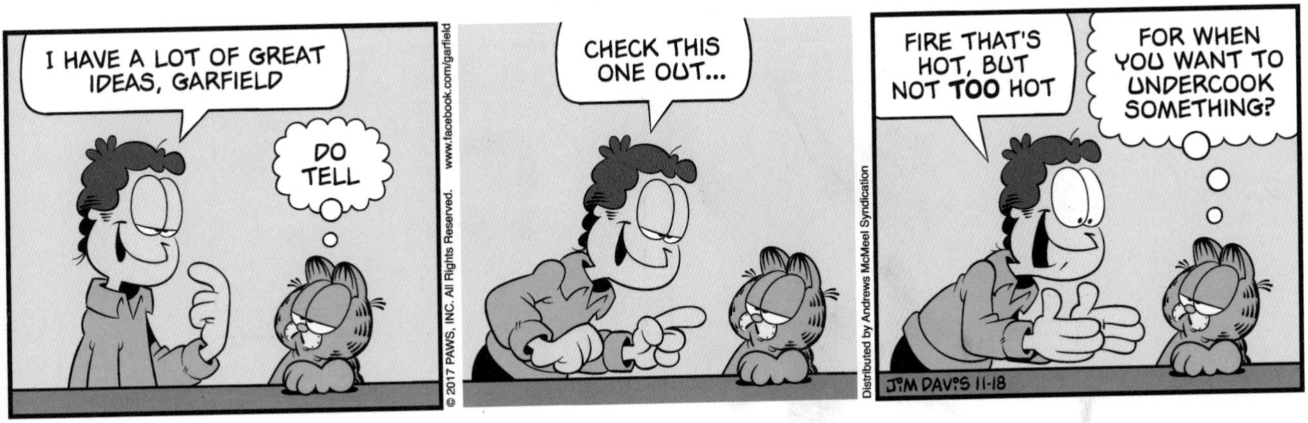
I HAVE A LOT OF GREAT IDEAS, GARFIELD
DO TELL
© 2017 PAWS, INC. All Rights Reserved. www.facebook.com/garfield
CHECK THIS ONE OUT...
Distributed by Andrews McMeel Syndication
FIRE THAT'S HOT, BUT NOT **TOO** HOT
FOR WHEN YOU WANT TO UNDERCOOK SOMETHING?
JIM DAVIS 11-18

garfield.com
GARFIELD
CRUNCH CRUNCH CRUNCH CRUNCH
www.facebook.com/garfield
HEY! NO DOUBLE-DIPPING!
© 2017 PAWS, INC. All Rights Reserved.
DON'T YOU KNOW HOW UNSANITARY THAT IS, YOU DISGUSTING PIG?!
DIP
JON, I WAS THINKING WE MIGHT GO TO DINNER AT...
JIM DAVIS 11-19
Distributed by Andrews McMeel Syndication
NEVER MIND

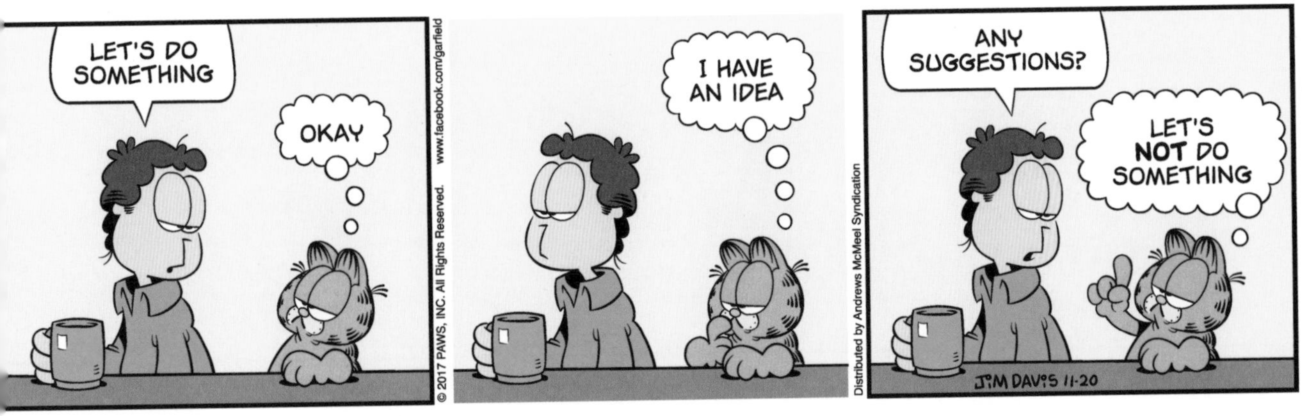
LET'S DO SOMETHING
OKAY
© 2017 PAWS, INC. All Rights Reserved. www.facebook.com/garfield
I HAVE AN IDEA
Distributed by Andrews McMeel Syndication
ANY SUGGESTIONS?
LET'S NOT DO SOMETHING
JIM DAVIS 11-20

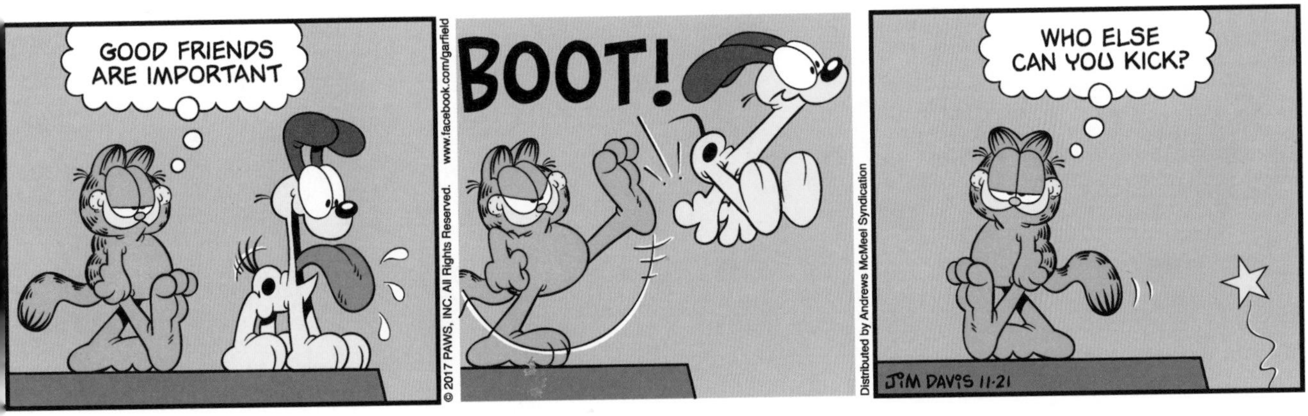
GOOD FRIENDS ARE IMPORTANT
© 2017 PAWS, INC. All Rights Reserved. www.facebook.com/garfield
BOOT!
Distributed by Andrews McMeel Syndication
WHO ELSE CAN YOU KICK?
JIM DAVIS 11-21

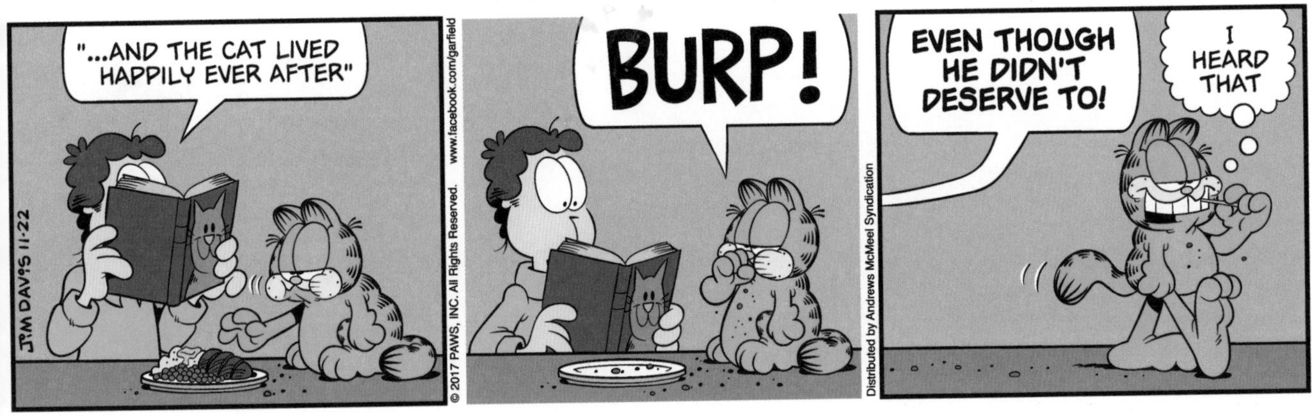
"...AND THE CAT LIVED HAPPILY EVER AFTER"
JIM DAVIS 11-22
© 2017 PAWS, INC. All Rights Reserved. www.facebook.com/garfield
BURP!
Distributed by Andrews McMeel Syndication
EVEN THOUGH HE DIDN'T DESERVE TO!
I HEARD THAT

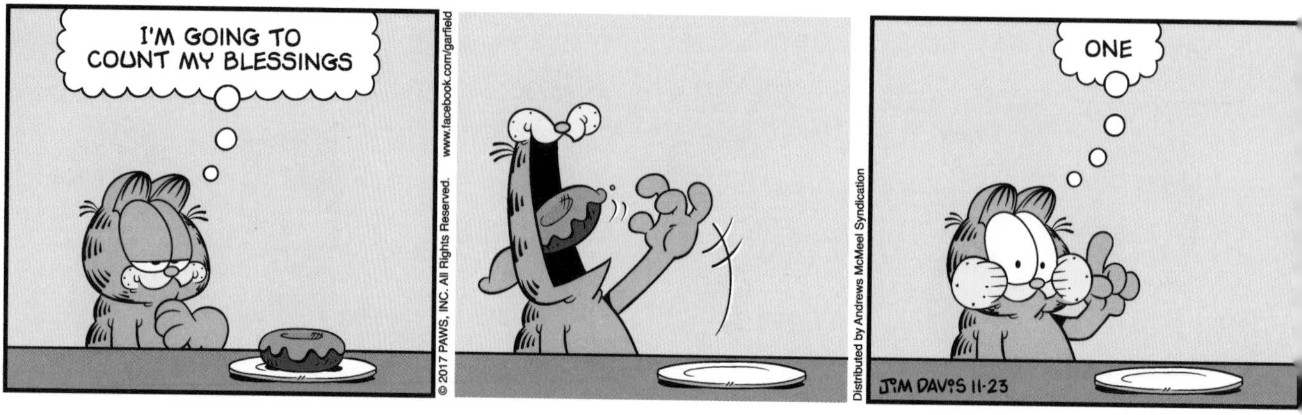
I'M GOING TO COUNT MY BLESSINGS
© 2017 PAWS, INC. All Rights Reserved. www.facebook.com/garfield
Distributed by Andrews McMeel Syndication
ONE
JIM DAVIS 11-23

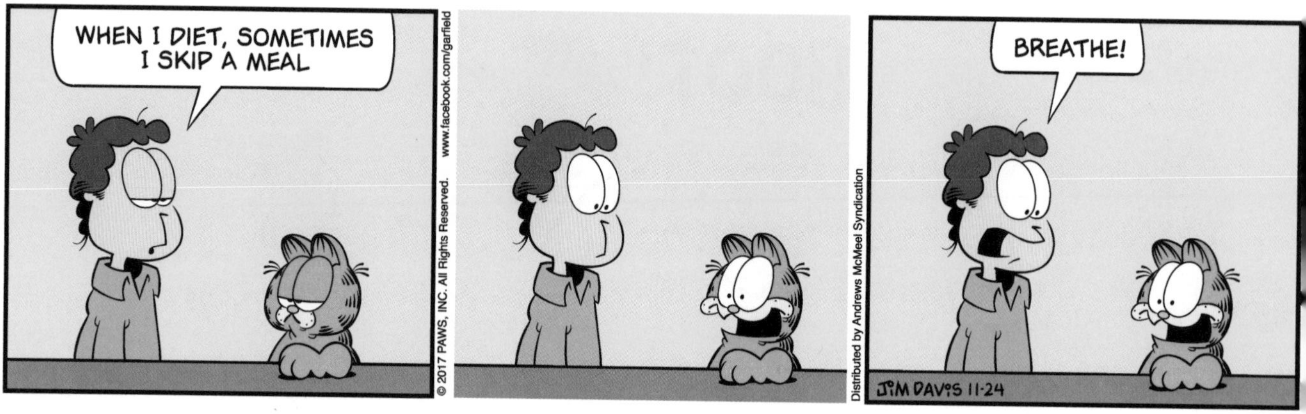
WHEN I DIET, SOMETIMES I SKIP A MEAL
© 2017 PAWS, INC. All Rights Reserved. www.facebook.com/garfield
Distributed by Andrews McMeel Syndication
BREATHE!
JIM DAVIS 11-24

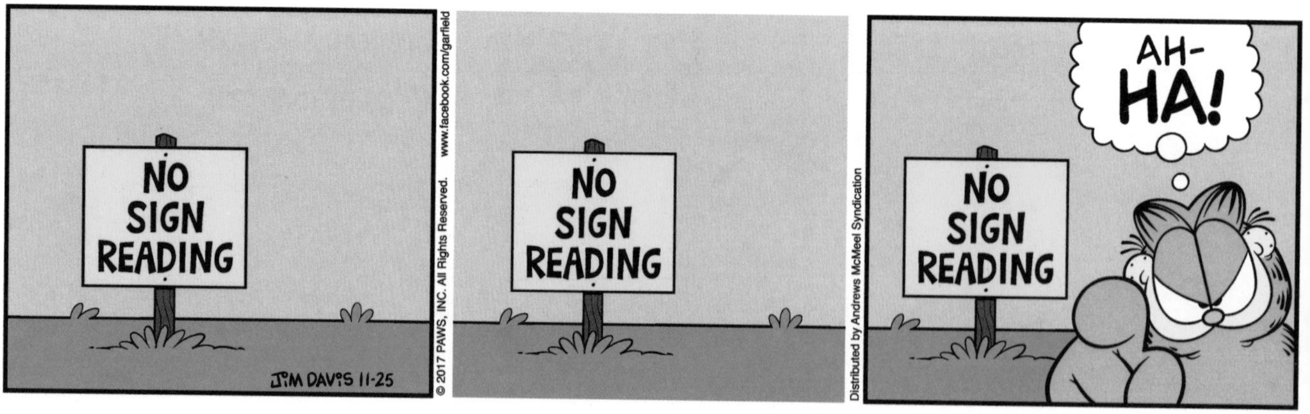
NO SIGN READING
JIM DAVIS 11-25
© 2017 PAWS, INC. All Rights Reserved. www.facebook.com/garfield
NO SIGN READING
Distributed by Andrews McMeel Syndication
AH-HA!
NO SIGN READING

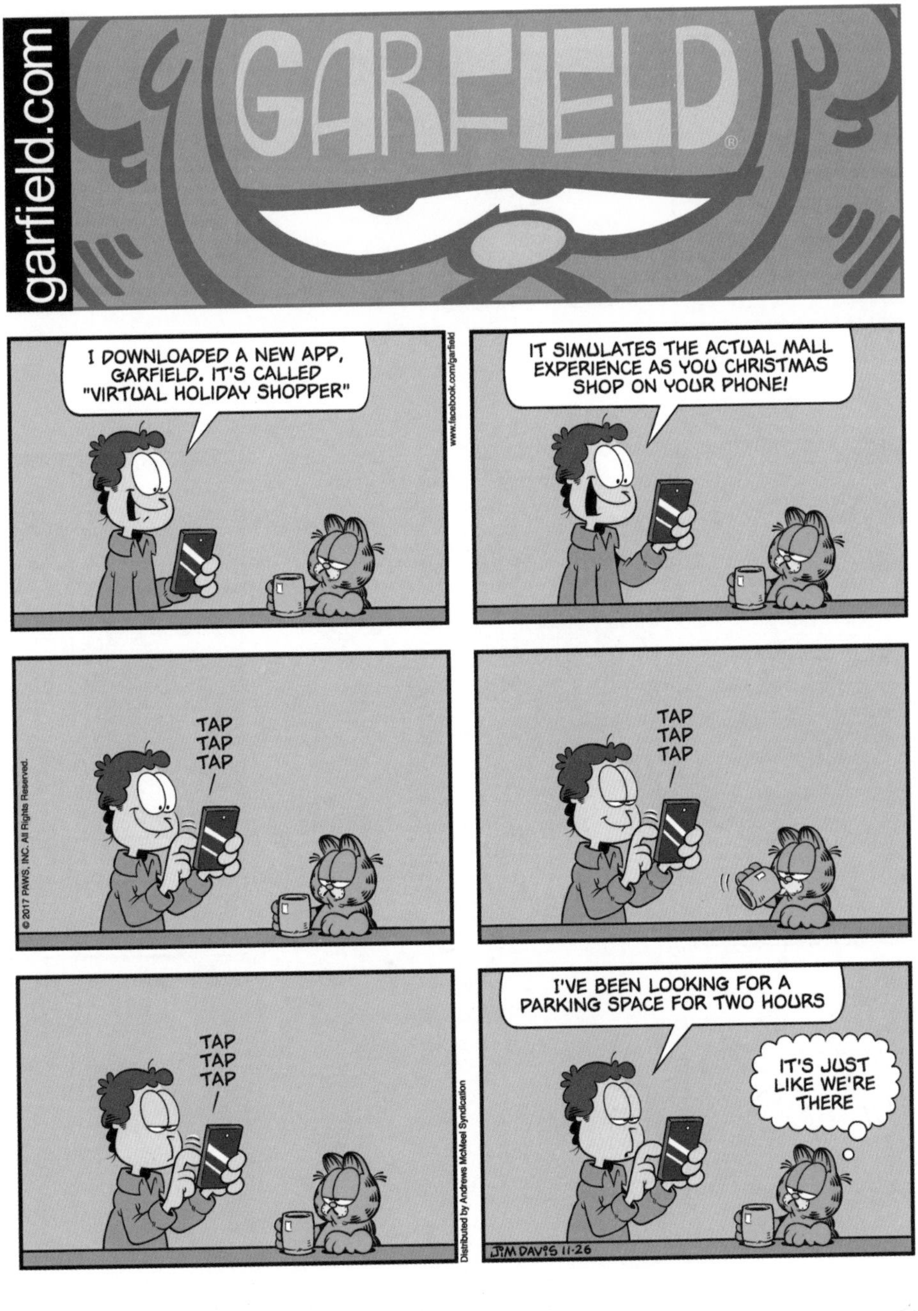
garfield.com
GARFIELD®
I DOWNLOADED A NEW APP, GARFIELD. IT'S CALLED "VIRTUAL HOLIDAY SHOPPER"
www.facebook.com/garfield
IT SIMULATES THE ACTUAL MALL EXPERIENCE AS YOU CHRISTMAS SHOP ON YOUR PHONE!
TAP TAP TAP
© 2017 PAWS, INC. All Rights Reserved.
TAP TAP TAP
TAP TAP TAP
Distributed by Andrews McMeel Syndication
I'VE BEEN LOOKING FOR A PARKING SPACE FOR TWO HOURS
IT'S JUST LIKE WE'RE THERE
JIM DAVIS 11-26

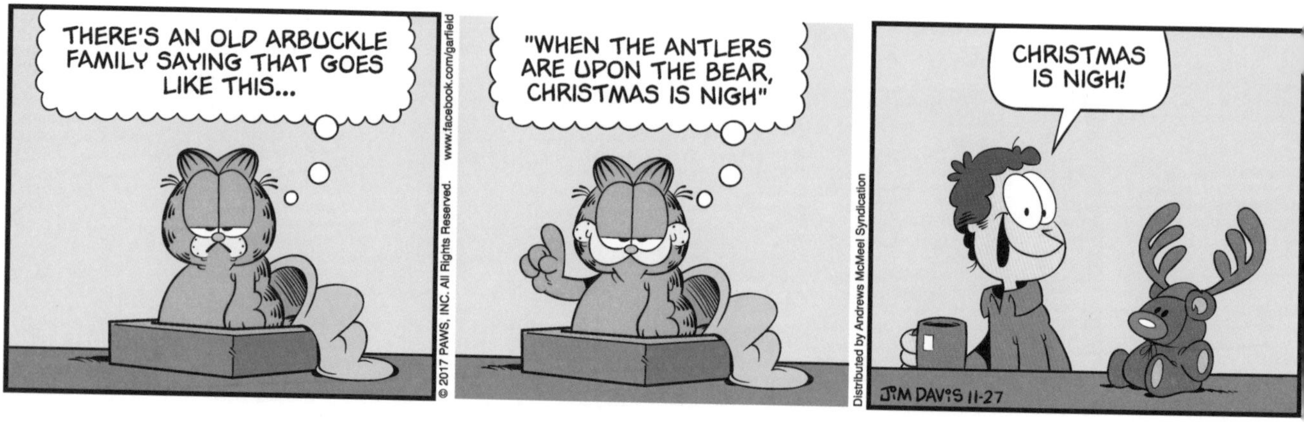
THERE'S AN OLD ARBUCKLE FAMILY SAYING THAT GOES LIKE THIS...
© 2017 PAWS, INC. All Rights Reserved. www.facebook.com/garfield
"WHEN THE ANTLERS ARE UPON THE BEAR, CHRISTMAS IS NIGH"
Distributed by Andrews McMeel Syndication
CHRISTMAS IS NIGH!
JIM DAVIS 11-27

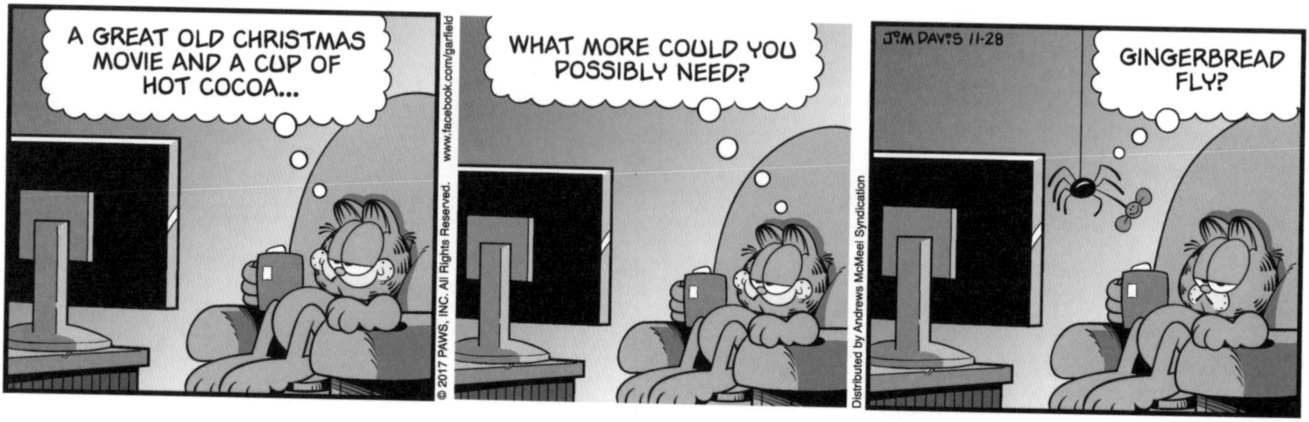
A GREAT OLD CHRISTMAS MOVIE AND A CUP OF HOT COCOA...
© 2017 PAWS, INC. All Rights Reserved. www.facebook.com/garfield
WHAT MORE COULD YOU POSSIBLY NEED?
Distributed by Andrews McMeel Syndication
JIM DAVIS 11-28
GINGERBREAD FLY?

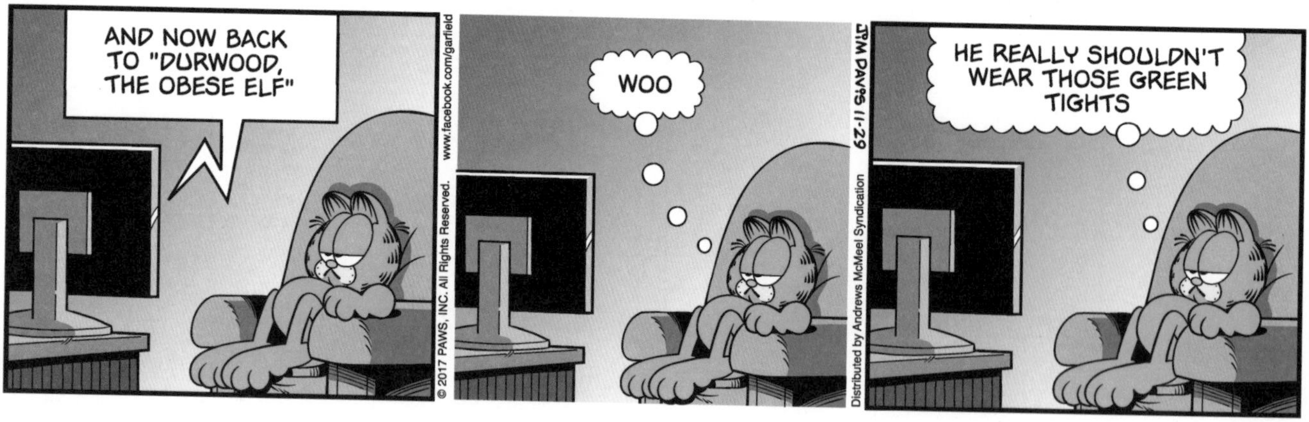
AND NOW BACK TO "DURWOOD, THE OBESE ELF"
© 2017 PAWS, INC. All Rights Reserved. www.facebook.com/garfield
WOO
JIM DAVIS 11-29
Distributed by Andrews McMeel Syndication
HE REALLY SHOULDN'T WEAR THOSE GREEN TIGHTS

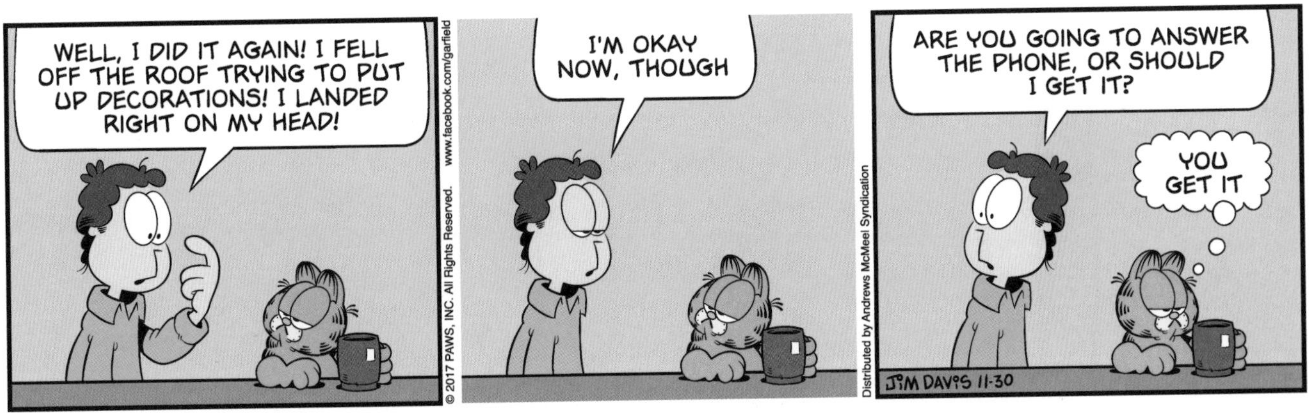
WELL, I DID IT AGAIN! I FELL OFF THE ROOF TRYING TO PUT UP DECORATIONS! I LANDED RIGHT ON MY HEAD!
© 2017 PAWS, INC. All Rights Reserved. www.facebook.com/garfield
I'M OKAY NOW, THOUGH
Distributed by Andrews McMeel Syndication
ARE YOU GOING TO ANSWER THE PHONE, OR SHOULD I GET IT?
YOU GET IT
JIM DAVIS 11-30

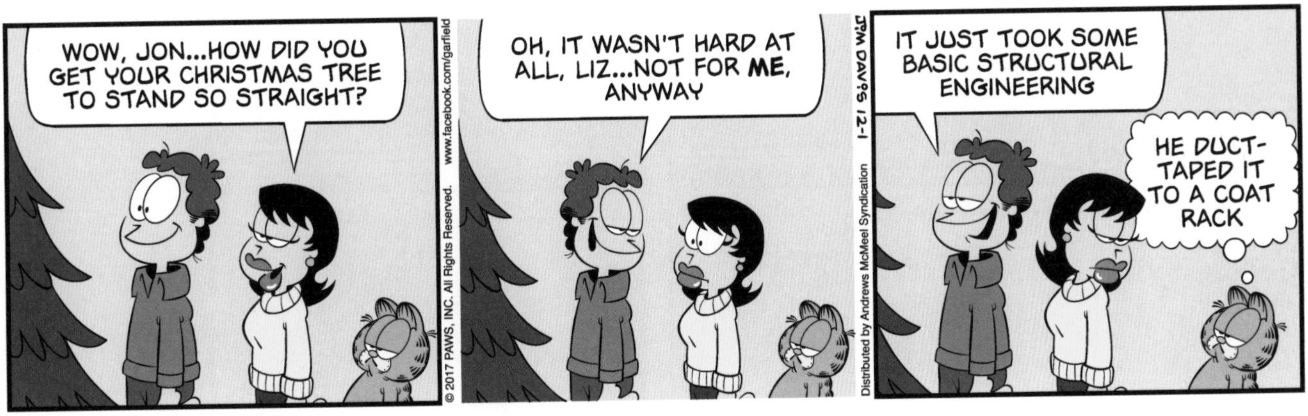
WOW, JON...HOW DID YOU GET YOUR CHRISTMAS TREE TO STAND SO STRAIGHT?
© 2017 PAWS, INC. All Rights Reserved. www.facebook.com/garfield
OH, IT WASN'T HARD AT ALL, LIZ...NOT FOR **ME**, ANYWAY
JIM DAVIS 12-1
Distributed by Andrews McMeel Syndication
IT JUST TOOK SOME BASIC STRUCTURAL ENGINEERING
HE DUCT-TAPED IT TO A COAT RACK

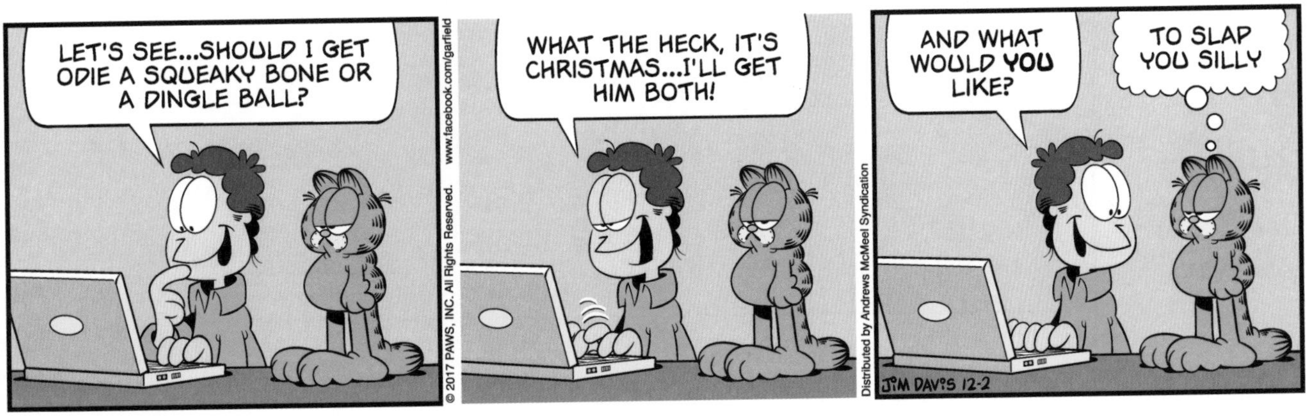
LET'S SEE...SHOULD I GET ODIE A SQUEAKY BONE OR A DINGLE BALL?
© 2017 PAWS, INC. All Rights Reserved. www.facebook.com/garfield
WHAT THE HECK, IT'S CHRISTMAS...I'LL GET HIM BOTH!
Distributed by Andrews McMeel Syndication
AND WHAT WOULD **YOU** LIKE?
TO SLAP YOU SILLY
JIM DAVIS 12-2

garfield.com
Garfield
www.facebook.com/garfield
© 2017 PAWS, INC. All Rights Reserved.
JIM DAVIS 12-3
Distributed by Andrews McMeel Syndication
OUR GIANT INFLATABLE RUDOLPH BLEW OVER AGAIN

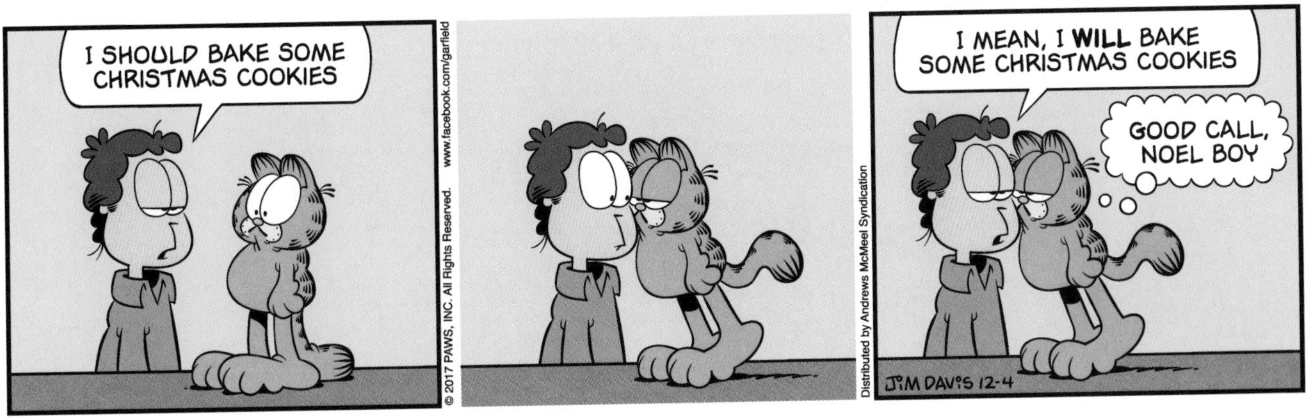
I SHOULD BAKE SOME CHRISTMAS COOKIES
© 2017 PAWS, INC. All Rights Reserved. www.facebook.com/garfield
Distributed by Andrews McMeel Syndication
I MEAN, I **WILL** BAKE SOME CHRISTMAS COOKIES
GOOD CALL, NOEL BOY
JIM DAVIS 12-4

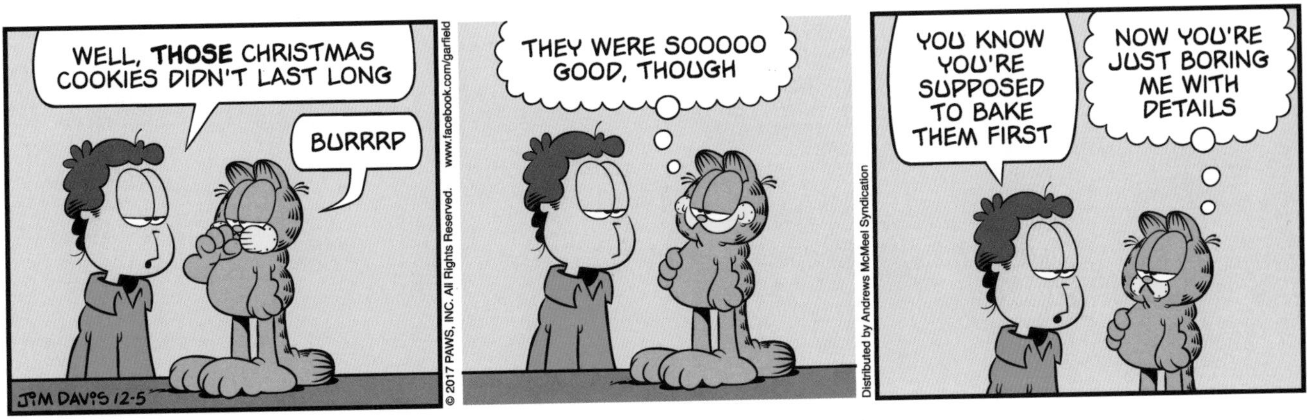
WELL, **THOSE** CHRISTMAS COOKIES DIDN'T LAST LONG
BURRRP
JIM DAVIS 12-5
© 2017 PAWS, INC. All Rights Reserved. www.facebook.com/garfield
THEY WERE SOOOOO GOOD, THOUGH
Distributed by Andrews McMeel Syndication
YOU KNOW YOU'RE SUPPOSED TO BAKE THEM FIRST
NOW YOU'RE JUST BORING ME WITH DETAILS

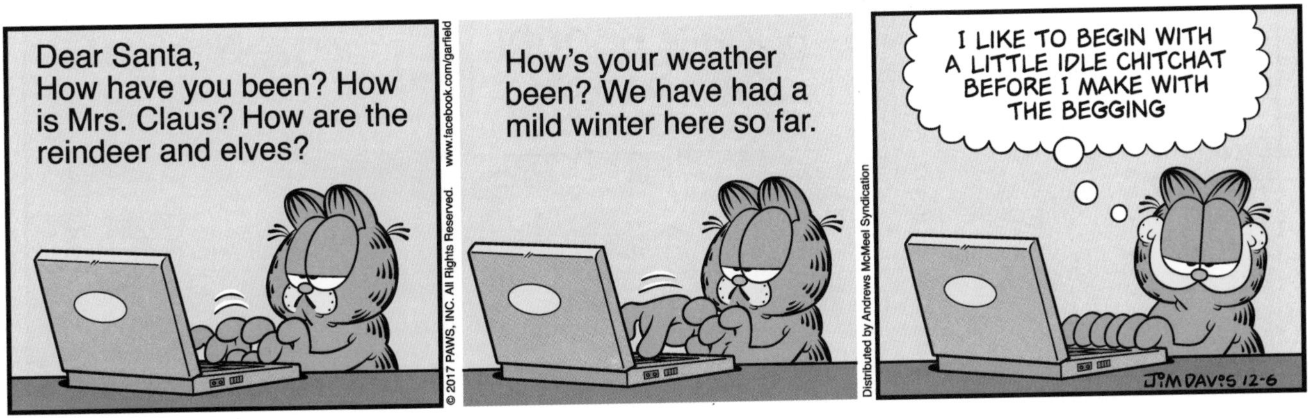
Dear Santa,
How have you been? How is Mrs. Claus? How are the reindeer and elves?
© 2017 PAWS, INC. All Rights Reserved. www.facebook.com/garfield
How's your weather been? We have had a mild winter here so far.
Distributed by Andrews McMeel Syndication
I LIKE TO BEGIN WITH A LITTLE IDLE CHITCHAT BEFORE I MAKE WITH THE BEGGING
JIM DAVIS 12-6

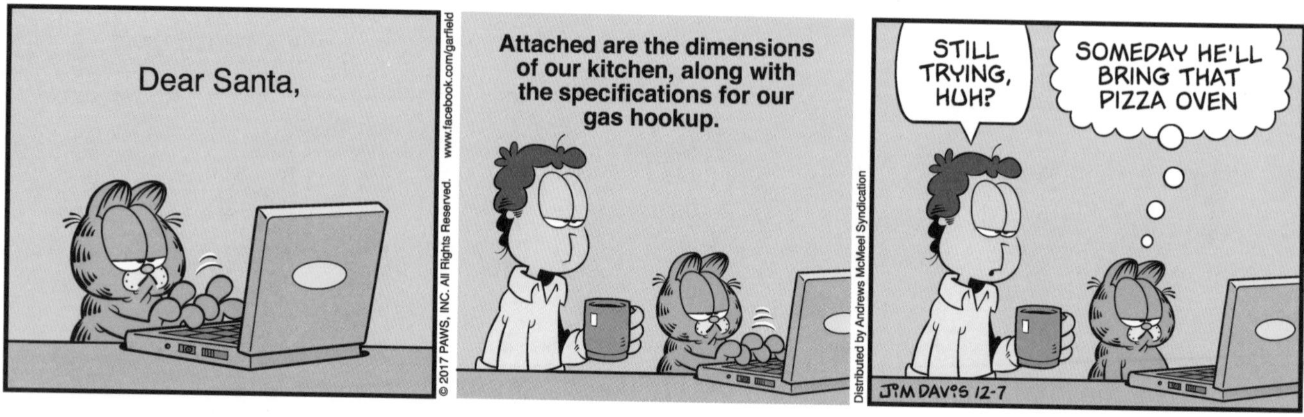
Dear Santa,
© 2017 PAWS, INC. All Rights Reserved. www.facebook.com/garfield
Attached are the dimensions of our kitchen, along with the specifications for our gas hookup.
Distributed by Andrews McMeel Syndication
STILL TRYING, HUH?
SOMEDAY HE'LL BRING THAT PIZZA OVEN
JIM DAVIS 12-7

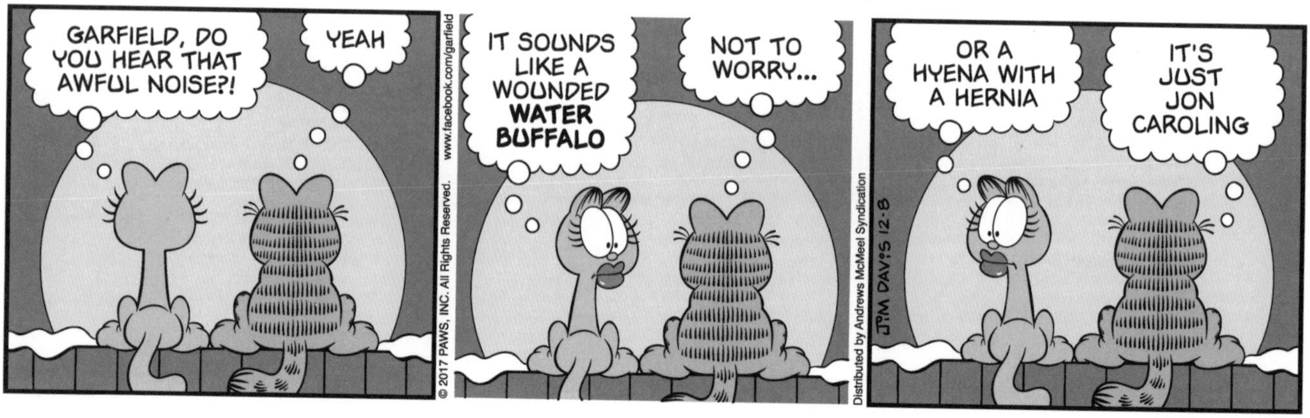
GARFIELD, DO YOU HEAR THAT AWFUL NOISE?!
YEAH
© 2017 PAWS, INC. All Rights Reserved. www.facebook.com/garfield
IT SOUNDS LIKE A WOUNDED WATER BUFFALO
NOT TO WORRY...
Distributed by Andrews McMeel Syndication
JIM DAVIS 12-8
OR A HYENA WITH A HERNIA
IT'S JUST JON CAROLING

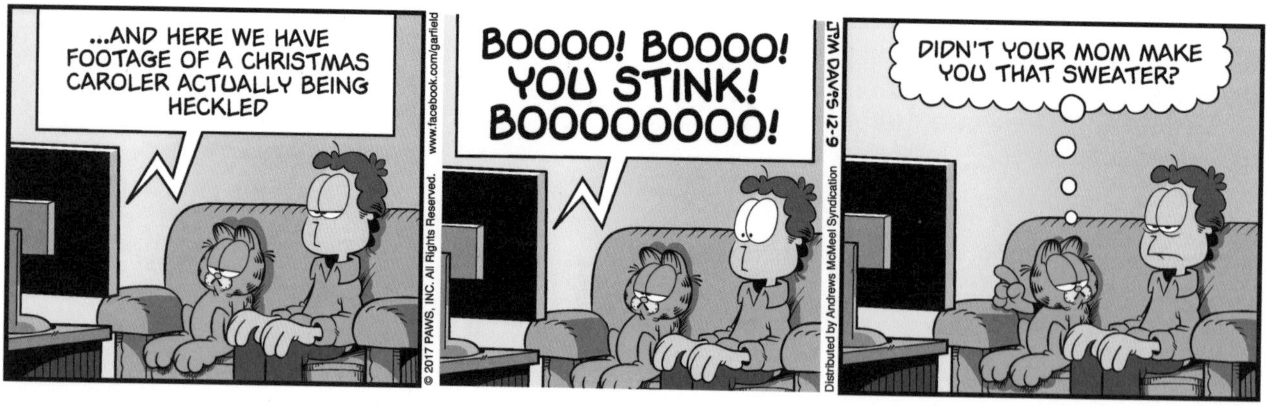
...AND HERE WE HAVE FOOTAGE OF A CHRISTMAS CAROLER ACTUALLY BEING HECKLED
© 2017 PAWS, INC. All Rights Reserved. www.facebook.com/garfield
BOOOO! BOOOO! YOU STINK! BOOOOOOOO!
JIM DAVIS 12-9
Distributed by Andrews McMeel Syndication
DIDN'T YOUR MOM MAKE YOU THAT SWEATER?

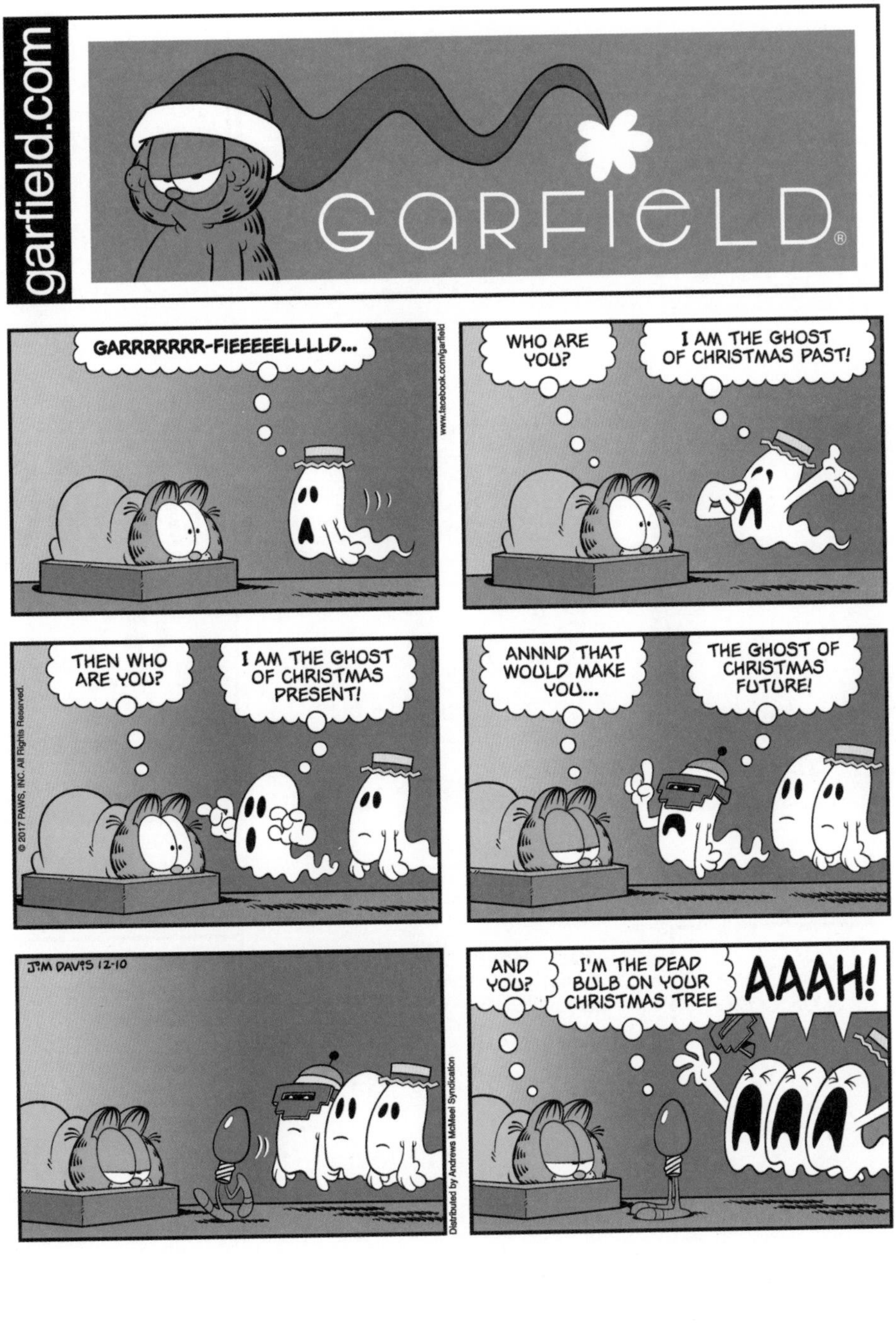
garfield.com
GARFIELD
GARRRRRRR-FIEEEEELLLLD...
www.facebook.com/garfield
WHO ARE YOU?
I AM THE GHOST OF CHRISTMAS PAST!
THEN WHO ARE YOU?
I AM THE GHOST OF CHRISTMAS PRESENT!
© 2017 PAWS, INC. All Rights Reserved.
ANNND THAT WOULD MAKE YOU...
THE GHOST OF CHRISTMAS FUTURE!
JIM DAVIS 12-10
Distributed by Andrews McMeel Syndication
AND YOU?
I'M THE DEAD BULB ON YOUR CHRISTMAS TREE
AAAH!

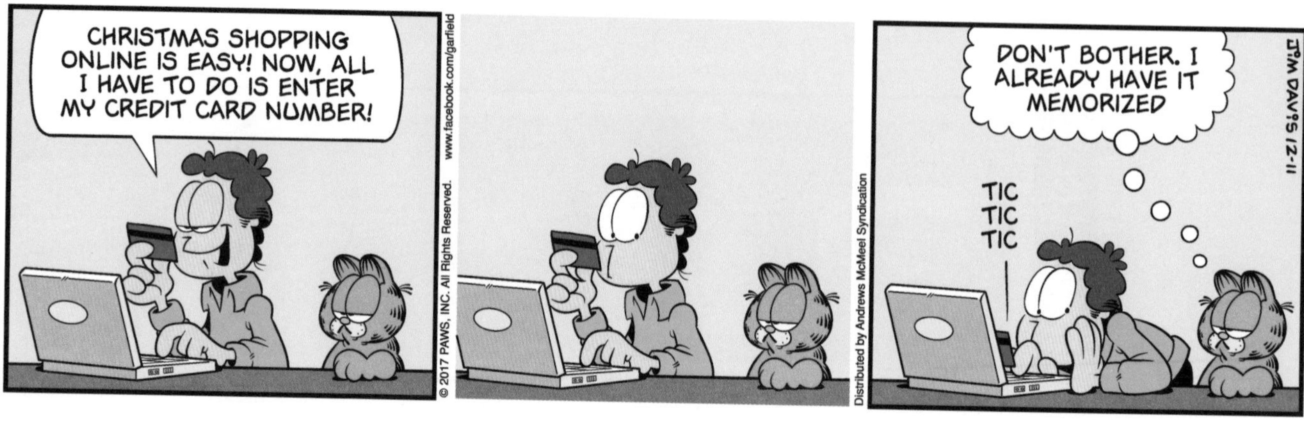
CHRISTMAS SHOPPING ONLINE IS EASY! NOW, ALL I HAVE TO DO IS ENTER MY CREDIT CARD NUMBER!
© 2017 PAWS, INC. All Rights Reserved. www.facebook.com/garfield
Distributed by Andrews McMeel Syndication
TIC TIC TIC
DON'T BOTHER. I ALREADY HAVE IT MEMORIZED
JIM DAVIS 12-11

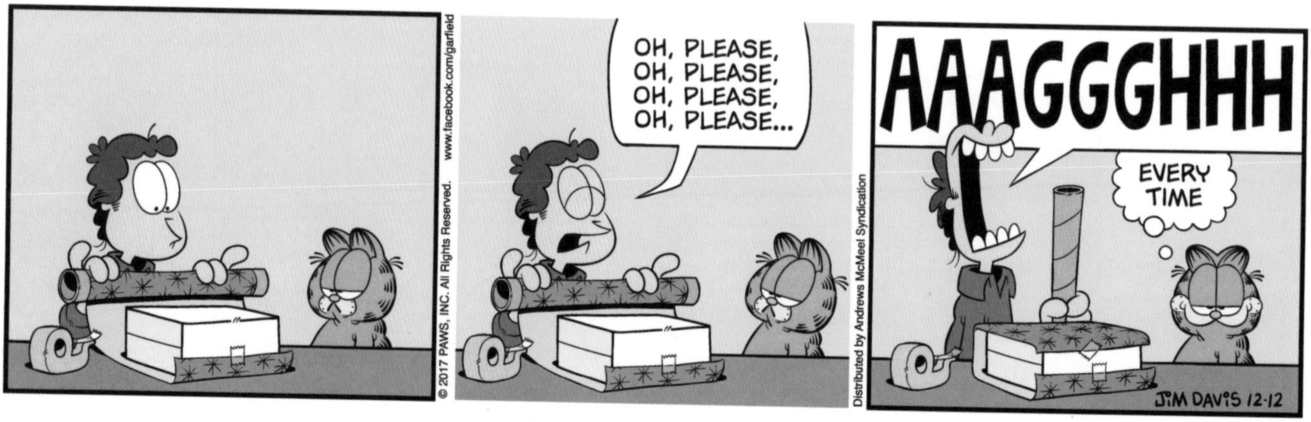
© 2017 PAWS, INC. All Rights Reserved. www.facebook.com/garfield
OH, PLEASE, OH, PLEASE, OH, PLEASE, OH, PLEASE...
Distributed by Andrews McMeel Syndication
AAAGGGHHH
EVERY TIME
JIM DAVIS 12-12

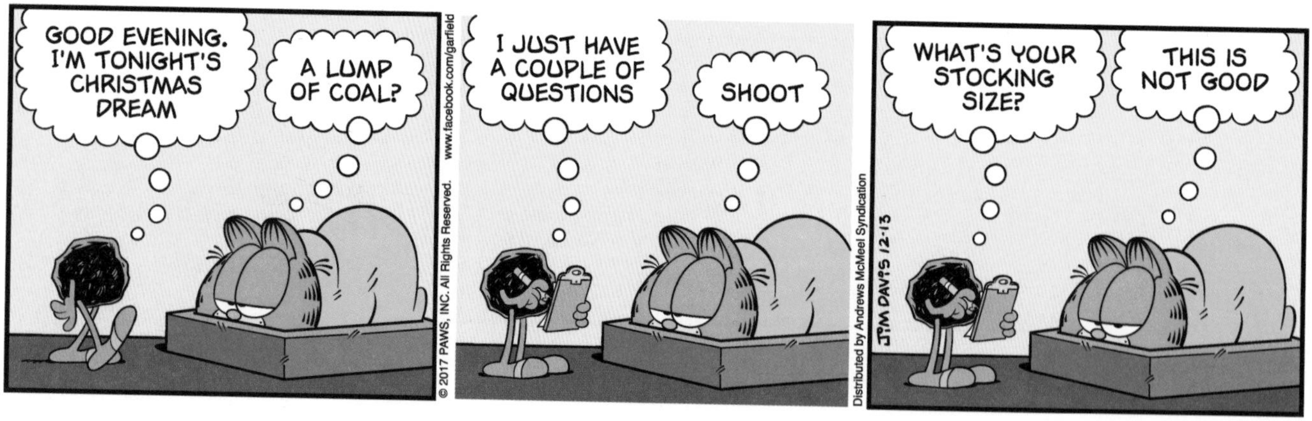
GOOD EVENING. I'M TONIGHT'S CHRISTMAS DREAM
A LUMP OF COAL?
© 2017 PAWS, INC. All Rights Reserved. www.facebook.com/garfield
I JUST HAVE A COUPLE OF QUESTIONS
SHOOT
Distributed by Andrews McMeel Syndication
JIM DAVIS 12-13
WHAT'S YOUR STOCKING SIZE?
THIS IS NOT GOOD

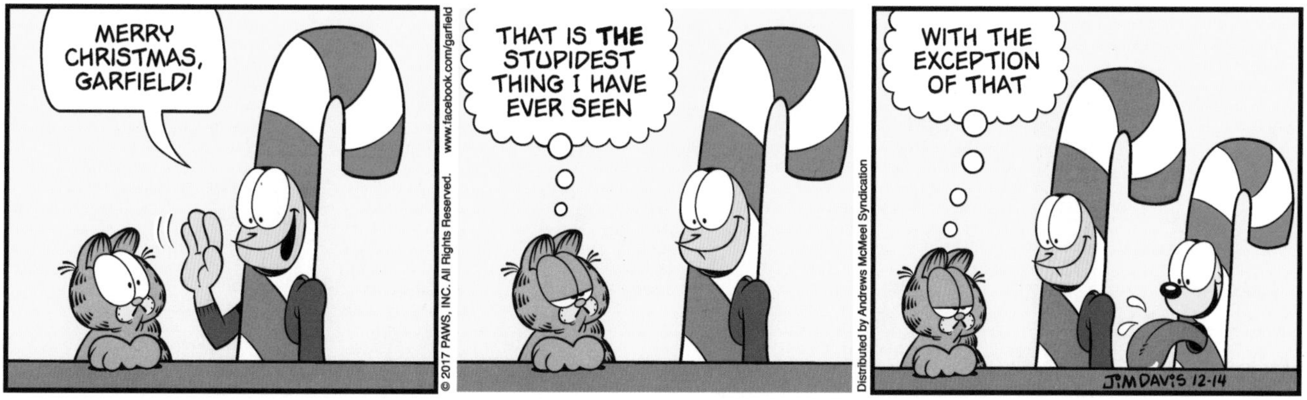
MERRY CHRISTMAS, GARFIELD!
THAT IS **THE** STUPIDEST THING I HAVE EVER SEEN
WITH THE EXCEPTION OF THAT
JIM DAVIS 12-14
© 2017 PAWS, INC. All Rights Reserved. www.facebook.com/garfield
Distributed by Andrews McMeel Syndication

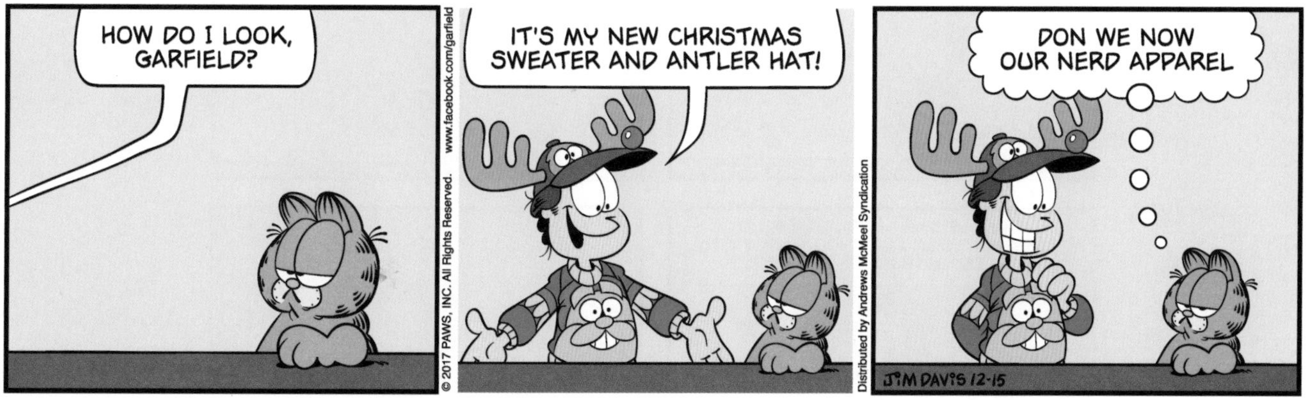
HOW DO I LOOK, GARFIELD?
IT'S MY NEW CHRISTMAS SWEATER AND ANTLER HAT!
DON WE NOW OUR NERD APPAREL
JIM DAVIS 12-15
© 2017 PAWS, INC. All Rights Reserved. www.facebook.com/garfield
Distributed by Andrews McMeel Syndication

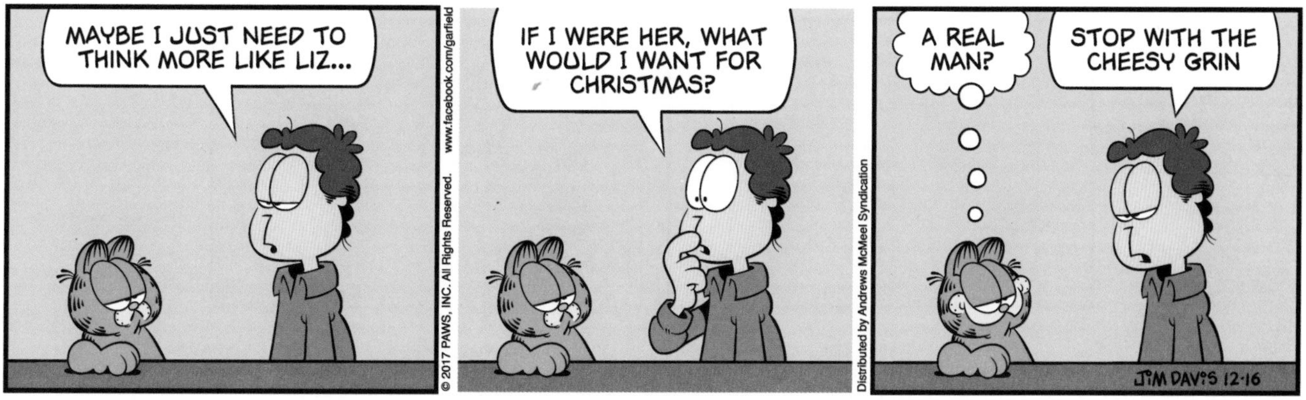
MAYBE I JUST NEED TO THINK MORE LIKE LIZ...
IF I WERE HER, WHAT WOULD I WANT FOR CHRISTMAS?
A REAL MAN?
STOP WITH THE CHEESY GRIN
JIM DAVIS 12-16
© 2017 PAWS, INC. All Rights Reserved. www.facebook.com/garfield
Distributed by Andrews McMeel Syndication

garfield.com
Garfield®
I DON'T KNOW WHAT TO GET YOU FOR CHRISTMAS, LIZ
OH, JON, YOU DON'T HAVE TO GET ME ANYTHING
www.facebook.com/garfield
YOU TELL ME THAT EVERY YEAR! AND THEN YOU GO OUT AND GET **ME** SOMETHING **REALLY** NICE, AND I FEEL LIKE A HORRIBLE BOYFRIEND!
I BET YOU'VE ALREADY DONE IT, HAVEN'T YOU?! I BET YOU'VE GOTTEN ME SOMETHING REALLY NICE!
© 2017 PAWS, INC. All Rights Reserved.
HAVEN'T YOU?
YES
Distributed by Andrews McMeel Syndication
YOU'RE EVIL
I LOVE YOU, TOO
JIM DAVIS 12-17

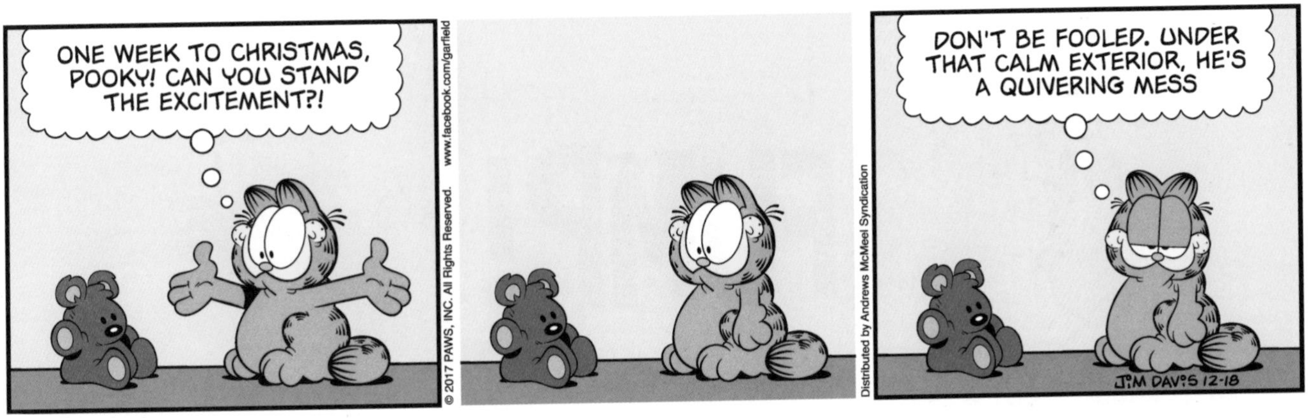
ONE WEEK TO CHRISTMAS, POOKY! CAN YOU STAND THE EXCITEMENT?!
DON'T BE FOOLED. UNDER THAT CALM EXTERIOR, HE'S A QUIVERING MESS
JIM DAVIS 12-18
© 2017 PAWS, INC. All Rights Reserved. www.facebook.com/garfield
Distributed by Andrews McMeel Syndication

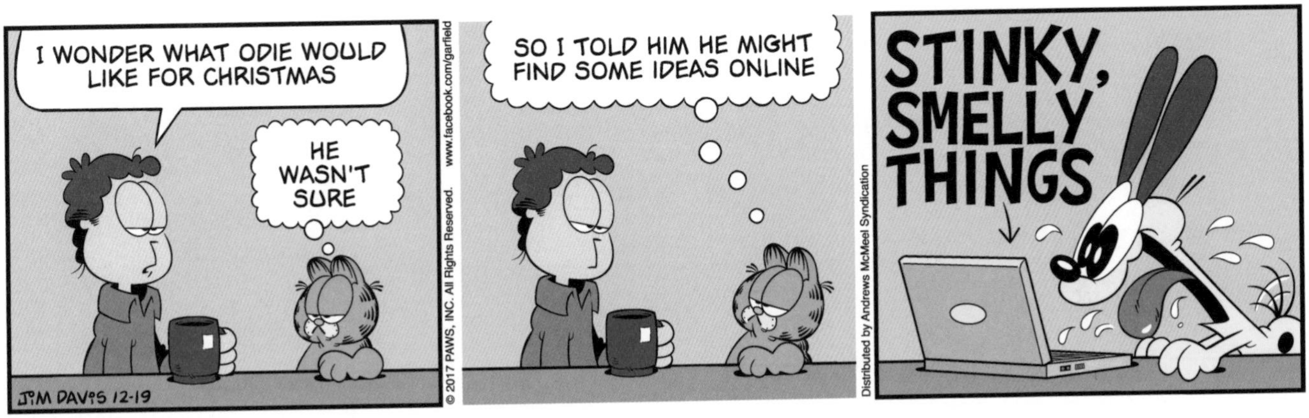
I WONDER WHAT ODIE WOULD LIKE FOR CHRISTMAS
HE WASN'T SURE
SO I TOLD HIM HE MIGHT FIND SOME IDEAS ONLINE
STINKY, SMELLY THINGS
JIM DAVIS 12-19
© 2017 PAWS, INC. All Rights Reserved. www.facebook.com/garfield
Distributed by Andrews McMeel Syndication

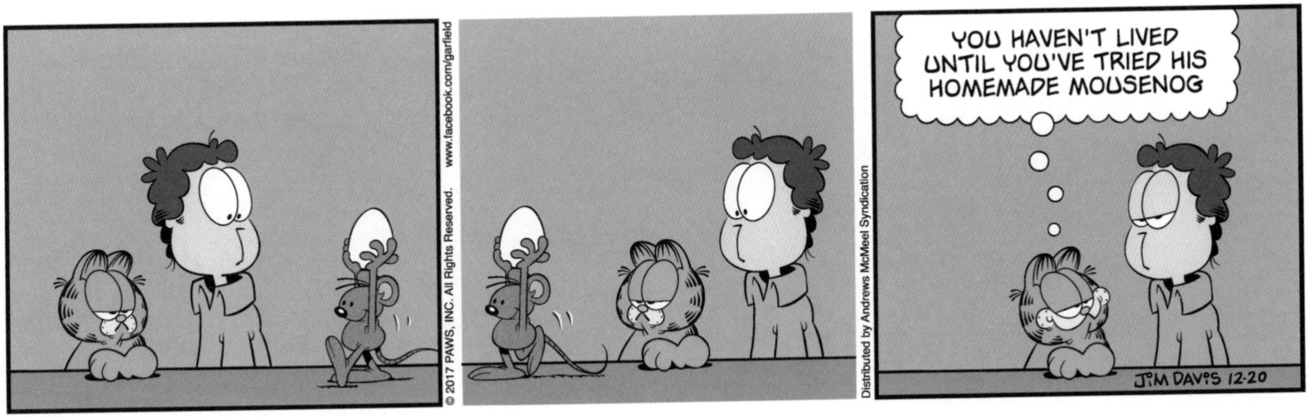
YOU HAVEN'T LIVED UNTIL YOU'VE TRIED HIS HOMEMADE MOUSENOG
JIM DAVIS 12-20
© 2017 PAWS, INC. All Rights Reserved. www.facebook.com/garfield
Distributed by Andrews McMeel Syndication

garfield.com
GARFIELD®
www.facebook.com/garfield
© 2017 PAWS, INC. All Rights Reserved.
WOO-HOO!
Distributed by Andrews McMeel Syndication
JIM DAVIS 12-24

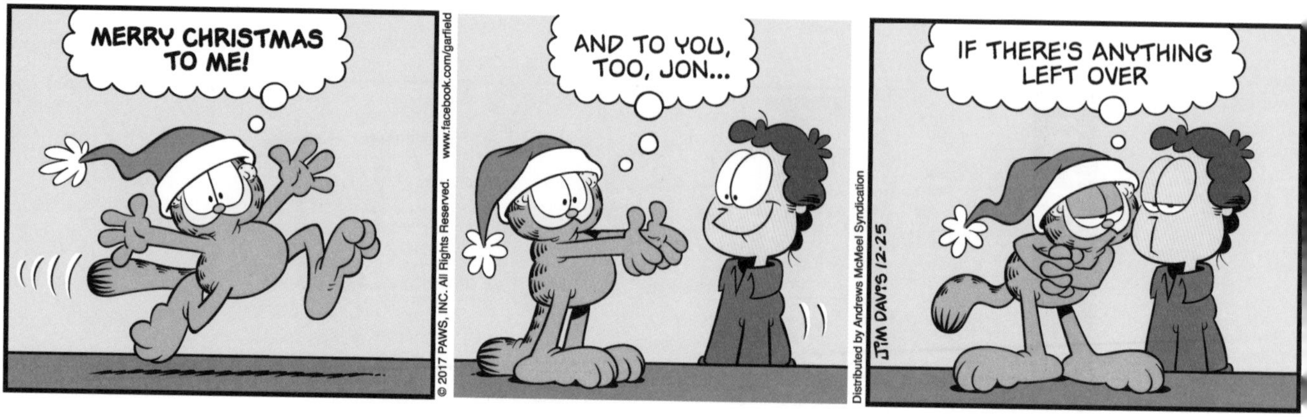
MERRY CHRISTMAS TO ME!
AND TO YOU, TOO, JON...
IF THERE'S ANYTHING LEFT OVER
JIM DAVIS 12-25
© 2017 PAWS, INC. All Rights Reserved. www.facebook.com/garfield
Distributed by Andrews McMeel Syndication

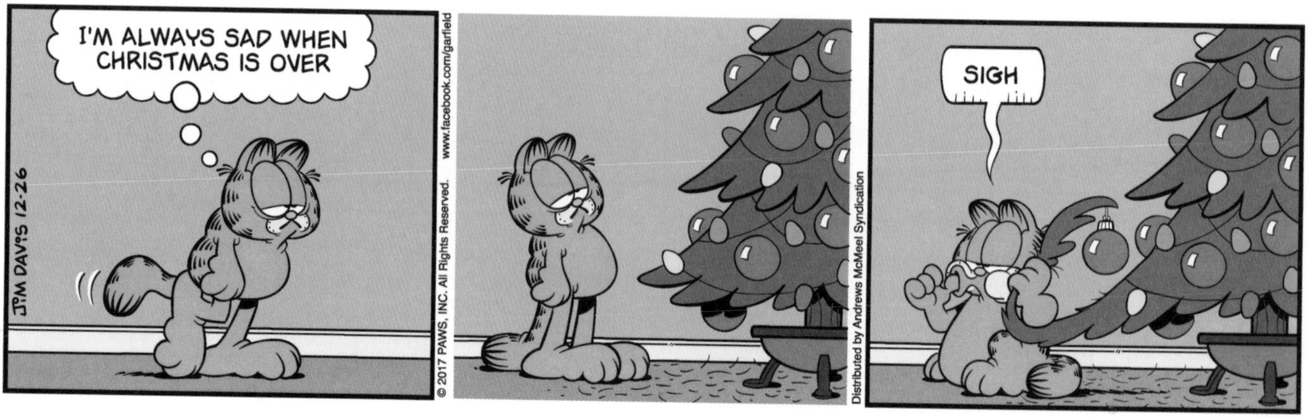
I'M ALWAYS SAD WHEN CHRISTMAS IS OVER
SIGH
JIM DAVIS 12-26
© 2017 PAWS, INC. All Rights Reserved. www.facebook.com/garfield
Distributed by Andrews McMeel Syndication

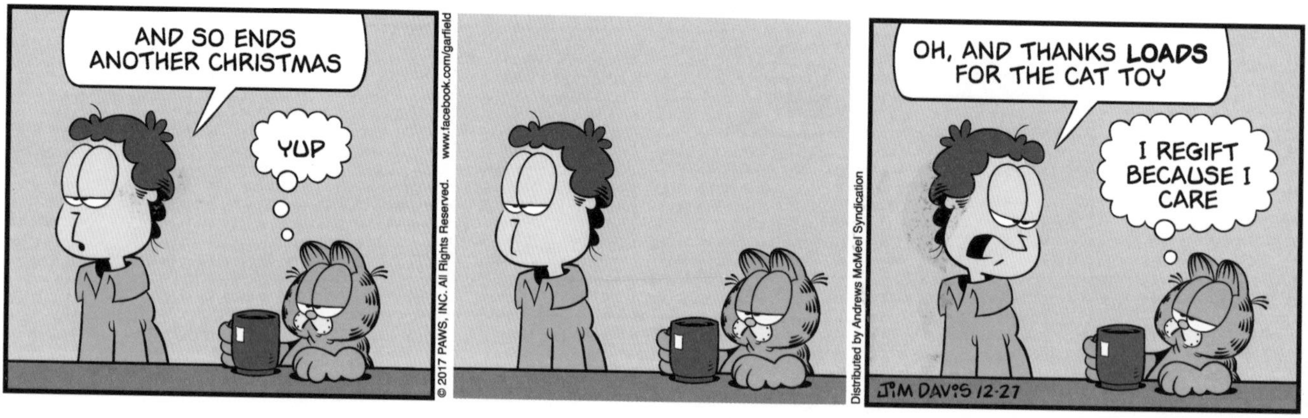
AND SO ENDS ANOTHER CHRISTMAS
YUP
OH, AND THANKS LOADS FOR THE CAT TOY
I REGIFT BECAUSE I CARE
JIM DAVIS 12-27
© 2017 PAWS, INC. All Rights Reserved. www.facebook.com/garfield
Distributed by Andrews McMeel Syndication

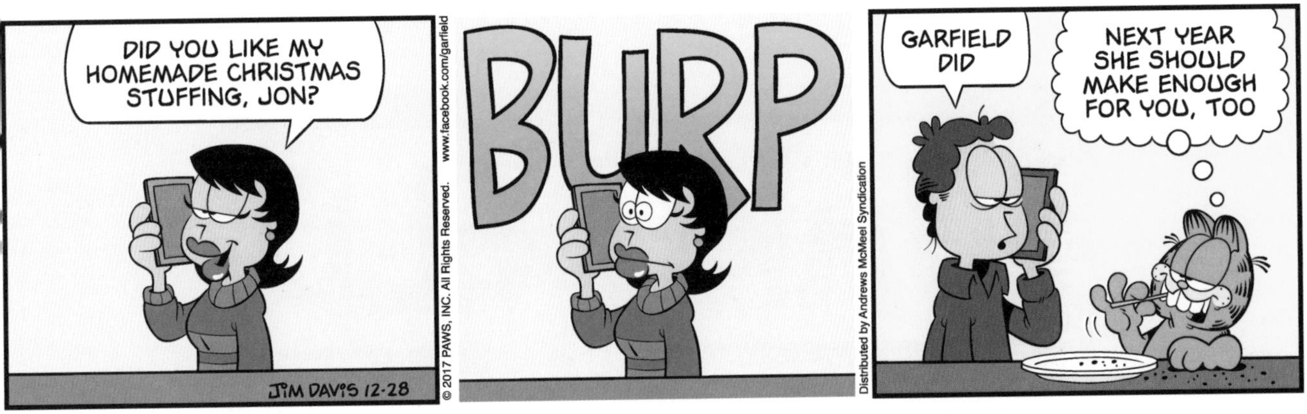
DID YOU LIKE MY HOMEMADE CHRISTMAS STUFFING, JON?
JIM DAVIS 12-28
© 2017 PAWS, INC. All Rights Reserved. www.facebook.com/garfield
BURP
Distributed by Andrews McMeel Syndication
GARFIELD DID
NEXT YEAR SHE SHOULD MAKE ENOUGH FOR YOU, TOO

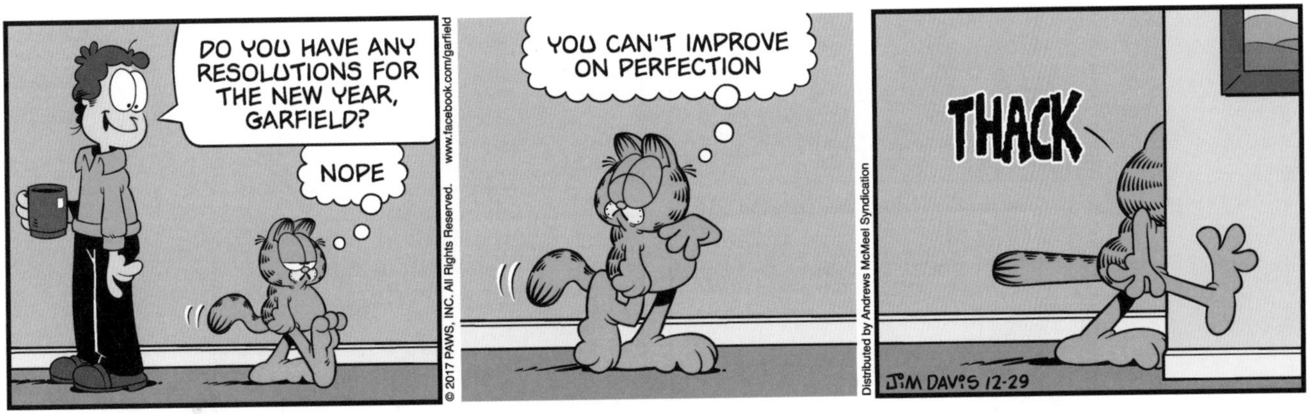
DO YOU HAVE ANY RESOLUTIONS FOR THE NEW YEAR, GARFIELD?
NOPE
© 2017 PAWS, INC. All Rights Reserved. www.facebook.com/garfield
YOU CAN'T IMPROVE ON PERFECTION
Distributed by Andrews McMeel Syndication
THACK
JIM DAVIS 12-29

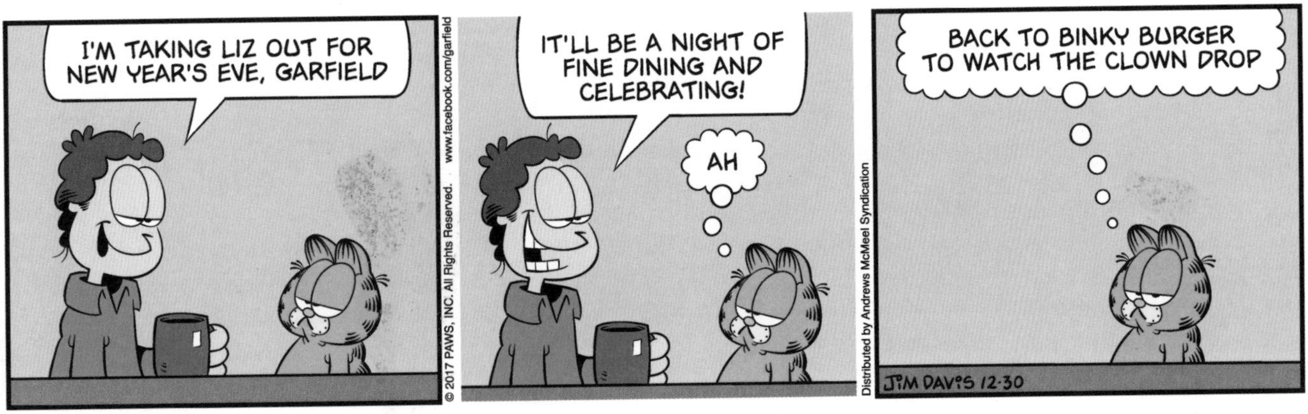
I'M TAKING LIZ OUT FOR NEW YEAR'S EVE, GARFIELD
© 2017 PAWS, INC. All Rights Reserved. www.facebook.com/garfield
IT'LL BE A NIGHT OF FINE DINING AND CELEBRATING!
AH
Distributed by Andrews McMeel Syndication
BACK TO BINKY BURGER TO WATCH THE CLOWN DROP
JIM DAVIS 12-30

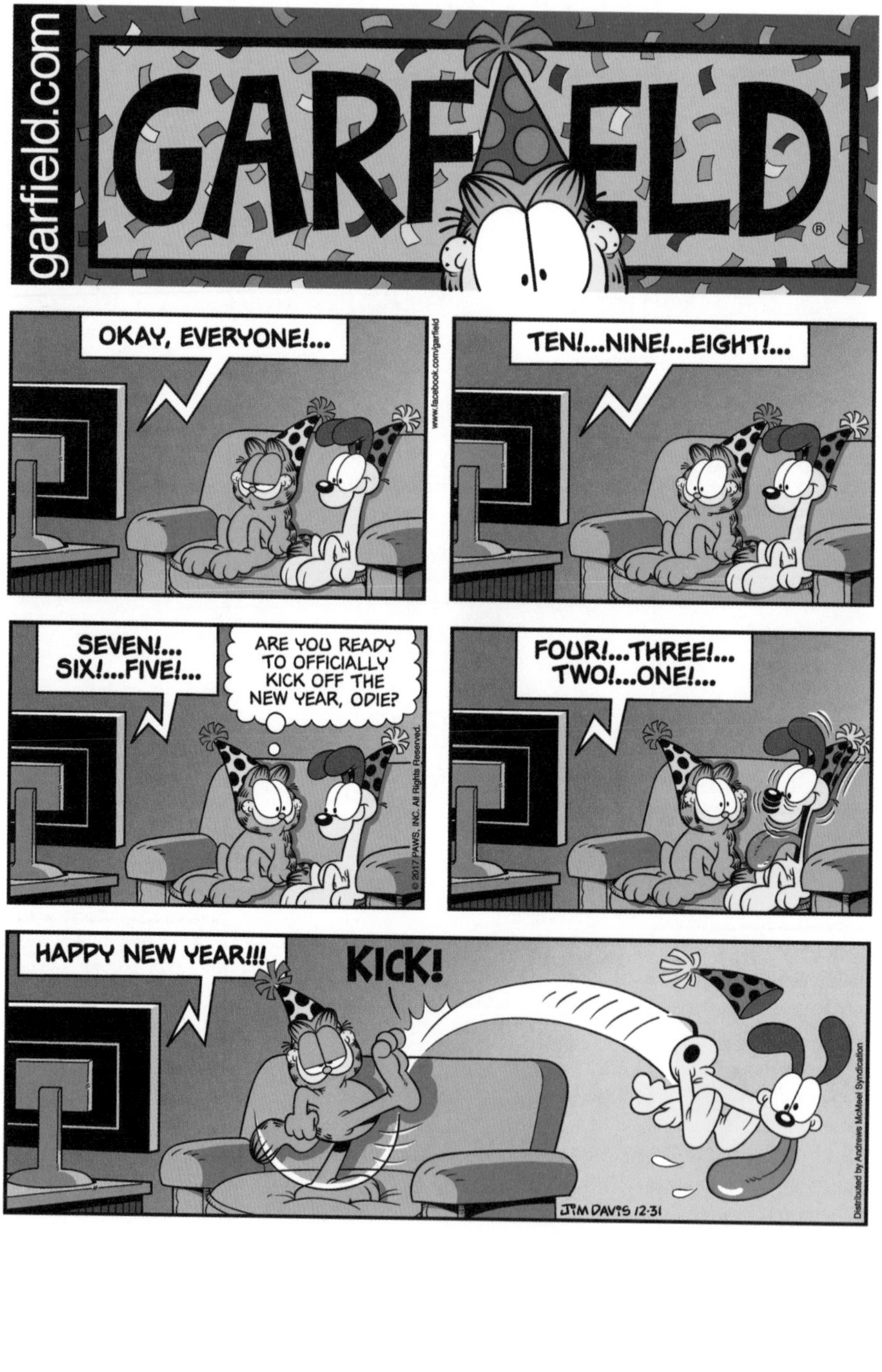
garfield.com
GARFIELD
www.facebook.com/garfield
OKAY, EVERYONE!...
TEN!...NINE!...EIGHT!...
SEVEN!... SIX!...FIVE!...
ARE YOU READY TO OFFICIALLY KICK OFF THE NEW YEAR, ODIE?
© 2017 PAWS, INC. All Rights Reserved.
FOUR!...THREE!... TWO!...ONE!...
HAPPY NEW YEAR!!!
KICK!
JIM DAVIS 12-31
Distributed by Andrews McMeel Syndication

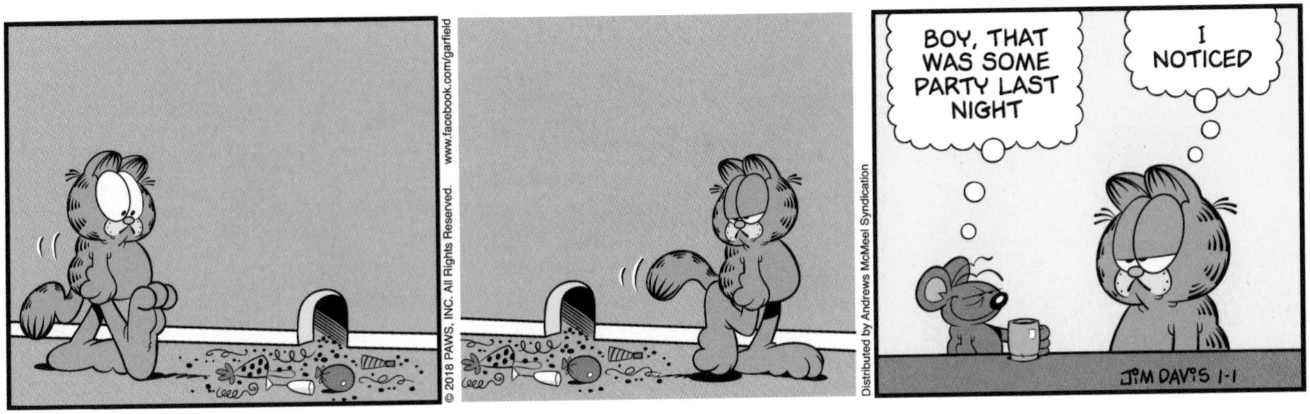
© 2018 PAWS, INC. All Rights Reserved. www.facebook.com/garfield
Distributed by Andrews McMeel Syndication
BOY, THAT WAS SOME PARTY LAST NIGHT
I NOTICED
JIM DAVIS 1-1

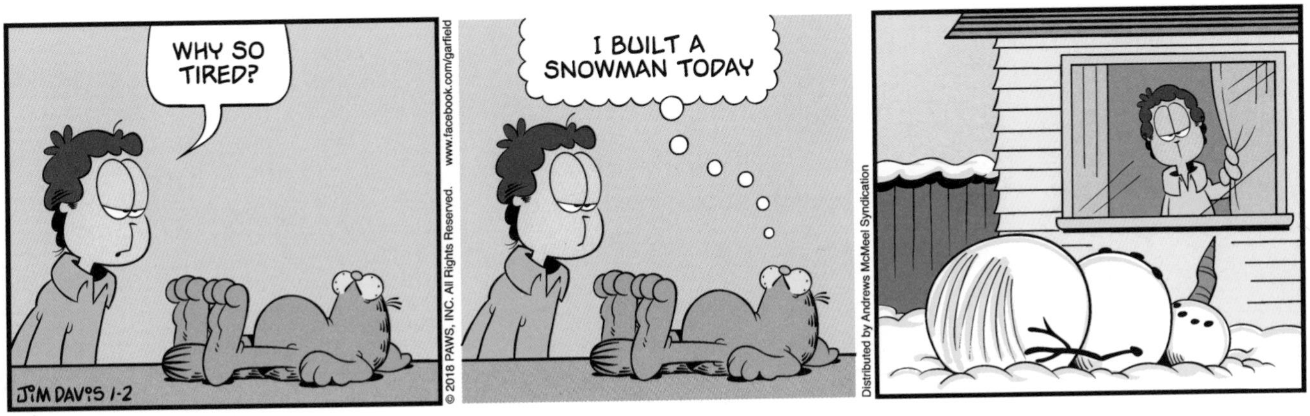
WHY SO TIRED?
JIM DAVIS 1-2
© 2018 PAWS, INC. All Rights Reserved. www.facebook.com/garfield
I BUILT A SNOWMAN TODAY
Distributed by Andrews McMeel Syndication

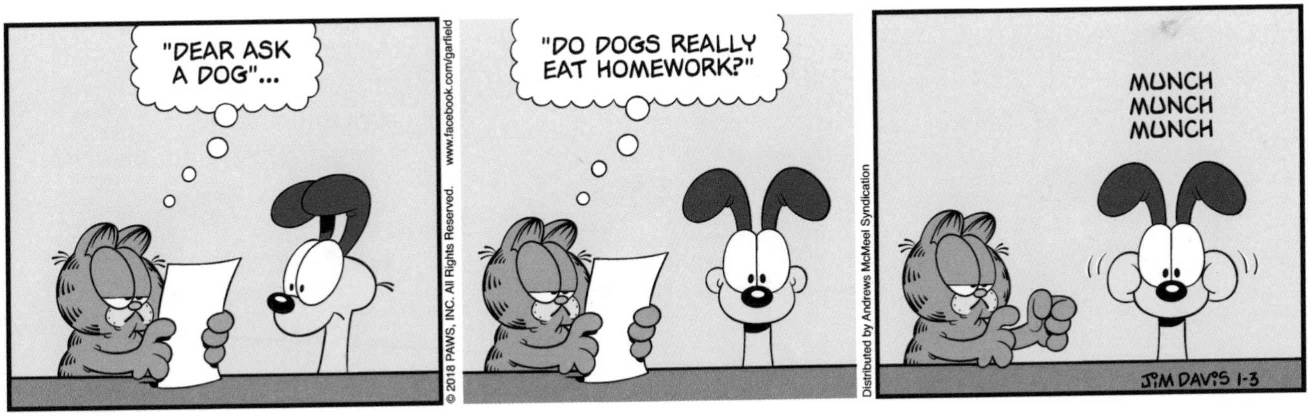
"DEAR ASK A DOG"...
© 2018 PAWS, INC. All Rights Reserved. www.facebook.com/garfield
"DO DOGS REALLY EAT HOMEWORK?"
Distributed by Andrews McMeel Syndication
MUNCH
MUNCH
MUNCH
JIM DAVIS 1-3

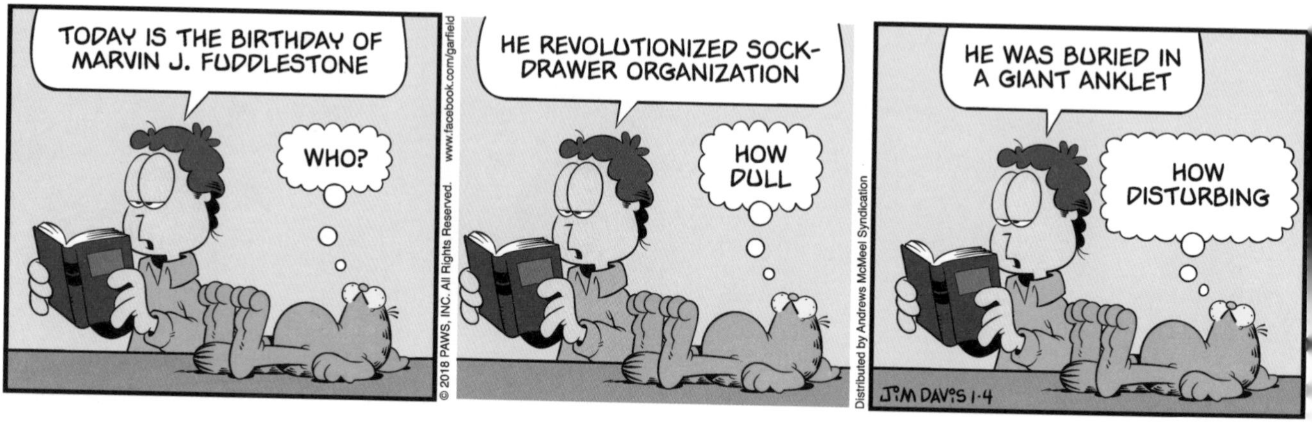
TODAY IS THE BIRTHDAY OF MARVIN J. FUDDLESTONE
WHO?
HE REVOLUTIONIZED SOCK-DRAWER ORGANIZATION
HOW DULL
HE WAS BURIED IN A GIANT ANKLET
HOW DISTURBING
JIM DAVIS 1-4


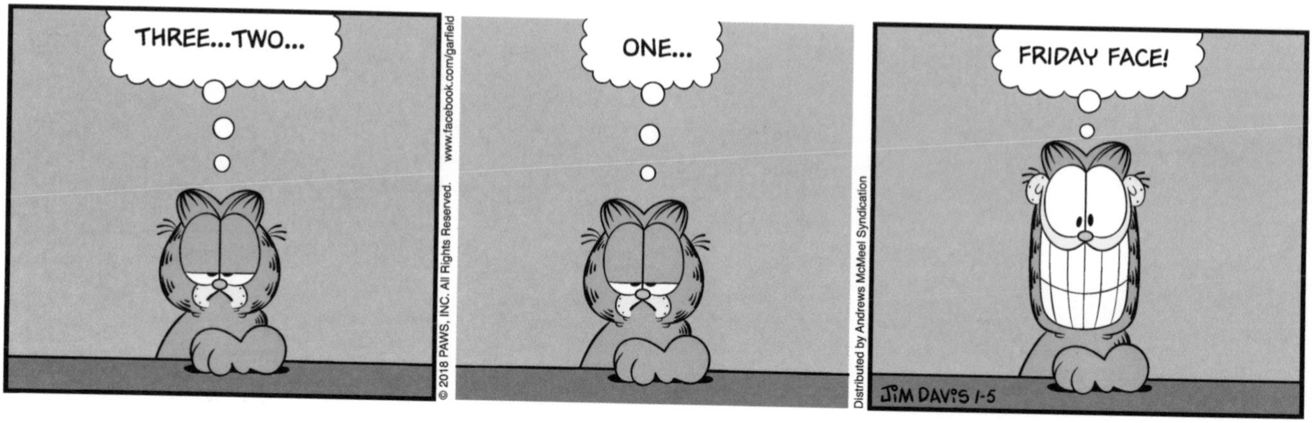
THREE...TWO...
ONE...
FRIDAY FACE!
JIM DAVIS 1-5


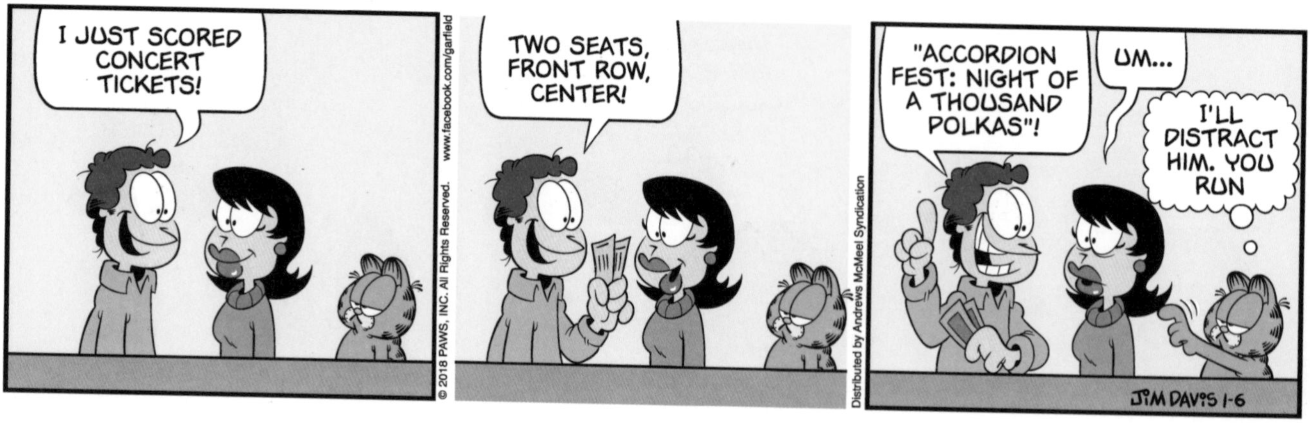
I JUST SCORED CONCERT TICKETS!
TWO SEATS, FRONT ROW, CENTER!
"ACCORDION FEST: NIGHT OF A THOUSAND POLKAS"!
UM...
I'LL DISTRACT HIM. YOU RUN
JIM DAVIS 1-6

garfield.com
GARFIELD
www.facebook.com/garfield
NO CATS ALLOWED
NONE
© 2018 PAWS, INC. All Rights Reserved.
THIS MEANS YOU!
HEY!
OKAY, OKAY
Distributed by Andrews McMeel Syndication
JUST ONE
JIM DAVIS 1-7

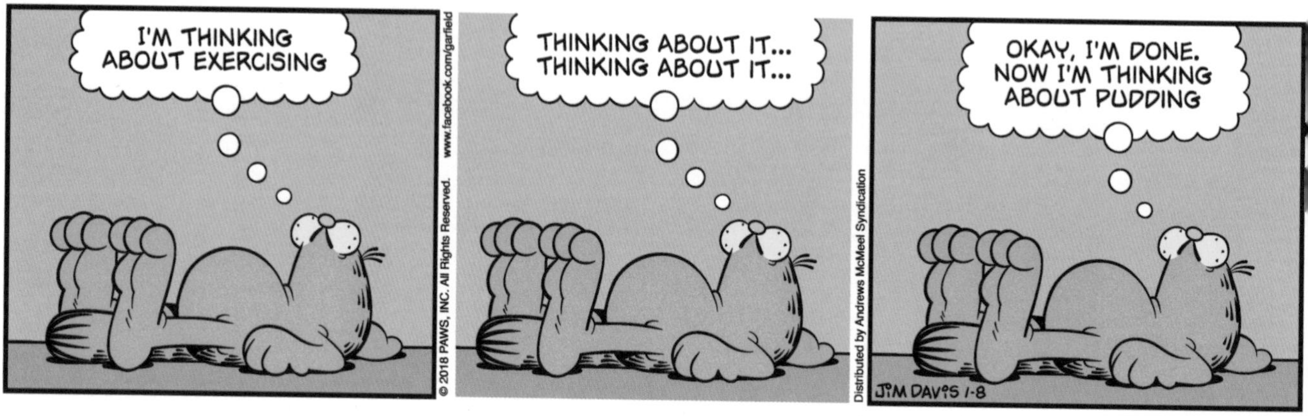
I'M THINKING ABOUT EXERCISING
© 2018 PAWS, INC. All Rights Reserved. www.facebook.com/garfield
THINKING ABOUT IT... THINKING ABOUT IT...
Distributed by Andrews McMeel Syndication
OKAY, I'M DONE. NOW I'M THINKING ABOUT PUDDING
JIM DAVIS 1-8

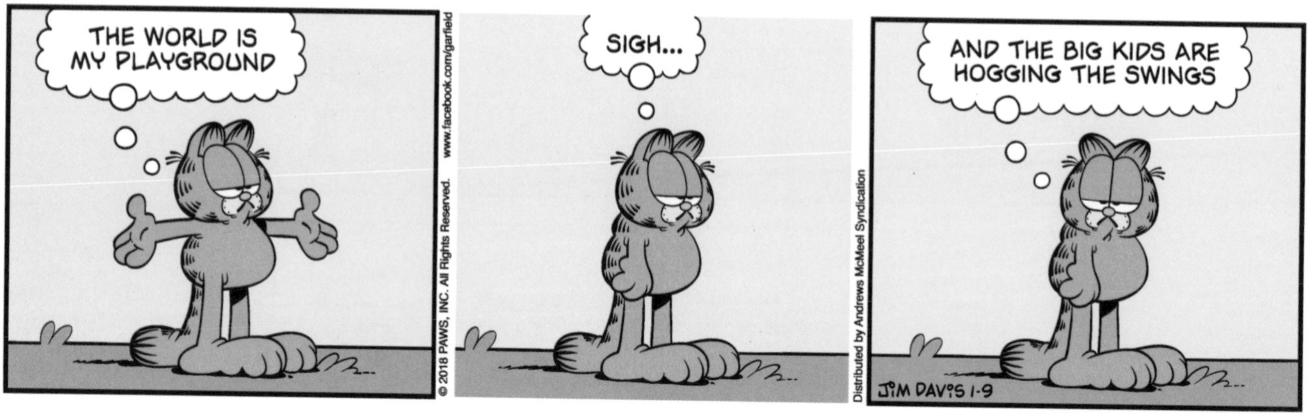
THE WORLD IS MY PLAYGROUND
© 2018 PAWS, INC. All Rights Reserved. www.facebook.com/garfield
SIGH...
Distributed by Andrews McMeel Syndication
AND THE BIG KIDS ARE HOGGING THE SWINGS
JIM DAVIS 1-9

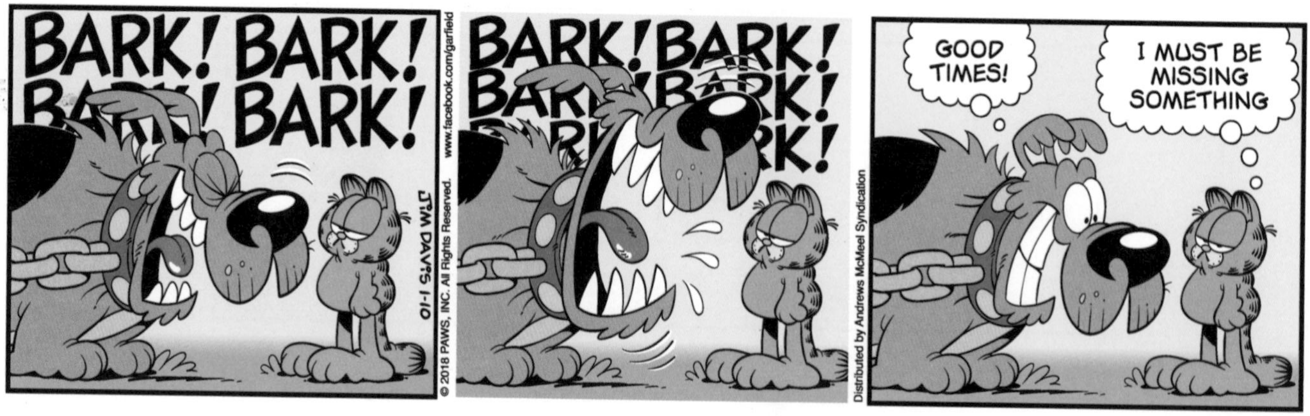
BARK! BARK!
BARK!
JIM DAVIS 1-10
© 2018 PAWS, INC. All Rights Reserved. www.facebook.com/garfield
BARK! BARK!
K!
Distributed by Andrews McMeel Syndication
GOOD TIMES!
I MUST BE MISSING SOMETHING

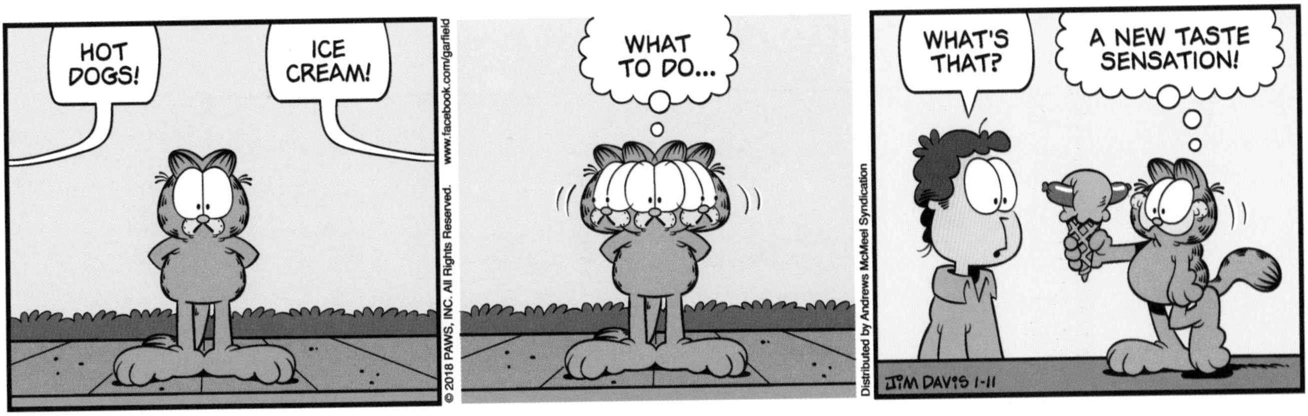
HOT DOGS!
ICE CREAM!
© 2018 PAWS, INC. All Rights Reserved. www.facebook.com/garfield
WHAT TO DO...
Distributed by Andrews McMeel Syndication
WHAT'S THAT?
A NEW TASTE SENSATION!
JIM DAVIS 1-11

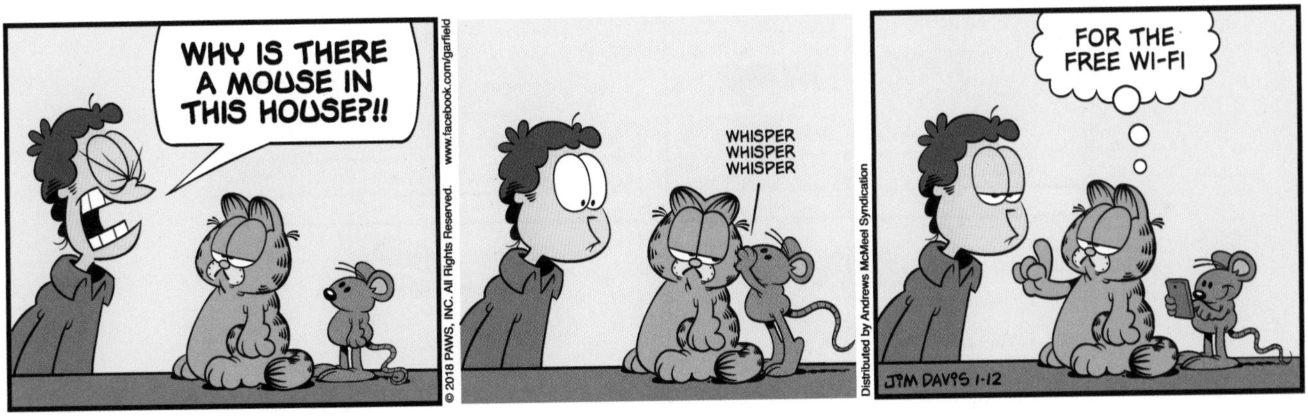
WHY IS THERE A MOUSE IN THIS HOUSE?!!
© 2018 PAWS, INC. All Rights Reserved. www.facebook.com/garfield
WHISPER WHISPER WHISPER
Distributed by Andrews McMeel Syndication
FOR THE FREE WI-FI
JIM DAVIS 1-12

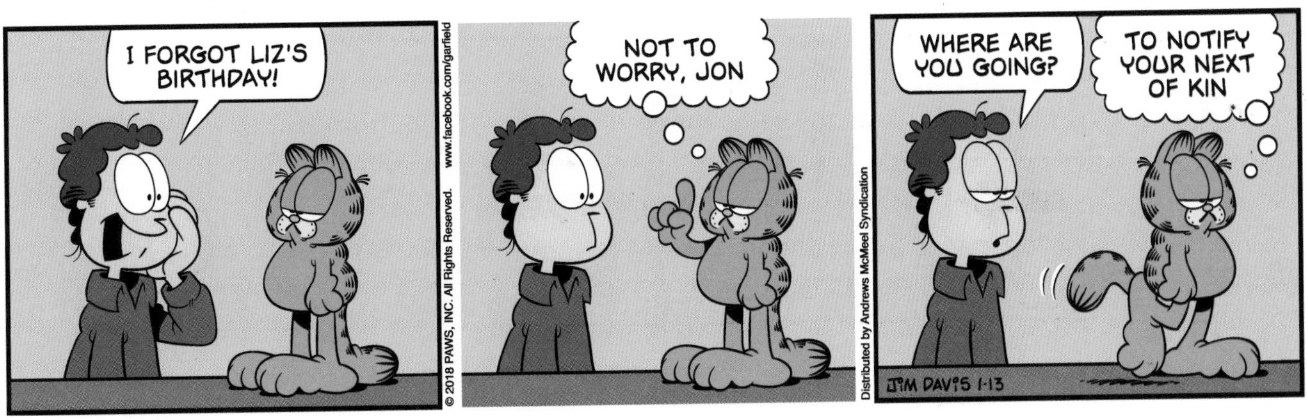
I FORGOT LIZ'S BIRTHDAY!
© 2018 PAWS, INC. All Rights Reserved. www.facebook.com/garfield
NOT TO WORRY, JON
Distributed by Andrews McMeel Syndication
WHERE ARE YOU GOING?
TO NOTIFY YOUR NEXT OF KIN
JIM DAVIS 1-13

garfield.com
Garfield
www.facebook.com/garfield
© 2018 PAWS, INC. All Rights Reserved.
FUN WITH RULE FOLLOWERS
Distributed by Andrews McMeel Syndication
JIM DAVIS 1-14

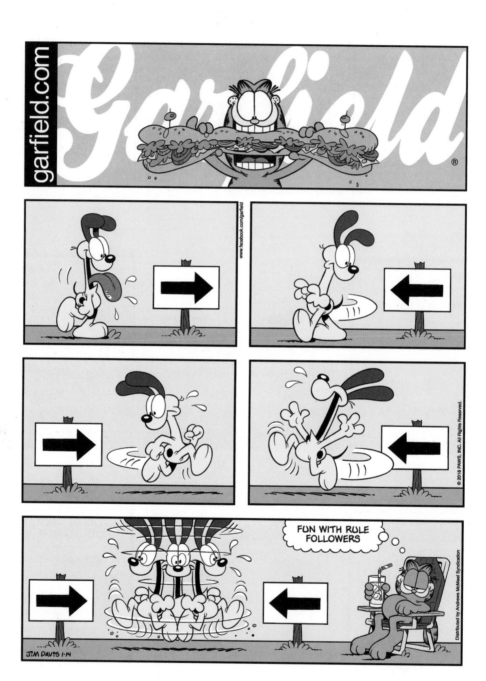

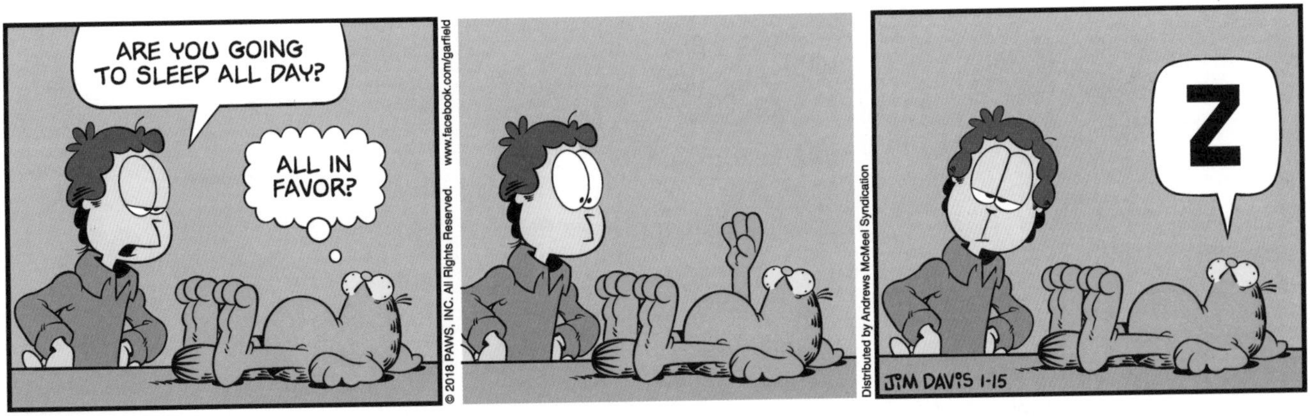
ARE YOU GOING TO SLEEP ALL DAY?
ALL IN FAVOR?
Z
JIM DAVIS 1-15
© 2018 PAWS, INC. All Rights Reserved. www.facebook.com/garfield
Distributed by Andrews McMeel Syndication

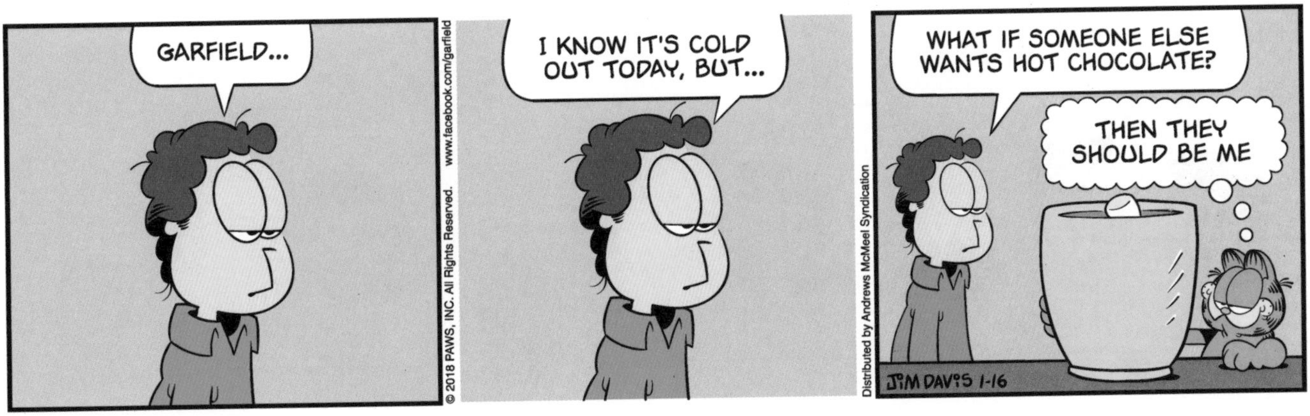
GARFIELD...
I KNOW IT'S COLD OUT TODAY, BUT...
WHAT IF SOMEONE ELSE WANTS HOT CHOCOLATE?
THEN THEY SHOULD BE ME
JIM DAVIS 1-16
© 2018 PAWS, INC. All Rights Reserved. www.facebook.com/garfield
Distributed by Andrews McMeel Syndication

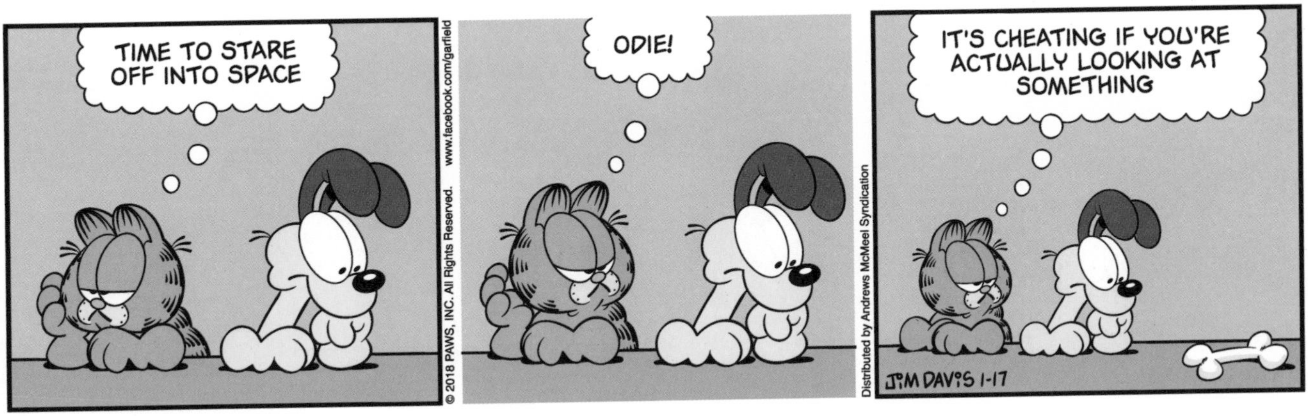
TIME TO STARE OFF INTO SPACE
ODIE!
IT'S CHEATING IF YOU'RE ACTUALLY LOOKING AT SOMETHING
JIM DAVIS 1-17
© 2018 PAWS, INC. All Rights Reserved. www.facebook.com/garfield
Distributed by Andrews McMeel Syndication

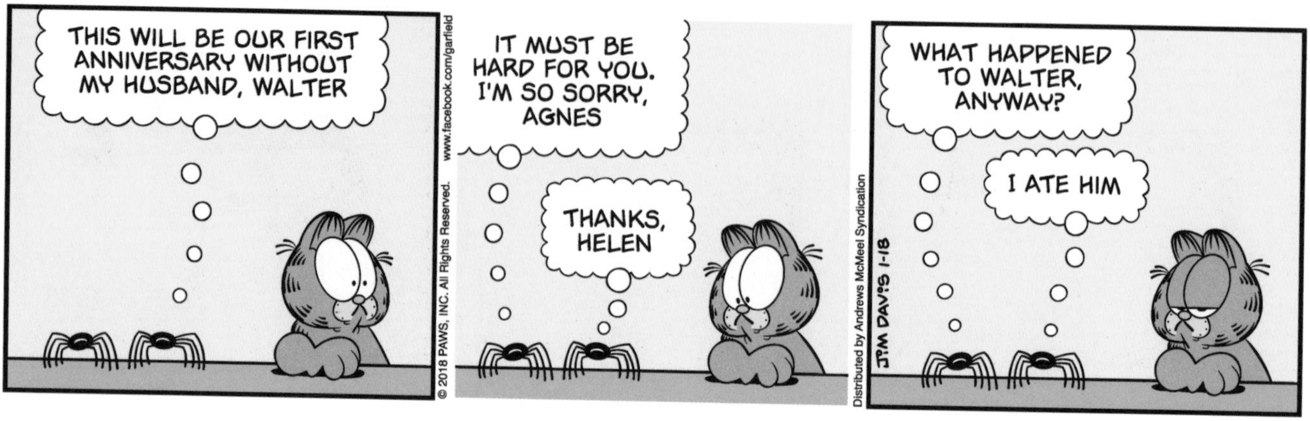
THIS WILL BE OUR FIRST ANNIVERSARY WITHOUT MY HUSBAND, WALTER
IT MUST BE HARD FOR YOU. I'M SO SORRY, AGNES
THANKS, HELEN
WHAT HAPPENED TO WALTER, ANYWAY?
I ATE HIM
JIM DAVIS 1-18
© 2018 PAWS, INC. All Rights Reserved. www.facebook.com/garfield
Distributed by Andrews McMeel Syndication

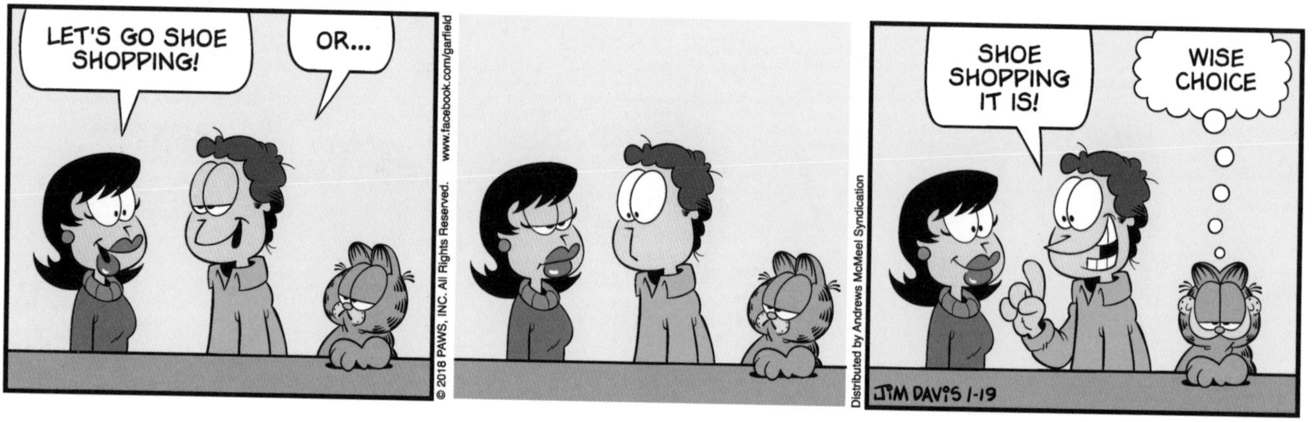
LET'S GO SHOE SHOPPING!
OR...
SHOE SHOPPING IT IS!
WISE CHOICE
JIM DAVIS 1-19
© 2018 PAWS, INC. All Rights Reserved. www.facebook.com/garfield
Distributed by Andrews McMeel Syndication

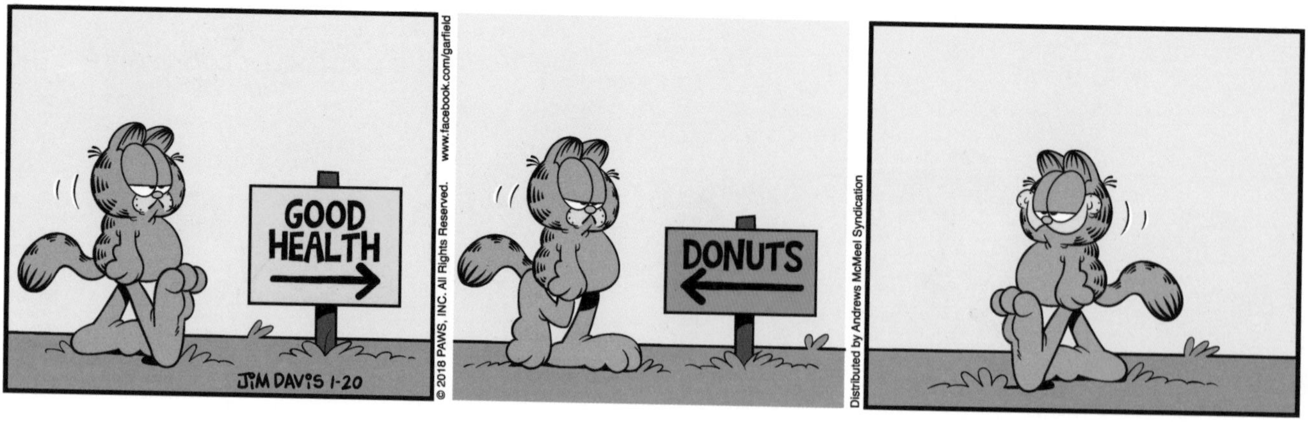
GOOD HEALTH
DONUTS
JIM DAVIS 1-20
© 2018 PAWS, INC. All Rights Reserved. www.facebook.com/garfield
Distributed by Andrews McMeel Syndication

garfield.com
DRUM COOKIES
GARFIELD
HEY! YOU CALL THAT "JUST SITTING THERE"?!
www.facebook.com/garfield
YOU DON'T LOOK **NEARLY** BORED ENOUGH, MISTER!
I'D LIKE TO SEE SOMETHING MORE ALONG **THESE** LINES...
© 2018 PAWS, INC. All Rights Reserved.
AND FOR PETE'S SAKE, **SLOUCH!**
THERE! THAT'S MORE LIKE IT!
JIM DAVIS 1-21
Distributed by Andrews McMeel Syndication
IT'S TOUGH LIVING WITH A CAT WITH SUCH LOW STANDARDS
ODIE! YOU CALL THAT DRINKING OUT OF THE TOILET?!

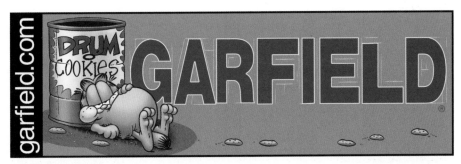

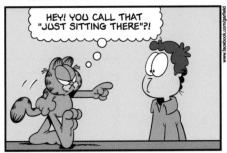

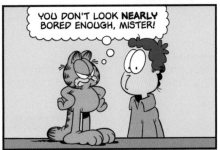

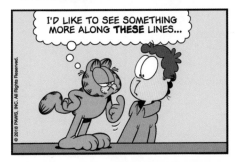

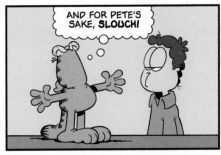

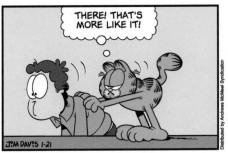

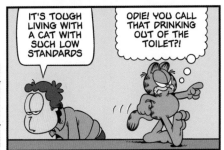

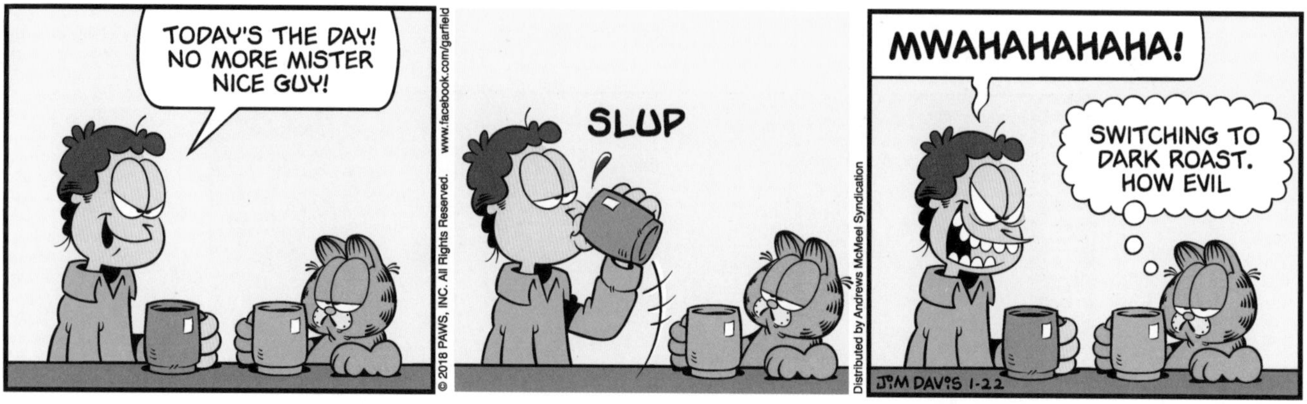
TODAY'S THE DAY! NO MORE MISTER NICE GUY!
© 2018 PAWS, INC. All Rights Reserved. www.facebook.com/garfield
SLUP
Distributed by Andrews McMeel Syndication
MWAHAHAHAHA!
SWITCHING TO DARK ROAST. HOW EVIL
JIM DAVIS 1-22

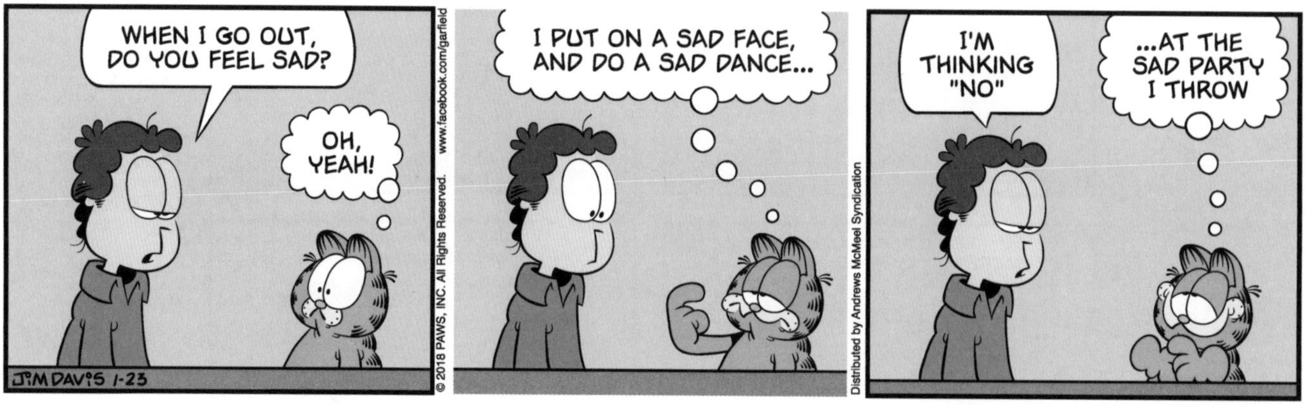
WHEN I GO OUT, DO YOU FEEL SAD?
OH, YEAH!
JIM DAVIS 1-23
© 2018 PAWS, INC. All Rights Reserved. www.facebook.com/garfield
I PUT ON A SAD FACE, AND DO A SAD DANCE...
Distributed by Andrews McMeel Syndication
I'M THINKING "NO"
...AT THE SAD PARTY I THROW

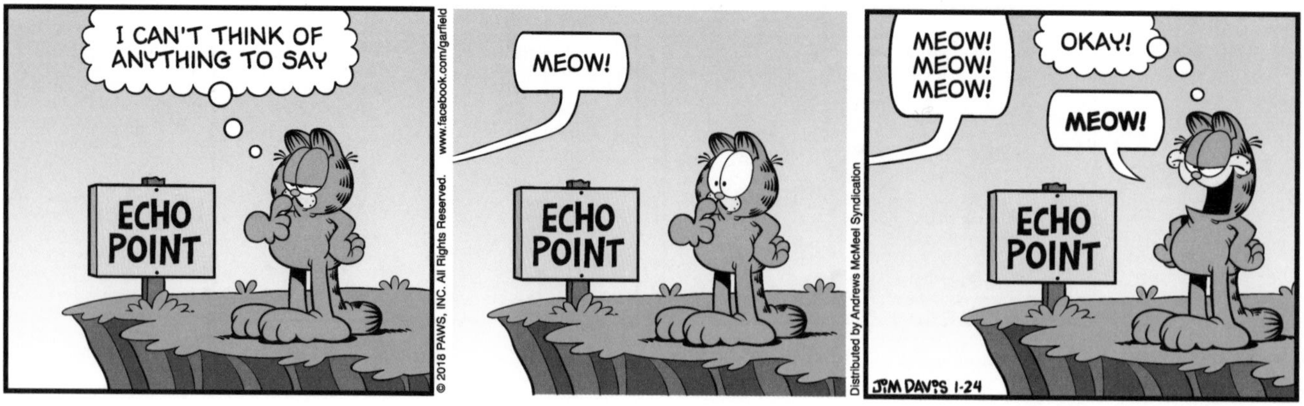
I CAN'T THINK OF ANYTHING TO SAY
ECHO POINT
© 2018 PAWS, INC. All Rights Reserved. www.facebook.com/garfield
MEOW!
ECHO POINT
Distributed by Andrews McMeel Syndication
MEOW! MEOW! MEOW!
OKAY!
MEOW!
ECHO POINT
JIM DAVIS 1-24

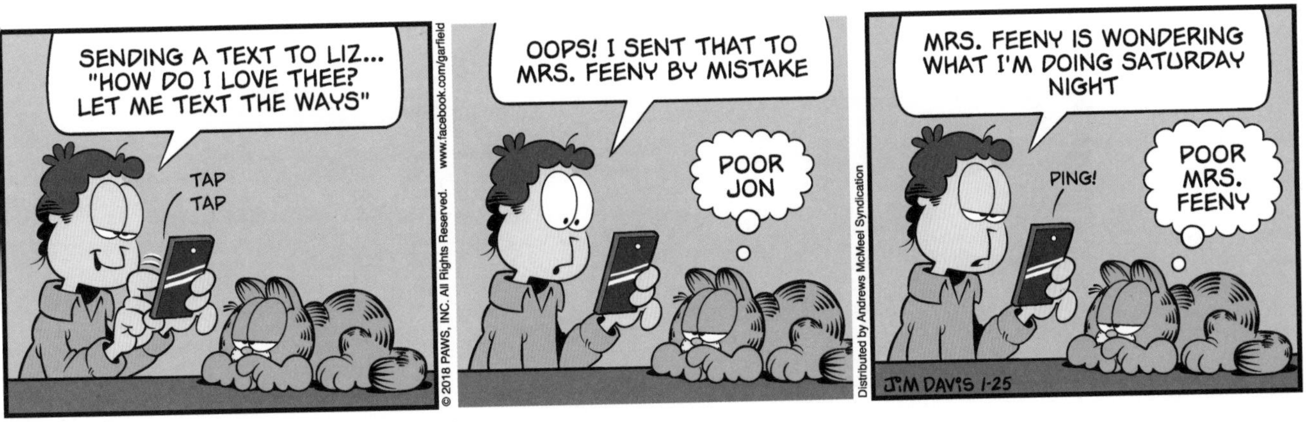
SENDING A TEXT TO LIZ... "HOW DO I LOVE THEE? LET ME TEXT THE WAYS"
TAP TAP
© 2018 PAWS, INC. All Rights Reserved. www.facebook.com/garfield
OOPS! I SENT THAT TO MRS. FEENY BY MISTAKE
POOR JON
Distributed by Andrews McMeel Syndication
MRS. FEENY IS WONDERING WHAT I'M DOING SATURDAY NIGHT
PING!
POOR MRS. FEENY
JIM DAVIS 1-25

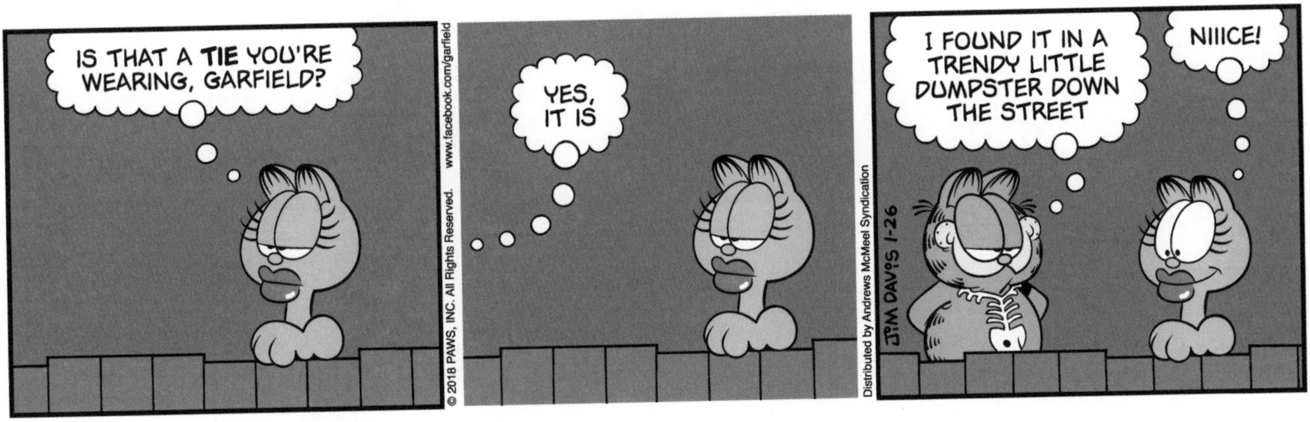
IS THAT A **TIE** YOU'RE WEARING, GARFIELD?
© 2018 PAWS, INC. All Rights Reserved. www.facebook.com/garfield
YES, IT IS
Distributed by Andrews McMeel Syndication
JIM DAVIS 1-26
I FOUND IT IN A TRENDY LITTLE DUMPSTER DOWN THE STREET
NIIICE!

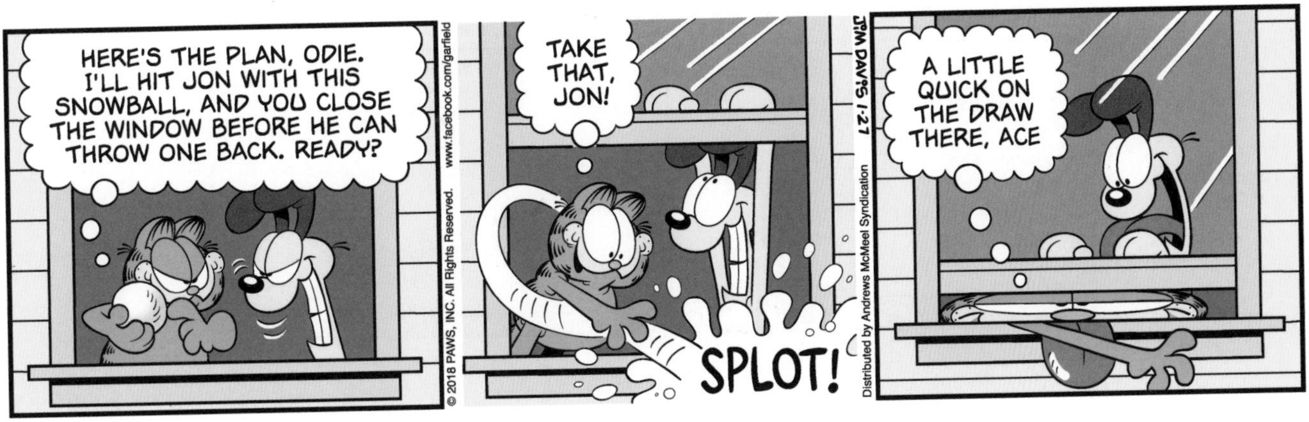
HERE'S THE PLAN, ODIE. I'LL HIT JON WITH THIS SNOWBALL, AND YOU CLOSE THE WINDOW BEFORE HE CAN THROW ONE BACK. READY?
© 2018 PAWS, INC. All Rights Reserved. www.facebook.com/garfield
TAKE THAT, JON!
SPLOT!
JIM DAVIS 1-27
Distributed by Andrews McMeel Syndication
A LITTLE QUICK ON THE DRAW THERE, ACE

garfield.com
GARFIELD®
NO, I DON'T WANT TO PLAY FETCH
www.facebook.com/garfield
NO, I DON'T NEED A HUG
© 2018 PAWS, INC. All Rights Reserved.
NO, I DON'T KNOW THE DOG SECRET HANDSHAKE
AND NO, YOU CAN BURY THAT YOURSELF
SEE YOU LATER, ODIE
Distributed by Andrews McMeel Syndication
SOME FRIENDS WEAR ME OUT
JIM DAVIS 1-28

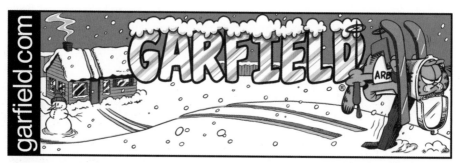

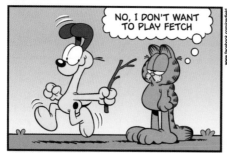

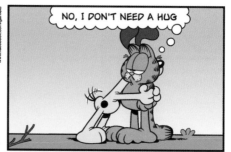

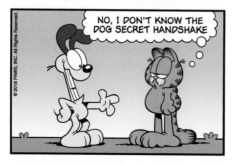

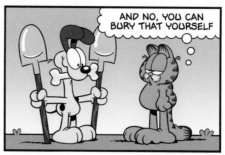

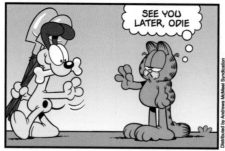

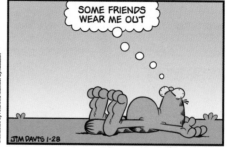

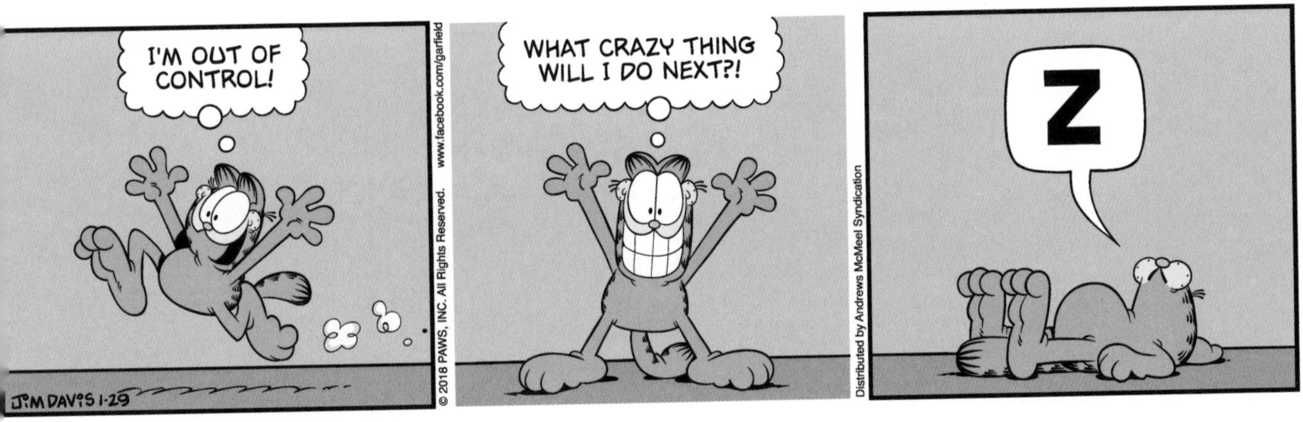
I'M OUT OF CONTROL!
JIM DAVIS 1-29
© 2018 PAWS, INC. All Rights Reserved. www.facebook.com/garfield
WHAT CRAZY THING WILL I DO NEXT?!
Distributed by Andrews McMeel Syndication
Z

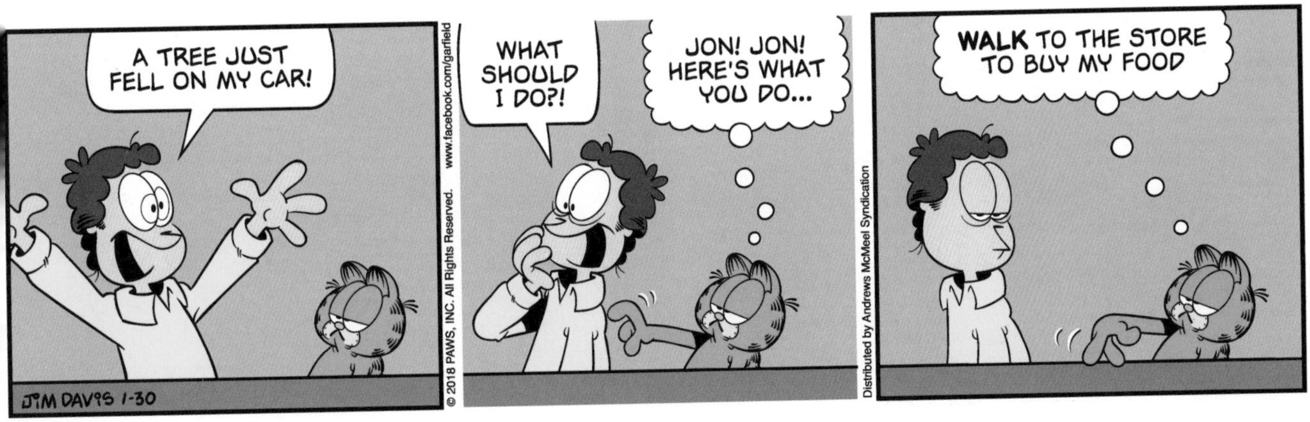
A TREE JUST FELL ON MY CAR!
JIM DAVIS 1-30
© 2018 PAWS, INC. All Rights Reserved. www.facebook.com/garfield
WHAT SHOULD I DO?!
JON! JON! HERE'S WHAT YOU DO...
Distributed by Andrews McMeel Syndication
**WALK** TO THE STORE TO BUY MY FOOD

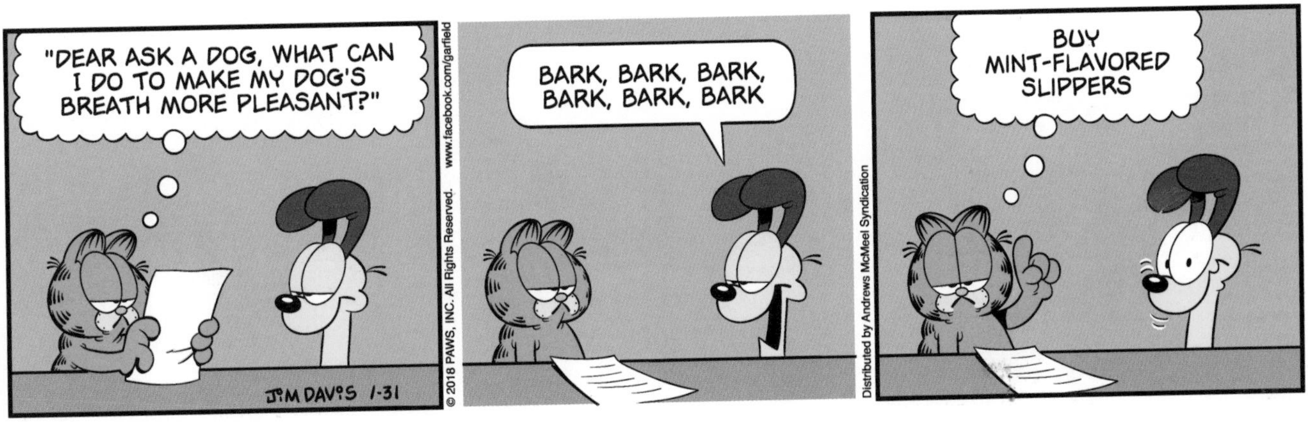
"DEAR ASK A DOG, WHAT CAN I DO TO MAKE MY DOG'S BREATH MORE PLEASANT?"
JIM DAVIS 1-31
© 2018 PAWS, INC. All Rights Reserved. www.facebook.com/garfield
BARK, BARK, BARK, BARK, BARK, BARK
Distributed by Andrews McMeel Syndication
BUY MINT-FLAVORED SLIPPERS

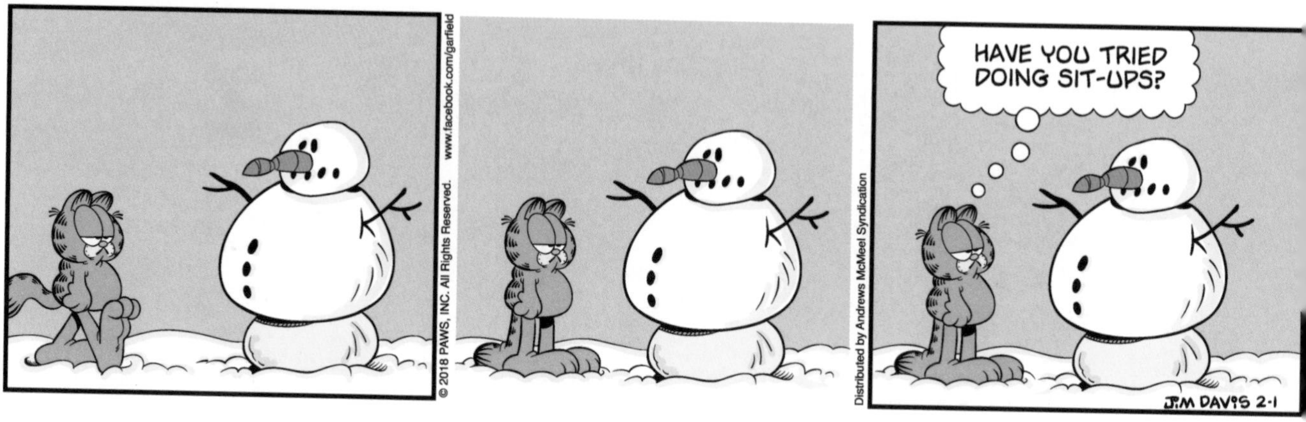
© 2018 PAWS, INC. All Rights Reserved. www.facebook.com/garfield
Distributed by Andrews McMeel Syndication
HAVE YOU TRIED DOING SIT-UPS?
JIM DAVIS 2-1

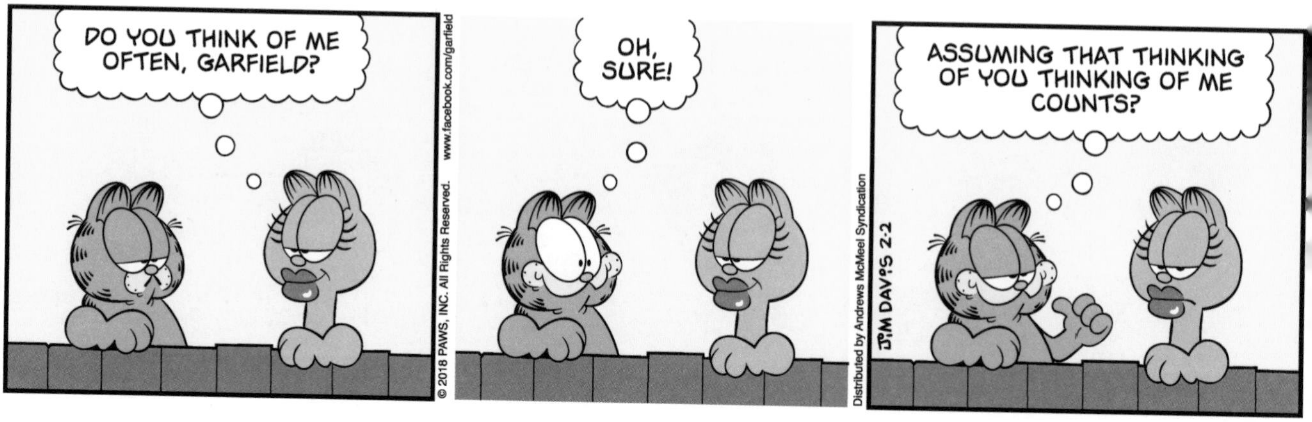
DO YOU THINK OF ME OFTEN, GARFIELD?
© 2018 PAWS, INC. All Rights Reserved. www.facebook.com/garfield
OH, SURE!
Distributed by Andrews McMeel Syndication
JIM DAVIS 2-2
ASSUMING THAT THINKING OF YOU THINKING OF ME COUNTS?

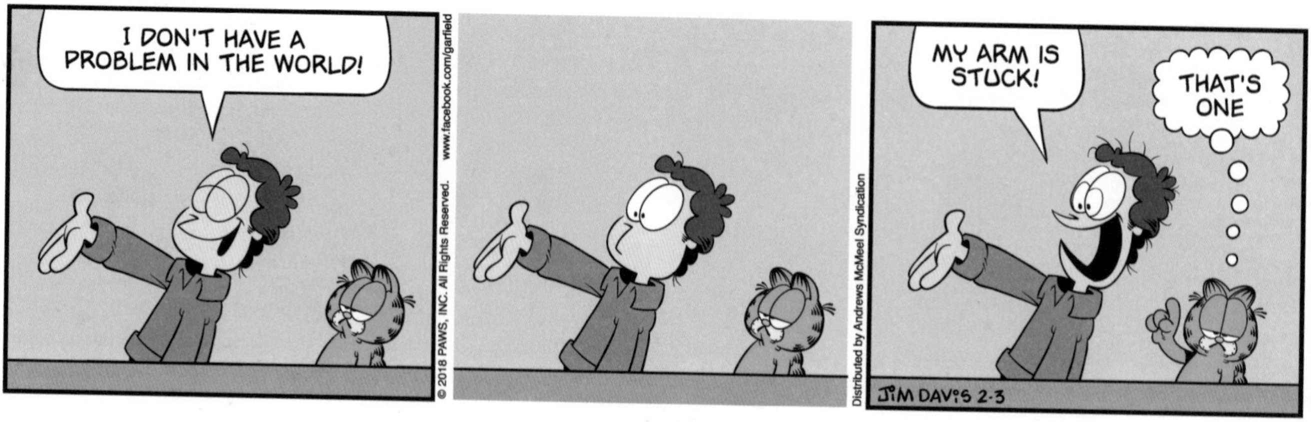
I DON'T HAVE A PROBLEM IN THE WORLD!
© 2018 PAWS, INC. All Rights Reserved. www.facebook.com/garfield
Distributed by Andrews McMeel Syndication
MY ARM IS STUCK!
THAT'S ONE
JIM DAVIS 2-3

# MORE WORDS TO LAUGH BY

If diet and exercise don't work out, there's always sumo wrestling.

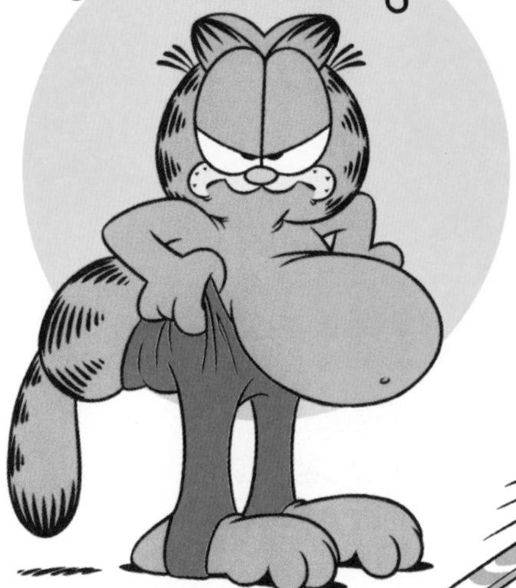

There's no love like your first love.

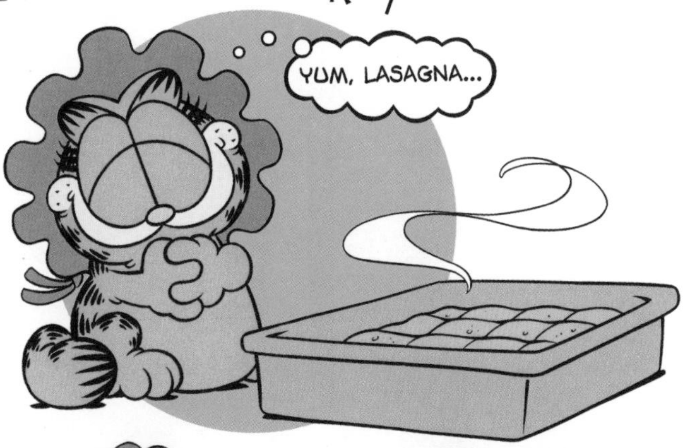
YUM, LASAGNA...

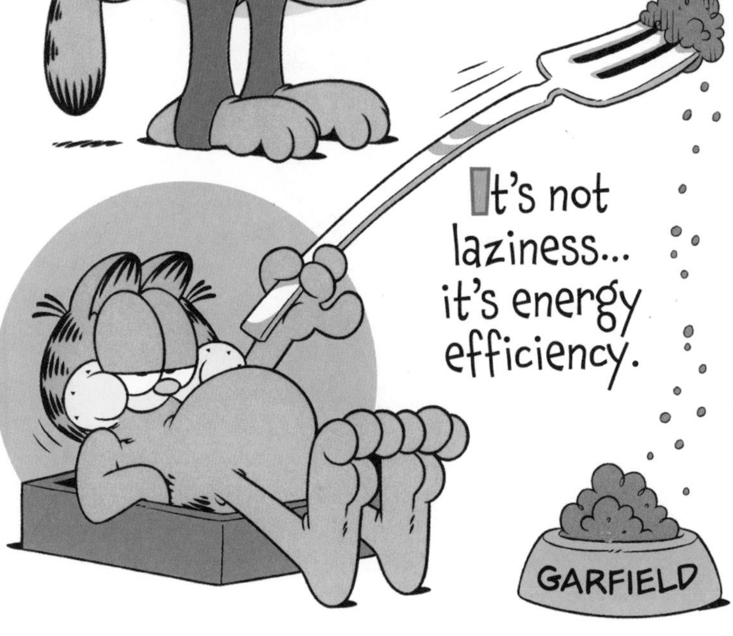
GARFIELD

It's not laziness... it's energy efficiency.

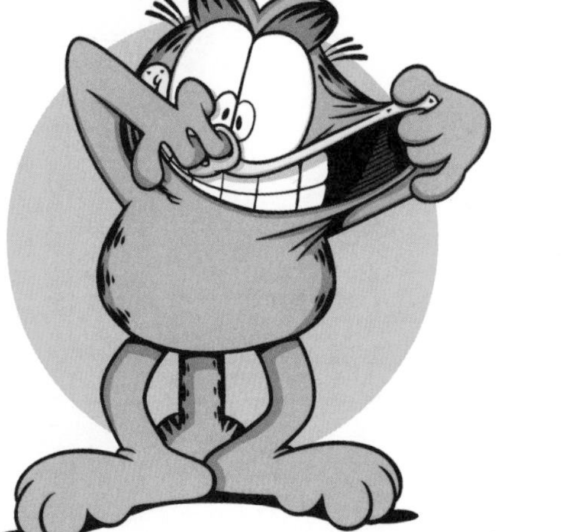

Goofing off. It's a silly job, but somebody's gotta do it.

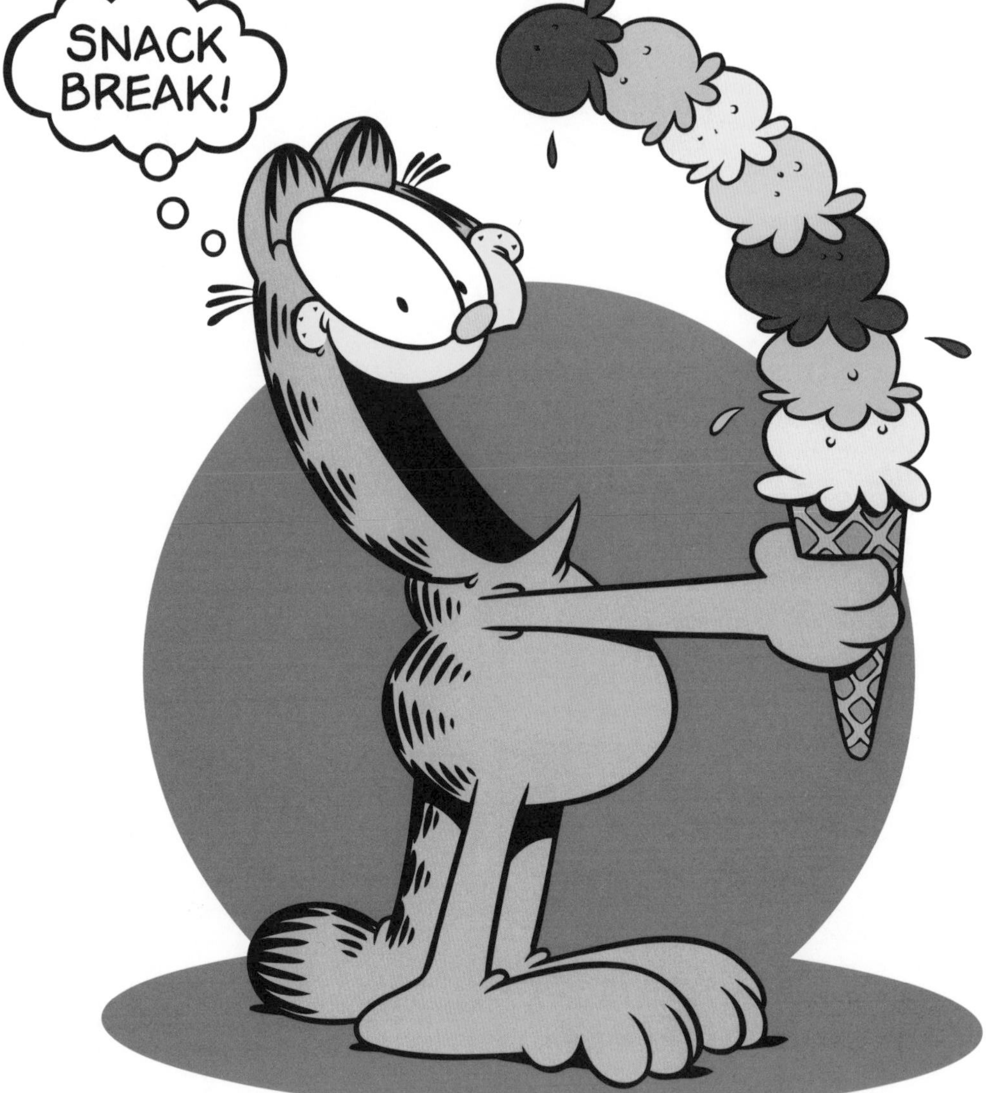
SNACK BREAK!

# Garfield
# EASY AS PIE

BY JIM DAVIS

**Ballantine Books** • **New York**

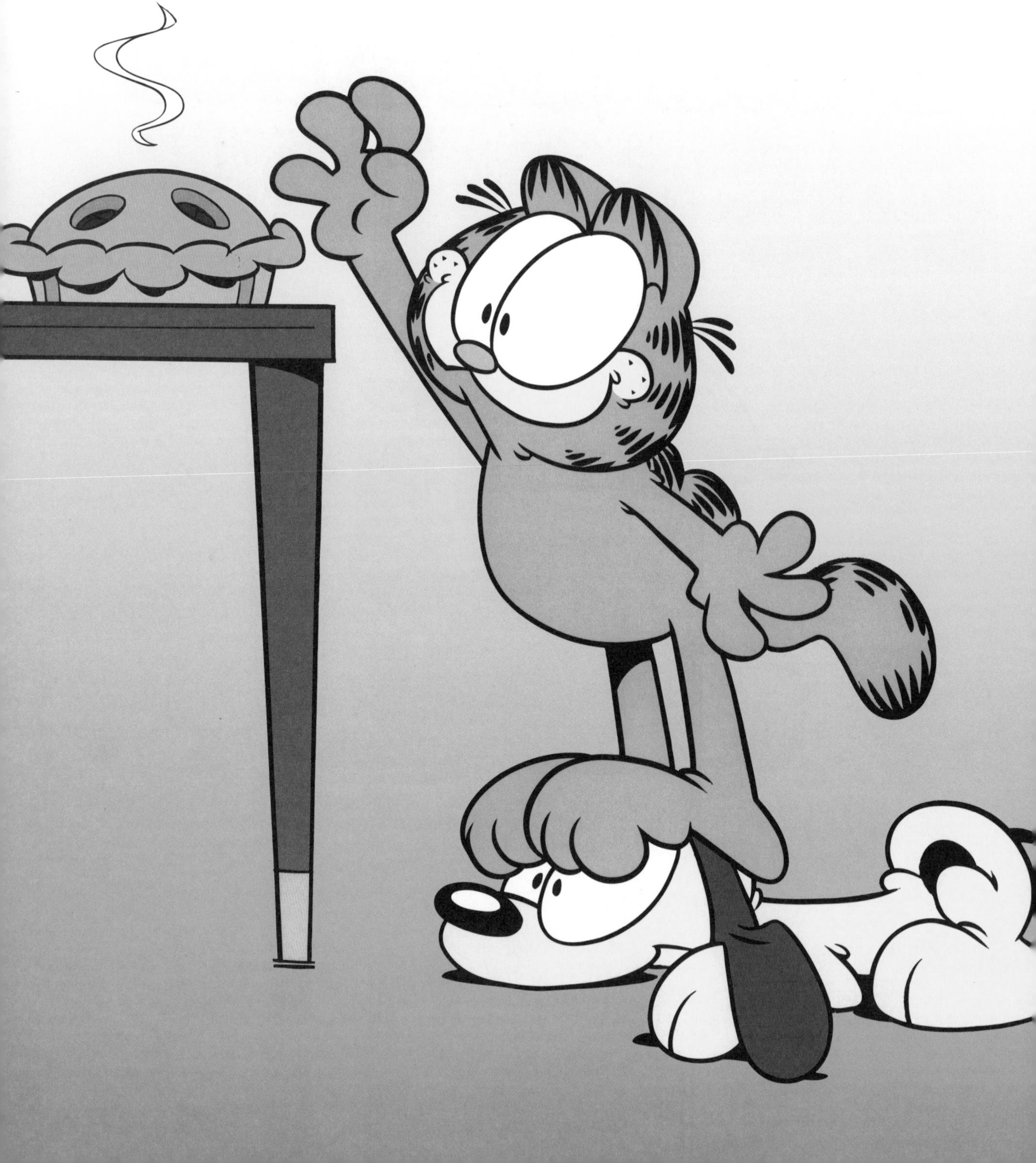

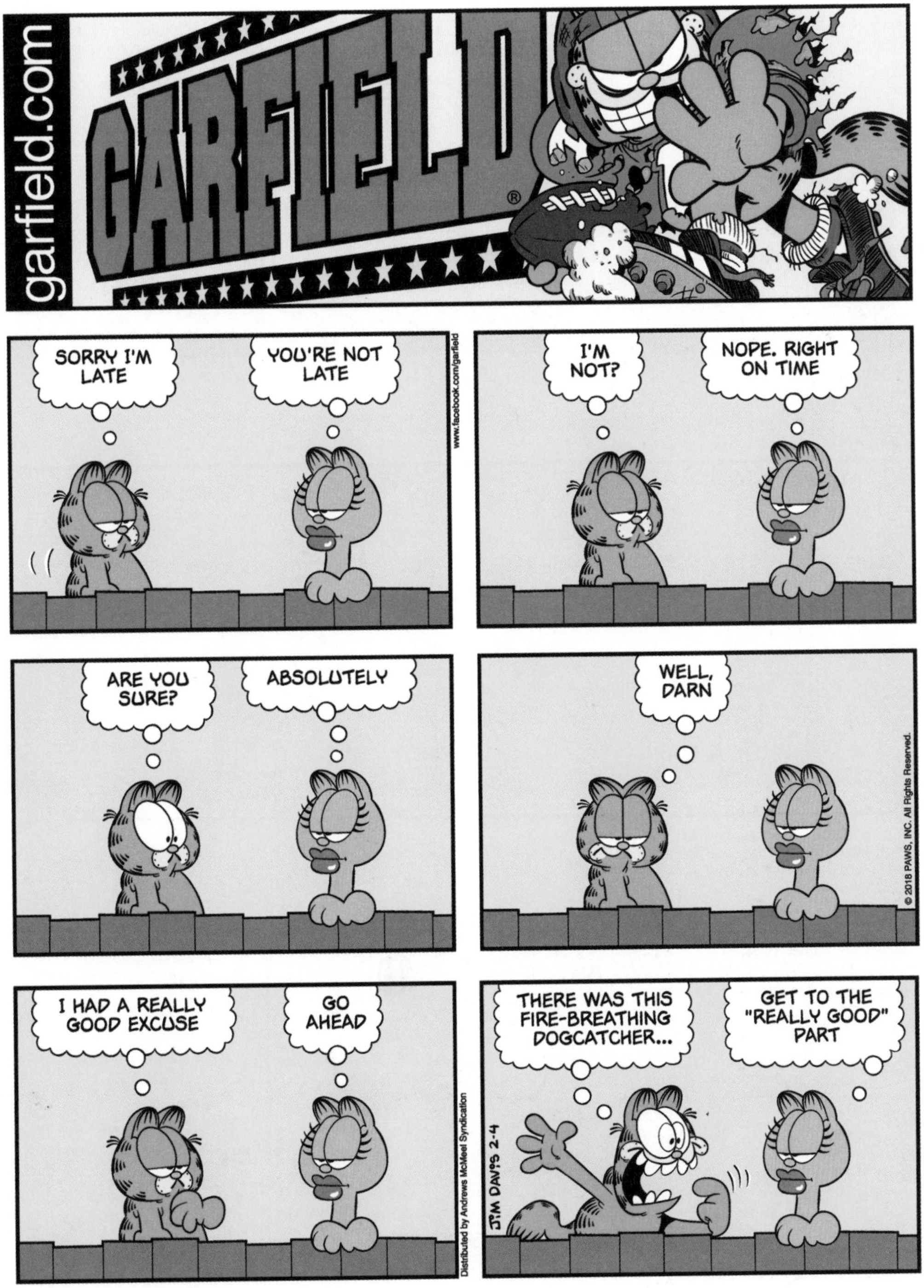
garfield.com
GARFIELD
SORRY I'M LATE
YOU'RE NOT LATE
I'M NOT?
NOPE. RIGHT ON TIME
ARE YOU SURE?
ABSOLUTELY
WELL, DARN
I HAD A REALLY GOOD EXCUSE
GO AHEAD
THERE WAS THIS FIRE-BREATHING DOGCATCHER...
GET TO THE "REALLY GOOD" PART
JPM DAVIS 2-4
www.facebook.com/garfield
© 2018 PAWS, INC. All Rights Reserved.
Distributed by Andrews McMeel Syndication

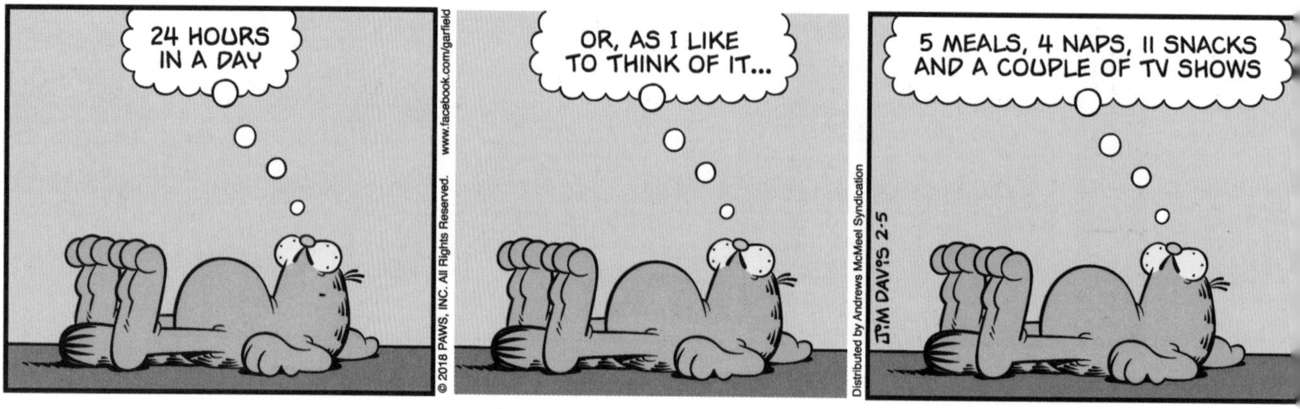
24 HOURS IN A DAY
OR, AS I LIKE TO THINK OF IT...
5 MEALS, 4 NAPS, 11 SNACKS AND A COUPLE OF TV SHOWS
JIM DAVIS 2-5
© 2018 PAWS, INC. All Rights Reserved. www.facebook.com/garfield
Distributed by Andrews McMeel Syndication

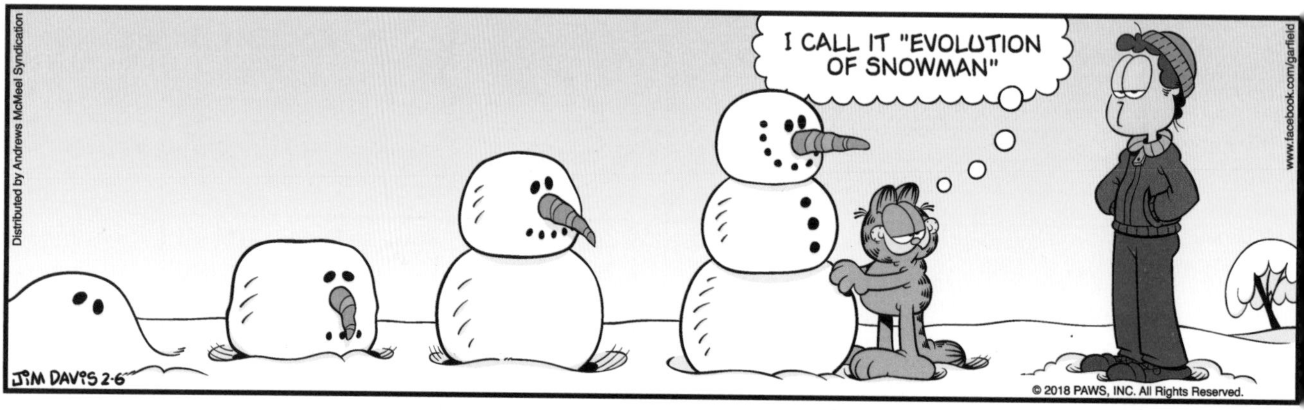
I CALL IT "EVOLUTION OF SNOWMAN"
JIM DAVIS 2-6
© 2018 PAWS, INC. All Rights Reserved.
Distributed by Andrews McMeel Syndication
www.facebook.com/garfield

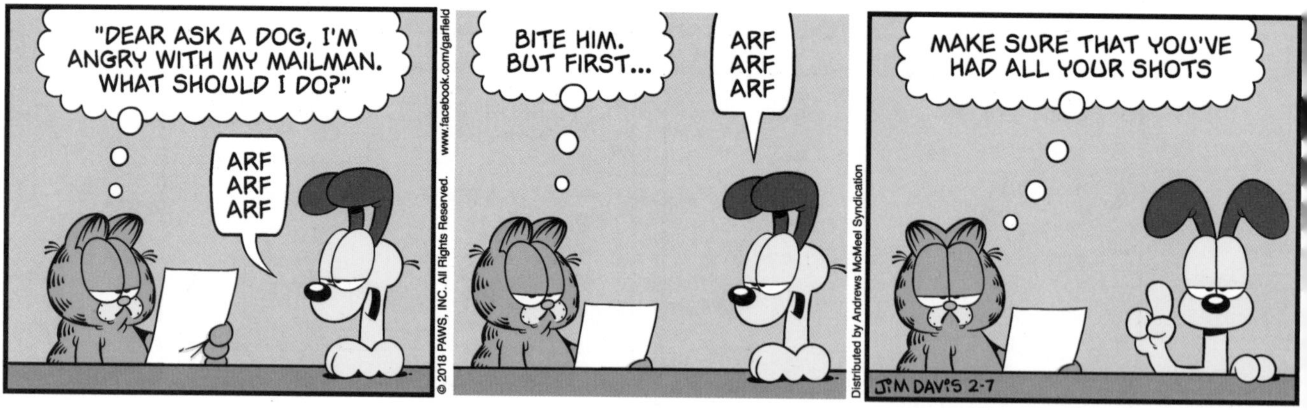
"DEAR ASK A DOG, I'M ANGRY WITH MY MAILMAN. WHAT SHOULD I DO?"
ARF ARF ARF
BITE HIM. BUT FIRST...
ARF ARF ARF
MAKE SURE THAT YOU'VE HAD ALL YOUR SHOTS
JIM DAVIS 2-7
© 2018 PAWS, INC. All Rights Reserved. www.facebook.com/garfield
Distributed by Andrews McMeel Syndication

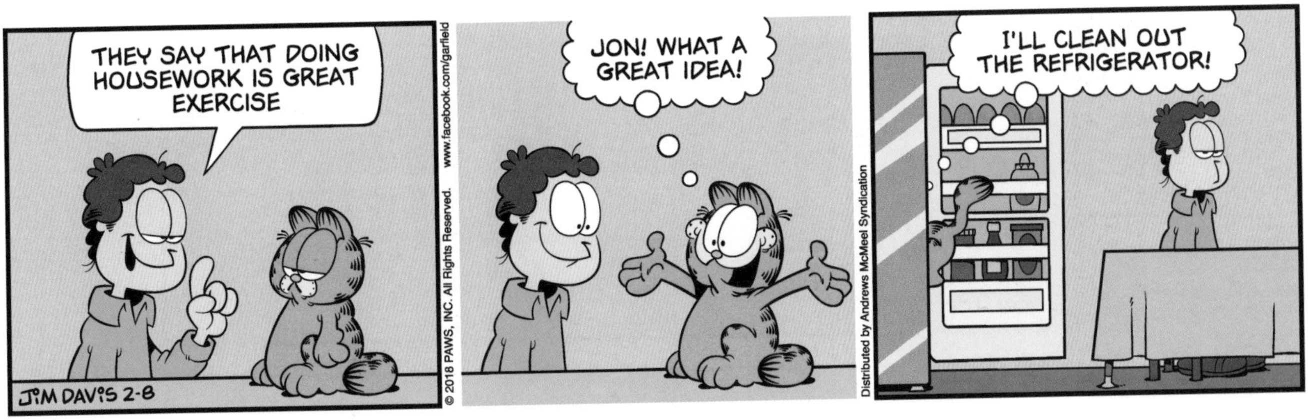
THEY SAY THAT DOING HOUSEWORK IS GREAT EXERCISE
JIM DAVIS 2-8
© 2018 PAWS, INC. All Rights Reserved. www.facebook.com/garfield
JON! WHAT A GREAT IDEA!
Distributed by Andrews McMeel Syndication
I'LL CLEAN OUT THE REFRIGERATOR!

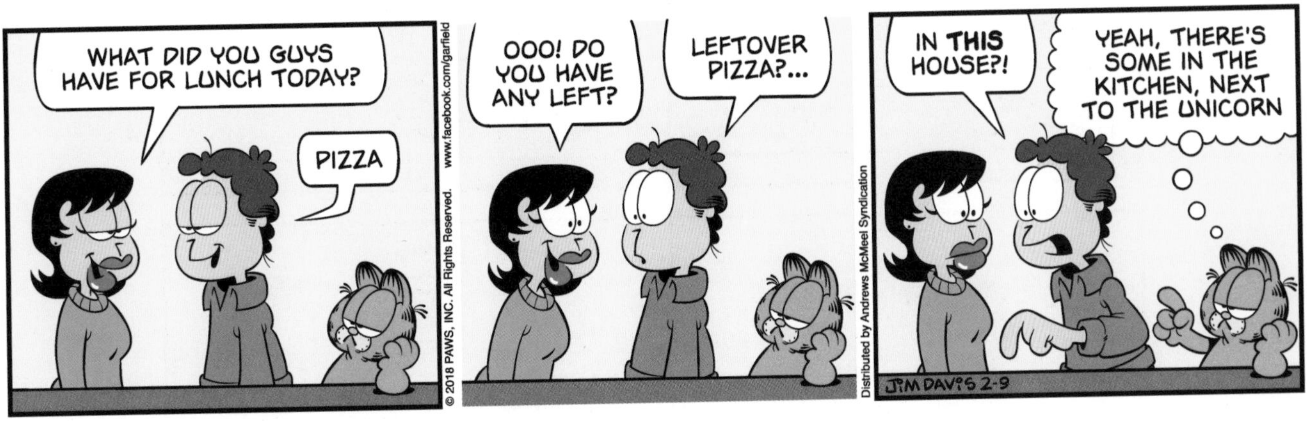
WHAT DID YOU GUYS HAVE FOR LUNCH TODAY?
PIZZA
© 2018 PAWS, INC. All Rights Reserved. www.facebook.com/garfield
OOO! DO YOU HAVE ANY LEFT?
LEFTOVER PIZZA?...
Distributed by Andrews McMeel Syndication
IN **THIS** HOUSE?!
YEAH, THERE'S SOME IN THE KITCHEN, NEXT TO THE UNICORN
JIM DAVIS 2-9

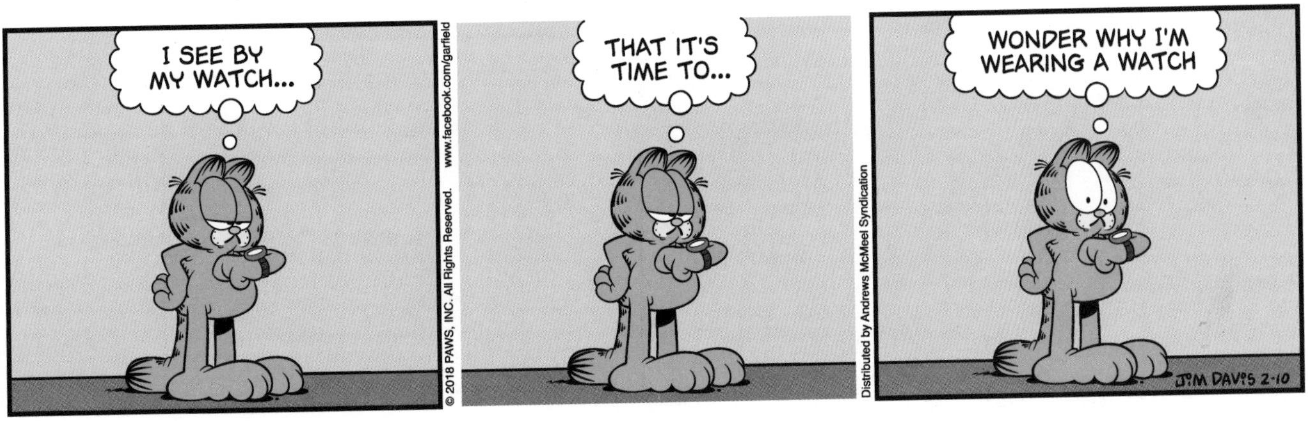
I SEE BY MY WATCH...
© 2018 PAWS, INC. All Rights Reserved. www.facebook.com/garfield
THAT IT'S TIME TO...
Distributed by Andrews McMeel Syndication
WONDER WHY I'M WEARING A WATCH
JIM DAVIS 2-10

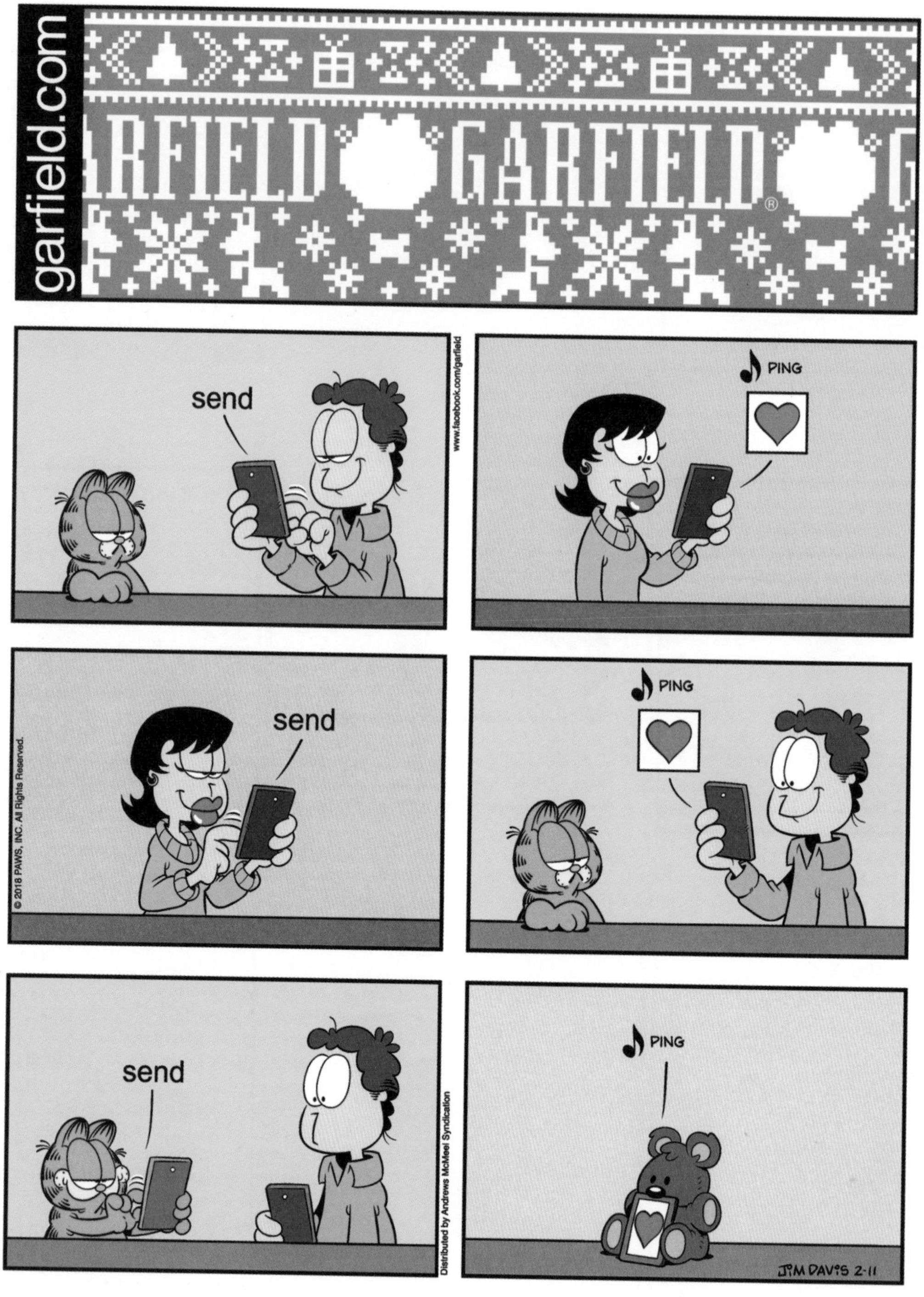
garfield.com
GARFIELD
GARFIELD®
www.facebook.com/garfield
send
PING
© 2018 PAWS, INC. All Rights Reserved.
send
PING
send
Distributed by Andrews McMeel Syndication
PING
JIM DAVIS 2-11

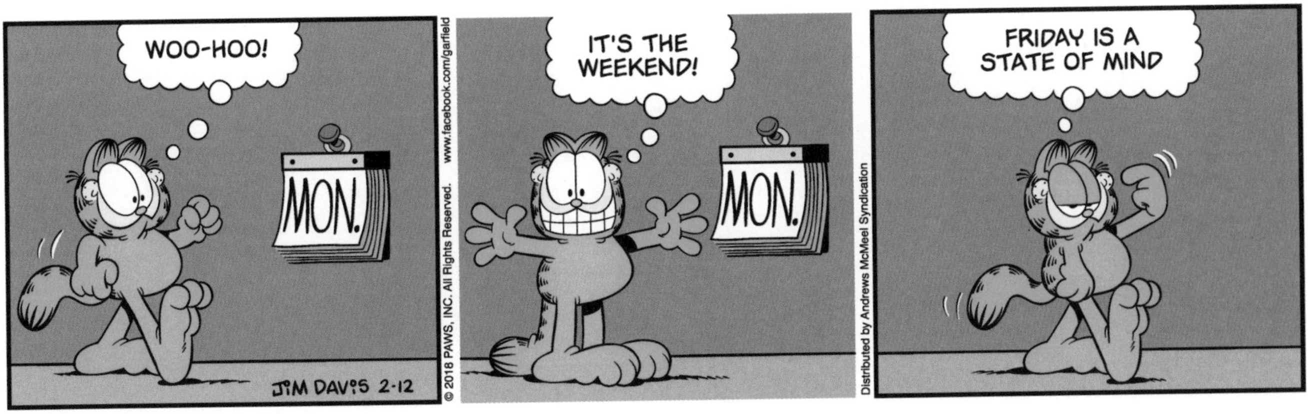
WOO-HOO!
MON.
JIM DAVIS 2-12
© 2018 PAWS, INC. All Rights Reserved. www.facebook.com/garfield
IT'S THE WEEKEND!
MON.
Distributed by Andrews McMeel Syndication
FRIDAY IS A STATE OF MIND

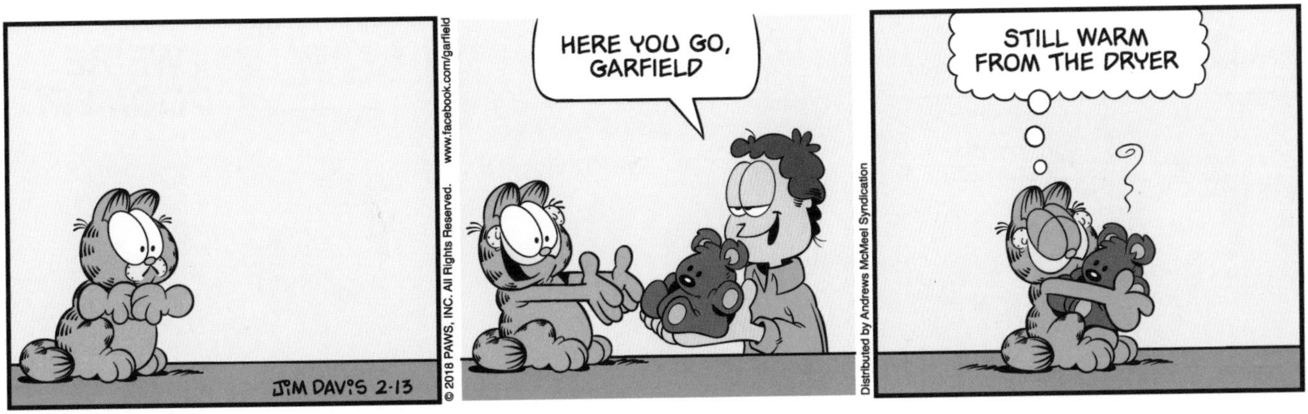
JIM DAVIS 2-13
© 2018 PAWS, INC. All Rights Reserved. www.facebook.com/garfield
HERE YOU GO, GARFIELD
Distributed by Andrews McMeel Syndication
STILL WARM FROM THE DRYER

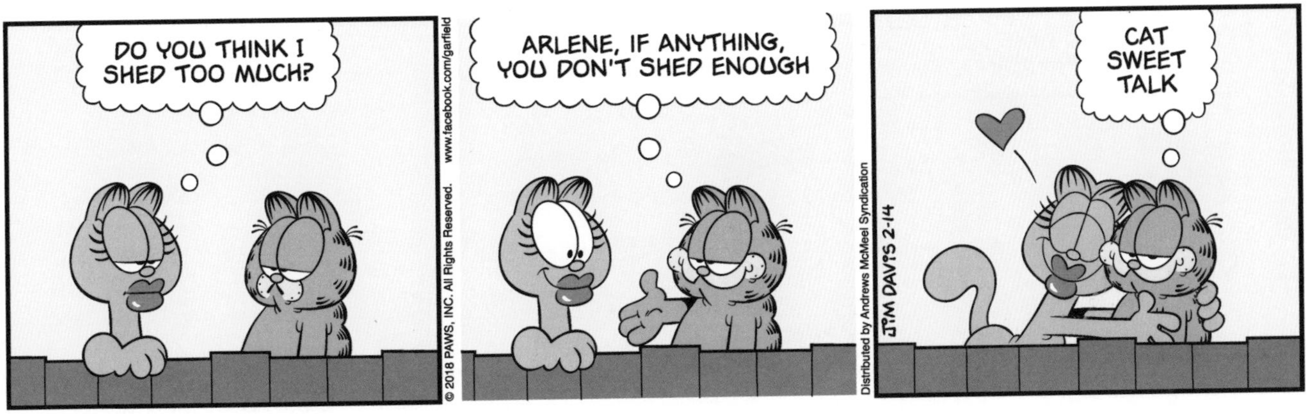
DO YOU THINK I SHED TOO MUCH?
© 2018 PAWS, INC. All Rights Reserved. www.facebook.com/garfield
ARLENE, IF ANYTHING, YOU DON'T SHED ENOUGH
Distributed by Andrews McMeel Syndication
JIM DAVIS 2-14
CAT SWEET TALK

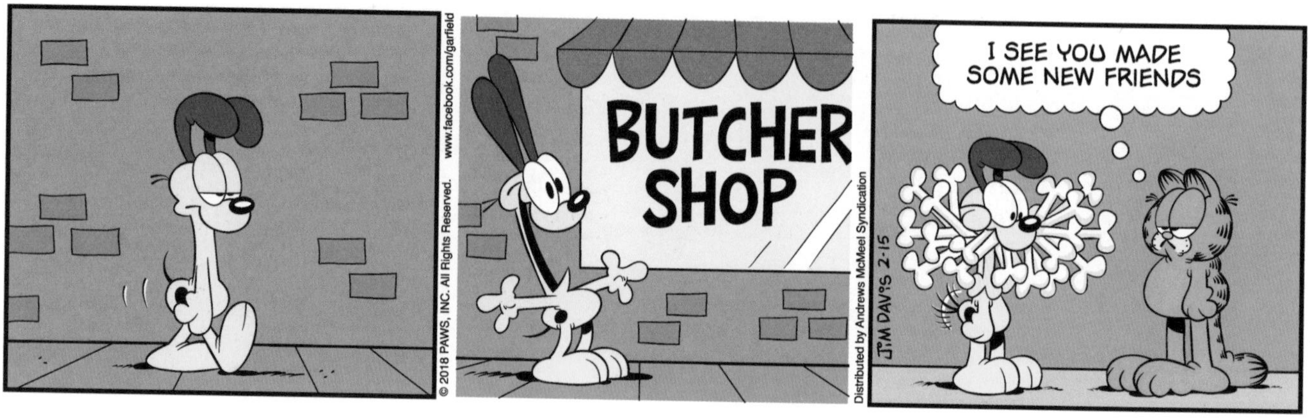
BUTCHER SHOP
I SEE YOU MADE SOME NEW FRIENDS
JIM DAVIS 2-15
© 2018 PAWS, INC. All Rights Reserved. www.facebook.com/garfield
Distributed by Andrews McMeel Syndication

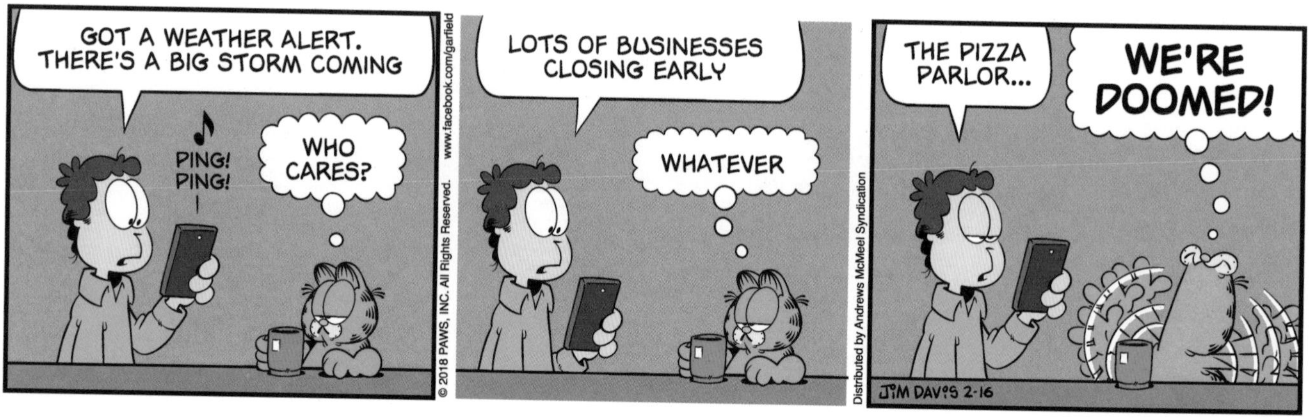
GOT A WEATHER ALERT. THERE'S A BIG STORM COMING
PING! PING!
WHO CARES?
LOTS OF BUSINESSES CLOSING EARLY
WHATEVER
THE PIZZA PARLOR...
WE'RE DOOMED!
JIM DAVIS 2-16
© 2018 PAWS, INC. All Rights Reserved. www.facebook.com/garfield
Distributed by Andrews McMeel Syndication

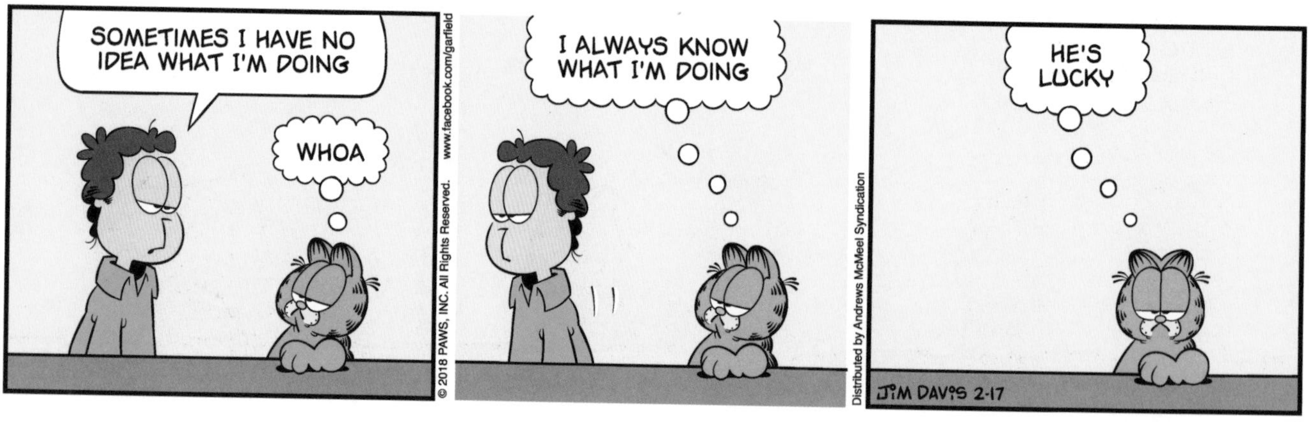
SOMETIMES I HAVE NO IDEA WHAT I'M DOING
WHOA
I ALWAYS KNOW WHAT I'M DOING
HE'S LUCKY
JIM DAVIS 2-17
© 2018 PAWS, INC. All Rights Reserved. www.facebook.com/garfield
Distributed by Andrews McMeel Syndication

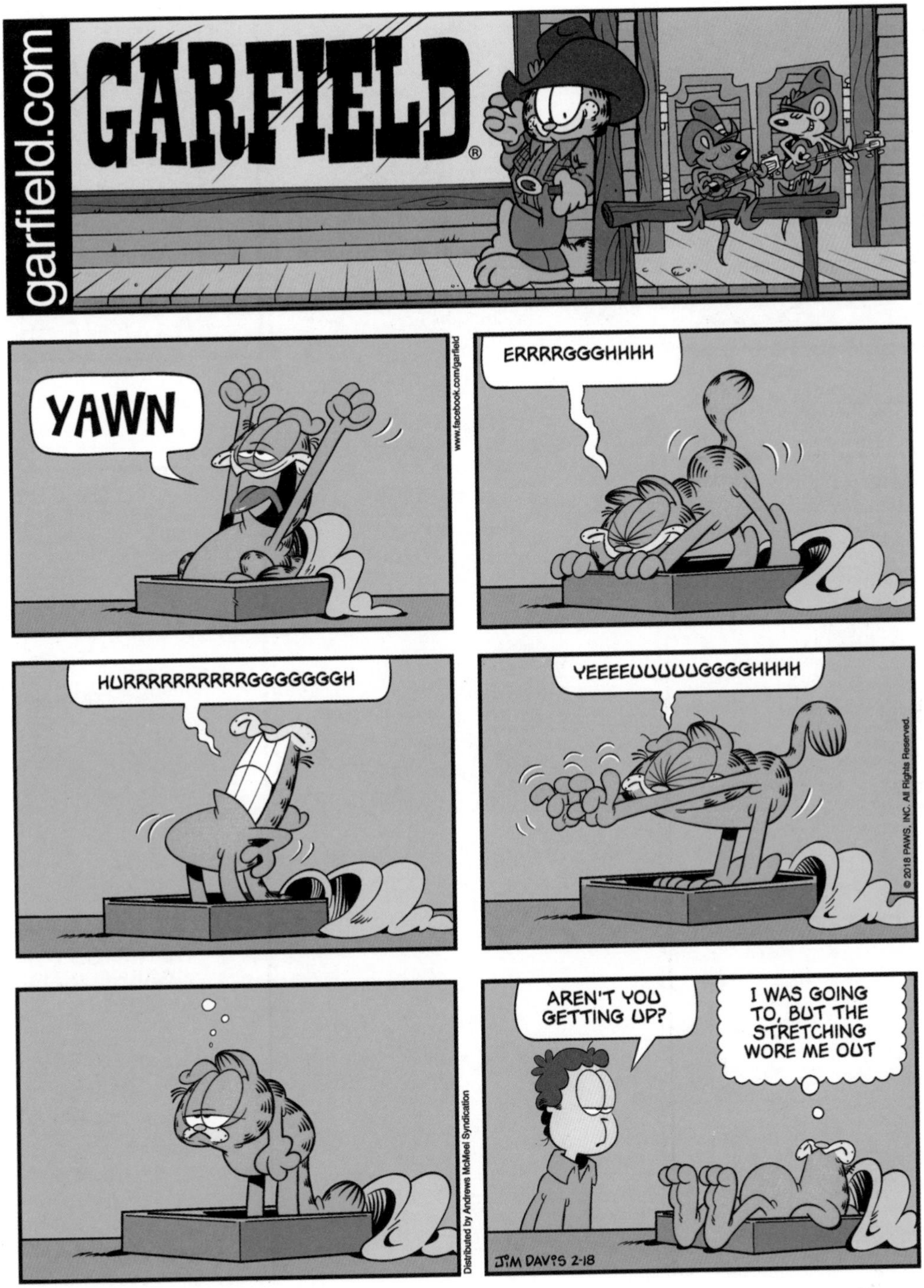
garfield.com
GARFIELD
www.facebook.com/garfield
YAWN
ERRRRGGGHHHH
HURRRRRRRRRRGGGGGGGH
YEEEEUUUUUGGGGHHHH
© 2018 PAWS, INC. All Rights Reserved.
Distributed by Andrews McMeel Syndication
ARE N'T YOU GETTING UP?
I WAS GOING TO, BUT THE STRETCHING WORE ME OUT
JIM DAVIS 2-18

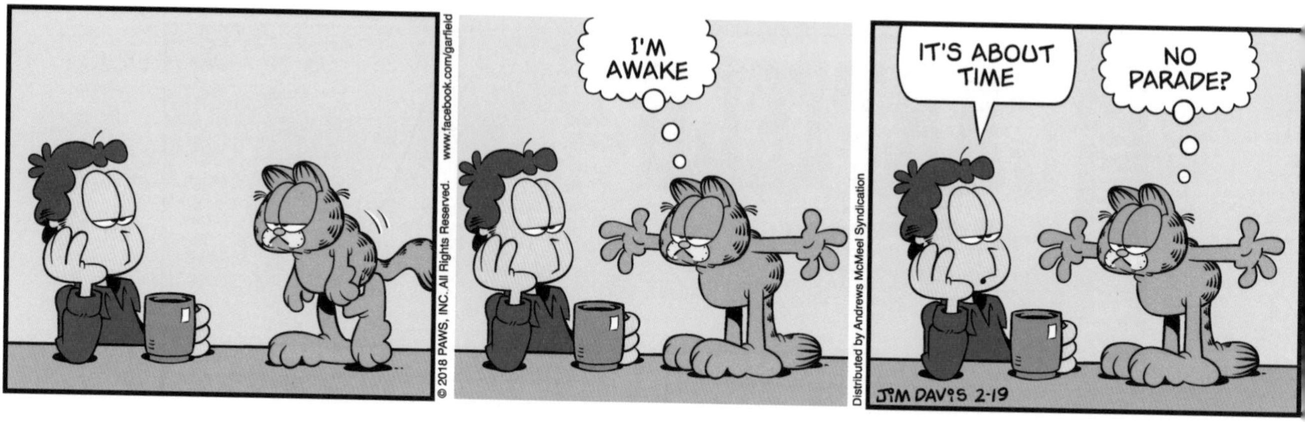
I'M AWAKE
IT'S ABOUT TIME
NO PARADE?
© 2018 PAWS, INC. All Rights Reserved. www.facebook.com/garfield
Distributed by Andrews McMeel Syndication
JIM DAVIS 2-19

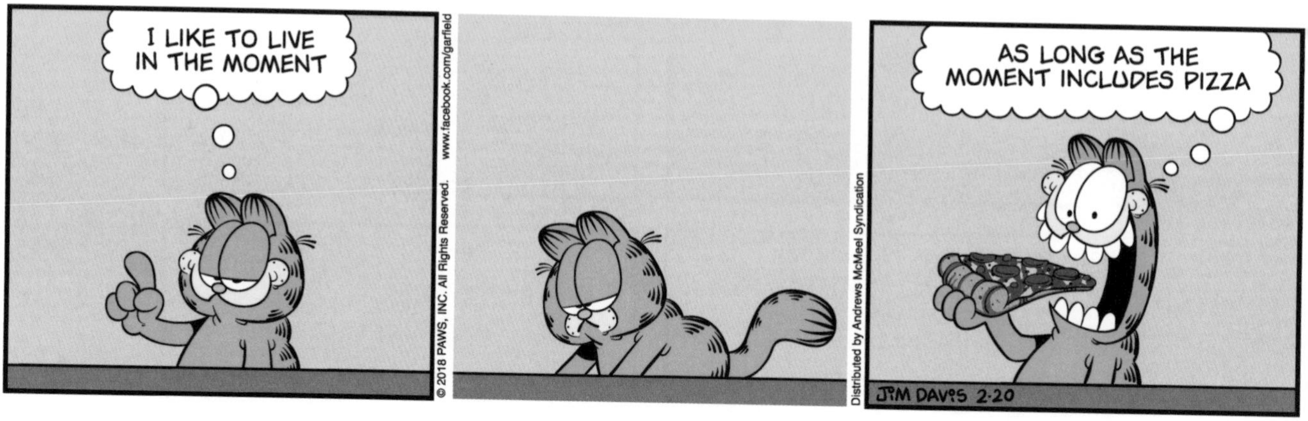
I LIKE TO LIVE IN THE MOMENT
AS LONG AS THE MOMENT INCLUDES PIZZA
© 2018 PAWS, INC. All Rights Reserved. www.facebook.com/garfield
Distributed by Andrews McMeel Syndication
JIM DAVIS 2-20

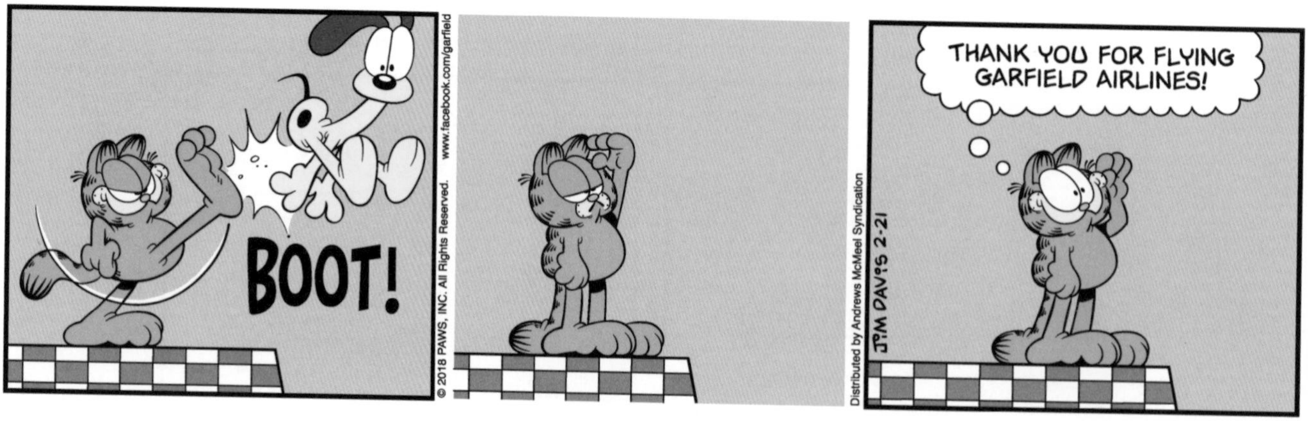
BOOT!
THANK YOU FOR FLYING GARFIELD AIRLINES!
© 2018 PAWS, INC. All Rights Reserved. www.facebook.com/garfield
Distributed by Andrews McMeel Syndication
JIM DAVIS 2-21

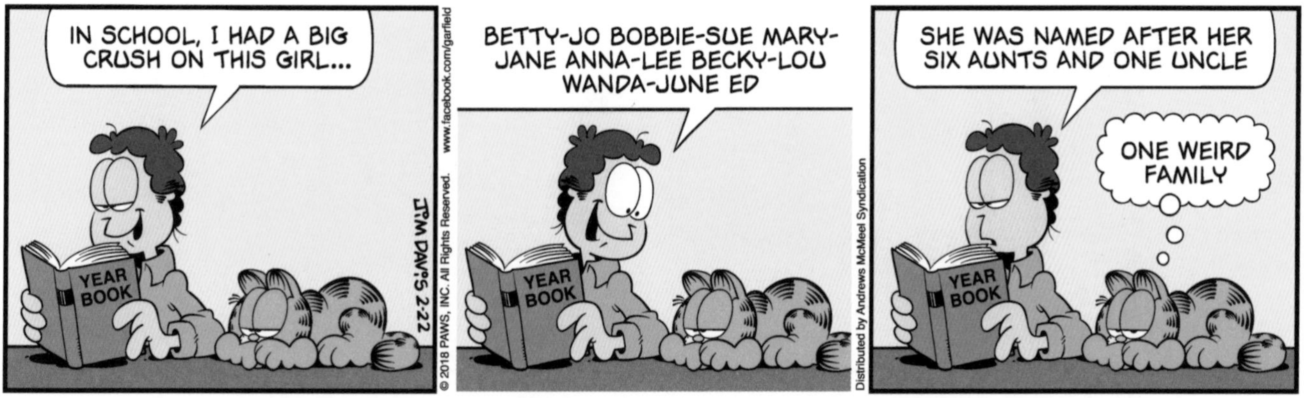
IN SCHOOL, I HAD A BIG CRUSH ON THIS GIRL...
YEAR BOOK
JIM DAVIS 2-22
BETTY-JO BOBBIE-SUE MARY-JANE ANNA-LEE BECKY-LOU WANDA-JUNE ED
SHE WAS NAMED AFTER HER SIX AUNTS AND ONE UNCLE
ONE WEIRD FAMILY


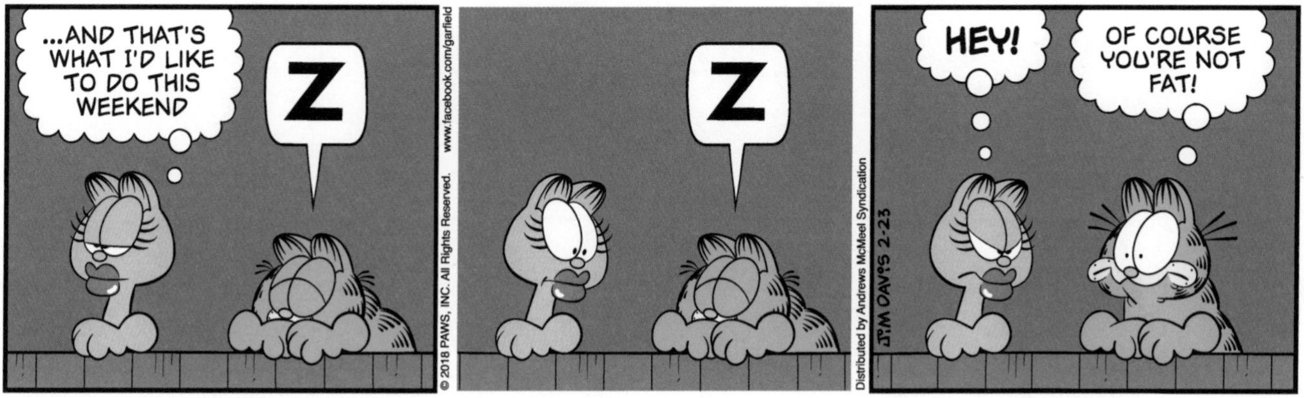
...AND THAT'S WHAT I'D LIKE TO DO THIS WEEKEND
Z
Z
JIM DAVIS 2-23
HEY!
OF COURSE YOU'RE NOT FAT!


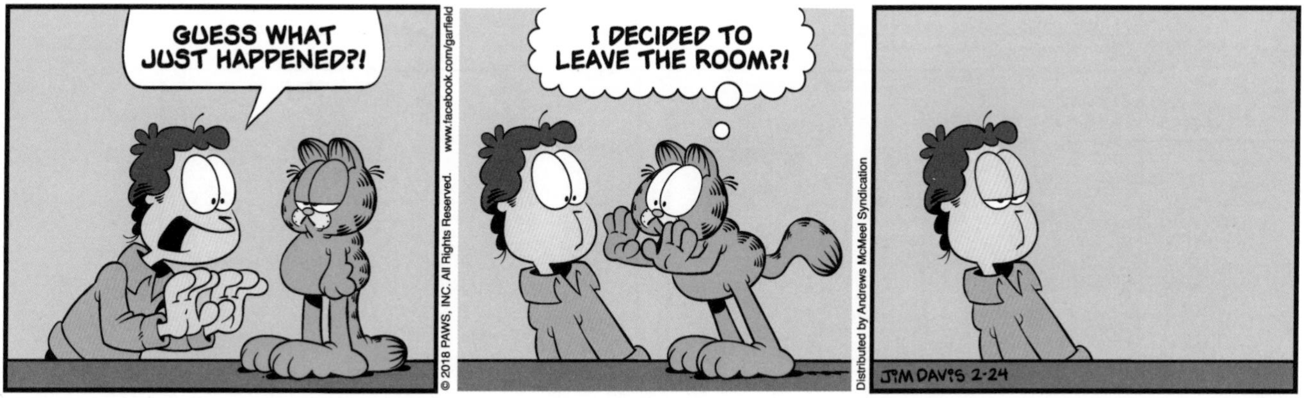
GUESS WHAT JUST HAPPENED?!
I DECIDED TO LEAVE THE ROOM?!
JIM DAVIS 2-24

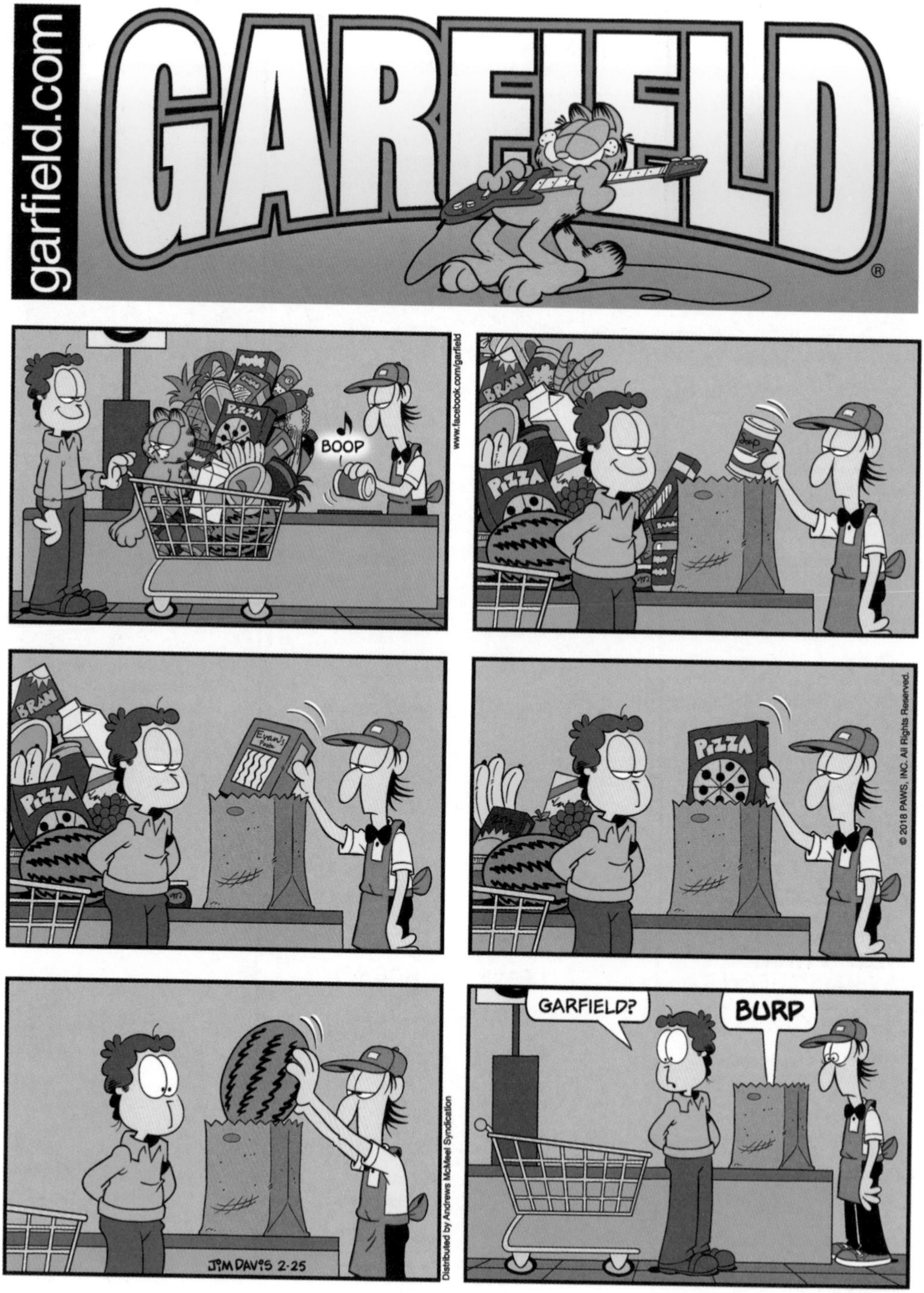
garfield.com
GARFIELD
BOOP
www.facebook.com/garfield
PIZZA
BRAN
© 2018 PAWS, INC. All Rights Reserved.
Distributed by Andrews McMeel Syndication
JIM DAVIS 2-25
GARFIELD?
BURP

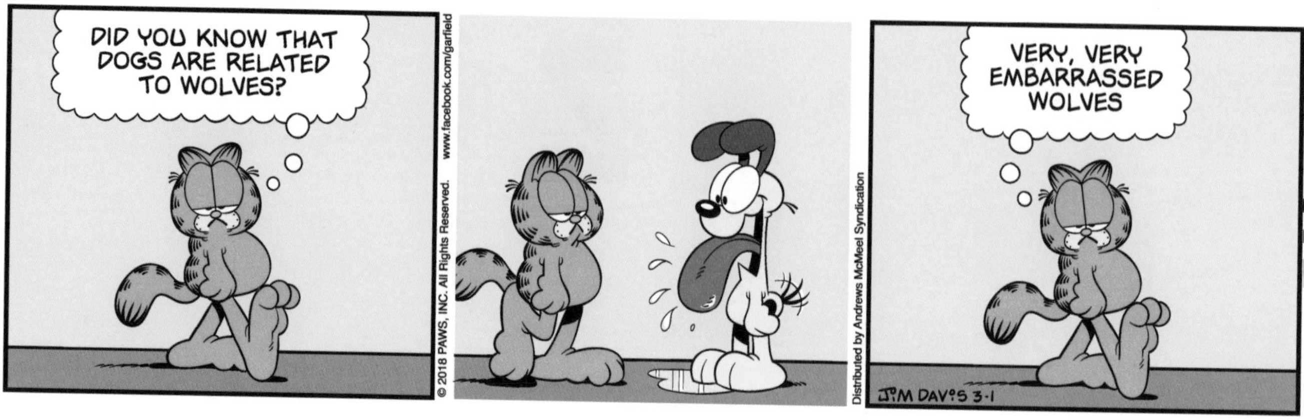
DID YOU KNOW THAT DOGS ARE RELATED TO WOLVES?
VERY, VERY EMBARRASSED WOLVES
© 2018 PAWS, INC. All Rights Reserved. www.facebook.com/garfield
Distributed by Andrews McMeel Syndication
JIM DAVIS 3-1

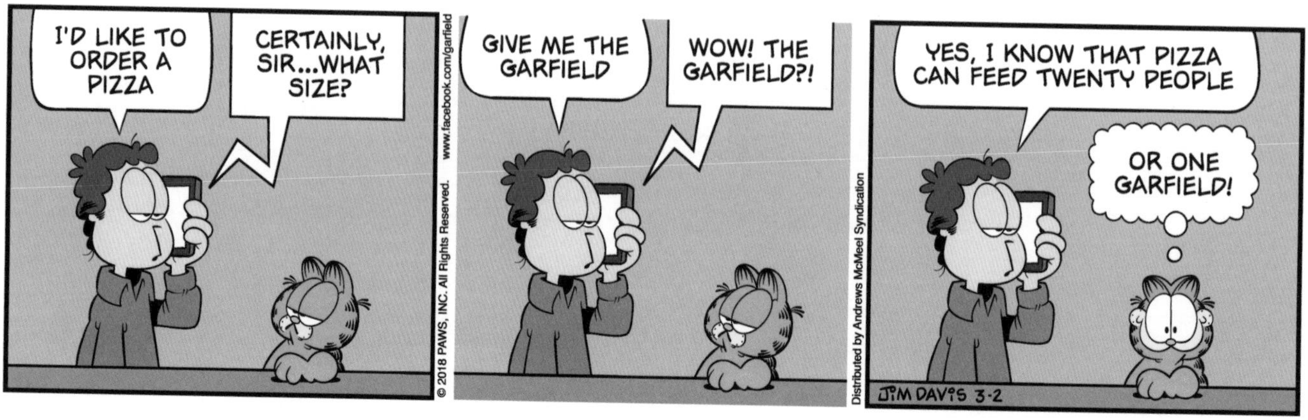
I'D LIKE TO ORDER A PIZZA
CERTAINLY, SIR...WHAT SIZE?
GIVE ME THE GARFIELD
WOW! THE GARFIELD?!
YES, I KNOW THAT PIZZA CAN FEED TWENTY PEOPLE
OR ONE GARFIELD!
© 2018 PAWS, INC. All Rights Reserved. www.facebook.com/garfield
Distributed by Andrews McMeel Syndication
JIM DAVIS 3-2

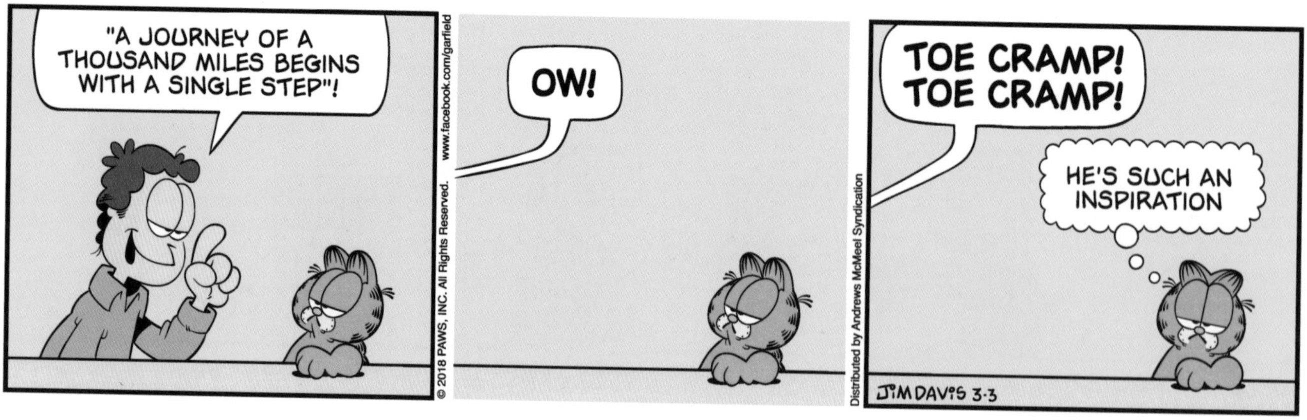
"A JOURNEY OF A THOUSAND MILES BEGINS WITH A SINGLE STEP"!
OW!
TOE CRAMP! TOE CRAMP!
HE'S SUCH AN INSPIRATION
© 2018 PAWS, INC. All Rights Reserved. www.facebook.com/garfield
Distributed by Andrews McMeel Syndication
JIM DAVIS 3-3

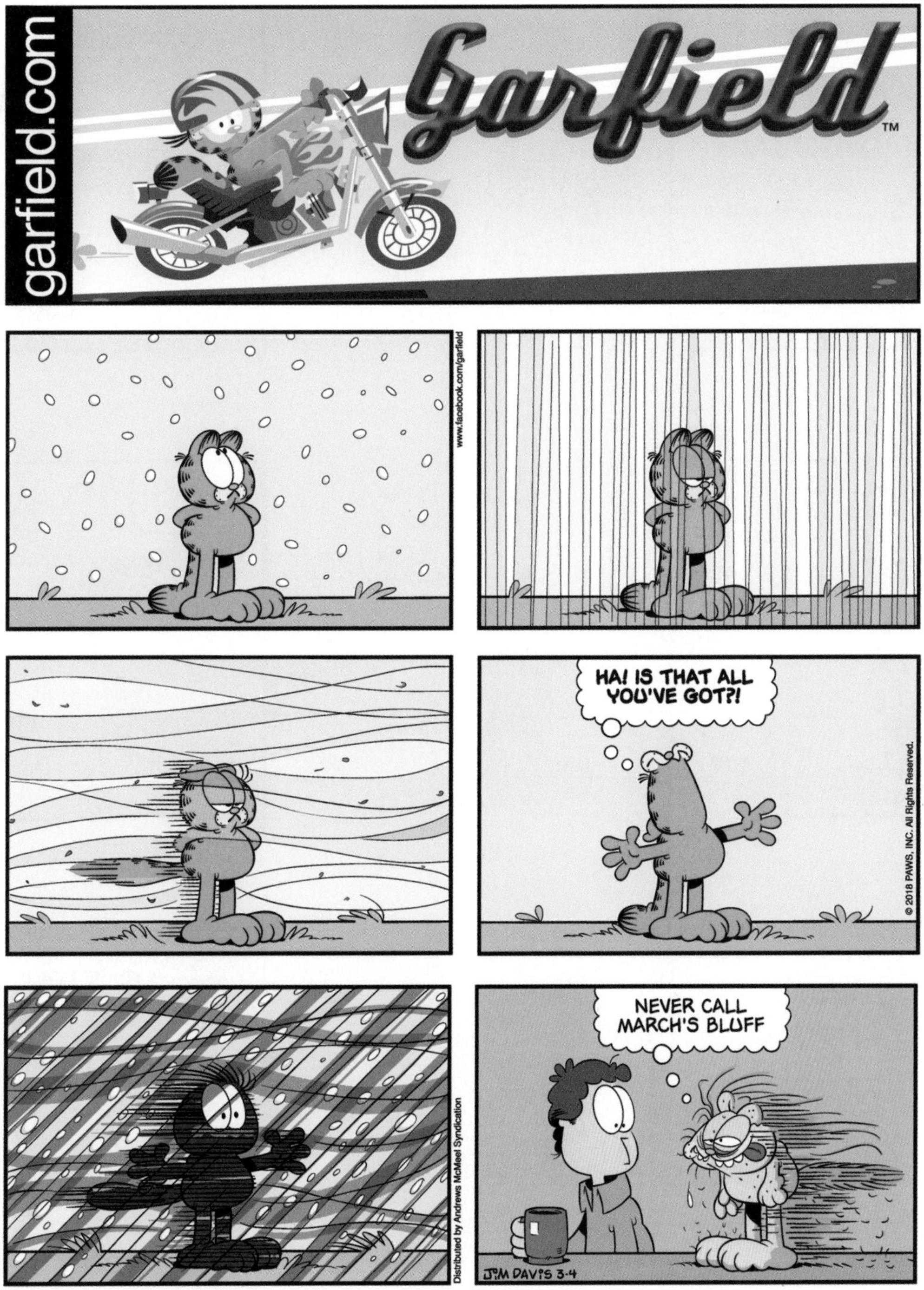
garfield.com
Garfield
TM
www.facebook.com/garfield
HA! IS THAT ALL YOU'VE GOT?!
© 2018 PAWS, INC. All Rights Reserved.
Distributed by Andrews McMeel Syndication
NEVER CALL MARCH'S BLUFF
JIM DAVIS 3-4

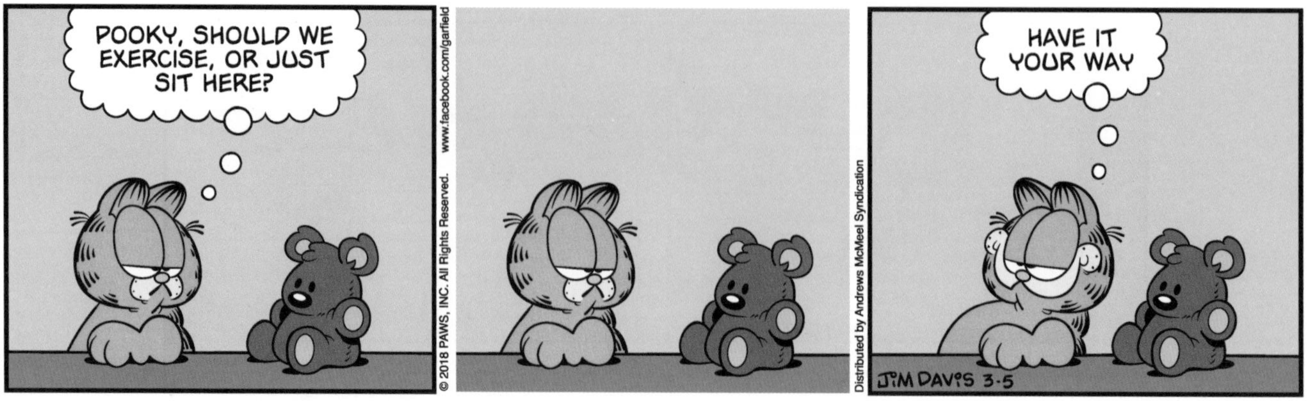
POOKY, SHOULD WE EXERCISE, OR JUST SIT HERE?
© 2018 PAWS, INC. All Rights Reserved. www.facebook.com/garfield
Distributed by Andrews McMeel Syndication
HAVE IT YOUR WAY
JIM DAVIS 3-5

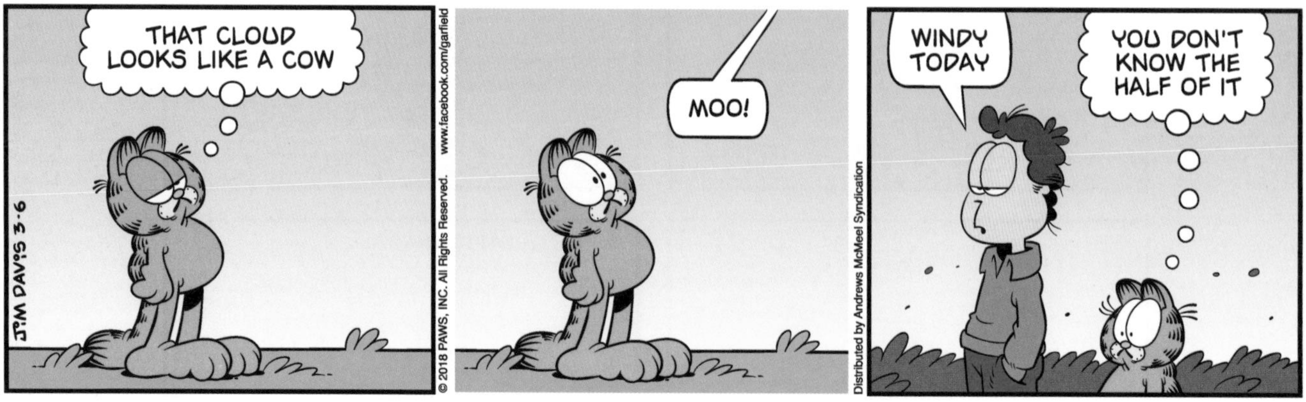
THAT CLOUD LOOKS LIKE A COW
JIM DAVIS 3-6
© 2018 PAWS, INC. All Rights Reserved. www.facebook.com/garfield
MOO!
Distributed by Andrews McMeel Syndication
WINDY TODAY
YOU DON'T KNOW THE HALF OF IT

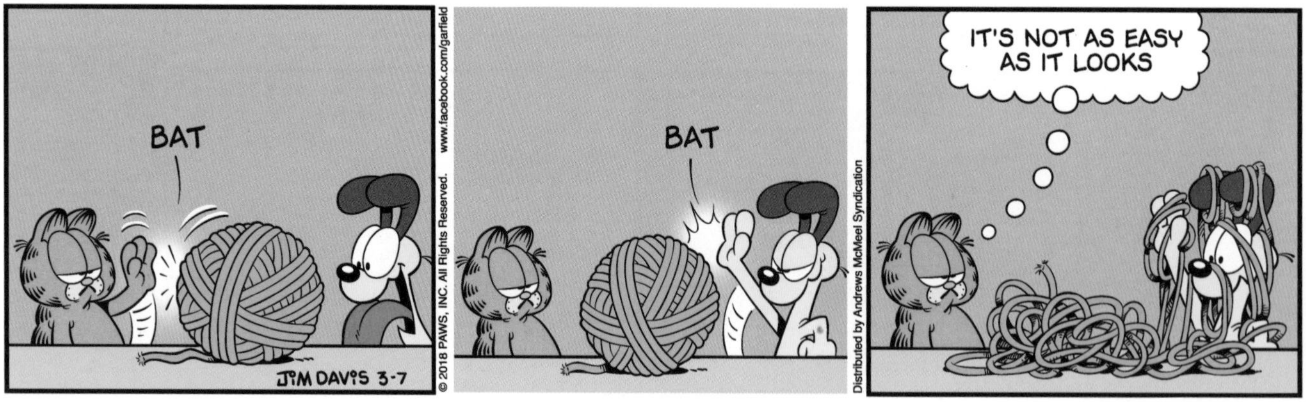
BAT
JIM DAVIS 3-7
© 2018 PAWS, INC. All Rights Reserved. www.facebook.com/garfield
BAT
Distributed by Andrews McMeel Syndication
IT'S NOT AS EASY AS IT LOOKS

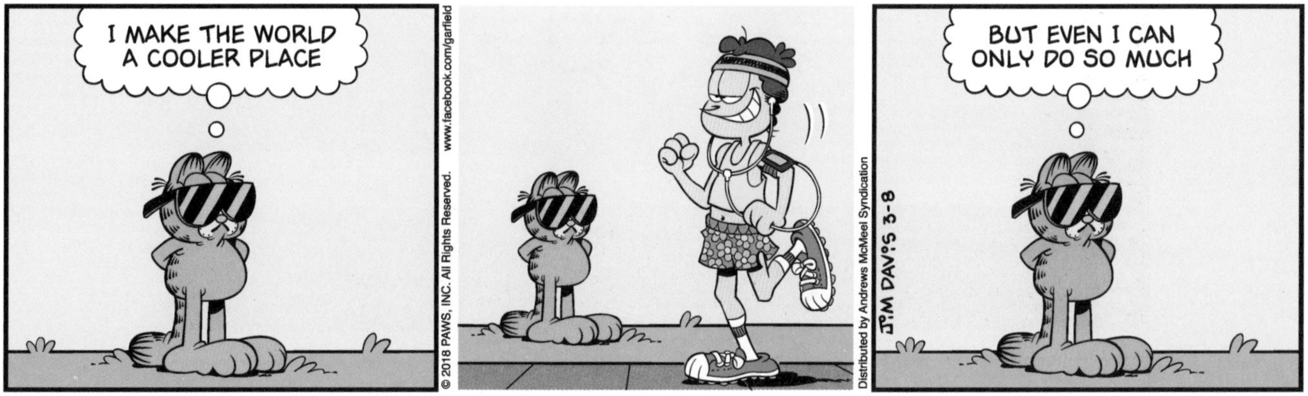
I MAKE THE WORLD A COOLER PLACE
BUT EVEN I CAN ONLY DO SO MUCH
© 2018 PAWS, INC. All Rights Reserved. www.facebook.com/garfield
Distributed by Andrews McMeel Syndication
JIM DAVIS 3-8

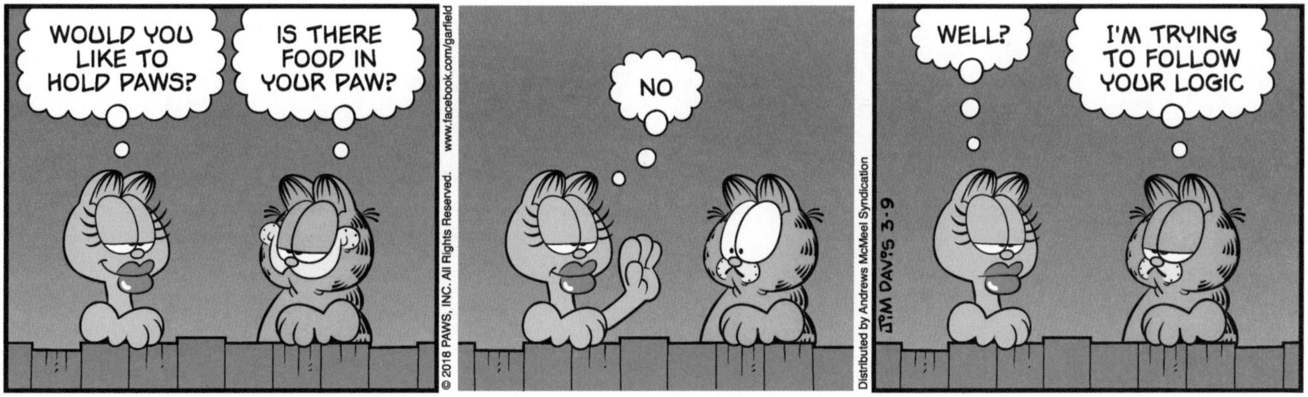
WOULD YOU LIKE TO HOLD PAWS?
IS THERE FOOD IN YOUR PAW?
NO
WELL?
I'M TRYING TO FOLLOW YOUR LOGIC
© 2018 PAWS, INC. All Rights Reserved. www.facebook.com/garfield
Distributed by Andrews McMeel Syndication
JIM DAVIS 3-9

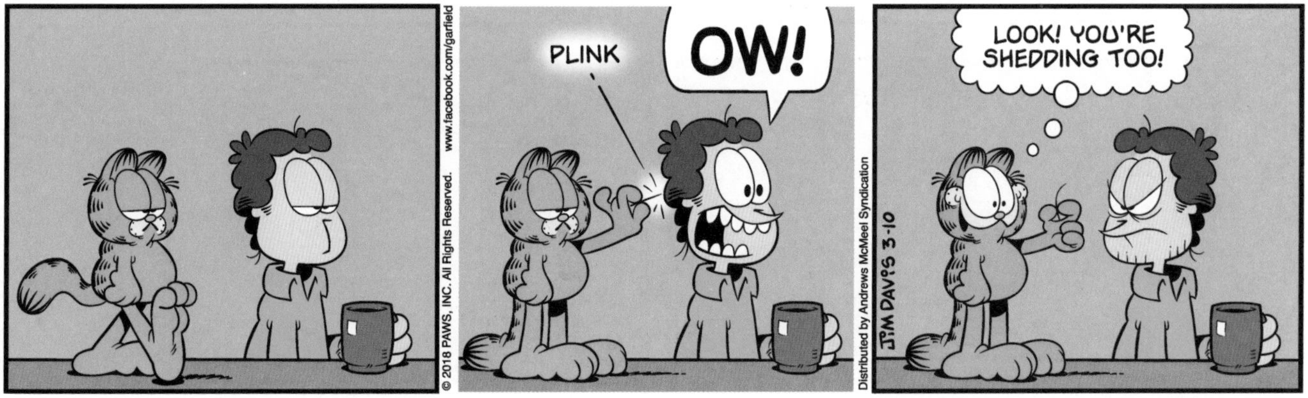
PLINK
OW!
LOOK! YOU'RE SHEDDING TOO!
© 2018 PAWS, INC. All Rights Reserved. www.facebook.com/garfield
Distributed by Andrews McMeel Syndication
JIM DAVIS 3-10

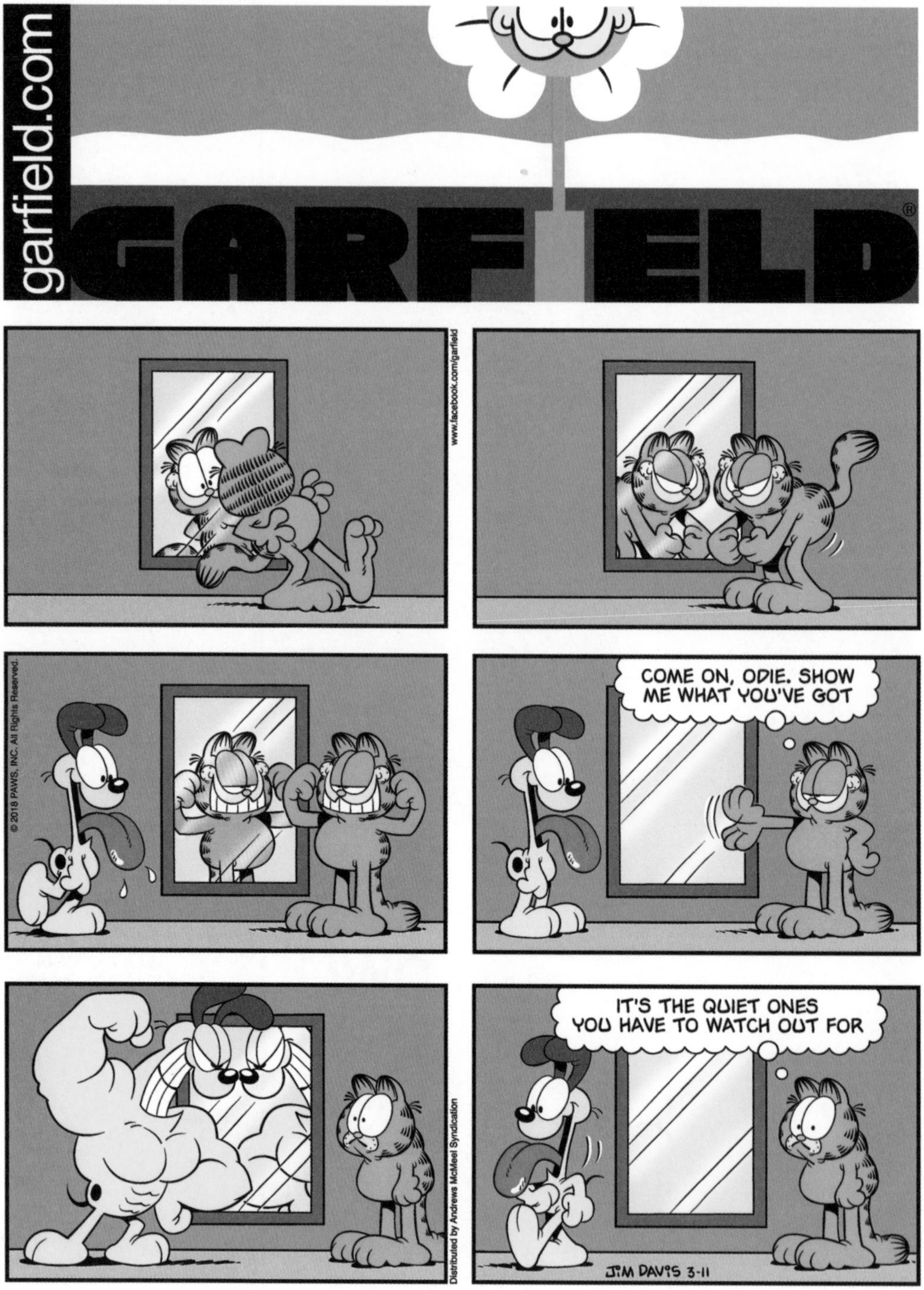
garfield.com
GARFIELD®
www.facebook.com/garfield
© 2018 PAWS, INC. All Rights Reserved.
COME ON, ODIE. SHOW ME WHAT YOU'VE GOT
Distributed by Andrews McMeel Syndication
IT'S THE QUIET ONES YOU HAVE TO WATCH OUT FOR
JIM DAVIS 3-11

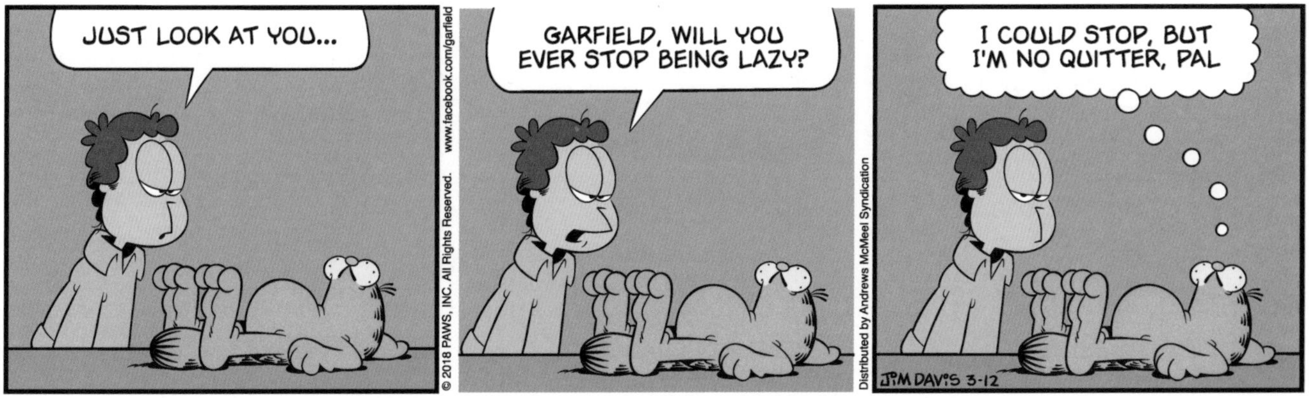
JUST LOOK AT YOU...
GARFIELD, WILL YOU EVER STOP BEING LAZY?
I COULD STOP, BUT I'M NO QUITTER, PAL
JIM DAVIS 3-12
© 2018 PAWS, INC. All Rights Reserved. www.facebook.com/garfield
Distributed by Andrews McMeel Syndication

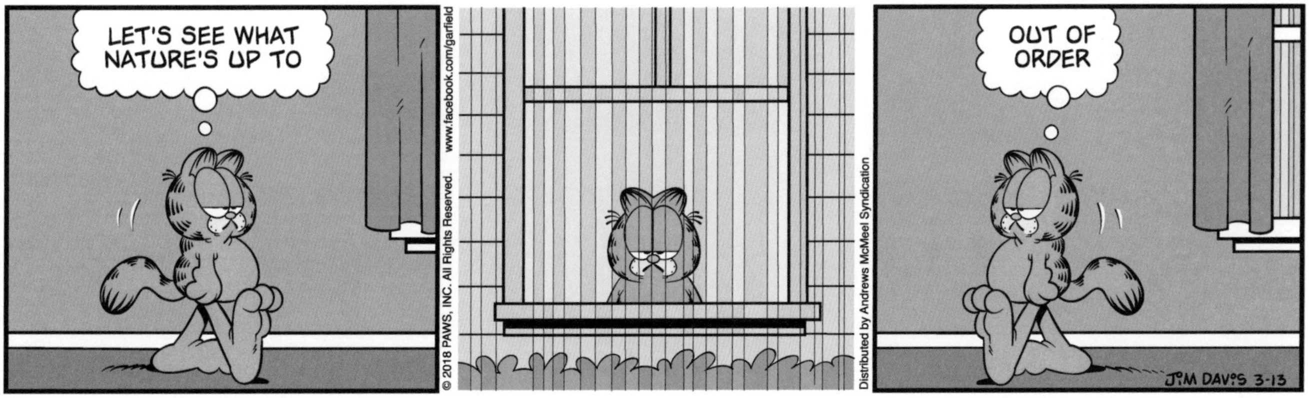
LET'S SEE WHAT NATURE'S UP TO
OUT OF ORDER
JIM DAVIS 3-13
© 2018 PAWS, INC. All Rights Reserved. www.facebook.com/garfield
Distributed by Andrews McMeel Syndication

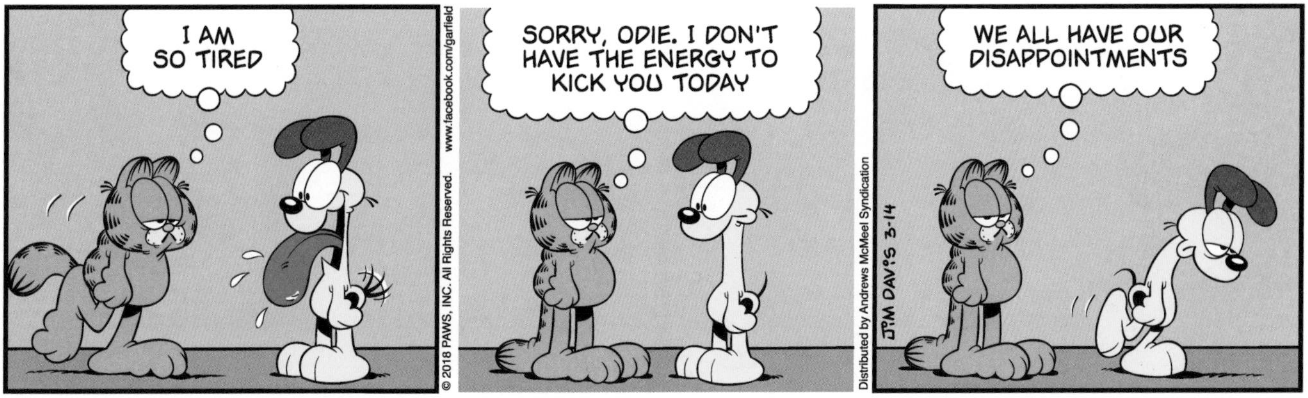
I AM SO TIRED
SORRY, ODIE. I DON'T HAVE THE ENERGY TO KICK YOU TODAY
WE ALL HAVE OUR DISAPPOINTMENTS
JIM DAVIS 3-14
© 2018 PAWS, INC. All Rights Reserved. www.facebook.com/garfield
Distributed by Andrews McMeel Syndication

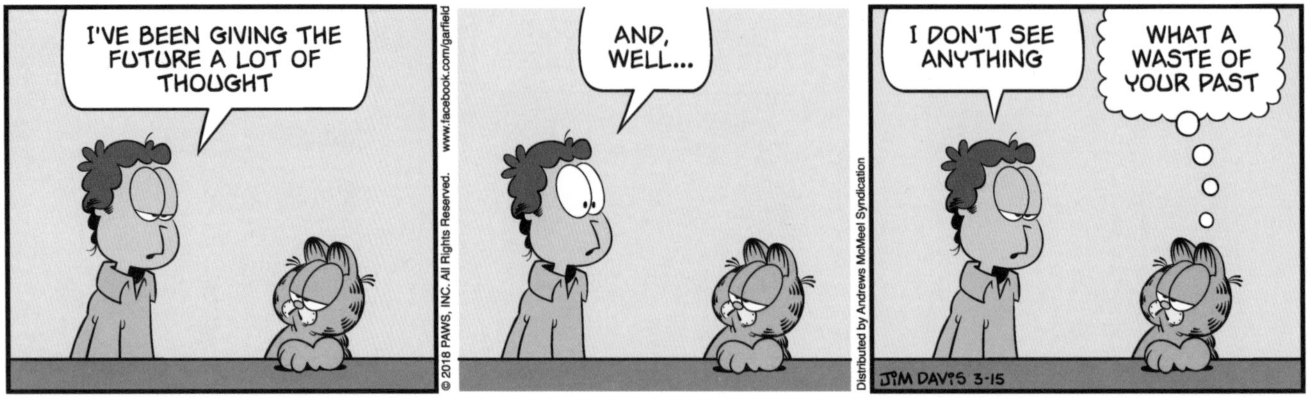
I'VE BEEN GIVING THE FUTURE A LOT OF THOUGHT
AND, WELL...
I DON'T SEE ANYTHING
WHAT A WASTE OF YOUR PAST
© 2018 PAWS, INC. All Rights Reserved. www.facebook.com/garfield
Distributed by Andrews McMeel Syndication
JIM DAVIS 3-15

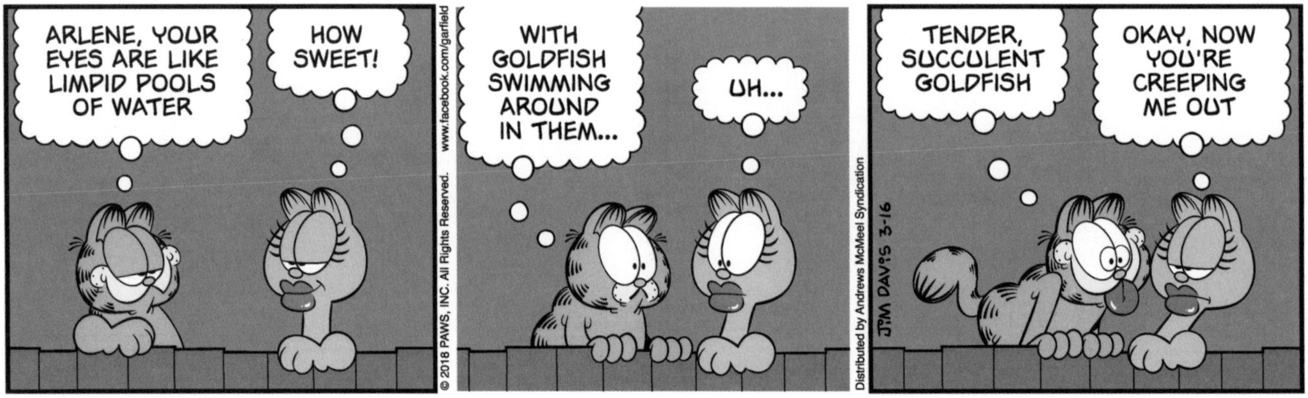
ARLENE, YOUR EYES ARE LIKE LIMPID POOLS OF WATER
HOW SWEET!
WITH GOLDFISH SWIMMING AROUND IN THEM...
UH...
TENDER, SUCCULENT GOLDFISH
OKAY, NOW YOU'RE CREEPING ME OUT
© 2018 PAWS, INC. All Rights Reserved. www.facebook.com/garfield
Distributed by Andrews McMeel Syndication
JIM DAVIS 3-16

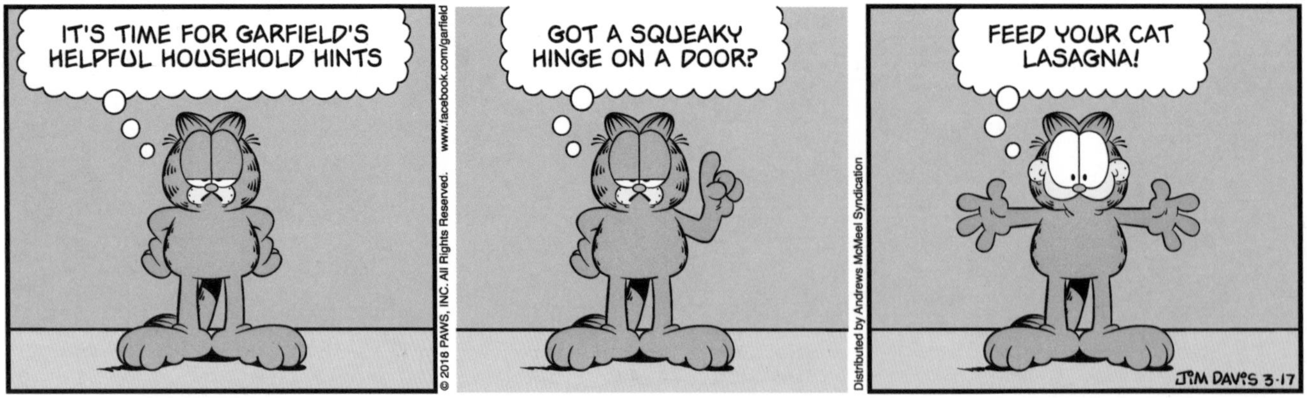
IT'S TIME FOR GARFIELD'S HELPFUL HOUSEHOLD HINTS
GOT A SQUEAKY HINGE ON A DOOR?
FEED YOUR CAT LASAGNA!
© 2018 PAWS, INC. All Rights Reserved. www.facebook.com/garfield
Distributed by Andrews McMeel Syndication
JIM DAVIS 3-17

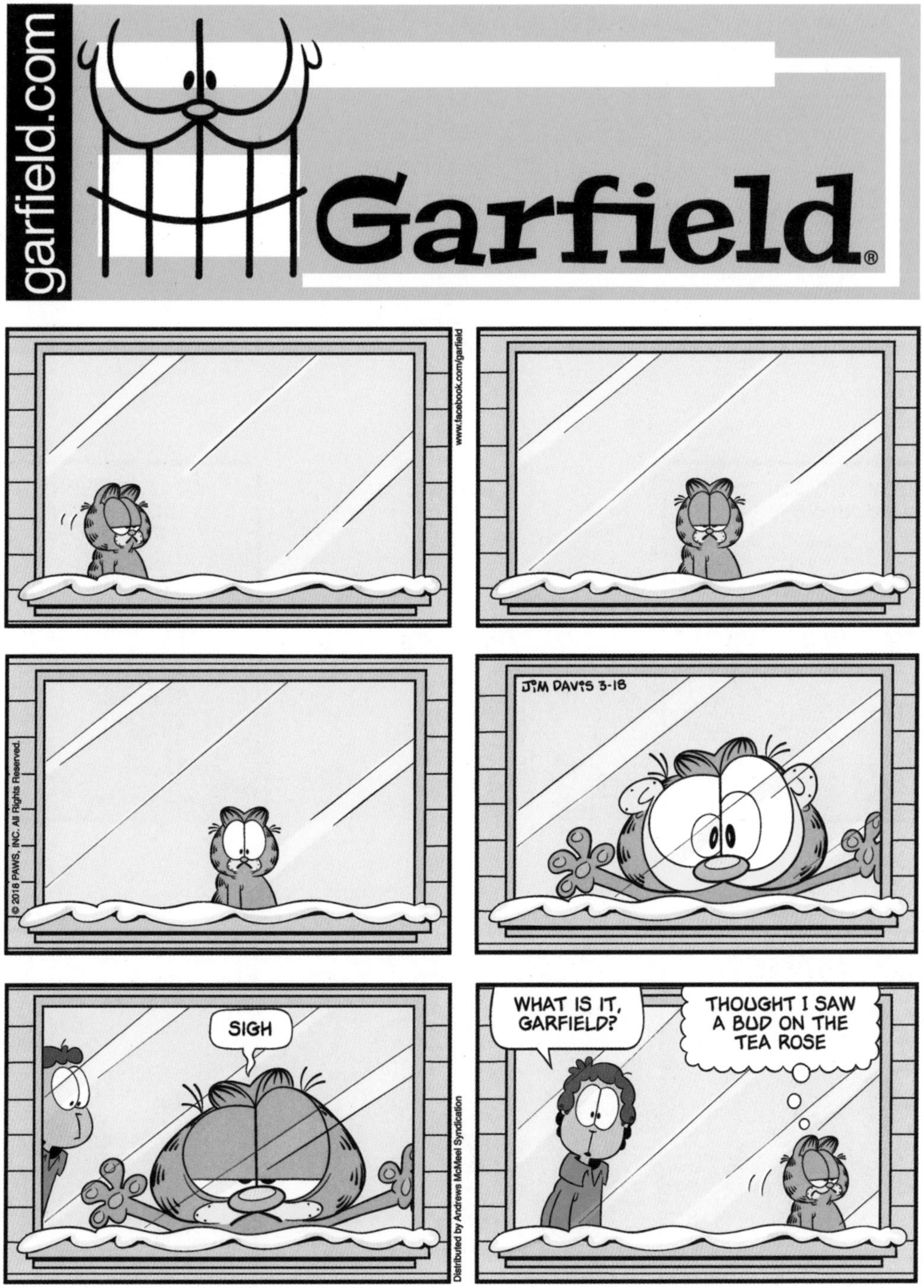
garfield.com
Garfield
www.facebook.com/garfield
© 2018 PAWS, INC. All Rights Reserved.
JIM DAVIS 3-18
SIGH
WHAT IS IT, GARFIELD?
THOUGHT I SAW A BUD ON THE TEA ROSE
Distributed by Andrews McMeel Syndication

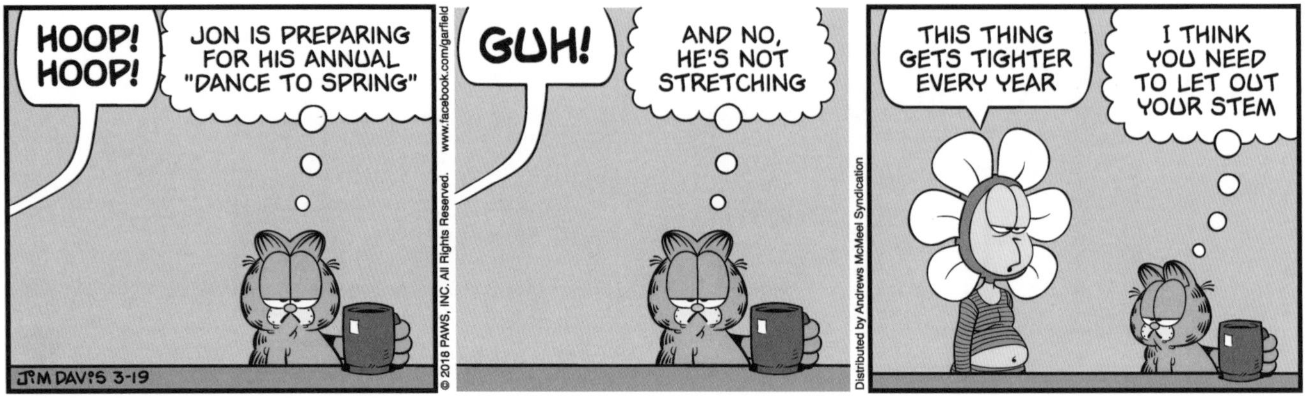
HOOP! HOOP!
JON IS PREPARING FOR HIS ANNUAL "DANCE TO SPRING"
JIM DAVIS 3-19
© 2018 PAWS, INC. All Rights Reserved. www.facebook.com/garfield
GUH!
AND NO, HE'S NOT STRETCHING
Distributed by Andrews McMeel Syndication
THIS THING GETS TIGHTER EVERY YEAR
I THINK YOU NEED TO LET OUT YOUR STEM

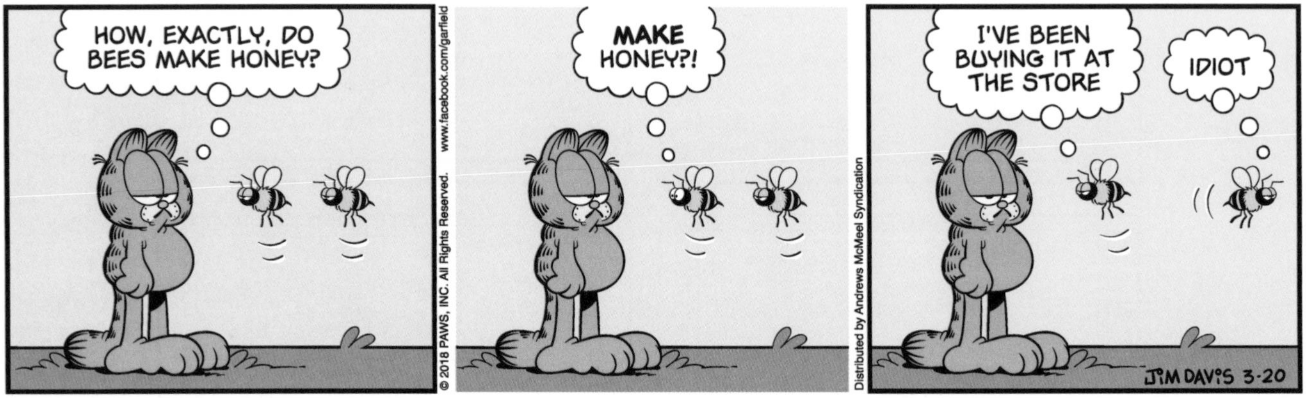
HOW, EXACTLY, DO BEES MAKE HONEY?
© 2018 PAWS, INC. All Rights Reserved. www.facebook.com/garfield
MAKE HONEY?!
Distributed by Andrews McMeel Syndication
I'VE BEEN BUYING IT AT THE STORE
IDIOT
JIM DAVIS 3-20

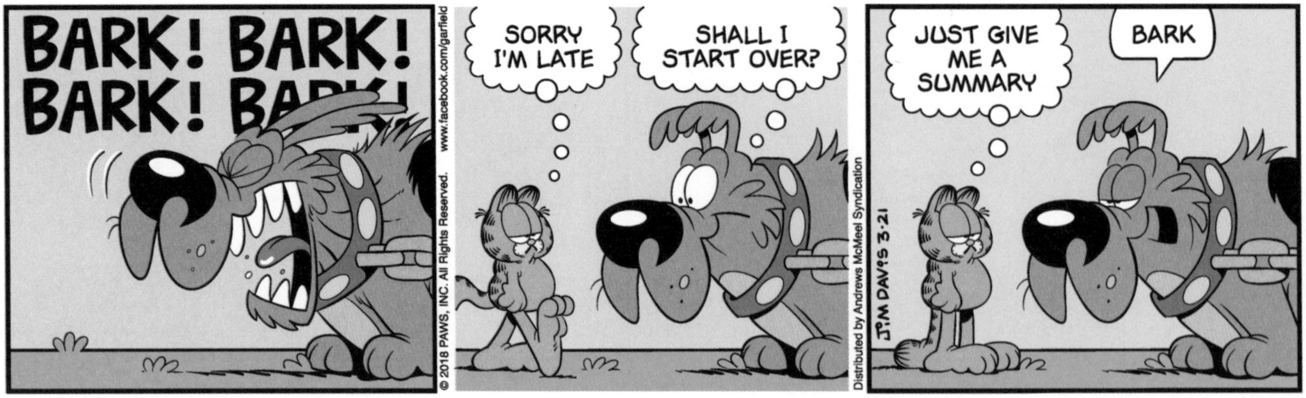
BARK! BARK! BARK! BARK!
© 2018 PAWS, INC. All Rights Reserved. www.facebook.com/garfield
SORRY I'M LATE
SHALL I START OVER?
Distributed by Andrews McMeel Syndication
JIM DAVIS 3-21
JUST GIVE ME A SUMMARY
BARK

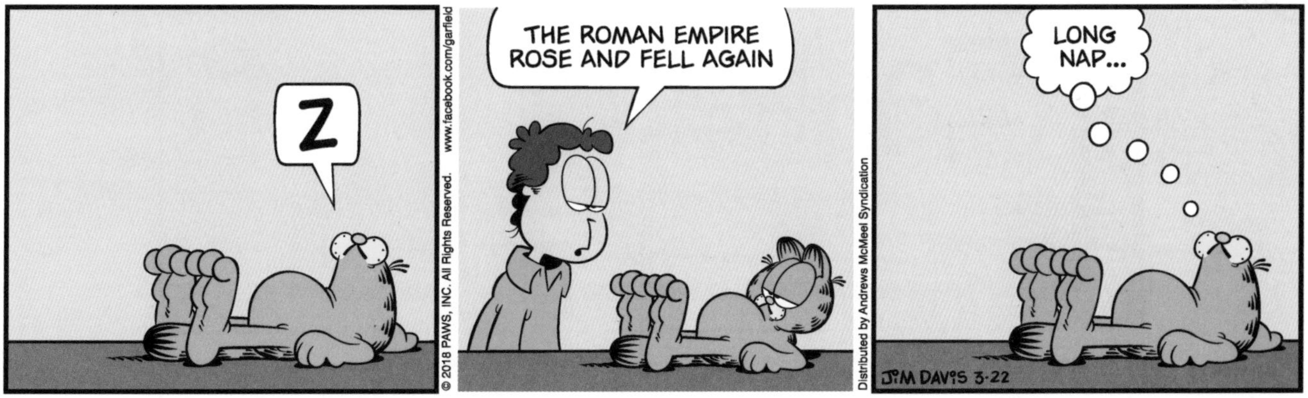
Z
THE ROMAN EMPIRE ROSE AND FELL AGAIN
LONG NAP...
© 2018 PAWS, INC. All Rights Reserved. www.facebook.com/garfield
Distributed by Andrews McMeel Syndication
JIM DAVIS 3-22

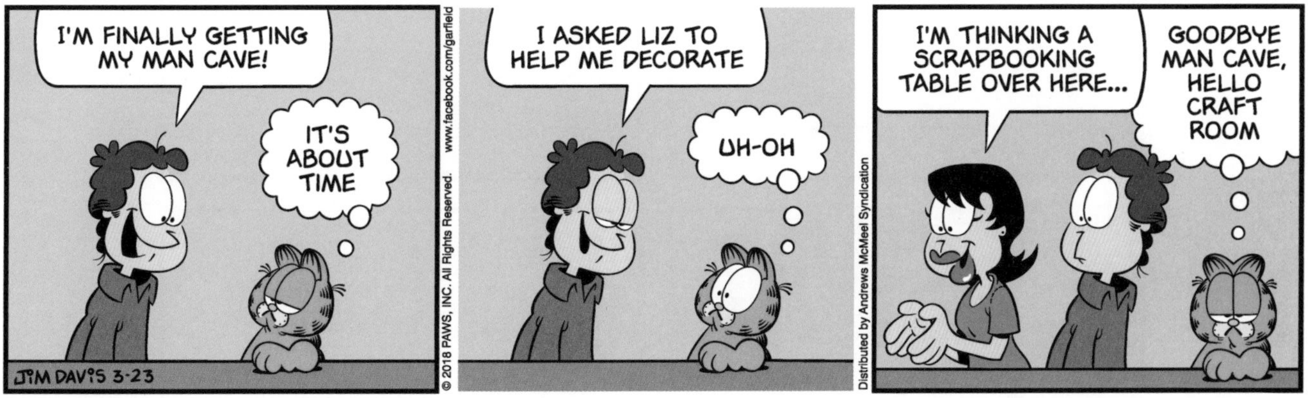
I'M FINALLY GETTING MY MAN CAVE!
IT'S ABOUT TIME
I ASKED LIZ TO HELP ME DECORATE
UH-OH
I'M THINKING A SCRAPBOOKING TABLE OVER HERE...
GOODBYE MAN CAVE, HELLO CRAFT ROOM
JIM DAVIS 3-23
© 2018 PAWS, INC. All Rights Reserved. www.facebook.com/garfield
Distributed by Andrews McMeel Syndication

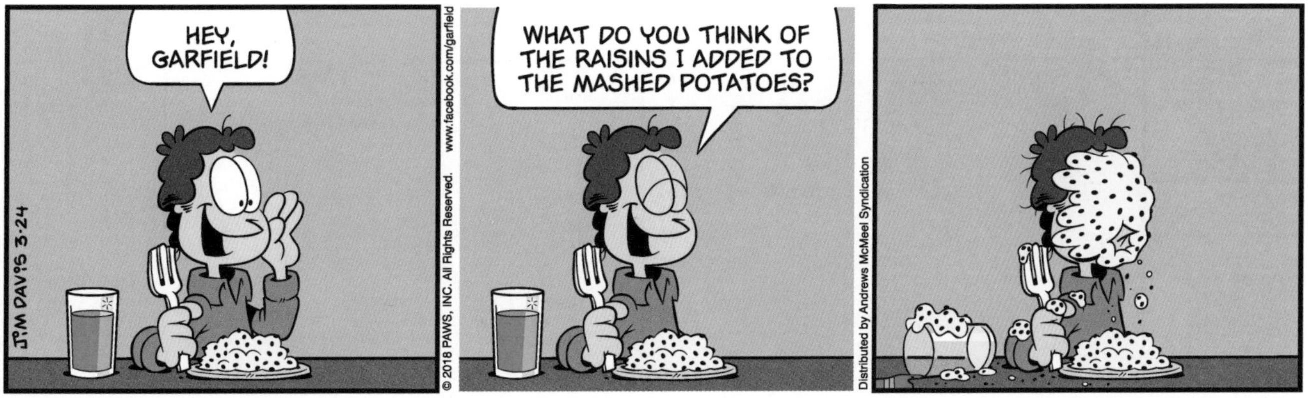
HEY, GARFIELD!
WHAT DO YOU THINK OF THE RAISINS I ADDED TO THE MASHED POTATOES?
JIM DAVIS 3-24
© 2018 PAWS, INC. All Rights Reserved. www.facebook.com/garfield
Distributed by Andrews McMeel Syndication

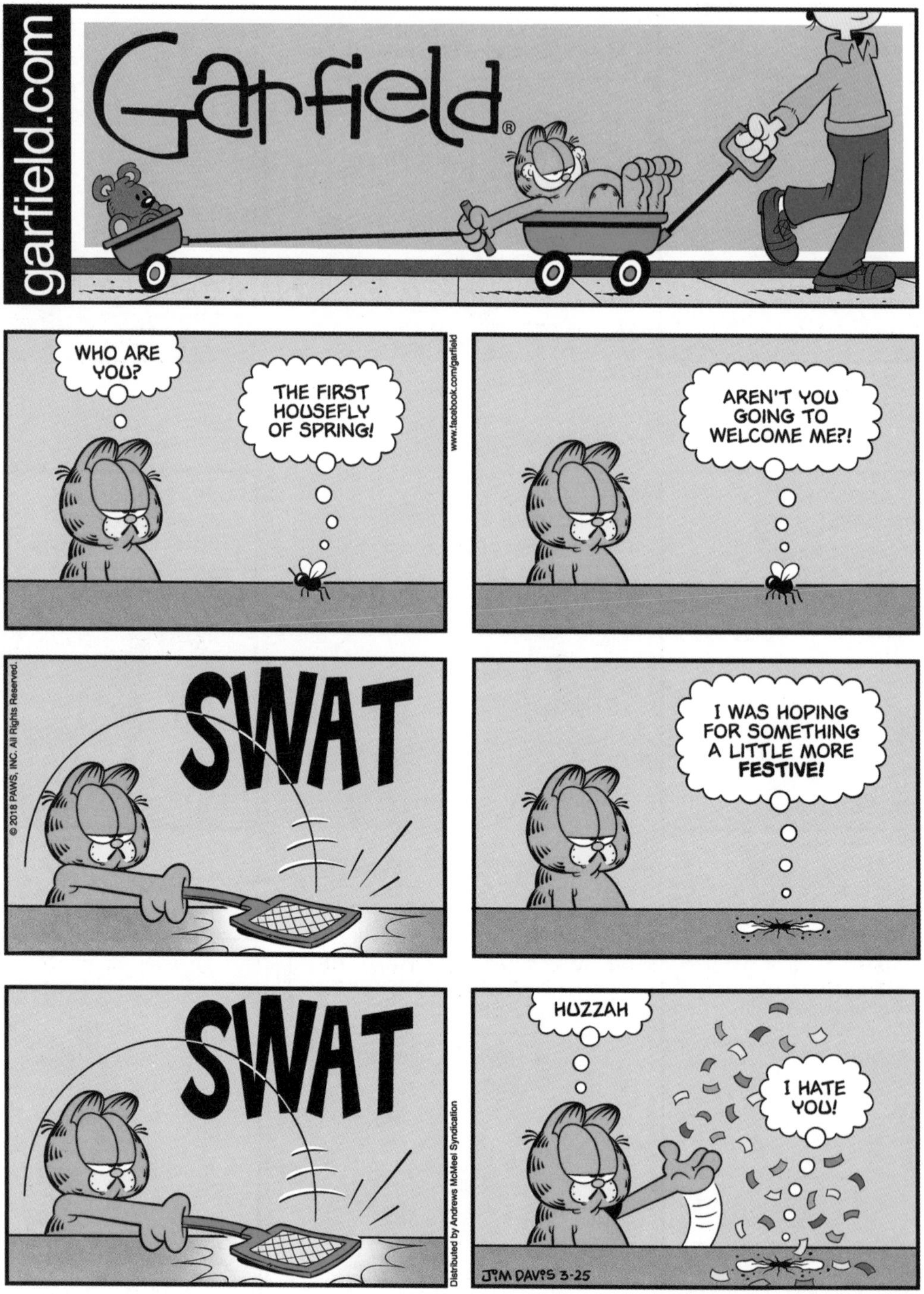
garfield.com
Garfield®
WHO ARE YOU?
THE FIRST HOUSEFLY OF SPRING!
www.facebook.com/garfield
AREN'T YOU GOING TO WELCOME ME?!
© 2018 PAWS, INC. All Rights Reserved.
SWAT
I WAS HOPING FOR SOMETHING A LITTLE MORE **FESTIVE!**
SWAT
Distributed by Andrews McMeel Syndication
HUZZAH
I HATE YOU!
JIM DAVIS 3-25

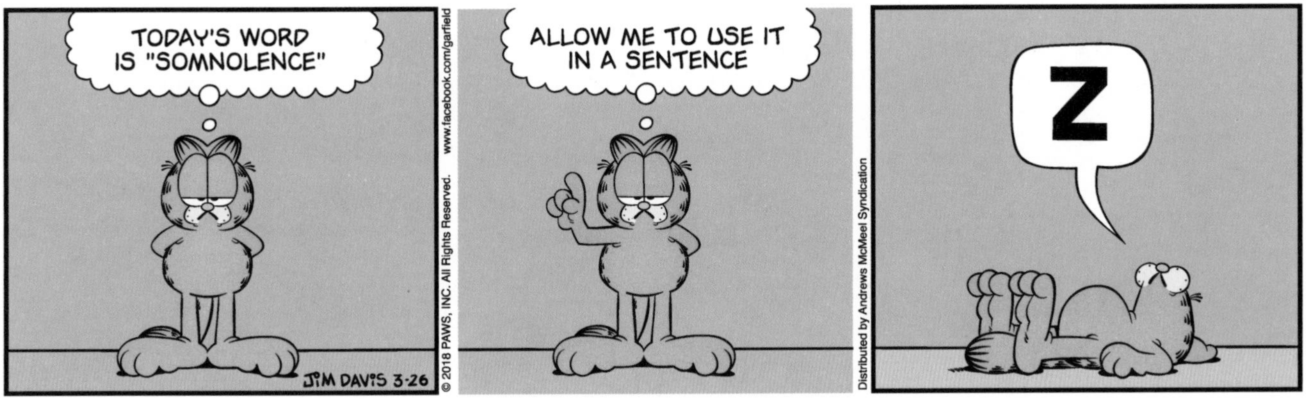
TODAY'S WORD IS "SOMNOLENCE"
JIM DAVIS 3-26
© 2018 PAWS, INC. All Rights Reserved. www.facebook.com/garfield
ALLOW ME TO USE IT IN A SENTENCE
Distributed by Andrews McMeel Syndication
Z

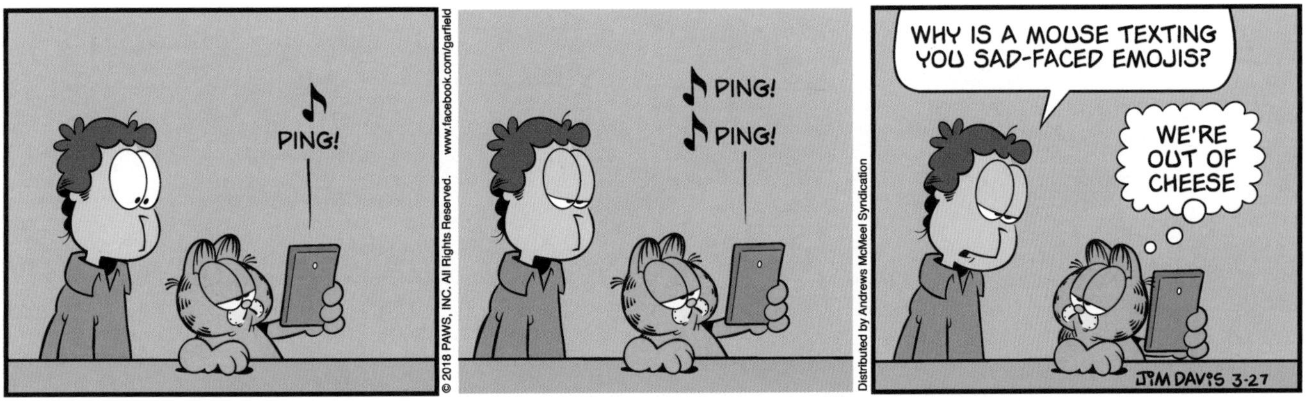
PING!
© 2018 PAWS, INC. All Rights Reserved. www.facebook.com/garfield
PING!
PING!
Distributed by Andrews McMeel Syndication
WHY IS A MOUSE TEXTING YOU SAD-FACED EMOJIS?
WE'RE OUT OF CHEESE
JIM DAVIS 3-27

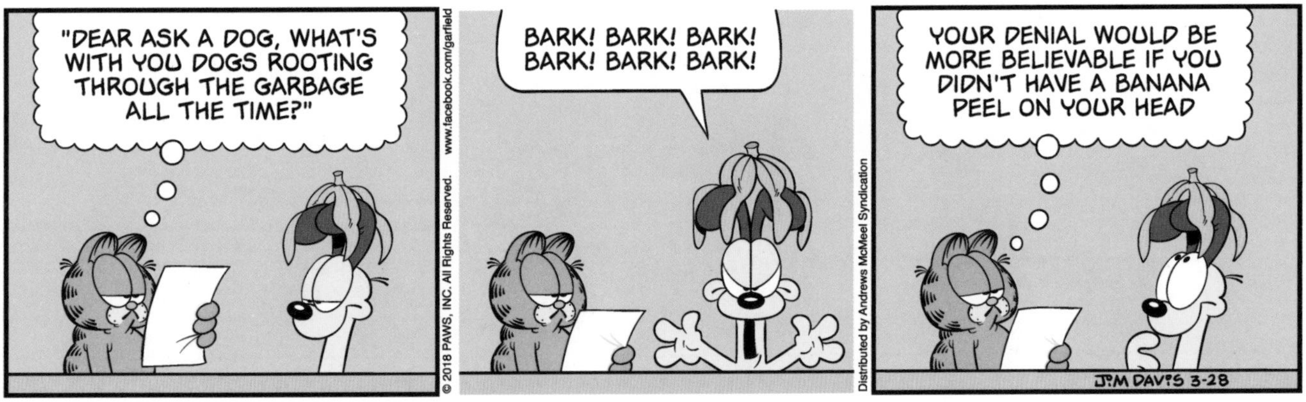
"DEAR ASK A DOG, WHAT'S WITH YOU DOGS ROOTING THROUGH THE GARBAGE ALL THE TIME?"
© 2018 PAWS, INC. All Rights Reserved. www.facebook.com/garfield
BARK! BARK! BARK! BARK! BARK! BARK!
Distributed by Andrews McMeel Syndication
YOUR DENIAL WOULD BE MORE BELIEVABLE IF YOU DIDN'T HAVE A BANANA PEEL ON YOUR HEAD
JIM DAVIS 3-28

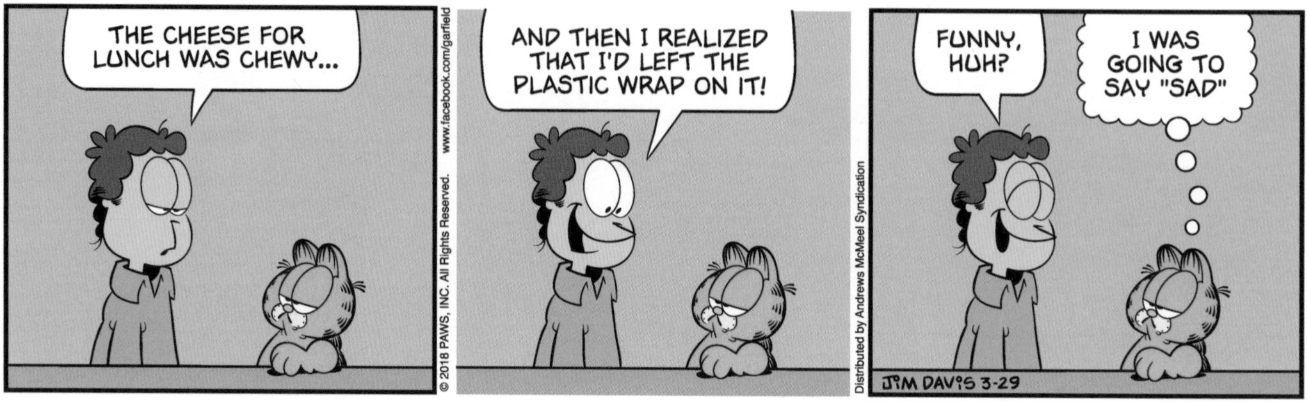
THE CHEESE FOR LUNCH WAS CHEWY...
© 2018 PAWS, INC. All Rights Reserved. www.facebook.com/garfield
AND THEN I REALIZED THAT I'D LEFT THE PLASTIC WRAP ON IT!
Distributed by Andrews McMeel Syndication
FUNNY, HUH?
I WAS GOING TO SAY "SAD"
JIM DAVIS 3-29

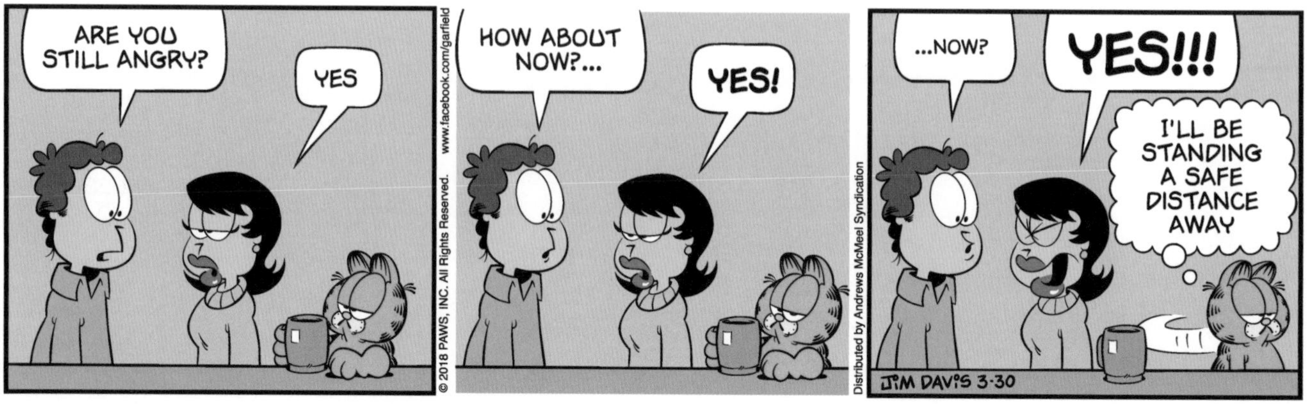
ARE YOU STILL ANGRY?
YES
© 2018 PAWS, INC. All Rights Reserved. www.facebook.com/garfield
HOW ABOUT NOW?...
YES!
Distributed by Andrews McMeel Syndication
...NOW?
YES!!!
I'LL BE STANDING A SAFE DISTANCE AWAY
JIM DAVIS 3-30

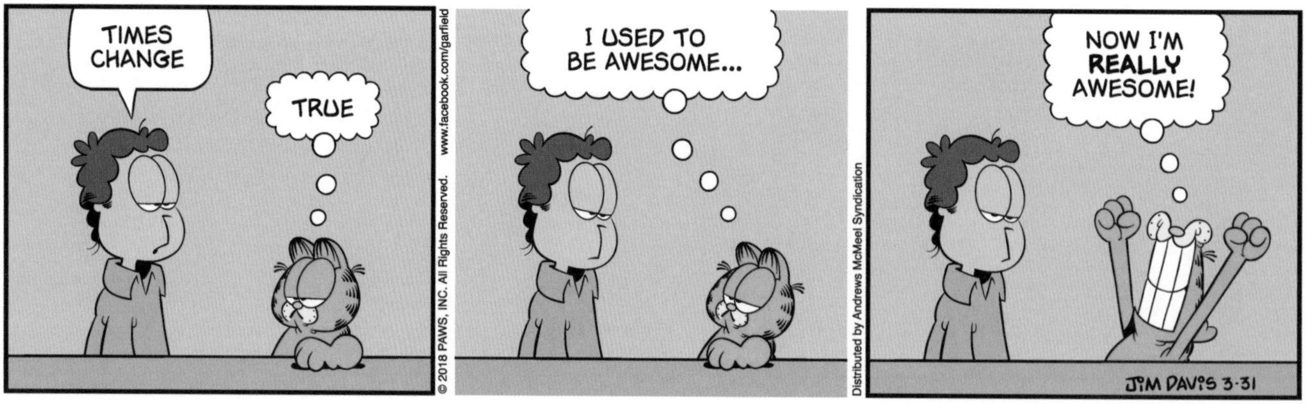
TIMES CHANGE
TRUE
© 2018 PAWS, INC. All Rights Reserved. www.facebook.com/garfield
I USED TO BE AWESOME...
Distributed by Andrews McMeel Syndication
NOW I'M REALLY AWESOME!
JIM DAVIS 3-31

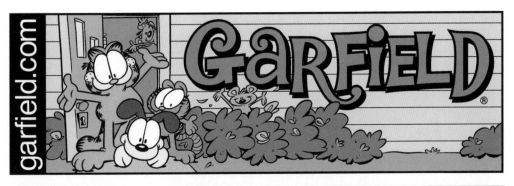

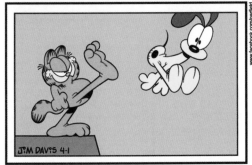

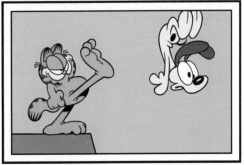

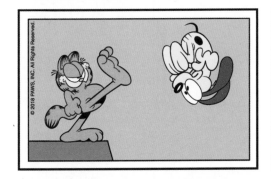

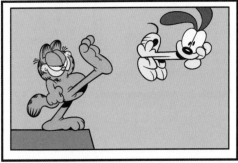

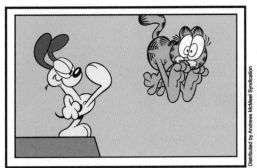

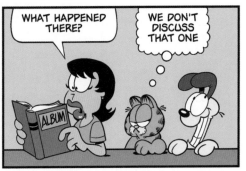

garfield.com
GARFIELD
JIM DAVIS 4-1
www.facebook.com/garfield
© 2018 PAWS, INC. All Rights Reserved.
Distributed by Andrews McMeel Syndication
WHAT HAPPENED THERE?
WE DON'T DISCUSS THAT ONE
ALBUM

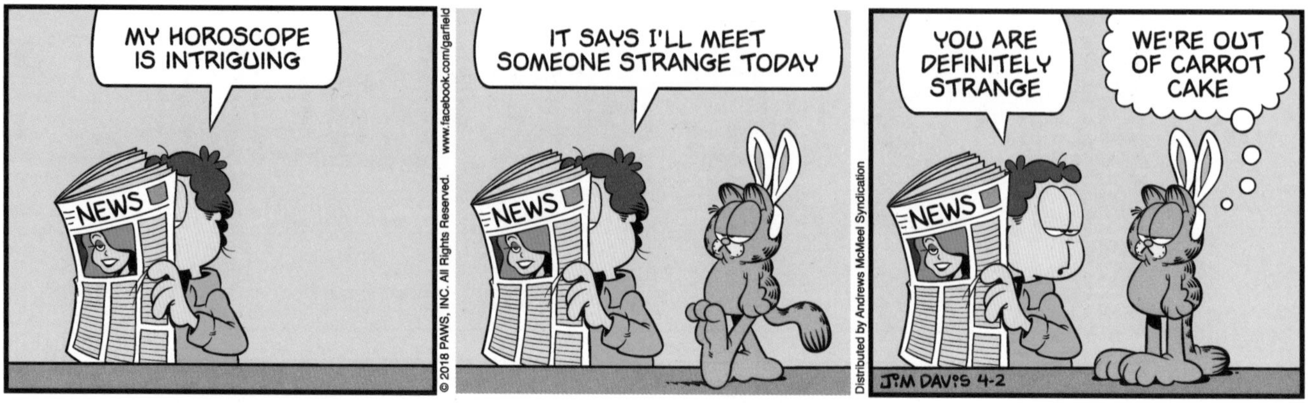
MY HOROSCOPE IS INTRIGUING
© 2018 PAWS, INC. All Rights Reserved. www.facebook.com/garfield
IT SAYS I'LL MEET SOMEONE STRANGE TODAY
Distributed by Andrews McMeel Syndication
YOU ARE DEFINITELY STRANGE
WE'RE OUT OF CARROT CAKE
JIM DAVIS 4-2

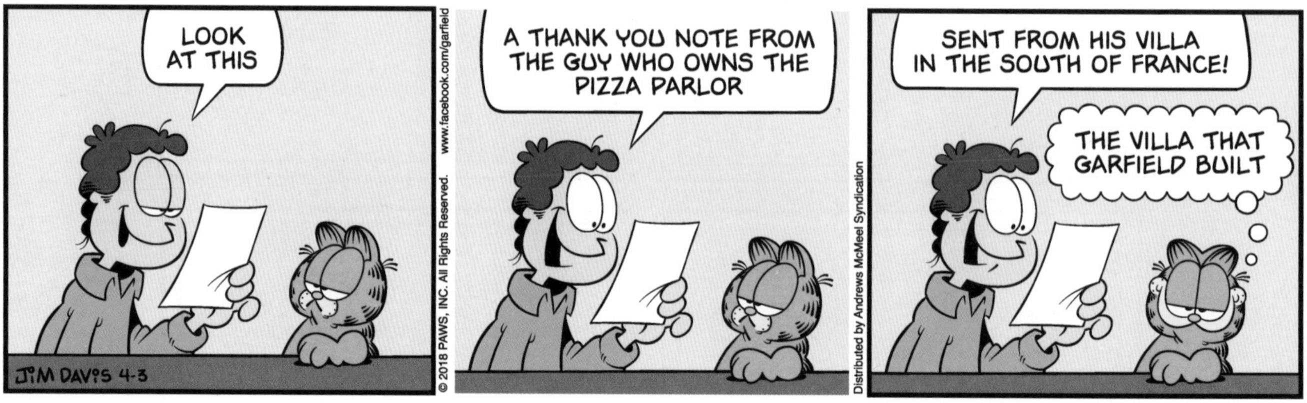
LOOK AT THIS
JIM DAVIS 4-3
© 2018 PAWS, INC. All Rights Reserved. www.facebook.com/garfield
A THANK YOU NOTE FROM THE GUY WHO OWNS THE PIZZA PARLOR
Distributed by Andrews McMeel Syndication
SENT FROM HIS VILLA IN THE SOUTH OF FRANCE!
THE VILLA THAT GARFIELD BUILT

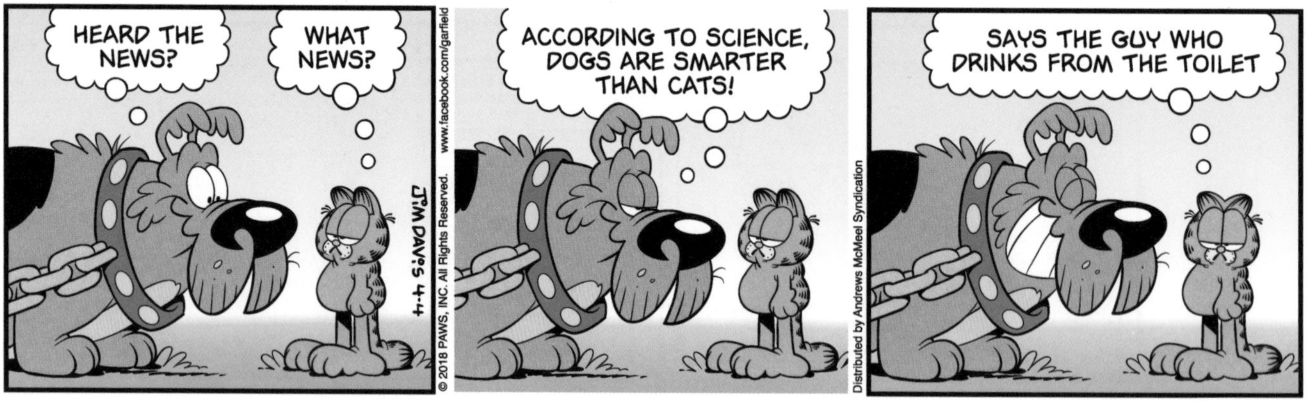
HEARD THE NEWS?
WHAT NEWS?
JIM DAVIS 4-4
© 2018 PAWS, INC. All Rights Reserved. www.facebook.com/garfield
ACCORDING TO SCIENCE, DOGS ARE SMARTER THAN CATS!
Distributed by Andrews McMeel Syndication
SAYS THE GUY WHO DRINKS FROM THE TOILET

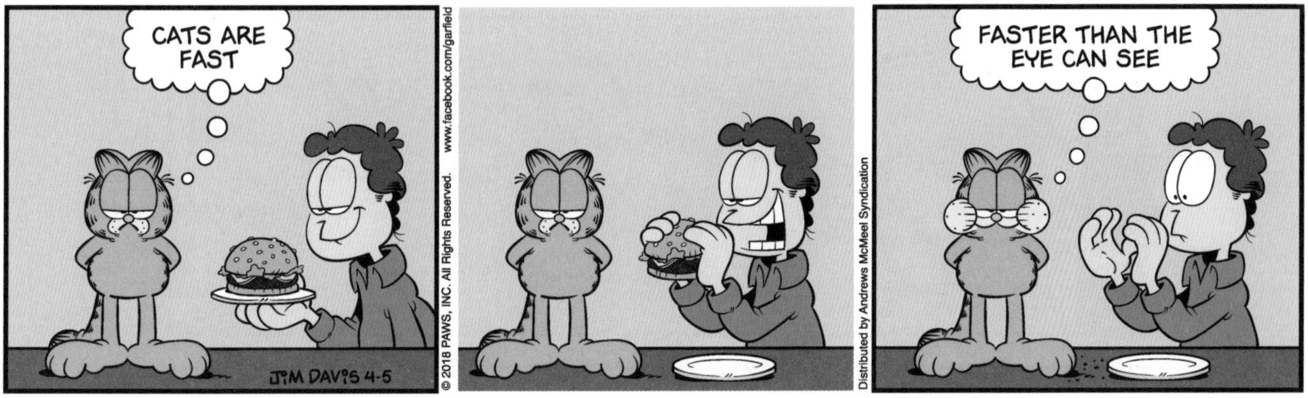
CATS ARE FAST
JIM DAVIS 4-5
© 2018 PAWS, INC. All Rights Reserved. www.facebook.com/garfield
FASTER THAN THE EYE CAN SEE
Distributed by Andrews McMeel Syndication

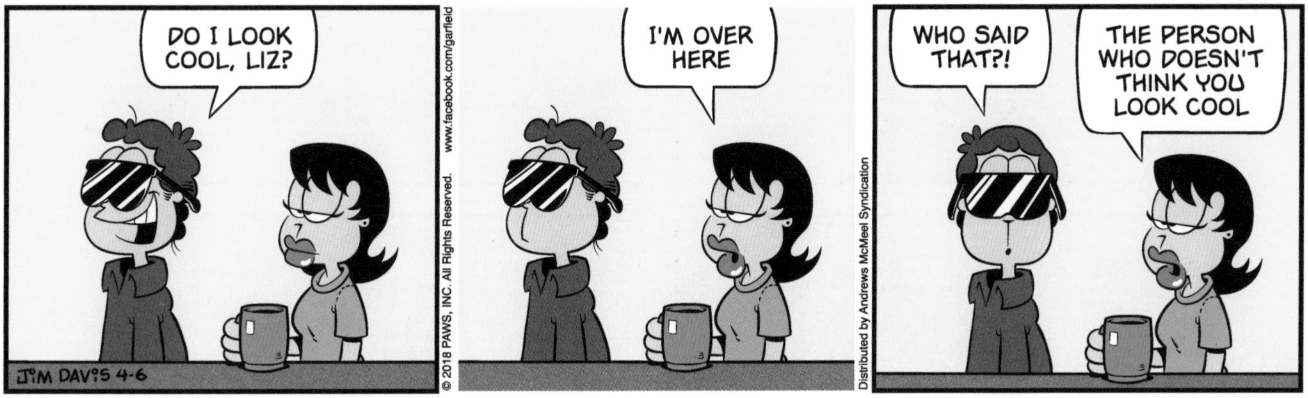
DO I LOOK COOL, LIZ?
JIM DAVIS 4-6
© 2018 PAWS, INC. All Rights Reserved. www.facebook.com/garfield
I'M OVER HERE
Distributed by Andrews McMeel Syndication
WHO SAID THAT?!
THE PERSON WHO DOESN'T THINK YOU LOOK COOL

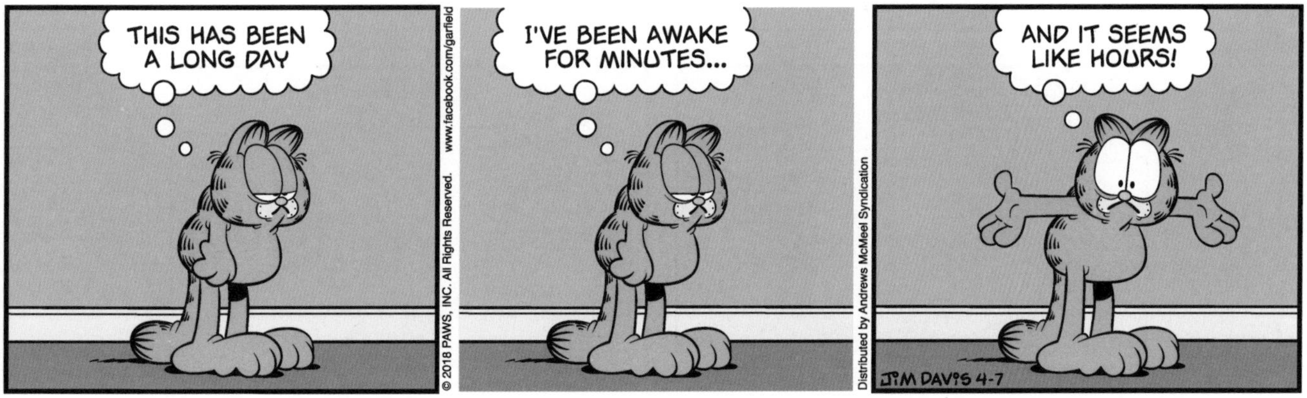
THIS HAS BEEN A LONG DAY
© 2018 PAWS, INC. All Rights Reserved. www.facebook.com/garfield
I'VE BEEN AWAKE FOR MINUTES...
Distributed by Andrews McMeel Syndication
AND IT SEEMS LIKE HOURS!
JIM DAVIS 4-7

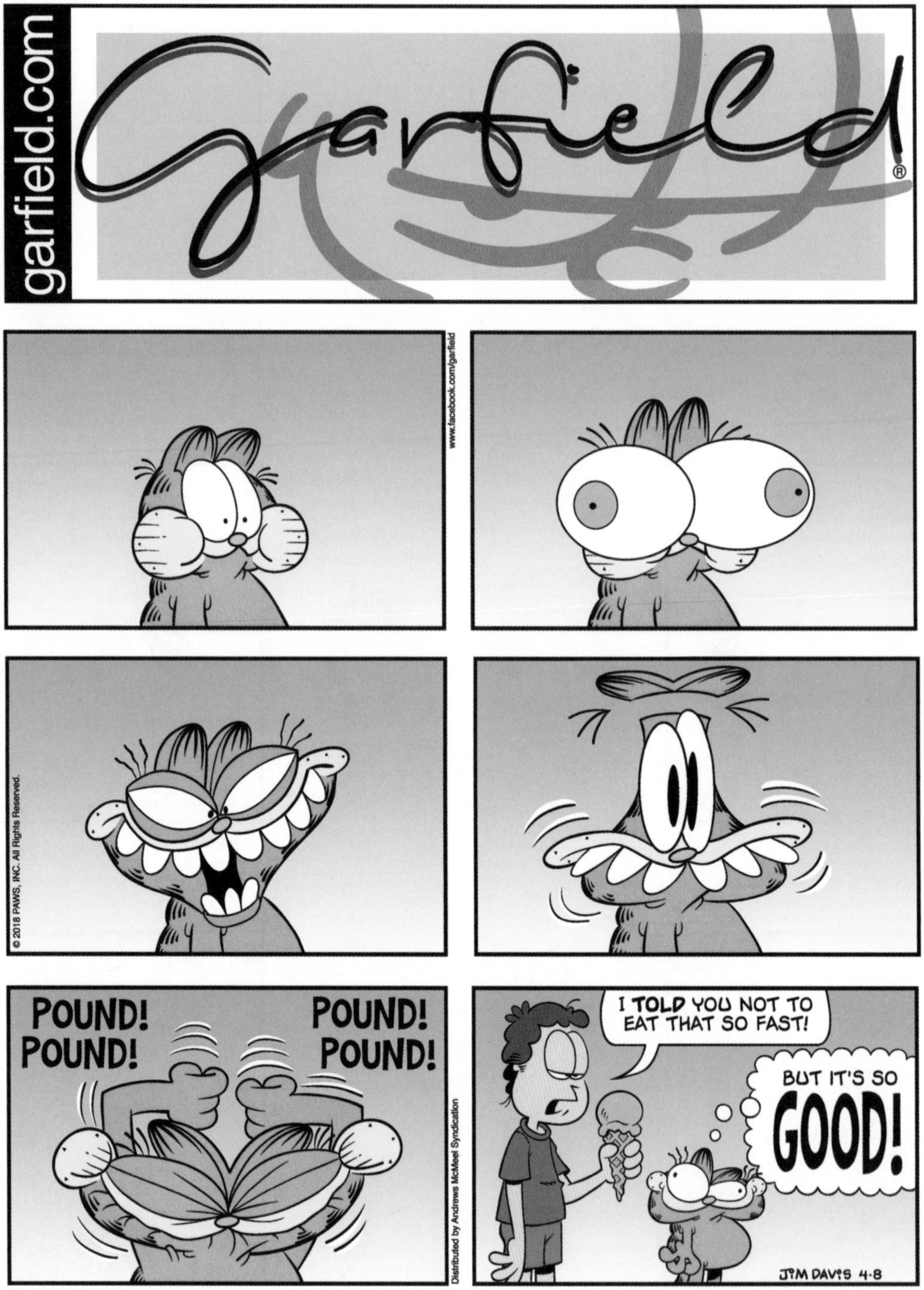
garfield.com
Garfield®
www.facebook.com/garfield
© 2018 PAWS, INC. All Rights Reserved.
POUND! POUND!
POUND! POUND!
Distributed by Andrews McMeel Syndication
I **TOLD** YOU NOT TO EAT THAT SO FAST!
BUT IT'S SO GOOD!
JIM DAVIS 4-8

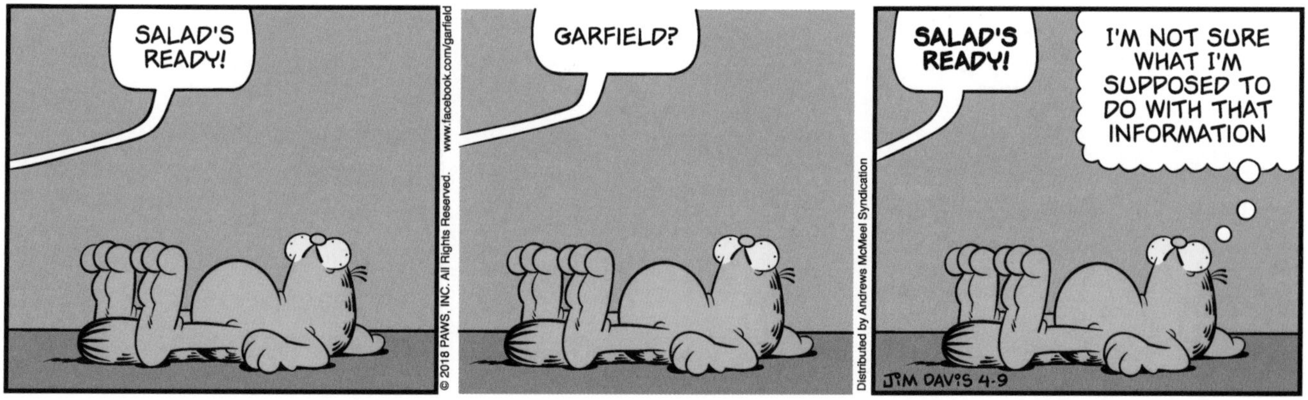
SALAD'S READY!
© 2018 PAWS, INC. All Rights Reserved. www.facebook.com/garfield
GARFIELD?
Distributed by Andrews McMeel Syndication
SALAD'S READY!
I'M NOT SURE WHAT I'M SUPPOSED TO DO WITH THAT INFORMATION
JIM DAVIS 4-9

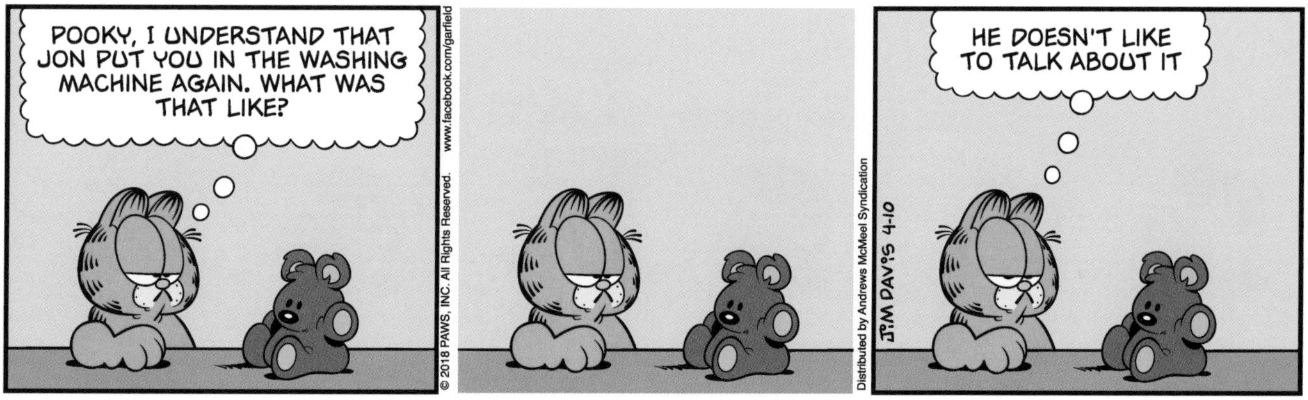
POOKY, I UNDERSTAND THAT JON PUT YOU IN THE WASHING MACHINE AGAIN. WHAT WAS THAT LIKE?
© 2018 PAWS, INC. All Rights Reserved. www.facebook.com/garfield
Distributed by Andrews McMeel Syndication
JIM DAVIS 4-10
HE DOESN'T LIKE TO TALK ABOUT IT

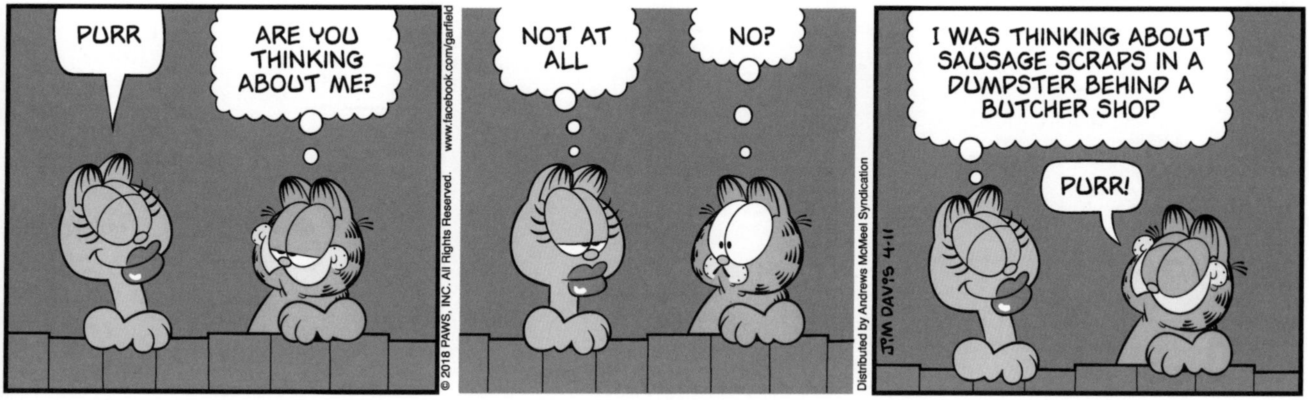
PURR
ARE YOU THINKING ABOUT ME?
© 2018 PAWS, INC. All Rights Reserved. www.facebook.com/garfield
NOT AT ALL
NO?
Distributed by Andrews McMeel Syndication
JIM DAVIS 4-11
I WAS THINKING ABOUT SAUSAGE SCRAPS IN A DUMPSTER BEHIND A BUTCHER SHOP
PURR!

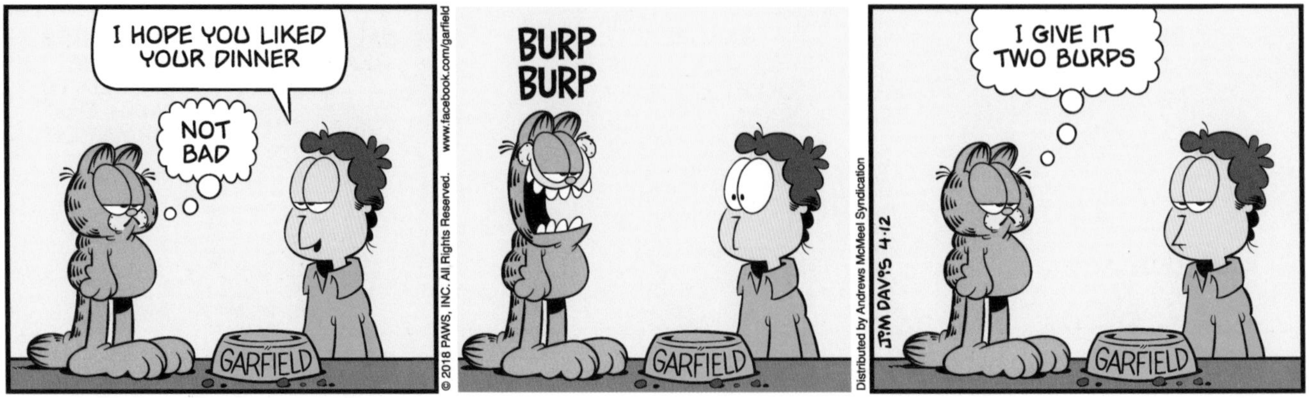
I HOPE YOU LIKED YOUR DINNER
NOT BAD
© 2018 PAWS, INC. All Rights Reserved. www.facebook.com/garfield
BURP BURP
Distributed by Andrews McMeel Syndication
I GIVE IT TWO BURPS
JIM DAVIS 4-12

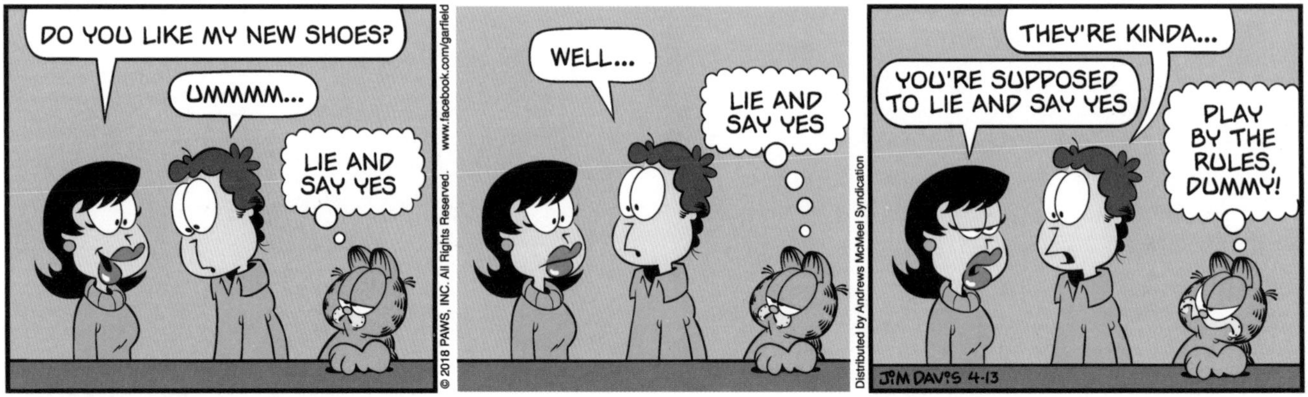
DO YOU LIKE MY NEW SHOES?
UMMMM...
LIE AND SAY YES
© 2018 PAWS, INC. All Rights Reserved. www.facebook.com/garfield
WELL...
LIE AND SAY YES
Distributed by Andrews McMeel Syndication
THEY'RE KINDA...
YOU'RE SUPPOSED TO LIE AND SAY YES
PLAY BY THE RULES, DUMMY!
JIM DAVIS 4-13

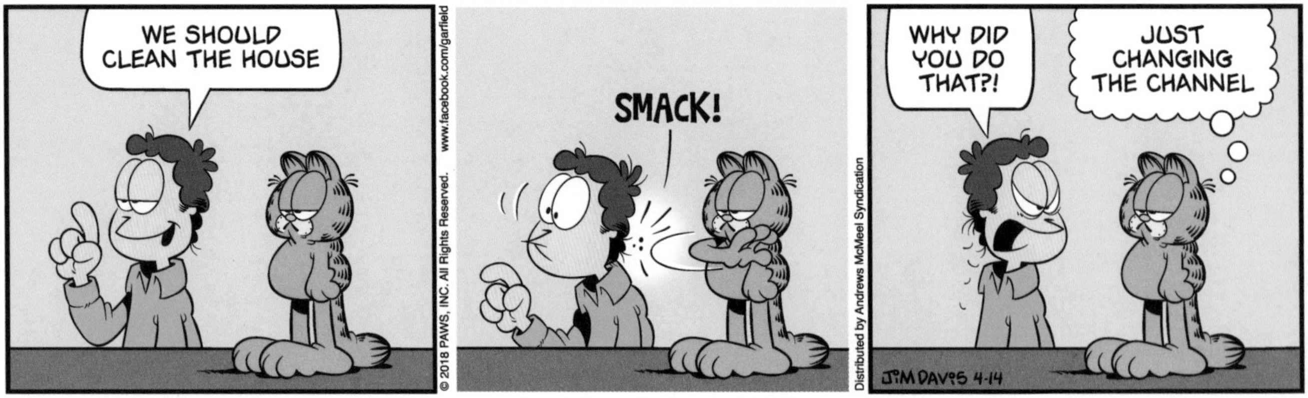
WE SHOULD CLEAN THE HOUSE
© 2018 PAWS, INC. All Rights Reserved. www.facebook.com/garfield
SMACK!
Distributed by Andrews McMeel Syndication
WHY DID YOU DO THAT?!
JUST CHANGING THE CHANNEL
JIM DAVIS 4-14

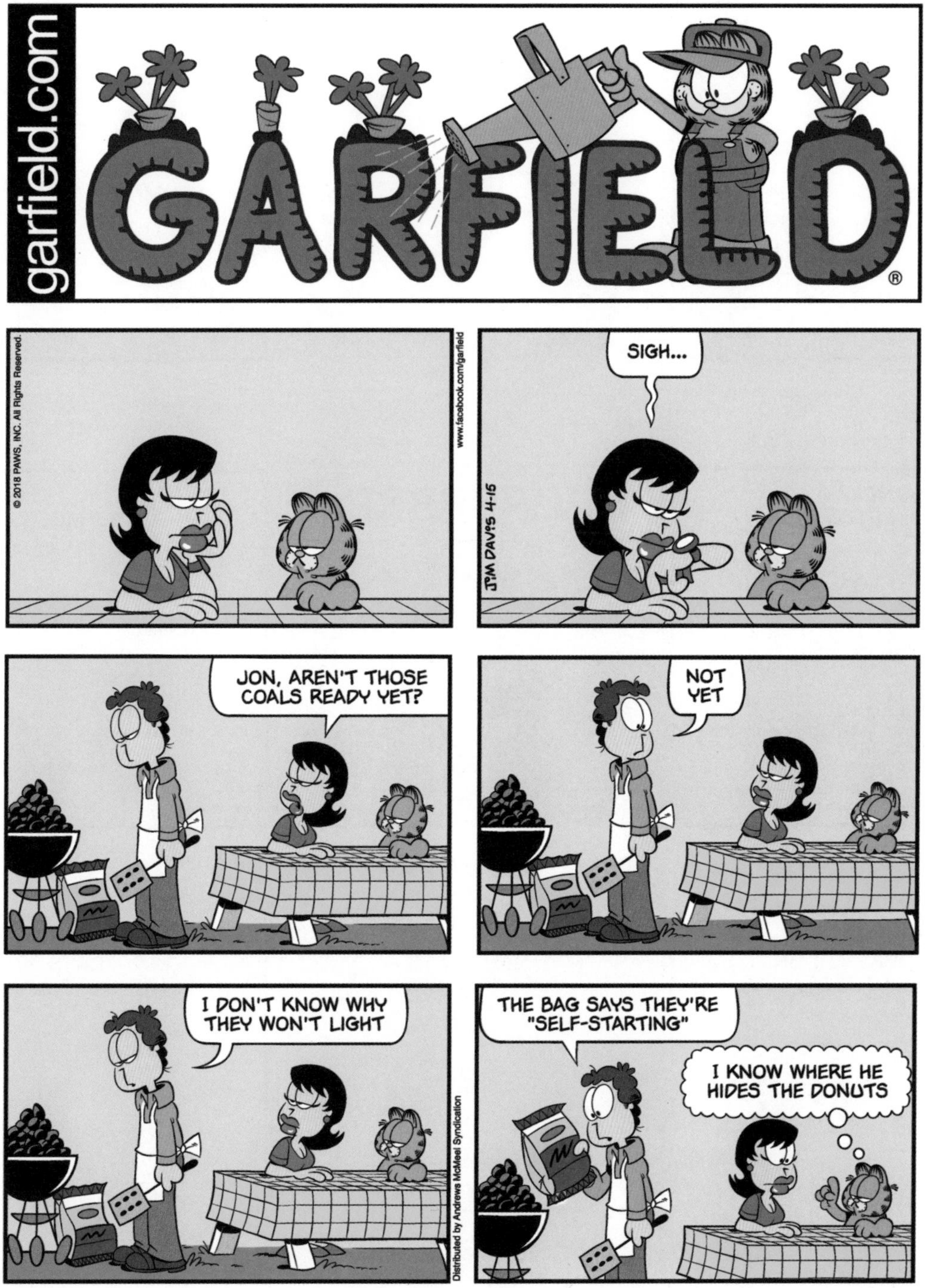
garfield.com
GARFIELD
© 2018 PAWS, INC. All Rights Reserved.
www.facebook.com/garfield
JPM DAVPS 4-15
SIGH...
JON, AREN'T THOSE COALS READY YET?
NOT YET
I DON'T KNOW WHY THEY WON'T LIGHT
Distributed by Andrews McMeel Syndication
THE BAG SAYS THEY'RE "SELF-STARTING"
I KNOW WHERE HE HIDES THE DONUTS

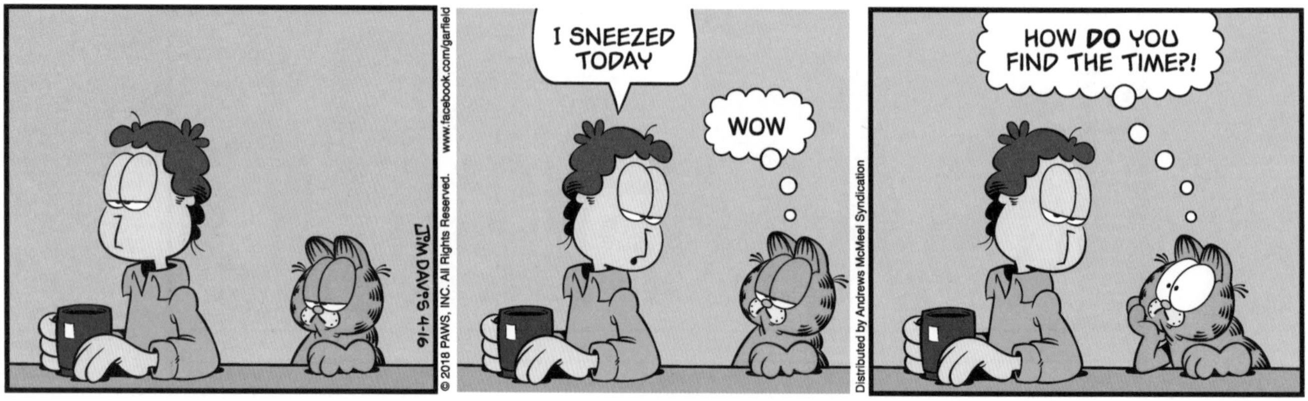
JIM DAVIS 4-16
© 2018 PAWS, INC. All Rights Reserved. www.facebook.com/garfield
I SNEEZED TODAY
WOW
Distributed by Andrews McMeel Syndication
HOW DO YOU FIND THE TIME?!

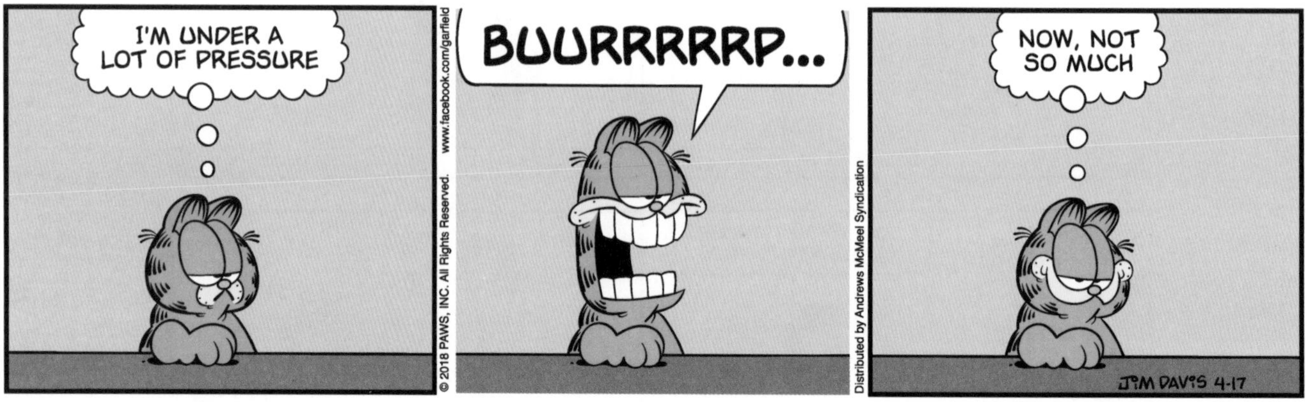
I'M UNDER A LOT OF PRESSURE
© 2018 PAWS, INC. All Rights Reserved. www.facebook.com/garfield
BUURRRRRP...
Distributed by Andrews McMeel Syndication
NOW, NOT SO MUCH
JIM DAVIS 4-17

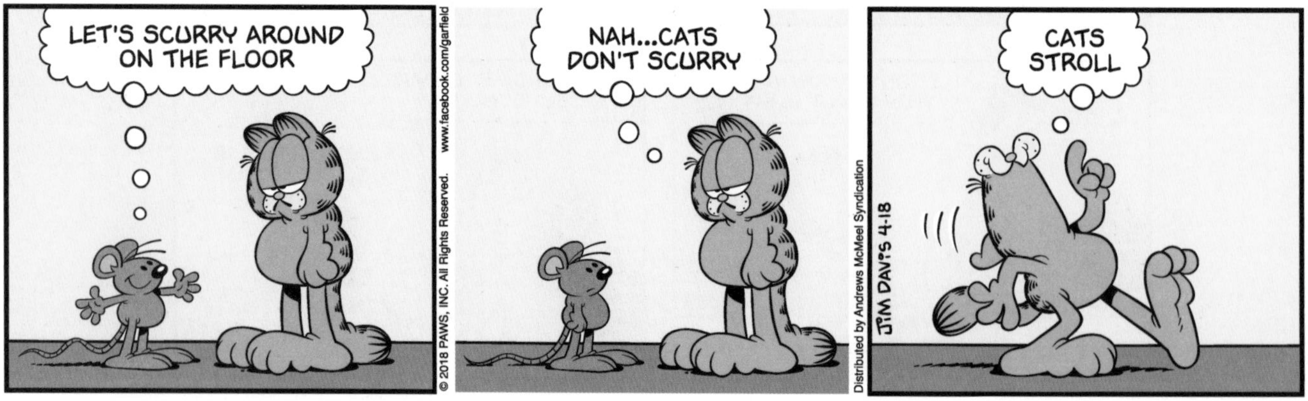
LET'S SCURRY AROUND ON THE FLOOR
© 2018 PAWS, INC. All Rights Reserved. www.facebook.com/garfield
NAH...CATS DON'T SCURRY
Distributed by Andrews McMeel Syndication
JIM DAVIS 4-18
CATS STROLL

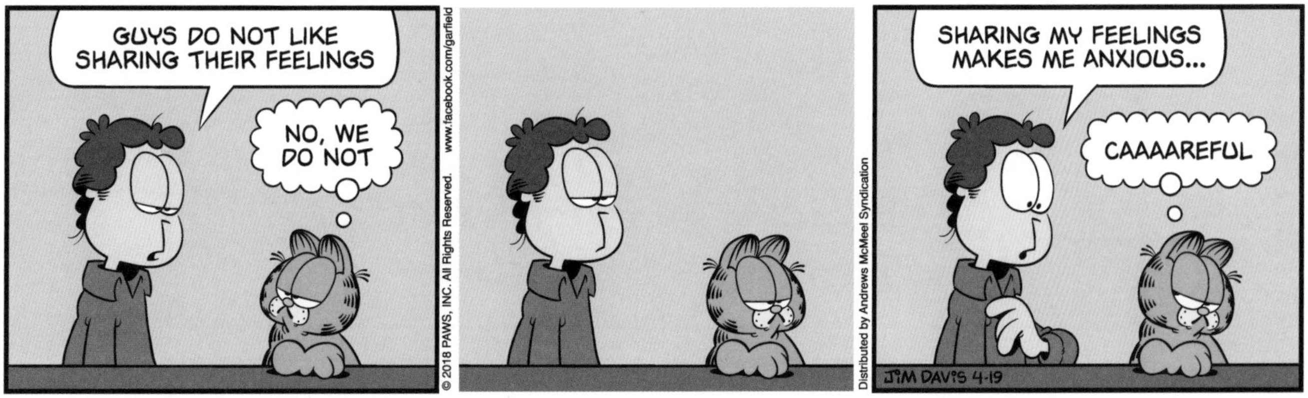
GUYS DO NOT LIKE SHARING THEIR FEELINGS
NO, WE DO NOT
SHARING MY FEELINGS MAKES ME ANXIOUS...
CAAAAREFUL
© 2018 PAWS, INC. All Rights Reserved. www.facebook.com/garfield
Distributed by Andrews McMeel Syndication
JIM DAVIS 4-19

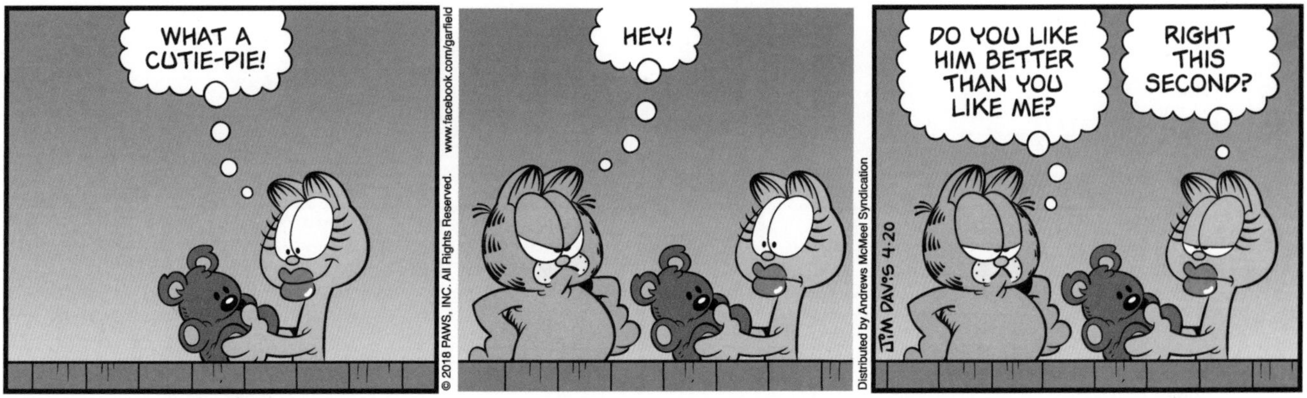
WHAT A CUTIE-PIE!
HEY!
DO YOU LIKE HIM BETTER THAN YOU LIKE ME?
RIGHT THIS SECOND?
© 2018 PAWS, INC. All Rights Reserved. www.facebook.com/garfield
Distributed by Andrews McMeel Syndication
JIM DAVIS 4-20

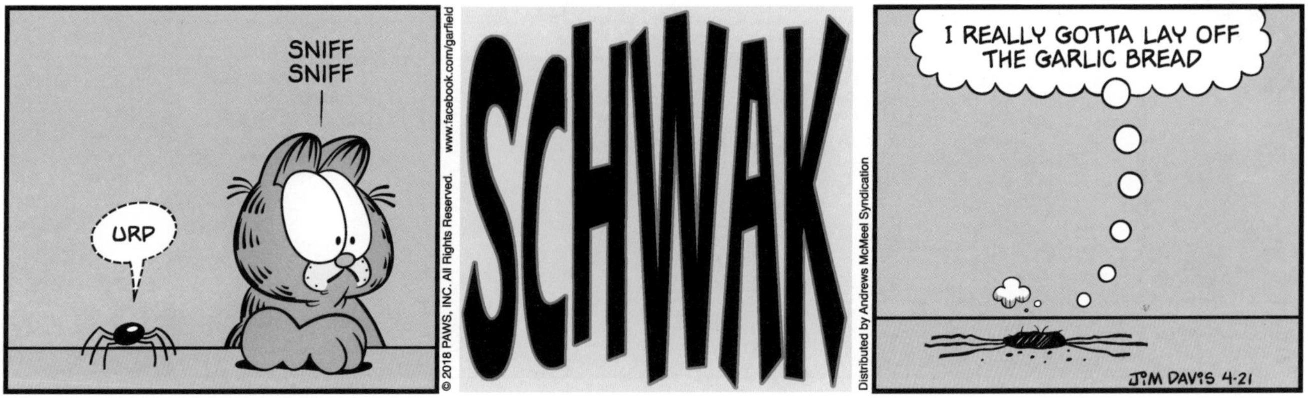
SNIFF SNIFF
URP
SCHWAK
I REALLY GOTTA LAY OFF THE GARLIC BREAD
© 2018 PAWS, INC. All Rights Reserved. www.facebook.com/garfield
Distributed by Andrews McMeel Syndication
JIM DAVIS 4-21

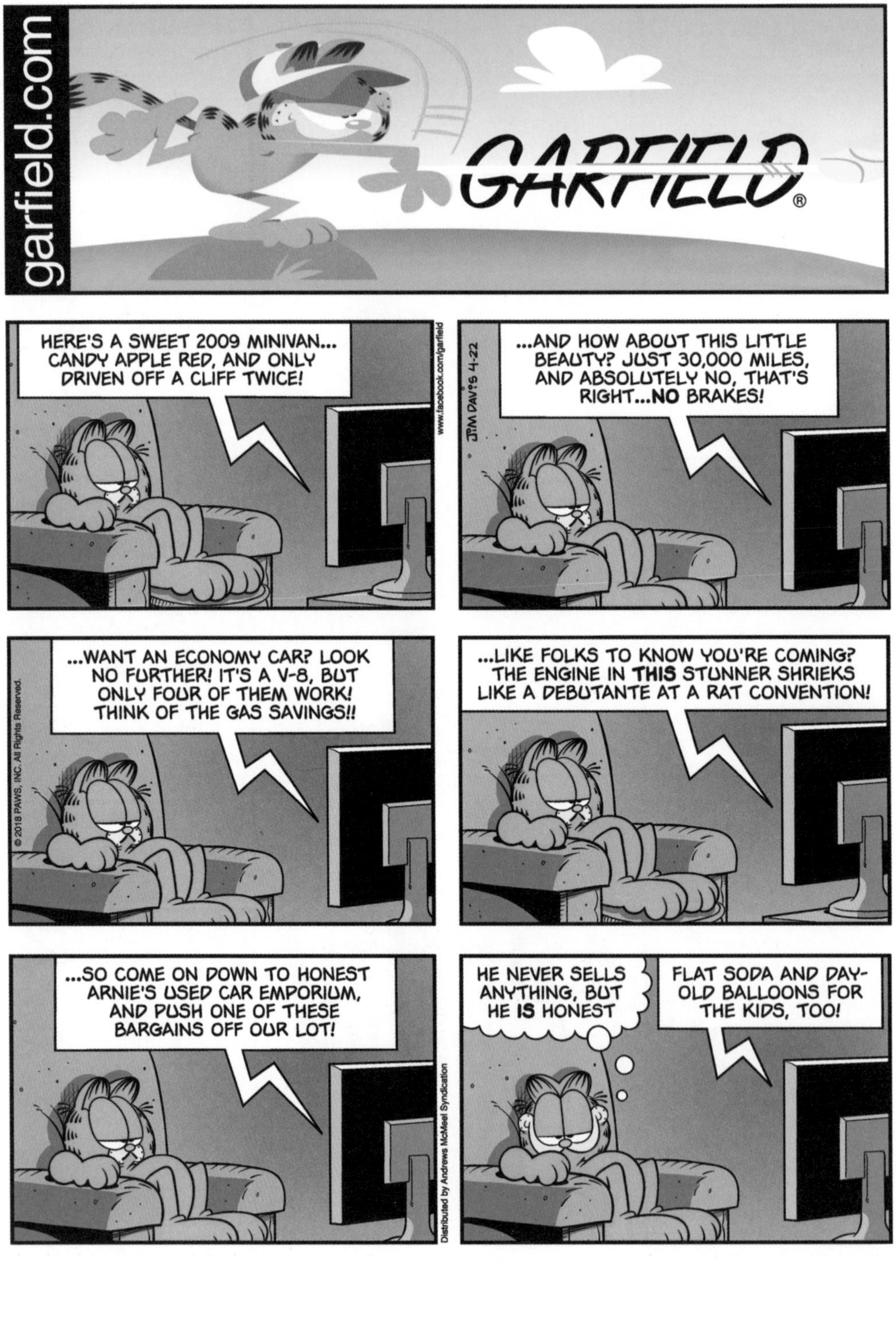
garfield.com
GARFIELD®
HERE'S A SWEET 2009 MINIVAN... CANDY APPLE RED, AND ONLY DRIVEN OFF A CLIFF TWICE!
www.facebook.com/garfield
JPM DAVPS 4-22
...AND HOW ABOUT THIS LITTLE BEAUTY? JUST 30,000 MILES, AND ABSOLUTELY NO, THAT'S RIGHT...NO BRAKES!
© 2018 PAWS, INC. All Rights Reserved.
...WANT AN ECONOMY CAR? LOOK NO FURTHER! IT'S A V-8, BUT ONLY FOUR OF THEM WORK! THINK OF THE GAS SAVINGS!!
...LIKE FOLKS TO KNOW YOU'RE COMING? THE ENGINE IN THIS STUNNER SHRIEKS LIKE A DEBUTANTE AT A RAT CONVENTION!
...SO COME ON DOWN TO HONEST ARNIE'S USED CAR EMPORIUM, AND PUSH ONE OF THESE BARGAINS OFF OUR LOT!
Distributed by Andrews McMeel Syndication
HE NEVER SELLS ANYTHING, BUT HE IS HONEST
FLAT SODA AND DAY-OLD BALLOONS FOR THE KIDS, TOO!

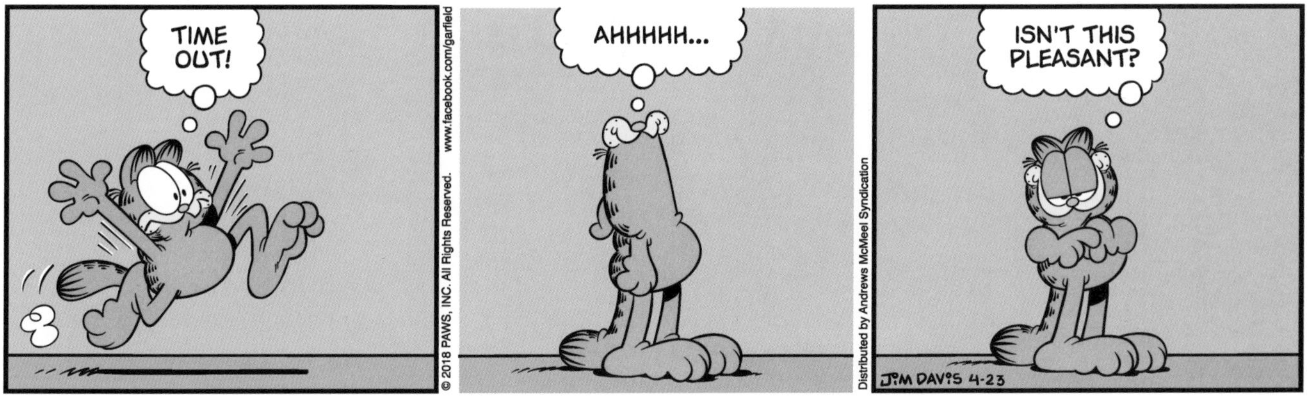
TIME OUT!
AHHHHH...
ISN'T THIS PLEASANT?
© 2018 PAWS, INC. All Rights Reserved. www.facebook.com/garfield
Distributed by Andrews McMeel Syndication
JIM DAVIS 4-23

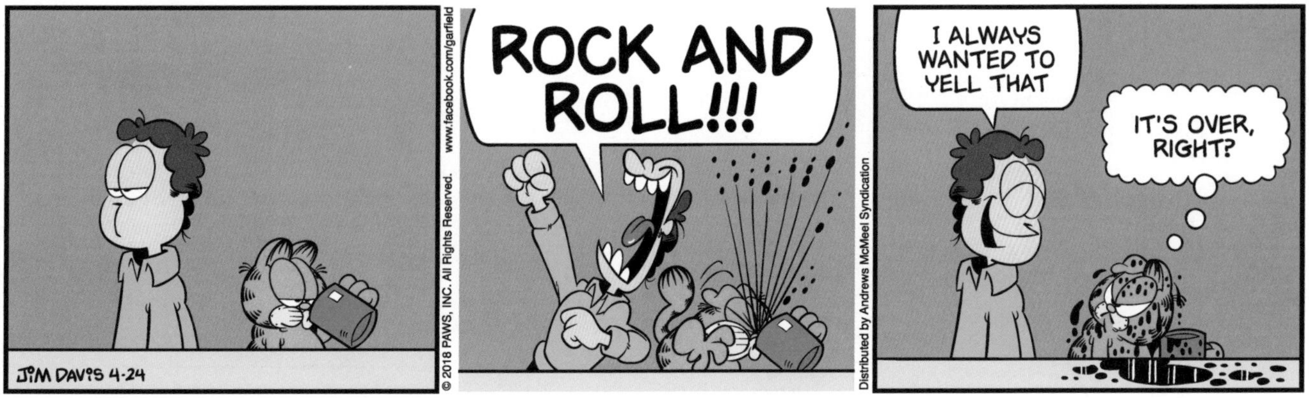
ROCK AND ROLL!!!
I ALWAYS WANTED TO YELL THAT
IT'S OVER, RIGHT?
JIM DAVIS 4-24
© 2018 PAWS, INC. All Rights Reserved. www.facebook.com/garfield
Distributed by Andrews McMeel Syndication

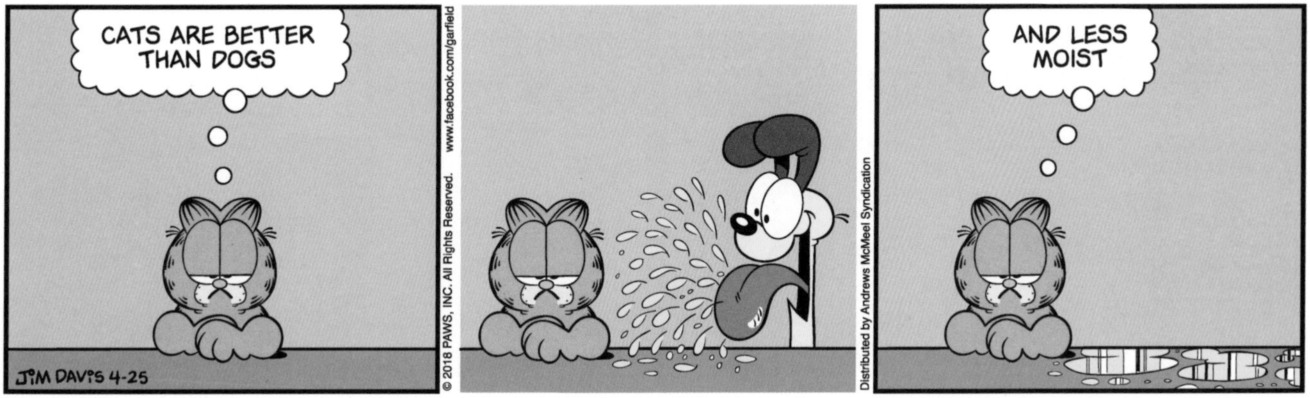
CATS ARE BETTER THAN DOGS
AND LESS MOIST
JIM DAVIS 4-25
© 2018 PAWS, INC. All Rights Reserved. www.facebook.com/garfield
Distributed by Andrews McMeel Syndication

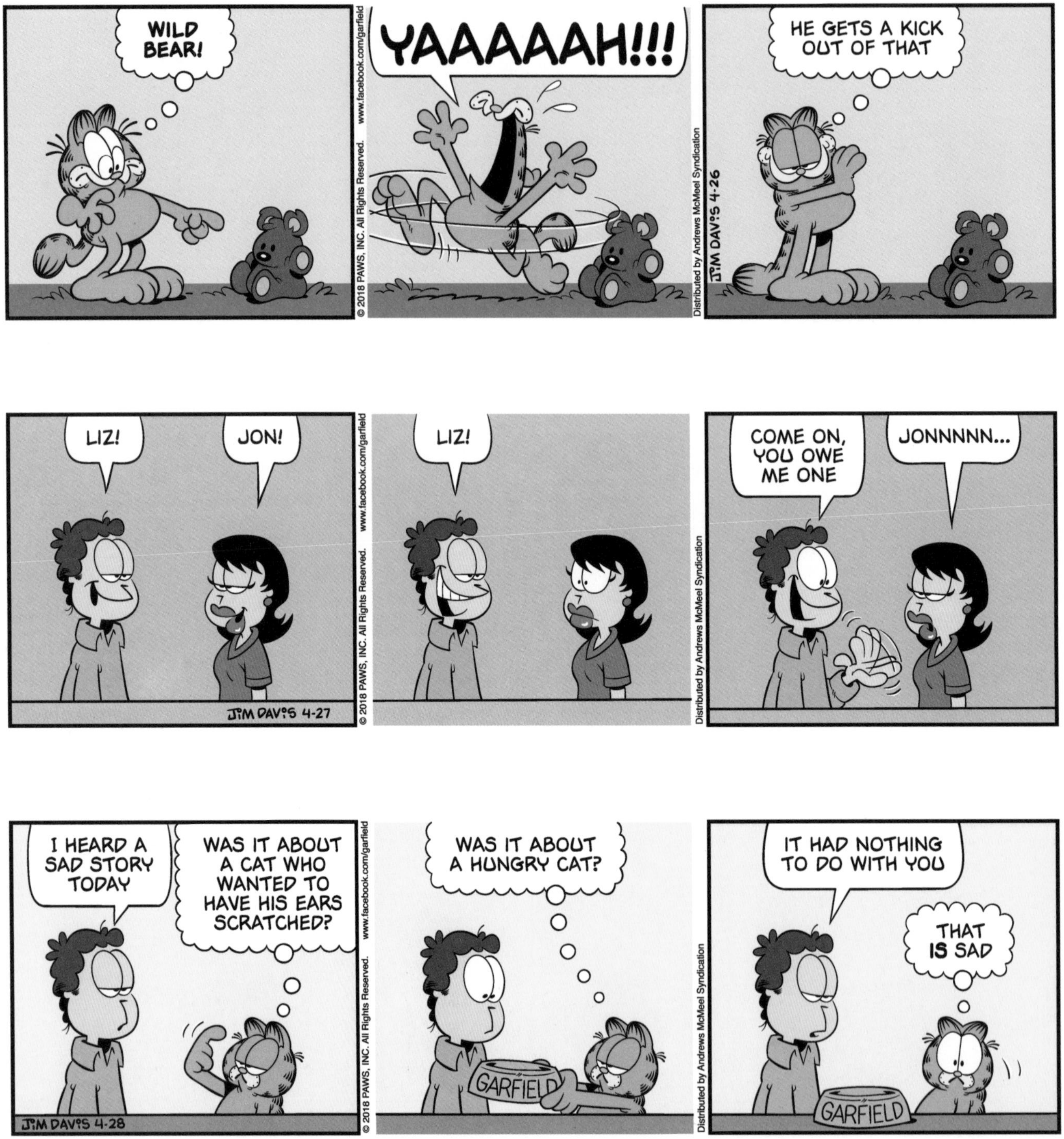
WILD BEAR!
YAAAAAH!!!
HE GETS A KICK OUT OF THAT
JIM DAVIS 4-26
© 2018 PAWS, INC. All Rights Reserved. www.facebook.com/garfield
Distributed by Andrews McMeel Syndication
LIZ!
JON!
LIZ!
COME ON, YOU OWE ME ONE
JONNNNN...
JIM DAVIS 4-27
© 2018 PAWS, INC. All Rights Reserved. www.facebook.com/garfield
Distributed by Andrews McMeel Syndication
I HEARD A SAD STORY TODAY
WAS IT ABOUT A CAT WHO WANTED TO HAVE HIS EARS SCRATCHED?
WAS IT ABOUT A HUNGRY CAT?
GARFIELD
IT HAD NOTHING TO DO WITH YOU
THAT **IS** SAD
GARFIELD
JIM DAVIS 4-28
© 2018 PAWS, INC. All Rights Reserved. www.facebook.com/garfield
Distributed by Andrews McMeel Syndication

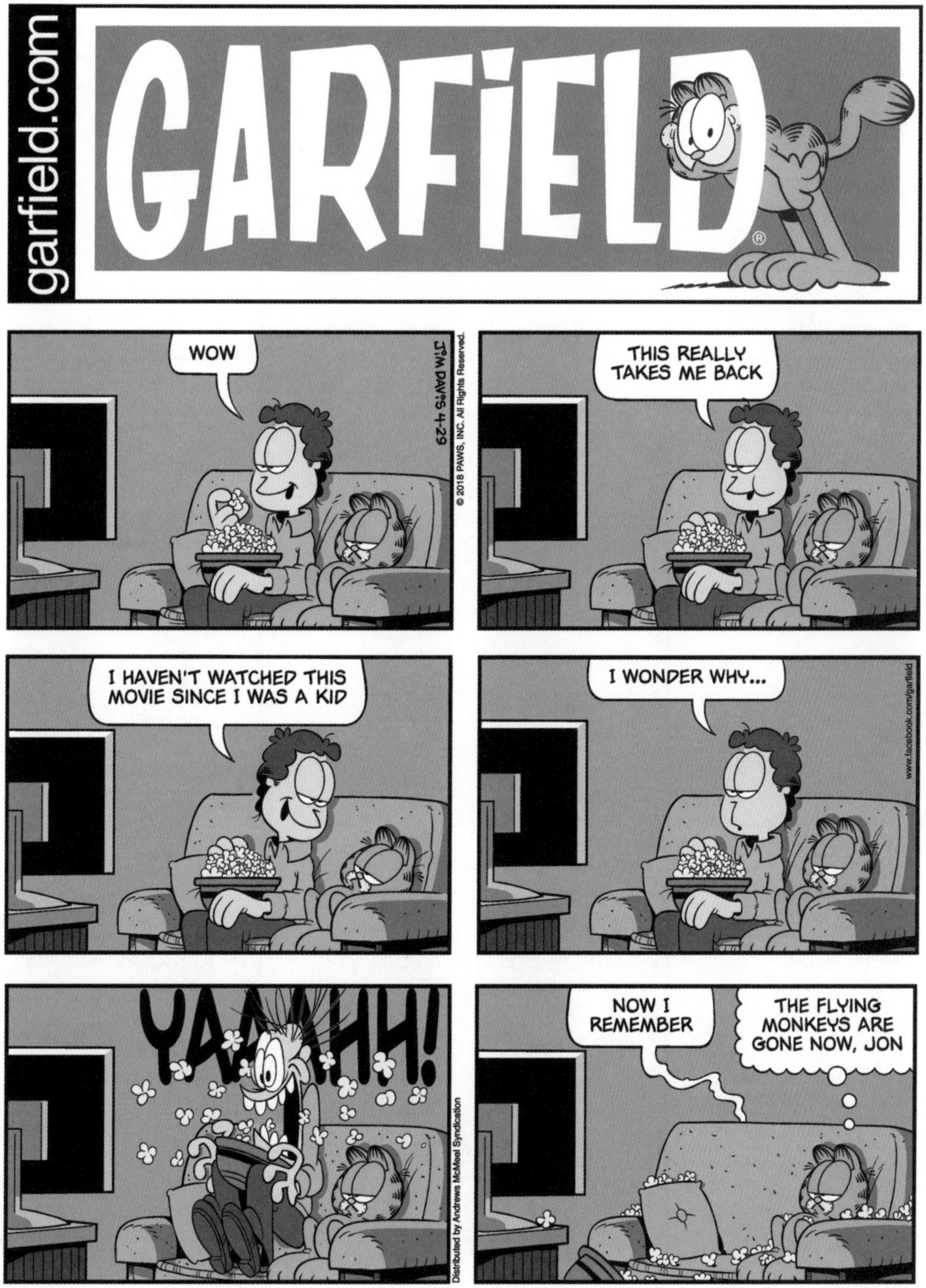

garfield.com
GARFIELD
WOW
JIM DAVIS 4-29
© 2018 PAWS, INC. All Rights Reserved.
THIS REALLY TAKES ME BACK
I HAVEN'T WATCHED THIS MOVIE SINCE I WAS A KID
I WONDER WHY...
www.facebook.com/garfield
YAAAHH!
Distributed by Andrews McMeel Syndication
NOW I REMEMBER
THE FLYING MONKEYS ARE GONE NOW, JON

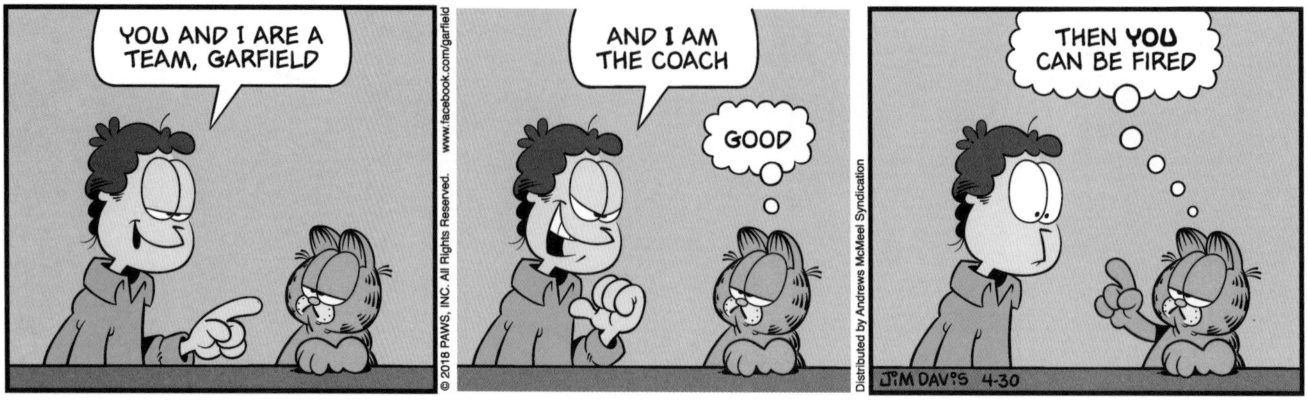
YOU AND I ARE A TEAM, GARFIELD
© 2018 PAWS, INC. All Rights Reserved. www.facebook.com/garfield
AND I AM THE COACH
GOOD
Distributed by Andrews McMeel Syndication
THEN YOU CAN BE FIRED
JIM DAVIS 4-30

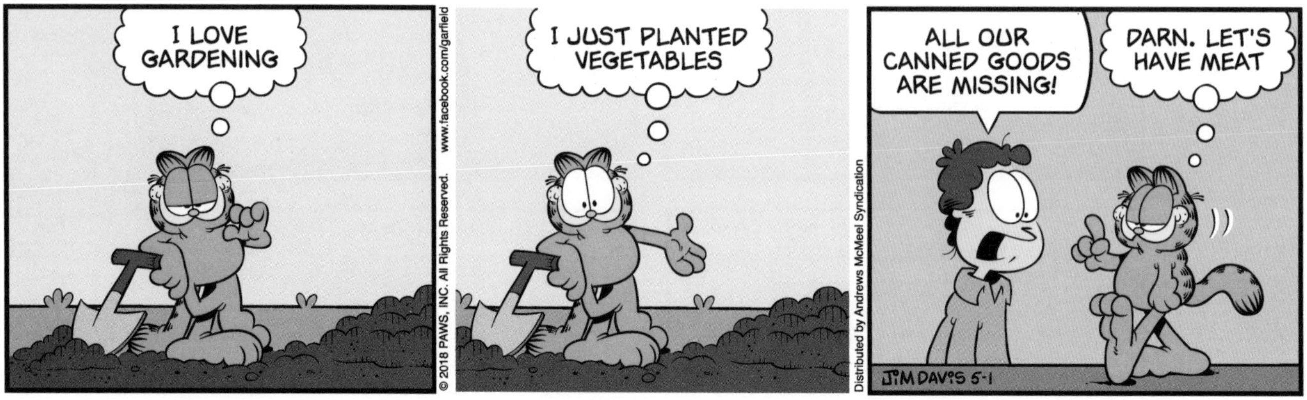
I LOVE GARDENING
© 2018 PAWS, INC. All Rights Reserved. www.facebook.com/garfield
I JUST PLANTED VEGETABLES
Distributed by Andrews McMeel Syndication
ALL OUR CANNED GOODS ARE MISSING!
DARN. LET'S HAVE MEAT
JIM DAVIS 5-1

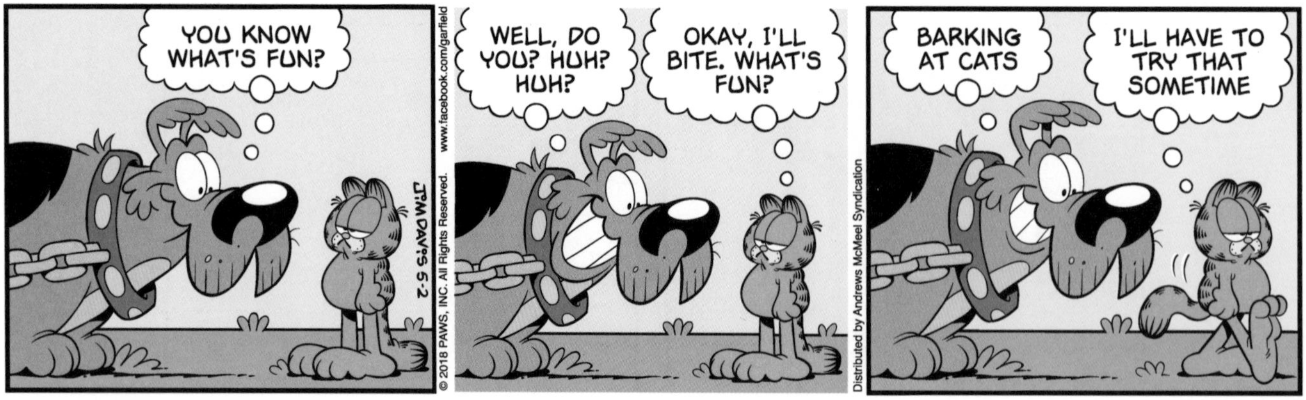
YOU KNOW WHAT'S FUN?
JIM DAVIS 5-2
© 2018 PAWS, INC. All Rights Reserved. www.facebook.com/garfield
WELL, DO YOU? HUH? HUH?
OKAY, I'LL BITE. WHAT'S FUN?
Distributed by Andrews McMeel Syndication
BARKING AT CATS
I'LL HAVE TO TRY THAT SOMETIME

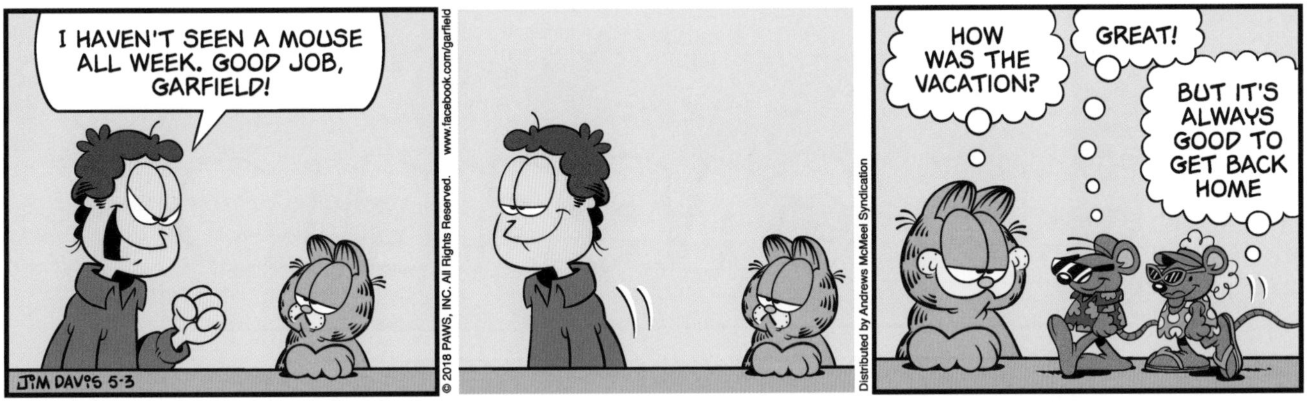
I HAVEN'T SEEN A MOUSE ALL WEEK. GOOD JOB, GARFIELD!
JIM DAVIS 5-3
© 2018 PAWS, INC. All Rights Reserved. www.facebook.com/garfield
Distributed by Andrews McMeel Syndication
HOW WAS THE VACATION?
GREAT!
BUT IT'S ALWAYS GOOD TO GET BACK HOME

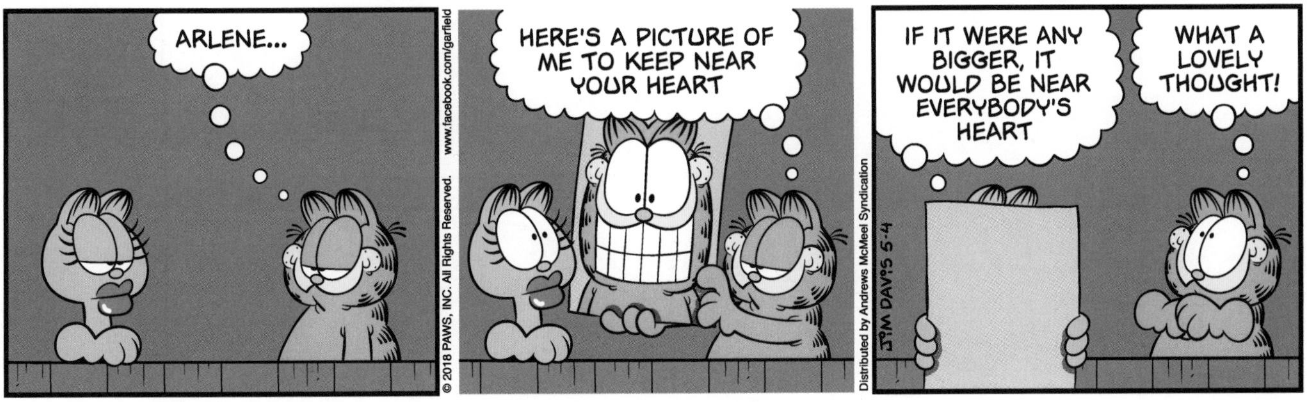
ARLENE...
© 2018 PAWS, INC. All Rights Reserved. www.facebook.com/garfield
HERE'S A PICTURE OF ME TO KEEP NEAR YOUR HEART
Distributed by Andrews McMeel Syndication
JIM DAVIS 5-4
IF IT WERE ANY BIGGER, IT WOULD BE NEAR EVERYBODY'S HEART
WHAT A LOVELY THOUGHT!

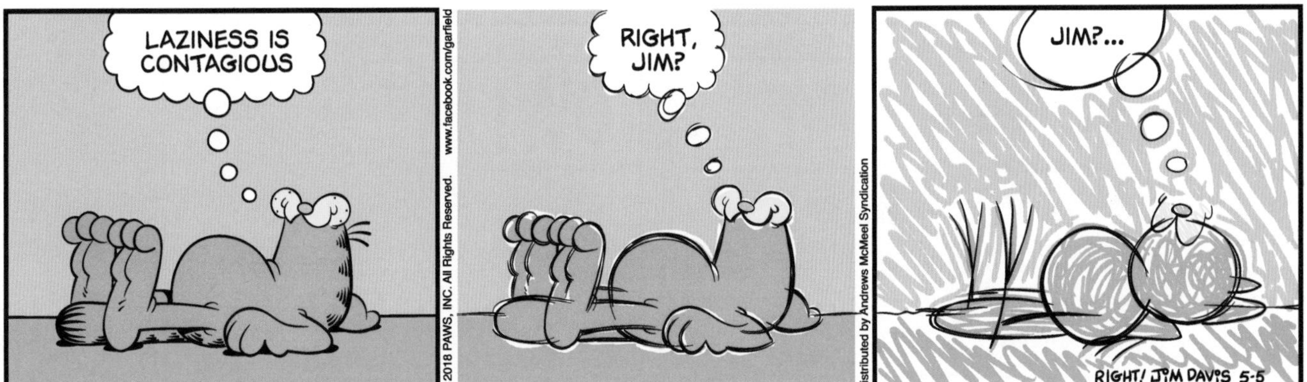
LAZINESS IS CONTAGIOUS
© 2018 PAWS, INC. All Rights Reserved. www.facebook.com/garfield
RIGHT, JIM?
Distributed by Andrews McMeel Syndication
JIM?...
RIGHT! JIM DAVIS 5-5

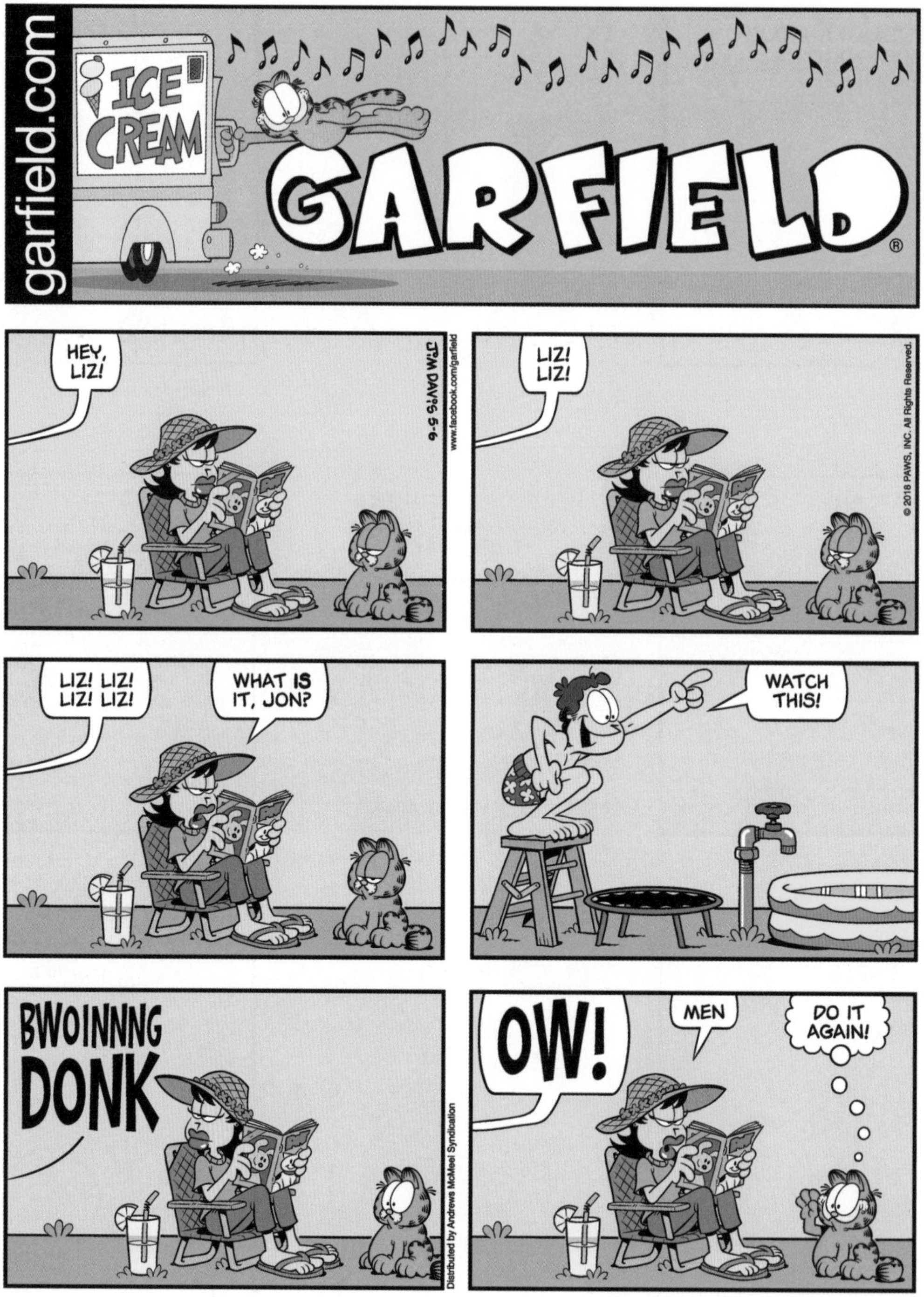
garfield.com
ICE CREAM
GARFIELD
HEY, LIZ!
JIM DAVIS 5-6
www.facebook.com/garfield
LIZ! LIZ!
© 2018 PAWS, INC. All Rights Reserved.
LIZ! LIZ! LIZ! LIZ!
WHAT IS IT, JON?
WATCH THIS!
BWOINNNG
DONK
Distributed by Andrews McMeel Syndication
OW!
MEN
DO IT AGAIN!

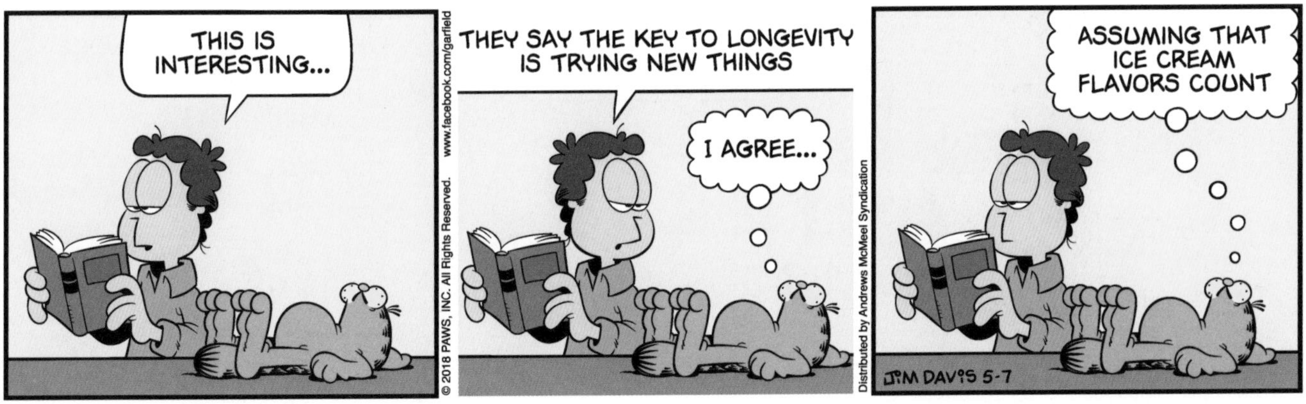
THIS IS INTERESTING...
THEY SAY THE KEY TO LONGEVITY IS TRYING NEW THINGS
I AGREE...
ASSUMING THAT ICE CREAM FLAVORS COUNT
JIM DAVIS 5-7
© 2018 PAWS, INC. All Rights Reserved. www.facebook.com/garfield
Distributed by Andrews McMeel Syndication

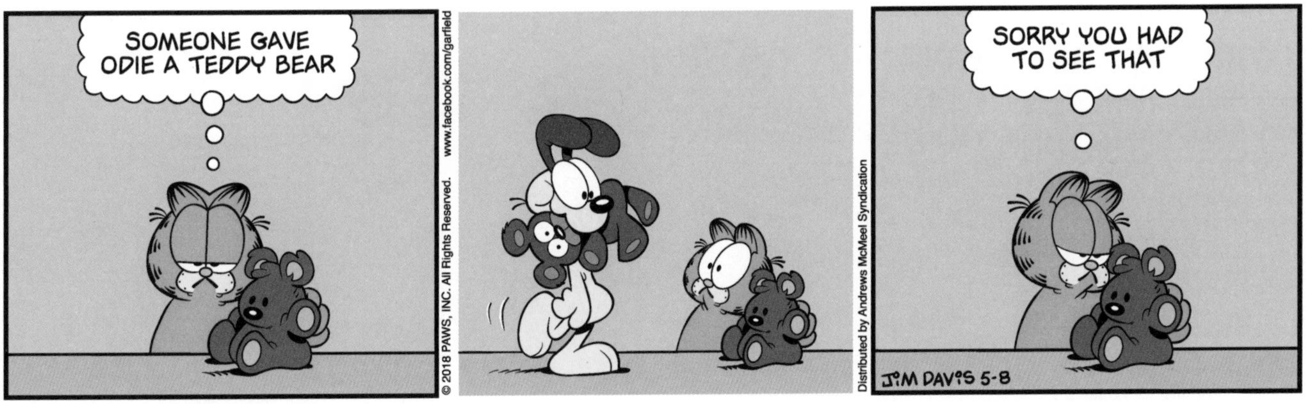
SOMEONE GAVE ODIE A TEDDY BEAR
SORRY YOU HAD TO SEE THAT
JIM DAVIS 5-8
© 2018 PAWS, INC. All Rights Reserved. www.facebook.com/garfield
Distributed by Andrews McMeel Syndication

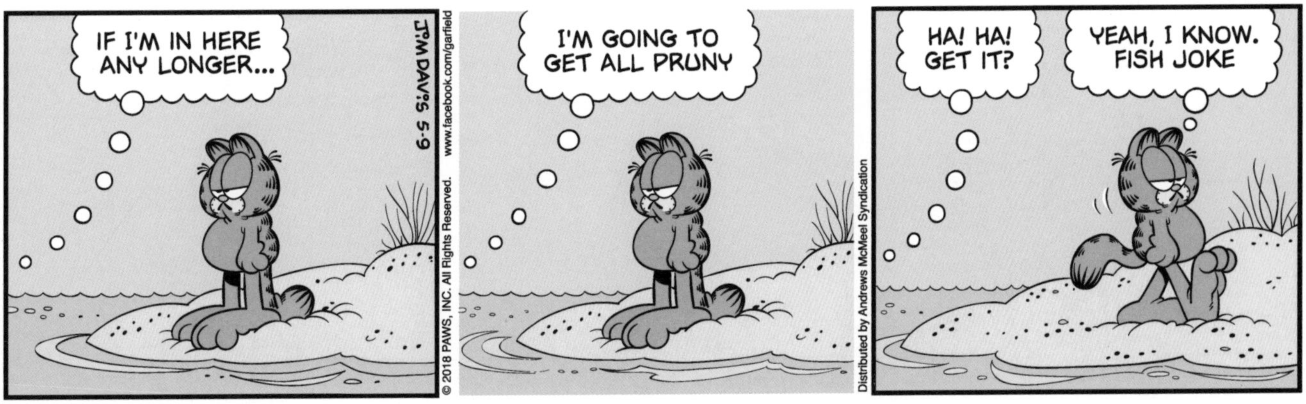
IF I'M IN HERE ANY LONGER...
JIM DAVIS 5-9
I'M GOING TO GET ALL PRUNY
HA! HA! GET IT?
YEAH, I KNOW. FISH JOKE
© 2018 PAWS, INC. All Rights Reserved. www.facebook.com/garfield
Distributed by Andrews McMeel Syndication

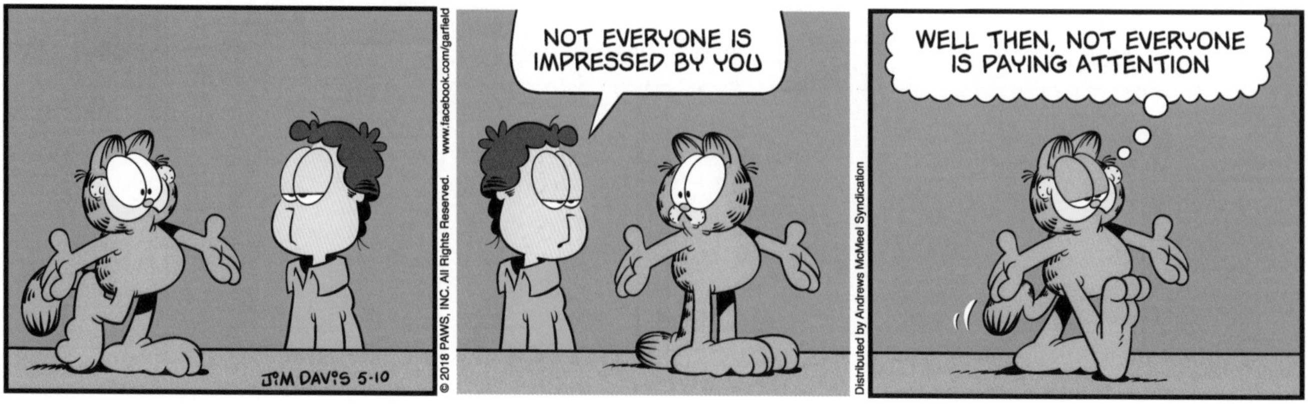
JIM DAVIS 5-10
© 2018 PAWS, INC. All Rights Reserved. www.facebook.com/garfield
NOT EVERYONE IS IMPRESSED BY YOU
Distributed by Andrews McMeel Syndication
WELL THEN, NOT EVERYONE IS PAYING ATTENTION

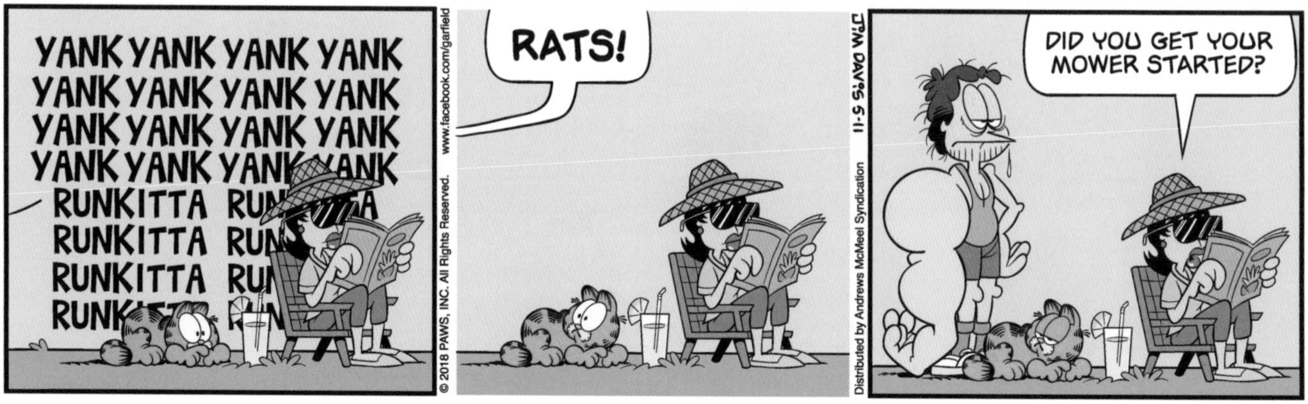
YANK YANK YANK YANK
YANK YANK YANK YANK
YANK YANK YANK YANK
YANK YANK
RUNKITTA
RUNKITTA
RUNKITTA
© 2018 PAWS, INC. All Rights Reserved. www.facebook.com/garfield
RATS!
JIM DAVIS 5-11
Distributed by Andrews McMeel Syndication
DID YOU GET YOUR MOWER STARTED?

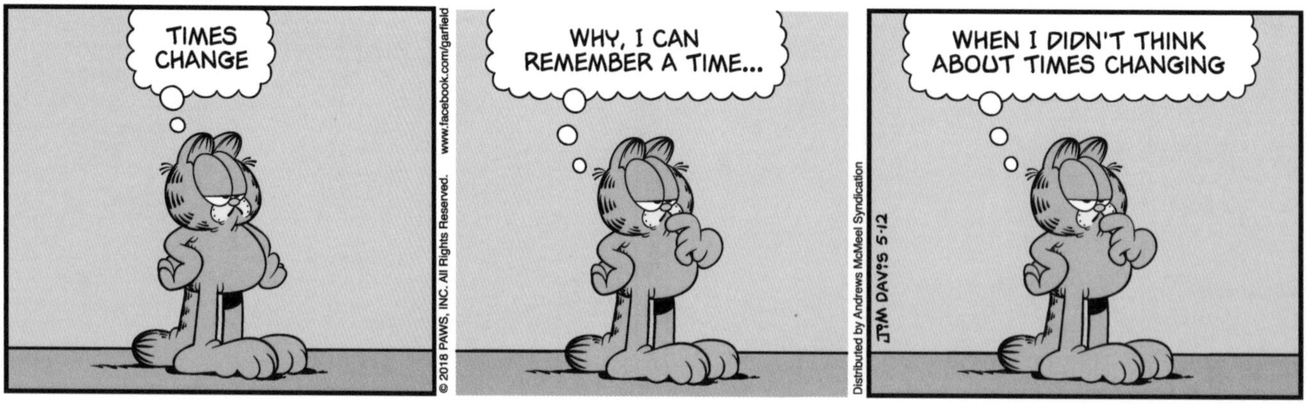
TIMES CHANGE
© 2018 PAWS, INC. All Rights Reserved. www.facebook.com/garfield
WHY, I CAN REMEMBER A TIME...
Distributed by Andrews McMeel Syndication
JIM DAVIS 5-12
WHEN I DIDN'T THINK ABOUT TIMES CHANGING

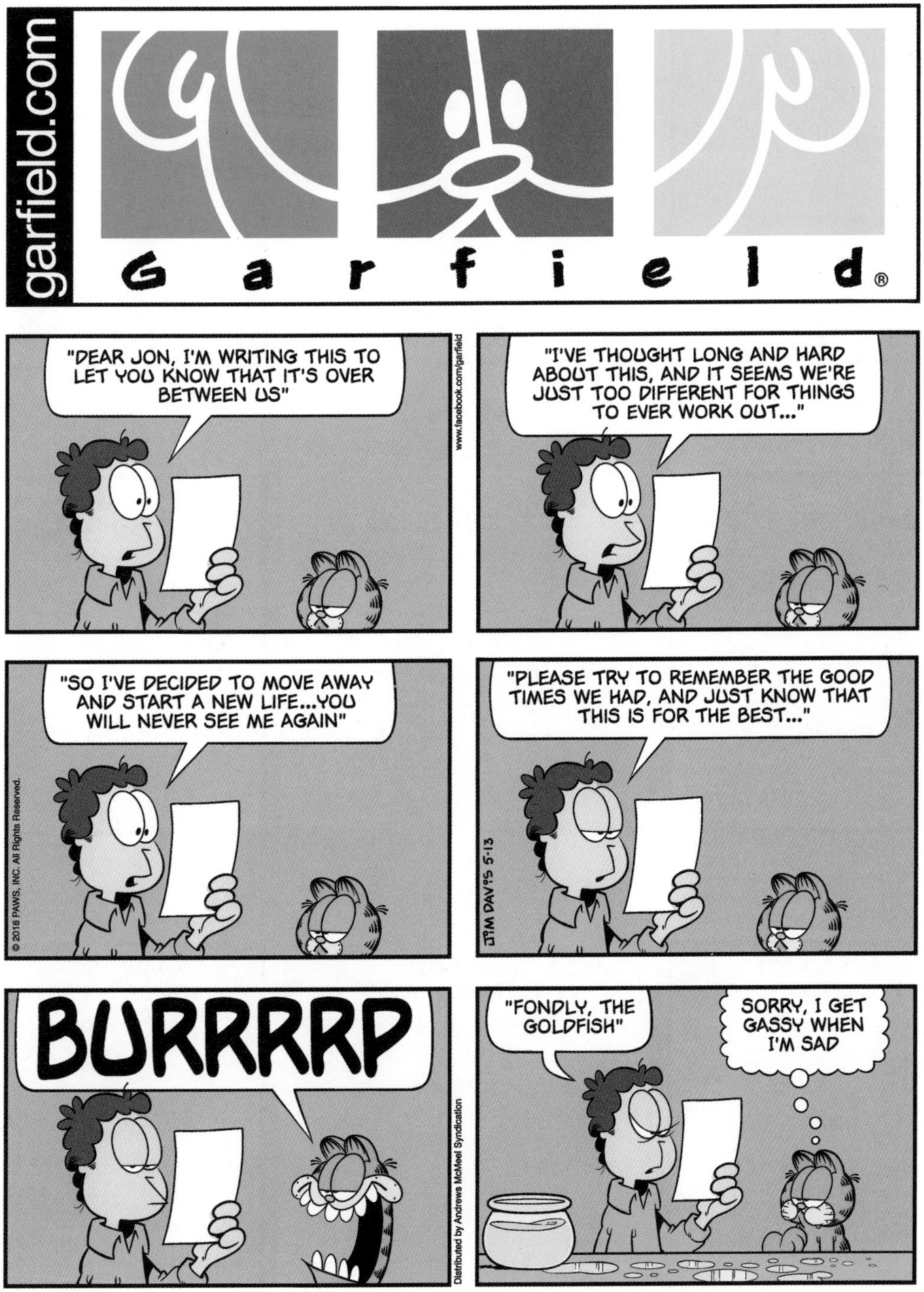
garfield.com
Garfield®
"DEAR JON, I'M WRITING THIS TO LET YOU KNOW THAT IT'S OVER BETWEEN US"
www.facebook.com/garfield
"I'VE THOUGHT LONG AND HARD ABOUT THIS, AND IT SEEMS WE'RE JUST TOO DIFFERENT FOR THINGS TO EVER WORK OUT..."
"SO I'VE DECIDED TO MOVE AWAY AND START A NEW LIFE...YOU WILL NEVER SEE ME AGAIN"
© 2018 PAWS, INC. All Rights Reserved.
"PLEASE TRY TO REMEMBER THE GOOD TIMES WE HAD, AND JUST KNOW THAT THIS IS FOR THE BEST..."
JIM DAVIS 5-13
BURRRRP
Distributed by Andrews McMeel Syndication
"FONDLY, THE GOLDFISH"
SORRY, I GET GASSY WHEN I'M SAD

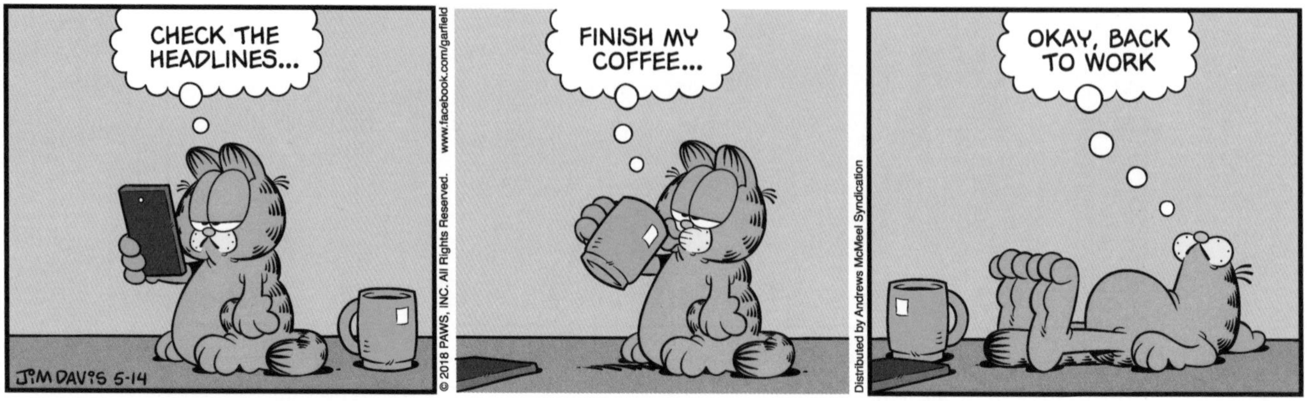
CHECK THE HEADLINES...
JIM DAVIS 5-14
© 2018 PAWS, INC. All Rights Reserved. www.facebook.com/garfield
FINISH MY COFFEE...
Distributed by Andrews McMeel Syndication
OKAY, BACK TO WORK

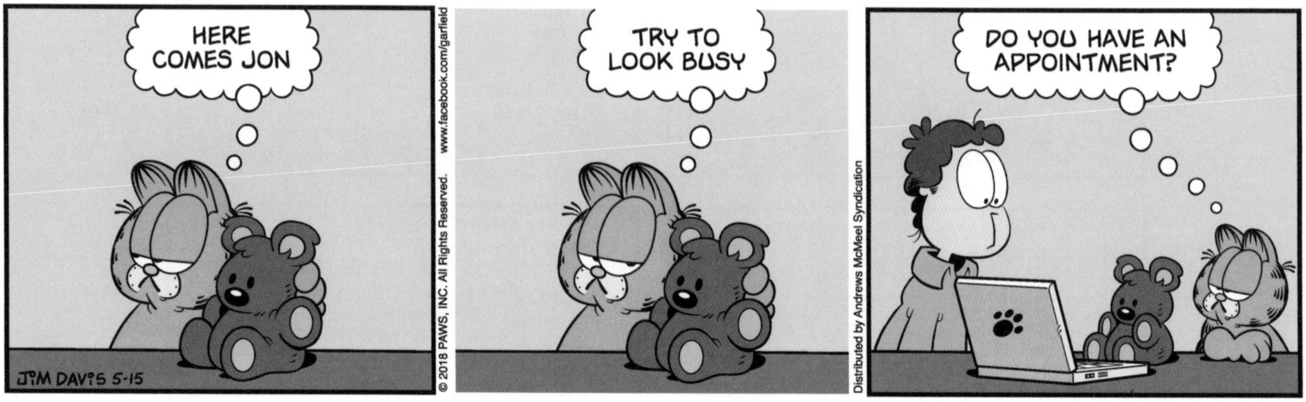
HERE COMES JON
JIM DAVIS 5-15
© 2018 PAWS, INC. All Rights Reserved. www.facebook.com/garfield
TRY TO LOOK BUSY
Distributed by Andrews McMeel Syndication
DO YOU HAVE AN APPOINTMENT?

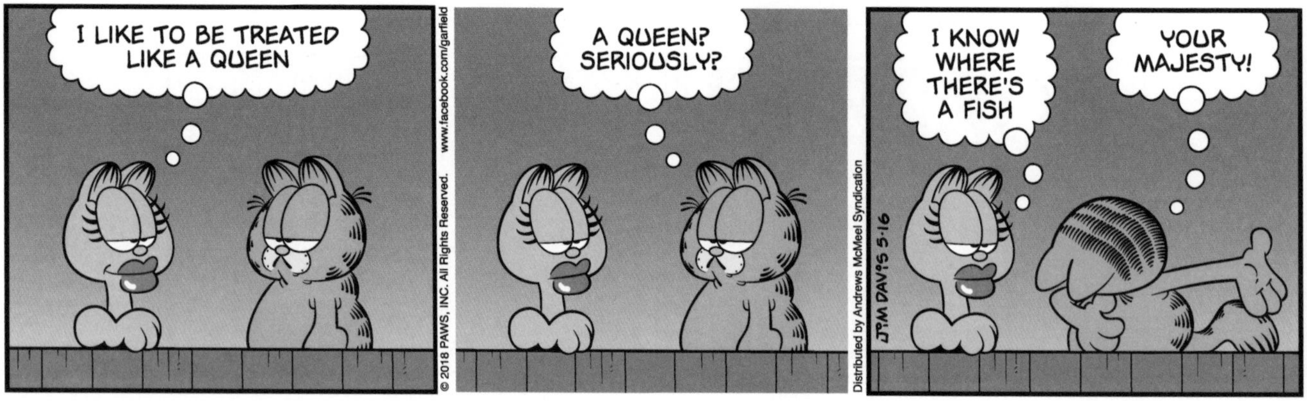
I LIKE TO BE TREATED LIKE A QUEEN
© 2018 PAWS, INC. All Rights Reserved. www.facebook.com/garfield
A QUEEN? SERIOUSLY?
Distributed by Andrews McMeel Syndication
JIM DAVIS 5-16
I KNOW WHERE THERE'S A FISH
YOUR MAJESTY!

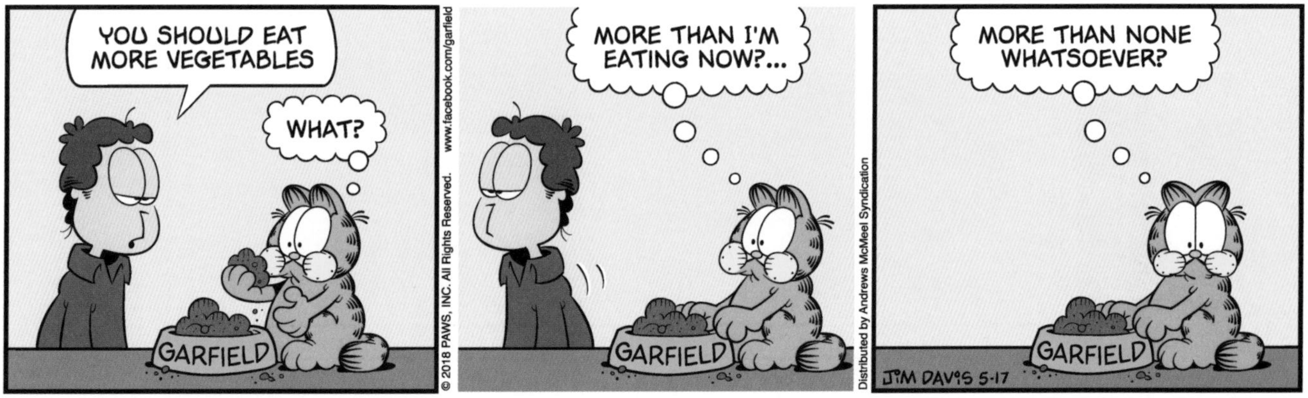
YOU SHOULD EAT MORE VEGETABLES
WHAT?
MORE THAN I'M EATING NOW?...
MORE THAN NONE WHATSOEVER?
GARFIELD
JIM DAVIS 5-17
© 2018 PAWS, INC. All Rights Reserved. www.facebook.com/garfield
Distributed by Andrews McMeel Syndication

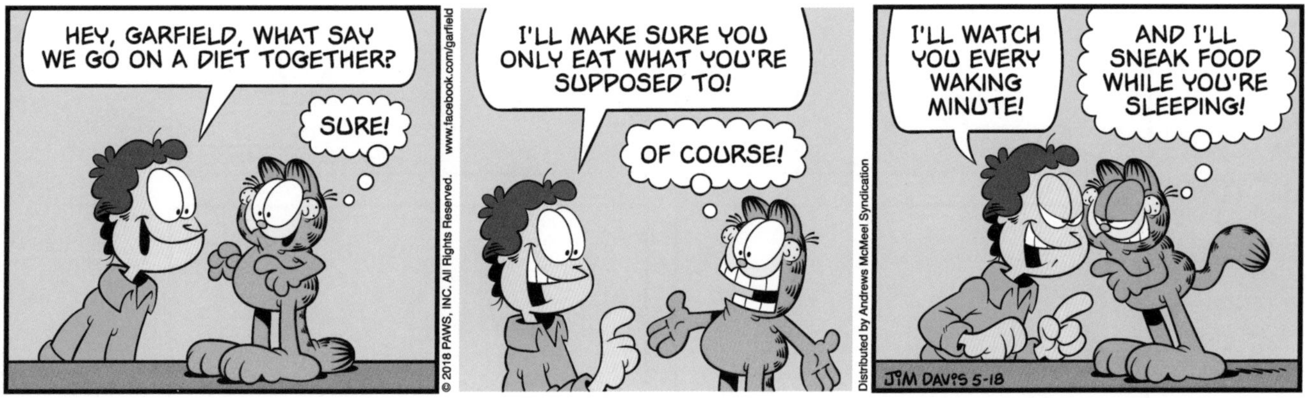
HEY, GARFIELD, WHAT SAY WE GO ON A DIET TOGETHER?
SURE!
I'LL MAKE SURE YOU ONLY EAT WHAT YOU'RE SUPPOSED TO!
OF COURSE!
I'LL WATCH YOU EVERY WAKING MINUTE!
AND I'LL SNEAK FOOD WHILE YOU'RE SLEEPING!
JIM DAVIS 5-18
© 2018 PAWS, INC. All Rights Reserved. www.facebook.com/garfield
Distributed by Andrews McMeel Syndication

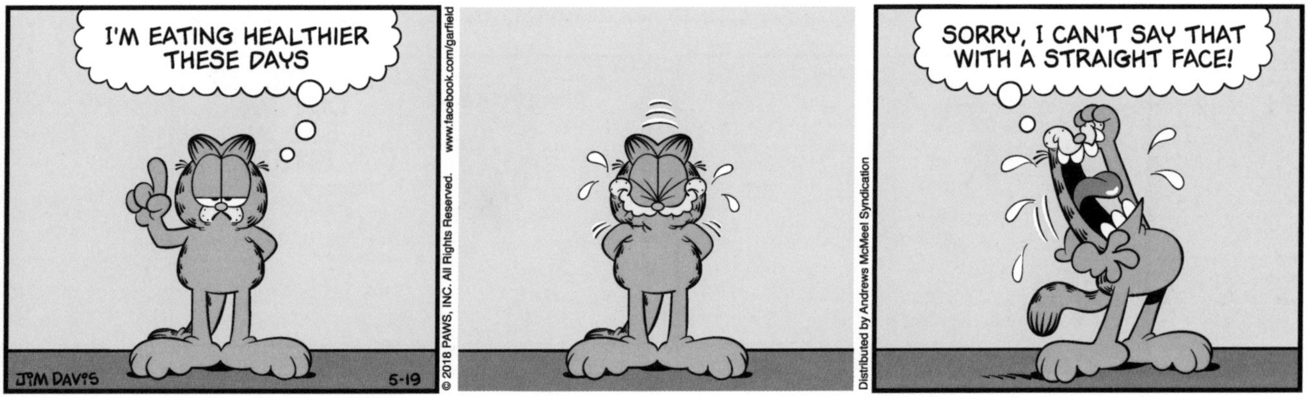
I'M EATING HEALTHIER THESE DAYS
SORRY, I CAN'T SAY THAT WITH A STRAIGHT FACE!
JIM DAVIS 5-19
© 2018 PAWS, INC. All Rights Reserved. www.facebook.com/garfield
Distributed by Andrews McMeel Syndication

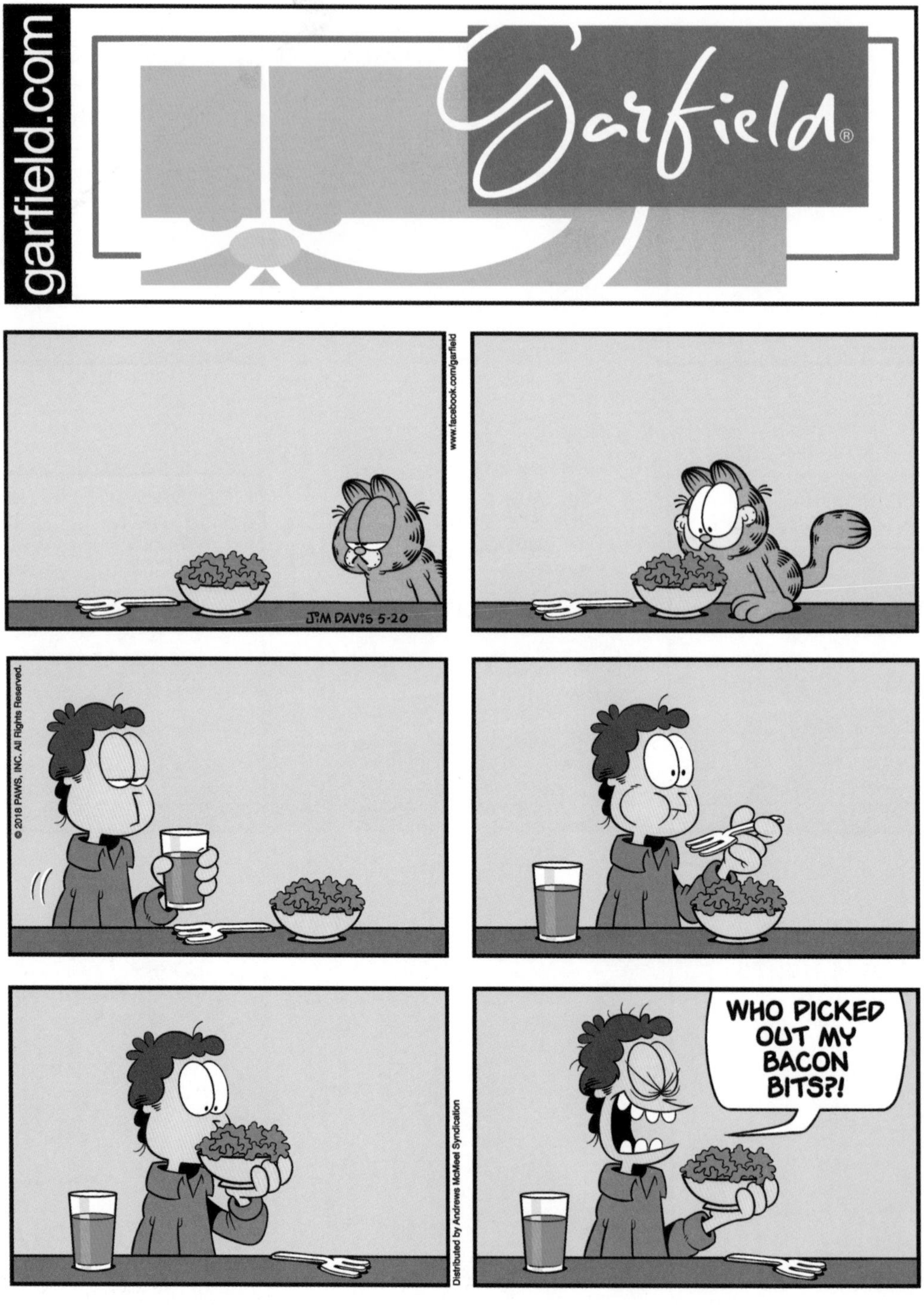
garfield.com
Garfield®
JIM DAVIS 5-20
www.facebook.com/garfield
© 2018 PAWS, INC. All Rights Reserved.
Distributed by Andrews McMeel Syndication
WHO PICKED OUT MY BACON BITS?!

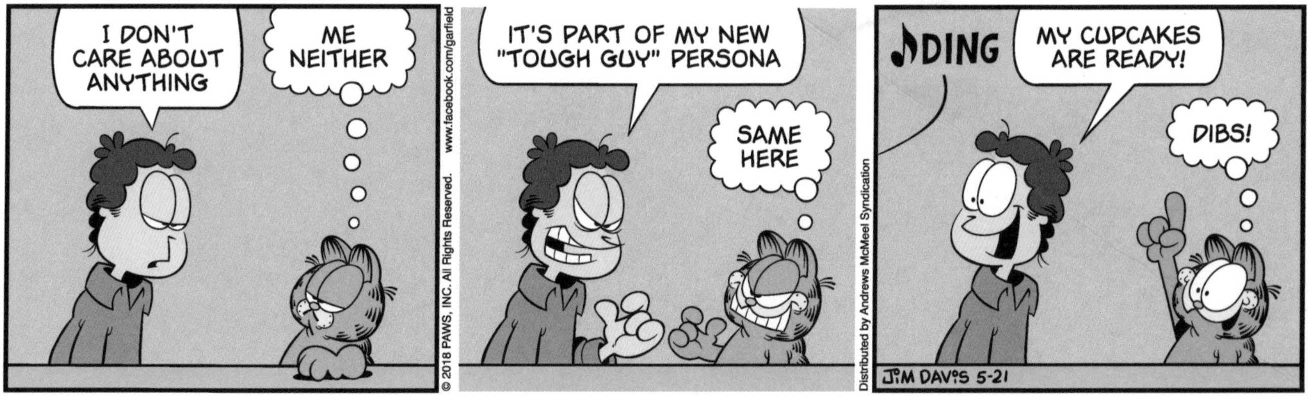
I DON'T CARE ABOUT ANYTHING
ME NEITHER
IT'S PART OF MY NEW "TOUGH GUY" PERSONA
SAME HERE
DING
MY CUPCAKES ARE READY!
DIBS!
JIM DAVIS 5-21
© 2018 PAWS, INC. All Rights Reserved. www.facebook.com/garfield
Distributed by Andrews McMeel Syndication

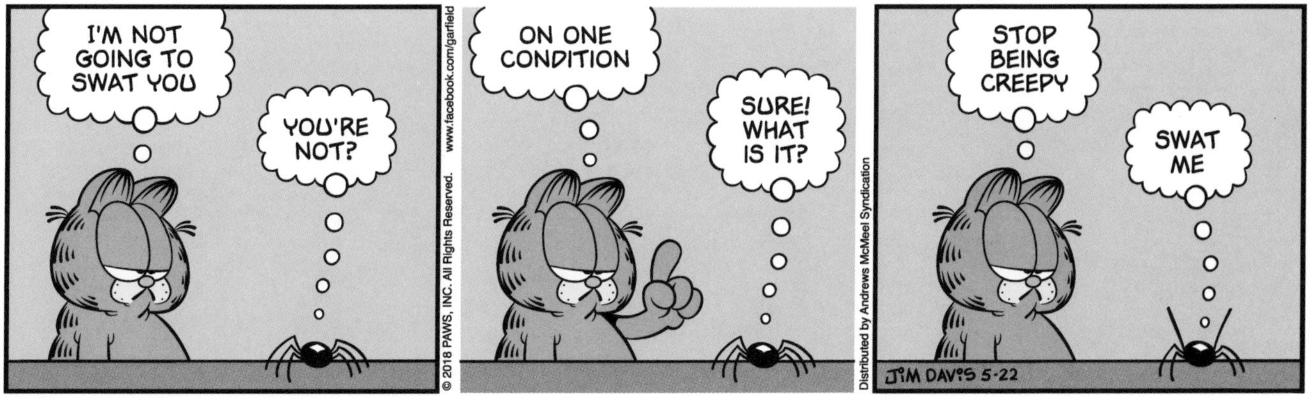
I'M NOT GOING TO SWAT YOU
YOU'RE NOT?
ON ONE CONDITION
SURE! WHAT IS IT?
STOP BEING CREEPY
SWAT ME
JIM DAVIS 5-22
© 2018 PAWS, INC. All Rights Reserved. www.facebook.com/garfield
Distributed by Andrews McMeel Syndication

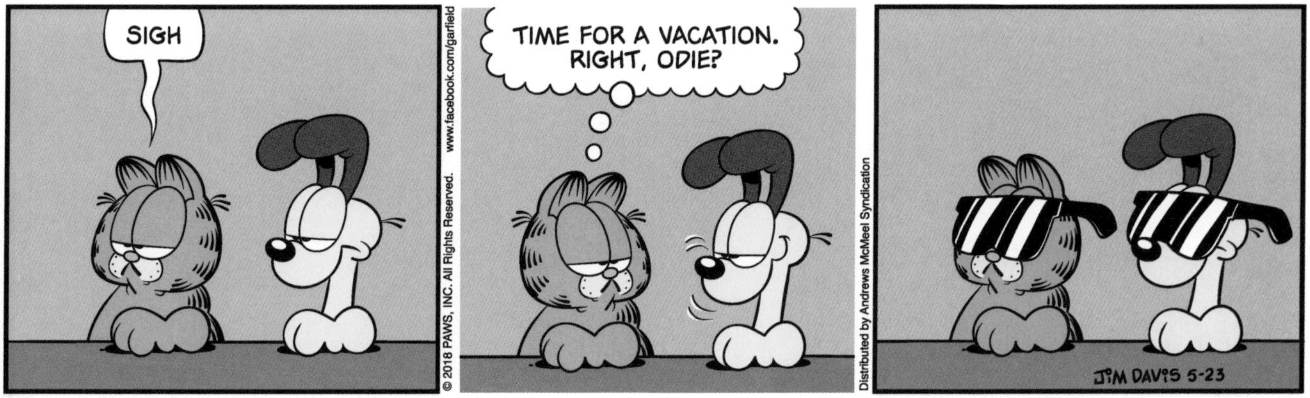
SIGH
TIME FOR A VACATION. RIGHT, ODIE?
JIM DAVIS 5-23
© 2018 PAWS, INC. All Rights Reserved. www.facebook.com/garfield
Distributed by Andrews McMeel Syndication

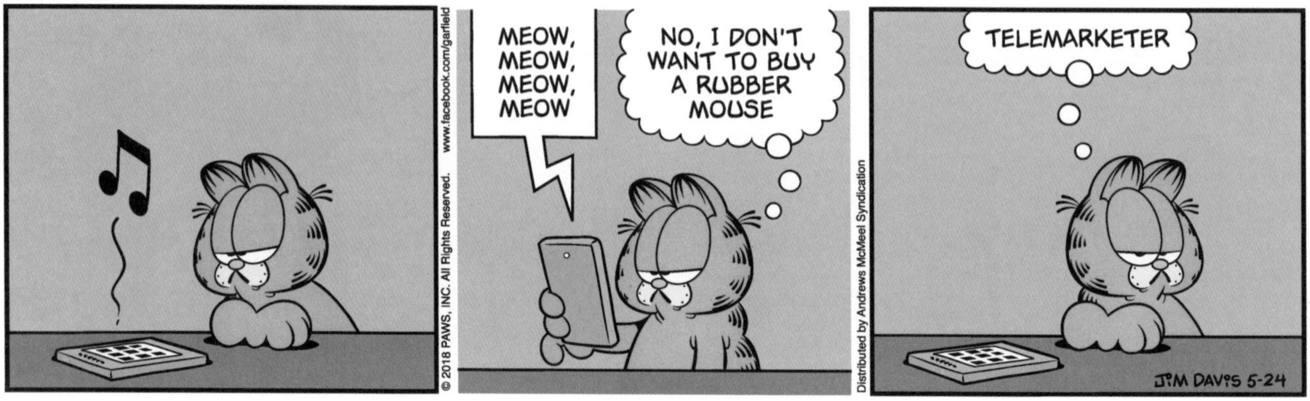
MEOW, MEOW, MEOW, MEOW
NO, I DON'T WANT TO BUY A RUBBER MOUSE
TELEMARKETER
© 2018 PAWS, INC. All Rights Reserved. www.facebook.com/garfield
Distributed by Andrews McMeel Syndication
JIM DAVIS 5-24

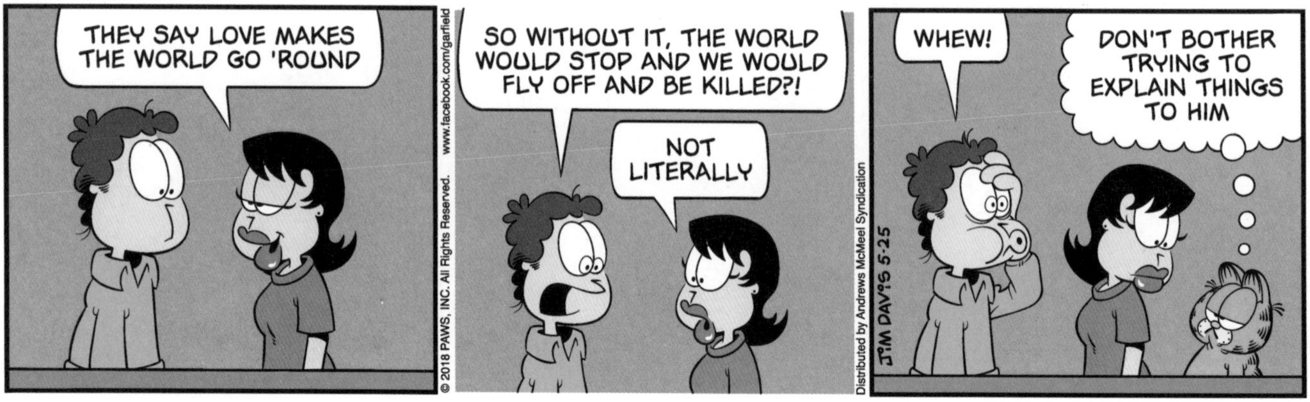
THEY SAY LOVE MAKES THE WORLD GO 'ROUND
SO WITHOUT IT, THE WORLD WOULD STOP AND WE WOULD FLY OFF AND BE KILLED?!
NOT LITERALLY
WHEW!
DON'T BOTHER TRYING TO EXPLAIN THINGS TO HIM
© 2018 PAWS, INC. All Rights Reserved. www.facebook.com/garfield
Distributed by Andrews McMeel Syndication
JIM DAVIS 5-25

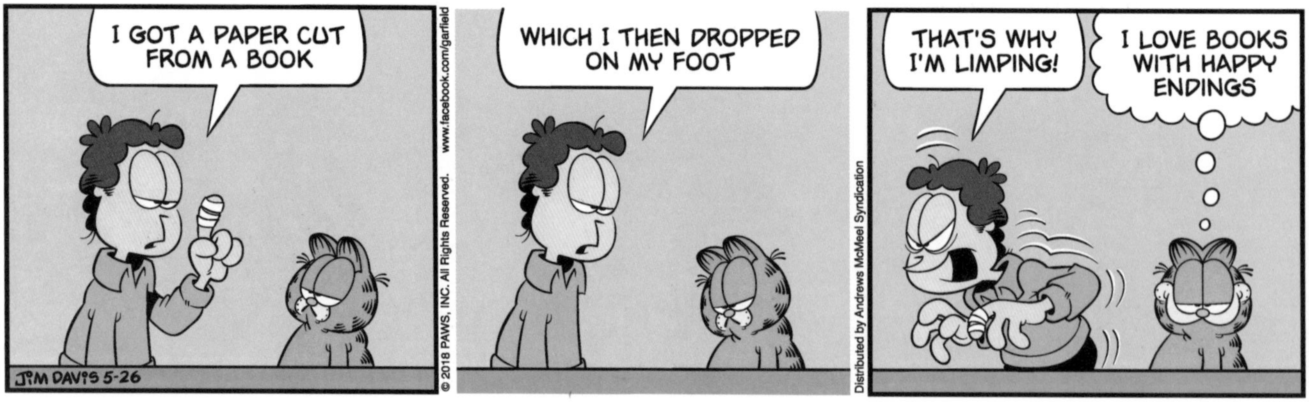
I GOT A PAPER CUT FROM A BOOK
WHICH I THEN DROPPED ON MY FOOT
THAT'S WHY I'M LIMPING!
I LOVE BOOKS WITH HAPPY ENDINGS
© 2018 PAWS, INC. All Rights Reserved. www.facebook.com/garfield
Distributed by Andrews McMeel Syndication
JIM DAVIS 5-26

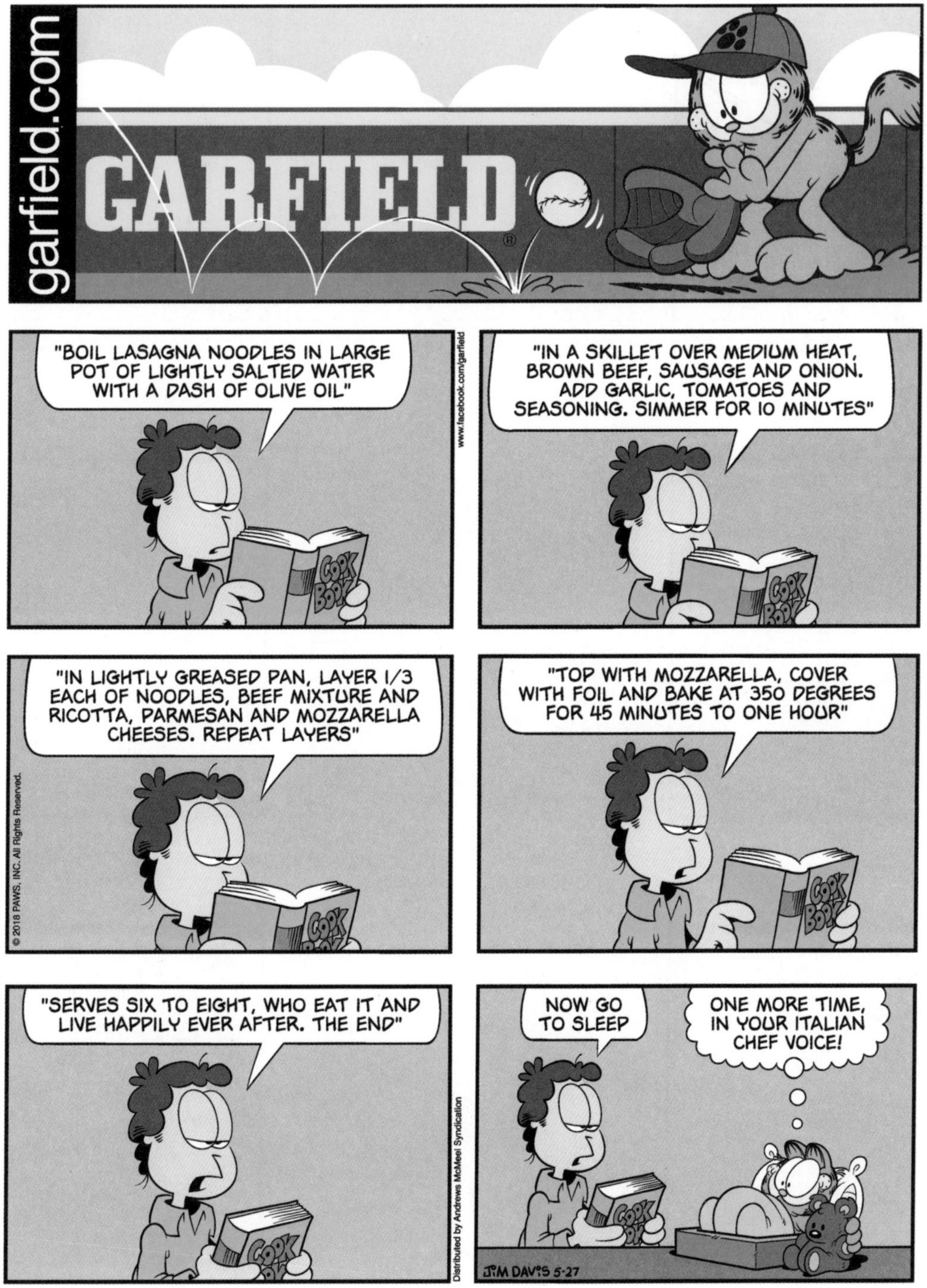
garfield.com
GARFIELD®
"BOIL LASAGNA NOODLES IN LARGE POT OF LIGHTLY SALTED WATER WITH A DASH OF OLIVE OIL"
www.facebook.com/garfield
"IN A SKILLET OVER MEDIUM HEAT, BROWN BEEF, SAUSAGE AND ONION. ADD GARLIC, TOMATOES AND SEASONING. SIMMER FOR 10 MINUTES"
COOK BOOK
"IN LIGHTLY GREASED PAN, LAYER 1/3 EACH OF NOODLES, BEEF MIXTURE AND RICOTTA, PARMESAN AND MOZZARELLA CHEESES. REPEAT LAYERS"
© 2018 PAWS, INC. All Rights Reserved.
"TOP WITH MOZZARELLA, COVER WITH FOIL AND BAKE AT 350 DEGREES FOR 45 MINUTES TO ONE HOUR"
"SERVES SIX TO EIGHT, WHO EAT IT AND LIVE HAPPILY EVER AFTER. THE END"
Distributed by Andrews McMeel Syndication
NOW GO TO SLEEP
ONE MORE TIME, IN YOUR ITALIAN CHEF VOICE!
JIM DAVIS 5-27

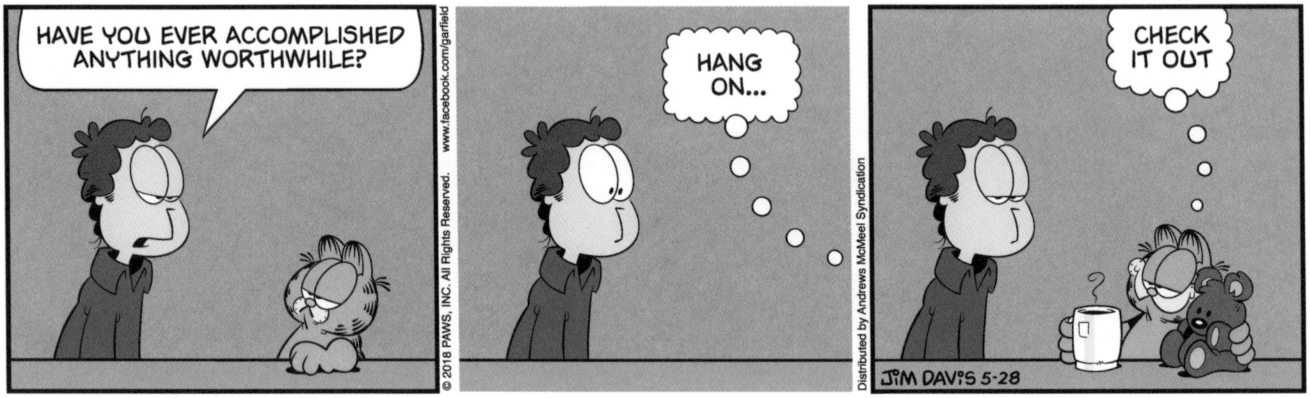
HAVE YOU EVER ACCOMPLISHED ANYTHING WORTHWHILE?
HANG ON...
CHECK IT OUT
JIM DAVIS 5-28
© 2018 PAWS, INC. All Rights Reserved. www.facebook.com/garfield
Distributed by Andrews McMeel Syndication

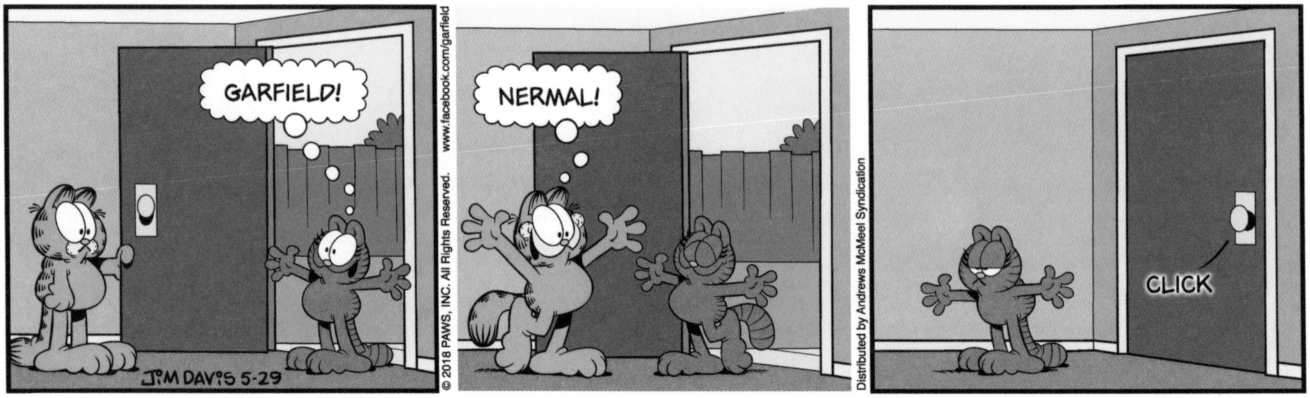
GARFIELD!
NERMAL!
CLICK
JIM DAVIS 5-29
© 2018 PAWS, INC. All Rights Reserved. www.facebook.com/garfield
Distributed by Andrews McMeel Syndication

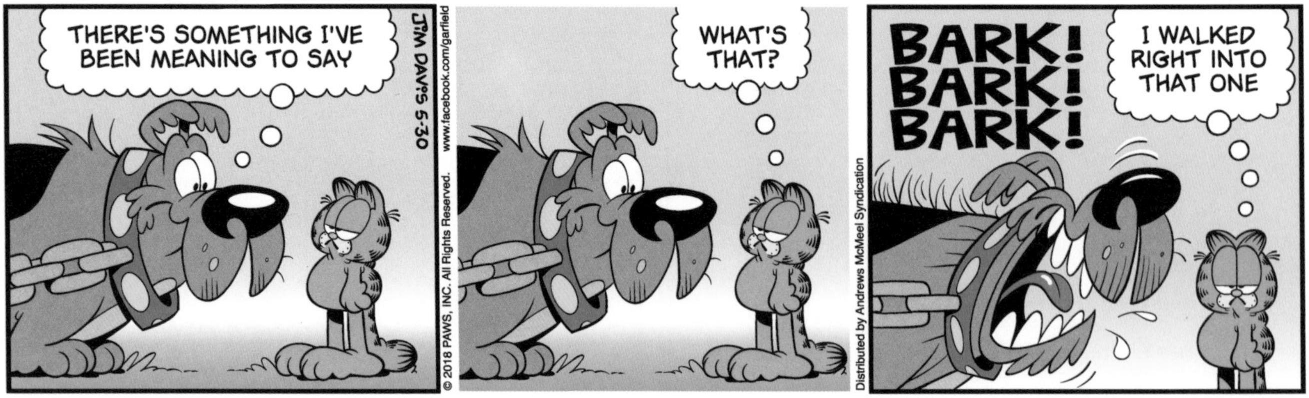
THERE'S SOMETHING I'VE BEEN MEANING TO SAY
WHAT'S THAT?
BARK! BARK! BARK!
I WALKED RIGHT INTO THAT ONE
JIM DAVIS 5-30
© 2018 PAWS, INC. All Rights Reserved. www.facebook.com/garfield
Distributed by Andrews McMeel Syndication

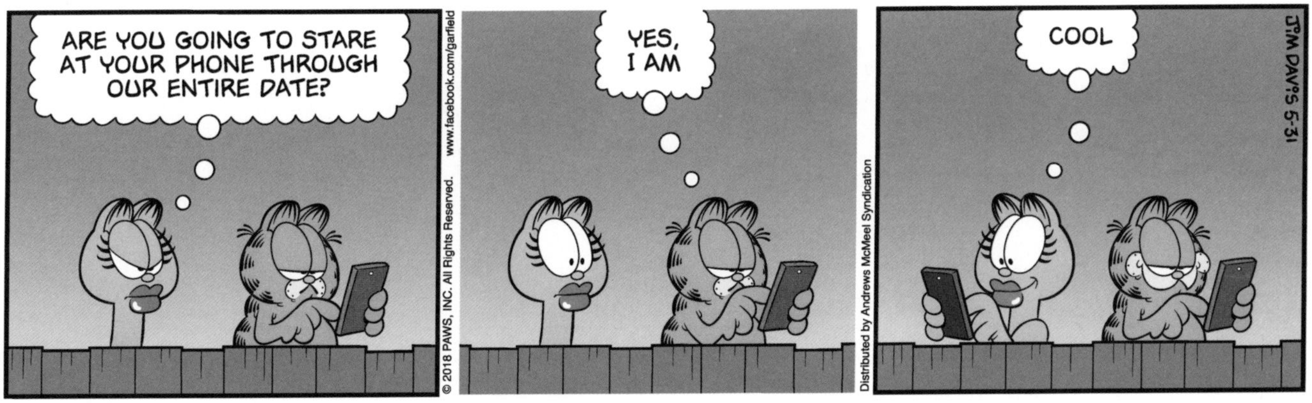
ARE YOU GOING TO STARE AT YOUR PHONE THROUGH OUR ENTIRE DATE?
YES, I AM
COOL
JIM DAVIS 5-31


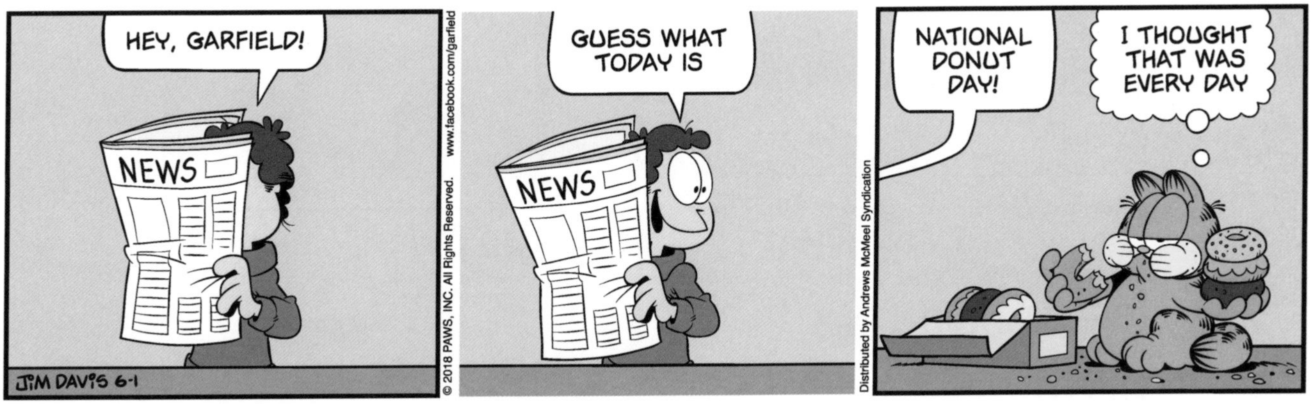
HEY, GARFIELD!
NEWS
GUESS WHAT TODAY IS
NEWS
NATIONAL DONUT DAY!
I THOUGHT THAT WAS EVERY DAY
JIM DAVIS 6-1


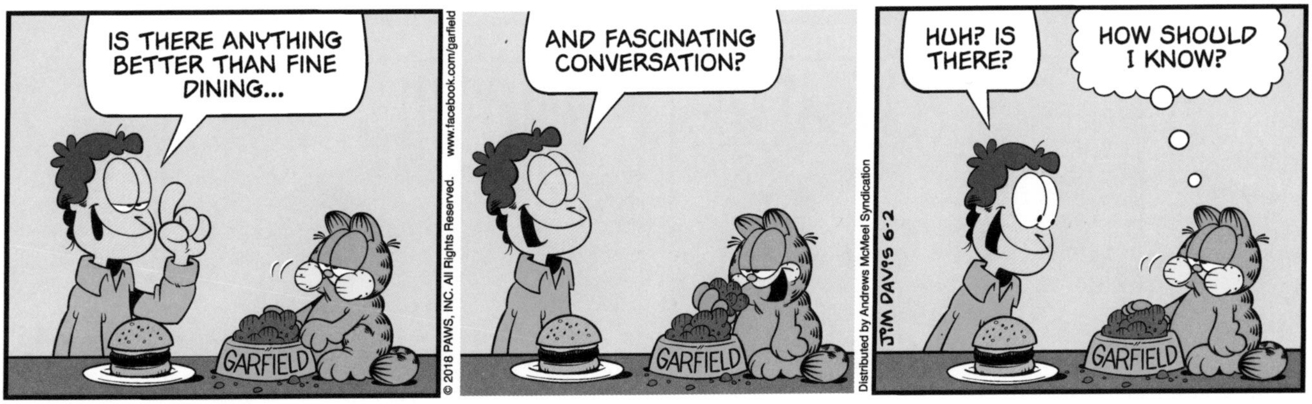
IS THERE ANYTHING BETTER THAN FINE DINING...
GARFIELD
AND FASCINATING CONVERSATION?
GARFIELD
HUH? IS THERE?
HOW SHOULD I KNOW?
GARFIELD
JIM DAVIS 6-2

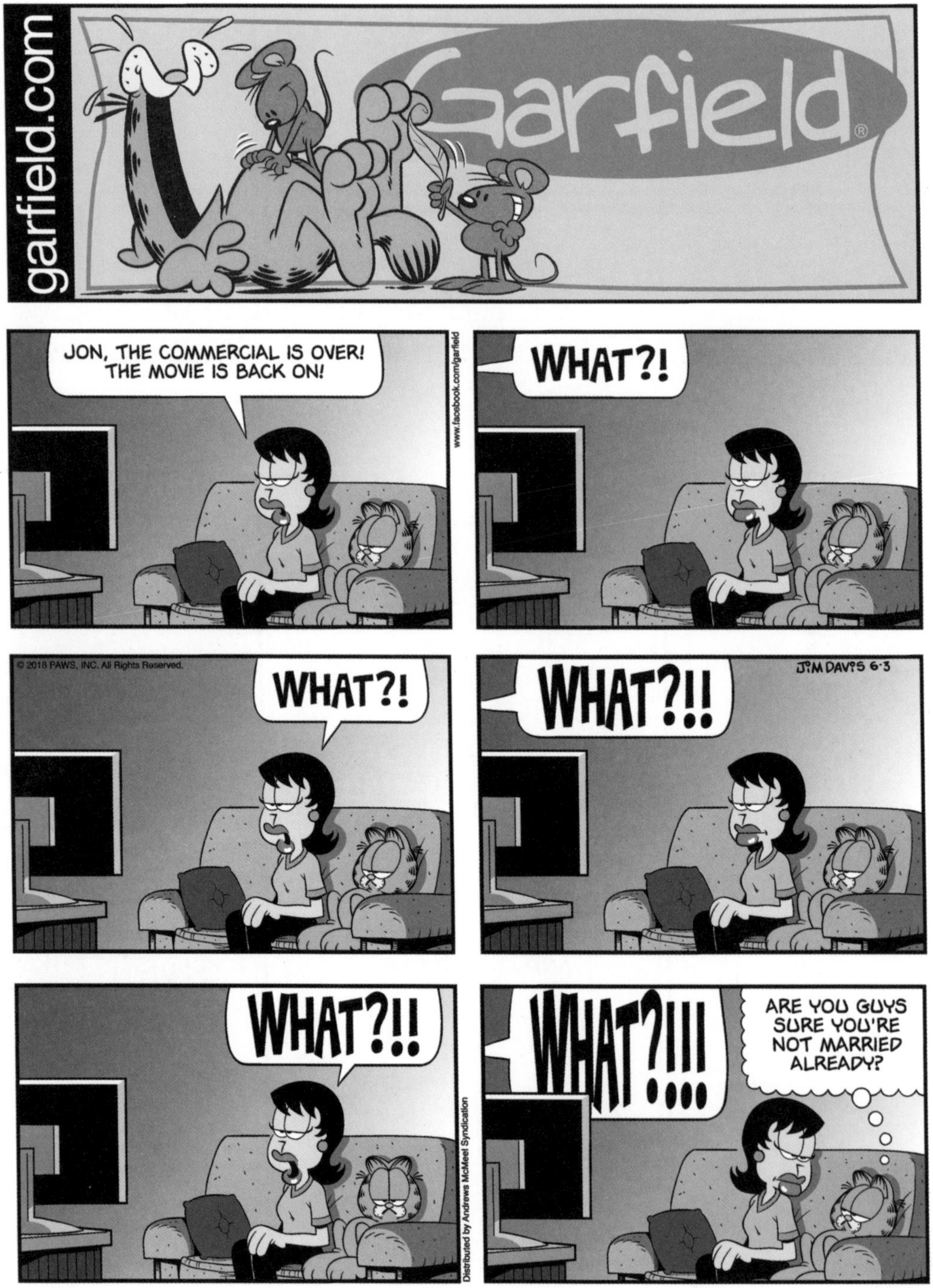

garfield.com
Garfield®
JON, THE COMMERCIAL IS OVER! THE MOVIE IS BACK ON!
www.facebook.com/garfield
WHAT?!
© 2018 PAWS, INC. All Rights Reserved.
WHAT?!
JIM DAVIS 6-3
WHAT?!!
WHAT?!!
Distributed by Andrews McMeel Syndication
WHAT?!!!
ARE YOU GUYS SURE YOU'RE NOT MARRIED ALREADY?

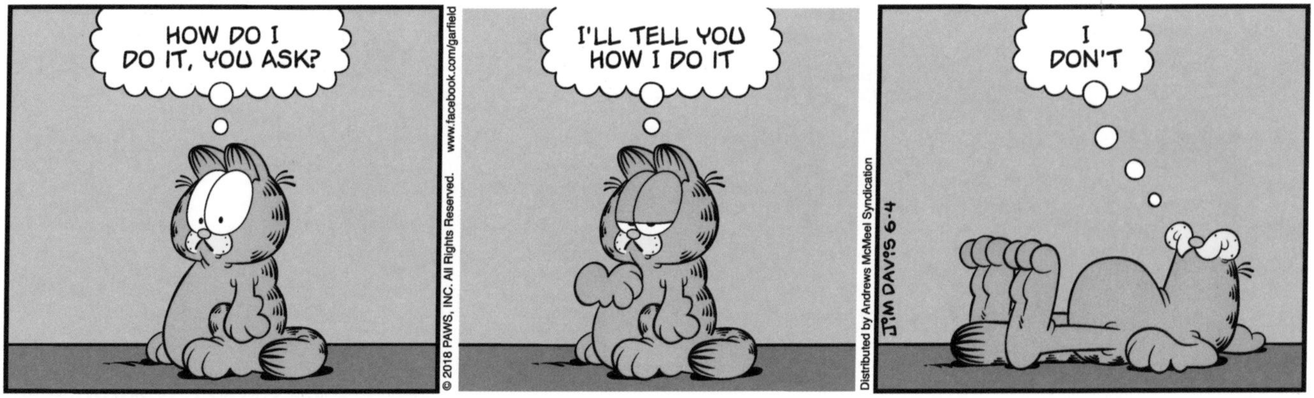
HOW DO I DO IT, YOU ASK?
© 2018 PAWS, INC. All Rights Reserved. www.facebook.com/garfield
I'LL TELL YOU HOW I DO IT
Distributed by Andrews McMeel Syndication
JIM DAVIS 6-4
I DON'T

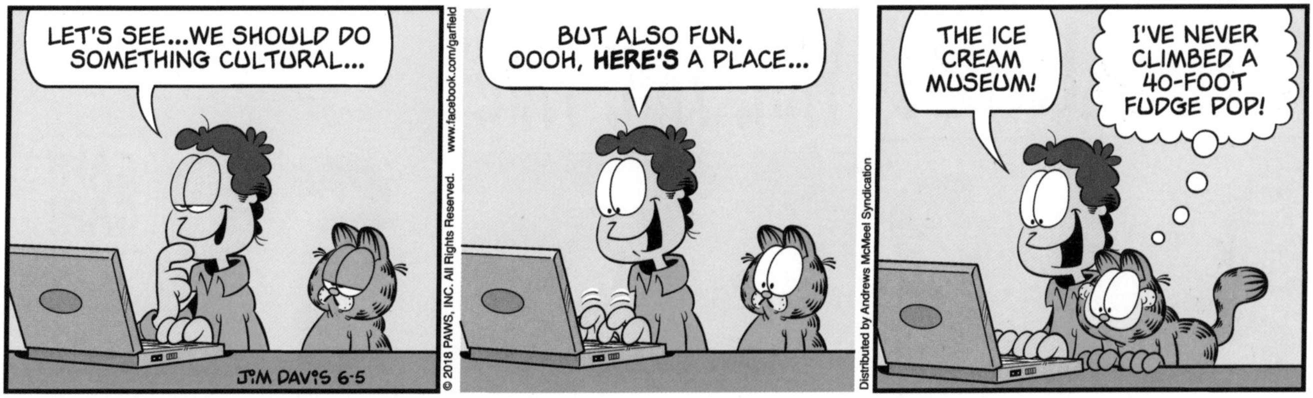
LET'S SEE...WE SHOULD DO SOMETHING CULTURAL...
JIM DAVIS 6-5
© 2018 PAWS, INC. All Rights Reserved. www.facebook.com/garfield
BUT ALSO FUN. OOOH, **HERE'S** A PLACE...
Distributed by Andrews McMeel Syndication
THE ICE CREAM MUSEUM!
I'VE NEVER CLIMBED A 40-FOOT FUDGE POP!

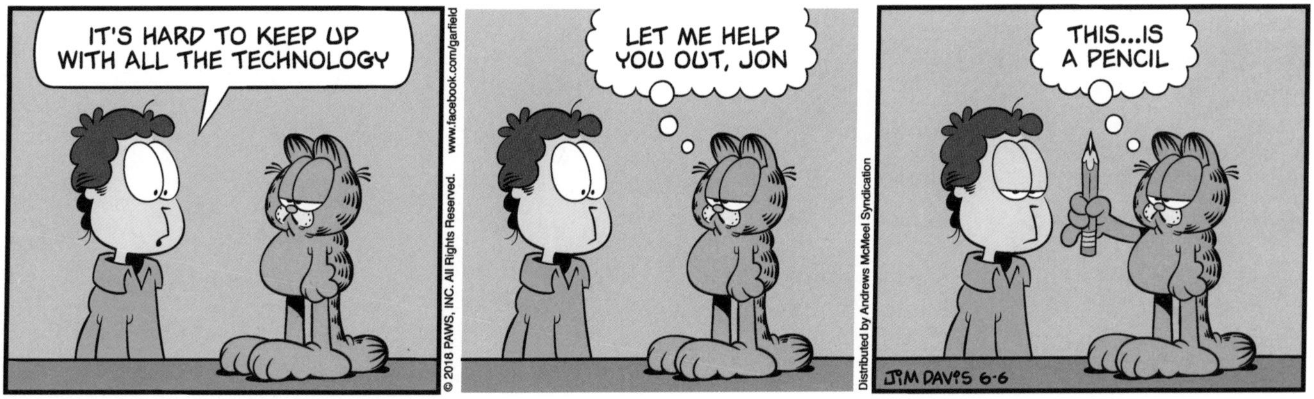
IT'S HARD TO KEEP UP WITH ALL THE TECHNOLOGY
© 2018 PAWS, INC. All Rights Reserved. www.facebook.com/garfield
LET ME HELP YOU OUT, JON
Distributed by Andrews McMeel Syndication
THIS...IS A PENCIL
JIM DAVIS 6-6

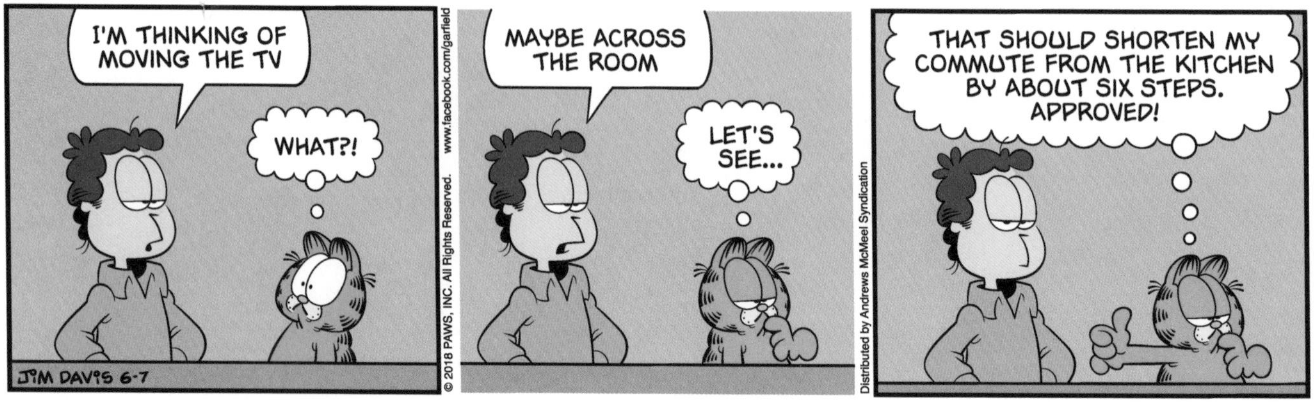
I'M THINKING OF MOVING THE TV
WHAT?!
MAYBE ACROSS THE ROOM
LET'S SEE...
THAT SHOULD SHORTEN MY COMMUTE FROM THE KITCHEN BY ABOUT SIX STEPS. APPROVED!
JIM DAVIS 6-7
© 2018 PAWS, INC. All Rights Reserved. www.facebook.com/garfield
Distributed by Andrews McMeel Syndication

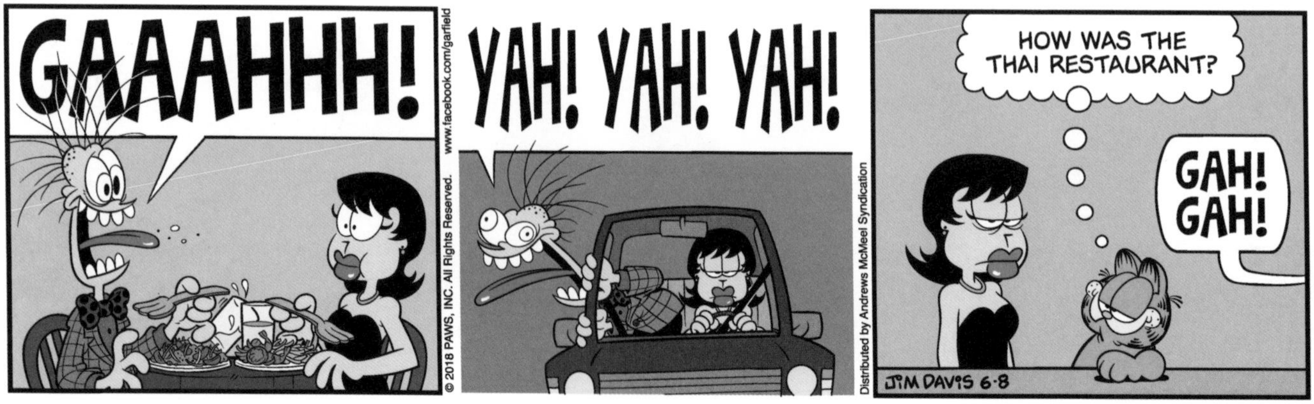
GAAAHHH!
YAH! YAH! YAH!
HOW WAS THE THAI RESTAURANT?
GAH! GAH!
JIM DAVIS 6-8
© 2018 PAWS, INC. All Rights Reserved. www.facebook.com/garfield
Distributed by Andrews McMeel Syndication

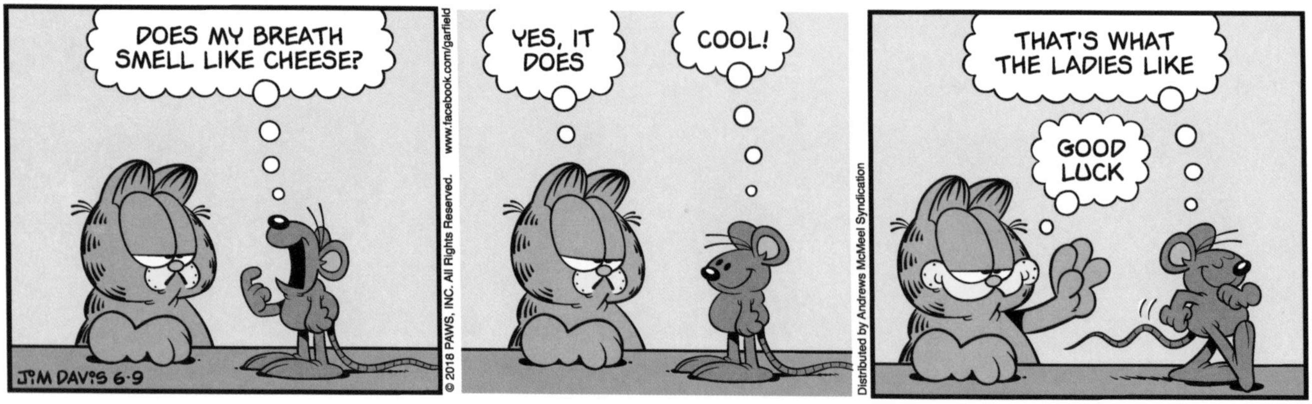
DOES MY BREATH SMELL LIKE CHEESE?
YES, IT DOES
COOL!
THAT'S WHAT THE LADIES LIKE
GOOD LUCK
JIM DAVIS 6-9
© 2018 PAWS, INC. All Rights Reserved. www.facebook.com/garfield
Distributed by Andrews McMeel Syndication

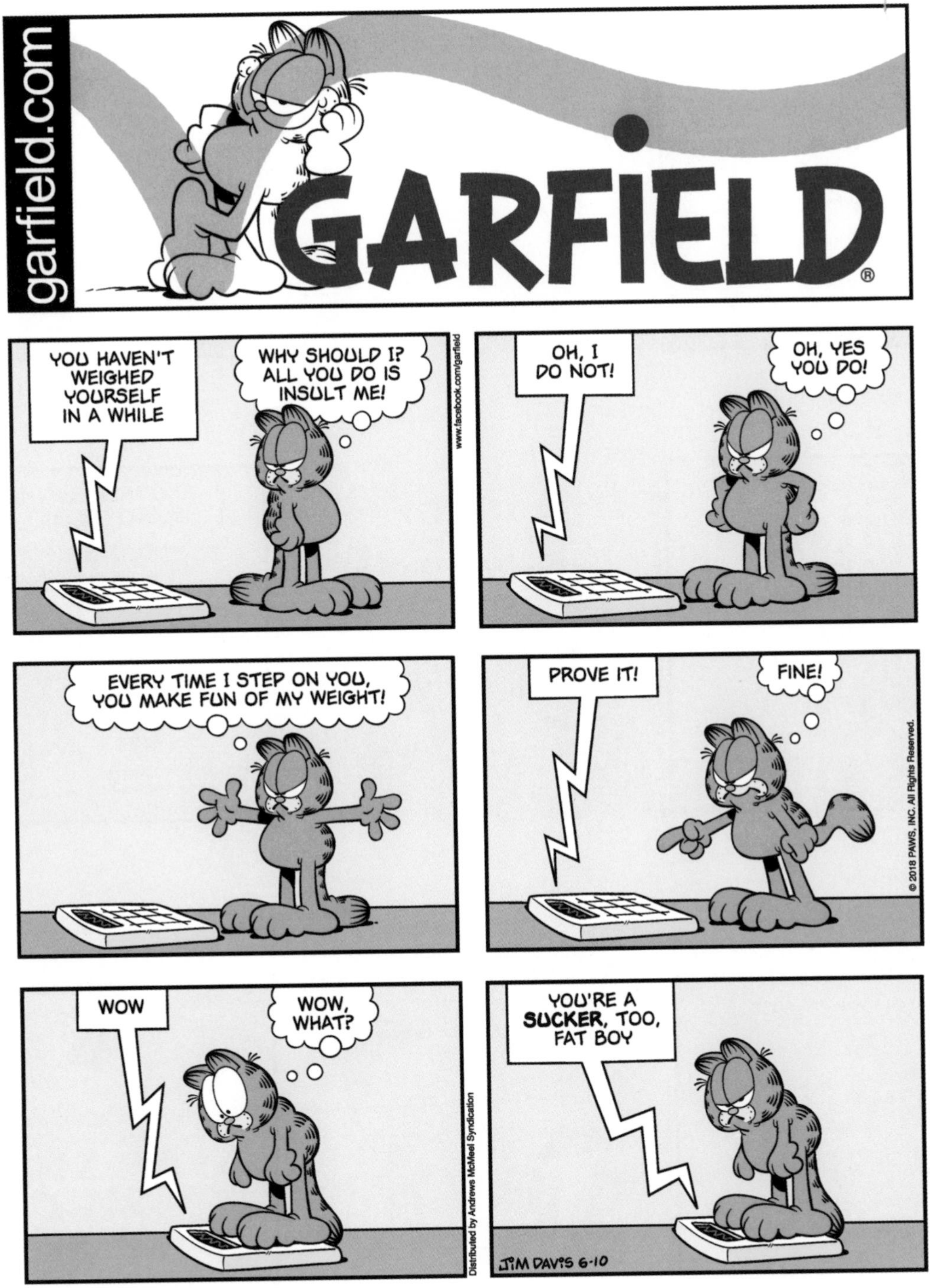
garfield.com
GARFIELD®
YOU HAVEN'T WEIGHED YOURSELF IN A WHILE
WHY SHOULD I? ALL YOU DO IS INSULT ME!
www.facebook.com/garfield
OH, I DO NOT!
OH, YES YOU DO!
EVERY TIME I STEP ON YOU, YOU MAKE FUN OF MY WEIGHT!
PROVE IT!
FINE!
© 2018 PAWS, INC. All Rights Reserved.
WOW
WOW, WHAT?
Distributed by Andrews McMeel Syndication
YOU'RE A **SUCKER**, TOO, FAT BOY
JIM DAVIS 6-10

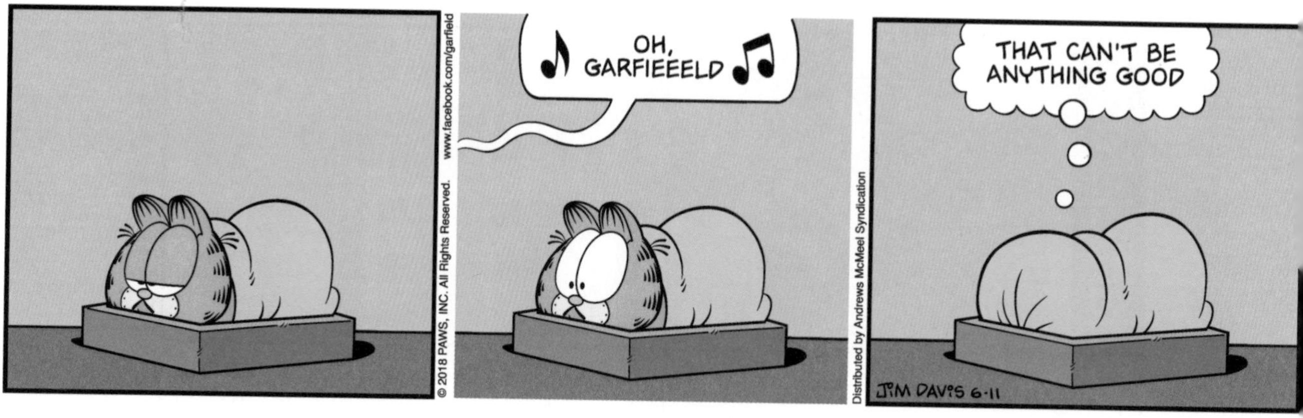
© 2018 PAWS, INC. All Rights Reserved. www.facebook.com/garfield
OH, GARFIEEELD
Distributed by Andrews McMeel Syndication
THAT CAN'T BE ANYTHING GOOD
JIM DAVIS 6-11

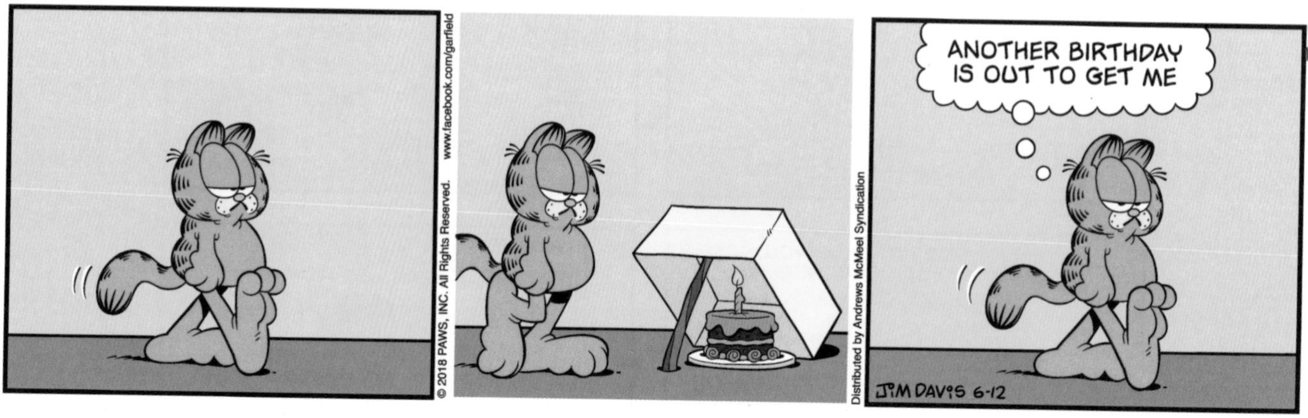
© 2018 PAWS, INC. All Rights Reserved. www.facebook.com/garfield
Distributed by Andrews McMeel Syndication
ANOTHER BIRTHDAY IS OUT TO GET ME
JIM DAVIS 6-12

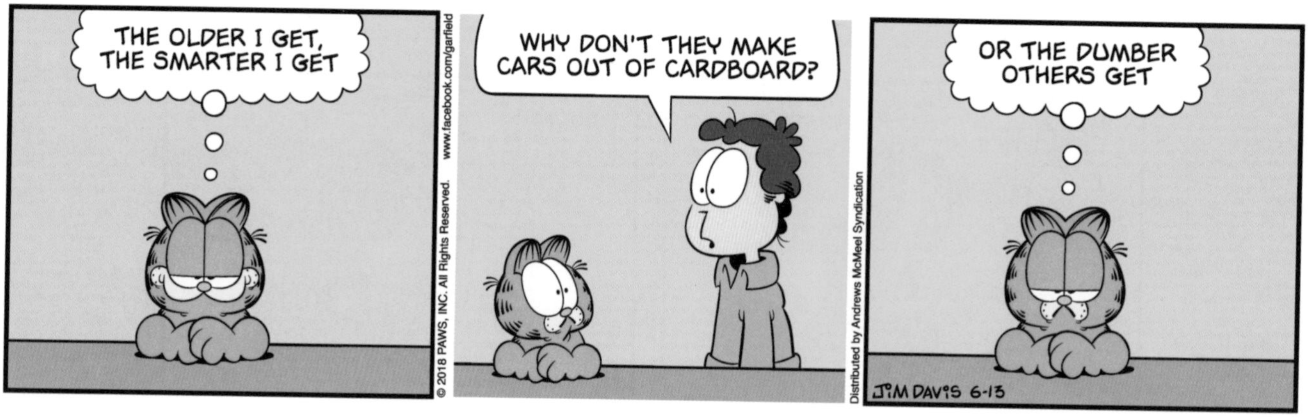
THE OLDER I GET, THE SMARTER I GET
© 2018 PAWS, INC. All Rights Reserved. www.facebook.com/garfield
WHY DON'T THEY MAKE CARS OUT OF CARDBOARD?
Distributed by Andrews McMeel Syndication
OR THE DUMBER OTHERS GET
JIM DAVIS 6-13

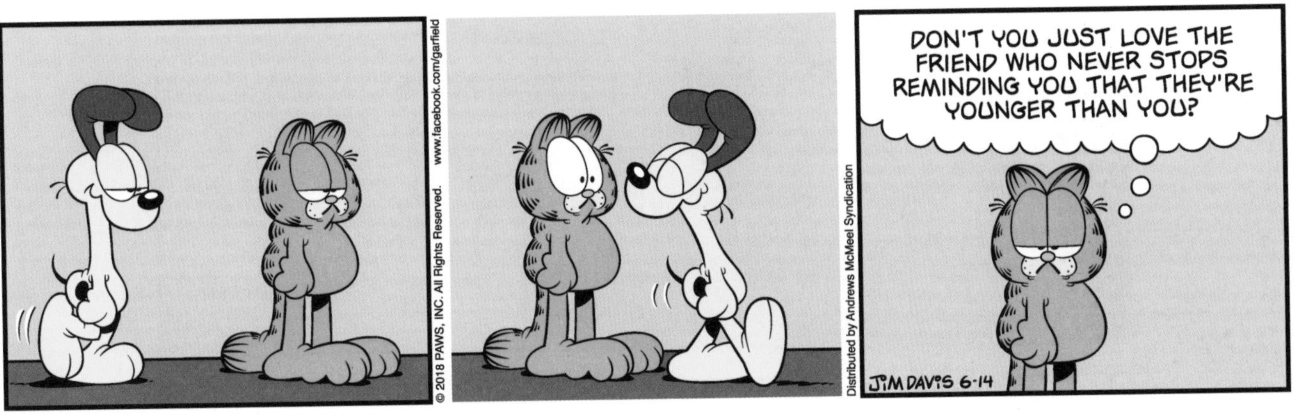
DON'T YOU JUST LOVE THE FRIEND WHO NEVER STOPS REMINDING YOU THAT THEY'RE YOUNGER THAN YOU?
JIM DAVIS 6-14
© 2018 PAWS, INC. All Rights Reserved. www.facebook.com/garfield
Distributed by Andrews McMeel Syndication

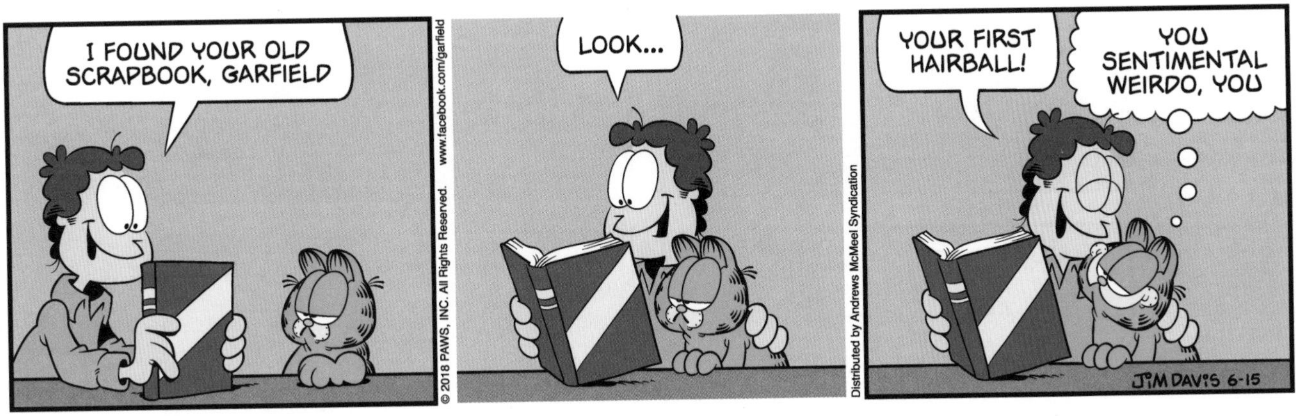
I FOUND YOUR OLD SCRAPBOOK, GARFIELD
LOOK...
YOUR FIRST HAIRBALL!
YOU SENTIMENTAL WEIRDO, YOU
JIM DAVIS 6-15
© 2018 PAWS, INC. All Rights Reserved. www.facebook.com/garfield
Distributed by Andrews McMeel Syndication

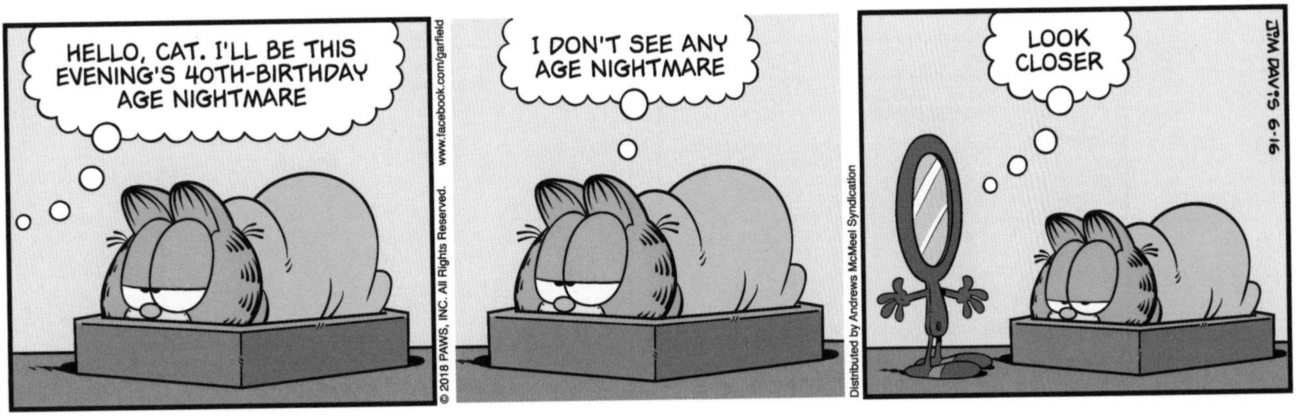
HELLO, CAT. I'LL BE THIS EVENING'S 40TH-BIRTHDAY AGE NIGHTMARE
I DON'T SEE ANY AGE NIGHTMARE
LOOK CLOSER
JIM DAVIS 6-16
© 2018 PAWS, INC. All Rights Reserved. www.facebook.com/garfield
Distributed by Andrews McMeel Syndication

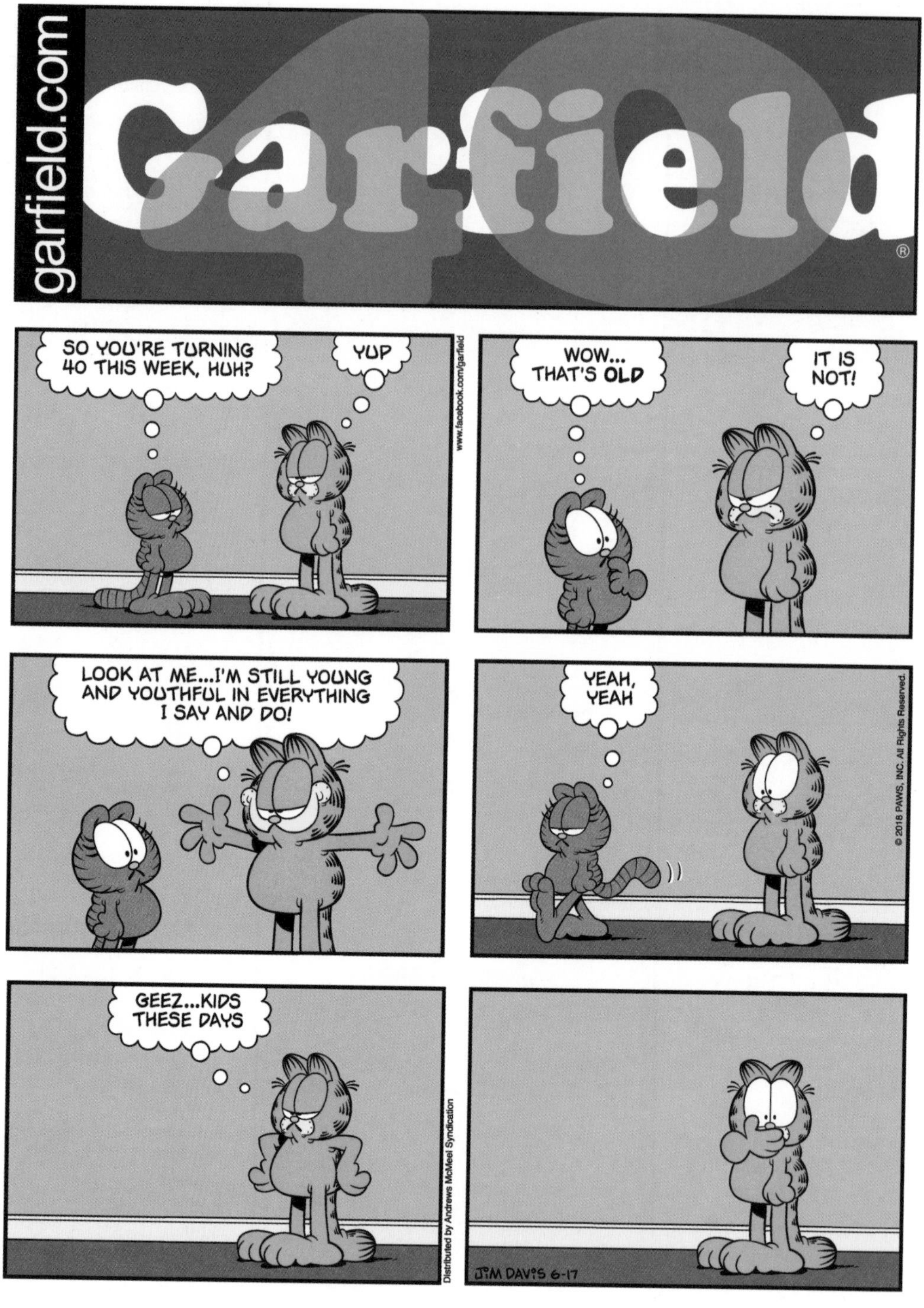
garfield.com
Garfield
SO YOU'RE TURNING 40 THIS WEEK, HUH?
YUP
www.facebook.com/garfield
WOW... THAT'S OLD
IT IS NOT!
LOOK AT ME...I'M STILL YOUNG AND YOUTHFUL IN EVERYTHING I SAY AND DO!
YEAH, YEAH
© 2018 PAWS, INC. All Rights Reserved.
GEEZ...KIDS THESE DAYS
Distributed by Andrews McMeel Syndication
JIM DAVIS 6-17

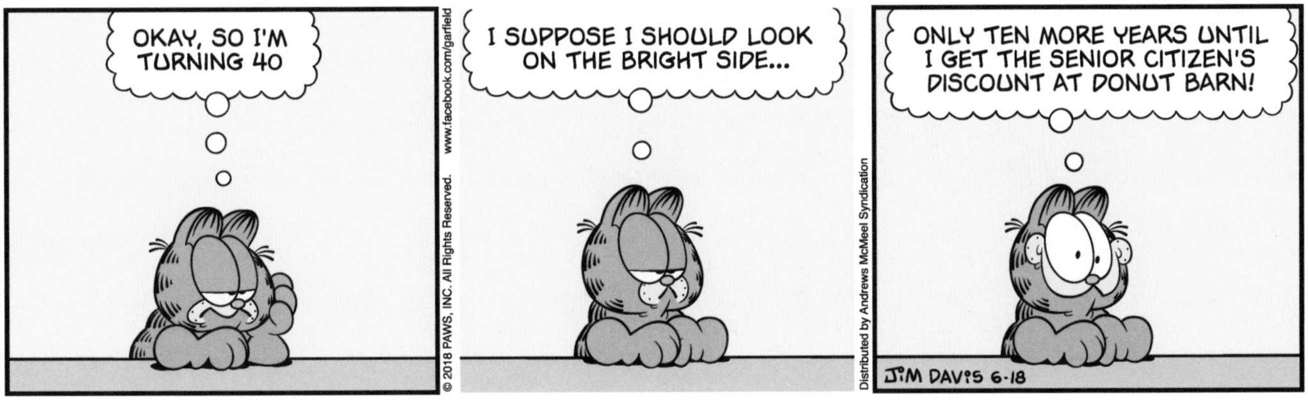
OKAY, SO I'M TURNING 40
I SUPPOSE I SHOULD LOOK ON THE BRIGHT SIDE...
ONLY TEN MORE YEARS UNTIL I GET THE SENIOR CITIZEN'S DISCOUNT AT DONUT BARN!
JIM DAVIS 6-18
© 2018 PAWS, INC. All Rights Reserved. www.facebook.com/garfield
Distributed by Andrews McMeel Syndication

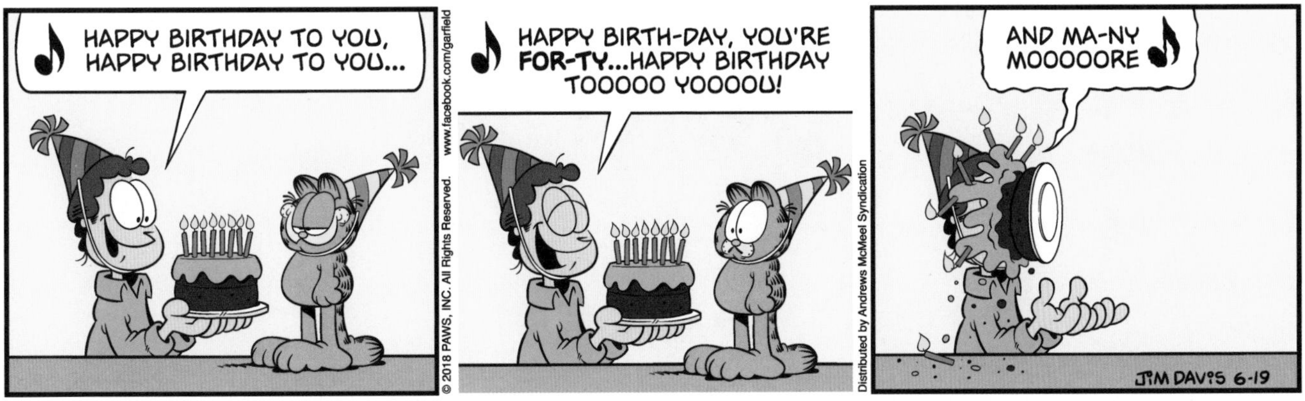
HAPPY BIRTHDAY TO YOU, HAPPY BIRTHDAY TO YOU...
HAPPY BIRTH-DAY, YOU'RE **FOR-TY**...HAPPY BIRTHDAY TOOOOO YOOOOU!
AND MA-NY MOOOOORE
JIM DAVIS 6-19
© 2018 PAWS, INC. All Rights Reserved. www.facebook.com/garfield
Distributed by Andrews McMeel Syndication

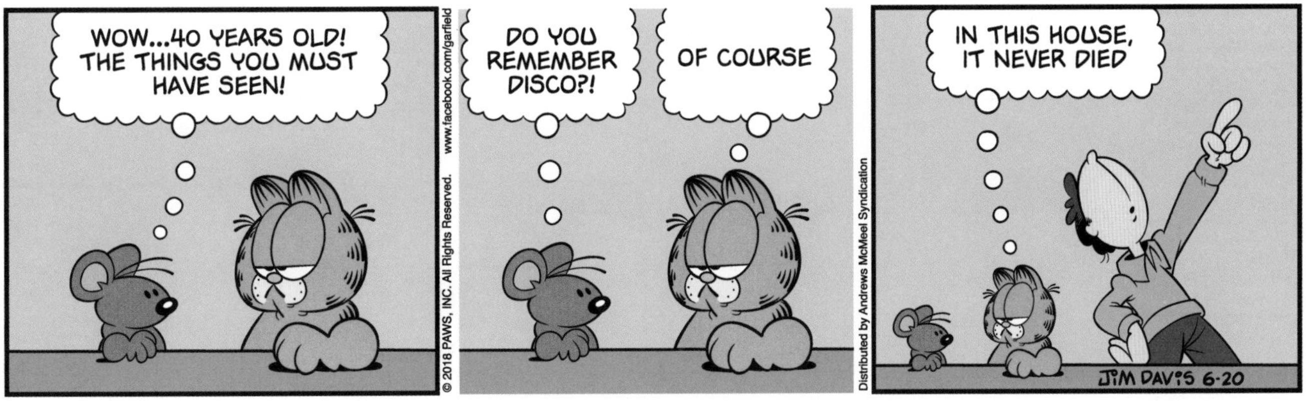
WOW...40 YEARS OLD! THE THINGS YOU MUST HAVE SEEN!
DO YOU REMEMBER DISCO?!
OF COURSE
IN THIS HOUSE, IT NEVER DIED
JIM DAVIS 6-20
© 2018 PAWS, INC. All Rights Reserved. www.facebook.com/garfield
Distributed by Andrews McMeel Syndication

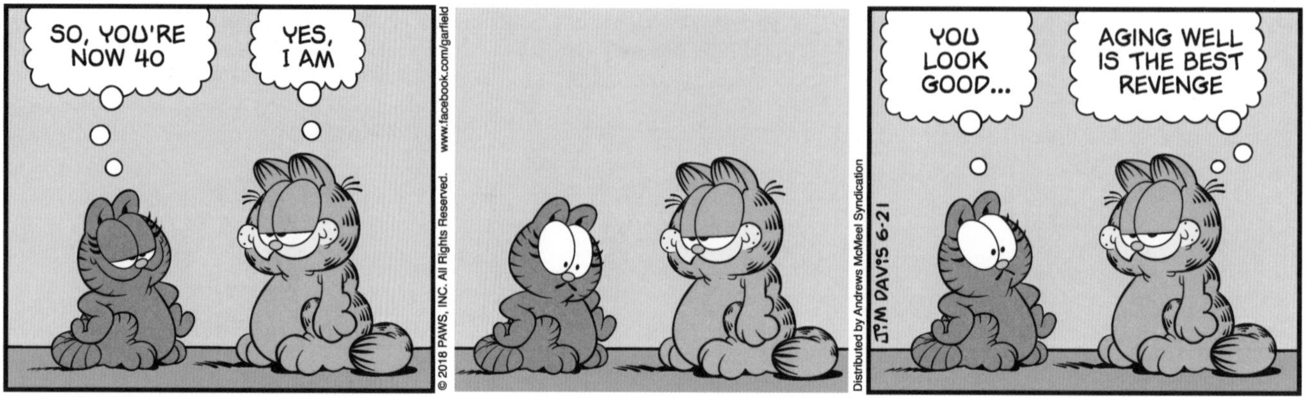
SO, YOU'RE NOW 40
YES, I AM
© 2018 PAWS, INC. All Rights Reserved. www.facebook.com/garfield
Distributed by Andrews McMeel Syndication
JIM DAVIS 6-21
YOU LOOK GOOD...
AGING WELL IS THE BEST REVENGE

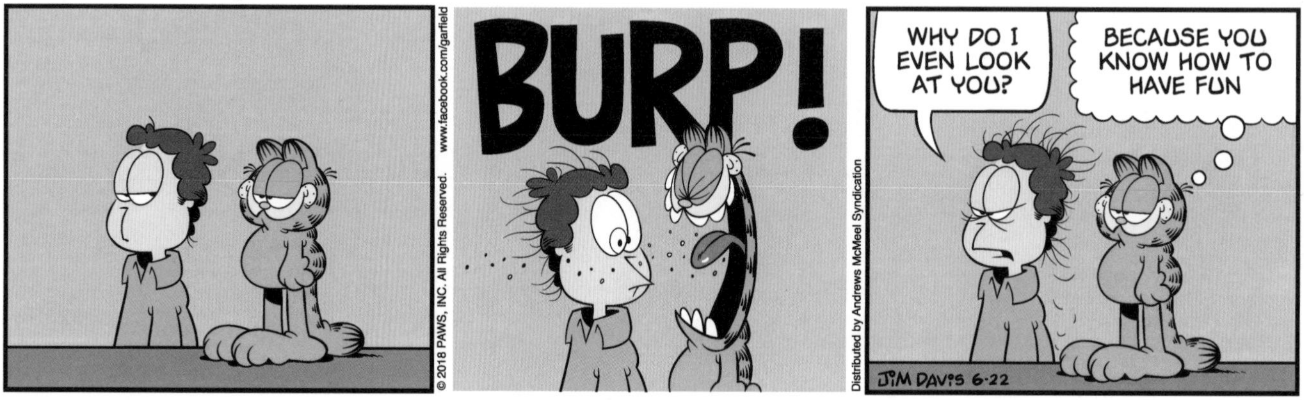
© 2018 PAWS, INC. All Rights Reserved. www.facebook.com/garfield
BURP!
Distributed by Andrews McMeel Syndication
WHY DO I EVEN LOOK AT YOU?
BECAUSE YOU KNOW HOW TO HAVE FUN
JIM DAVIS 6-22

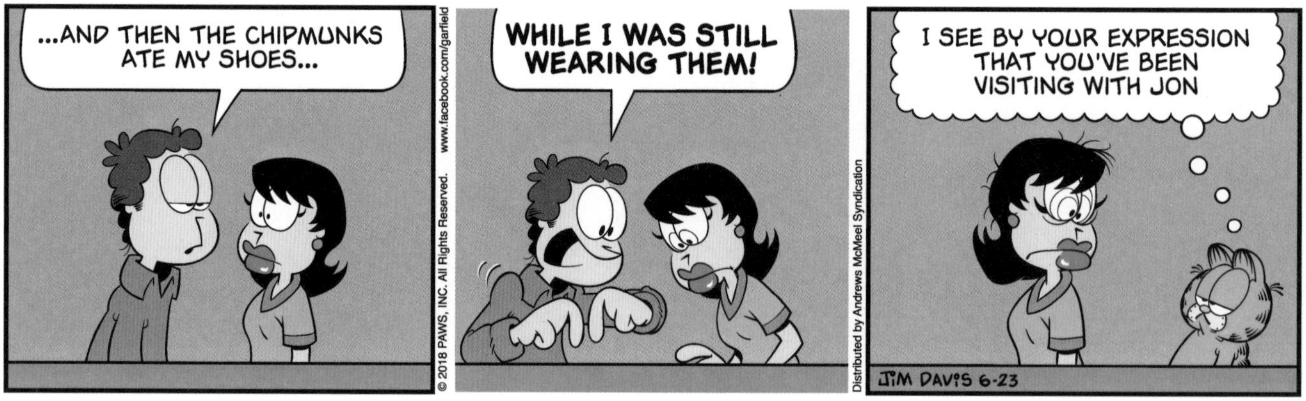
...AND THEN THE CHIPMUNKS ATE MY SHOES...
© 2018 PAWS, INC. All Rights Reserved. www.facebook.com/garfield
WHILE I WAS STILL WEARING THEM!
Distributed by Andrews McMeel Syndication
I SEE BY YOUR EXPRESSION THAT YOU'VE BEEN VISITING WITH JON
JIM DAVIS 6-23

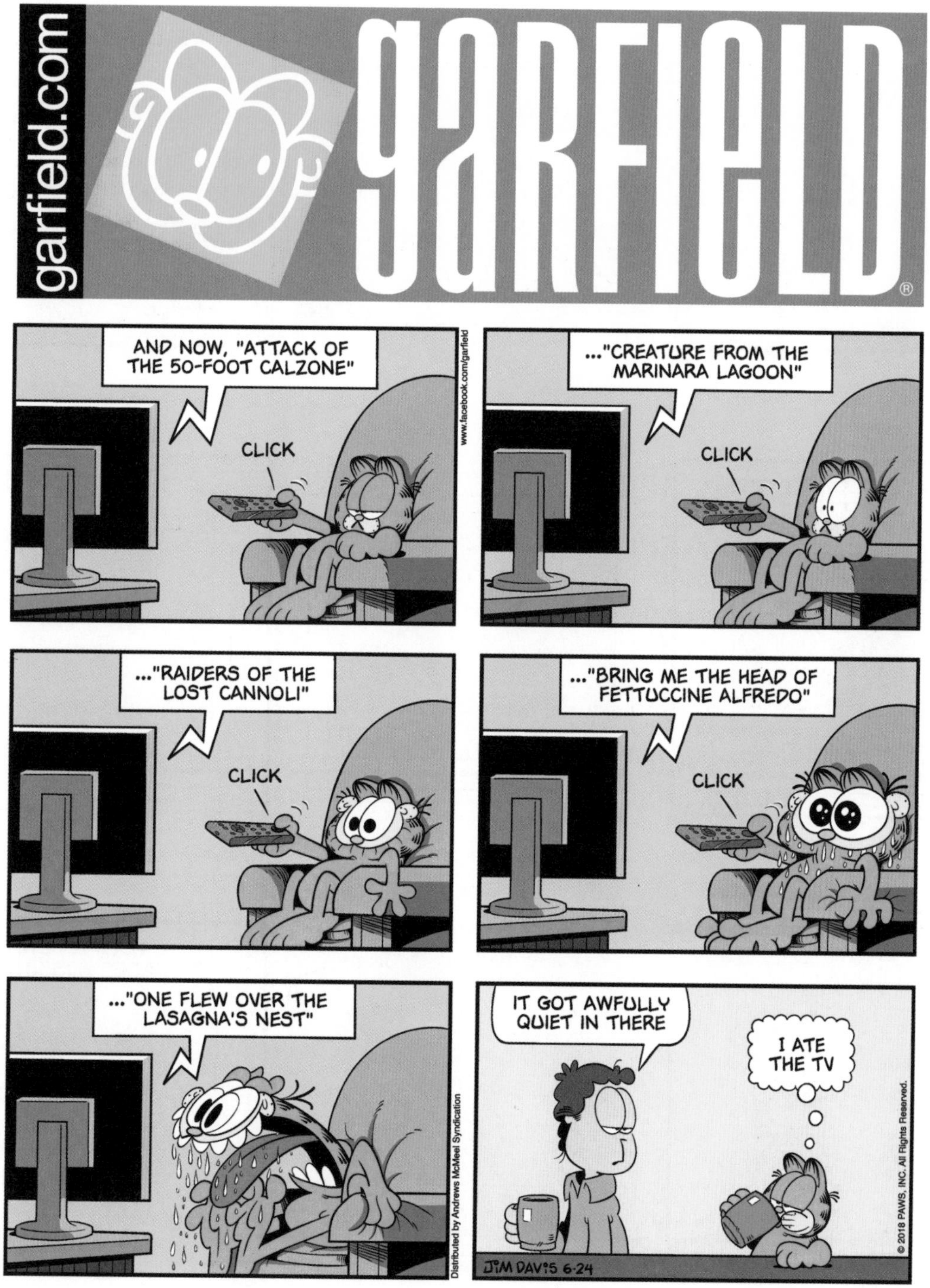
garfield.com
GARFIELD
AND NOW, "ATTACK OF THE 50-FOOT CALZONE"
CLICK
www.facebook.com/garfield
..."CREATURE FROM THE MARINARA LAGOON"
CLICK
..."RAIDERS OF THE LOST CANNOLI"
CLICK
..."BRING ME THE HEAD OF FETTUCCINE ALFREDO"
CLICK
..."ONE FLEW OVER THE LASAGNA'S NEST"
Distributed by Andrews McMeel Syndication
IT GOT AWFULLY QUIET IN THERE
I ATE THE TV
© 2018 PAWS, INC. All Rights Reserved.
JIM DAVIS 6-24

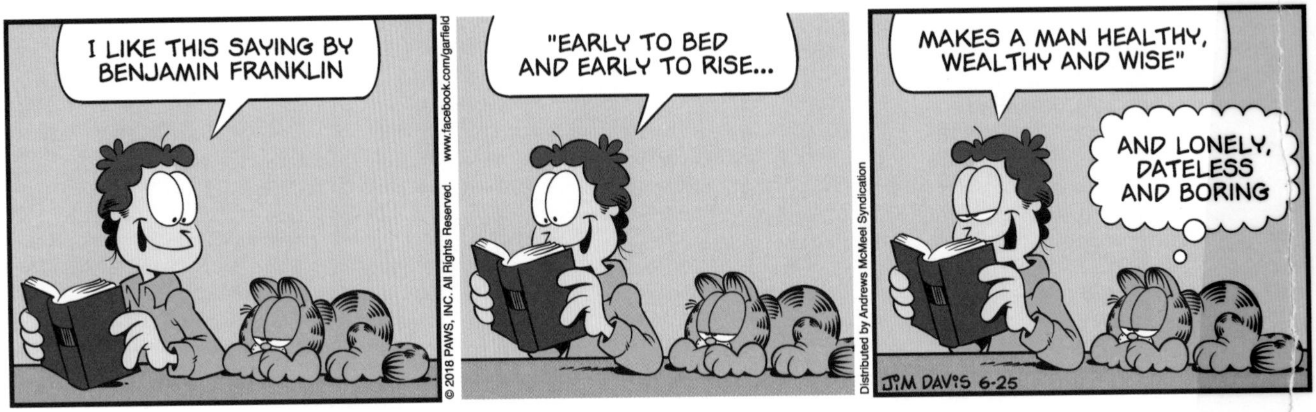
I LIKE THIS SAYING BY BENJAMIN FRANKLIN
"EARLY TO BED AND EARLY TO RISE...
MAKES A MAN HEALTHY, WEALTHY AND WISE"
AND LONELY, DATELESS AND BORING
JIM DAVIS 6-25
© 2018 PAWS, INC. All Rights Reserved. www.facebook.com/garfield
Distributed by Andrews McMeel Syndication

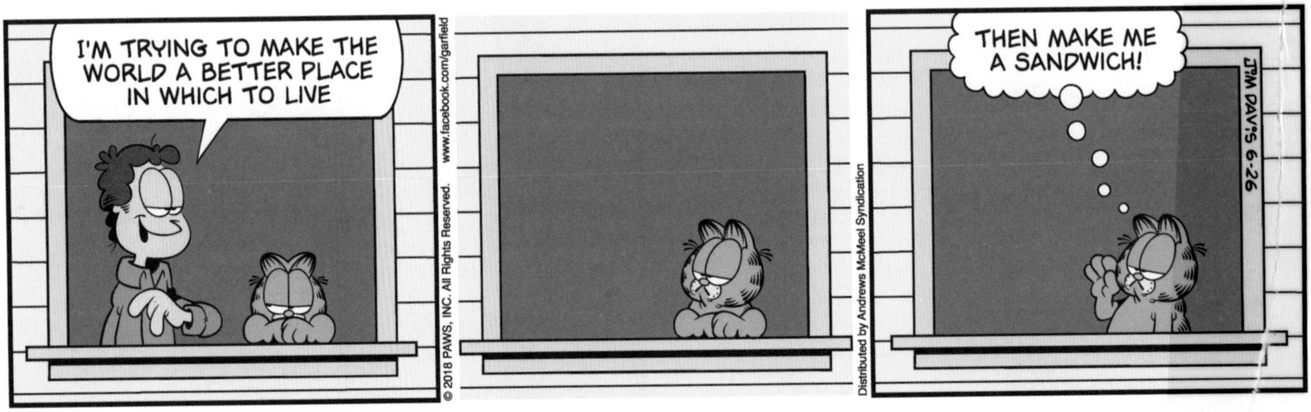
I'M TRYING TO MAKE THE WORLD A BETTER PLACE IN WHICH TO LIVE
THEN MAKE ME A SANDWICH!
JIM DAVIS 6-26
© 2018 PAWS, INC. All Rights Reserved. www.facebook.com/garfield
Distributed by Andrews McMeel Syndication

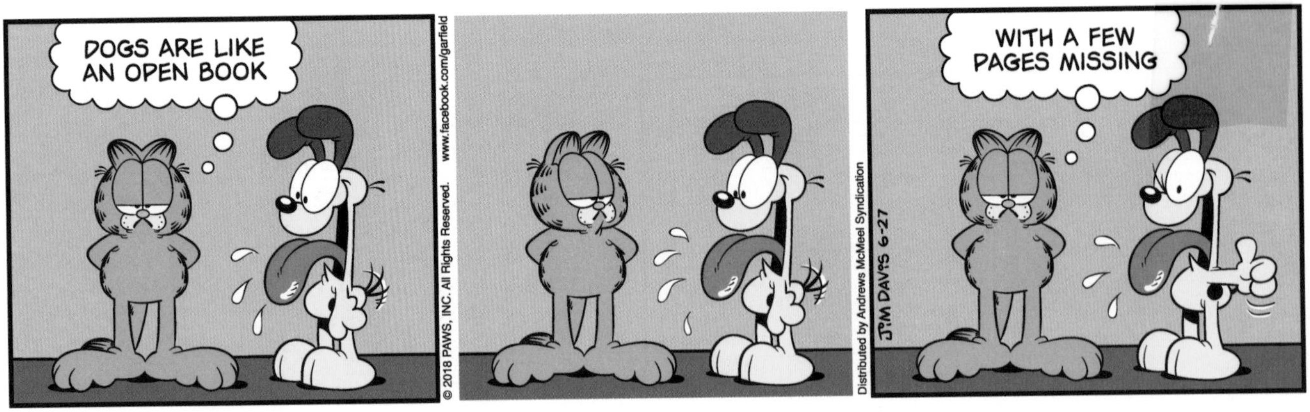
DOGS ARE LIKE AN OPEN BOOK
WITH A FEW PAGES MISSING
JIM DAVIS 6-27
© 2018 PAWS, INC. All Rights Reserved. www.facebook.com/garfield
Distributed by Andrews McMeel Syndication

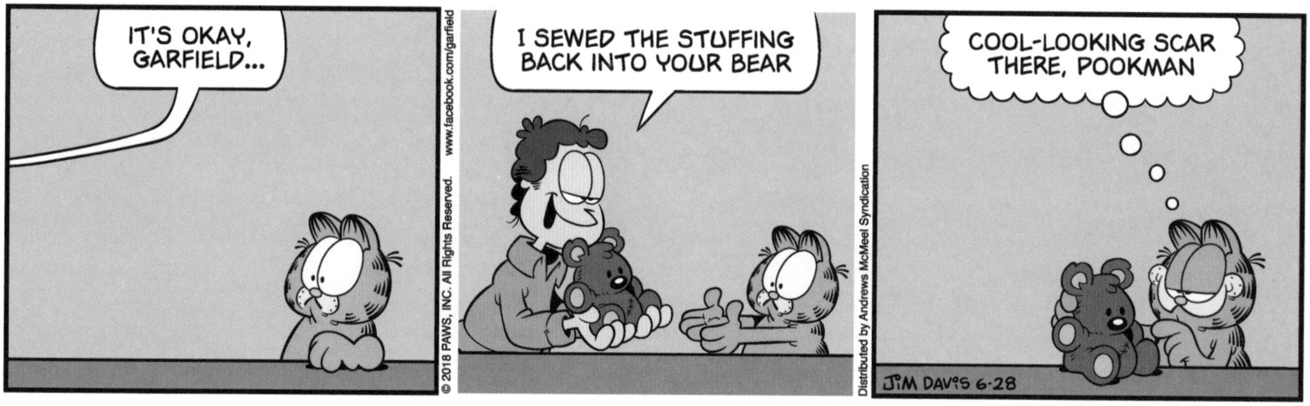
IT'S OKAY, GARFIELD...
I SEWED THE STUFFING BACK INTO YOUR BEAR
COOL-LOOKING SCAR THERE, POOKMAN
JIM DAVIS 6-28


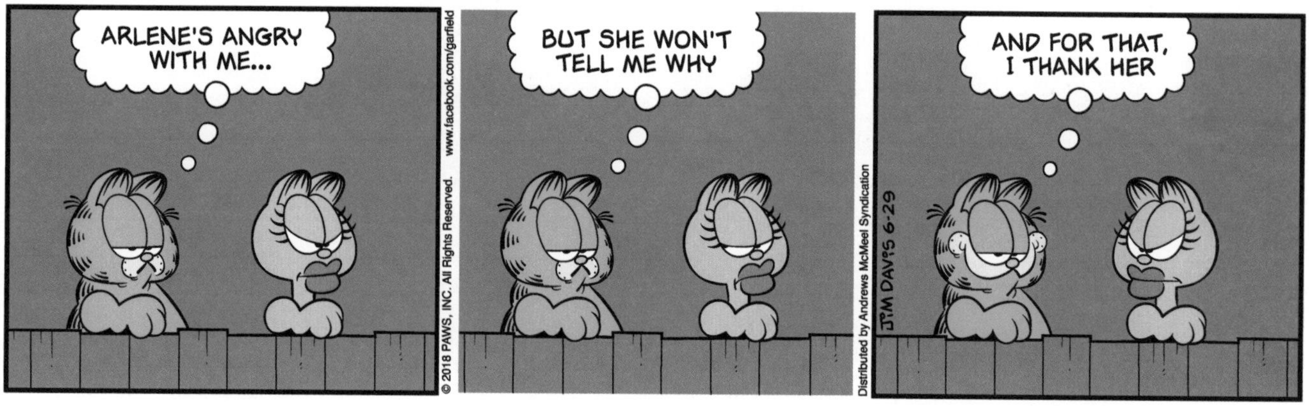
ARLENE'S ANGRY WITH ME...
BUT SHE WON'T TELL ME WHY
AND FOR THAT, I THANK HER
JIM DAVIS 6-29


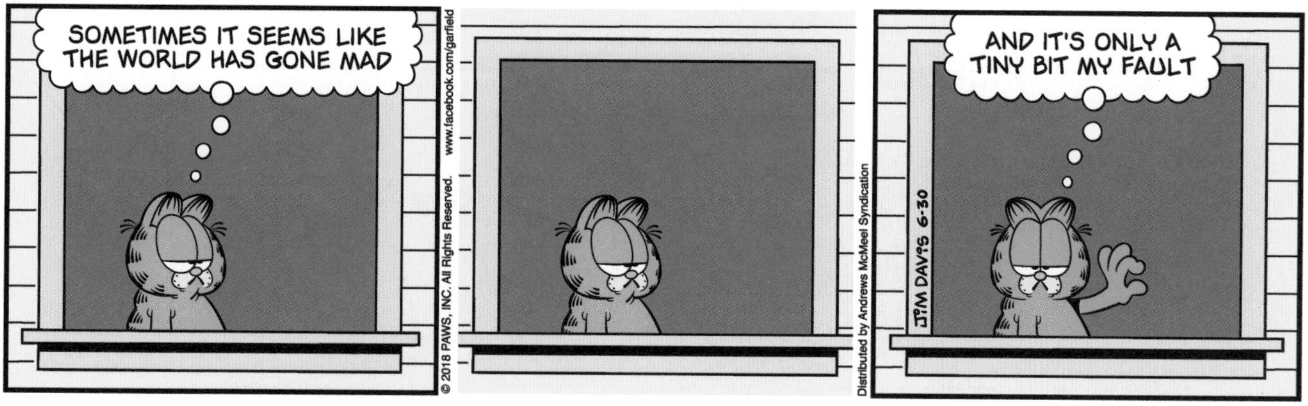
SOMETIMES IT SEEMS LIKE THE WORLD HAS GONE MAD
AND IT'S ONLY A TINY BIT MY FAULT
JIM DAVIS 6-30

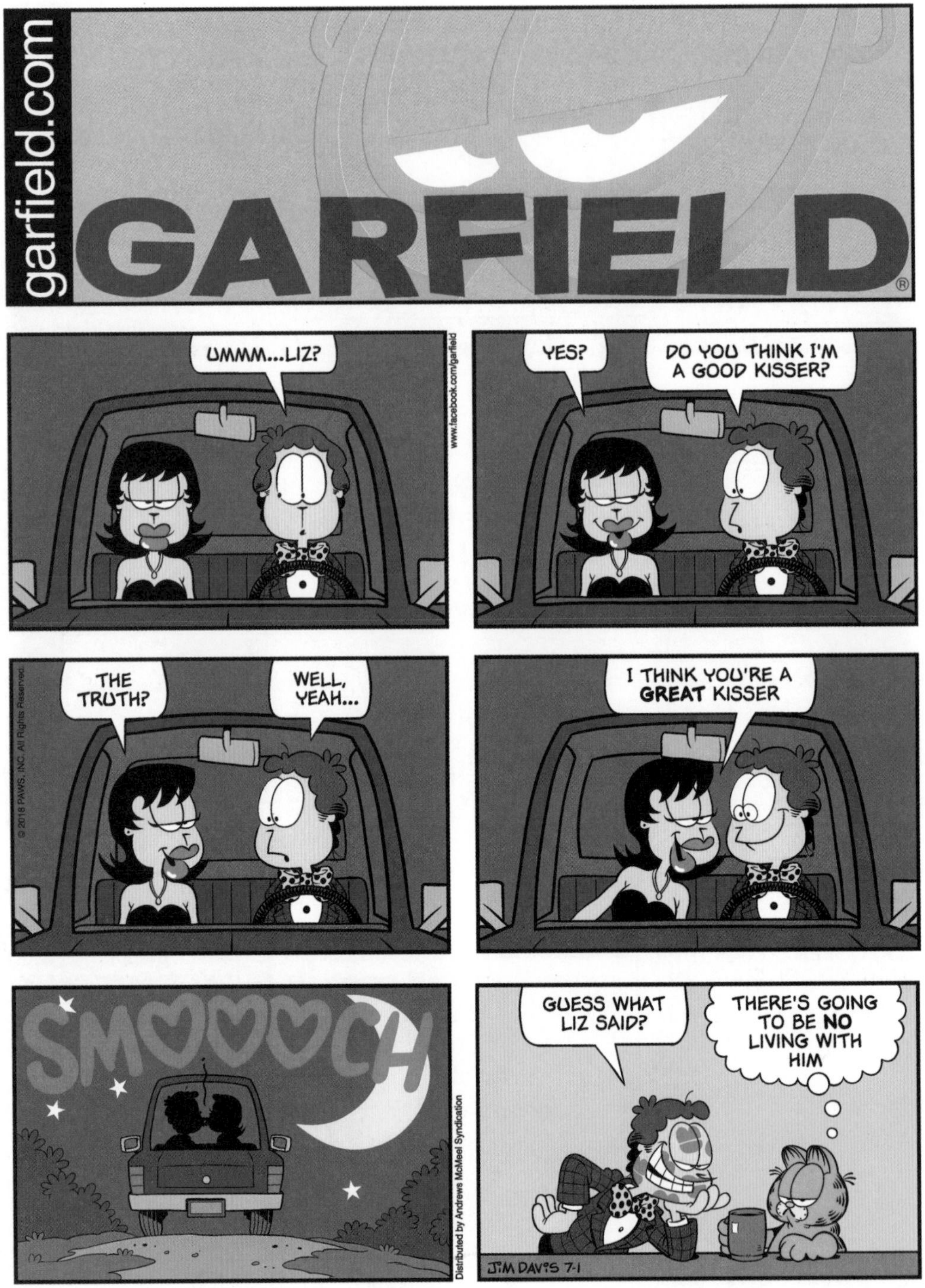

garfield.com
GARFIELD
UMMM...LIZ?
www.facebook.com/garfield
YES?
DO YOU THINK I'M A GOOD KISSER?
© 2018 PAWS, INC. All Rights Reserved.
THE TRUTH?
WELL, YEAH...
I THINK YOU'RE A GREAT KISSER
SMOOOCH
Distributed by Andrews McMeel Syndication
GUESS WHAT LIZ SAID?
THERE'S GOING TO BE NO LIVING WITH HIM
JIM DAVIS 7-1

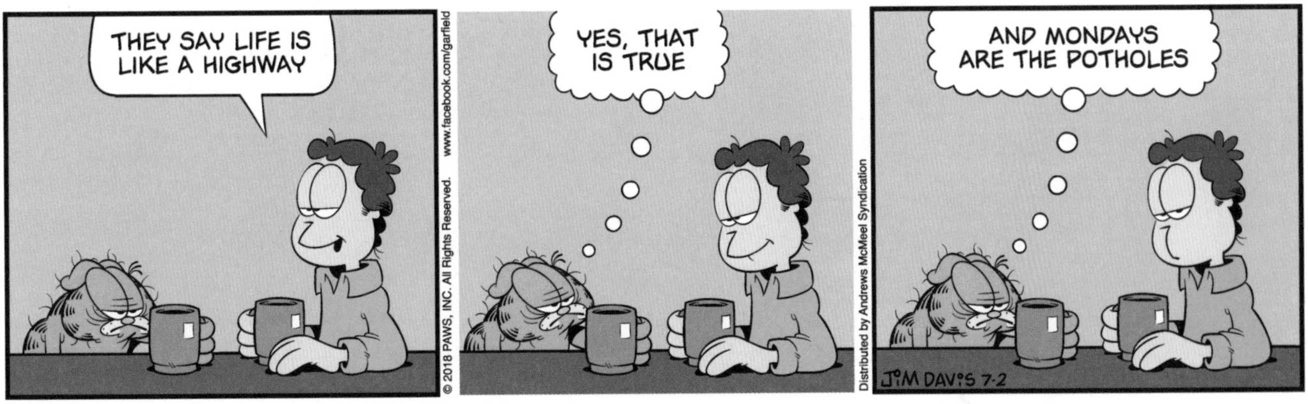
THEY SAY LIFE IS LIKE A HIGHWAY
YES, THAT IS TRUE
AND MONDAYS ARE THE POTHOLES
© 2018 PAWS, INC. All Rights Reserved. www.facebook.com/garfield
Distributed by Andrews McMeel Syndication
JIM DAVIS 7-2

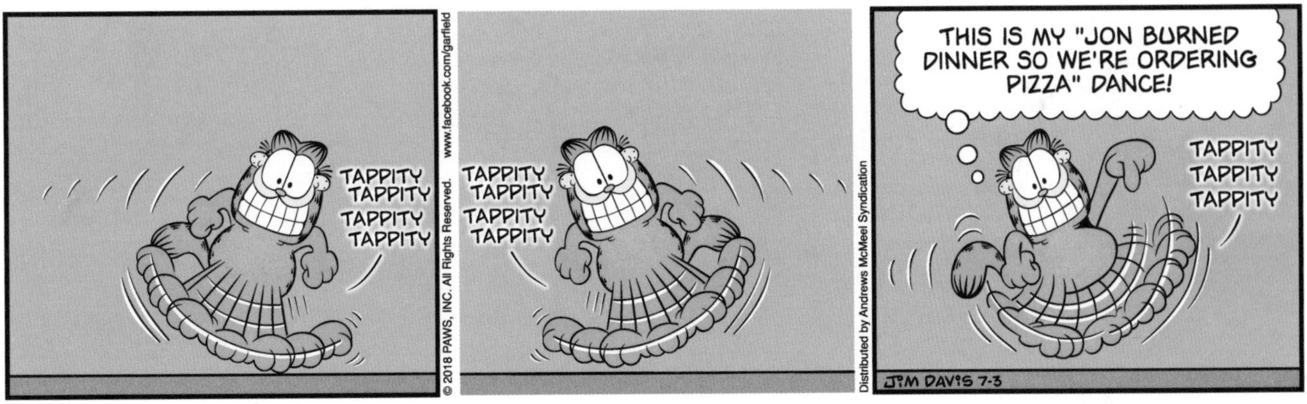
TAPPITY TAPPITY TAPPITY TAPPITY
TAPPITY TAPPITY TAPPITY TAPPITY
THIS IS MY "JON BURNED DINNER SO WE'RE ORDERING PIZZA" DANCE!
TAPPITY TAPPITY TAPPITY
© 2018 PAWS, INC. All Rights Reserved. www.facebook.com/garfield
Distributed by Andrews McMeel Syndication
JIM DAVIS 7-3

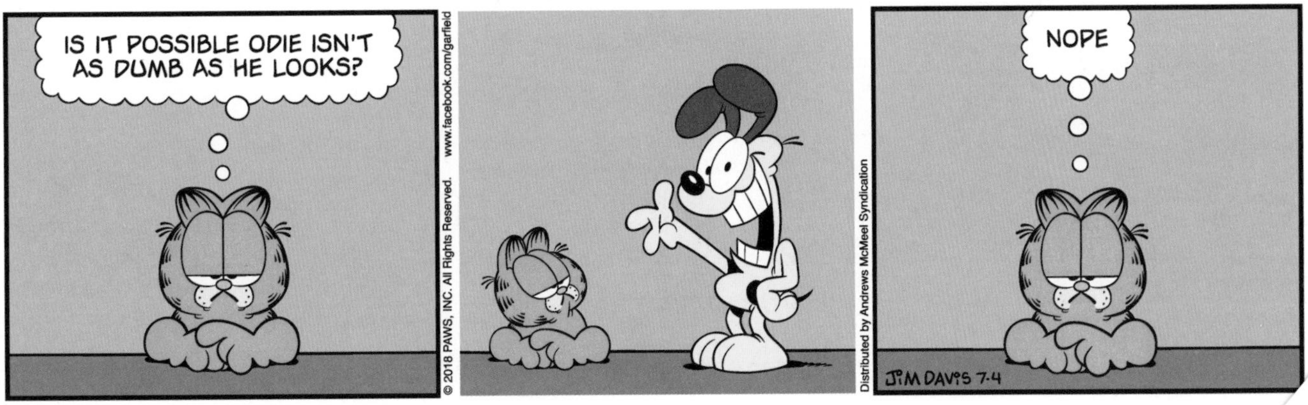
IS IT POSSIBLE ODIE ISN'T AS DUMB AS HE LOOKS?
NOPE
© 2018 PAWS, INC. All Rights Reserved. www.facebook.com/garfield
Distributed by Andrews McMeel Syndication
JIM DAVIS 7-4

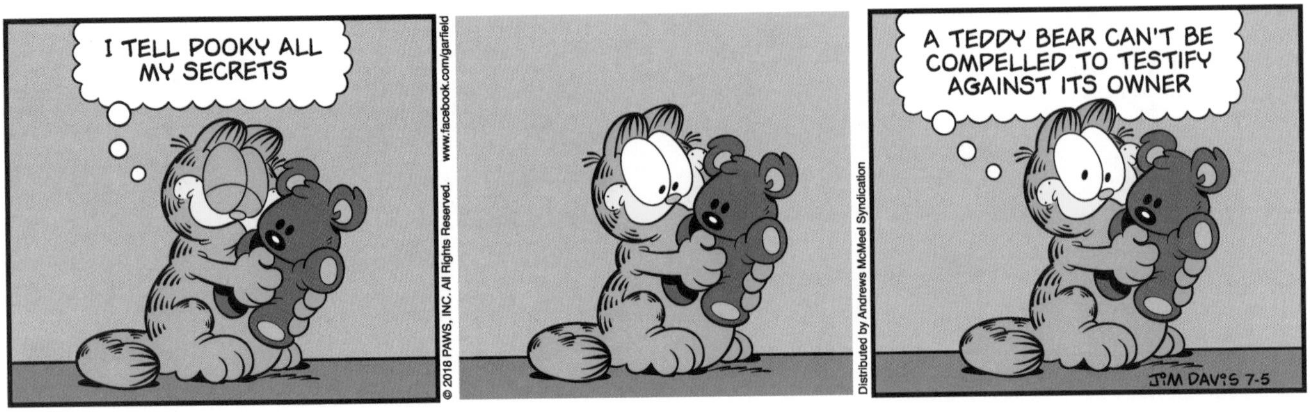
I TELL POOKY ALL MY SECRETS
A TEDDY BEAR CAN'T BE COMPELLED TO TESTIFY AGAINST ITS OWNER
© 2018 PAWS, INC. All Rights Reserved. www.facebook.com/garfield
Distributed by Andrews McMeel Syndication
JIM DAVIS 7-5

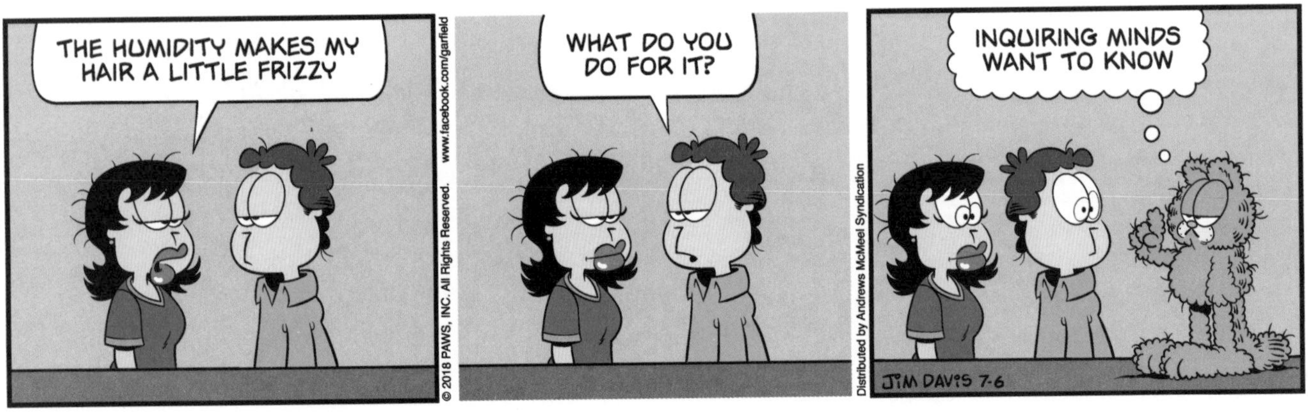
THE HUMIDITY MAKES MY HAIR A LITTLE FRIZZY
WHAT DO YOU DO FOR IT?
INQUIRING MINDS WANT TO KNOW
© 2018 PAWS, INC. All Rights Reserved. www.facebook.com/garfield
Distributed by Andrews McMeel Syndication
JIM DAVIS 7-6

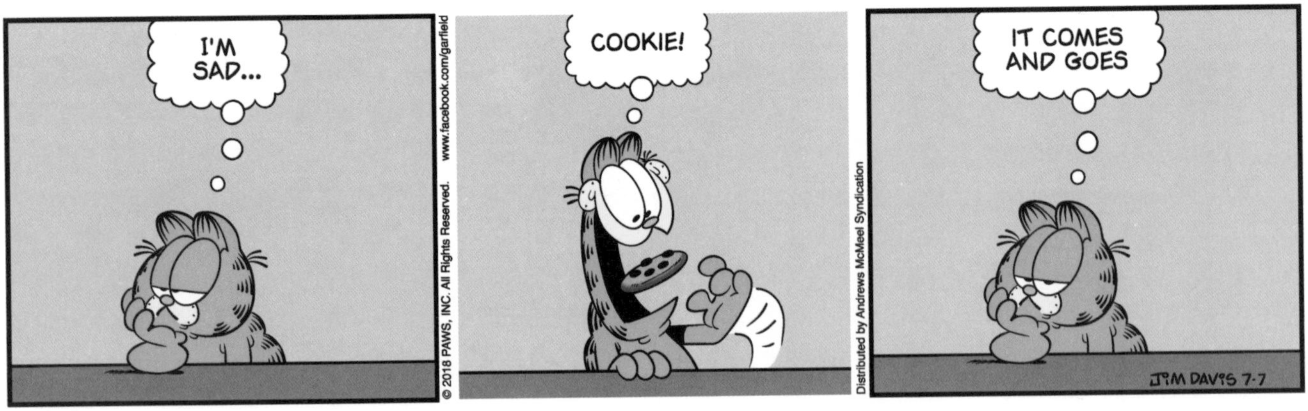
I'M SAD...
COOKIE!
IT COMES AND GOES
© 2018 PAWS, INC. All Rights Reserved. www.facebook.com/garfield
Distributed by Andrews McMeel Syndication
JIM DAVIS 7-7

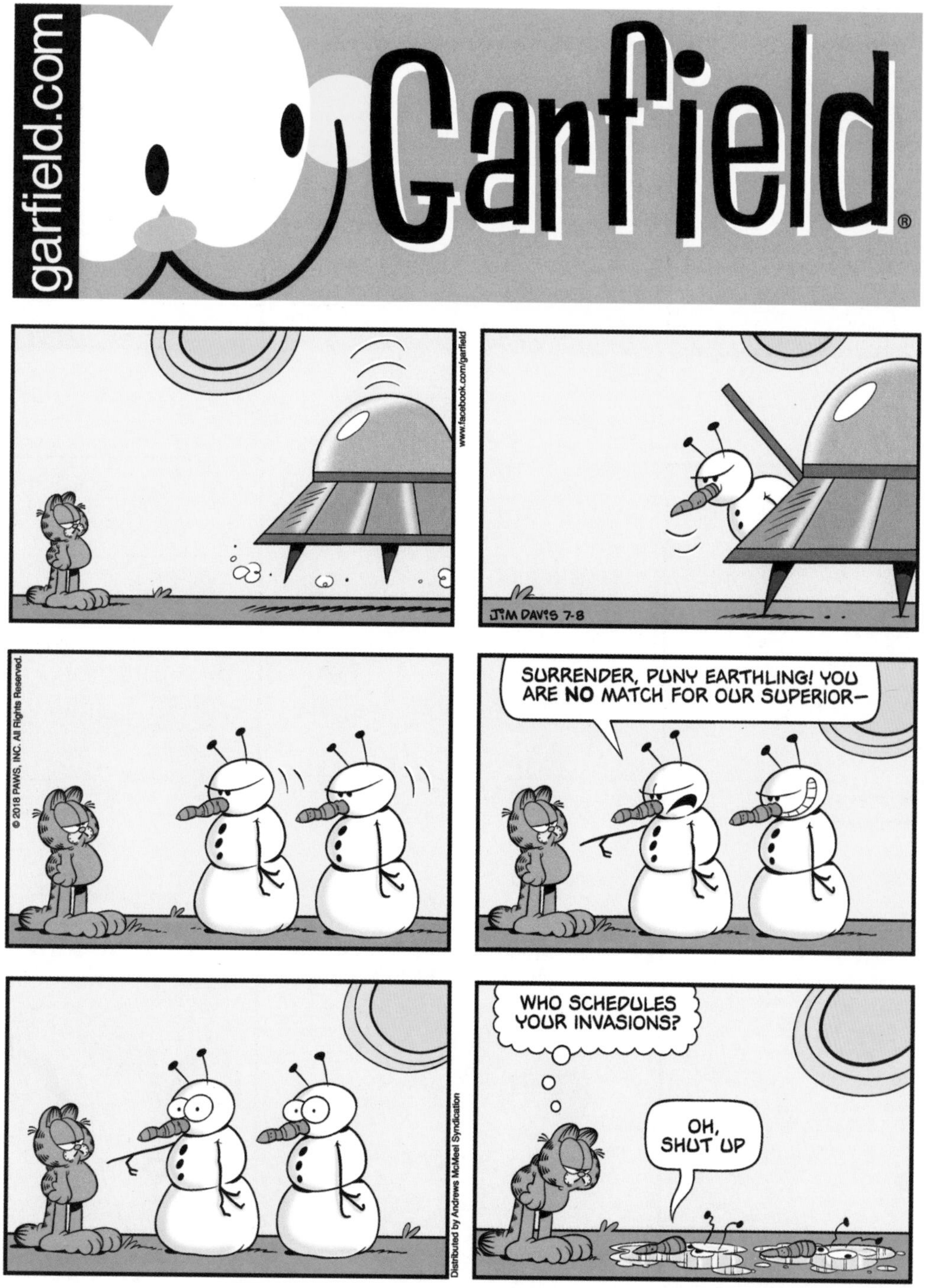
garfield.com
Garfield®
www.facebook.com/garfield
JIM DAVIS 7-8
© 2018 PAWS, INC. All Rights Reserved.
SURRENDER, PUNY EARTHLING! YOU ARE **NO** MATCH FOR OUR SUPERIOR—
Distributed by Andrews McMeel Syndication
WHO SCHEDULES YOUR INVASIONS?
OH, SHUT UP

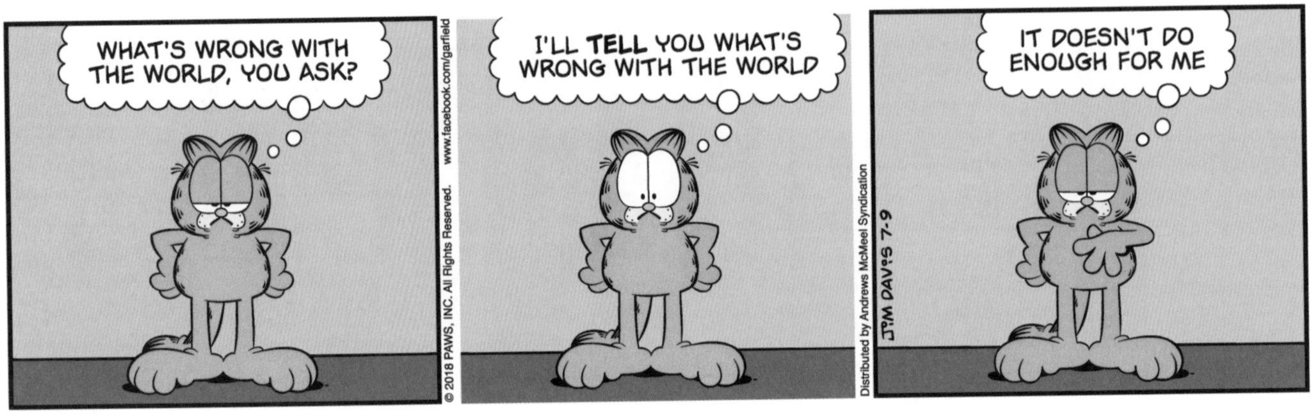
WHAT'S WRONG WITH THE WORLD, YOU ASK?
I'LL **TELL** YOU WHAT'S WRONG WITH THE WORLD
IT DOESN'T DO ENOUGH FOR ME
JIM DAVIS 7-9
© 2018 PAWS, INC. All Rights Reserved. www.facebook.com/garfield
Distributed by Andrews McMeel Syndication

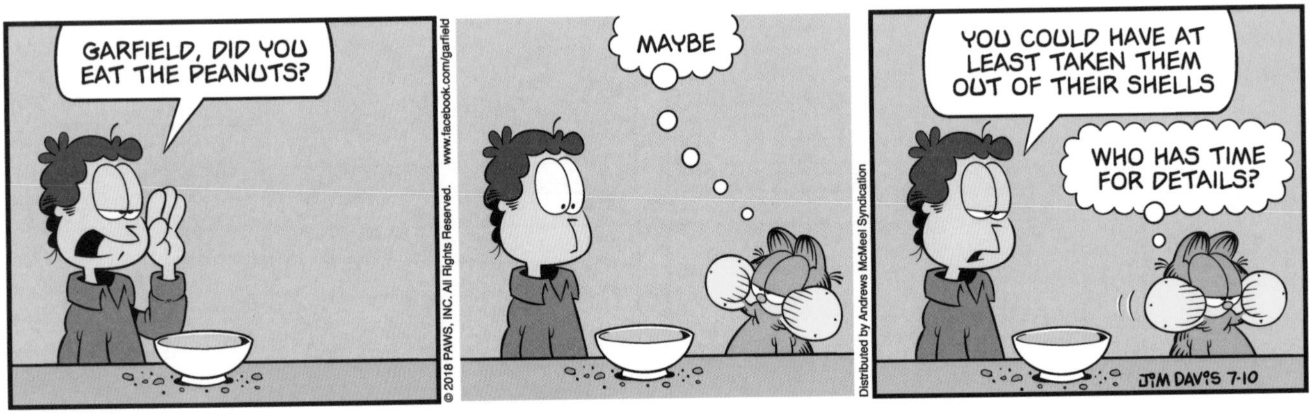
GARFIELD, DID YOU EAT THE PEANUTS?
MAYBE
YOU COULD HAVE AT LEAST TAKEN THEM OUT OF THEIR SHELLS
WHO HAS TIME FOR DETAILS?
JIM DAVIS 7-10
© 2018 PAWS, INC. All Rights Reserved. www.facebook.com/garfield
Distributed by Andrews McMeel Syndication

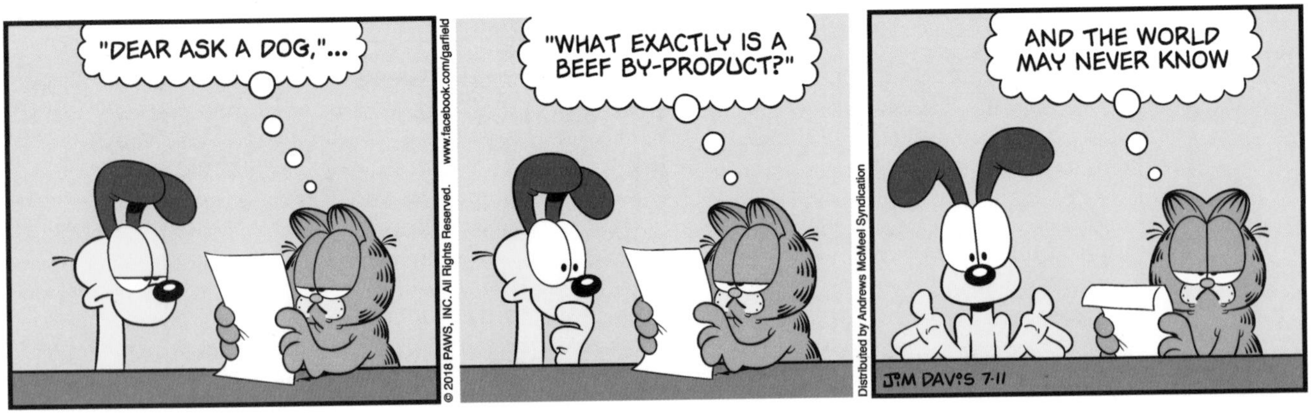
"DEAR ASK A DOG,"...
"WHAT EXACTLY IS A BEEF BY-PRODUCT?"
AND THE WORLD MAY NEVER KNOW
JIM DAVIS 7-11
© 2018 PAWS, INC. All Rights Reserved. www.facebook.com/garfield
Distributed by Andrews McMeel Syndication

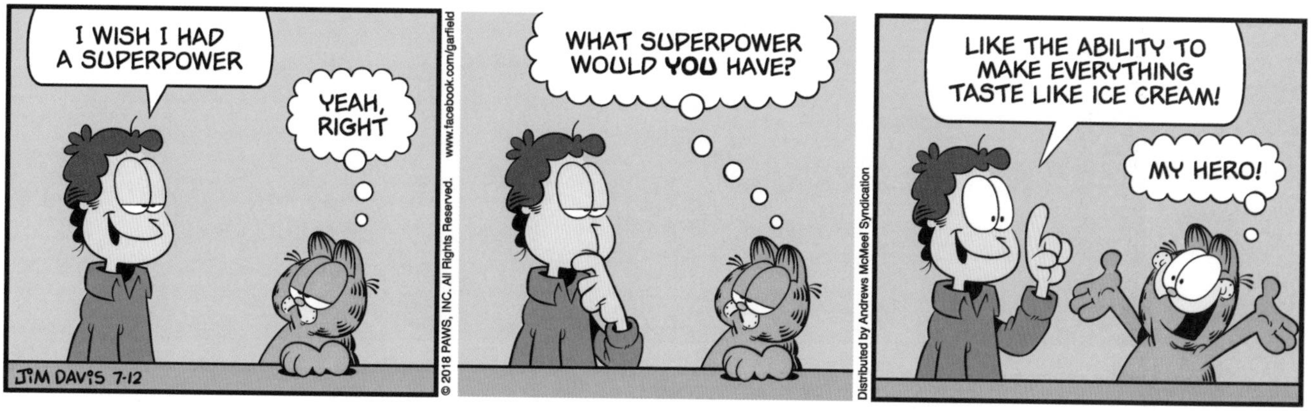
I WISH I HAD A SUPERPOWER
YEAH, RIGHT
WHAT SUPERPOWER WOULD **YOU** HAVE?
LIKE THE ABILITY TO MAKE EVERYTHING TASTE LIKE ICE CREAM!
MY HERO!
JIM DAVIS 7-12

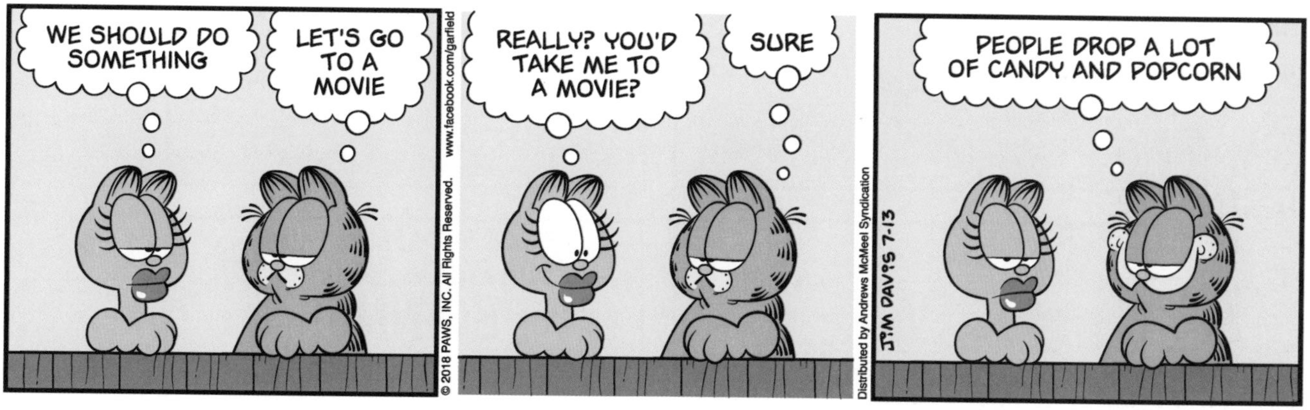
WE SHOULD DO SOMETHING
LET'S GO TO A MOVIE
REALLY? YOU'D TAKE ME TO A MOVIE?
SURE
PEOPLE DROP A LOT OF CANDY AND POPCORN
JIM DAVIS 7-13

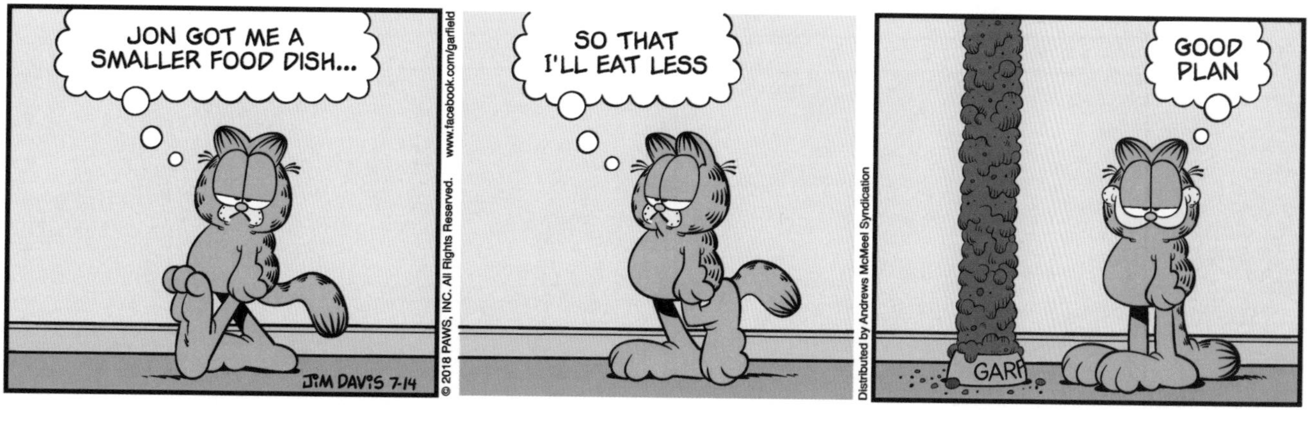
JON GOT ME A SMALLER FOOD DISH...
SO THAT I'LL EAT LESS
GOOD PLAN
GARF
JIM DAVIS 7-14

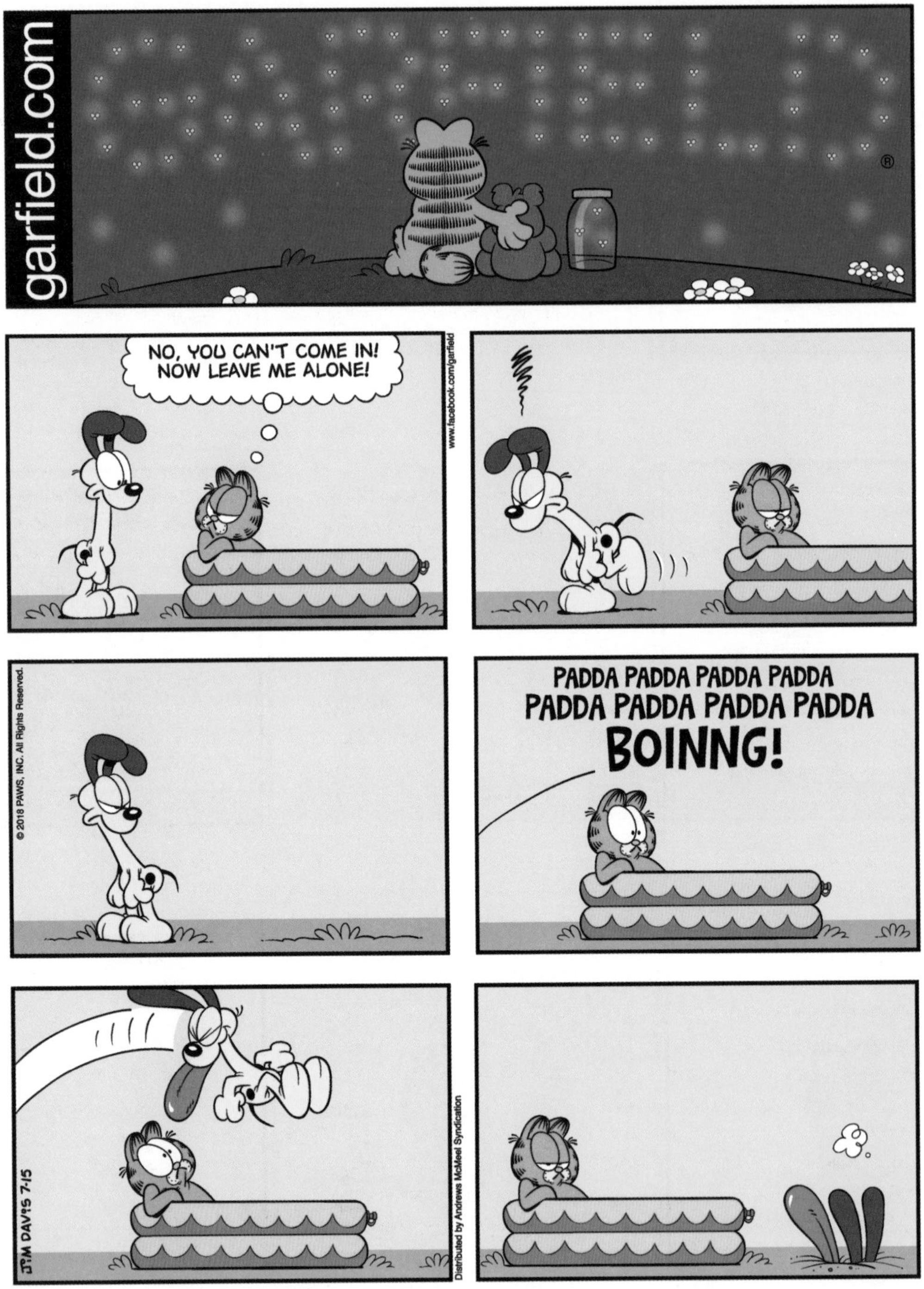
garfield.com
NO, YOU CAN'T COME IN! NOW LEAVE ME ALONE!
www.facebook.com/garfield
© 2018 PAWS, INC. All Rights Reserved.
PADDA PADDA PADDA PADDA
PADDA PADDA PADDA PADDA
BOINNG!
JIM DAVIS 7-15
Distributed by Andrews McMeel Syndication

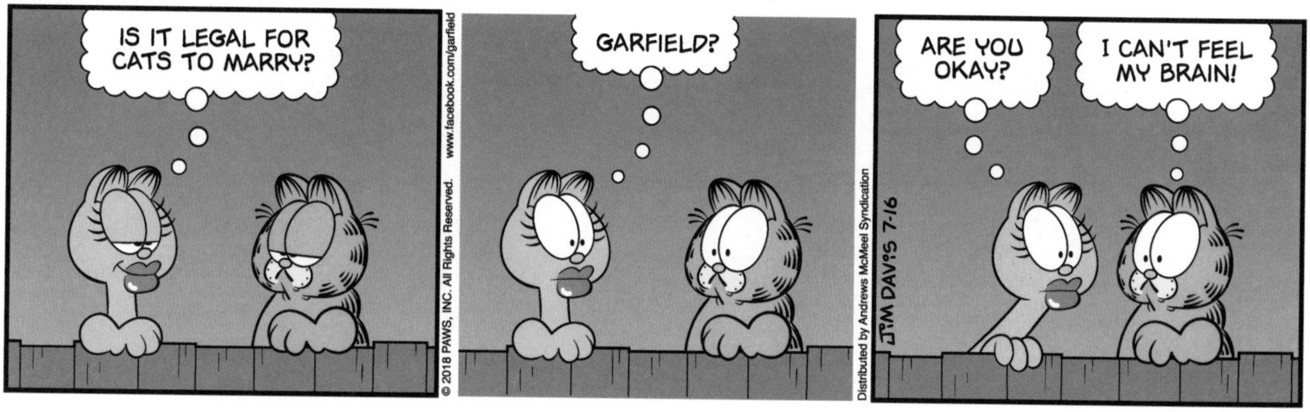
IS IT LEGAL FOR CATS TO MARRY?
GARFIELD?
ARE YOU OKAY?
I CAN'T FEEL MY BRAIN!
JIM DAVIS 7-16
© 2018 PAWS, INC. All Rights Reserved. www.facebook.com/garfield
Distributed by Andrews McMeel Syndication

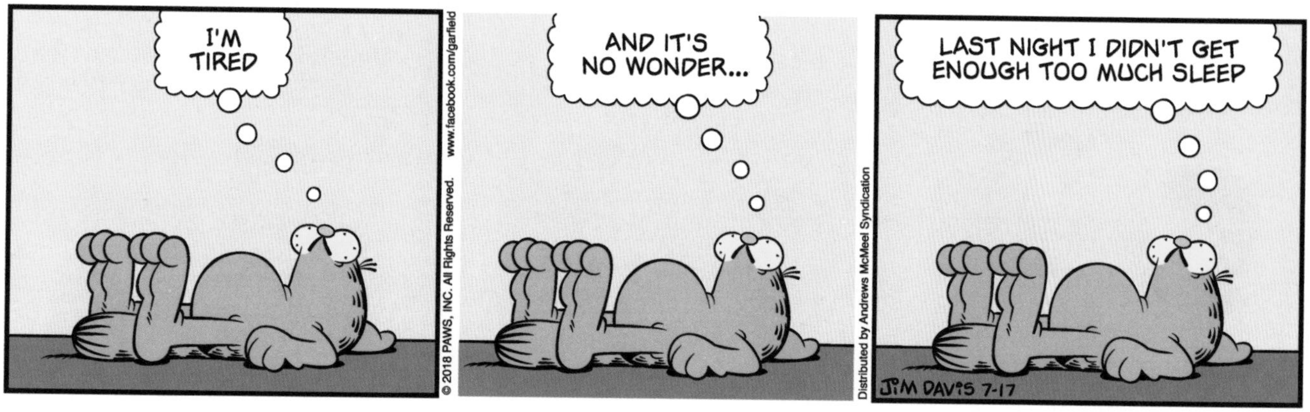
I'M TIRED
AND IT'S NO WONDER...
LAST NIGHT I DIDN'T GET ENOUGH TOO MUCH SLEEP
JIM DAVIS 7-17
© 2018 PAWS, INC. All Rights Reserved. www.facebook.com/garfield
Distributed by Andrews McMeel Syndication

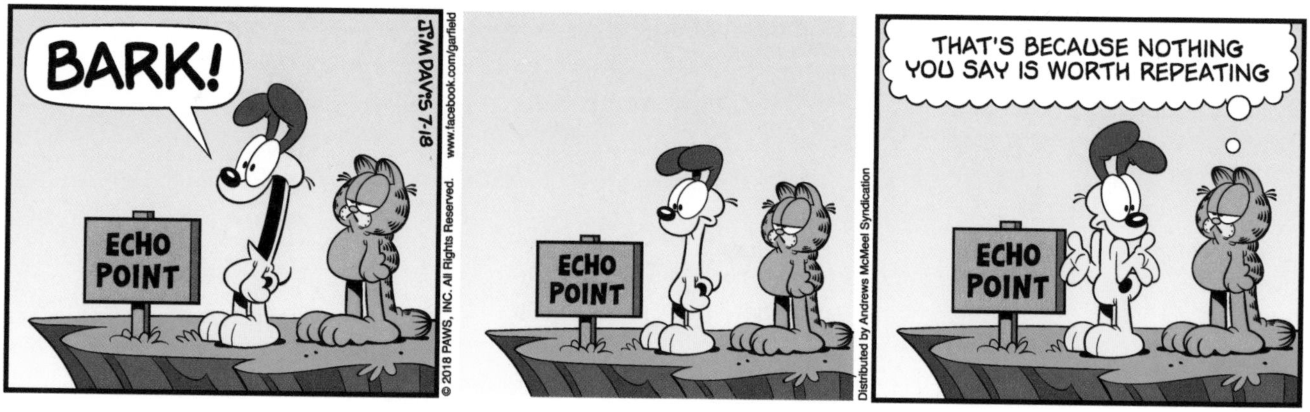
BARK!
ECHO POINT
JIM DAVIS 7-18
ECHO POINT
ECHO POINT
THAT'S BECAUSE NOTHING YOU SAY IS WORTH REPEATING
© 2018 PAWS, INC. All Rights Reserved. www.facebook.com/garfield
Distributed by Andrews McMeel Syndication

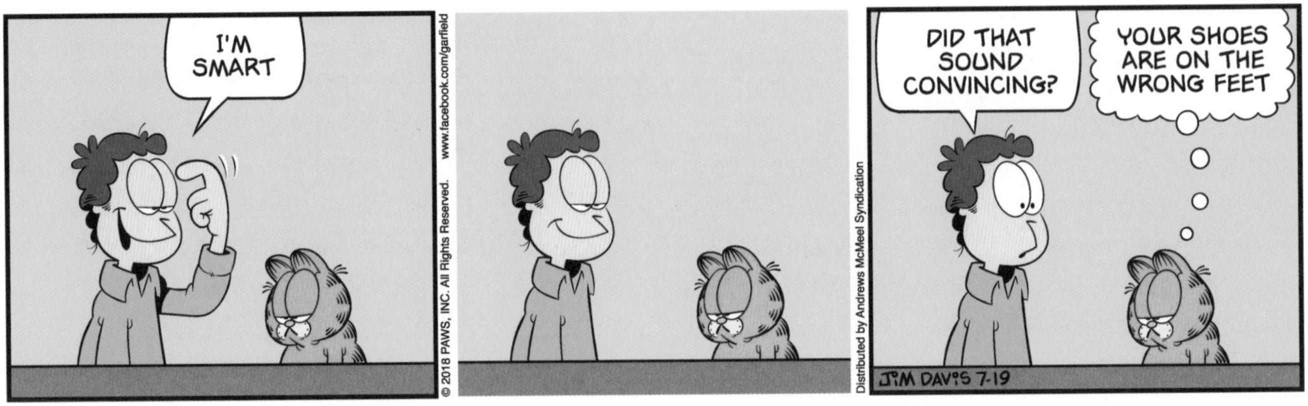
I'M SMART
DID THAT SOUND CONVINCING?
YOUR SHOES ARE ON THE WRONG FEET
JIM DAVIS 7-19
© 2018 PAWS, INC. All Rights Reserved. www.facebook.com/garfield
Distributed by Andrews McMeel Syndication

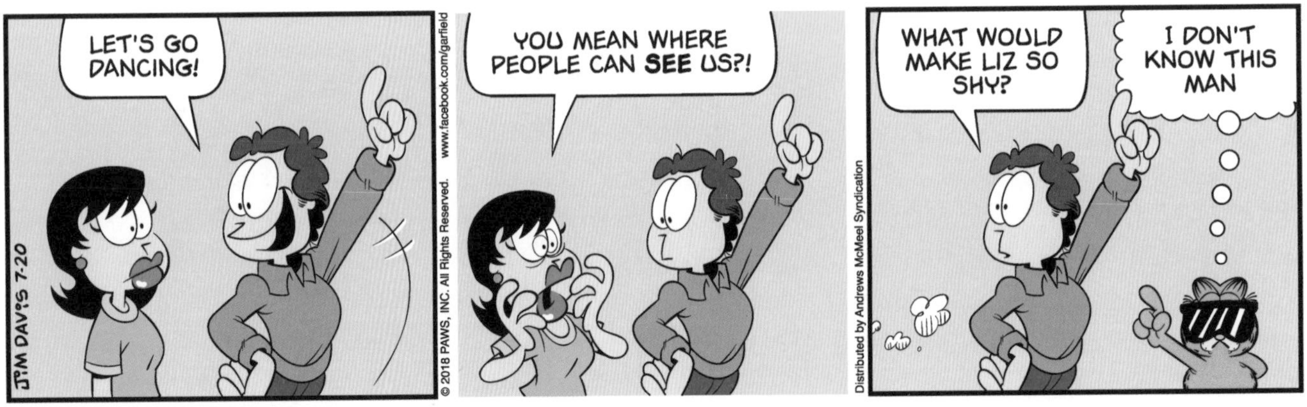
LET'S GO DANCING!
YOU MEAN WHERE PEOPLE CAN **SEE** US?!
WHAT WOULD MAKE LIZ SO SHY?
I DON'T KNOW THIS MAN
JIM DAVIS 7-20
© 2018 PAWS, INC. All Rights Reserved. www.facebook.com/garfield
Distributed by Andrews McMeel Syndication

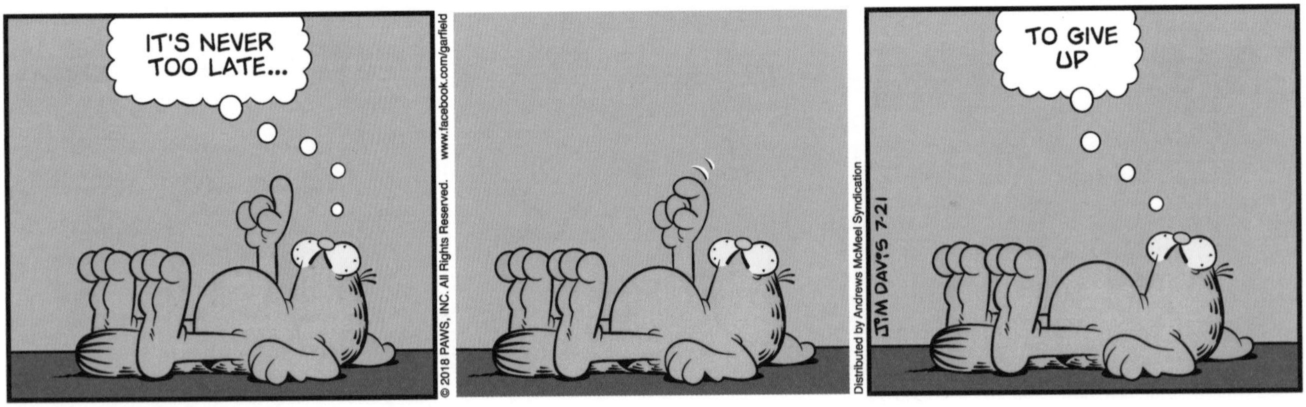
IT'S NEVER TOO LATE...
TO GIVE UP
JIM DAVIS 7-21
© 2018 PAWS, INC. All Rights Reserved. www.facebook.com/garfield
Distributed by Andrews McMeel Syndication

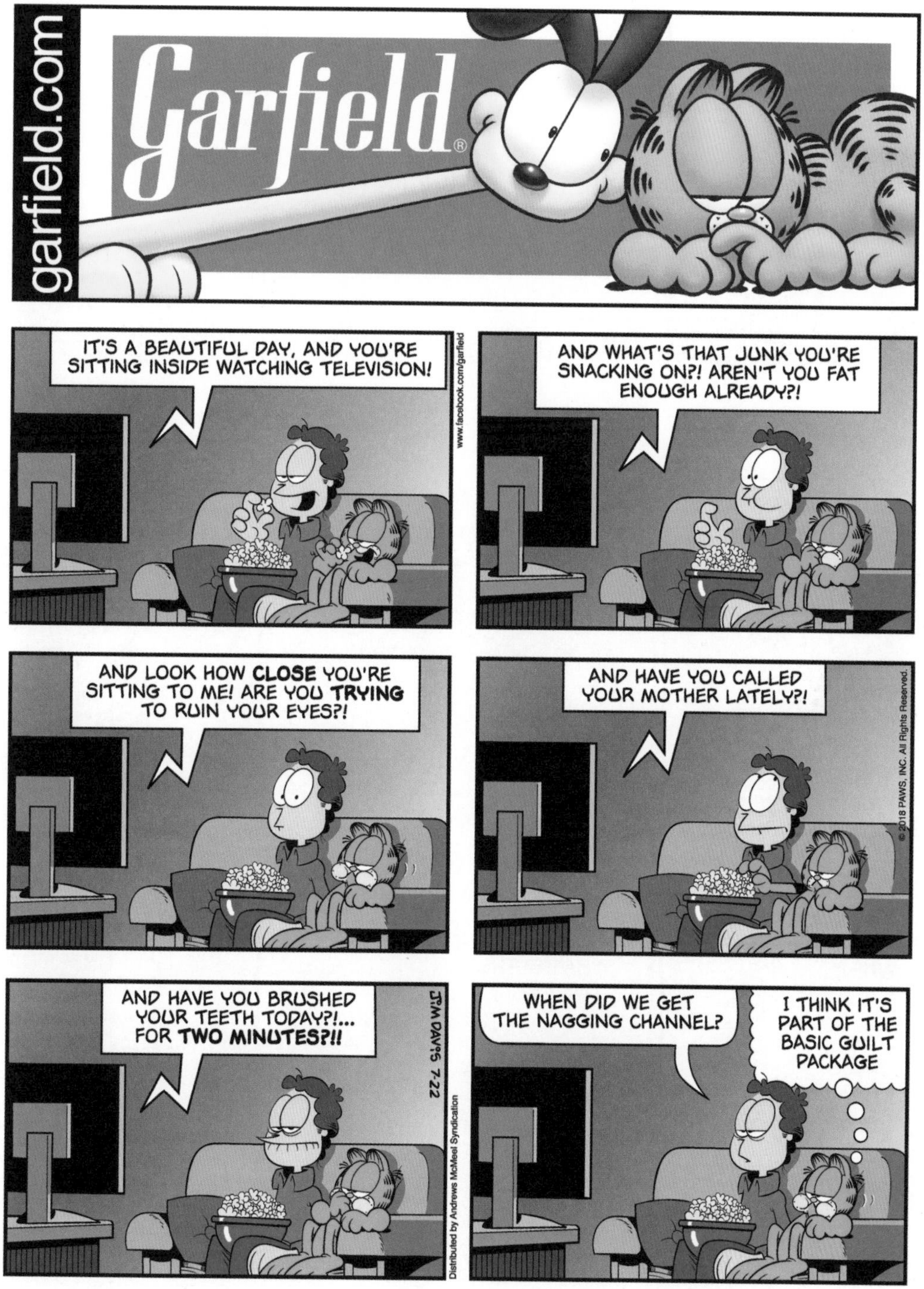
garfield.com
Garfield®
IT'S A BEAUTIFUL DAY, AND YOU'RE SITTING INSIDE WATCHING TELEVISION!
www.facebook.com/garfield
AND WHAT'S THAT JUNK YOU'RE SNACKING ON?! AREN'T YOU FAT ENOUGH ALREADY?!
AND LOOK HOW **CLOSE** YOU'RE SITTING TO ME! ARE YOU **TRYING** TO RUIN YOUR EYES?!
AND HAVE YOU CALLED YOUR MOTHER LATELY?!
© 2018 PAWS, INC. All Rights Reserved.
AND HAVE YOU BRUSHED YOUR TEETH TODAY?!... FOR **TWO MINUTES?!!**
JIM DAVIS 7-22
Distributed by Andrews McMeel Syndication
WHEN DID WE GET THE NAGGING CHANNEL?
I THINK IT'S PART OF THE BASIC GUILT PACKAGE

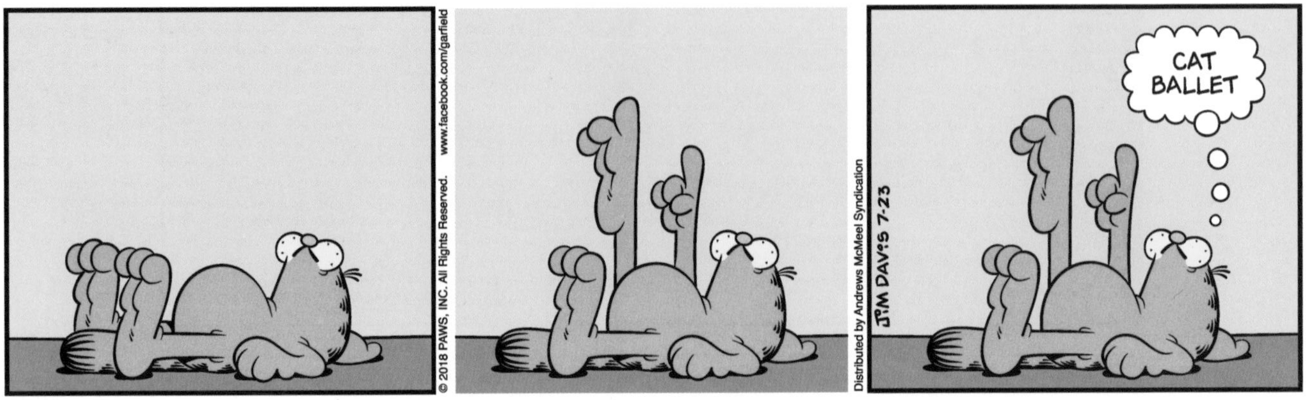
© 2018 PAWS, INC. All Rights Reserved. www.facebook.com/garfield
Distributed by Andrews McMeel Syndication
JIM DAVIS 7-23
CAT BALLET

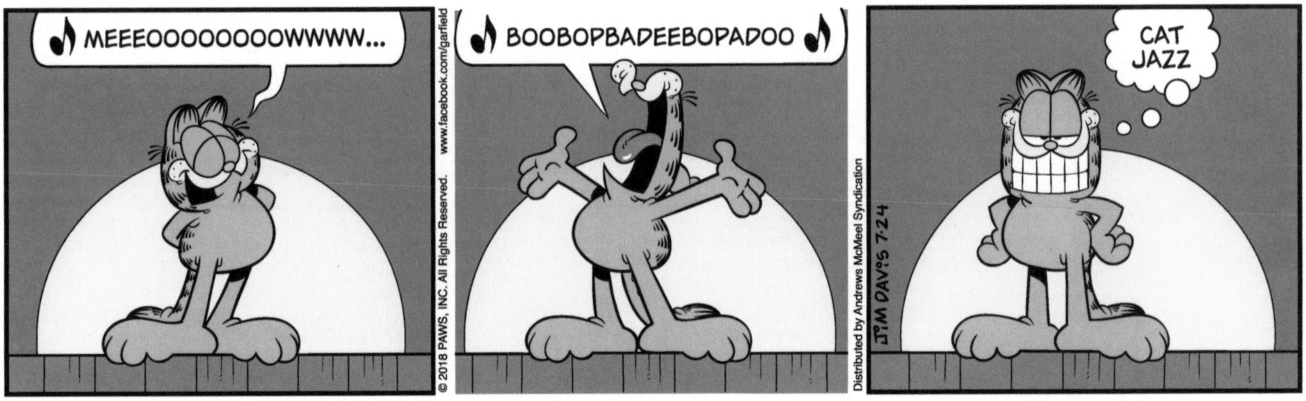
MEEEOOOOOOOOWWWW...
© 2018 PAWS, INC. All Rights Reserved. www.facebook.com/garfield
BOOBOPBADEEBOPADOO
Distributed by Andrews McMeel Syndication
JIM DAVIS 7-24
CAT JAZZ

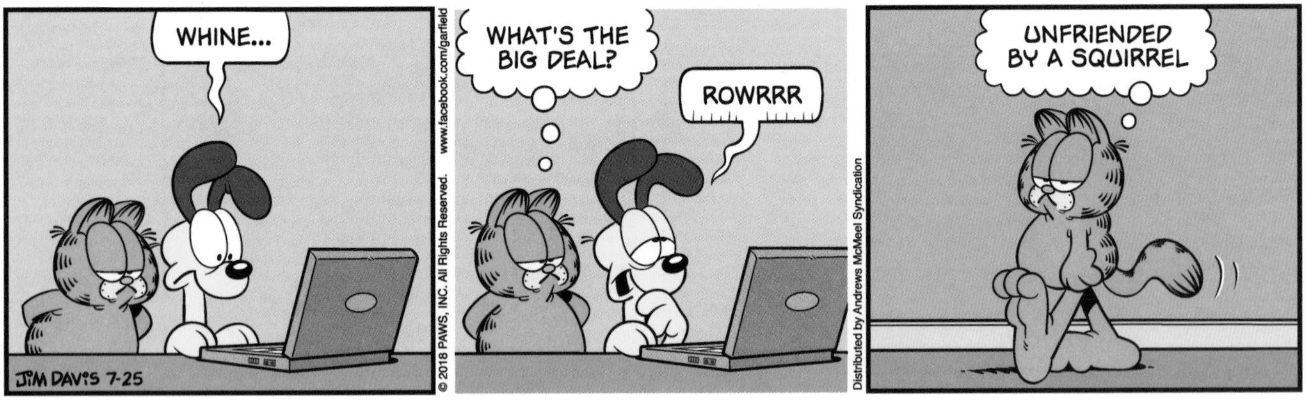
WHINE...
JIM DAVIS 7-25
© 2018 PAWS, INC. All Rights Reserved. www.facebook.com/garfield
WHAT'S THE BIG DEAL?
ROWRRR
Distributed by Andrews McMeel Syndication
UNFRIENDED BY A SQUIRREL

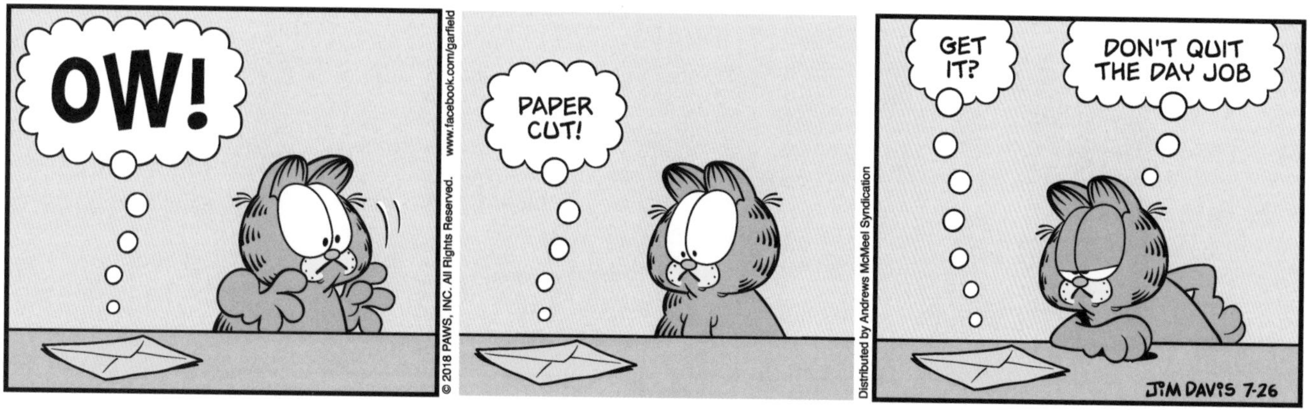
OW!
PAPER CUT!
GET IT?
DON'T QUIT THE DAY JOB
JIM DAVIS 7-26
© 2018 PAWS, INC. All Rights Reserved. www.facebook.com/garfield
Distributed by Andrews McMeel Syndication

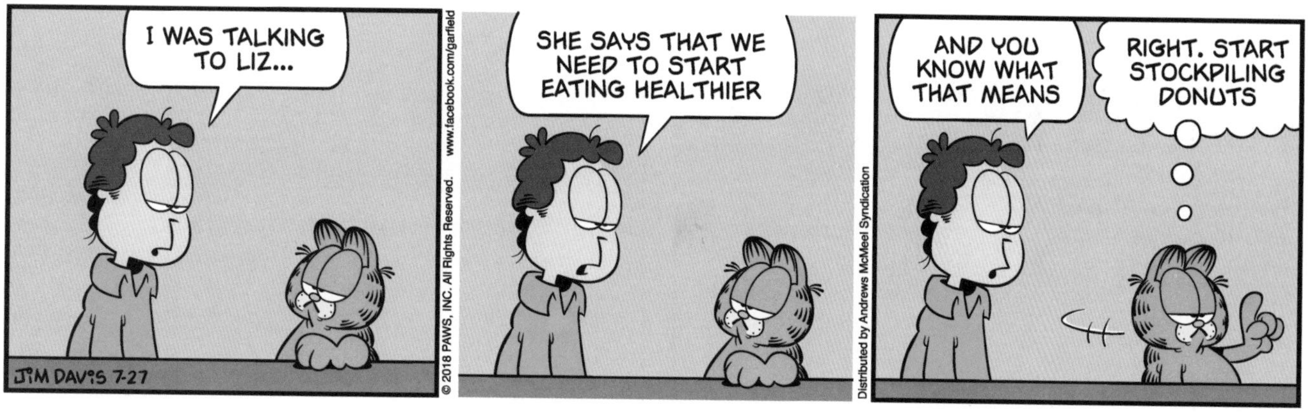
I WAS TALKING TO LIZ...
SHE SAYS THAT WE NEED TO START EATING HEALTHIER
AND YOU KNOW WHAT THAT MEANS
RIGHT. START STOCKPILING DONUTS
JIM DAVIS 7-27
© 2018 PAWS, INC. All Rights Reserved. www.facebook.com/garfield
Distributed by Andrews McMeel Syndication

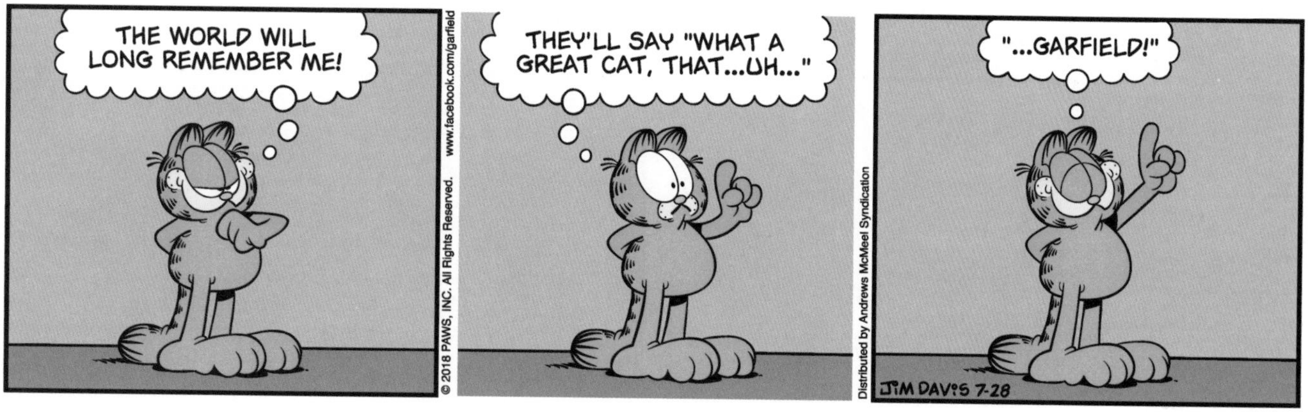
THE WORLD WILL LONG REMEMBER ME!
THEY'LL SAY "WHAT A GREAT CAT, THAT...UH..."
"...GARFIELD!"
JIM DAVIS 7-28
© 2018 PAWS, INC. All Rights Reserved. www.facebook.com/garfield
Distributed by Andrews McMeel Syndication

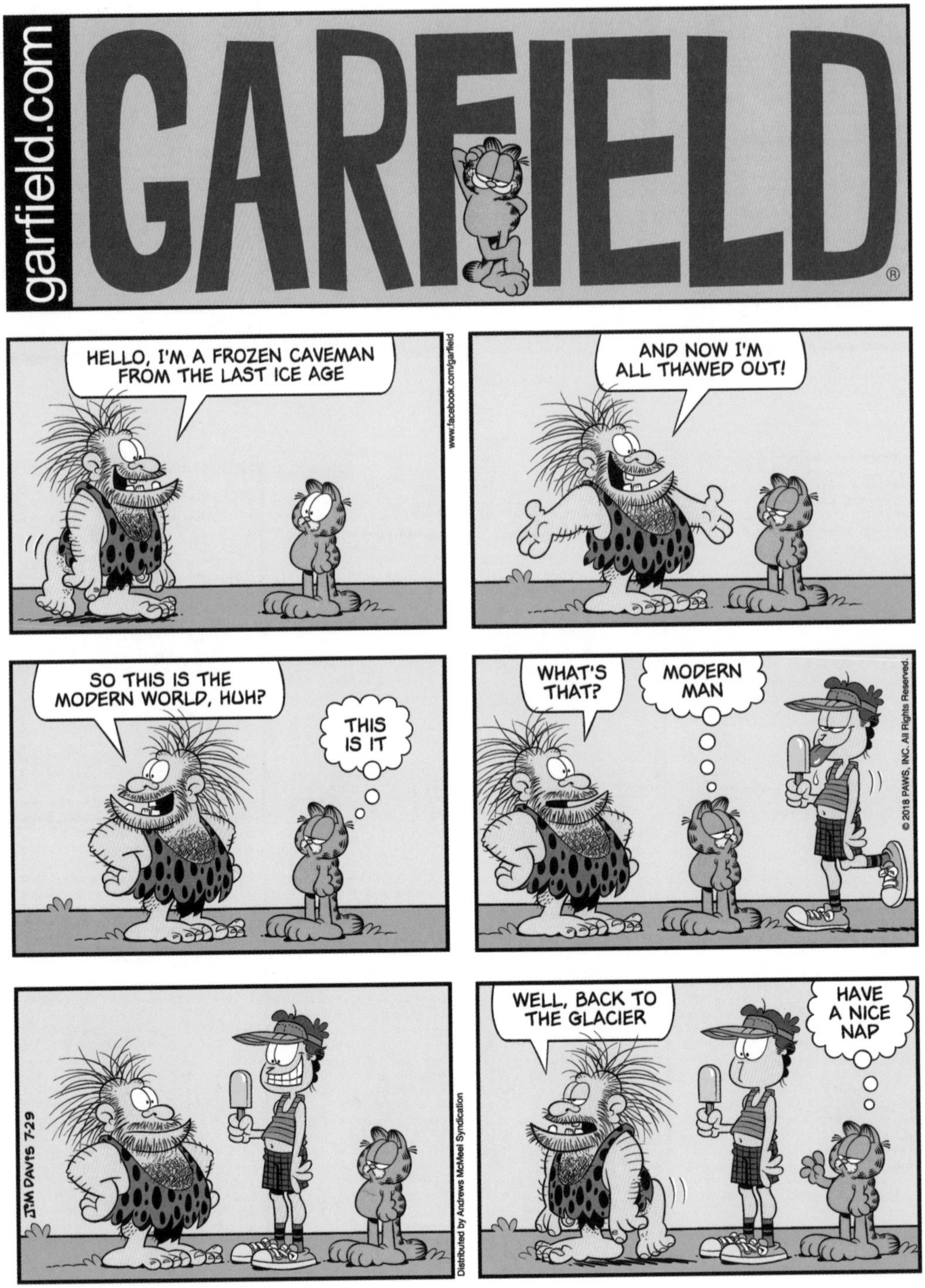
garfield.com
GARFIELD
HELLO, I'M A FROZEN CAVEMAN FROM THE LAST ICE AGE
www.facebook.com/garfield
AND NOW I'M ALL THAWED OUT!
SO THIS IS THE MODERN WORLD, HUH?
THIS IS IT
WHAT'S THAT?
MODERN MAN
© 2018 PAWS, INC. All Rights Reserved.
JIM DAVIS 7-29
Distributed by Andrews McMeel Syndication
WELL, BACK TO THE GLACIER
HAVE A NICE NAP

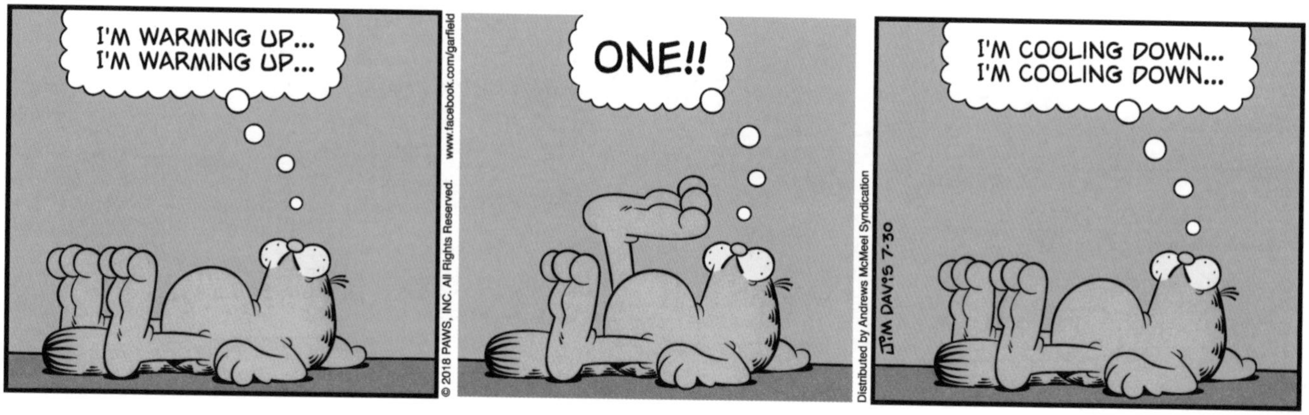
I'M WARMING UP...
I'M WARMING UP...
ONE!!
I'M COOLING DOWN...
I'M COOLING DOWN...
JIM DAVIS 7-30
© 2018 PAWS, INC. All Rights Reserved. www.facebook.com/garfield
Distributed by Andrews McMeel Syndication

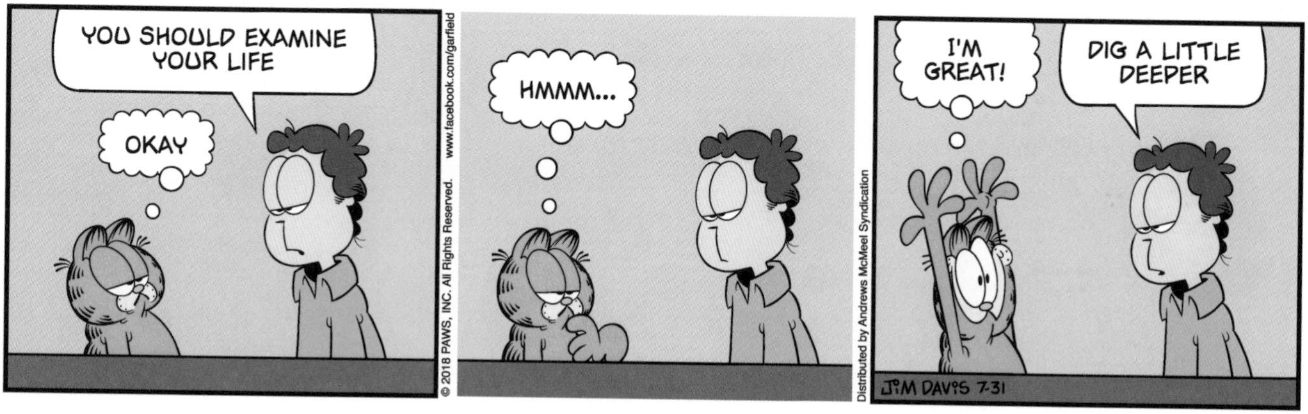
YOU SHOULD EXAMINE YOUR LIFE
OKAY
HMMM...
I'M GREAT!
DIG A LITTLE DEEPER
JIM DAVIS 7-31
© 2018 PAWS, INC. All Rights Reserved. www.facebook.com/garfield
Distributed by Andrews McMeel Syndication

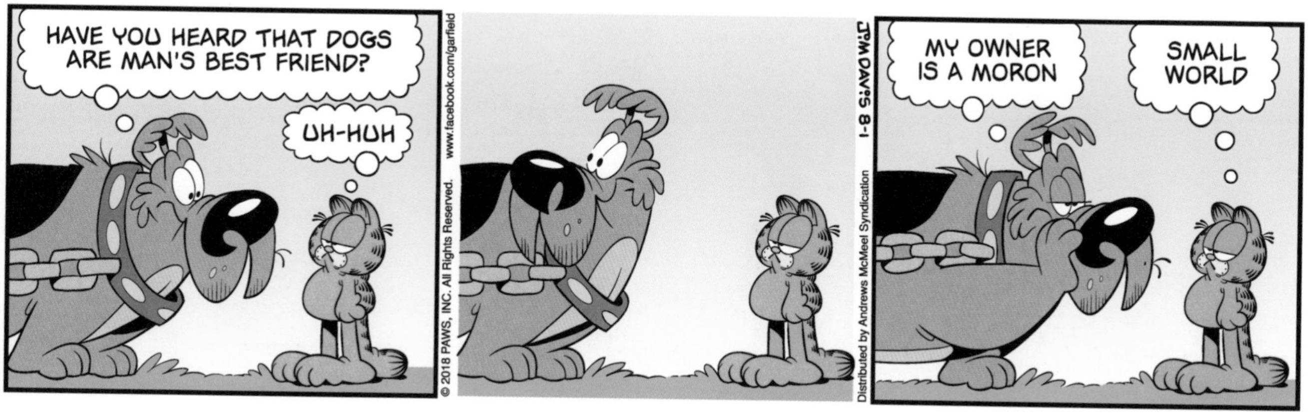
HAVE YOU HEARD THAT DOGS ARE MAN'S BEST FRIEND?
UH-HUH
MY OWNER IS A MORON
SMALL WORLD
JIM DAVIS 8-1
© 2018 PAWS, INC. All Rights Reserved. www.facebook.com/garfield
Distributed by Andrews McMeel Syndication

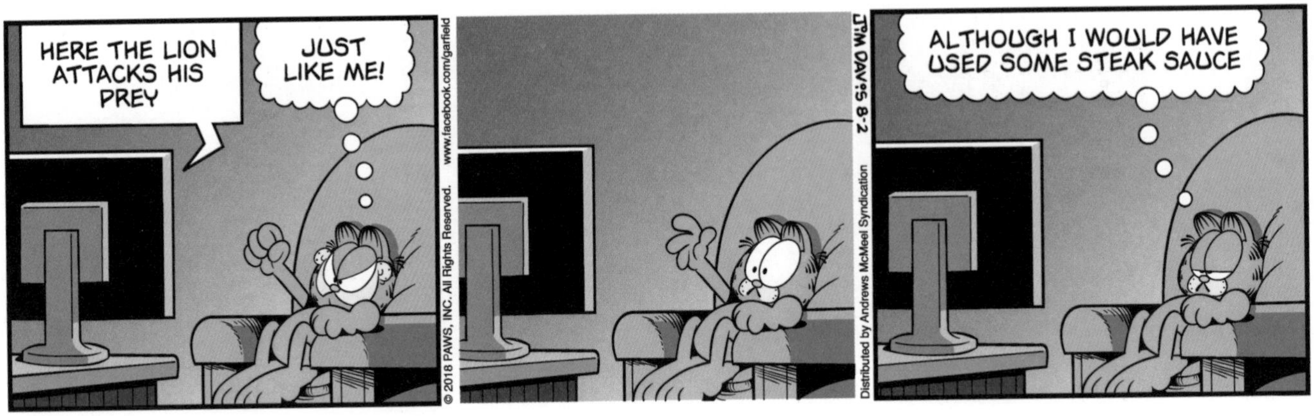
HERE THE LION ATTACKS HIS PREY
JUST LIKE ME!
© 2018 PAWS, INC. All Rights Reserved. www.facebook.com/garfield
JIM DAVIS 8-2
Distributed by Andrews McMeel Syndication
ALTHOUGH I WOULD HAVE USED SOME STEAK SAUCE

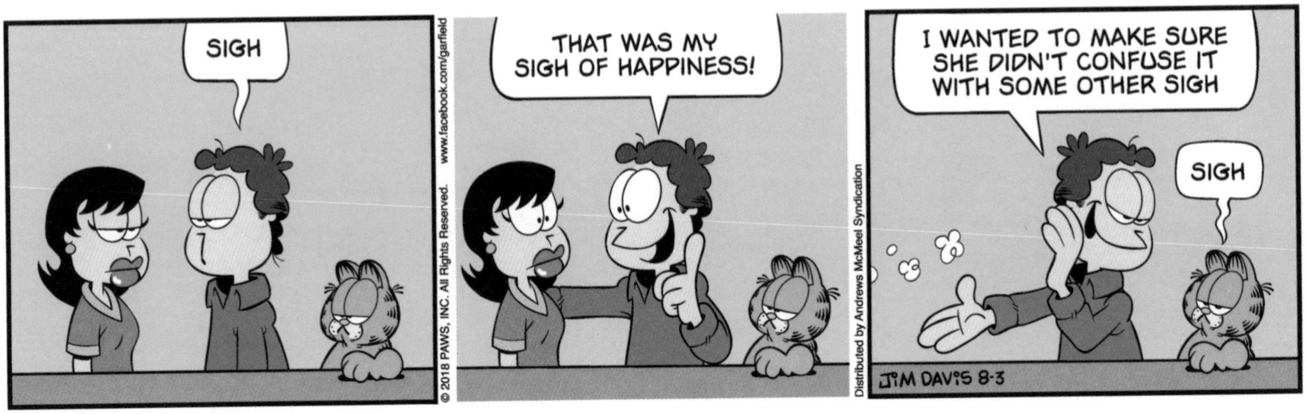
SIGH
© 2018 PAWS, INC. All Rights Reserved. www.facebook.com/garfield
THAT WAS MY SIGH OF HAPPINESS!
Distributed by Andrews McMeel Syndication
I WANTED TO MAKE SURE SHE DIDN'T CONFUSE IT WITH SOME OTHER SIGH
SIGH
JIM DAVIS 8-3

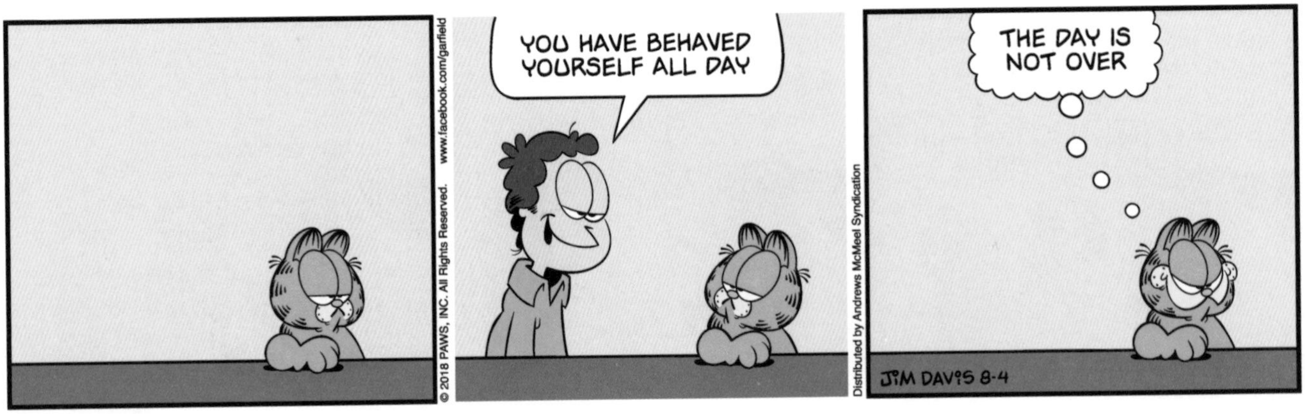
© 2018 PAWS, INC. All Rights Reserved. www.facebook.com/garfield
YOU HAVE BEHAVED YOURSELF ALL DAY
Distributed by Andrews McMeel Syndication
THE DAY IS NOT OVER
JIM DAVIS 8-4

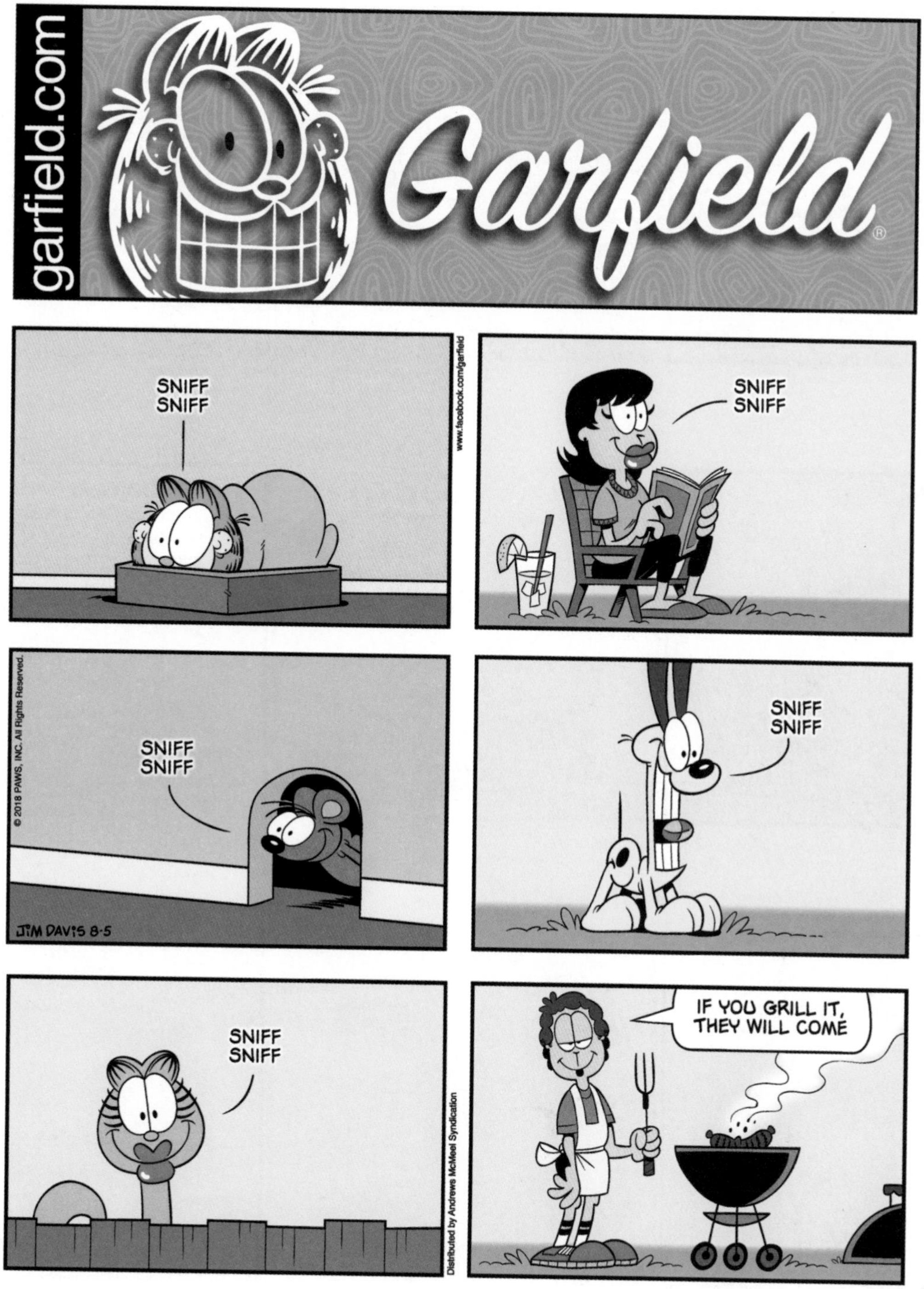
garfield.com
Garfield
SNIFF SNIFF
www.facebook.com/garfield
SNIFF SNIFF
© 2018 PAWS, INC. All Rights Reserved.
SNIFF SNIFF
JIM DAVIS 8-5
SNIFF SNIFF
SNIFF SNIFF
Distributed by Andrews McMeel Syndication
IF YOU GRILL IT, THEY WILL COME

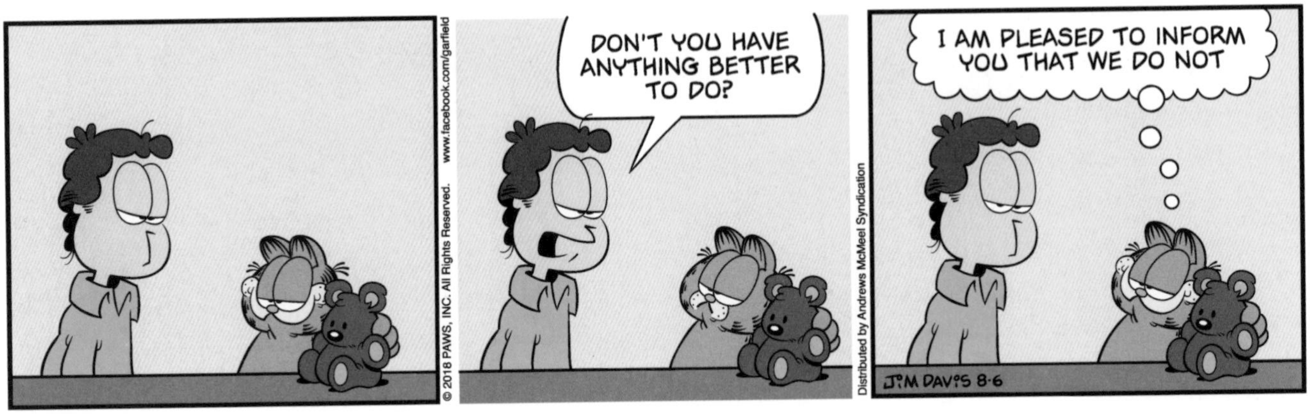
© 2018 PAWS, INC. All Rights Reserved. www.facebook.com/garfield
DON'T YOU HAVE ANYTHING BETTER TO DO?
Distributed by Andrews McMeel Syndication
I AM PLEASED TO INFORM YOU THAT WE DO NOT
JIM DAVIS 8-6

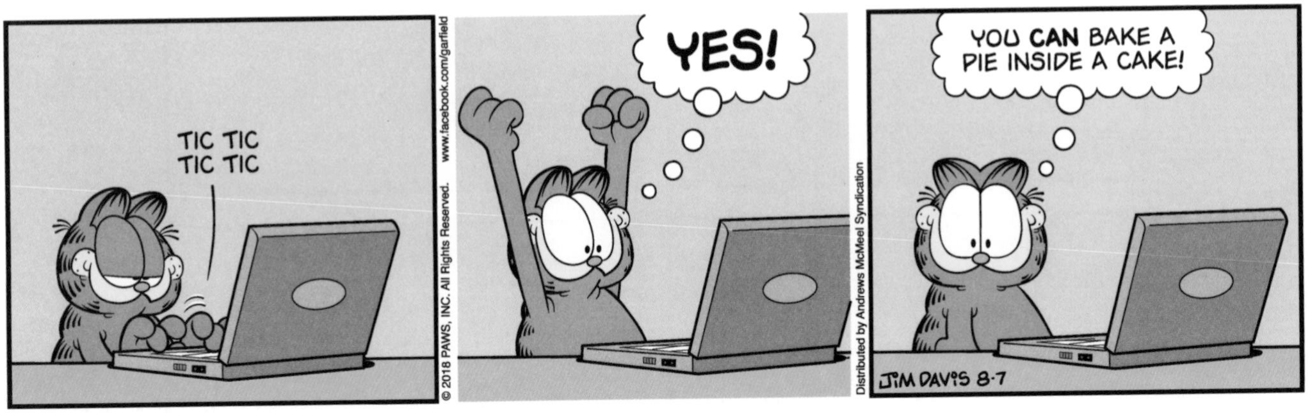
TIC TIC
TIC TIC
© 2018 PAWS, INC. All Rights Reserved. www.facebook.com/garfield
YES!
Distributed by Andrews McMeel Syndication
YOU **CAN** BAKE A PIE INSIDE A CAKE!
JIM DAVIS 8-7

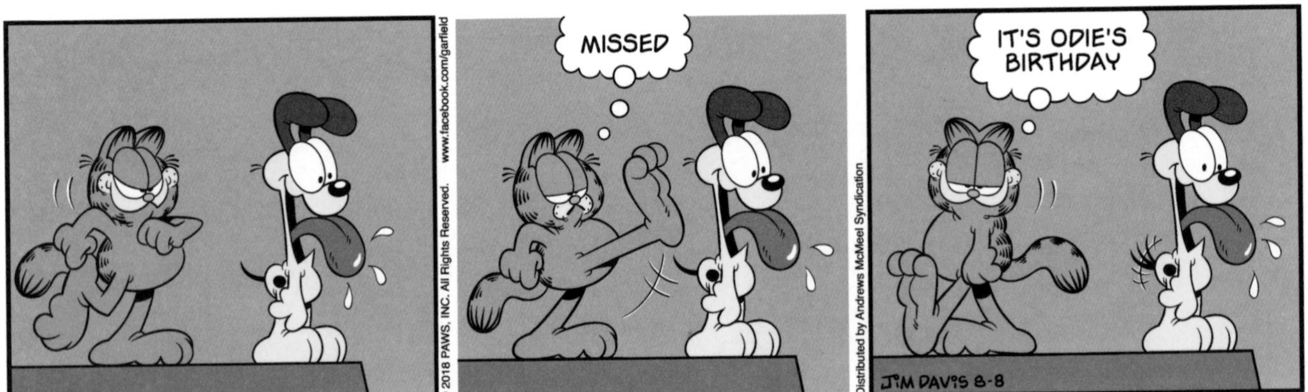
© 2018 PAWS, INC. All Rights Reserved. www.facebook.com/garfield
MISSED
Distributed by Andrews McMeel Syndication
IT'S ODIE'S BIRTHDAY
JIM DAVIS 8-8

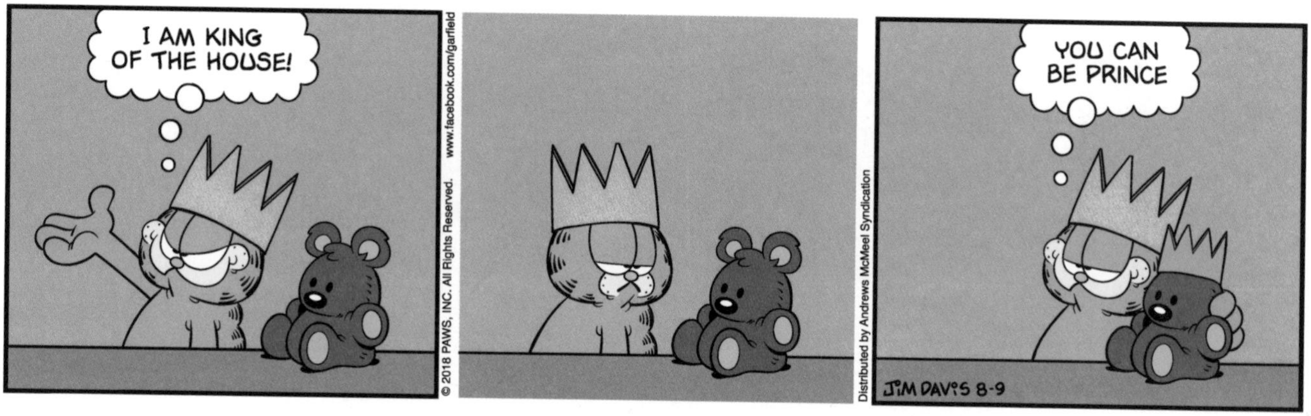
I AM KING OF THE HOUSE!
© 2018 PAWS, INC. All Rights Reserved. www.facebook.com/garfield
Distributed by Andrews McMeel Syndication
YOU CAN BE PRINCE
JIM DAVIS 8-9

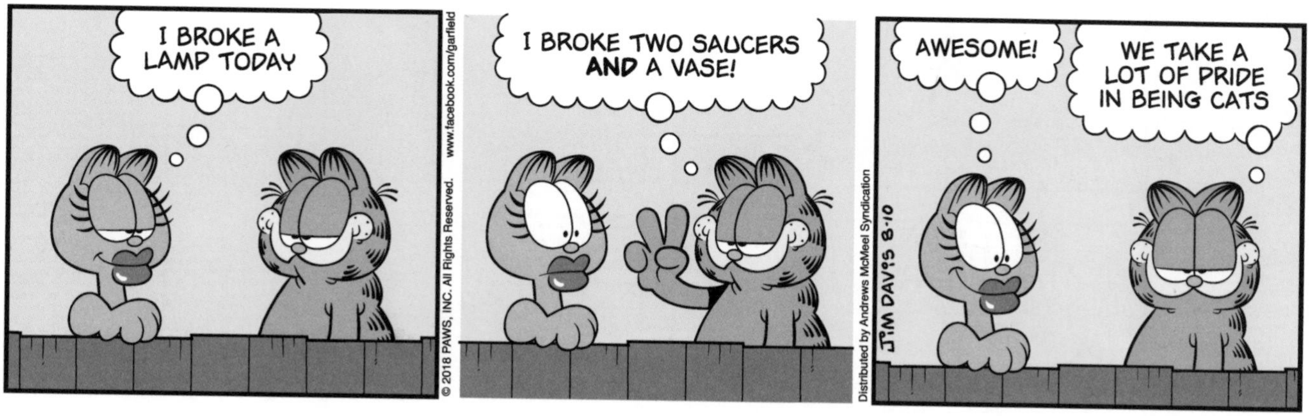
I BROKE A LAMP TODAY
© 2018 PAWS, INC. All Rights Reserved. www.facebook.com/garfield
I BROKE TWO SAUCERS **AND** A VASE!
Distributed by Andrews McMeel Syndication
JIM DAVIS 8-10
AWESOME!
WE TAKE A LOT OF PRIDE IN BEING CATS

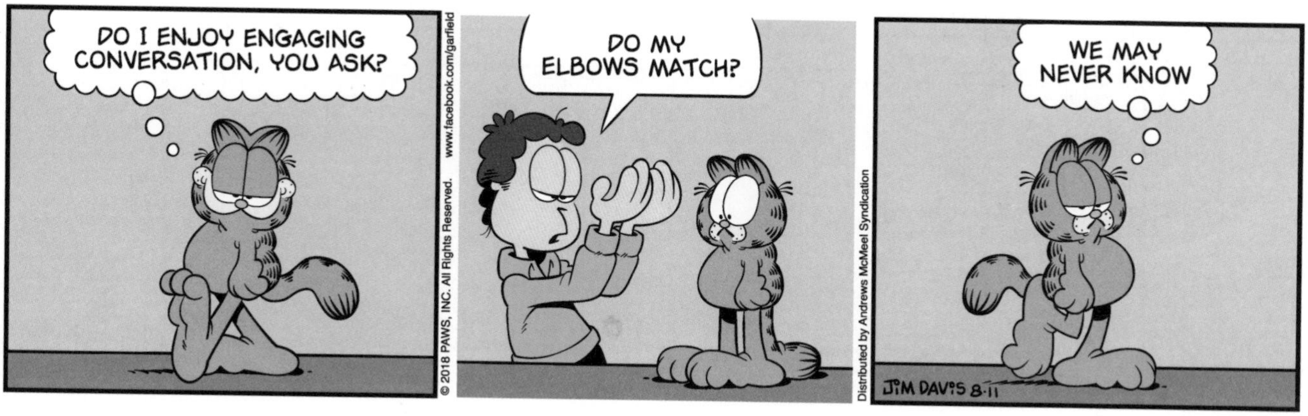
DO I ENJOY ENGAGING CONVERSATION, YOU ASK?
© 2018 PAWS, INC. All Rights Reserved. www.facebook.com/garfield
DO MY ELBOWS MATCH?
Distributed by Andrews McMeel Syndication
WE MAY NEVER KNOW
JIM DAVIS 8-11

garfield.com
Garfield®
GARFIELD! GARFIELD!
JIM DAVIS 8-12
www.facebook.com/garfield
GARFIELD! COME QUICK!
© 2018 PAWS, INC. All Rights Reserved.
HURRY!! HURRY!!
Distributed by Andrews McMeel Syndication
I HAPPEN TO THINK RAINBOWS ARE SPECIAL!
SO ARE MY NAPS

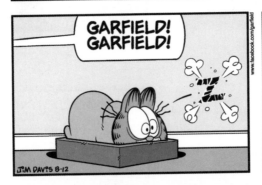

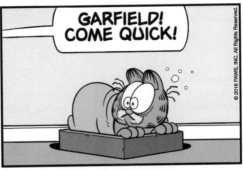

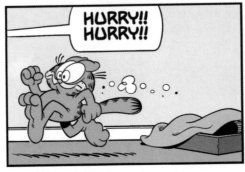

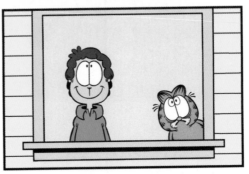

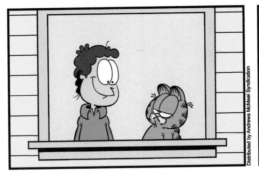

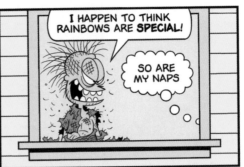

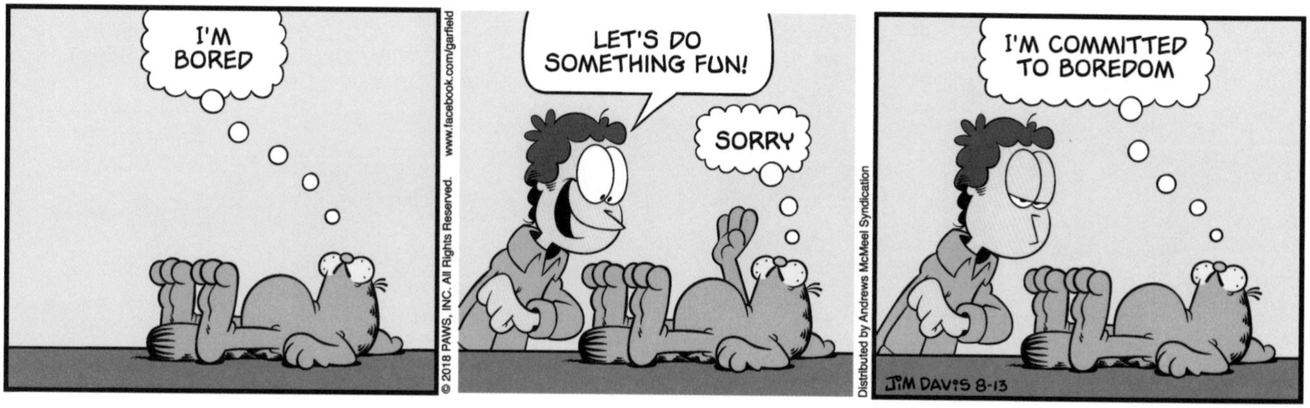
I'M BORED
LET'S DO SOMETHING FUN!
SORRY
I'M COMMITTED TO BOREDOM
© 2018 PAWS, INC. All Rights Reserved. www.facebook.com/garfield
Distributed by Andrews McMeel Syndication
JIM DAVIS 8-13

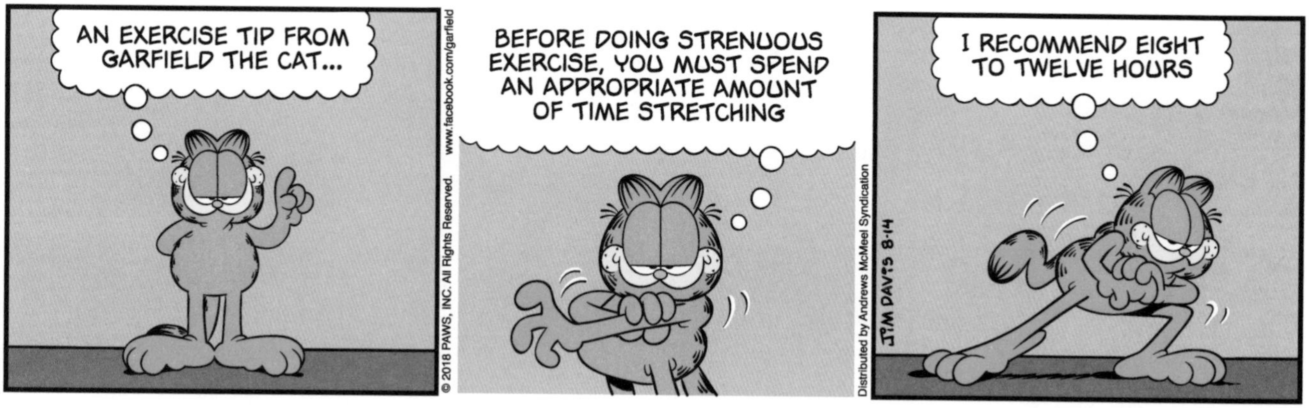
AN EXERCISE TIP FROM GARFIELD THE CAT...
BEFORE DOING STRENUOUS EXERCISE, YOU MUST SPEND AN APPROPRIATE AMOUNT OF TIME STRETCHING
I RECOMMEND EIGHT TO TWELVE HOURS
© 2018 PAWS, INC. All Rights Reserved. www.facebook.com/garfield
Distributed by Andrews McMeel Syndication
JIM DAVIS 8-14

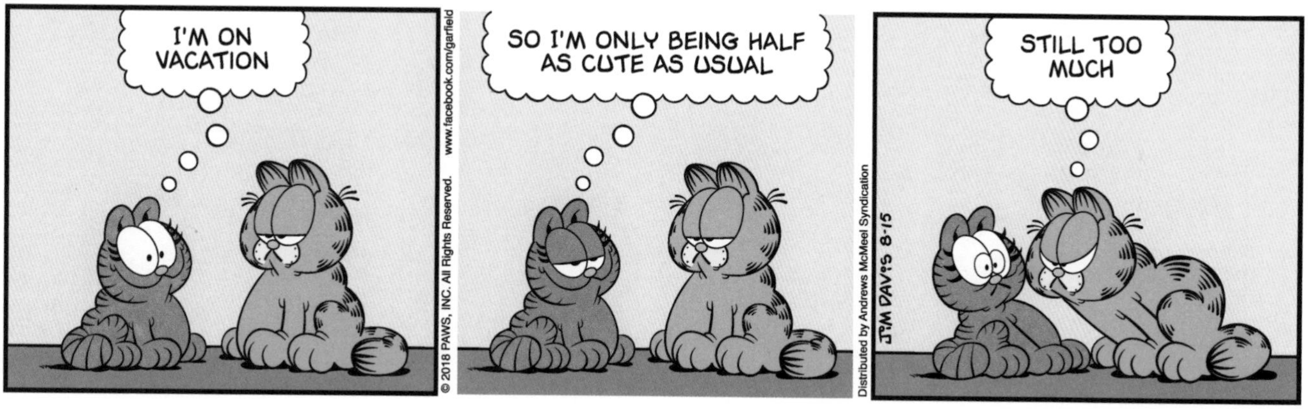
I'M ON VACATION
SO I'M ONLY BEING HALF AS CUTE AS USUAL
STILL TOO MUCH
© 2018 PAWS, INC. All Rights Reserved. www.facebook.com/garfield
Distributed by Andrews McMeel Syndication
JIM DAVIS 8-15

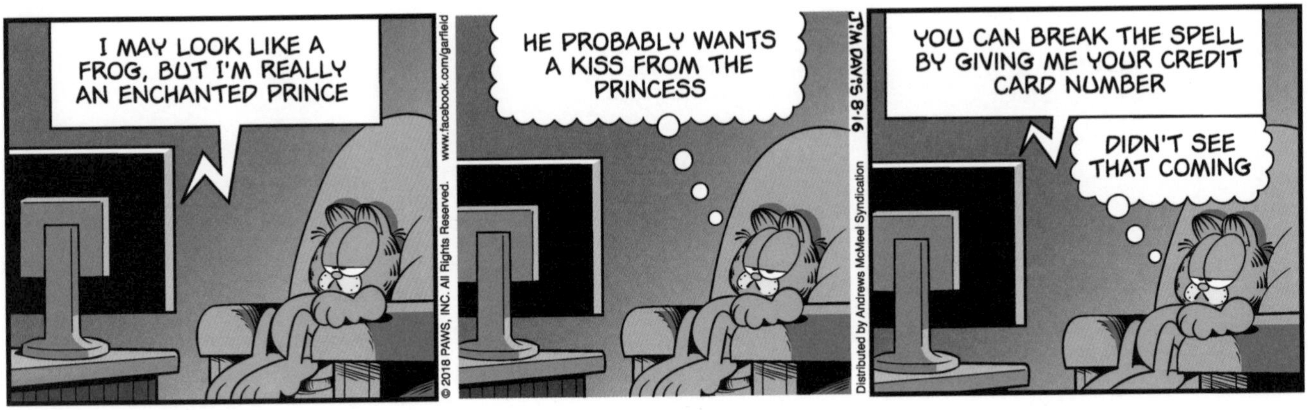
I MAY LOOK LIKE A FROG, BUT I'M REALLY AN ENCHANTED PRINCE
HE PROBABLY WANTS A KISS FROM THE PRINCESS
YOU CAN BREAK THE SPELL BY GIVING ME YOUR CREDIT CARD NUMBER
DIDN'T SEE THAT COMING
JIM DAVIS 8-16
© 2018 PAWS, INC. All Rights Reserved. www.facebook.com/garfield
Distributed by Andrews McMeel Syndication

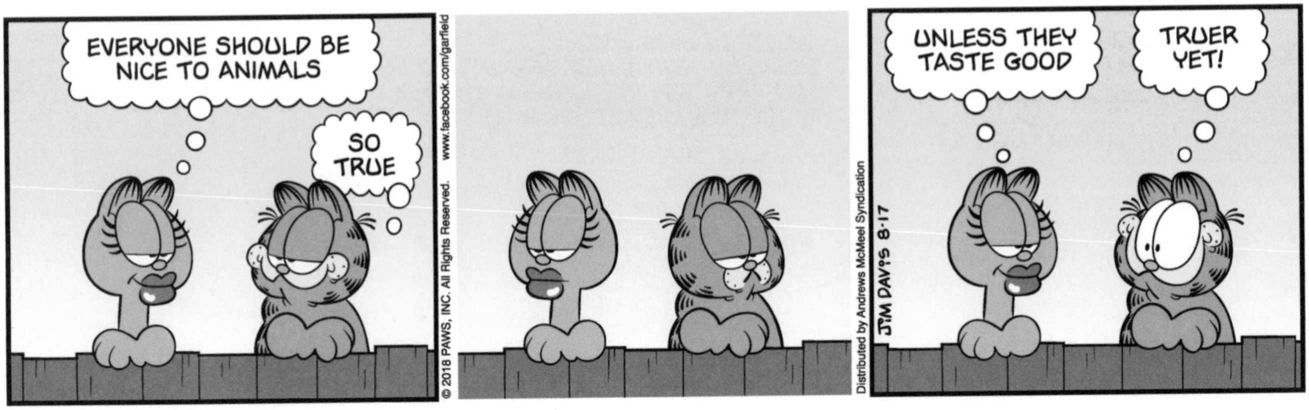
EVERYONE SHOULD BE NICE TO ANIMALS
SO TRUE
UNLESS THEY TASTE GOOD
TRUER YET!
JIM DAVIS 8-17
© 2018 PAWS, INC. All Rights Reserved. www.facebook.com/garfield
Distributed by Andrews McMeel Syndication

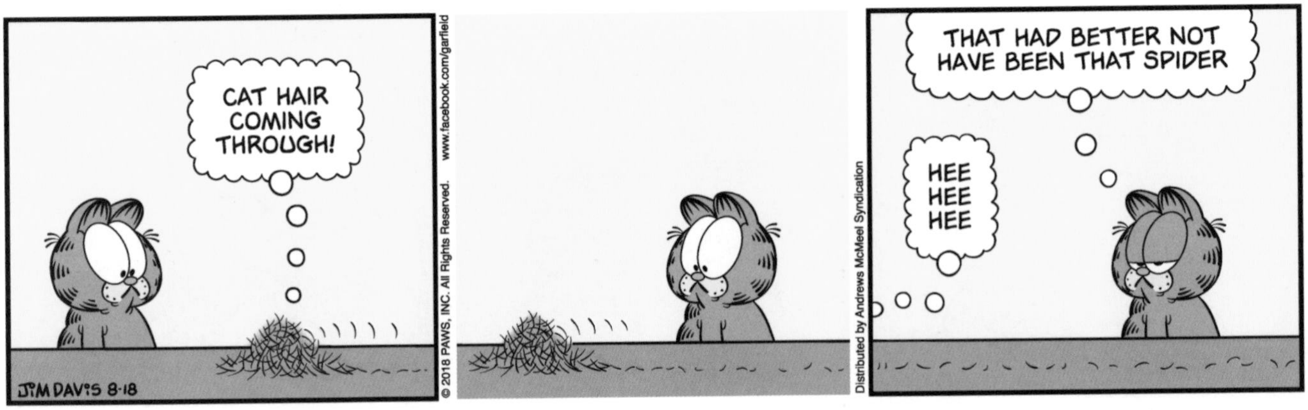
CAT HAIR COMING THROUGH!
THAT HAD BETTER NOT HAVE BEEN THAT SPIDER
HEE HEE HEE
JIM DAVIS 8-18
© 2018 PAWS, INC. All Rights Reserved. www.facebook.com/garfield
Distributed by Andrews McMeel Syndication

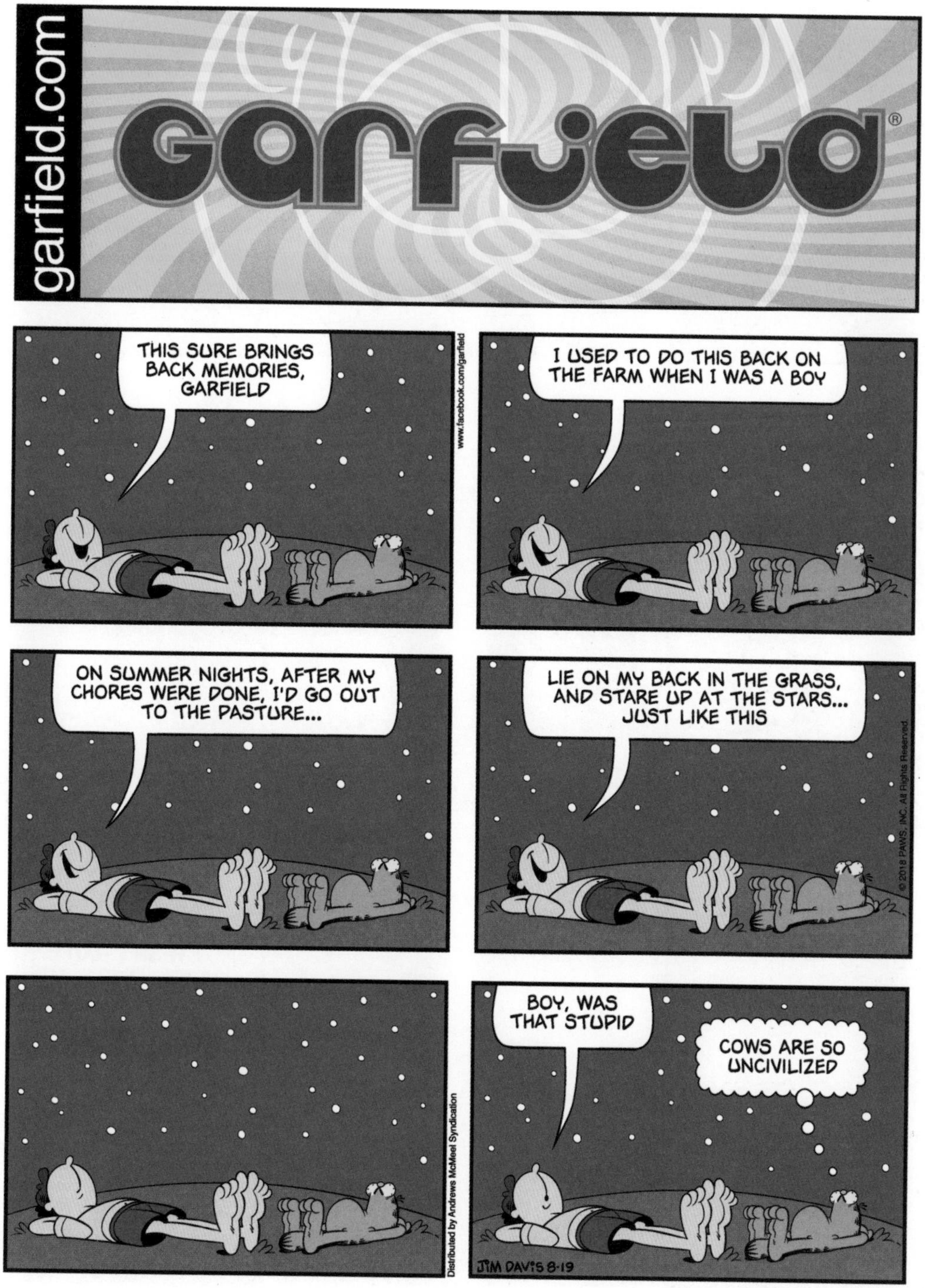
garfield.com
GARFIELD®
THIS SURE BRINGS BACK MEMORIES, GARFIELD
www.facebook.com/garfield
I USED TO DO THIS BACK ON THE FARM WHEN I WAS A BOY
ON SUMMER NIGHTS, AFTER MY CHORES WERE DONE, I'D GO OUT TO THE PASTURE...
LIE ON MY BACK IN THE GRASS, AND STARE UP AT THE STARS... JUST LIKE THIS
© 2018 PAWS, INC. All Rights Reserved.
Distributed by Andrews McMeel Syndication
BOY, WAS THAT STUPID
COWS ARE SO UNCIVILIZED
JIM DAVIS 8-19

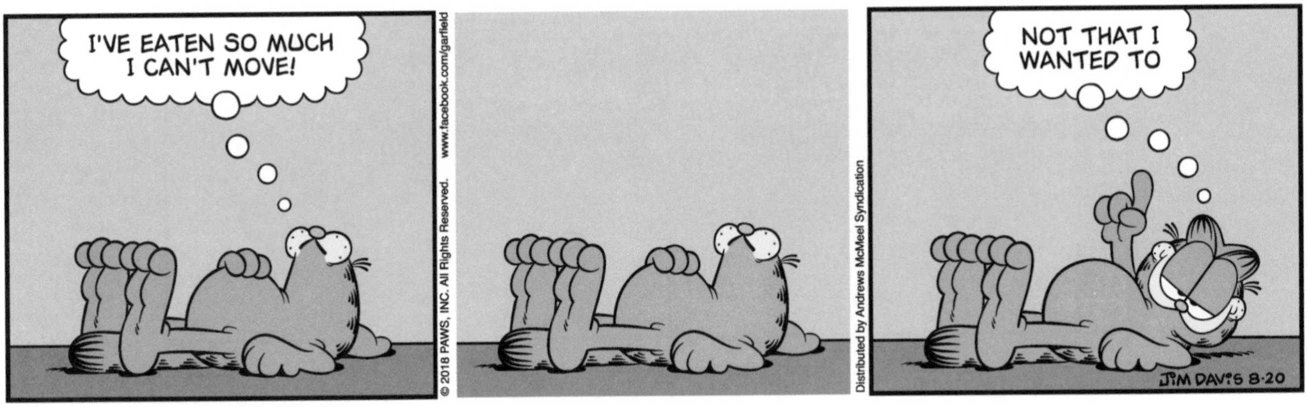
I'VE EATEN SO MUCH I CAN'T MOVE!
NOT THAT I WANTED TO
© 2018 PAWS, INC. All Rights Reserved. www.facebook.com/garfield
Distributed by Andrews McMeel Syndication
JIM DAVIS 8-20

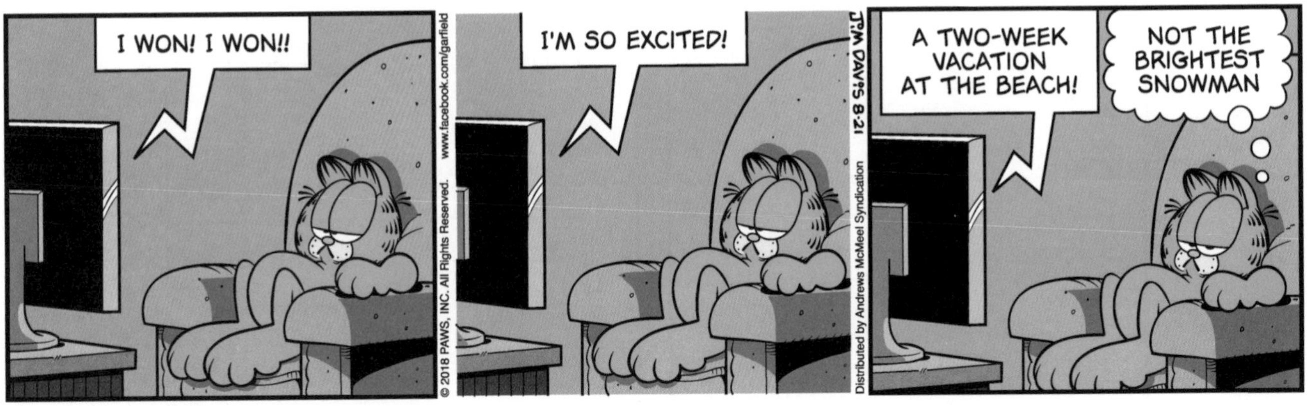
I WON! I WON!!
I'M SO EXCITED!
A TWO-WEEK VACATION AT THE BEACH!
NOT THE BRIGHTEST SNOWMAN
© 2018 PAWS, INC. All Rights Reserved. www.facebook.com/garfield
Distributed by Andrews McMeel Syndication
JIM DAVIS 8-21

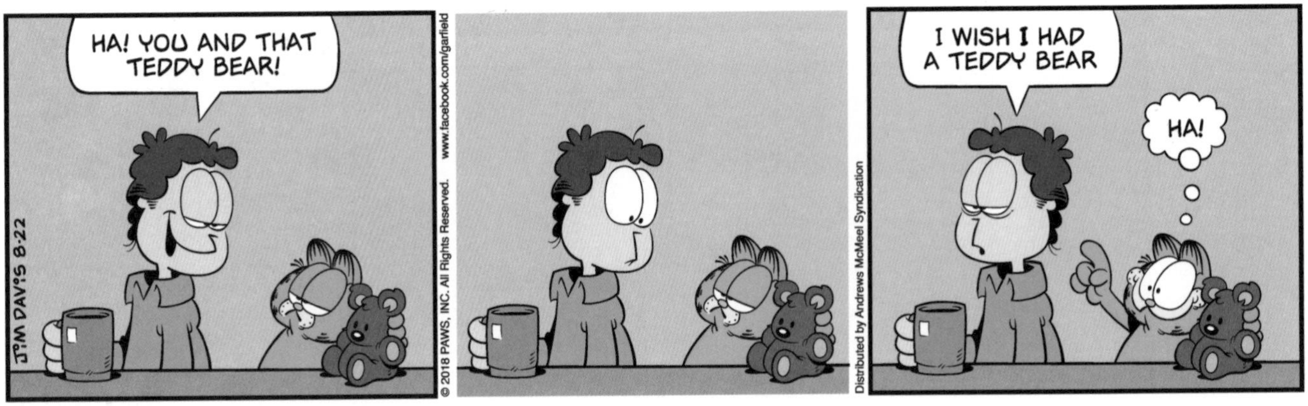
HA! YOU AND THAT TEDDY BEAR!
I WISH I HAD A TEDDY BEAR
HA!
© 2018 PAWS, INC. All Rights Reserved. www.facebook.com/garfield
Distributed by Andrews McMeel Syndication
JIM DAVIS 8-22

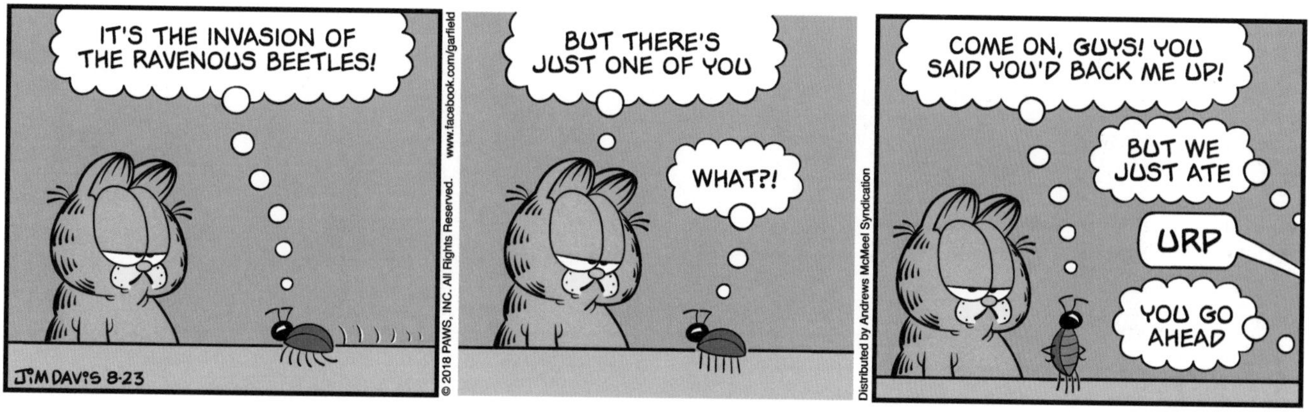
IT'S THE INVASION OF THE RAVENOUS BEETLES!
JIM DAVIS 8-23
© 2018 PAWS, INC. All Rights Reserved. www.facebook.com/garfield
BUT THERE'S JUST ONE OF YOU
WHAT?!
Distributed by Andrews McMeel Syndication
COME ON, GUYS! YOU SAID YOU'D BACK ME UP!
BUT WE JUST ATE
URP
YOU GO AHEAD

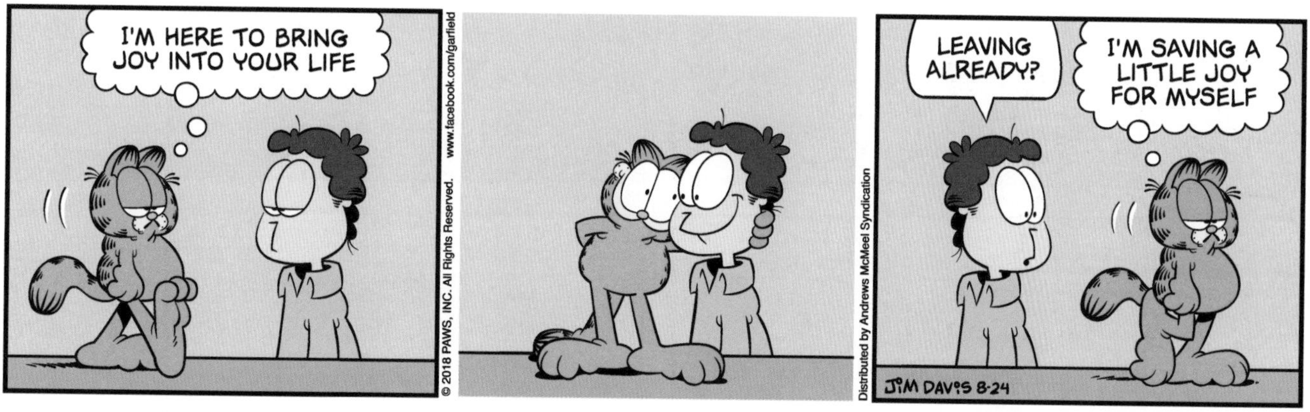
I'M HERE TO BRING JOY INTO YOUR LIFE
© 2018 PAWS, INC. All Rights Reserved. www.facebook.com/garfield
Distributed by Andrews McMeel Syndication
LEAVING ALREADY?
I'M SAVING A LITTLE JOY FOR MYSELF
JIM DAVIS 8-24

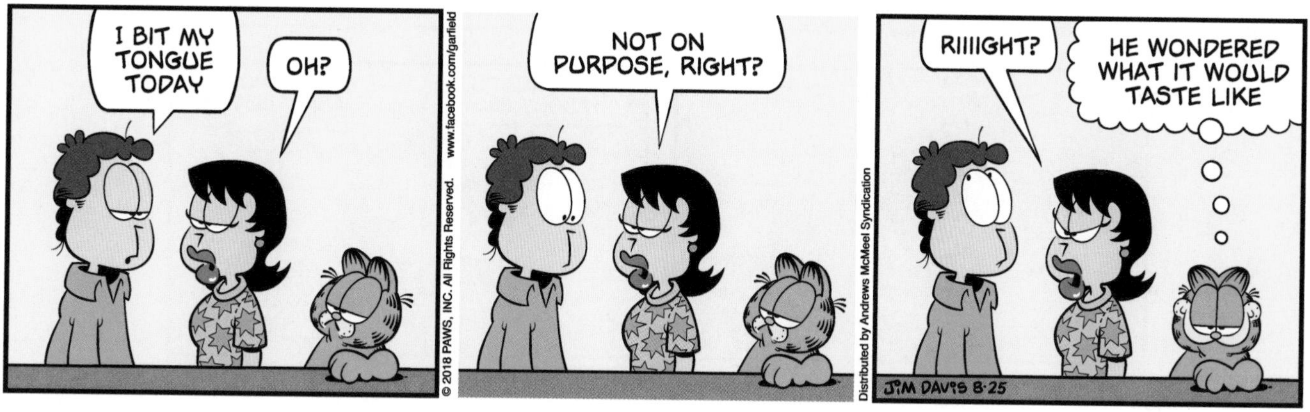
I BIT MY TONGUE TODAY
OH?
© 2018 PAWS, INC. All Rights Reserved. www.facebook.com/garfield
NOT ON PURPOSE, RIGHT?
Distributed by Andrews McMeel Syndication
RIIIIGHT?
HE WONDERED WHAT IT WOULD TASTE LIKE
JIM DAVIS 8-25

garfield.com
GARFIELD
WHY SO GLUM, GARFIELD?
www.facebook.com/garfield
LOOK ON THE BRIGHT SIDE...
YOU HAVE SO MUCH TO BE HAPPY ABOUT!
PLENTY OF FOOD...
© 2018 PAWS, INC. All Rights Reserved.
Distributed by Andrews McMeel Syndication
OKAY, THAT'S ABOUT IT
THAT'S NOT A BAD LIST
JIM DAVIS 8-26

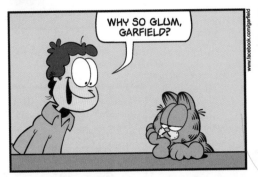

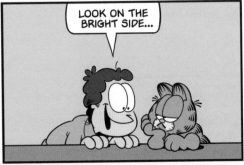

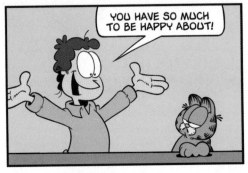

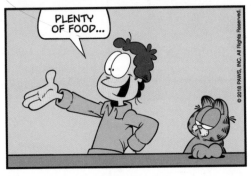

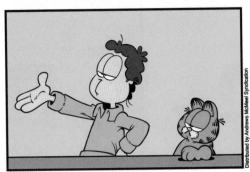

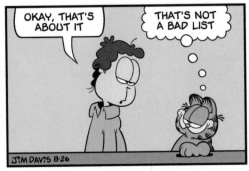

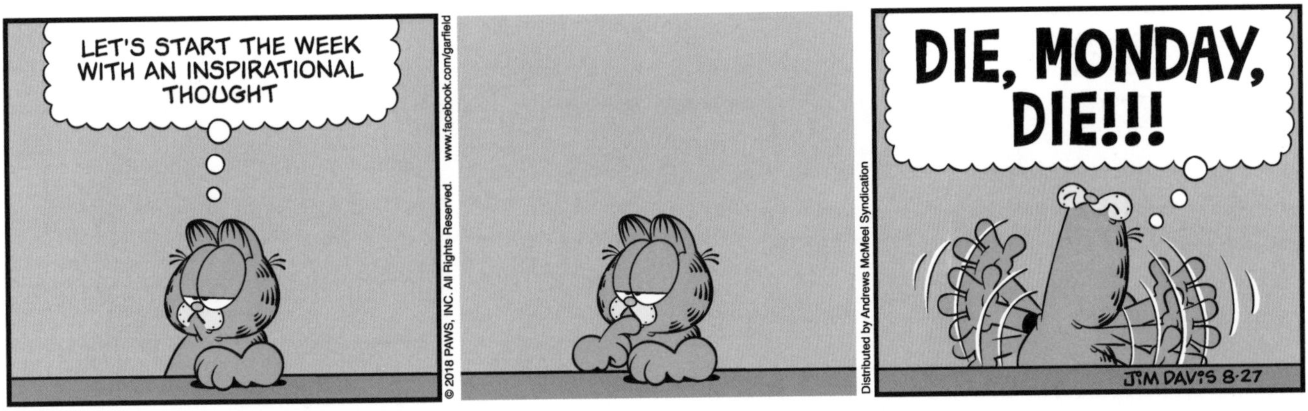
LET'S START THE WEEK WITH AN INSPIRATIONAL THOUGHT
DIE, MONDAY, DIE!!!
JIM DAVIS 8-27
© 2018 PAWS, INC. All Rights Reserved. www.facebook.com/garfield
Distributed by Andrews McMeel Syndication

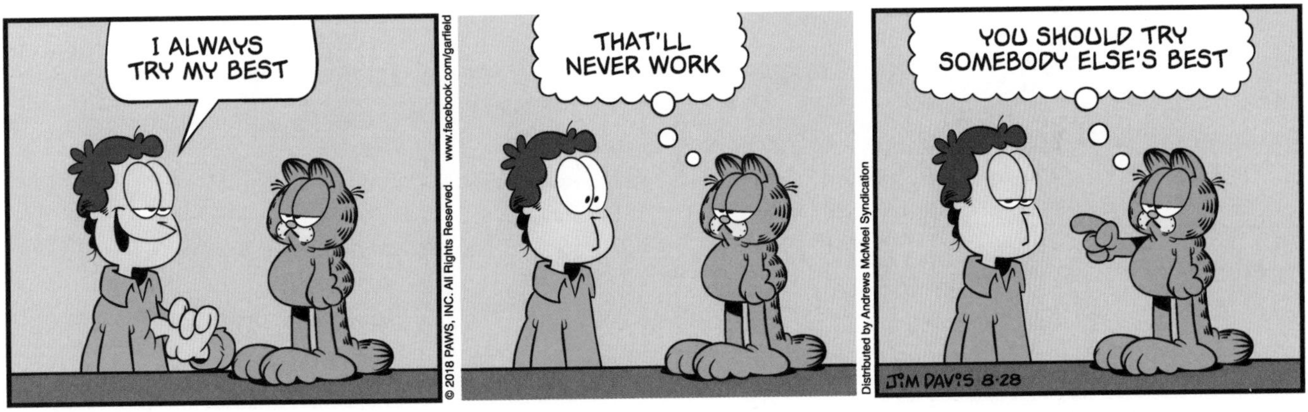
I ALWAYS TRY MY BEST
THAT'LL NEVER WORK
YOU SHOULD TRY SOMEBODY ELSE'S BEST
JIM DAVIS 8-28
© 2018 PAWS, INC. All Rights Reserved. www.facebook.com/garfield
Distributed by Andrews McMeel Syndication

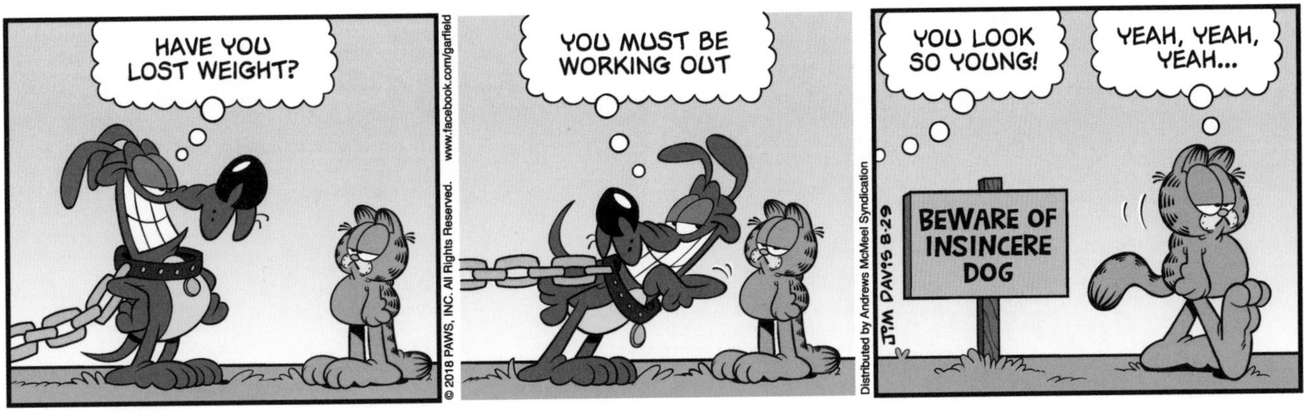
HAVE YOU LOST WEIGHT?
YOU MUST BE WORKING OUT
YOU LOOK SO YOUNG!
YEAH, YEAH, YEAH...
BEWARE OF INSINCERE DOG
JIM DAVIS 8-29
© 2018 PAWS, INC. All Rights Reserved. www.facebook.com/garfield
Distributed by Andrews McMeel Syndication

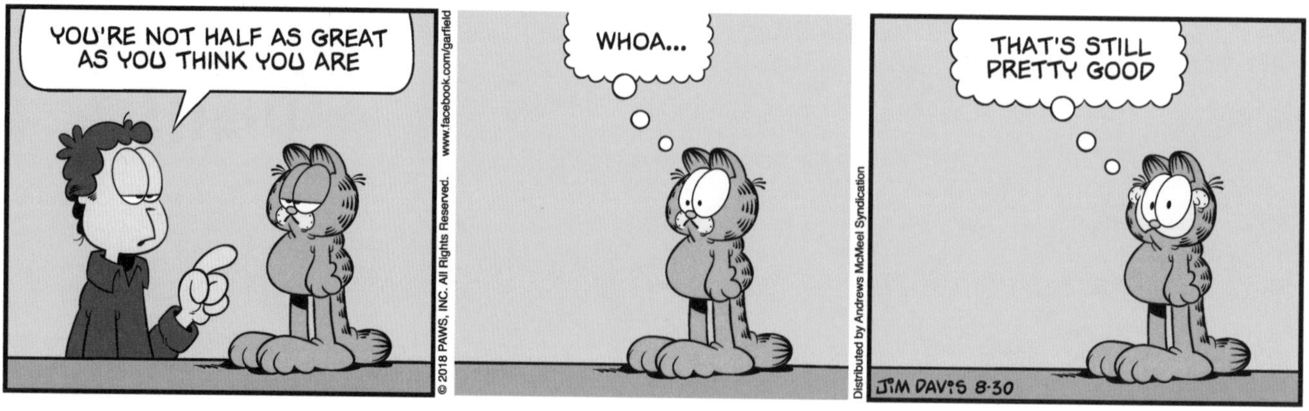
YOU'RE NOT HALF AS GREAT AS YOU THINK YOU ARE
WHOA...
THAT'S STILL PRETTY GOOD
JIM DAVIS 8-30
© 2018 PAWS, INC. All Rights Reserved. www.facebook.com/garfield
Distributed by Andrews McMeel Syndication

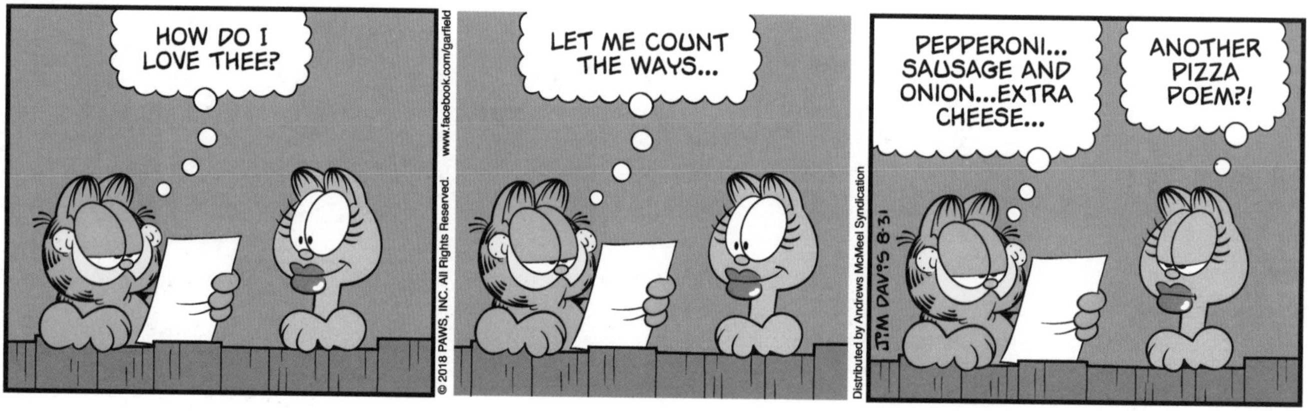
HOW DO I LOVE THEE?
LET ME COUNT THE WAYS...
PEPPERONI... SAUSAGE AND ONION...EXTRA CHEESE...
ANOTHER PIZZA POEM?!
JIM DAVIS 8-31
© 2018 PAWS, INC. All Rights Reserved. www.facebook.com/garfield
Distributed by Andrews McMeel Syndication

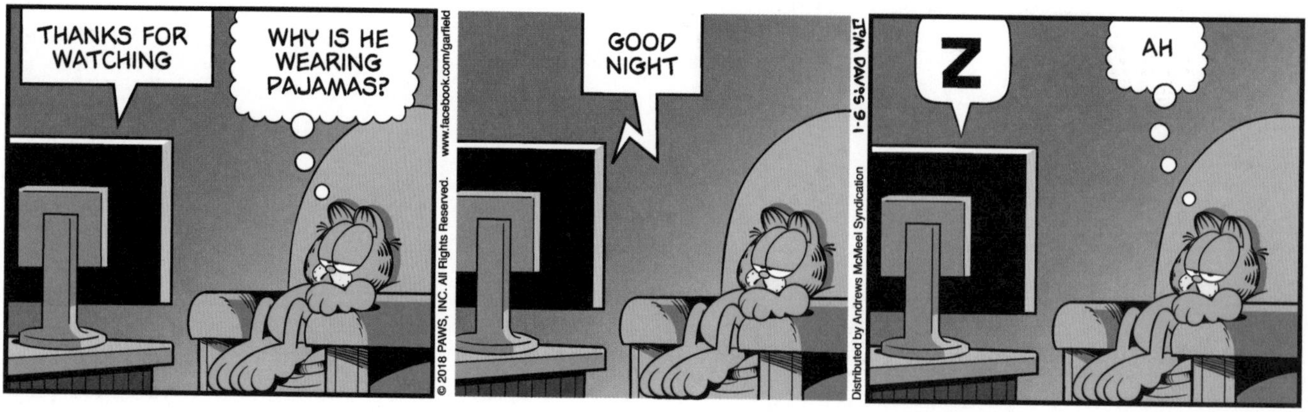
THANKS FOR WATCHING
WHY IS HE WEARING PAJAMAS?
GOOD NIGHT
Z
AH
JIM DAVIS 9-1
© 2018 PAWS, INC. All Rights Reserved. www.facebook.com/garfield
Distributed by Andrews McMeel Syndication

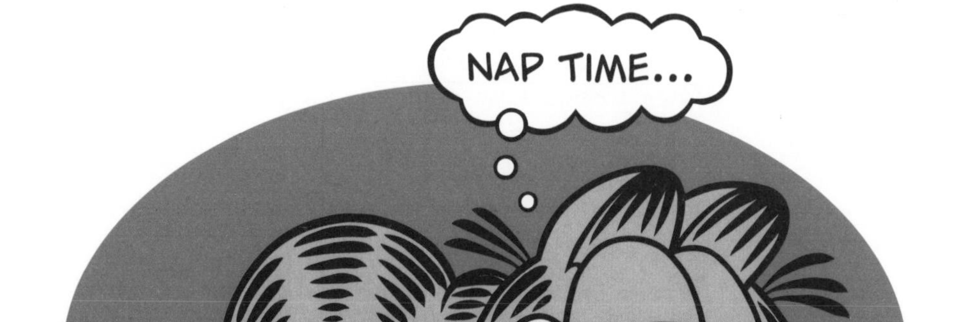
NAP TIME...

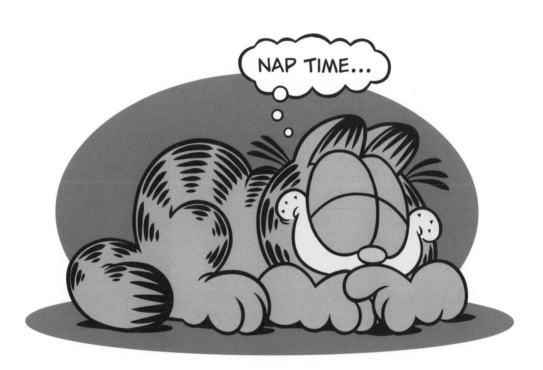

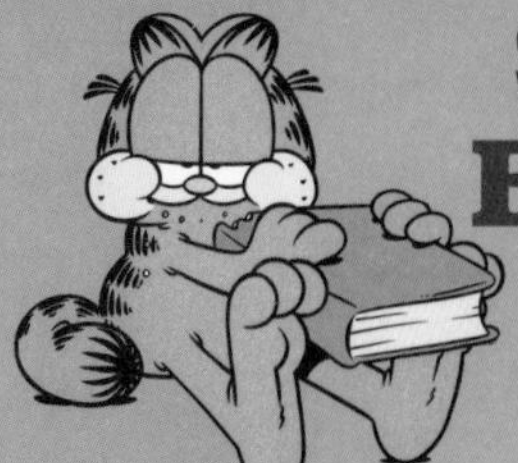

# STRIPS, SPECIALS OR BESTSELLING BOOKS...

# GARFIELD'S ON EVERYONE'S MENU.

***Don't miss even one episode in the Tubby Tabby's hilarious series!***

GARFIELD AT LARGE . . . (#1) 978-0-345-44382-3
GARFIELD GAINS WEIGHT . . . (#2) 978-0-345-44975-7
GARFIELD BIGGER THAN LIFE . . . (#3) 978-0-345-45027-2
GARFIELD WEIGHS IN . . . (#4) 978-0-345-45205-4
GARFIELD TAKES THE CAKE . . . (#5) 978-0-345-44978-8
GARFIELD EATS HIS HEART OUT . . . (#6) 978-0-345-46459-0
GARFIELD SITS AROUND THE HOUSE . . . (#7) 978-0-345-46463-7
GARFIELD TIPS THE SCALES . . . (#8) 978-0-345-46909-0
GARFIELD LOSES HIS FEET . . . (#9) 978-0-345-46467-5
GARFIELD MAKES IT BIG . . . (#10) 978-0-345-46468-2
GARFIELD ROLLS ON . . . (#11) 978-0-345-47561-9
GARFIELD OUT TO LUNCH . . . (#12) 978-0-345-47562-6
GARFIELD FOOD FOR THOUGHT . . . (#13) 978-0-345-47563-3
GARFIELD SWALLOWS HIS PRIDE . . . (#14) 978-0-345-91386-9
GARFIELD WORLDWIDE . . . (#15) 978-0-345-91754-6
GARFIELD ROUNDS OUT . . . (#16) 978-0-345-49169-5
GARFIELD CHEWS THE FAT . . . (#17) 978-0-345-49170-1
GARFIELD GOES TO WAIST . . . (#18) 978-0-345-49173-2
GARFIELD HANGS OUT . . . (#19) 978-0-345-49174-9
GARFIELD TAKES UP SPACE . . . (#20) 978-0-345-49178-7
GARFIELD SAYS A MOUTHFUL . . . (#21) 978-0-345-49179-4
GARFIELD BY THE POUND . . . (#22) 978-0-345-52558-1
GARFIELD KEEPS HIS CHINS UP . . . (#23) 978-0-345-52559-8
GARFIELD TAKES HIS LICKS . . . (#24) 978-0-345-52587-1
GARFIELD HITS THE BIG TIME . . . (#25) 978-0-345-52589-5
GARFIELD PULLS HIS WEIGHT . . . (#26) 978-0-345-52594-9
GARFIELD DISHES IT OUT . . . (#27) 978-0-345-52595-6
GARFIELD LIFE IN THE FAT LANE . . . (#28) 978-0-345-52600-7
GARFIELD TONS OF FUN . . . (#29) 978-0-345-52601-4
GARFIELD BIGGER AND BETTER . . . (#30) 978-0-345-52605-2
GARFIELD HAMS IT UP . . . (#31) 978-0-345-52606-9
GARFIELD THINKS BIG . . . (#32) 978-0-425-28516-9
GARFIELD THROWS HIS WEIGHT AROUND . . . (#33) 978-0-425-28559-6
GARFIELD LIFE TO THE FULLEST . . . (#34) 978-0-425-28564-0
GARFIELD FEEDS THE KITTY . . . (#35) 978-0-425-28569-5
GARFIELD HOGS THE SPOTLIGHT . . . (#36) 978-0-425-28574-9
GARFIELD BEEFS UP . . . (#37) 978-0-345-44109-6
GARFIELD GETS COOKIN' . . . (#38) 978-0-345-44582-7
GARFIELD EATS CROW . . . (#39) 978-0-345-45201-6
GARFIELD SURVIVAL OF THE FATTEST . . . (#40) 978-0-345-46458-3
GARFIELD OLDER AND WIDER . . . (#41) 978-0-345-46462-0
GARFIELD PIGS OUT . . . (#42) 978-0-345-46466-8
GARFIELD BLOTS OUT THE SUN . . . (#43) 978-0-345-46615-0
GARFIELD GOES BANANAS . . . (#44) 978-0-345-91346-3
GARFIELD LARGE & IN CHARGE . . . (#45) 978-0-345-49172-5
GARFIELD SPILLS THE BEANS . . . (#46) 978-0-345-49177-0
GARFIELD GETS HIS JUST DESSERTS . . . (#47) 978-0-345-91387-6
GARFIELD WILL EAT FOR FOOD . . . (#48) 978-0-345-49176-3
GARFIELD WEIGHS HIS OPTIONS . . . (#49) 978-0-345-49181-7
GARFIELD POTBELLY OF GOLD . . . (#50) 978-0-345-52244-3
GARFIELD SHOVELS IT IN . . . (#51) 978-0-345-52419-5
GARFIELD LARD OF THE JUNGLE . . . (#52) 978-0-345-52584-0
GARFIELD BRINGS HOME THE BACON . . . (#53) 978-0-345-52586-4
GARFIELD GETS IN A PICKLE . . . (#54) 978-0-345-52590-1
GARFIELD SINGS FOR HIS SUPPER . . . (#55) 978-0-345-52593-2
GARFIELD CAUTION: WIDE LOAD . . . (#56) 978-0-345-52596-3
GARFIELD SOUPED UP . . . (#57) 978-0-345-52598-7

**New larger, full-color format!**

GARFIELD GOES TO HIS HAPPY PLACE . . . (#58) 978-0-345-52602-1
GARFIELD THE BIG CHEESE . . . (#59) 978-0-345-52604-5
GARFIELD CLEANS HIS PLATE . . . (#60) 978-0-345-52608-3
GARFIELD CHICKENS OUT . . . (#61) 978-0-425-28515-2
GARFIELD LISTENS TO HIS GUT . . . (#62) 978-0-425-28557-2
GARFIELD COOKS UP TROUBLE . . . (#63) 978-0-425-28562-6
GARFIELD FEEDS HIS FACE . . . (#64) 978-0-425-28567-1
GARFIELD EATS AND RUNS . . . (#65) 978-0-425-28572-5
GARFIELD NUTTY AS A FRUITCAKE . . . (#66) 978-0-425-28576-3
GARFIELD SLURPS AND BURPS . . . (#67) 978-1-9848-1773-0
GARFIELD BELLY LAUGHS . . . (#68) 978-1-9848-1777-8
GARFIELD EASY AS PIE . . . (#69) 978-0-593-15640-7
GARFIELD GOES HOG WILD . . . (#70) 978-0-593-15642-1

**DVD TIE-INS**

GARFIELD AS HIMSELF . . . 978-0-345-47805-4
GARFIELD HOLIDAY CELEBRATIONS . . . 978-0-345-47930-3
GARFIELD TRAVEL ADVENTURES . . . 978-0-345-48087-3

**AND DON'T MISS . . .**

GARFIELD AT 25: IN DOG YEARS I'D BE DEAD . . . 978-0-345-45204-7
GARFIELD'S JOKE ZONE/INSULTS . . . 978-0-345-46263-3
GARFIELD FAT CAT 3-PACK/ VOL. 1 . . . 978-0-345-46455-2
GARFIELD FAT CAT 3-PACK/ VOL. 2 . . . 978-0-345-46465-1
GARFIELD FAT CAT 3-PACK/ VOL. 3 . . . 978-0-345-48088-0
GARFIELD FAT CAT 3-PACK/ VOL. 4 . . . 978-0-345-49171-8
GARFIELD FAT CAT 3-PACK/ VOL. 5 . . . 978-0-345-49180-8
GARFIELD FAT CAT 3-PACK/ VOL. 6 . . . 978-0-345-52420-1
GARFIELD FAT CAT 3-PACK/ VOL. 7 . . . 978-0-345-52588-8
GARFIELD FAT CAT 3-PACK/ VOL. 8 . . . 978-0-345-52599-4
GARFIELD FAT CAT 3-PACK/ VOL. 9 . . . 978-0-345-52607-6
GARFIELD FAT CAT 3-PACK/ VOL. 10 . . . 978-0-425-28558-9
GARFIELD FAT CAT 3-PACK/ VOL. 11 . . . 978-0-425-28566-4
GARFIELD FAT CAT 3-PACK/ VOL. 12 . . . 978-0-425-28578-7
GARFIELD FAT CAT 3-PACK/ VOL. 13 . . . 978-0-345-46460-6
GARFIELD FAT CAT 3-PACK/ VOL. 14 . . . 978-0-345-49175-6
GARFIELD FAT CAT 3-PACK/ VOL. 15 . . . 978-0-345-52585-7
GARFIELD FAT CAT 3-PACK/ VOL. 16 . . . 978-0-345-52592-5
GARFIELD FAT CAT 3-PACK/ VOL. 17 . . . 978-0-345-52603-8
GARFIELD FAT CAT 3-PACK/ VOL. 18 . . . 978-0-399-59440-3
GARFIELD FAT CAT 3-PACK/ VOL. 19 . . . 978-0-425-28561-9
GARFIELD FAT CAT 3-PACK/ VOL. 20 . . . 978-0-425-28571-8
GARFIELD FAT CAT 3-PACK/ VOL. 21 . . . 978-1-9848-1775-4
GARFIELD FAT CAT 3-PACK/ VOL. 22 . . . 978-0-593-15638-
GARFIELD'S 20TH ANNIVERSARY COLLECTION . . . 978-0-345-42126-
SEASON'S EATINGS: A VERY MERRY GARFIELD CHRISTMAS . . . 978-0-345-47560-
GARFIELD'S GUIDE TO EVERYTHING . . . 978-0-345-46461-
ODIE UNLEASHED! . . . 978-0-345-46464-
GARFIELD'S BOOK OF CAT NAMES . . . 978-0-345-48516-
THE GARFIELD JOURNAL . . . 978-0-345-46469-
LIGHTS, CAMERA, HAIRBALLS!: GARFIELD AT THE MOVIES . . . 978-0-345-49134
30 YEARS OF LAUGHS AND LASAGNA . . . 978-0-345-50379
GARFIELD MINUS GARFIELD . . . 978-0-345-51387
GARFIELD FROM THE TRASH BIN . . . 978-0-345-5188
GARFIELD LEFT SPEECHLESS . . . 978-0-345-5305
MY LAUGHABLE LIFE WITH GARFIELD . . . 978-0-345-5259
GARFIELD'S SUNDAY FINEST . . . 978-0-345-5259
AGE HAPPENS: GARFIELD HITS THE BIG 4-0 . . . 978-0-345-5260
GARFIELD COMPLETE WORKS: VOLUME ONE: 1978 & 1979 . . . 978-0-425-2871
GARFIELD COMPLETE WORKS: VOLUME TWO: 1980 & 1981 . . . 978-0-425-2871